ARMIN LANGE, Dr. theol. (1995), University of Münster, is ⟨…⟩
Temple Judaism at the University of Vienna and a member of the international team editing the Dead Sea Scrolls. He has recently published the first volume of his *Handbuch der Textfunde vom Toten Meer* (Mohr Siebeck 2009).

EMANUEL TOV, Ph.D. (1974) in Biblical Studies, Hebrew University, is J.L. Magnes Professor of Bible at the Hebrew University and the former Editor-in-Chief of the Dead Sea Scrolls Publication Project. He has published several books on textual criticism and on the Scrolls.

MATTHIAS WEIGOLD is a member of the research project 'The Meaning of Ancient Jewish Quotations and Allusions for the Textual History of the Hebrew Bible' at the University of Vienna.

The Dead Sea Scrolls in Context

Supplements

to

Vetus Testamentum

Edited by the Board of the Quarterly

H.M. BARSTAD – R.P. GORDON – A. HURVITZ – J. JOOSTEN

G.N. KNOPPERS – A. VAN DER KOOIJ – A. LEMAIRE – C.A. NEWSOM

H. SPIECKERMANN – J. TREBOLLE BARRERA – H.G.M. WILLIAMSON

VOLUME 140/1

The Dead Sea Scrolls in Context

Integrating the Dead Sea Scrolls
in the Study of Ancient Texts, Languages,
and Cultures

Volume One

Edited by

Armin Lange, Emanuel Tov, and Matthias Weigold

In association with Bennie H. Reynolds III

BRILL

LEIDEN • BOSTON
2011

This book is printed on acid-free paper.

Library of Congress Cataloging-in-Publication Data

The Dead Sea scrolls in context : integrating the Dead Sea scrolls in the study of ancient texts, languages, and cultures / edited by Armin Lange, Emanuel Tov, and Matthias Weigold in association with Bennie H. Reynolds III.
     p. cm. – (Supplements to Vetus Testamentum, ISSN 0083 5889 ; v. 140)
Proceedings of a conference jointly organized by the Hebrew University of Jerusalem and the University of Vienna in Vienna on February 11-14, 2008.
   Includes bibliographical references.
   ISBN 978-90-04-18903-4 (hardback : alk. paper)
1. Dead Sea scrolls–Congresses. 2. Qumran community–Congresses. 3. Judaism–History–Post-exilic period, 586 B.C.-210 A.D.–Congresses. I. Lange, Armin, 1961- II. Tov, Emanuel. III. Weigold, Matthias. IV. Universitah ha-'Ivrit bi-Yerushalayim. V. Universität Wien. VI. Title. VII. Series.

BM487.D44958 2011
296.1'55–dc22

2010037469

ISSN   0083-5889
ISBN   978 90 04 18903 4 (set)

MIX
Paper from
responsible sources
FSC
www.fsc.org FSC® C004472

PRINTED BY DRUKKERIJ WILCO B.V. - AMERSFOORT, THE NETHERLANDS

CONTENTS

ANCIENT SEMITIC LANGUAGES
AND THE DEAD SEA SCROLLS

THE HEBREW BIBLE AND OTHER SECOND TEMPLE JEWISH
LITERATURE IN LIGHT OF THE DEAD SEA SCROLLS

INTRODUCTION

In the framework of the cooperation between the Hebrew University of Jerusalem and the University of Vienna, Armin Lange, Emanuel Tov, and Matthias Weigold organized in February of 2008 the international conference "The Dead Sea Scrolls in Context: Integrating the Dead Sea Scrolls in the Study of Ancient Texts, Languages, and Cultures" at Vienna University.

It was a special honor for the conference organizers that the Federal President of the Republic of Austria, Dr. Heinz Fischer, and his Excellency, the Ambassador of the State of Israel to Austria, Dan Ashbel, addressed words of greeting to the conference. We would like to use this opportunity to reiterate our gratitude to both President Fischer and Ambassador Ashbel. We are also grateful to the Embassy of the State of Israel to Austria, Brill Publishers, the Faculty of Historical and Cultural Studies of Vienna University, the Österreichische Gesellschaft der Freunde der Hebräischen Universität Jerusalem, the Rectorate of Vienna University, and Vandenhoeck & Ruprecht publishers for sponsoring our conference. The active help of Professor Dr. Alfred Ebenbauer and Professor Dr. Dr. Dr. Peter Landesmann in fundraising were instrumental for the success of the conference. We would also like to thank Dara Fischer, Katharina Gabor, Daniela Hanin, Maria Kelm, Nikolaus Keusch, Kerstin Mayerhofer, and Olivia Rogowski for their help in organizing the conference. Furthermore, we are obliged to the departments Public Relations and Event Management as well as Research Service and International Relations of Vienna University.

The present volume is the first of two volumes in which the proceedings of our conference will be published. We are grateful to Ms. Maria Kelm for her support in editing the proceedings. We are grateful to Hans Barstad and the editorial board of Supplements to Vetus Testamentum for accepting our proceedings for publication. Liesbeth Hugenholtz, Machiel Kleemans, and Suzanne Mekking of Brill publishers have guided us through the publication process in preparing the manuscript of this volume.

In addition to twenty presentations by faculty members of the Hebrew University and the University of Vienna, thirty eight colleagues from all over the world answered our call for papers and contributed presentations to the Vienna "Dead Sea Scrolls in Context" conference. The topic of the conference responded to the completion of the publication of the scrolls from the Judean Desert. Except for some small fragments, all of the Dead Sea Scrolls have been published and are now easily accessible. The time has therefore come to integrate the Dead Sea Scrolls fully into the various disciplines that benefit from the discovery of these very important ancient texts. The Dead Sea Scrolls enrich many areas of biblical research, as well as the study of ancient Jewish, early Christian and other ancient literatures, languages, and cultures. In addition to Dead Sea Scrolls specialists, the Vienna conference was, therefore, also attended by specialists from these other fields. We made it a requirement for both the presentations of the Vienna conference and the contributions to its proceedings that contributors address both the Dead Sea Scrolls themselves as well as one of the contexts mentioned above.

The first volume of the Vienna conference proceedings contains articles that discuss new methodologies applied to the Dead Sea Scrolls, and articles that address the relevance of the Dead Sea Scrolls for the textual history of the Hebrew Bible, for ancient Semitic languages, the Hebrew Bible and Second Temple Jewish literature, and for ancient Jewish literature in Greek.

The first part of the present volume ("Methodological Contexts: The Dead Sea Scrolls Beyond Historical Criticism") puts the Dead Sea Scrolls into the context of new methodologies and approaches beyond the constraints of historical criticism. *Emanuel Tov* ("The Sciences and the Reconstruction of the Ancient Scrolls: Possibilities and Impossibilities") surveys and discusses various scientific methodologies which were applied to the Dead Sea Scrolls, such as radiocarbon dating, ink research, analysis of parchment shrinkage, DNA-analysis, elemental composition analysis, analysis of stitching material, the use of advanced photographic techniques, computer assisted fragment identification, research of hair follicles and fibers, and the so-called Stegemann method of reconstructing ancient scrolls. Of these scientific approaches, Tov finds radiocarbon analysis, ink research, research of leather follicles and papyrus fibers, elemental composition analysis, and infrared color photographing the most promising methods. *James A. Loader* ("Creating New Contexts: On the Possibilities of Biblical Studies in Contexts Generated by the Dead Sea Scrolls") carries the methodological question into the realm of intertextuality. The Dead Sea Scrolls lend a striking topicality to the concept of intertextuality. Not only was Qumran literature written in the context of the Hebrew Bible, but it created in turn contexts for the reading of the Hebrew Bible that did not exist before the Dead Sea Scrolls. The example of the Dead Sea Scrolls shows thus that pre-texts do not remain unaffected by their post-texts. *Jeff S. Anderson* ("Curses and Blessings: Social Control and Self Definition in the Dead Sea Scrolls") reflects on blessings and curses in covenant renewals and expulsions, war prayers, and parenetic exhortations based on J.L. Austin's notion of performative utterances.[1] Blessings and curses uttered in ritual contexts at Qumran were potent and effective performatives. The community employed these utterances in multiple contexts using speech laced with intertextual references to blessings and curses from the Hebrew Bible. In the framework of the Qumran community's dualistic world view, blessings and curses enhanced social solidarity, marginalized outsiders, and coerced obedience to social sanctions. Based on the example of 1QSa, *Tal Ilan* ("Reading for Women in 1QSa [*Serekh ha-Edah*]") shows how individual Dead Sea Scrolls can be interpreted from a feminist standpoint. Ilan reads the constructions of gender in 1QSa not in isolation, but in light of other texts that existed simultaneously. She shows that in 1QSa, the council of the Yaḥad comprises both women and men of honor. Ilan asks: if 1QSa is thus interested in both men and women, why did research ignore the role of women in the Qumran community for so long?

The second part of the present volume is dedicated to "The Textual History of the Hebrew Bible in Light of the Dead Sea Scrolls." The three articles of this part exemplify how the Dead Sea Scrolls help to better understand the pre-canonical textual history of the biblical books. *John Elwolde* ("The *Hodayot*'s Use of the Psalter: Text-Critical Contributions [Book 2: Pss 42–72]") analyzes the text-critical importance of allusions to Pss 42–72 in the Qumran *Hodayot*. Out of twenty-one passages, he finds only the allusion to Ps 57:5 in 1QHᵃ V:6–7 (XIII:8–9) of text-critical interest. The *Hodayot* attest to the regular form לָבִיא instead of MT's *hapax legomenon* לְבָא, Peshitta's ܠܒܐ, and *Tg. Ps.*'s שלהובין. Furthermore, in the *Hodayot* no equivalent for MT's לְהָטִים אֶשְׁכְּבָה or LXX's ἐκοιμήθην τεταραγμένος can be found. Based on the example of Mal 3:22–24, *Russell Fuller* ("Hebrew and Greek Biblical Manuscripts: Their Interpretations and their Interpreters") demonstrates that the redactional history of biblical compositions cannot be reconstructed based on their Masoretic texts. In Mal 3:22–24, the text sequence of the Greek version is older than the Masoretic one. It has its origin no later than the middle of the sec-

---

[1] J.L. Austin, *How to Do Things with Words* (Cambridge: Harvard University Press, 1962).

ond century B.C.E as attested by the paleographic date of 4QXII^a (4Q76). The sequence of the Masoretic text highlights the eschatological perspective in the last section of Malachi and emphasizes thus the eschatological imagery used in contemporary compositions like the book of *Jubilees*. Based on the example of Judg 6:7–10, *Alexander Rofé* ("Studying the Biblical Text in the Light of Historico-Literary Criticism: The Reproach of the Prophet in Judg 6:7–10 and 4QJudg^a") discusses the relationship between textual criticism ("lower criticism") and the historical-critical approach ("higher criticism"). The absence of Judg 6:7–10 from 4QJudg^a is due to *parablepsis*. But this short text was favored by the contents of the pericope in question. Judges 6:7–10 is an addition aiming to reply to Gideon's complaint "why has all this befallen us" (Judg 6:13). The example shows that various textual witnesses reveal the textual vicissitudes of the late history of biblical texts but do not provide information about their early history.

The third part of the present volume, "Ancient Semitic Languages and the Dead Sea Scrolls," is dedicated to the contribution of the Dead Sea Scrolls to the understanding of Hebrew and Aramaic. *Steven E. Fassberg* ("The Dead Sea Scrolls and Their Contribution to the Study of Hebrew and Aramaic") surveys the history of research on the study of Hebrew and Aramaic in light of the Dead Sea Scrolls. The Dead Sea Scrolls have left an indelible mark on Hebrew linguistic research in 1) pointing to the existence of different Hebrew dialects in ancient Coele-Syria, 2) in providing evidence for vernacular Hebrew during the Second Temple period, and 3) in highlighting the history of the Hebrew verbal system. Similarly, the Dead Sea Scrolls provide new insights into the Aramaic of the Second Temple period by highlighting the literary nature of the Aramaic texts from Qumran (standard literary Aramaic), by arguing for a Palestinian setting and middle Aramaic date of *Targum Onqelos*, and by allowing for a new periodization of the Aramaic language, i.e. Old, Official, Middle, Late, and Modern Aramaic. The Aramaic Dead Sea Scrolls belong to the Middle Aramaic period (200 B.C.E.–200 C.E.). Furthermore, the coexistence of Hebrew and Aramaic documents at the various sites in the Judean Desert as well as the Hebraisms in the Aramaic documents and the Aramaisms in the Hebrew documents prove the bilingualism of Palestinian Jews before and after the turn of the Common Era.

Five other papers underline the significance of the Dead Sea Scrolls for Hebrew and Aramaic research. *Moshe Bar-Asher* ("Two Issues in Qumran Hebrew: Synchronic and Diachronic Perspectives") studies the transition from Qumran to Mishnaic Hebrew by way of the examples of מבואי/מבוי and העשה in Qumran and Mishnaic Hebrew. The transitions between different forms of Hebrew take place at different times for different features. In some cases Qumran may line up with biblical Hebrew and against later Mishnaic Hebrew, while in other cases Qumran and Mishnaic Hebrew are set off from biblical Hebrew. *Francesco Zanella* ("The Lexemes תרומה and מנה in the Poetic Texts of Qumran: Analysis of a Semantic Development") explains the semantic development of the lexemes תרומה and מנה in the context of ancient Jewish perceptions of speech. In Qumran texts, speech is no longer linked to perversion, falsehood, and mischief. Speech acts, rather, have the purpose of praising and exalting the true nature of God, which must be at first fully comprehended. The act of praising, therefore, originates from a cognitive (perhaps mystical) process that brings the speaker/petitioner to a deeper level of knowledge. In their new meanings of "contribution of knowledge" (תרומה) and "selected prayer" (מנה), תרומה and מנה lexicalize the innovative relations between praise, true knowledge, and "oral sacrifice." Two ostraca from pagan Mareshah highlight, according to *Esther Eshel* ("Aramaic Texts from Qumran in Light of New Epigraphical Finds"), the use of two Aramaic lexemes in Qumran texts. The use of the noun מחשא in the Mareshah ostraca demonstrates that in 4Q211 משחתה might refer to a luminous phenomenon made by stars or meteors. Furthermore, that the Mareshah ostraca use the verb נזח to describe the movement of Halley's comet argues for a similar usage in the "Birth of Noah" text. These linguistic observations point to the knowledge of Mesopotamian astrology, astronomy, and demonology in Coele-Syria during the Persian and Hellenistic periods. *Aaron Koller* ("Four Dimensions of Linguistic Variation: Aramaic Dialects in and around Qumran") explains the dialectological variation of Middle Aramaic in considering geography, textual genres, and linguistic ideologies. By comparing the linguistic features of *Targum Onqelos* and *Targum Pseudo-Jonathan* with Aramaic texts from Qumran, *Christa Müller-Kessler* ("The Linguistic Heritage of Qumran Aramaic") shows that both Targumim belong to the dialect geography of Babylonia. Although Targumic Aramaic preserves features of Qumran Aramaic, it is far more developed than the latter. Therefore its placement within the group of Middle Aramaic has to be reconsidered. The diversity in the linguistic elements of Qumran Aramaic presents a non-homogeneous language style that differs from text to text.

The fourth part of the present volume, "The Hebrew Bible and Other Second Temple Jewish Literature in Light of the Dead Sea Scrolls," is devoted to another important context of the Dead Sea Scrolls. *Mila Gins-burskaya* ("Leviticus in the Light of the Dead Sea Scrolls: Atonement and Purification from Sin") explores the concept of atonement and the related ideas of purification and divine forgiveness in cultic and non-cultic texts of the Hebrew Bible and the Dead Sea Scrolls. While the connection between atonement, forgiveness, and purification from sin is particularly enhanced in the Dead Sea Scrolls, the synthesis of cultic and non-cultic trends in the Dead Sea Scrolls supports the view that there is no ideological discontinuity between the Dead Sea Scrolls and the Hebrew Bible. *Bennie H. Reynolds III* ("Adjusting the Apocalypse: How the *Apocryphon of Jeremiah C* Updates the Book of Daniel") argues that *Apocryphon of Jeremiah C* updated some prophecies of the book of Daniel approximately sixty years after it was written, i.e. during the reign of John Hyrcanus (134–104 B.C.E.). The writer of the *Apocryphon* renewed and actuated Daniel's failed prophecy, placing the eschaton near the beginning of the first century B.C.E. *Michael Segal* ("Identifying Biblical Interpretation in Parabiblical Texts") identifies interpretative techniques as markers for the "post-canonical" nature of a textual composition. He exemplifies his theory based on the re-narrations of the story of the sojourn to Egypt (Gen 12:10–20) in the book of *Jubilees* and the *Genesis Apocryphon*. In both texts, Segal observes an implicit interpretative thrust to harmonize the story of Abram's and Sarai's sojourn to Egypt with Israel's exile in Egypt. This interpretative thrust became explicit much later in *Genesis Rabbah*. In her comparison of 4Q377 2 i 9 with Demetrius the Chronographer, Philo's *Legum allegoriae* (1.76; 2.66–67; 3.103), *m. Soṭah* 1:7, 9, and *Sipre Num* 99, *Hanna Tervanotko* ("Miriam Misbehaving? The Figure of Miriam in 4Q377 in Light of Ancient Jewish Literature") shows that 4Q377 2 i 9 preserves an allusion to Num 12. The brevity of this allusion implies that this text was written for the use of audiences who could relate to it with such a subtle hint. *Pierpaolo Bertalotto* ("Qumran Messianism, Melchizedek, and the Son of Man") observes that both the Melchizedek of 11QMelch and the Son of Man in the Enochic *Book of Parables* are linked by way of the angelic appellative אלוהים, that both are interpretative developments of the "one like a son of man" in Dan 7:13–14, and that being identified with the "Anointed of the Spirit," both perform revelatory tasks. Bertalotto concludes that the Melchizedek of 11QMelch was created against the background of the Son of Man in the *Book of Parables*. *J. Harold Ellens* ("The Dead Sea Scrolls and the Son of Man in Daniel, 1 Enoch, and the New Testament Gospels: An Assessment of 11QMelch [11Q13]") reads the Melchizedek figure of 11QMelch in the context of the book of Daniel, *1 Enoch*, and the New Testament Gospels. At Qumran, the *Hodayot*, the *War Scroll*, and the *Rule of the Community* attest to a messianic figure that is not only a virtual Son of Man but also a suffering servant. In 11QMelch, Melchizedek becomes a messianic figure that combines the *exousia* of the eschatological judge with the savior of the people of God. Because the suffering messiah and the eschatological judge contradict Qumran determinist thought, Ellens suggests that a heretical movement existed within the community envisioning the possibility of hope and salvation beyond the scope of the predestined elect.

The fifth and last part of the first volume of the conference proceedings is devoted to "Ancient Jewish Literature in Greek and the Dead Sea Scrolls." *Jamal-Dominique Hopkins* ("The Dead Sea Scrolls and the Greco-Roman World: Examining the Essenes' View of Sacrifice in Relation to the Scrolls") argues that in light of the Dead Sea Scrolls, remarks of both Josephus (*Ant.* 18.19) and Philo (*Prob.* 75) point to a spiritualized understanding of sacrifice in the Essene movement. Philo, *Prob.* 80–82, makes it probable that studying was viewed as such a form of spiritualized sacrifice by the Essenes. *Ekaterina Matusova* ("*1 Enoch* in the Context of Philo's Writings") finds allusions to Enochic literature in Philo's treatises *De gigantibus (On Giants)* and *Quod Deus sit immutabilis (That God Is Unchangeable)*. Based on these allusions she is able to establish a *terminus ante quem* for the date of the Greek translation of *1 Enoch* in the first century B.C.E. The allusions show furthermore that *1 Enoch* was accepted not only by the Qumran community but widely in ancient Judaism.

Noah Hacham ("Where Does the Shekhinah Dwell? Between the Dead Sea Sect, Diaspora Judaism, Rabbinic Literature, and Christianity") shows that the idea of the Divine Presence dwelling among God's people originated in the (Babylonian) Diaspora due to its separation from the nation's religious center. Later, Hellenism exercised, especially among Diaspora Jews, great influence on the development of the concept of Shekhinah. When the Second Temple was destroyed, the Diaspora concept of Shekhinah enabled Jews to live without a religious and national center. Even before the destruction of the Second Temple, the Qumran community viewed itself as a human temple in which God would dwell removed from his physical sanctuary. In comparison with the priestly personification of wisdom in Wisdom of Solomon 18, *Ulrike Mittmann* ("11QMelch im Spiegel der Weisheit") shows that 11QMelch understands Melchizedek as a priestly figure of personified wisdom. Different from 11QMelch, the early Christian interpretation of Melchizedek identifies the priestly wisdom that is personified in the priestly figure of Melchizedek with the Davidic Messiah and the Son of Man. *Loren T. Stuckenbruck* ("The 'Heart' in the Dead Sea Scrolls: Negotiating between the Problem of Hypocrisy and Conflict within the Human Being") compares the *Hodayot*, the Exhortation of *1 Enoch*, Ben Sira, and the *Treatise of the Two Spirits* with regard to the problems of hypocrisy and conflict within human beings with each other. On the one hand, with regard to "hypocritical" behavior, the *Hodayot*, the Exhortation of *1 Enoch*, and Ben Sira are less interested in what happens within human beings. Their claims to piety should not be confused with authentic religiosity. For these texts, the demarcation between the pious and the sinners is a socially discernible contrast. On the other hand, for the *Treatise of the Two Spirits*, a recognizable distinction between "the sons of light/righteousness" and "the sons of iniquity" is not guaranteed. It regards "the heart" of each human being as a combat zone where the powers of good and evil struggle to assert their control. As God has apportioned to each human being a certain measure of the spirit of "truth" and the spirit of "iniquity," an apocalyptic act of divine clearance at the end will reveal the people of God as they have been predetermined from the beginning.

The second volume of the *Dead Sea Scrolls in Context* proceedings will explore further areas which illuminate the Dead Sea Scrolls and are illuminated by them: "Jewish History, Culture, and Archeology and the Dead Sea Scrolls," "Jewish Thought and Religion in Light of the Dead Sea Scrolls," "The Dead Sea Scrolls and the Ancient Mediterranean and Ancient Near Eastern Worlds," "The Dead Sea Scrolls and Jewish Literature and Culture of the Rabbinic and Medieval Periods," as well as "The Dead Sea Scrolls and Early Christianity."

Unless otherwise indicated, abbreviations follow *The SBL Handbook of Style: For Ancient Near Eastern, Biblical, and Early Christian Studies* (ed. P.H. Alexander et al.; Peabody: Hendrickson, 1999).

Armin Lange, Bennie H. Reynolds III,
Emanuel Tov, and Matthias Weigold
Chapel Hill, Jerusalem, and Vienna, June 2010

METHODOLOGICAL CONTEXTS:
THE DEAD SEA SCROLLS BEYOND
HISTORICAL CRITICISM

THE SCIENCES AND
THE RECONSTRUCTION OF THE ANCIENT SCROLLS:
POSSIBILITIES AND IMPOSSIBILITIES

Emanuel Tov

The Hebrew University of Jerusalem

The study of the Qumran scrolls is the study of fragments and sheets rather than that of complete scrolls. For example, 4QJer[a] consists of fifty fragments covering parts, sometimes very minute, of sixteen chapters. 4Q509 consists of 313 fragments, and 4QSam[a] has 346 fragments covering parts of fifty chapters. I have no idea how many fragments altogether have been found in the Qumran caves, but it must be a large number. Some scholars speak of 15,000 fragments for cave 4 alone,[1] while others estimate the total number of fragments as 10,000[2] or as many as 100,000.[3] If we set the *average* number of fragments per scroll randomly at forty, we are dealing with 37,000 fragments covering 930 fragmentary scrolls. The actual number will remain unknown unless one dedicates many weeks to counting.

When dealing with a topic like the sciences and the ancient scrolls, scientists often forget that these fragments are parts, however minute, of once complete sheets, and that each medium-sized scroll consisted of a number of sheets. A fragment does not constitute an independent unit for a material investigation, since the information about fragments needs to be supplemented by that in other fragments deriving from the same sheet. Each sheet forms an independent unit, not necessarily of the same nature as the sheet that is now stitched to it. Therefore, in the material analysis of the fragments it is necessary to know more about each sheet or the scroll as a whole. The scroll is the overriding unit, but since many scrolls are composed of different sheets, we have to base our remarks on these sheets. Single-column sheets like 4QTest

---

[1] R. de Vaux, quoted by P. Benoit in *DJD* VI (1977): v.

[2] Thus S.R. Woodward et al., "Analysis of Parchment Fragments from the Judean Desert Using DNA Techniques," in *Current Research and Technological Developments in the Dead Sea Scrolls—Conference on the Texts from the Judean Desert, Jerusalem, 30 April 1995* (ed. D.W. Parry and S.D. Ricks; STDJ 20; Leiden: Brill, 1996), 215–238 (222).

[3] J.T. Milik, oral communication.

(4Q175) and single-sheet scrolls are rare in Qumran. Most scrolls are composed of a number of sheets, seventeen in the case of the large Isaiah scroll.

Over the past five decades, the sciences have come to our aid in examining several material aspects of scroll fragments, their coverings, stitching material, etc. The first such study was that included in *DJD* I (1955), viz., examinations by Crowfoot of the linen textiles, some of which must have covered scrolls.[4] Further, according to investigations made in 1958 and the early 1960s by Ryder on the one hand and Poole and Reed on the other,[5] the leather scrolls found at Qumran were made mainly from skins of sheep and goats.[6] A more detailed study of the scroll material mentioned the following four species: calf, fine-wooled sheep, medium-wooled sheep, and a hairy animal that was either a sheep or a goat.[7]

There are many ways in which the sciences helped or *could* help us to gain a better understanding of the scroll fragments and aid us in their reconstruction. The main areas are: (1) determining the date of the scrolls (based on the age of the leather and ink [?]), (2) determining whether fragments derive from the same sheet (Carbon-14, DNA research, the chemical composition of the leather and ink; follicle patterns in leather, and fibers in papyrus), (3) retrieving previously unreadable letters with the aid of advanced photographic techniques, (4) and identifying fragments and determining the relation between fragments with the aid of computer-assisted research. At the same time, we should also be able to determine where these sciences are *unable* to help us.[8]

---

[4] G.M. Crowfoot in *DJD* I (1955): 18–38. The tests themselves were carried out under the direction of W.F. Libby at the University of Chicago in 1950.

[5] M.L. Ryder, "Follicle Arrangement in Skin from Wild Sheep, Primitive Domestic Sheep and in Parchment," *Nature* 182 (1958): 1–6; J. Poole and R. Reed, "The Preparation of Leather and Parchment by the Dead Sea Scrolls Community," *Technology and Culture* 3 (1962): 1–26; repr. in *Technology and Culture: An Anthology* (ed. M. Kranzberg and W.H. Davenport; New York: Schocken, 1972), 143–168; idem, "A Study of Some Dead Sea Scrolls and Leather Fragments from Cave 4 at Qumran: Part I, Physical Examination; Part II, Chemical Examination," *Proceedings of the Leeds Philosophical and Literary Society, Scientific Section* 9/1 (1962): 1–13; 9/6 (1964): 171–182.

[6] Ibid., "Part I, Physical Examination," 1–13, especially 8.

[7] M.L. Ryder, "Remains Derived from Skin," in *Science in Archaeology: A Comprehensive Survey of Progress and Research* (ed. D. Brothwell and E.S. Higgs; London: Thames & Hudson, 1963), 539–554.

[8] For an earlier survey, see M. Broshi, "The Dead Sea Scrolls, the Sciences and New Technologies," *DSD* 11 (2004): 133–142.

This study refers solely to the scientific examination of the fragments, and not to the identification and reconstruction on the basis of content. Further, it refers only to scientific aid in the reconstruction and understanding of the scrolls, and not to the contribution of these examinations to the archeology of Qumran or the understanding of life at Qumran. Thus, we do not deal with ground-penetrating radar locating caves, examination of parasites in combs, Qumran skeletons, or pottery, nor do we deal with the study of metals, wood, glass, etc. The latter list of examinations is very important for many aspects of Qumran archeology and Qumran research, and sometimes also of scroll research, but does not contribute directly to the reading and reconstruction of scroll fragments, which is our immediate aim.

Over the past four decades, many types of scientific investigation have been carried out, providing help for the research of the scrolls.

This paper focuses on the following areas:

1. Topics examined and results reached with the aid of the sciences
2. Some technical data about the scrolls
3. Scientific aid in the reconstruction of ancient scrolls: possibilities and impossibilities.

1. Topics Examined and Results Reached with the Aid of the Sciences

Individual scholars as well as groups of scholars[9] advanced the scientific investigation of the scrolls in individual and collective publications dealing with the sciences.[10] Progress has been made in the following areas.

---

[9] Note especially the Jerusalem "Taskforce for science and the scrolls" on behalf of the Orion Center at the Hebrew University.

[10] Parry and Ricks, *Current Research*; J.-B. Humbert and J. Gunneweg, eds., *Khirbet Qumrân et ʿAïn Feshkha: Études d'anthropologie, de physique et de chimie* (NTOA.SA 3; Fribourg: Academic Press, 2003); K. Galor, J.-B. Humbert, and J. Zangenberg, eds., *Qumran, the Site of the Dead Sea Scrolls: Archaeological Interpretations and Debates: Proceedings of a Conference Held at Brown University, November 17–19, 2002* (STDJ 57; Leiden: Brill, 2006); J. Gunneweg, C. Greenblatt, and A. Adriaens, eds., *Bio- and Material Cultures at Qumran: Papers from a COST Action G8 Working Group Meeting Held in Jerusalem, Israel on 22–23 May 2005* (Stuttgart: Fraunhofer IRB, 2006).

a. *Dating the Scrolls*

(1) *Carbon-14*

The first system used for dating scrolls was that of *paleography* (dating on the basis of the type of handwriting), and this is still our major resource for dating.[11] At the same time, at an early stage in the study of the scrolls, C-14 examinations[12] of the leather and papyrus fragments became instrumental in determining their dates,[13] usually corroborating paleographical dating.[14] These examinations have been applied only to a small number of scrolls.[15]

The paleographical dates applied to the documents range from the fourth century B.C.E. to the first century C.E. for the Jericho documents, from 250 B.C.E. to 68 C.E. for the Qumran texts, from 150 B.C.E. to 70 C.E. for the Masada texts, and from 75 B.C.E. to 135 C.E. for the texts from Wadi Murabbaʿat, Naḥal Ḥever, and Naḥal Ṣeelim.

---

[11] For a summary of the paleographical dates given to the scrolls, see B. Webster, "Chronological Index of the Texts from the Judaean Desert," in *DJD* XXXIX (2002): 351–446.

[12] C-14 analysis is based on the fact that the animal hides contained carbon-14 atoms when the animal was alive, and that the number of these atoms decreased at a measurable rate after its death, when they became carbon-12 atoms, all compared with the C-14 atoms in tree rings.

[13] The best non-technical explanation of C-14 is probably by G. Doudna, "Dating the Scrolls on the Basis of Radiocarbon Analysis," in *The Dead Sea Scrolls after Fifty Years: A Comprehensive Assessment* (ed. P.W. Flint and J.C. VanderKam; 2 vols.; Leiden: Brill, 1998–1999), 1:430–471. See also *Methods of Investigation of the Dead Sea Scrolls and the Khirbet Qumran Site: Present Realities and Future Prospects* (ed. M.O. Wise et al.; Annals of the New York Academy of Sciences 722; New York: New York Academy of Sciences, 1994), 441–453 ("Report and Discussion Concerning Radiocarbon Dating of Fourteen Dead Sea Scrolls").

[14] For comparative tables recording the paleographical and C-14 data, see Webster, "Chronological Index" (362–368). 1QIsaᵃ was tested in the laboratories of Zurich and Tucson with similar results (see n. 15).

[15] The report of the first C-14 tests (14 texts) carried out in Zurich is that of G. Bonani et al., "Radiocarbon Dating of the Dead Sea Scrolls," *Atiqot* 20 (1991): 27–32 = *Radiocarbon* 34 (1992): 843–849. The second group of carbon-tests was carried out on 28 texts, of which one (1QIsaᵃ) had also been sampled by Bonani et al.: A.J.T. Jull et al., "Radiocarbon Dating of Scrolls and Linen Fragments from the Judean Desert," *Radiocarbon* 37 (1995): 11–19 = *Atiqot* 28 (1996): 85–91. Some individual texts were examined as well: M. Broshi and H. Eshel, "Radiocarbon Dating and 'The Messiah Before Jesus,'" *RevQ* 20 (2001): 310–317 (4Q427 and 4Q491) = *Tarbiz* 70 (2001): 133–138; J. Charlesworth in his publications of XJoshua (MS Schøyen 2713) in *DJD* XXXVIII (2000): 231–239 and XJudges (MS Schøyen 2861) in *DJD* XXVIII (2001): 231–233.

With the aid of a C-14 test, 1QIsa[a] was dated to between 250 and 103 B.C.E. (paleographical date: 125–100 B.C.E.)[16] and 11QT[a] between 97 B.C.E. and 1 C.E. (paleographical date: late first century B.C.E. to early first century C.E.).[17] However, there are also a few texts for which the paleographical and C-14 dates differ greatly. This pertains to 4QTQahat, C-14 dated to 385–349 B.C.E. This date is earlier than the dates of all other Qumran scrolls.[18] By the same token, one of the fragments of 4QS[d] (4Q258) dated to 134–230 C.E. at the one-sigma range, after the destruction of Qumran, is later than expected.[19] Some scholars ascribe the deviating dates of these documents—either too early or too late according to the common view about Qumran—to the applying of castor oil to the leather in the 1950s in order to improve the clarity of the written text.[20] This claim is made especially by G. Doudna; Doudna's own view is that all the scrolls date from the period before 40 B.C.E.[21] On the other hand, according to Broshi, the possible influence of such

---

[16] Jull et al., "Radiocarbon Dating"; Bonani et al., "Radiocarbon Dating": 202–107 B.C.E.

[17] Ibid.

[18] Ibid. The fragment was probably contaminated, offsetting the precision of the C-14 analysis.

[19] Jull et al., "Radiocarbon Dating." Another fragment of the same scroll was dated to 11 B.C.E.–78 C.E.

[20] See J. Strugnell, "On the History of the Photographing of the Discoveries in the Judean Desert for the International Group of Editors," in E. Tov with the collaboration of S.J. Pfann, *Companion Volume to The Dead Sea Scrolls Microfiche Edition* (2nd rev. ed.; Leiden: Brill, 1995), 125: "Next came some cleaning of the darker patches with oil, to bring out the writing—something chemically harmless, I am told, but some of us used it too generously in the early days."

[21] "Dating the Scrolls on the Basis of Radiocarbon Analysis," 430–465; idem, *Redating the Dead Sea Scrolls Found at Qumran* (QC 8.4; Cracow: Enigma Press, 1999); idem, "The Legacy of an Error in Archaeological Interpretation: The Dating of the Qumran Cave Scroll Deposits," in Galor, Humbert, and Zangenberg, *Qumran, the Site of the Dead Sea Scrolls*, 147–157. See also K.L. Rasmussen et al., "Cleaning and Radiocarbon Dating of Material from Khirbet Qumran," in Gunneweg, Greenblatt, and Adriaens, *Bio- and Material Cultures*, 139–163; idem et al., "The Effects of Possible Contamination on the Radiocarbon Dating of the Dead Sea Scrolls I: Castor Oil," *Radiocarbon* 43 (2001): 127–132 (note that the great majority of the samples taken are not from parchments); R. van der Water, "Reconsidering Palaeographic and Radiocarbon Dating of the Dead Sea Scrolls," *RevQ* 19 (1999–2000): 213–216; J. Atwill and S. Braunheim, "Redating the Radiocarbon Dating of the Dead Sea Scrolls," *DSD* 11 (2004): 143–157; see also the reactions to this paper by J. van der Plicht, "Radiocarbon Dating and the Dead Sea Scrolls: A Comment on 'Redating,'" *DSD* 14 (2007): 77–89; T. Higham, J.E. Taylor, and D. Green, "New Radiocarbon Determination," in Humbert and Gunneweg, *Khirbet Qumrân*, 197–200; S. Pfann, "Relative Agreement and Systematic Error of Radiocarbon Tests Applied to the Dead Sea Scrolls," *Radiocarbon*, forthcoming.

oil is negligible.[22] The last word has not been said on this issue, and the presence of castor oil on the margins of the leather (from which samples were taken) as opposed to the inscribed surface itself, has yet to be proven. This discussion is important, since C-14 examinations are very significant for scroll research. A. Masic has developed a new technique to identify such oil.[23]

(2) *Ink Research*

So far ink has not been dated.

(3) *Parchment Shrinkage*

In a little-known study, Burton, Poole, and Reed suggested dating the scroll fragments according to the pattern of the shrinkage temperature of the collagen fibers in the leather (1959).[24] To the best of my knowledge, this method has not been applied to the Qumran fragments.

b. *Relation between Fragments*

When reconstructing scrolls there are many unknowns. The question of whether two or more fragments should be joined as adjacent fragments or designated as belonging to the same column or sheet, remains a major issue in scrolls research. Information about the content is usually insufficient in fragmentary scrolls. The analysis of script is often equally unsatisfying when analyzing small fragments. We would appreciate some help from the sciences in either linking fragments or excluding such a connection, but such help is still being developed. In short, we would like to have objective criteria for making a connection between any two fragments or excluding such a possibility. The first steps in exploring some possibilities have been made, but scholars are in need of a database incorporating

---

[22] Broshi, "The Dead Sea Scrolls," 135: "To 16 of the 34 samples no castor oil was applied; in the other, samples were taken from margins never touched by castor oil. Even if there were traces of oil they would have been eliminated by the pre-treatment." See also I. Carmi, "Are the 14C Dates of the Dead Sea Scrolls Affected by Castor Oil Contamination," *Radiocarbon* 44 (2002): 127–132.

[23] "Dead Sea Scrolls: Non-Invasive Characterisation of Conservation Treatment Materials by Means of IR-ERS," in *Israeli-Italian Bi-national Workshop*, Ramat-Gan, 2007 (unpublished in the meantime).

[24] D. Burton, J.B. Poole, and R. Reed, "A New Approach to the Dating of the Dead Sea Scrolls," *Nature* 184 (1959): 533–534.

alternative scientific data referring to a large number of fragments. The techniques that come to mind relating to the possible joining of fragments are DNA research, ink research, research of leather follicles and papyrus fibers, and elemental composition analysis. However, it should be remembered that these examinations can only determine whether or not two fragments belong to the same sheet. A fragment is not a unit. The real unit is the sheet, because the information gathered by the aforementioned examinations pertains to the sheet as a whole. This examination is further complicated by the fact that skins of different animals were used as writing material for one scroll (see below). To the best of my knowledge, all these techniques would produce the same results for fragments taken from any part of the sheet (C-14, DNA, research of leather follicles, ink research[25]), with the exception of the examination of fibers in papyri, a technique that is not yet developed.

In all these cases, the sciences may help us in determining whether a frg. a and frg. b derive from the same sheet or of the same animal, no more and no less. If they derived from the same sheet, the exact relation between these fragments cannot be determined with the aid of the sciences. Since the fragments could be three columns apart, multiple possibilities should be envisaged. Furthermore, if two completely different compositions were written on skins deriving from the same animal, wrong conclusions could be drawn if we were to be guided solely by the scientific examinations.

(1) *DNA*

DNA research of ancient texts is still in its infancy. Scholars have succeeded in extracting aDNA (ancient DNA) from ancient sources such as mummies, scrolls, and ancient animal bones. The main research in this area was carried out by Kahila Bar-Gal in her Hebrew University dissertation supervised by P. Smith, E. Tchernov, and S. Woodward.[26] The technique has been applied to fragments of several scrolls

---

[25] The results of ink research, as yet unexplored, would be less compelling, since two different scribes could have used the same ink in different compositions.

[26] "Genetic Change in the *Capra* Species of Southern Levant over the Past 10,000 Years as Studied by DNA Analysis of Ancient and Modern Populations" (Ph.D. diss., The Hebrew University of Jerusalem, 2000). See further Kahila Bar-Gal's paper "What Can Fragments of the Dead Sea Scrolls Teach Us of Ancient Animal Husbandry?" (abstract of paper presented at the Symposium on the Role of Analytical Methods in the Study, Restoration, and Conservation of Ancient Manuscripts, with Emphasis on the Dead

that have been mentioned by name: 4QS^b (4Q256), 4QS^d (4Q258), 4QS^e (4Q259), 4QIsa^a (4Q161), 11QT^a (fragments from six different sheets as well as stitching material)[27] together with a host of uninscribed fragments from caves 3 and 4. Examinations of 1QH^a and 4QpHos^b (4Q167) did not yield DNA.[28] The techniques used were described by Woodward.[29]

This type of investigation can (1) determine the species of animal from which the leather derived, (2) distinguish between the DNA signature of individual animals, and (3) determine groups of animals (herds) from which the hides derived.[30] Ideally, these herds should be linked with bones of individual animals or herds, ancient or modern, since the DNA signature has not changed from antiquity to modern times. These links between hides and herds have hardly been made,[31] and researchers are still waiting for the construction of databases that link specific fragments and bones.

(2) *Ink Research*

The study of the composition of ink could give us some clues regarding the relationship between scroll fragments. So far, ink has not been dated but its composition has been analyzed, to a limited extent, by Nir-El

---

Sea Scrolls, Prague, 14 April 1999; online: http://orion.mscc.huji.ac.il/orion/programs/taskforce.shtml); eadem et al., "The Genetic Signature of the Dead Sea Scrolls," in *Historical Perspectives: From the Hasmoneans to Bar Kokhba in Light of the Dead Sea Scrolls: Proceedings of the Fourth International Symposium of the Orion Center for the Study of the Dead Sea Scrolls and Associated Literature, 27–31 January 1999* (ed. D. Goodblatt, A. Pinnick, and D.R. Schwartz; STDJ 37; Leiden: Brill, 2001) 165–171.

[27] More precise data on the texts sampled are listed in Bar-Gal, "Genetic Change," 70.

[28] As implied by the discussion of the results ibid., 71–76.

[29] Woodward et al., "Analysis of Parchment Fragments"; idem in D.W. Parry et al., "New Technological Advances: DNA, Databases, Imaging Radar," in *The Dead Sea Scrolls after Fifty Years*, 1:496–515; idem, "DNA Analysis of Ancient Parchment" (abstract of paper presented at the Symposium on the Role of Analytical Methods in the Study, Restoration, and Conservation of Ancient Manuscripts, with Emphasis on the Dead Sea Scrolls, Prague, 14 April 1999; online: http://orion.mscc.huji.ac.il/orion/programs/taskforce.shtml).

[30] See the summary by Woodward et al., "Analysis of Parchment Fragments," 216: "The precision of the DNA analysis will allow us to identify at least three levels of hierarchy: the species, population, and individual animal from which the parchment was produced."

[31] Thus Bar-Gal, "Genetic Change," 75, noting that the Qumran bones cannot be traced. The existence of such bones, including those of goats, is mentioned in Y. Magen and Y. Peleg, "The Qumran Excavations 1993–2004, Preliminary Report," *Judea and Samaria Publications* 6 (2007): 1–74 (42–43).

and Broshi[32] (pertaining to both inscribed papyrus and leather) and a German research group (I. Rabin, O. Hahn et al.).[33] On the basis of examinations carried out in 1995 at the Soreq Nuclear Research Centre on fragments from caves 1 and 4, Nir-El and Broshi concluded that no metal ink was used in writing the Qumran scrolls under investigation.[34] The examinations were made with the EDXRF (Energy Dispersive X-Ray Fluorescence) procedure. These scholars assumed that the copper elements in the ink derived from copper inkwells used by scribes, and that the ink used was carbon-based.[35] A similar suggestion had been made earlier by H.J. Plenderleith,[36] Steckoll (see n. 32), and Haran,[37] mainly for the texts from cave 1.

In the future, study of the components of ink may help us to pinpoint different types of ink. Rabin believes that a basic distinction can be made between ink prepared at Qumran and ink prepared elsewhere because of an analysis of the water component in ink.[38] In particular, she points out that the chlorium/bromium ratio is lower in places near

---

[32] Y. Nir-El and M. Broshi, "The Black Ink of the Qumran Scrolls," *DSD* 3 (1996): 157–167. For earlier studies, see among others S.H. Steckoll, "Investigations of the Inks Used in Writing the Dead Sea Scrolls," *Nature* 220 (1968): 91–92. Other examinations are mentioned by Nir-El and Broshi. See also the discussion in my *Scribal Practices and Approaches Reflected in the Texts Found in the Judean Desert* (STDJ 54; Leiden: Brill, 2004), 53–55.

[33] See the summary by I. Rabin et al., "Characterization of the Writing Media of the Dead Sea Scrolls," in *Holistic Qumran: Trans-disciplinary Research of Qumran and the Dead Sea Scrolls* (ed. J. Gunneweg, A. Adriaens, and J. Dik; STDJ 87; Leiden: Brill, 2010), 123–134. The techniques used are micro X-ray fluorescence, FT-IR spectroscopy, mass spectrometry, and scanning electron microscopy. See also O. Hahn et al., "Non-destructive Investigation of the Scroll Material: 4QComposition Concerning Divine Providence (4Q413)," *DSD* 15 (2007): 359–364 (described below).

[34] The sources sampled are listed in Nir-El and Broshi, "Black Ink," 157 n. 1. See further Y. Nir-El, "מקורו של הצבען בדיו שחורה בכתיבת ספרים, תפילין ומזוזות," *Sinai* 57 (1993–1994): 261–268 (Hebrew).

[35] On the other hand, according to the editors of 4QpaleoExod^m, the ink used in that manuscript contained iron: P.W. Skehan, E. Ulrich, and J.E. Sanderson in *DJD* IX (1992): 18.

[36] "Technical Note on Unwrapping of Dead Sea Scroll Fragments," in *DJD* I (1955): 39.

[37] M. Haran, "Scribal Workmanship in Biblical Times: The Scrolls and Writing Implements," *Tarbiz* 50 (1980–1981): 65–87 (81–84) (Hebrew with English summary). According to Haran, metal-based ink was used only from the second century C.E. onwards.

[38] I. Rabin et al., "Non-Destructive Methods in the Study of the Dead Sea Scrolls" (paper presented at the Israeli-Italian Bi-national Workshop on Materials, Time, and Stability: Applications in Archaeology and Conservation, Bar-Ilan University, Ramat-Gan, 2007). Thanks are due to the author for showing me the material ahead of its publication.

the Dead Sea than in other localities. Studies like this could help us differentiate between groups of scrolls penned at different locations, even if the locations themselves cannot be named. Other areas of investigation are the ink of corrections in the text as opposed to that of the main text as well as possible distinctions between the scrolls found in the different caves.

(3) Elemental Composition Analysis

A study by Hahn et al. based on the contaminants present in the parchment and ink showed how two fragments cannot have belonged to the same sheet.[39] According to these scholars, "Scroll and ink are organic materials, consisting mainly of carbon, hydrogen, oxygen and nitrogen. In addition to these main elements a variety of contaminants are found. Their kind, type and quantity depend on the details of the preparation process and storage conditions. For example, minerals dissolved in the water used for the preparation of the scroll material and inks are a source of a specific contamination that would normally be distributed evenly throughout the material. On the other hand, the contaminants deposited on a scroll surface, due to its storage, (e.g., on the floor of a cave), would be mainly restricted to the surface areas and more likely to appear as patches." This examination makes use of a micro X-ray fluorescence spectrometer (XRF) as well as a micro-focus confocal XRF. The authors use this approach in an examination of two small fragments published as 4Q413 that belong to the top of the same column of a sheet.[40] They were separated and renamed 4Q413 and 4Q413a by T. Elgvin on the basis of paleography and microscopic parchment analysis.[41] Elgvin's microscopic analysis showed that the surface of 4Q413a "is more scraped than that of 4Q413, so that the hair structure is not visible, while it is clearly seen on 4Q413." The *elemental composition analysis* of the leather and ink executed by Hahn et al. now confirmed these findings, demonstrating that the two fragments could not have belonged to the same sheet.[42] This type of analysis may well be better

---

[39] O. Hahn et al., "Non-Destructive Investigation of the Scroll Material: 4QComposition Concerning Divine Providence (4Q413)," *DSD* 15 (2007): 359–364.

[40] E. Qimron in *DJD* XX (1997): 169–171.

[41] T. Elgvin, "4Q413—A Hymn *and* a Wisdom Instruction," in *Emanuel: Studies in Hebrew Bible, Septuagint, and Dead Sea Scrolls in Honor of Emanuel Tov* (ed. S.M. Paul et al.; VTSup 94; Leiden: Brill, 2003) 205–214.

[42] Hahn et al., "Non-Destructive Investigation."

suited for negative than positive conclusions, but the authors do not say this in their paper. In any event, a similar approach followed by Rabin et al. in the study mentioned in n. 38 provides much promise for positive results. These authors study the composition analysis of the surface and inner layers of the leather, and we wait for more specific results.

Scribes probably prepared their own ink. It is not known whether ink prepared from the same components deposited in different inkwells would produce a different type of chemical signature. On the whole, the identification of scribes or compositions on the basis of the ink used has not even begun.

(4) Stitching Material

Sheets in parchment scrolls were joined with different stitching materials. DNA and C-14 analysis of the stitching materials may aid us in understanding the background of the different scrolls. So far, one such examination has been carried out (see n. 46).

According to rabbinic prescriptions, scroll sheets are to be joined with sinews from the same ritually clean cattle or wild animals from which the scroll itself was prepared.[43] The evidence suggests that most of the stitching material used in the scrolls from Qumran indeed consists of sinews. Further investigation should help us to determine which threads were made of animal sinews and which, contrary to rabbinic ruling, were of flax. In their 1962 research, Poole and Reed claimed that the stitching material examined was of vegetable origin and most probably flax.[44] It is not known, however, which specific scrolls were examined for this purpose. At the same time, more recent examinations have been applied to four specific scrolls.[45] Further research is needed regarding

---

[43] See b. Menaḥ. 31b "only with sinews, but not with thread"; y. Meg. 1.71d "It is also an oral prescription delivered to Moses at Sinai that ⟨scrolls⟩ shall be written on the skins of ritually clean cattle or ritually clean wild animals, and be sewn together with their sinews." This was indeed the case with the stitch material and the sheets of 11QTᵃ (domestic goat), see n. 45 below.

[44] Poole and Reed, "The Preparation of Leather," 22.

[45] The following conclusions have been reached:

1QIsaᵃ: M. Burrows with the assistance of J.C. Trever and W.H. Brownlee, *The Dead Sea Scrolls of St. Mark's Monastery*, vol. 1: *The Isaiah Manuscript and the Habakkuk Commentary* (New Haven: ASOR, 1950), xiv: "linen thread."

4QNumᵇ: N. Jastram in *DJD* XII (1994 [repr. 1999]): 217: flax.

4QcryptA Words of the Maskil (4Q298): S.J. Pfann in *DJD* XX (1997): 2: flax.

the consistency of the use of the stitching material in the same scroll. The animal stitching material may also be used for DNA-examinations.[46]

c. Retrieving Previously Illegible Letters with the Aid of Advanced Photographic Techniques[47]

For their time, the black/white infrared photographs taken by Najib Anton Albina, the photographer at the Palestine Archeological Museum (PAM) in the 1950s and 1960s, were extraordinarily good.[48] Other early photographs were equally good: the infrared black/white photographs by the Biberkrauts of the scrolls purchased by the State of Israel, and those of 1QIsaᵃ, 1QS, and 1QpHab by John Trever.[49] The three series of PAM photographs, more than the fragments themselves, formed the basis for the study and publication of the scrolls in *DJD*. Often, the photographs reveal more details than the fragments themselves, although the fragments need always to be consulted because only they reveal the distinctions between ink and shadow.

4QApocryphal Pentateuch A (4Q368): J. VanderKam and M. Brady in *DJD* XXVIII (2001): 131: flax.

[46] In the meantime, see A. Gorski, "Analysis of Microscopic Material and the Stitching of the Dead Sea Scrolls: A Preliminary Study" (abstract of paper presented at the Symposium on the Role of Analytical Methods in the Study, Restoration, and Conservation of Ancient Manuscripts, with Emphasis on the Dead Sea Scrolls, Prague, 14 April 1999; online: http://orion.mscc.huji.ac.il/orion/programs/taskforce.shtml). This paper refers to the stitching of 1QpHab and 1QIsaᵃ (no conclusions). See also by the same author "Analysis of Microscopic Material and the Stitching of the Dead Sea Scrolls: A Preliminary Study," in *Historical Perspectives*, 173–178. Bar-Gal, "Genetic Change," 72 and Table 3.6 mentions the sampling of stitch material of the 11QTᵃ (domestic goat).

[47] For good summaries of all aspects relating to the imaging of the scrolls, see G. Bearman, S.J. Pfann, and S.A.I. Spiro, "Imaging the Scrolls: Photographic and Direct Digital Acquisition," in *The Dead Sea Scrolls after Fifty Years*, 1:472–495; B. and K. Zuckerman, "Photography and Computer Imaging," *Encyclopedia of the Dead Sea Scrolls* (ed. L.H. Schiffman and J.C. VanderKam; 2 vols.; Oxford: Oxford University Press, 2000) 2:669–675.

[48] See F.M. Cross, "On the History of the Photography," and J. Strugnell, "On the History of the Photographing of the Discoveries in the Judean Desert for the International Group of Editors," in Tov, *Companion Volume*, 121–122 and 123–134.

[49] Additional early photographs by David Shinhav, Ruth Yekutiel, Tsila Sagiv, and Robert Schlosser are described by J.C. VanderKam and P.W. Flint, *The Meaning of the Dead Sea Scrolls: Their Significance for Understanding the Bible, Judaism, Jesus, and Christianity* (San Francisco: HarperSanFrancisco, 2002), 69–70.

In later years, with the advancement of technology, better photographs were taken, revealing additional parts of letters, complete letters, and in rare cases complete words.[50] The following innovative techniques were used.

1. Use of filters in infrared photography (B. and K. Zuckerman).

2. High density digitization. This technique was applied to the *Genesis Apocryphon* in 1993 by Bearman and the Zuckermans using a "new tunable filter that could be set to any wavelength in the IR ⟨the infrared spectrum⟩ with a very narrow bandpass."[51] A second imaging expedition was launched by these scholars in 1997, producing new digital infrared images of approximately 900 fragments (not scrolls).[52] Some of these photographs revealed additional letters in darkened areas.[53] Additional letters were revealed on the leather in separate projects by Bearman[54] and Zuckerman.[55] Likewise, Johnston also revealed additional letters,

---

[50] The collection as a whole has not been re-photographed although in 2008 plans were underway for such an enterprise.

[51] Bearman, Pfann, and Spiro, "Imaging," 488.

[52] Ibid.

[53] See the photograph of 4QCant[b] by G. Bearman and S. Spiro on behalf of the Ancient Biblical Manuscript Center as presented by E. Tov in *DJD* XVI (2000): 209 and pl. XXV.

[54] G.H. Bearman and S.I. Spiro, "Imaging: Clarifying the Issues," *DSD* 3 (1996): 321–328; idem, "Archaeological Applications of Advanced Imaging Techniques. Reading Ancient Documents," *BA* 59 (1996): 56–66; idem, "Imaging Clarified," in *The Provo International Conference on the Dead Sea Scrolls: Technological Innovations, New Texts, and Reformulated Issues* (ed. D.W. Parry and E. Ulrich; STDJ 30; Leiden: Brill, 1999), 5–12; D.M. Cabries, S.W. Booras, and G.H. Bearman, "Imaging the Past: Recent Applications of Multispectral Imaging Technology to Deciphering Manuscripts," *Antiquity: A Quarterly Review of Archaeology* 77 (2003): 359–372.

[55] B. Zuckerman in collaboration with S.A. Reed, "A Fragment of an Unstudied Column of 11QtgJob," *The Comprehensive Aramaic Lexicon Newsletter* 10 (1993): 1–7 (online: http://cal1.cn.huc.edu/newsletter/Zuckreed.html); M.J. Lundberg and B. Zuckerman, "When Images Meet: The Potential of Photographic and Computer Imaging Technology for the Study of the Copper Scroll," in *Copper Scroll Studies* (ed. G.J. Brooke and P.R. Davies; JSPSup 40; London: Sheffield Academic Press, 2002), 45–55; B. Zuckerman, "Bringing the Dead Sea Scrolls Back to Life: A New Evaluation of Photographic and Electronic Imaging of the Dead Sea Scrolls," *DSD* 3 (1996): 178–207. Lists of new readings revealed by Zuckerman's techniques are included in "The Targums of Job (4QtgJob and 11QtgJob)," in *The Dead Sea Scrolls: Hebrew, Aramaic, and Greek Texts with English Translation* (ed. J. Charlesworth; The Princeton Theological Seminary Dead Sea Scrolls Project; Tübingen: Mohr Siebeck, forthcoming).

especially in 11QT^a.[56] Puech was able to improve the reading of the *Copper Scroll* with the aid of radiographs and photographs of the flattened replica of the scroll.[57]

3. Lange's method of Computer Aided Text-Reconstruction and Transcription (CATT)[58] offers a new software option for the reconstruction of fragments based on digitized images of scrolls.[59] The author suggests that each scholar digitizes his or her own images of the scrolls, and he guides the reader in the use of software programs that can be used in order to improve the readability of these images.[60] The author also shows how to scan individual letters and combine them into units that can be electronically placed in *lacunae*, thus examining the correctness of reconstructions.

d. *Identifying Fragments and Determining the Relation between Fragments*

(1) *Computer-Assisted Identifications*

To the best of my knowledge, little use has been made of computer-assisted research in the identification of small fragments. Parry identified a number of minute fragments of 4QSam^a with the help of the Word-

---

[56] J.H. Charlesworth, "The Dead Sea Scrolls and Scientific Methodologies," in *Optics and Imaging in the Information Age* (IS&T: The Society for Imaging Science and Technology, 1997), 266–274; K. Knox, R. Johnston, and R.L. Easton, "Imaging the Dead Sea Scrolls," *Optics and Photonics News* 8 (1997): 30.

[57] É. Puech, "Some Results of the Restoration of the Copper Scroll by EDF Mécénat," in *The Dead Sea Scrolls Fifty Years After Their Discovery: Proceedings of the Jerusalem Congress, July 20–25, 1997* (ed. L.H. Schiffman et al.; Jerusalem: Israel Exploration Society, 2000), 889–894; D. Brizemeure, N. Lacoudre, and É. Puech, *Le Rouleau de cuivre de la grotte 3 de Qumrân: Expertise, Restauration, Epigraphie* (2 vols.; STDJ 55; Leiden: Brill, 2006).

[58] A. Lange, *Computer-Aided Text-Reconstruction and Transcription—CATT Manual* (Tübingen: Mohr Siebeck, 1993). For a review, see G. Bearman in *DSD* 1 (1994): 373–375.

[59] Lange describes his own technique as follows (p. 3): "... uses image editing software in dealing with the several different types of damage done to manuscripts and inscriptions. Image editing programs try to transfer the photographic darkroom into the desktop computer."

[60] When this book was written, digitized images were not yet available in commercial databases such as *The Dead Sea Scrolls Electronic Library* (rev. ed.; Brigham Young University, 2006), part of the *Dead Sea Scrolls Electronic Reference Library* of Brill Publishers (ed. E. Tov; Leiden: Brill, 2006).

cruncher program.[61] Pike and Skinner recognized many of the hitherto
unidentified fragments with the aid of the same program.[62] Tigchelaar
identified many fragments with the aid of the Accordance program.[63]
Undoubtedly, the use of Accordance or Wordcruncher could produce
many additional identifications. Optical Character Recognition (OCR)
could have been employed for the analysis of script or the identification
of partially preserved letters, but to the best of my knowledge, this technique has not been used.[64]

(2) Research of Hair Follicles in Leather and Fibers in Papyri

The analysis of hair follicles and papyrus fibers could indicate that two
or more scroll fragments derived from either the same or a different
sheet. Barns provided the first description of the procedure followed for
papyrus fragments,[65] described in greater detail by Pfann.[66] Pfann likewise briefly described the procedure followed for the study of hair follicles in leather.[67] In both cases, much more detailed research is needed.

---

[61] See F.M. Cross, D.W. Parry, and R.J. Saley in *DJD* XVII (2005): 3.

[62] D. Pike and A. Skinner, in consultation with J. VanderKam and M. Brady, *Qumran
Cave 4.XXIII: Unidentified Fragments* (DJD XXXIII; Oxford: Clarendon, 2001).

[63] E.J.C. Tigchelaar, "4Q499 48 + 47 (par 4Q369 1 ii): A Forgotten Identification," *RevQ*
18 (1997): 303–306; idem, "Minuscula Qumranica I," *RevQ* 21 (2004): 643–648; idem,
"On the Unidentified Fragments of *DJD* XXXIII and PAM 43.680: A New Manuscript of
4QNarrative and Poetic Composition, and Fragments of 4Q13, 4Q269, 4Q525 and 4QSb
(?)," *RevQ* 21 (2004): 477–485; idem, "A Cave 4 Fragment of *Divre Mosheh* (4QDM) and
the Text of 1Q22 I:7–10 and Jubilees 1:9, 14," *DSD* 12 (2005): 303–312.

[64] One could teach the computer the various shapes of the letters of each scroll, so that
the program would suggest readings for partially preserved letters.

[65] J.W.B. Barns, "Note on Papyrus Fibre Pattern," in *DJD* VI (1977): 29.

[66] S.J. Pfann in *DJD* XXXVI (2000): 517–523.

[67] S.J. Pfann, "Hair Follicle Analysis of Primitive Parchments: An Essential Tool for
the Reconstruction of Fragmentary Dead Sea Scrolls" (abstract of paper presented at the
Symposium on the Role of Analytical Methods in the Study, Restoration, and Conservation of Ancient Manuscripts, with Emphasis on the Dead Sea Scrolls, Prague, 14 April
1999; online: http://orion.mscc.huji.ac.il/orion/programs/taskforce.shtml]): "The pattern,
form, size and density of hair follicles which occur over the hides of various animals do
so with a fair degree of consistency. Those hides which preserve their epidermis and are
used in the preparation of scrolls maintain these hair follicle patterns. These same follicle
patterns preserved on the surfaces of disjointed fragments of the Dead Sea Scrolls has
proven to contain important clues aiding in their reconstruction (and thus their meaning and interpretation). This form of analysis was developed by the author while working
with the edition of the various Dead Sea Scrolls assigned to him for publication over the
past decade. With the aid of the binocular microscope many proposed links between disjointed fragments have been either confirmed of disproved based on this work."

The research of leather and papyrus sheets is promising, but at this stage it is unclear whether the various parameters identified in the fragments are distinctive enough in order to identify and differentiate between individual sheets. Research needs to proceed from the features of known sheets of complete scrolls to fragmentary texts, and such studies have not yet been written.

In the case of papyrus fragments, examining each papyrus strip involves the color, thickness, density, variability, and angle of the intersection between the horizontal and vertical strips of papyrus.

Research carried out so far by Pfann, focusing on fragmentary texts, shows the possibilities this research has in store. Pfann analyzed the papyrus texts in the cryptic script 4Qpap cryptA Midrash Sefer Moshe (4Q249)[68] and 4Q249a–z and 4Q250a–j,[69] focusing on the special features of each papyrus fragment. In the case of leather fragments, Pfann likewise analyzed the special hair follicle features of each individual fragment of 4QCryptA Words of the Maskil to All Sons of Dawn (4Q298).[70] This analysis enabled him to support the reconstruction of fragments belonging to the same sheet. The hair structure of 4Q413 and 4Q413a was found to be different by Elgvin (see n. 41 above).

Each single feature of the papyrus or leather, and definitely the combined features may give guidance regarding the placement of fragments in a particular sheet. However, this type of research is rather limited. Pfann examined the fragments that had been identified at an earlier stage as belonging to specific scrolls. Within those parameters, he separated the papyrus fragments into many different compositions based on the criteria mentioned above. This research enabled him to surmise that specific fragments belonged to the same sheet of papyrus, but no more than that. In the case of leather, the fragments could be placed anywhere in the sheet, either in the same column or one or two columns apart. In the case of papyrus, the guidance of the horizontal and vertical strips may aid in a more specific location alongside the horizontal or vertical strips, but further research on the known complete papyri has to consolidate the criteria used. Probably the strongest merit of this and any similar procedure is the ability to disprove that two fragments belonged to the same leather or papyrus sheet.

---

[68] S.J. Pfann in *DJD* XXXV (1999): 1–24.
[69] S.J. Pfann in *DJD* XXXVI (2000): 515–701.
[70] S.J. Pfann and M. Kister, "4Q298: The Maskil's Address to All Sons of Dawn," *JQR* 85 (1994): 203–235; idem in *DJD* XX (1997): 1–30.

(3) *The Stegemann System of Reconstructing*

The so-called "Stegemann system of reconstructing fragmentary scrolls"[71] belongs here only partially since it is based not on the sciences but on logical inference of destruction patterns of the leather or papyrus. Among other things, on the basis of the supposed measurements of the scroll and the increase in size between revolutions of the scroll starting with its innermost end, this system tries to establish the distance between the fragments (columns) based on identical destruction patterns, if any, repeated in each revolution of the scroll.

2. Some Technical Data about the Scrolls

When integrating data from the sciences into the reconstruction of the scrolls, we have to take into consideration the data known about them. Otherwise, we are in danger of applying the wrong types of conclusions. The following parameters relate to this reconstruction.[72]

1. The first stage in the preparation of parchment was the slaughtering of an animal and the preparation of its hide for the production of the scroll material. Even the leftovers were used for writing: contrary to practice in later centuries, most of the *tefillin* found at Qumran were written on irregularly shaped pieces that were leftovers from the preparation of large skins. Upon preparation, most skins were inscribed on

---

[71] H. Stegemann, "Methods for the Reconstruction of Scrolls from Scattered Fragments," in *Archaeology and History in the Dead Sea Scrolls: The New York Conference in Memory of Yigael Yadin* (ed. L.H. Schiffman; JSPSup 8; JSOT/ASOR Monograph Series 2; Sheffield: JSOT Press, 1990), 189–220; A. Steudel, "Assembling and Reconstructing Manuscripts," in *The Dead Sea Scrolls after Fifty Years*, 1:516–534; E. Chazon, "The Qumran Community, The Dead Sea Scrolls and The Physical Method of Scrolls' Reconstruction" (abstract of paper presented at the Symposium on the Role of Analytical Methods in the Study, Restoration, and Conservation of Ancient Manuscripts, with Emphasis on the Dead Sea Scrolls, Prague, 14 April 1999; online: http://orion.mscc.huji.ac.il/orion/programs/taskforce.shtml). See also D. Stoll, "Die Schriftrollen vom Toten Meer—mathematisch oder Wie kann man einer Rekonstruktion Gestalt verleihen?" in *Qumranstudien: Vorträge und Beiträge der Teilnehmer des Qumranseminars auf dem internationalen Treffen der Society of Biblical Literature, Münster, 25.–26. Juli 1993* (ed. H.-J. Fabry, A. Lange, and H. Lichtenberger; Göttingen: Vandenhoeck & Ruprecht, 1996), 205–217.

[72] For a detailed description of each issue, see my *Scribal Practices*.

the (hairy) outside layer, while 11QT[a] was inscribed on the inside of the skin (the flesh side).[73]

2. The *length* of the composition was calculated approximately before commencing the writing, so that the required number of sheets could be ordered from a manufacturer or could be prepared to fit the size of the composition. Subsequently, the individual sheets were ruled and inscribed and only afterwards stitched together. The fact that some ruled sheets were used as uninscribed handle sheets (e.g. the last sheets of 11QT[a] and 11QShirShabb) and that some uninscribed top margins were ruled (the second sheet of 1QpHab) shows that the ruling was sometimes executed without relation to the writing of a specific scroll. The numbering of a few sheets preserved in the Judean Desert probably indicates that some or most sheets were inscribed separately, and joined subsequently according to the sequence of these numbers (however, the great majority of the sheets were not numbered).

3. The first step in the preparation of scrolls for writing was the *ruling* (scoring), which facilitated the execution of the inscription in straight lines. The scroll was written by hanging the letters from the lines. This ruling provided graphical guidance for the writing, horizontal ruling for the lines, and vertical ruling for the beginning and/or end of the columns. In very few cases, the ruling was indicated by diluted ink.

4. Almost all Qumran and Masada texts written on leather in the square script had ruled horizontal lines in accordance with the practice for most literary texts written on parchment in Semitic languages and in Greek. On the other hand, texts written on papyrus were not ruled. The horizontal and vertical fibers of the papyrus probably provided some form of guidance for the writing.

5. The ruling was sometimes applied with the aid of guide dots/strokes, or with a grid-like device, while in other instances no device was used. These guide dots ("points jalons"), or sometimes strokes, were drawn in order to guide the drawing of dry lines. The ruling might have been executed by the scribes, but it is more likely that it was applied by the scroll manufacturers without reference to the text to be inscribed, as

---

[73] For parallels in rabbinic literature, see *y. Meg.* 1.71d: "One writes on the hairy side of the skin" (cf. *Massekhet Sefer Torah* 1.4).

indicated by several discrepancies between the inscribed text and the ruled lines, such as a larger number of ruled lines than inscribed text (see 4QDeut[n]).

6. The preparation of the material for writing included not just the ruling, but also the preparation of the surface for writing in columns. The number of columns per sheet and their sizes differed from scroll to scroll, sometimes from sheet to sheet, and they depended much on the size of the sheets and the scroll.

7. The size of the scroll depended on the dimensions of the sheets. At Qumran, the length of most leather sheets varied between 21 and 90 cm, usually 30–40 cm.[74] The natural limitations of the sizes of animal hides determined the different lengths of these sheets, which varied more in some scrolls than in others.

8. The sizes of the hides derived from the different animals differ, but the animals that have been identified (calf, sheep, ibex, goat) would not yield more than one hide of 90 × 60 cm or two or three short ones. In some cases, more than one composition could be written on the material provided by a single animal, while in other cases several animals would be needed for a long composition, such as 11QT[a] and the large Isaiah scroll.

9. There is a positive correlation between the length and width of columns: as a rule the higher the column, the wider the lines, and the longer the scroll.

10. The sizes of the columns differ in accordance with the number of columns per sheet, the scope of the sheets, and the conventions developed by the scroll manufacturers. The different parameters of the columns pertain to their width and length as well as to the top, bottom, and intercolumnar margins. In some Qumran scrolls, the height and width of the columns are fairly consistent, while in most scrolls these parameters varied from sheet to sheet as well as within each sheet, in accordance with the measurements of the sheets. The average number of lines per

---

[74] For example, 1QIsa[a] consists of seventeen sheets (ten sheets measuring 35–47.7 cm, five 48.7–62.8 cm, and two 25.2–26.9 cm). 11QT[a] is composed of nineteen sheets (eight measuring 37–43 cm, ten 47–61 cm, and the final sheet measuring 20 cm). For additional details, see my *Scribal Practices*, 79–81.

column in Qumran scrolls is probably 20, with a height of approximately
14–15 cm (including the top and bottom margins). Larger scrolls contained columns with between 25 and as many as 60 lines. Scrolls of the
smallest dimensions contained merely 5–13 lines and their height was
similarly small. Among the scrolls with a large writing block, one finds
many texts from Qumran, as well as *all* the scrolls from Masada, Naḥal
Ḥever, Sdeir, and Murabbaʿat that can be measured. The same compositions were often written on scrolls of differing sizes, although in some
cases a degree of regularity is visible.

11. All biblical texts were inscribed on one side only, while several
nonbiblical texts were inscribed on both sides (opisthographs).

12. With one possible exception, all compositions were written on separate scrolls. Some biblical scrolls contain more than one book (the Torah,
Minor Prophets).

13. Some, mainly long, manuscripts were written by more than one
scribe.

3. Aid from the Sciences for the Reconstruction of Ancient Scrolls: Possibilities and Impossibilities

In previous examinations, the reconstruction of the missing parts of the
ancient scrolls was based mainly on content. In the case of biblical scrolls
or other known compositions, content is our main guide, but even in
these compositions small fragments with partial or frequently occurring
words cannot be identified easily. In other cases, with fragmentary contents and the fertile minds of scholars, there are many possibilities and
therefore it would be good to be aided by additional methods. Such aid
may come from an exact or almost exact physical join, but such joins are
rare. Some fragments of similar shape reflect subsequent layers or revolutions of a scroll (see n. 71), but such cases are also rare. In many cases,
we would like to look to the sciences for help. Our main interest would
be in proving or disproving a link already made between two fragments
or in searching for a scroll to which a given fragment may have belonged.
In such cases, we would like to resort to the sciences for objective criteria. The sciences have been invoked often, with high expectations, so it is
time to be a little realistic.

It would not be feasible to send all the fragments to C-14 analysis only in order to know if their C-14 dates match. Ink analysis, if advanced sufficiently, would be easier and may be very relevant. In my view, the so-called elemental composition analysis sounds promising, and it is non-destructive, but we wait for the verdict of scientists. DNA will provide some answers, as will the follicle research on leather, and fiber research on papyri. It should be remembered that the maximum results we would receive refer to the identity of the complete sheet(s) from which the fragments derived, and not to the placing of individual fragments. These sheets were 21 to 90 cm long at Qumran, mostly 30–40 cm, and the placing of a fragment in such a large space would leave many options open. Most animals would not yield more than one hide of 90 × 60 cm.

On the other hand, in the descriptions of the DNA method, especially that of Woodward,[75] the expectations for DNA analysis have been very high. This scholar, who together with Kahila Bar-Gal was able to derive aDNA from ancient objects, was not sufficiently aware of the limitations of DNA in the case of the scrolls. In a programmatic paper published in 1998, he lists five questions for which DNA was supposed to provide answers.

1. "How many different manuscripts are represented in the collection of fragments at the Rockefeller and Israel Museums? … Obtaining DNA signatures unique to each manuscript will make it possible to sort out the physical relationships of scroll fragments." At most, however, we would be able to list the individual animals, from whose skins the hides were derived. When naming these animals "animal 1," "animal 2," etc., we would have an important summary list, but that list would provide only a few clues for researchers. Thus, if two different compositions were written on the hide of animal 1, DNA alone would not suffice to distinguish between them. Further, multi-sheet compositions required more than one animal, sometimes ten or more, so that DNA signatures alone would not be able to distinguish between Qumran manuscripts.

2. "Which pieces can be grouped together as originating from the same scroll because they are from identical or related manuscripts? … This should assist both in the reconstruction of manuscripts and in the

---

[75] Woodward, "New Technological Advances."

verification of assemblies that were previously already made." It seems to me that all these are idle hopes as explained in my reply to item 1.

3. "Did more than one scribe work on a single document, or did different scribes use parchment that originated from the same source for different manuscripts?" In my view, neither question can be answered with DNA.

4. "Is the parchment for the patch from the same herd as the original manuscript? Does the patch represent a herd from a different region, reflecting mobility of either the original scroll or the herd?" These suggestions are helpful,[76] but impractical. Most importantly, the number of patches in the scrolls can be counted on one hand.

5. "Does the collection represent a library from a single locality, or is it a collection representing contributions from a wide region?" In general it is true that DNA analysis will help us to know more about the provenance of the hides, if only the connections between hides and bones can be made.

The expectations expressed in the Introduction to the Qumran scrolls by VanderKam and Flint, which run parallel to those of Woodward, are equally as utopian.[77]

4. Conclusions

Summarizing the various types of expectations for scroll research, we note that they may help us with regard to some issues.

  a. C-14 examinations should be continued as a useful tool for dating in spite of the uncertainty regarding the contamination of castor oil.
  b. If performed on a large scale, C-14 examinations could also help us understand the relationship between many individual fragments. For example, two or more fragments assigned to the same column or sheet should not have different C-14 dates.

---

[76] The patch in 4Q22 and its main text were dated to different periods with C-14 analysis, see Jull et al., "Radiocarbon Dating," 86.

[77] VanderKam and Flint, *The Meaning of the Dead Sea Scrolls*, 55–84 (57–58). 1. "Assembling scrolls in the Rockefeller and Israel Museums." 2. "Making new reconstructions and assembling earlier ones." 3. "Parchment used for patches." 4. "Scrolls made from more than one animal." 5. "The species of animals used for production." 6. "Assembling the scope of the collection." "Does the collection found at Qumran represent a library from one location or from a wider region?"

c. Ink research, research of leather follicles and papyrus fibers, and elemental composition analysis such as the chlorium/bromium ratio should be encouraged as non-destructive examinations that may help us understand the relation between individual fragments. The merits of these examinations should be reviewed by scientists, since we humanists lack the means to review the methods used.

d. The infrared color photographing of all the fragments with new techniques should be encouraged.

At the same time, expectations from these techniques should be realistic, taking into consideration the realia of scroll production such as described above, in particular the fact that the sheet and not the fragment is the unit of reference.

In an ideal world, we would have access to a database providing information of all the types described above about all the scroll fragments. Undoubtedly, this information would help us to solve some questions that face researchers. For example, by examining the technical data about the scrolls, we may be able to create clusters[78] of scrolls of a certain nature, such as Qumran scrolls as opposed to non-Qumran scrolls (based on elemental composition analysis). We may be able to find that scrolls written on a specific type of leather (DNA analysis) or with a specific type of ink have something in common, or that the Hebrew scrolls somehow differ from those written in Aramaic.

In the analysis of individual fragments, this database would help especially in negative aspects, namely the suggestion that two fragments that were joined in the past should not be ascribed to the same manuscript, as in the case of 4Q413 and 4Q413a discussed above.

In an ideal world we should have access to a database like this, but we are also realistic enough to realize that the keepers of the scrolls would have to agree to all these procedures, some of which are destructive. We keep our fingers crossed.

---

[78] The idea was expressed already by K. Bar-Gal, "Genetic Change," 76: "These findings show the ability of the aDNA method to contribute in matching and grouping together scroll fragments. These results also stress the possibility to solve the problem of the 10,000 unmatched fragments using genetic analysis."

CREATING NEW CONTEXTS:
ON THE POSSIBILITIES OF
BIBLICAL STUDIES IN CONTEXTS
GENERATED BY THE DEAD SEA SCROLLS

JAMES ALFRED LOADER
University of Vienna

A. INTRODUCTION

The overall theme of this volume, "The Dead Sea Scrolls in Context: Integrating the Dead Sea Scrolls in the Study of Ancient Texts, Languages and Cultures," with its title and subtitle, assumes at least two levels of meaning when referring to "context." First, we can obviously understand the main title by itself to mean that the Dead Sea Scrolls can and should be seen in their own historical context, that is, in the context of the time in which they were written, the community within which they originated and the religious framework which gave rise to them. Nothing can fault this time-honoured and established aspect of context, since the achievement of sixty years of scholarship has demonstrated it impressively. But the subtitle of the conference significantly extends the scope of the "context" notion to the situation in which we who study them find ourselves. Studying the various aspects of the Scrolls in our scholarly context means that we and our disciplines now become involved with them. I would like to develop this notion to show that the Scrolls not only "have" their ancient contexts, but that they become part of "our" context and at the same time provide us with a new context by drawing us into theirs. This reciprocity between the Scrolls and the contexts in which they become involved, entails that they *create* new contexts for biblical Studies. By the same token, they demand creativity from all who wish to come to terms with them. This demand can be addressed by means of the concept of intertextuality.

I therefore propose to devote this paper to the perspective invoked by the conference subtitle. I shall focus on contexts generated by the literary character of the Dead Sea Scrolls as a text group of translucent intertextual disposition. In my view this applies in both the so-called "narrow" and "broad" senses of the concept of intertextuality.

The "narrow" concept of intertextuality can even be called a dominant feature of Qumran studies, whether the word itself is used or not. The well-known phenomenon that texts themselves influence other texts is usually understood in a *direct* sense, that is, when a text is influenced by another or several others as it is created. But the biblical texts and the texts from the Dead Sea area also influence each other *indirectly*. As with all texts, this happens to the texts of interest to us through the reading subject who receives both sets of texts. When read, all texts are intertextual in this sense because they border on one another in the consciousness of the reader. The reader has a literary competence, a frame of reference that cannot be disabled or otherwise ignored. Any biblical scholar who reads the Dead Sea Scrolls has no choice but to read them in the context of the Bible. And any Qumran scholar reading the Bible must read it in the context of the Dead Sea Scrolls. In both cases texts echo other texts and are echoed in other texts. How seriously biblical influence on the Dead Sea Scrolls has been taken since their discovery is patently obvious in the self-evident orientation of scholarship towards the direction of the impact "Bible → Scrolls." But the other side of the coin should be taken equally seriously—intertextuality is not merely a matter of one-way influence. It should also be taken into consideration that the Bible is likewise influenced by these texts. The "inter" in intertextuality is a reciprocal relationship because the biblical text, its reading and the way it is understood are bordered by the Dead Sea Scrolls.

B. INTERTEXTUALITY

In order to clarify the concepts and terminology that I employ in this paper, let us briefly consider the fundamental ways in which the nouns "intertext" and "intertextuality" and the adjective "intertextual" are used in contemporary literary criticism.

The first to be mentioned is the radical and highly provocative meaning of the concept, in order to make clear what I shall not pursue further in this paper: The concept, which was coined together with the terminology by Julia Kristeva, is that "every text is made up as a mosaic of citations, every text is the absorption and transformation of another text."[1]

---

[1] J. Kristeva, *Semeiotikè: Recherches pour une Sémanalyse* (Paris: Seuil, 1969), 146.

The radical nature of this sweeping understanding has sometimes been heightened (e.g. by Harold Bloom[2]) and sometimes curbed (e.g. by Ulrich Broich[3]). Although the effect of texts as perpetual echoes, the meaning of which is continually deferred, is in itself an intriguing topic, it will not be pursued further in this paper. To be sure, there is some resemblance to my own metaphor of texts bordering on each other, but for the purposes of elucidating the contribution of the concept of intertextuality to our theme of the Dead Sea Scrolls in Context, I shall not here come back to it.

Second, an outline of the concept as it will be used here: Where a text can be demonstrated to refer or relate to another text or group of texts[4] or to a genre,[5] it can be said to have a direct intertextual relationship to that text or text type. This is usually called "influence," but the reciprocal relationship referred to above should also be borne in mind. This model entails the presence of a *pre-text* from which the influence stems, and a *post-text* that is influenced. There are different degrees of intertextual intensity ("Dichte" in German jargon), and—as intimated above—in the case of the Dead Sea Scrolls this is very high.

What interests us now is the various types of this kind of intertextuality, since they are not only all found in the Dead Sea Scrolls, but the intensity of their presence is such that they often defy endeavours to classify and pigeonhole them in terms of the usual literary categories. Apart from the Dead Sea biblical manuscripts themselves, the scrolls contain many writings that must be called both innovative in terms of their inventive ideas *and* epigonic in terms of their intertextual dependence on other texts, especially the Hebrew Bible. The usual types identified for this kind of intertextuality are hypertextual (imitative), metatextual (commenting), or palintextual (repetitive) relationships.

---

[2] H. Bloom, *Poetry and Repression: Revisionism from Blake to Stevens* (New Haven: Yale University Press, 1976), 3.

[3] U. Broich, "Intertextuality," in *International Postmodernism: Theory and Practice* (ed. H. Bertens and D. Fokkema; A Comparative History of Literatures in European Languages 11; Amsterdam: Benjamins, 1997), 249–256.

[4] U. Broich, "Intertextualität," *Reallexikon der deutschen Literaturwissenschaft* (ed. H. Fricke et al.; 3 vols.; Berlin: de Gruyter, 2007), 2:175–179, 176.

[5] M. Pfister, "Konzepte der Intertextualität," in *Intertextualität: Formen, Funktionen, anglistische Fallstudien* (ed. U. Broich and M. Pfister; Konzepte der Sprach- und Literaturwissenschaft 35; Tübingen: Niemeyer, 1985), 1–30; idem, "Zur Systemreferenz," in *Intertextualität* (ed. Broich and Pfister), 52–58.

In the light of these considerations I would now like to submit the threefold thesis to be argued on the basis of representative texts:

a. The Dead Sea Scrolls provide highly fruitful terrain for the literary study of intertextuality,
b. while at the same time resisting attempts at the application of clear-cut intertextual categories in literary criticism.
c. Their intertextuality enables us to develop the integration of this research into the broader study of texts and cultures in several directions.

C. Types of Intertextuality in the Dead Sea Scrolls

We shall now consider cases of hypertexts, metatexts and palintexts in the Dead Sea Scrolls.[6]

1. *Hypertexts*

The term "hypertext," as first introduced by Gerard Genette and now coined to refer the non-linear association of texts by electronic means,[7] can also be applied generally to denote an intertextuality where interrelationships exist between texts on a par with each other. It does appear, however, at least in biblical studies, that a linear relationship between the texts involved is difficult to avoid. Thus, in the often applied definition of Stocker,[8] a hypertext is a text that imitates another. It is therefore a transformation of the pre-text without explicit comment. Accordingly, the imitated text is the pre-text, whereas the intertextuality of the hypertext consists of its being modelled on the pre-text. It is perhaps more neutral to speak of the "modelling" of texts on others than of imitation, since

---

[6] I use the terminology as developed by P. Stocker, *Theorie der intertextuellen Lektüre: Modelle und Fallstudien* (Paderborn: Schöningh, 1998) and applied in biblical studies (e.g. O. Wischmeyer, *Hermeneutik des Neuen Testaments* [Tübingen: Francke, 2004]), which had been influenced by the proposals of Gerard Genette dating from 1982. Genette did influence German theories in the early nineties, but the concepts and terminology have not remained static, certainly not in biblical studies (cf. G. Genette, *Palimpseste: Die Literatur auf zweiter Stufe* [Frankfurt am Main: Suhrkamp, 1993], 13–16 on meta- and hypertextuality and the use of the concepts involved in the following paragraphs).

[7] Cf. R.S. Kamzelak, "Hypertext," *Reallexikon der deutschen Literaturwissenschaft* (ed. Fricke et al.) 2:110–112.

[8] Stocker, *Theorie*, 60; cf. Wischmeyer, *Hermeneutik*, 189.

the latter term suggests pedantry or a derogatory value judgement, which does not necessarily have to apply at all, especially where the pre-text is a group or type of texts.[9] Moreover, the important aspect of this kind of relationship is that *the very existence of a pre- and a hypertext involves a reciprocal relationship from the vantage point of the reader.* The post-text presents the pre-text in a new light and therefore both augments it and accepts the pretext—somewhat with the same logic as the claim of Jesus to accept and confirm the Torah by presenting it in a new light. There are many clear cases of hypertextuality in this sense to be found in the Dead Sea Scrolls, which can be illustrated by some representative cases.

1.1.

An obvious instance would be the *Hodayot*, or the *Thanksgiving Hymns* in 1QH[a]. Leaving aside both the question of who the first person singular speaker was and the question of their liturgical or private use, the literary status of their intertextuality by itself is interesting enough. Consider the Fourth Hodayah at 1QH[a] II:31–39, which I use as a representative case:

> I thank you, O Lord,
>   for your eye s[tood watching] over my soul
>   and you rescued me from the jealousy of liars.
> From the congregation of those who seek the smooth way
>   you saved the soul of the poor they planned to destroy
>   by spilling his blood because of his service to you.
>
> Only, they did not know that my steps come from you,
>   and they made me to scorn and ridicule
>   the mouth of those who seek deception.
>
> But you, my God, helped the soul of the poor and the weak
>   from the hand of those who were stronger that him.
> You redeemed my soul from the hand of the powerful
>   and by their taunts you did not let me lose heart
>   so as to give up your service through fear of the wicked ...[10]

This is clearly modelled on the individual thanksgiving hymns of the biblical Psalter. Apart from linguistic affinities, several typical features are well represented in these biblical psalms:

---

[9] Cf. Pfister, "Zur Systemreferenz," 52–58.

[10] Own translation. The last half of line 36 and the following fragmented lines until the end of the column are left untranslated.

- An opening with a declaration of thanks addressed to God,
- the use of [א]כי as link to a series of statements on God's intervention,
- the extended reference to a crisis,
- the character of God's intervention as help and salvation,
- the presentation of God's help as substantiation for the praise,
- the identification of the speaker's enemies with the wicked,
- the self-identification of the speaker as the servant of God,
- the characterisation of the enemies as strong and
- the speaker as weak and poor (אביון),
- the motifs of spilling the speaker's blood and
- of derision and ridicule for the pious,
- the association of thanksgiving and lamenting motifs,
- the use of parallelism and stichs (although written continuously).

If we now compare this to typical individual thanksgiving songs in the biblical Psalter, we find practically all of them in this genre. For practical reasons I use Ps 9 as a basis for presenting the picture:

Hodayah 4	Psalm 9
Similarities	*Similarities*
Opening with ידה	Opening with ידה (v. 2)
Substantiation linked by כיא	Substantiation linked by כי (v. 5)
Extended reference to a crisis (passim)	Extended reference to a crisis (passim)
Detailed account of God's intervention (passim)	Detailed account of God's intervention (passim)
Polarisation with enemies (plural) (passim)	Polarisation with enemies (plural) (passim)
Enemies called רשע	Enemies called רשע (vv. 6, 17)
Enemies aggressive and strong	Enemies aggressive, should not become stronger (v. 20)
Speaker weak (רש, עני)	Speaker weak (אביון) (vv. 17, 18, 19)
Saved from "spilling of blood"	Saved from the "gates of death" (v. 14)
Piety expressly mentioned (עבודה)	Piety expressly mentioned (דרש, בטח) (v. 11)
Individual speaker associated with group (line 39)	Individual speaker associated with group (vv. 11–12, 19)

Hodayah 4	Psalm 9
Absent in Hodayah II ...	*... but prominent in Ps 9*
Zion absent	Zion prominent (vv. 12, 15)
Lament-type supplications absent	Lament-supplications combined with praise (passim)
Motif of God's name absent	Motif of God's name prominent (vv. 3, 11)
Motif of "own pit" absent	Motif of "own pit" prominent (vv. 16ab, 17b)
Prominent in Hodayah II ...	*... but absent in Ps 9*
Motif of lies prominent	Motif of lies absent
Scorn motif prominent	Scorn motif absent
Structural difference	*Structural difference*
Single praise motif with כיא substantiation	Duplicated praise motif with כי substantiation (vv. 12, 13)

This kind of relationship can be recognised between the Hodayah and other so-called individual songs of thanksgiving in the Psalter, as well as between this biblical group and the other Hodayot in 1QHᵃ.[11] Nowhere do we find a direct quotation from Ps 9, neither is the Psalm or any other among the individual thanksgiving songs copied or blandly plagiarised. On the contrary, the Fourth Hodayah is clearly an autonomous composition that can be understood very well in the context of the Dead Sea Scrolls and what we know from them—whether the speaking first person singular is understood as the Teacher of Righteousness or not.[12] But this autonomy is not absolute. The individual thanksgiving songs in the Bible, being as they are contained in the Holy Scriptures of the community, provide a pre-text on which the author could model his post-text as

---

[11] The Psalms in question are 18; 22; 30; 31; 32; 34; 35; 40; 41; 50; 51; 56; 57; 61; 66; 71; 92; 107; 109; 116; 118; 138. Cf. also J. Maier and K. Schubert, *Die Qumran-Essener: Texte der Schriftrollen und Lebensbild der Gemeinde* (3rd ed.; UTB 224; München: Reinhardt, 1992), 194.

[12] Cf. J.J. Collins, "Amazing Grace: The Transformation of the Thanksgiving Hymn at Qumran," in *Psalms in Community: Jewish and Christian Textual, Liturgical and Artistic Traditions* (ed. H.W. Attridge and M.E. Fassler; SBLSymS 25; Atlanta: SBL, 2003), 75–85, 76–77, who points out that the answer—whether positive or not—to the question of authorship by the Teacher has no impact on issues such as "the relationship between psalms that bear the strong imprint of an individual and communal liturgical usage." Similarly, I argue that this issue does not impact on the hypertextual relationship between the Hodayot and their biblical antecedents.

an expression of his understanding of the conflict and the experience of vindication as well as the faith on which he based it. So here we have an instance of the relationship of a text with a whole genre or textual type, including its typical thought pattern, rhetorical character and style, that is, what is often called "system reference."[13] The imitation is there, but it is not pedantic. Therefore it is not plausible to call the hypertexts of the Hodayot "imitations" without qualifying the statement, so that the presence of the hypertextual element can be neither denied nor found to describe the intertextuality adequately.[14]

1.2.

My second example comes from a completely different type of text, namely a prose narrative from Qumran Cave 4 about the prophet Jeremiah, edited by Devorah Dimant[15] and to which she had earlier also devoted a paper.[16] In her edition she reconstructs the whole *Apocryphon of Jeremiah C* from the fragments:[17]

---

[13] Cf. Pfister, "Konzepte der Intertextualität," 1–30, idem, "Zur Systemreferenz," 52–58.

[14] Collins, "Amazing Grace," 85, though not discussing hypertextuality as a literary phenomenon, seems to suggest a similar situation when he points out the different nuances and unique characteristics of the *Hodayot* over against the biblical Psalms, e.g., the rare call to worship in the *Hodayot* and its typical use in what I have called the *pre-text*. That is, they do not simply imitate the biblical thanksgiving psalms, but are modeled on them. This principle had already been noted and shown in detail by G. Morawe, "Vergleich des Aufbaus der Danklieder und hymnischen Bekenntnislieder (1QH) von Qumran mit dem Aufbau der Psalmen im Alten Testament und im Spätjudentum," *RevQ* 4 (1963–1964): 323–356, viz. that, apart from the clear quotations and references to the biblical psalms as well as the imitation of the structure of hymns found in the pre-text, there are also clear differences, e.g. formulary diction, less rejoicing and more reflection; cf. his summary ibid., 355 and his still earlier dissertation of 1956 (*Aufbau und Abgrenzung der Loblieder von Qumran: Studien zur gattungsgeschichtlichen Einordnung der Hodajôth* [Theologische Arbeiten 16; Berlin: Evangelische Verlagsanstalt, 1960], 168–172). *A fortiori*, the imitating feature has therefore to be qualified.

[15] D. Dimant in *DJD* XXX (2001): 91–260. Here the text has a new identification, viz. 4Q385a 18, i.e., the last fragment of the reconstructed *Apocryphon of Jeremiah C*.

[16] D. Dimant, "An Apocryphon of Jeremiah from Cave 4 (4Q385B = 4Q385 16)," in *New Qumran Texts and Studies: Proceedings of the First Meeting of the International Organization for Qumran Studies, Paris 1992* (ed. G.J. Brooke and F. García Martínez; STDJ 15; Leiden: Brill, 1994), 11–30.

[17] Dimant in *DJD* XXX (2001): 99–100, where she identifies the relevant fragments as she pieces together the *Apocryphon* text.

Introduction:
> An account of world history sent by Jeremiah from Egypt is read by Jews in Babylonia

Review:
> *The Biblical Period in the past tense*
> Israel's journeys in the desert, taking possession of Canaan, the beginning of the monarchy, the times of David and Solomon and the sins of the period are reviewed

> *The Second Temple Period in the future tense*
> The termination of the monarchy, the increasing sins of Israel, further punishment and destruction of the land by enemies, corruption of the priests, disregard for God's laws and inner division of Israel are foretold

> *The Eschatological Era in the future tense, revealed to Jeremiah by God*[18]
> The downfall of Greek and Egyptian powers, the coming of bliss and the effect of the Tree of Life are foretold

Conclusion:
> Jeremiah's activities after the fall of Jerusalem.

As the title of the *DJD* edition ("Parabiblical Texts") suggests, all of this material would qualify to study our topic of intertextuality, but—again for practical reasons—we shall concentrate on the conclusion in 4Qapo-crJer Cᵃ (4Q385a) 18, since here we have a clear instance of a hypertext that again offers more than mere imitation. The text is continuous enough to enable a clear reading, but also fragmentary enough to warrant a paraphrase for our purposes:

> Column i: After the destruction of Jerusalem Jeremiah goes to Babylon with the Jewish captives in order to teach them what to do so that, in contradistinction to what they had done in their own land, they could keep the covenant (ברית) while in Babylon.

> Column ii: Jeremiah is in Tahpanes in Egypt (cf. Jer 43:8), where the Jews as well as God want him to inquire of God. He receives divine instruction to tell the children of Judah and Benjamin to keep his commandments and to refrain from idolatry.

In the main body of the reconstructed *Apocryphon*, the sweeping review of Israel's history since the exodus is especially dependent on the books of Deuteronomy and Jeremiah, although also affinities with Baruch and the Epistle of Jeremiah can be detected. But the thrust of the quasi-historical review is encompassing and therefore involves an intertextual

---

[18] According to Dimant in *DJD* XXX (2001): 98, the most probable understanding of the receiver of the revelation is Jeremiah himself.

relationship with large sections of the Hebrew Bible—from the stories of Israel's wandering in the desert through the Former Prophets down to the sack of Jerusalem.

How should we typify this relationship? It can be called a hypertextual relationship, since the post-text can be said to imitate the extended narrative line of Israel's journey through the desert, the occupation of the Promised Land, the institution and early stages of the monarchy as these are narrated in the books of Samuel, and the rest of its history as recounted in the books of Kings. But on the other hand "imitation" sits uncomfortably as a qualification, since the post-text has its own scope and tendency. Moreover, it is a repetition of sorts, since it offers a reiteration of mainly the same story line as that of the pre-text. But then it is not a replication of a relatively extended text such as the two Decalogues in Exod 20 and Deut 5 or the poems in Pss 14 and 53, so that it cannot be called a palintext. Therefore Timothy Lim is to be agreed with when, in speaking of the "dependence" of the *Apocryphon* on biblical books, he at the same time judges that

> it [the Jeremiah Apocryphon] did not simply adopt the biblical narrative wholesale but wove a new compositional garment from the diverse strands of the biblical sources.[19]

This cannot be said of "dependence" in the sense of a repetition or an imitation. To be sure, his type of intertextuality contains elements of both imitation and repetition, but its character is more accurately described as *amplificatory*. What determines the relationship of the post-text with its pre-text is the fact that the features of running over the same terrain and emulating the same critical narrative of the pre-text are taken further in that the pre-text is amplified, that is, a new dimension is created by means of the repetitive imitation. For instance, there are motifs in the post-text that pick up one strand in the pre-text and strengthen it. The pre-text offers the explanation of Israel's exile in terms of the deed-consequence nexus, that is, as the punishment for her sins. The post-text expands this to show that not only did Israel sin and receive punishment, but she continued sinning and became worse so that also the punishment is aggravated. In addition to their state they now also lose their identity as a people, the land itself is chastised by further punishment due to the "Angels of Mastemot."

---

[19] T. Lim, review of *DJD XXX*, *JBL* 123 (2004): 153–154, 154.

The conclusion further contributes to the augmentation of the biblical pre-text. The Bible is not quoted, but the language is given a biblical flavour. In col. i there are allusions to 2 Kgs 25:8–9, 25, Jer 24:1; 42:6, 13, 21; 43:7; 44:23; 51:59; 52:12–13, 21 and several parallels in 2 Chronicles, whereas the "underlying biblical model" of col. ii is Jer 41–42, with echoes of the admonition by Jeremiah in Jer 44–45.[20]

Here too the biblical pre-text is amplified. Jeremiah is not only associated with the conquered Jews, but, whereas the biblical text has Jeremiah remain in the land (Jer 40:4–6), in the *Apocryphon* he actually accompanies them to Babylonia. He returns in time for the following events, according to which he is forced to accompany the Jews who went to Egypt (Jer 43). The *Apocryphon* can therefore use the tradition of a letter by Jeremiah to the Babylonian exiles (cf. Jer 29) to enable him to accompany and instruct both communities. From the conclusion of the *Apocryphon*

> Jeremiah emerges as the national religious leader and teacher, whose moral and intellectual stature invested him with the authority necessary to lead his people at that crucial hour and to lay the foundations for the future.[21]

In 4Q385a 18 i 7–8 Jeremiah is portrayed as invested with the same kind of authority that Moses has in Exod 19:7.[22] The broad strokes of the historical review in this way do confirm the main thrust of the large biblical pre-text, but the threads taken from it are woven into a new garment (in Lim's metaphor) in which Jeremiah assumes Mosaic features so that it could be explained how Israel in the end did survive not only the initial catastrophe, but also the worsening of its situation during the exile, so that hope for an eschatological paradise could be kept alive.

All of this is achieved with a perspectival skill, since the review of events that predated Jeremiah are formulated in the past tense, whereas the events which were known to the author but happened after Jeremiah, are formulated in the future tense so that they could be revealed beforehand and therefore attain stature.

The biblical pre-text is therefore affirmed, even where it is altered for the purpose of highlighting the Mosaic function and status of Jeremiah. Far from rejecting the pre-text or presenting it against its own grain, the pre-text is enhanced and strengthened. The form of intertextuality that we have here, I would submit, is neither bland imitation nor repetition, but rather amplification. If we need to swim with the stream of

---

[20] So Dimant in her earlier article ("An Apocryphon of Jeremiah from Cave 4," 22, 24).
[21] Ibid., 26.
[22] Ibid., 21.

neologisms in scholarly jargon, I would submit the label *amplitext* instead of hypertext or palintext for this kind of intertextuality. My example only gives one instance, but this kind of intertextuality is common in the Dead Sea Scrolls and in other "parabiblical" texts, which seem to exist for this very reason.

1.3.

As a last case of evidence for the polyvalent character of intertextual relationships between the Dead Sea Scrolls and the Hebrew Bible, I refer to the well-known imitation of the Priestly Blessing from Num 6:24–26 in the *Community Rule* (1QS II:1–9), where the biblical blessing is used in an extensive way. Whereas in our first two cases we have several texts in a collection intertextually related to several texts in another collection and (assuming the reconstruction of Dimant to be correct) a large connected text intertextually related to another large connected text, we here have a specific relationship of one coherent unit within a larger body of text with one other coherent unit within another totally different text (albeit with a further development based on a structural model from yet another pre-text).

The intertextuality operates on three levels: First, the biblical text from Numbers is quoted; second, it is then turned on its head by means of parody; third, the parody follows the structural example of another blessing and a curse in Deuteronomy 27:12–26 and 28:1–68.[23] It is obvious that the biblical texts are together used as models for the text in the *Community Rule*. Here too it is insufficient to merely declare the adapted use of the pre-texts for the admission ceremony to constitute a hypertextual imitation, or to register the words quoted from the biblical texts as a simple repetition (since verb forms are changed etc.). Neither is the interpretative amplification of the concomitant curse formulae adequate to declare the use of the passages from both Numbers and Deuteronomy a metatextual commentary on the meaning of the biblical passages. It is all of this simultaneously: Not only the Priestly Blessing, but a whole group of texts together become pre-texts and as such serve several purposes, notably as *models* for new applications, as material from which substantial portions can be *repeated*, and as objects of interpretation so that the

---

[23] I only briefly refer to this case, as I have already discussed it in more detail elsewhere; cf. J.A. Loader, "Qumran, Text and Intertext: On the Significance of the Dead Sea Scrolls for Theologians Reading the Old Testament," *OTE* 19 (2006): 892–911, 905–907.

whole section can be read as *comment* on the meaning of the pre-texts. So the literary-theoretical categories of hypertextuality, palintextuality and metatextuality are simultaneously present and at work.

2. Metatexts

When intertextuality entails explicit comment on other texts without being transformations of the pre-texts, they are called "metatexts."[24] They explain, expound and claim to lead to the meaning of or the sense made by the text. It stands to reason that the pre-text or portions from it will often be cited or appear as quotations in the metatext. But the definitive aspect is that the pronouncements made on the pre-text intend to reveal the sense it makes. In biblical studies this would of course be a very prominent phenomenon, because commentaries on biblical texts and other interpretative literature would relate to the biblical pre-text(s) in this way.

Of course here too the relationship is by nature one of reciprocity. The comments totally depend on the pre-text, since they are only made for the sake of understanding the pre-text. But the pre-text is also influenced by its metatextual post-text, since the way it is read and understood is affected—and may even be decisively determined—by the post-text.

Also this form of intertextuality is typical of the Dead Sea Scrolls, the most obvious manifestation being the Pesharim. By nature they explicitly take up one text and create another one around it. The biblical commentaries therefore have a clear intertextual character. They quote the pre-text quite extensively, and in this regard do not sit comfortably with Stocker's contention that quotations are only an incidental characteristic of metatexts (as opposed to palintexts, where he finds them essential). In the Dead Sea commentaries, the quotation of the texts to be expounded are very important and even constitutive for the structure and introductory formulae of the distinct expositions. After a quotation of the pre-text, the post-text would follow an introductory formula ("its commentary [פשר] is"). So the distinction between the two is quite clear and consistently present in the extended commentaries on Habakkuk (1QpHab) and Nahum (4QpNah [4Q169]).

We also have a text type which further illustrates the difficulty of keeping the different literary categories separated. This is the case in

---

[24] Stocker, *Theorie*, 15; Wischmeyer, *Hermeneutik*, 189.

the *Florilegium* from Cave 4 (4QFlor [4Q174]).[25] Here texts from 2 Sam 7:10–14, Ps 1:1, and Ps 2:1–2 are quoted and amplified with shorter quotations from other passages in the Hebrew Bible. Then they are commented upon in the same style as the Pesharim in an exposition relating them all to the eschatological expectations of the community. Brought together from different pre-texts, they are recontextualised in a new post-text and then commented upon by a metatext. So here we have a type of intertextuality halfway between typical metatexts and typical palintexts.

3. *Palintexts*

A palintext is the repetition of another text or other texts so as to form yet another text.[26] This phenomenon should not be confused with the regular scribal task of copying manuscripts. Especially the *testimonia* and *florilegia*, or testimonies and anthologies, among the Dead Sea Scrolls are obvious cases. As an example, I take the compendium of messianic texts from the Fourth Cave (4QTest [4Q175]).[27] In this text a number of passages from the Hebrew Bible are arranged in a specific order and rounded off with a quotation from another Qumran text, the *Apocryphon of Joshua* (4Q379; olim *Psalms of Joshua*).[28] This organization reveals several levels of intertextual relationships:

- A text from Exodus is repeated in a new document (4Q175).
- It is related to the repetition of a passage from the book of Numbers.

---

[25] Also called "4QMidrEschat" in view of its eschatological orientation. In her edition and interpretation of the relationship of two fragmentary midrashic manuscripts, notably 4Q174 and 4Q177, A. Steudel (*Der Midrasch zur Eschatologie aus der Qumrangemeinde [4QMidrEschat^{a.b}]: Materielle Rekonstruktion, Textbestand, Gattung und traditionsgeschichtliche Einordnung des durch 4Q174 ["Florilegium"] und 4Q177 ["Catena A"] repräsentierten Werkes aus den Qumranfunden* [STDJ 13; Leiden: Brill, 1994], 5–56 and 57–124) brings them together as "4QMidrEschat^{a, b}" and defines the literary type as a thematic midrash parallel to early pesharim (ibid., 190–192). This categorization does not directly affect my discussion of intertextuality in general, but it does seem to confirm the view of the metatextual phenomenon presented here.

[26] Cf. Stocker, *Theorie*, 50–51.

[27] First published by J.M. Allegro and A.A. Anderson in *DJD* V (1968): 57–60; discussed more extensively in Loader, "Qumran, Text and Intertext," 892–911.

[28] For this text cf., e.g., E. Tov, "The Rewritten Book of Joshua," in *Biblical Perspectives: Early Use and Interpretation of the Bible in Light of the Dead Sea Scrolls: Proceedings of the First International Symposium of the Orion Center for the Study of the Dead Sea Scrolls and Associated Literature, 12–14 May, 1996* (ed. M.E. Stone and E.G. Chazon; STDJ 28; Leiden: Brill, 1998), 233–256.

- This is related to a further passage copied from Deuteronomy.
- Finally, all of these palintexts are grafted onto the *Apocryphon of Joshua*,
- which itself is an intertextual fabric of psalm-material and the book of Joshua.

The *Testimonia* (4Q175) is a short document from Cave 4 dated to the early first century B.C.E. and consists of four sections built around four quotations or repetitions of biblical texts from a pre-text of the Samaritan type (not from the tradition handed on in the Masoretic line, but in line with the Samaritan Pentateuch's version of Exod 20).[29] The last quotation, from Josh 6:26, is followed by an extended contextualisation of yet another intertextual relationship, namely from the book of Joshua as the pre-text of the *Apocryphon of Joshua*.

- The first section consists of a quotation from Exod 20:18 or 22[30] referring to *a prophet similar to Moses*.
- The second is from a prophecy of Balaam about *a future royal figure* (Num 24:15–17). This prophecy predicts that "a star shall stride forth from Jacob, and a sceptre shall rise out of Israel; he shall crush the borderlands of Moab, and destroy all the sons of Sheth," which is usually interpreted as a prophecy of the coming of the royal messiah.[31]
- The third section is a blessing for Levi, and implicitly for *the priestly messiah* (Deut 33:8–11).
- The last section opens with a verse from Joshua (6:26), which is then expounded by means of a quotation from the sectarian *Apocryphon of Joshua* (cf. 4Q379).

---

[29] Note Deut 5:28–29 plus 18:18–19, Exod 20:18, where the Deuteronomy verses occur together (cf. D.W. Parry and E. Tov, eds., *The Dead Sea Scrolls Reader* [6 vols.; Leiden: Brill, 2004–2005], 2:135), 20:21/22 (London Polyglot; P.W. Skehan, "The Period of the Biblical Texts from Khirbet Qumran," *CBQ* 19 [1957]: 435–440, 435; cf. Allegro in *DJD* V [1968]: 57, who also refers to the Samaritan text, but makes no further use of the fact); at its end this verse also has a marking similar to the division sign at the endings of lines 8, 13 and 20 in 4Q175.

[30] It is often taken for granted that we here have four sections built on five quotations (or palintexts), e.g. Allegro in *DJD* V [1968]: 57; G. Vermes, *The Dead Sea Scrolls: Qumran in Perspective* (London: Collins, 1977), 80; cf. J. Lübbe, "A Reinterpretation of 4Q Testimonia," *RevQ* 12 (1986): 187–197, 193, who speaks of a "conflation of the biblical texts forming the first section of this document, viz Dt 5:28–29 and 18:18–19."

[31] Cf. J.J. Collins, *The Scepter and the Star: The Messiahs of the Dead Sea Scrolls and Other Ancient Literature* (ABRL; New York: Doubleday, 1995) and below, n. 34.

The prophet from the *Exodus quotation* is obviously singular and is distinguished from "among their own people." The expectation of a prophet to herald the coming of the two messiahs is well known in Qumran,[32] so that it is natural to expect the quotations that follow to have something to do with this.

The star and sceptre of the *Numbers quotation*[33] similarly signify one person, since the verbs following to describe his actions are singular. In its contextual relationship to the Exodus quotation, the Numbers passage is flanked by the obviously singular prophetic figure and the singular priestly figure in the blessing invoked on Levi (Deut 33:8, 11). Their intertextual relationship rules out any identification with the collective community in a prophetic role.

The *Deuteronomy quotation* refers to an "eschatological priest" from Levi, who is obviously the priestly messiah.[34] After the clearly messianic Numbers quotation, this must also be messianic, for which the figure of the priestly messiah in Qumran is the evident candidate.

The last section concerns the *curse of Joshua* on the rebuilding of the city of Jericho, intertextually made to refer to Jerusalem and the eschatological conflict, which can certainly be associated with the messiah.[35] The passage does refer to the eschatological struggle, as Albl claims, but this is also a messianic matter.

For these reasons the text before us is not just a "conflation," but a palintextual interpretation of different aspects of the eschatological

---

[32] E.g. 1QS IX:14–15, 1QpHab VII:4–5; cf. also Mal 3:23–24.

[33] The Numbers passage is so often used with messianic reference in the Dead Sea Scrolls (and the *Testaments of the Twelve Patriarchs*) that Maier and Schubert, *Qumran-Essener*, 102 call it the very basis for the Qumran teaching of two messiahs. Cf. also A.S. van der Woude, *Die messianischen Vorstellungen der Gemeinde von Qumran* (Assen: Van Gorcum, 1957), passim, with a summary and list of references in the Dead Sea Scrolls, as well as the more recent study of the whole issue of the two messiahs under the significant title *The Scepter and the Star* by Collins (1995).

[34] That is, the messiah clearly juxtaposed to the royal messiah in 1QS IX:10–11: "... until the coming of the prophet and the messiahs from Aaron and Israel."

[35] M.C. Albl, *The Form and Function of the Early Christian Testimonia Collections* (SNT 96; Leiden: Brill, 1999), 89, suggests that the last quotation cannot be squared messianic, but the Dead Sea Scrolls contain no rounded-off messianic theology, so that it is difficult to bracket out the last section of the Testimony for not fitting into "the" messianic picture of Qumran. On the sceptre, cf. Gen 49:10 and 4QCommGen A (4Q252) V; CD 7:18–21 and G.J. Brooke, "Isaiah 40:3 and the Wilderness Community," in *New Qumran Texts and Studies* (ed. idem and García Martínez), 117–132, 123–124; further 1QSa II:14–15, where the royal messiah sits with his military officers in a subordinate position to the priestly messiah and the priests; cf. Maier and Schubert, *Qumran-Essener*, 102. Cf. further Loader, "Qumran, Text and Intertext," 902–903.

future expected by the community.[36] The verses taken from the Bible thus exemplify the interest of the Qumran community in the Old Testament prophecies expected to be fulfilled in their own day, which was experienced as eschatological time. In any event, the intertextuality of our texts provides details about the motif. The messianic expectation comprised persons representing three facets: prophetic, royal and priestly. In accordance with 1QS IX:10–15, the *Testimony* documents this construct from the Scriptures by means of a palintextual network from the perspective of the faith of the community (for which reason the term "Testimony" for this genre of texts from the Fourth Qumran Cave is quite appropriate).

As far as I can see, the relevance of the concept of intertextuality is rarely noticed with reference to these texts.[37] What becomes apparent here is that there is a mutual relationship in the repetition of biblical texts, but these together form a palintext to several pre-texts at once. Thereby they reciprocally contribute to each other's significance by limiting, extending, focusing and emending what they would mean in isolation—even within the canon of the same community. The intertextuality affords the text meanings that are not otherwise present in the same words. Since the genre of the Testimony is present in Classical literature, the New Testament and in Patristic texts, its presence in Qumran becomes very interesting.

It seems to me that this extensive and intensive use of the biblical tradition works both ways in a highly creative manner. First, central aspects of

---

[36] So G.J. Brooke, *Exegesis at Qumran: 4Florilegium in its Jewish Context* (JSOTSup 29; Sheffield: JSOT Press, 1985), 311–319, Albl, *Form and Function*, 89–90, who see the figure of the royal messiah represented here, and Steudel, who regards all three figures as messianic ("Testimonia," *Encyclopedia of the Dead Sea Scrolls* [ed. L.H. Schiffman and J.C. VanderKam; 2 vols.; Oxford: Oxford University Press, 2000], 2:936–938, 937). The latter also makes the following important observation: "Interestingly, all three eschatological figures, prophet, king, and high priest, are also and exclusively in the Qumran literature found in 1QRule of the Community (1QS ix.11), in a manuscript that was copied by the same scribe who also wrote Testimonia (the passage represented by 1QS ix.11 is missing in earlier stages of the Rule of the Community redaction; see Rule of the Community[e] [4Q259])." Cf. also CD 12:23–24; 14:19; 19:10–11; 20:1).

[37] Cf., however, Collins, *The Scepter and the Star*, 61; G.J. Brooke, "Shared Intertextual Interpretations in the Dead Sea Scrolls and the New Testament," in *Biblical Perspectives* (ed. Stone and Chazon), 35–57 (on Old Testament texts in Qumran and in the New Testament); R.B. Hays, *Echoes of Scripture in the Letters of Paul* (New Haven: Yale University Press, 1989) (on the New Testament); B. Embry, "The 'Psalms of Solomon' and the New Testament: Intertextuality and the Need for a Re-evaluation," *JSP* 13 (2002): 99–136 (on pseudepigrapha); and M.A. Sweeny, *Form and Intertextuality in Prophetic and Apocalyptic Literature* (FAT 45; Tübingen: Mohr Siebeck, 2005) (on apocalyptic).

the community's theology are obviously given a biblical base.[38] Remind-
ing ourselves again of the hypertextual use of the Priestly Blessing, the
doctrine of the dualism between light and darkness, good and evil, is
expressed in terms of Num 6 through the lens of Deut 27 and 28. But
by the same token the community's self-understanding is established on
the same biblical foundation, since its self-understanding is the social
expression of the principle of light. By virtue of its exclusivity, those outside the community must be the expression of the principle of darkness,
that is, evil in the flesh. To achieve this type of effect, which is found all
over the Scrolls, a large measure of creativity, and the courage and will to
put it to practice are necessary aspects of the interpreter's approach to his
material.

D. New Contexts

The Dead Sea Scrolls perhaps afford one of the best instances of the
meaning of the concept of intertextuality in biblical studies. They have
a special relevance for scholarship interested in the *literary* study of
these texts because by their very nature they lend a striking topicality
to the concept of intertextuality. This is in evidence all over the Dead Sea
Scrolls and—since mainly biblical texts are concerned in this respect—
biblical scholarship cannot but pay more attention to the phenomenon
of intertextuality as it is exemplified in these texts.

The Dead Sea Scrolls create new contexts for reading the texts of the
Hebrew Bible. They do so because they are texts the origin of which was
determined by a particular understanding of the pre-existing Hebrew
Bible texts. Therefore, there is a reciprocal relationship between the Dead
Sea Scrolls and the Hebrew Bible: Having come about under the impact
of the Hebrew Bible, the Dead Sea Scrolls in turn impact on the Hebrew
Bible by virtue of impacting on its reception. The interactivity between
texts is not just a constitutive element of electronic hypertexts, but of
all intertextual relationships—consisting as they do of pre-texts that are
by definition integrated into new contexts. In the case of the Dead Sea
Scrolls, it means that they have not only originated in the context of the
Hebrew Bible, but have in turn *created* contexts for the reading of the

---

[38] R. Kugler, "Making all Experience Religious: The Hegemony of Ritual at Qumran,"
JSJ 33 (2002): 131–152, argues for scriptural exegesis at Qumran as the basis of its ritual
practices generally.

Hebrew Bible that were not there before the Dead Sea Scrolls. The pre-texts do not remain unaffected by their post-texts.

There are several forms of intertextuality which the extensive and concentrated presence of the phenomenon in the Dead Sea Scrolls suggests. On the literary and theological levels they offer us much more than materials for religio-historial comparison. Having undergone the influence of earlier biblical texts, they have also *reciprocated* this influence:

- Our example of hypertextuality suggests that rash judgements as to epigonism are to be avoided, since dependence on pre-texts may yield extremely creative post-texts in their own right. Even Shakespeare was, after all, dependent on pre-existing poetic forms on which he modelled his sonnets.
- Our example of palintextuality showed how rich the contextualisation of repetitions can be in terms of meaning. Far from being "mere" repetitions or conflations, texts are made to border on each other, therefore limit each other's possibilities to mean some things and extend their possibilities to mean others.
- Since it is so simple, our metatextual example is perhaps the least intriguing in this regard. The pre-text quoted and its meaning being provided in the new formulation of the metatext is straightforward and in principle no different from what we do when we write our commentaries on these texts and/or their biblical pre-texts. But they also show to what degree the expounding of pre-texts share characteristics with other forms of intertextual relationships.
- All forms of intertextuality involve the power of creativity, In the case of the Dead Sea Scrolls specifically, this creativity is a matter of relating to the Holy Scriptures of faith communities. The reciprocity involved in the use of texts in other texts becomes a major issue when texts are projected through the prism of faith.
- Although the community from which the Dead Sea Scrolls sprang probably themselves believed the contrary, their way of expressing this faith by means of intertextual use of the Scriptures illustrates that truth is not encoded in the biblical text waiting to be decoded, but that the faith of the reader is the prism through which both their and our texts respond to biblical pre-texts.

CURSES AND BLESSINGS: SOCIAL CONTROL
AND SELF DEFINITION IN THE DEAD SEA SCROLLS

JEFF S. ANDERSON
Wayland Baptist University

Nearly fifty years ago, J.L. Austin's *How To Do Things with Words* developed the notion of performative utterances that do not merely describe or report events, but are simultaneously a verbal utterance and a deed performed.[1] With these illocutions, to say something is literally to do something. For Austin, performatives become effective to the extent that they are uttered in appropriate ways and in appropriate social circumstances.[2] As it pertains to ritual speech acts of blessings and curses, Austin's work has tended to shift the discussion away from a Frazerian dichotomy between magic and religion, as well as away from the magical power of words or notions of power of the soul. Social anthropologists have widely applied Austin's theory of performative utterances and illocutionary speech actsto functional models of societal social control and self definition.[3] Performative language thus enables one to approach

---

[1] J.L. Austin, *How to Do Things with Words* (Cambridge: Harvard University Press, 1962). Austin's distinction between words that describe things and words that do something proved insufficient and the theory was modified by John Searle, *Speech Acts: An Essay on the Philosophy of Language* (Cambridge: Cambridge University Press, 1970).

[2] Austin posits four conditions for effective performatives: There must be an accepted conventional procedure having a certain conventional effect. Second, the particular personas and circumstances in a given case must be appropriate for the invocation of the particular procedure. Third, the procedure must be executed by all participants, both correctly and completely. Finally, if a procedure is designed for use by persons having certain thoughts and feelings, then the person participating in so invoking the procedure must in fact have those thoughts and feelings (Austin, *How to Do Things with Words*, 14–15).

[3] See R. Finnegan, "How to Do Things with Words: Performative Utterances among the Limba of Sierra Leone," *Man* 4 (1969): 537–552; B. Ray, "Performative Utterances in African Rituals," *HR* 13 (1973): 16–35; S.G.A. Onibere, "Potent Utterance: An Essay on the Bini View of a Curse," *East Asia Journal of Theology* 4 (1986): 161–169; S.J. Tambiah, "Form and Meaning of Magical Acts: A Point of View," in *Modes of Thought: Essays on Thinking in Western and non-Western Societies* (ed. R. Horton and R. Finnegan; London: Faber & Faber, 1973), 199–229; C.A. Kratz, "Genres of Power: A Comparative Analysis of Okiek Blessings, Curses, and Oaths," *Man* 24 (1989): 636–656.

ritual words from the fundamental linguistic level to see how words actually can accomplish certain ends, apart from magical or symbolic notions alone.[4]

Biblical scholars have applied the notion of speech acts to blessings and curses, viewing them as illocutionary utterances whose power lies in the nature of human language uttered under appropriate circumstances by appropriate individuals.[5] The words of blessing and curse are not magically self-fulfilling yet are nevertheless incredibly potent in proper social contexts. These performatives can at once both maintain and challenge social structures, serving as social propagandists and iconoclasts alike. When associated with legal collections, these illocutions can coerce the community to conform to a rigid set of social norms at the same time as they maintain the distinct social solidarity and identity of that community. Blessings and curses often employ stereotypical language combined with vividly enacted intramural rituals that evoke the powers of the blessing or curse.[6] While no destructive ritual acts typically accompanied these biblical utterances, they were nonetheless powerful. When paired together, the typically lopsided sanctions of the curses evoke effective social functions of these rituals.

The covenant community at Qumran employed ritual blessings and curses widely in ways consistent with the witness of the Hebrew Bible, acting out biblical traditions, but also modifying them significantly according to the Yaḥad's own halakhah. Consistent with their use of other traditions of the Bible, the community acted out biblical rituals, conflated

---

[4] Austin discusses three categories of fallacies which render speech acts impotent: misinvocations, misapplications, and misexecutions (*How to Do Things with Words*, 14–15).

[5] A. Thiselton, "The Supposed Power of Words in Biblical Writings," *JTS* 25 (1974): 283–299; C.W. Mitchell. *The Meaning of BRK "to Bless" in the Old Testament* (SBLDS 95; Atlanta: Scholars Press, 1987); J.S. Anderson, "The Social Function of Curses in the Hebrew Bible," *ZAW* 110 (1998): 1–15. Thiselton has applied speech act theory to the study of hermeneutics in *New Horizons in Hermeneutics* (Grand Rapids: Zondervan, 1992), 283–307.

[6] M. Weinfeld mentions a number of dramatic acts that typically accompany curses in ancient treaties including burning wax figurines, breaking bows and arrows, scattering salt, cutting up animals, and covenantal sacrifices, "The Loyalty Oath in the Ancient Near East," *UF* (1976): 400–402. See also C.A. Faraone, "Molten Wax, Spilt Wine, and Mutilated Animals: Sympathetic Magic in Near Eastern and Early Greek Oath Ceremonies," *JHS* 113 (1993): 60–80.

texts from multiple contexts, reused and rewrote familiar biblical texts and literary forms at will.[7]

Robert Kugler has recently argued that the study of ritual density and change at Qumran has received sparing attention, in spite of overwhelming textual and artifactual evidence of ritual practice there.[8] Following designations of Catherine Bell,[9] Kugler presents a preliminary inventory of six types of Qumran ritual: rites of passage, calendrical rites, rites of exchange and consequence, rites of affliction, feasting and fasting rites, and political rites. In Kugler's inventory, blessings and curses are present in nearly every category.[10]

Ritually enacted blessings and curses are present at Qumran in two broad public contexts with highly stylized rituals: rites of initiation and expulsion (1 QS II:1–18; 4QCurses [4Q280]; CD 7:4–10; 4QD[a] [4Q266]) and battle liturgies (1QM [1Q33] XIII:2–13, 4QShir[a–b] [4Q510–511]). Additionally, like the biblical blessings and curses in Leviticus and Deuteronomy that follow immediately after legal collections, 4QMMT, the *Damascus Document* and the *Temple Scroll* contain examples of blessings and curses immediately following legislation that were likely to have been performed in public contexts (4QD[a] [4Q266] also follows halakhic material). Associating blessings and curses with these three social contexts is not unusual when compared to other cultures in the Ancient Near East and Israel's own culture in the biblical tradition, yet the community's own adaptation and modification of blessings and curses is consistent with the community of the renewed covenant.

---

[7] This methodology of interpretation birthed a community that had affinities to both Essenes and Sadducees. In terms of the community's self perception, however, they were nothing less than biblical Israel, and consequently a socio-religious phenomenon *sui generis* among the Judaisms of the Second Temple period. S. Talmon, "The Community of the Renewed Covenant: Between Judaism and Christianity," in *The Community of the Renewed Covenant: The Notre Dame Symposium on the Dead Sea Scrolls* (ed. E. Ulrich and J. VanderKam; Christianity and Judaism in Antiquity 10; Notre Dame: University of Notre Dame Press, 1994), 3–26.

[8] R. Kugler, "Making all Experience Religious: The Hegemony of Ritual at Qumran," *JSJ* 33 (2002): 131–152.

[9] C. Bell, *Ritual Theory, Ritual Practice* (Oxford: Oxford University Press, 1992).

[10] I follow Mary Douglas' definition of ritual as "symbolic action concerning the sacred." M. Douglas, *Purity and Danger: An Analysis of Concept of Pollution and Taboo* (London: Routledge, 1966), 66.

RITES OF INITIATION AND EXPULSION (1 QS II:1–18; 4QCURSES
[4Q280]; 4QBER[a–d] [4Q286–289]; 4QD[a] [4Q266])

About the same time as the Dead Sea Scrolls were discovered, biblical scholars were beginning to examine the influence of suzerainty and parity treaties on the biblical covenant tradition in the Decalogue, Deuteronomy, and the covenant renewal ceremony of Josh 24.[11] As texts were published from Qumran, insights from these studies on covenant treaties informed work on the scrolls themselves.[12] The blessings and curses in the covenant renewal ceremony of 1QS II, 4QCurses (4Q280), and 4QBer[a–d] (4Q286–290) reflect rich intertextuality with various traditions of the Hebrew Bible, including the priestly blessing in Numbers, the blessings and curses of Leviticus and Deuteronomy, and the covenant renewal ceremony in Josh 24. These blessings and curses are uttered within a theatrical ritual with clearly defined elements of a processional, stylized recitation of the blessing and curse by proper leaders of the ritual, and an affirmation of acceptance by the participants by means of a self-curse, or oath.[13] This intramural event was repeated every year, probably the day of or before *Shavuʿot*, "all the days of Belial's dominion," for

---

[11] G. Mendenhall, *Law and Covenant in Israel and the Ancient Near East* (Pittsburgh: The Biblical Colloquium, 1955); D.J. Wiseman, "The Vassal-Treaties of Esarhaddon," *Iraq* 20 (1958): 1–110; S. Gevirtz, "West Semitic Curses and the Problem of the Origins of Hebrew Law," *VT* (1961): 137–158; F.C. Fensham, "Malediction and Benediction in Ancient Near Eastern Vassal-Treaties and the Old Testament," *ZAW* 74 (1962): 1–9; J.A. Fitzmyer, *The Aramaic Inscriptions of Sefire* (Rome: Pontifical Biblical Institute, 1967); D. Hillers, *Treaty Curses and Old Testament Prophets* (Rome: Pontifical Biblical Institute, 1964).

[12] K. Baltzer, e.g., argued that of all the elements of these ancient treaties, the blessings and curses underwent the most far-reaching transformation in Israel. He maintained that the blessings or curses were originally presented as two equal possibilities which were historicized over time. Early on in the history of Israel, the blessing constituted present experience and the curse threatened the future. After the destruction by Babylon, the blessing represented the promise of the future and the curse constituted the present experience of Israel. Baltzer also contended that the texts of covenant renewal at Qumran portrayed curses and blessings eschatalogically. K. Baltzer, *The Covenant Formulary in Old Testament, Jewish, and Early. Christian Writings* (trans. D.E. Green; Philadelphia: Fortress, 1971), 92–93, 179–180.

[13] Contrast M. Weinfeld who argues that the ceremony of the Qumran community is freed altogether of ritual action and left only with the fealty oath sworn by the participants of the covenant, "The Covenant in Qumran," in *The Bible and the Dead Sea Scrolls: The Second Princeton Symposium on Judaism and Christian Origins*, vol. 2: *The Dead Sea Scrolls and the Qumran Community* (ed. J.H. Charlesworth; Waco: Baylor University Press, 2006), 59–69, 61.

veterans and new initiates alike.[14] While the ceremony is patterned after the one at Gerizim and Ebal, the community adapted both content and form of blessings and curses to its own needs.[15] Like the blessings and curses of Deut 27, there is no mention of blood or sacrifice, a common element in many ancient treaties. The context is clearly one of covenant renewal, as language in 1QS I: 16–20 employs a stock phrase to establish a covenant (העוברים בברית) from Deut 30:18 and 29:11.

The initial blessing (1QS II:1–4a) is uttered by the priests upon all the men of God's lot who walk unblemished in all his paths. Since there is no mention of blessing in Deut 27 this blessing adapts the only priestly blessing that the Yaḥad had to draw from, the Aaronic blessing of Num 6. The *Community Rule* follows the Aaronic blessing narrowly. The themes of protection, illumination, and peace highlight the blessing, but with an eschatological connotation: the peace that is to be obtained is an eternal peace (לשלום עולמים). The single blessing is followed by a double curse (1QS II:4b–10, 11–18), first uttered by the Levites alone against the men of the lot of Belial followed by a curse uttered by both priests and Levites against those who might seek to enter the covenant but hide an unregenerate heart. The threefold theme of no mercy, no forgiveness, no peace, also present in 4QCurses (4Q280) below, is reminiscent of the prologue and epistles of Enoch and is directed against outsiders.[16]

Bilhah Nitzan argues that 4Q280 also belongs to the annual covenant renewal ceremony and notes parallels with 1QS II:15–17, 25–26 that deal with members of the Yaḥad who did not keep the covenant.[17] The order of 1QS is interrupted with the Melki-resha curse, the same pattern of cursing Melki-resha that the *War Scroll* and *Berakhot* (4Q286–290) adopt toward Belial. Because the liturgical form of 4Q280 is less developed than 1QS, Nitzan suggests that this curse probably represents an earlier stage of the ceremony.

In the *Community Rule*, both curse and blessing are combined with an oath in which adherents affirm maledictions against themselves with a

---

[14] The association with *Shavuʿot* may be a play on שבוע.

[15] B. Nitzan, *Quman Prayer and Religious Poetry* (trans. J. Chapman; STDJ 12; Leiden: Brill, 1994), 123–171.

[16] J.S. Anderson, "Two-Way Instruction and Covenantal Theology in the Epistle of Enoch," *Hen* 28 (2006): 161–176.

[17] B. Nitzan, "Blessings and Curses," *Encyclopedia of the Dead Sea Scrolls* (ed. L.H. Schiffman and J.C. VanderKam; 2 vols.; Oxford: Oxford University Press, 2000), 1:97–98.

double amen (1QS II:10, 18). In essence the ritual introduces a modified single blessing, a double curse, double invokers of the curse, and a double amen. Like the blessing of eternal peace, the curse is also viewed eschatologically, ארורי עולמים (1QS II:17).[18]

What social function do these curses and blessings of the *Community Rule* and 4Q280 convey? The first and perhaps most obvious is the delineation of socio-religious boundaries. This is nothing new. Pedersen argued a century ago that the *qal* passive participle of ארר denoted separation of the one who utters the curse from its object as well as a separation of the object from the community.[19] Scharbert depicted the curse formula as the "most severe means of separating the community from the evildoer."[20] One can point to a host of texts in and outside the Hebrew Bible where the purpose of curses and blessings was to define social and ethnic boundaries by the exclusion or humiliation of the individual or group under the curse.[21] In the first curse, the expression ארור אתה is uttered against the lot of Belial.[22] Additionally, the language employed in this ceremony, "to cross over," is clearly boundary language. Unlike the ceremony in Deut 27 where the nation of Israel is given the possibility of both blessing and curse, here the notion is noticeably intramural. The outgroup-ingroup, ingroup-innergroup boundaries are clearly defined by curses and blessings. Whether the sons of Belial represent individuals outside the community or backslidden members of the community, the result is the same. The curses not only made explicit a known division between competing communities but actually enacted that relationship

---

[18] For the eternal curse, see also *1 En.* 5:5–7; 102:3.

[19] J. Pedersen expresses the curse as "Ausstoßung aus der Gesellschaft, Beraubung des Glückes und der Ehre, Bann und Besessenheit." J. Pedersen, *Der Eid bei den Semiten in seinem Verhältnis zu verwandten Erscheinungen sowie die Stellung des Eides im Islam* (Studien zur Geschichte und Kultur des islamischen Orients 3; Strassbourg: Trübner, 1914), 78.

[20] J. Scharbert, "Fluchen und Segnen im Alten Testament," *Bib* 39 (1958): 1–26; idem, *Solidarität in Segen und Fluch im Alten Testament und in seiner Umwelt*, vol. 1: *Väterfluch und Vätersegen* (BBB 14; Bonn: Hanstein, 1958).

[21] Curses against, Cain, Canaan, Esau, Simeon, Levi in the ancestral narratives; Moab, Edom, and several other groups in the Balaam narrative, and the curses against the Gibeonites, and Shechemites in the Deuteronomistic History are some examples.

[22] Similar language is used in 4QCurses (4Q280) against Melki-resha, "[... Accur]sed are you, Melki-resha, in all the pla[ns of your blameworthy inclination. May] God not be merciful ... May there be no peace for you by the mouth of those who intercede" (4Q280 2 2–4, according to F. García Martínez and E.J.C. Tigchelaar, *The Dead Sea Scrolls Study Edition* [2 vols.; Leiden: Brill, 1997–1998], 2:637).

each time the ritual was performed.[23] In 4QCurses (4Q280), this ritualized curse separated the object (Melki-resha) from the Sons of Light.
Such projection of threat onto an Outgroup served as a back-handed
blessing to the Ingroup which uttered the curse and as a force to deny
others participation in that community.

Second, in cultures of the ancient Near East, blessings and curses were
often a private law of the vulnerable when the enforcing arm of the
law was limited. Boundary inscriptions were a common Ancient Near
Eastern example of this use of curses, a metaphor alluded to often in
the scrolls, not only here, but also in the *War Scroll* and the *Damascus
Document*. As such, curses were a last resort of the weak based on a
transcendental principle of justice which covered the limited arm of the
legal system. As Weber retorts, "the curse of the poor is the weapon
of democracy."[24] Such denouncement rhetoric promoted egalitarianism
and had a leveling effect to broader society. It may be that the Yaḥad
viewed itself as oppressed with limited resources for justice.

Finally, the ceremony functioned as a tool of social control and a way
to convey social values. According to some social control models, people
are more willing to conform to social norms of a community because of
a latent fear of retaliation. Due to the theological nature of this renewal
text, fear of divine retribution is a strong deterrent to antisocial behavior.
Note the divine force behind a three fold blessing and seven fold curse:
May he bless you with everything, may he illuminate your heart, may he
lift upon you his countenance—followed by—may God hand you over
to terror, may he bring upon you destruction, may God not be merciful,
may he not forgive, may he lift up the countenance of his anger, may God's
anger and wrath consume him, may God separate him for evil.[25]

The community's double affirmation (אמן אמן) is telling. Speech act
theorists have argued that virtually all illocutionary speech acts are con-
ditional. They must be uttered in appropriate contexts by appropriate

---

[23] Mowinckel organizes his discussion by examining curses directed against those
outside the community versus curses directed against those inside the community (S. Mowinckel, *Psalmenstudien*, vol. V: *Segen und Fluch in Israels Kult und Psalmdichtung* [1924;
repr. Amsterdam: Schippers, 1961], 80).

[24] M. Weber, *Ancient Judaism* (trans. D. Martindale; New York: Free Press, 1952), 256–
257.

[25] R. Werline argues that God's refusal to listen to the prayers of the condemned in
the moment of punishment constitute the curses' vitality, "The Curses of the Covenant
Renewal Ceremony in 1QS 1.16–2.19," in *For a Later Generation: The Transformation
of Tradition in Israel, Early Judaism and Early Christianity* (ed. R. Argall, B. Bow, and
R. Werline; Harrisburg: Trinity, 2000), 280–288.

individuals or they will ultimately be unsuccessful. James Harris called this the "cornerstone of speech act analysis."[26] The procedure must be executed by all participants correctly and completely. While curses can at times be uttered in secret without the knowledge of their object, the curse within the contexts of an oath must be acknowledged in some way by the individual who agrees to the oath. With a reenactment every year, the double curse invoked by double personas, and a double affirmation strengthen the viability of that oath.

WAR PRAYERS (1QM XIII:2–13, 4QSHIR[a–b] [4Q510–511])

In 1 Sam 17 Goliath cursed David by his gods prior to their infamous battle at Socoh and in Num 22–24 Balak summoned Balaam to curse Israel in a verbal buildup to an actual war. Many ancient texts supply examples of gathering omens before battle to ascertain the will of the gods, employing professional sorcerers to curse the enemy, and gathering an entire army in public contexts to swear an oath of military allegiance.[27] The *War Scroll* (1QM) offers detailed ritual instructions for the final battle between the Sons of Light and the Sons of Darkness. The Sons of Light were to prepare as if they were taking part in a holy ritual. Yet the outcome of the war had already been predetermined and that victorious outcome was specifically foreshadowed in the text. In the heart of the *War Scroll* (cols. X–XIV) are a series of varied liturgical pieces in the context of warfare. The prayers of this section are not necessarily homogenous but reflect parallels with other ritualized texts, most notably the covenant renewal ceremony.[28]

The context of reciting this text occurs at the time of the eschatological war between the Sons of Light and the Sons of Darkness, but Nitzan observes that it is unclear at what stage of the war the recitation was to be uttered.[29] For example, in col. XIV the blessings and curses are recited near the corpses of slain enemies, presumably after the actual

---

[26] J. Harris, "Speech Acts and God Talk," *International Journal for the Philosophy of Religion* 11 (1980): 167–183, 169.

[27] C.A. Faraone, "Curses and Blessings in Ancient Greek Oaths," *Journal of Ancient Near Eastern Religion* 5 (2006): 139–156.

[28] P.R. Davies, "War of the Sons of Light Against the Sons of Darkness," *Encyclopedia of the Dead Sea Scrolls* 2:965–968, 967.

[29] Nitzan, *Qumran Prayer*, 138.

battle is over.[30] Assuming that the *War Scroll* entails preparation for a physical battle, if the blessings and curses are uttered prior to the battle they are employed similarly to other war curses. If they are employed after the battle, these performatives still draw important lines of demarcation between God, Belial, and their respective lots.

While not expressed in covenantal language, many of the same stylized ceremonial elements in the *Community Rule* are presented here in the *War Scroll* as a liturgical ceremony. There is a processional, or at the least, a clearly defined order of priests, levites and elders. The invokers are the priests, levites, and elders who bless the God of Israel and damn (זעם) Belial and all the spirits of his lot. God is blessed for his holy plan, Belial cursed for his hostile plan and the spirits of his lot are cursed for their wicked plan. The use of חשב is similar here to the reconstructed text of 4QCurses (4Q280), where Melki-resha is cursed for the plans of his blameworthy inclination. In 1QM the ארור formula is employed against these foes. The word "lot" (גורל), is referential to the boundary of allotment, evoking curses associated with the violation of boundaries, like the covenant renewal texts. But unlike the covenant renewal ceremony, words of curse written first, the ritual ends with a blessing.

Sometimes blessings and curses served as a *substitute* for political action. When there were no available channels through which an individual or group could seek justice, curses often were a means of seeking revenge. In the context of warfare, rather than a literal confrontation in which one was sure to be defeated, the curse often substituted for an actual battle.[31] This not only provided a socially sanctioned outlet for

---

[30] J. Duhaime outlines the War Prayers this way: Prayers at the camp (cols. IX–XII), prayers on the battlefield (col. XII–XIV:1), prayers after the victory (col. XIV:2–end). J. Duhaime, "War Scroll," in *The Dead Sea Scrolls: Hebrew Aramaic, and Greek Texts with English Translations*, vol. 2: *Damascus Document, War Scroll, and Related Documents* (ed. J.H. Charlesworth et al.; The Princeton Theological Seminary Dead Sea Scrolls Project; Tübingen: Mohr Siebeck, 1995), 80–203, 80. See also Y. Yadin, *The Scroll of the War of the Sons of Light against the Sons of Darkness* (Oxford: Oxford University Press, 1962), 223.

[31] Ya'ari and Friedman argue that in Arab societies warfare has actually been averted when antagonists vent their frustrations by cursing the enemy: "While the curse-and-bless prelude was originally designed to gear enemies up for an armed clash, it has also had the effect of substituting for physical combat." E. Ya'ari and I. Friedman, "Curses in Verses," *The Atlantic* (Feb. 1991): 26. Additionally, note the revealing quote: "They curse us because they cannot kill us." K. Thomas, *Religion and the Decline of Magic: Studies in Popular Belief in Sixteenth and Seventeenth Century England* (New York: Scribner, 1971), 509.

aggressive impulses, but was also a powerful means of effecting revenge.[32] Regardless, these blessings and curses strengthened the resolve of those who participated in the ritual.

The language of blessing and curse is also employed in 4QShir[a–b] (4Q510–511). In framework similar to the *War Scroll*, the text portrays the struggle between the forces of light and darkness. These songs indicate that the one reciting the text is declaring the glories of God to frighten the spirits of the ravaging angels and demons.[33] Although the manuscripts are severely damaged, the associated text in 4Q511 demonstrates the tension of blessing and curse. The text is highly fragmented, but essentially reflects a ritual that opens the same way that 1QM does, praising God who is the source of both blessings and curses. This text expresses the dualistic and deterministic position that God is the irresistible source of both blessing and curse. Nitzan states, "the blessing and corresponding curse serve as a kind of magical weapon intended to protect the children of light from the spirits of Belial in warring activities ..."[34] For Nitzan, while the blessing and curse of covenantal ceremony was a means if identifying and separating from the lot of Belial, the use in this context resembles the practice of using recitations which carry magical powers.[35] Rather than magical recitations, perhaps instead both the covenant renewal ceremonies and the battle curses combine speech and ritual act as performative utterances. In both contexts the effect of blessings and curses is the same. They fortify the self identity of the community, coerce behavior, and define actions that are sanctioned by the community.

HORTATORY EXHORTATIONS FOLLOWING
LEGAL MATERIALS (4QMMT, 4Q266, 11QT)

4QMMT, the *Damascus Document*, and the *Temple Scroll* all contain curses and blessings which follow legal or halakhic instruction, thus rein-

---

[32] Duhaime, "War Scroll," 87.

[33] See A. Lange, "The Essene Position on Magic and Divination," in *Legal Texts and Legal Issues: Proceedings of the Second Meeting of the International Organization for Qumran Studies, Cambridge 1995* (ed. M. Bernstein, F. García Martínez, and J. Kampen; STDJ 23; Leiden: Brill, 1997), 377–435.

[34] Nitzan, *Qumran Prayer*, 138.

[35] Ibid., 139.

forcing legal sanctions.[36] While there is probably no literary relationship between these three documents, their content is remarkably similar.[37] The reconstructed text of 4QMMT as it is presented in the composite text and translation by Strugnell and Qimron contains three sections: a calendar at the beginning (A), a list of laws (B), and a hortatory conclusion (C). It is the conclusion that alludes to the blessings and curses. The blessings and curses of the text above are replete with biblical allusions from Deut 31:29; 30:1–2; 4:30; and possibly Deuteronomic language in Hos 3:4–5.[38] Deuteronomy 30:1–3 states that after the time of blessings and curses has run its course, Israel will return to God with all their heart and soul. An allusion to Deut 4:30 or 31:29 anchors the time of this return to the end of days. The expressions (באחרית הימים), (באחרית העת), and (אחרית הימים) are significant. The phrase is probably not used eschatologically as 4QMMT C 22 expressly states, "this is the last days." The Torah uses the expression, "the last days" in only two occasions; both are in the context of blessings and curses. In Gen 49:1, Jacob asks his sons to "gather around, so I can tell you what will happen at the end of days." The context here is a blessing on most of his sons and the curses on Simeon and Levi. In Num 24:14, just prior to Balaam's fourth and unsolicited oracle, Balaam says to Balak, "let me warn you what this people will do to your people at the end of days." In context, the fourth oracle turns out to be nothing less that a curse on Moab. Both of these texts in the Torah are not eschatological. Collins notes that one of the supplements to 1QS, 1QSa (1Q28a), states, "the rule for all the congregation of Israel at the end of days."[39] Unlike the blessings and curses of 1QS and the *War Scroll*, there is probably no eschatological connotation in 4QMMT.

But to what extent is the language of 4QMMT part of a ritual? Fraade suggests that there is an unmistakable link to the covenantal ceremony enacted after crossing the Jordan.[40] Wise, Abegg, and Cook nicely

---

[36] J.P. Meier argues that the noun halakhah is used only in a general sense at Qumran (1QS III:9). J.P. Meier, "Is there *Halaka* (the Noun) at Qumran?" *JBL* 122 (2003): 150–155.

[37] L.H. Schiffman, "*Miqṣat Maʿaśe Ha-Torah* and the *Temple Scroll*," *RevQ* 14 (1989–1990): 435–457.

[38] M. Bernstein states that the language becomes more biblical in the hortatory section of 4QMMT. M. Bernstein, "The Employment and Interpretation of Scripture in 4QMMT: Preliminary Observations," in *Reading 4QMMT: New Perspectives on Qumran Law and History* (ed. J. Kampen and M. Bernstein; SBLSymS 2; Atlanta: Scholars Press, 1996), 29–51, 46.

[39] J.J. Collins, "Eschatology," *Encyclopedia of the Dead Sea Scrolls* 1:256–261, 258.

[40] S.D. Fraade, "Rhetoric and Hermeneutics in Miqṣat Maʿaśe Ha-Torah (4QMMT): The Case of the Blessings and Curses," *DSD* 10 (2003): 150–161, 160.

organize the material into two units that each contain a warning, exhortation, and illustration. Such a construction could, but does not necessarily have to lend itself to a ritualized setting.[41] Multiple copies of 4QMMT suggest that the treatise functioned intramurally and was likely used to instruct new members and to reaffirm the unique halakhic perspectives to veterans of the community. The message seems clear: obey this set of laws and blessing will return.[42]

The rite of expulsion in 4QD[a] (4Q266) 11 15–18, a fragmentary copy of the *Damascus Document* without parallel in the Cairo Genizah, also contains blessings and curses which follow halakhic instruction.[43] With the eight MSS from Cave 4 taken into account, over two-thirds of the *Damascus Document* contains halakhic instruction.[44] The rite of expulsion apparently follows CD 14:8–21. The timing of this expulsion ceremony is significant as it also coincides with Shavu'ot and is probably part of a covenant renewal ceremony. The expulsion applies to everyone who despises the regulations in accordance with all the statutes that are found in the Law of Moses. The ritual includes a community assembly, a prayer uttered by a priest who is appointed over the Many, and a written verdict. Even those associated with the expelled man were to leave with him. Again, as seen above, the language of border violations is reminiscent of the curse. The author uses covenantal language of "crossing over," yet with a twist. The expelled has crossed over the boundaries set by God.

Last, another parallel to 4QMMT is the Law of the King in the *Temple Scroll* (11QT[a] LIX:2–21). Like 4QMMT, it concludes a section of halakhic materials by invoking a relatively long list of curses against those who might not keep the covenant, presumably due to the disobedience of the king. The *Temple Scroll* alludes to the covenant blessings and curses of Deut 17; 28; 31; and Lev 26 by describing the scattering and disgrace of the people, destruction of cities, and the humiliation of exile. Like 4QMMT, once the curses have run their course, a return follows, "afterwards they shall come back to me with all their heart and with all their soul, in agreement with all the words of this law." Thus the period of curse

---

[41] M. Wise, M. Abegg, and E. Cook, *The Dead Sea Scrolls: A New Translation* (San Francisco: HarperSanFrancisco, 1996), 363–364.

[42] G.W.E. Nickelsburg, *Ancient Judaism and Christian Origins: Diversity, Continuity, and Transformation* (Minneapolis: Fortress, 2003), 48.

[43] J.C. VanderKam, "Covenant," *Encyclopedia of the Dead Sea Scrolls* 1:151–155, 153.

[44] J.M. Baumgarten and M.T. Davis, "Cave IV, V, VI Fragments Related to the Damascus Document (4Q266–273 = 4QD[a–h], 5Q12 = 5QD, 6Q15 = 6QD)," in *The Dead Sea Scrolls* (ed. Charlesworth et al.), 2:59–79, 59.

is followed by a time of blessing. The implication is remarkably similar to 4QMMT C 23–26, which implies that obedience to a certain interpretation of the Torah will spare the ruler from the misfortunes of the curse.[45]

CONCLUSION

The counterposing of blessings and curses played a central role in the ritual life of the Qumran community in ceremonies and literary compositions. Such ritual density was intramural, public, and consensual. Examples from three arenas—covenant renewals and expulsions, war prayers, and paranetic exhortations—demonstrate that blessings and curses uttered in ritual contexts at Qumran were potent and effective performatives. The community employed these utterances in multiple contexts by rich intertextuality with the blessings and curses from the Hebrew Bible. The threat of curse and promise of blessing enhanced social solidarity, marginalized outsiders, and coerced obedience to social sanctions. These performatives were uttered in intramural contexts consistent with the Hebrew Bible, but went beyond biblical utterances as their rhetoric affirmed the dualistic and deterministic ideology of the Yaḥad concerning the identity and struggle between light and darkness, between the lots of God and Belial.[46] This community adapted a "new covenant" for themselves that did not apply to all nations, or even to all Israel for that matter, but only those who remained faithful to the community itself and adhered to its strictest codes. All others were cursed. Such rituals, "entangled community members inextricably with God's will for the cosmos and drew them away from the profane world of their Jewish and non-Jewish neighbors."[47] These blessings and curses were potent, but not because of the magical power of words or the soul, but as performatives uttered in proper ritual contexts.[48]

The approach in this essay is indebted to Shemaryahu Talmon's sociological models for understanding the distinctive self understanding and

---

[45] L.H. Schiffman, "The Place of 4QMMT in the Corpus of Qumran Manuscripts," in *Reading 4QMMT*, 81–98, 96.

[46] Nitzan, "Blessings and Curses," 95.

[47] Kugler, "Making All Experience Religious," 152.

[48] Thiselton, "The Supposed Power of Words in Biblical Writings," 296, states, "illocutionary speech acts no more depend on primitive notions of word-magic than a modern judge and jury do when their words actually consign a man to prison or to freedom."

world view of the community at Qumran.[49] For Talmon, historical critical methodology alone is insufficient to a full understanding of Qumran
and these sociological models bear directly on the life and faith of the
Yaḥad. As such, sociological method represents a promising approach
for analyzing the Dead Sea Scrolls.

---

[49] S. Talmon, "The Transmission History of the Text of the Hebrew Bible in the Light
of Biblical Manuscripts from Qumran and Other Sites in the Judean Desert," in *The Dead
Sea Scrolls Fifty Years After Their Discovery: Proceedings of the Jerusalem Congress, July 20–
25, 1997* (ed. L.H. Schiffman et al.; Jerusalem: Israel Exploration Society, 2000), 40–50;
idem, "The Community of the Renewed Covenant."

READING FOR WOMEN IN 1QSA (*SEREKH HA-EDAH*)

TAL ILAN

Freie Universität Berlin

Before the 1990s there were no women in Qumran. All agreed (and most continue to agree) that the Qumranites were Josephus' Essenes, and these were male celibates.[1] The excavations at Qumran, carried out by Dominican monks, only confirmed this. Like in the all-male monasteries they knew, they found a refectory and a scriptorium,[2] and they found no jewels or cosmetics.[3] The few possible female skeletons that may have been found in the cemeteries were made to disappear, or masculinized.[4] Unwanted feminine subjects in the texts were emended out (like the wife, made to testify against her husband in *Serekh ha-Edah*)[5] or allegorized (or should I say pesherized, as the women of the wicked

---

[1] There is no need to repeat this premise in detail. For a summary, see H. Stegemann, "The Qumran Essenes: Local Members of the Main Jewish Union in Late Second Temple Times," in *The Madrid Qumran Congress: Proceedings of the International Congress on the Dead Sea Scrolls, Madrid 18–21 March, 1991* (ed. J. Trebolle Barrera and L. Vegas Montaner; 2 vols.; STDJ 11; Leiden: Brill, 1992), 1:83–166.

[2] See R. de Vaux, *Archaeology and the Dead Sea Scrolls* (Oxford: Oxford University Press, 1973), e.g. 29–30.

[3] See particularly J. Magness, *The Archaeology of Qumran and the Dead Sea Scrolls* (Grand Rapids: Eerdmans, 2002), 182–185.

[4] See J.E. Taylor, "The Cemeteries of Khirbet Qumran and Women's Presence at the Site," *DSD* 6 (1999): 285–323 and my *Integrating Women into Second Temple History* (TSAJ 76; Tübingen: Mohr Siebeck 1999), 206–207. This topic has been the subject of much recent debate, see e.g., O. Röhrer-Ertel, F. Rohrhirsch, and D. Hahn, "Über die Gräberfelder von Khirbet Qumran, inbesondere die Funde der Campagne 1956, I: Anthropologische Datenvorlage und Erstauswertung aufgrund der Collection Kurth," *RevQ* 19 (1999): 3–46; J. Zias, "The Cemeteries of Qumran and Celibacy: Confusion Laid to Rest?" *DSD* 7 (2000): 220–253; S.G. Sheridan, "Scholars, Soldiers, Craftsmen, Elites? Analysis of French Collection of Human Remains from Qumran," *DSD* 9 (2002): 199–248; A. Baumgarten, "Who Cares and Why Does it Matter? Qumran and the Essenes Once Again," *DSD* 11 (2004): 174–190; H. Eshel et al., "New Data of the Cemetery East of Khirbet Qumran," *DSD* 9 (2002): 135–165; J. Zias, "Qumran Archaeology: Skeletons with Multiple Personality Disorders and Other Grave Errors," *RevQ* 21 (2003): 83–98. The last has not yet been said on this matter.

[5] See on this matter below.

wiles),[6] or marginalized (like the wives of the *Damascus Document* who were interpreted as married to lesser members of the sect).[7]

But the women in Qumran wanted out; not just the skeletons in the cupboard, the ones mentioned in the texts too. Since the late 1990s there has been an explosion of studies on women and gender in Qumran. In a cursory study I have conducted I have come up with at least 40 articles, and at least two books, all dating to after 1992.[8] In fact, in my opinion, it is getting to the point where studies on the topic unwittingly repeat what has already been stated elsewhere, both because the options are not endless, and because scholars fail to read what their predecessors have written. This criticism applies to myself as well, but since I cannot demonstrate in my scholarship what works of others I have failed to consult, I will instead demonstrate how some of my own works have been ignored.

In general one can divide the topics being discussed into two basic questions: How are women viewed by the texts found in Qumran, and were there real women in the Qumran community. The first question requires that one read texts that fall outside of the purely sectarian literature, to include other compositions found in Qumran, such as

---

[6] See e.g. H. Burgman, "'The Wicked Woman': Der Makkabäer Simon?" *RevQ* 8 (1974): 323–359.

[7] On this premise see e.g. E. Qimron, "Celibacy in the Dead Sea Scrolls and the Two Kinds of Sectarians," in *The Madrid Qumran Congress* (ed. Trebolle Barrera and Vegas Montaner), 1:287–294; and much more recently A. Shemesh, "The Halakhic and Social Status of Women According to the Dead Sea Scrolls," *Bar Ilan* 30–31 (2006): 533–535 (Hebrew).

[8] In the interest of space I only list here a sample of these publications, particularly those not mentioned in other bibliographical references in this article: L. Schiffman, "Laws Pertaining to Women in the Temple Scroll," in *The Dead Sea Scrolls: Forty Years of Research* (ed. D. Dimant and U. Rappaport; STDJ 10; Leiden: Brill, 1992), 210–228; L. Cansdale, "Women Members in the *Yahad* According to the Qumran Scrolls," in *Proceedings of the Eleventh World Congress of Jewish Studies* (Jerusalem: World Union of Jewish Studies, 1994), A:215–222; L. Elder-Bennet, "The Woman Question and Female Ascetics among Essenes," *BA* 57 (1994): 220–234; M.I. Gruber, "Women in the Religious System of Qumran," in *Judaism in Late Antiquity*, part 5: *The Judaism of Qumran: A Systemic Reading of the Dead Sea Scrolls*, vol. 1: *Theory of Israel* (ed. A. Avery-Peck, J. Neusner, and B. Chilton; HO 56; Leiden: Brill, 2001), 173–195; S. White-Crawford, "Not According to Rule: Women, the Dead Sea Scrolls and Qumran," in *Emanuel: Studies in Hebrew Bible, Septuagint and the Dead Sea Scrolls in Honor of Emanuel Tov* (ed. S.M. Paul et al.; VTSup 94; Leiden: Brill, 2003), 127–150; M.J. Bernstein, "Women and Children in Legal and Liturgical Texts from Qumran," *DSD* 11 (2004): 191–211. The books are: C. Wassen, *Women in the Damascus Document* (SBL Academia Biblica 21; Leiden: Brill, 2005) and the highly eccentric I. Sheres and A. Kohn Blau, *Sex and Ritual in the Dead Sea Scrolls: The Truth about the Virgin* (New York: Continuum, 1995).

biblical, para-biblical, apocryphal and pseudepigraphical writings.[9] The second question, while concentrating on the sectarian texts, requires that these be more rigorously defined and leads the inquirer beyond the texts to archaeology of the site, particularly with regard to the cemetery.[10]

Following E. Schuller, who in 1997 raised the possibility that there were women in Qumran, and that they may have played a role in the community beyond that of wives of lesser members,[11] this topic has been continuously explored, first with doubts and misgivings but recently with more and more conviction. Women in Qumran are said to have served as "mothers" (אמות) of the congregation and to have something called רוקמה in it which, for lack of a better term, has been translated as "authority." Women in Qumran were expected to give evidence against their husbands (I will return to this issue presently) and were allowed a broader latitude for their vows than in other Jewish denominations. They were responsible for the examination of other women, to determine their virginity.[12] Supporters of the Essene hypothesis have produced a new consensus that these women, wives of lesser members, did not reside in Qumran. Instead, they hold that Qumran remained the stronghold of the more steadfast, celibate Essenes. According to this new consensus, the scrolls point to two sort of Essenes: those married and those not. This basic picture finds some marginal support in Josephus.[13] For lack of space, I do not present here the texts in which these issues emerge,

---

[9] See e.g. S. White Crawford, "Lady Wisdom and Dame Folly at Qumran," *DSD* 5 (1998): 355–366; J.E. Taylor, *Jewish Women Philosophers of First Century Alexandria: Philo's "Therapeutae" Reconsidered* (Oxford: Oxford University Press, 2003), 329–334; B.G. Wright, "Wisdom and Women in Qumran," *DSD* 11 (2004): 240–261; B.G. Wold, *Women, Men and Angels: The Qumran Wisdom Document* Musar leMevin *and its Allusions to Genesis Creation Traditions* (WUNT 2/201; Tübingen: Mohr Siebeck, 2005).

[10] And see n. 4, above.

[11] E. Schuller, "Women in the Dead Sea Scrolls," in *Methods of Investigation of the Dead Sea Scrolls and the Khirbet Qumran Site: Present Realities and Future Prospects* (ed. M.O. Wise et al.; Annals of the New York Academy of Sciences 722; New York: New York Academy of Sciences, 1994), 115–131 and in a revised version in "Women in the Dead Sea Scrolls," in *The Dead Sea Scrolls after Fifty Years: A Comprehensive Assessment* (ed. P.W. Flint and J.C. VanderKam; 2 vols.; Leiden: Brill, 1998–1999), 1:117–144.

[12] V. Hurowitz, "רוקמה in Damascus Document 4QD^e (4Q270) 7 i 14," *DSD* 9 (2002): 34–37; G.J. Brooke, "Between Qumran and Corinth: Embroidered Allusions to Women's Authority," in *The Dead Sea Scrolls as Background to Postbiblical Judaism and Early Christianity* (ed. J.R. Davila; STDJ 46; Leiden: Brill 2003), 157–176; S. White-Crawford, "Mothers, Sisters, and Elders: Titles for Women in Second Temple Jewish and Early Christian Communities," in *The Dead Sea Scrolls as Background to Postbiblical Judaism and Early Christianity* (ed. Davila), 177–179.

[13] See most forcefully Shemesh, "Halakhic and Social Status of Women," 533–546.

and which have meanwhile become a corpus repeatedly quoted in the scholarly articles where these issues are debated.

Instead, I wish to concentrate on one single composition: *Serekh ha-Edah* (*Rule of the Congregation*). It is a short composition appended to the end of the scroll of the larger *Serekh ha-Yaḥad* (*Rule of the Community*). The methodological rational for this approach is an attempt to move beyond the corpus just mentioned, which is an artificial one created by scholars, to an organic composition, understood as a whole by at least the copyist who produced 1QS. If this text is read for gender, it reveals not scattered references but a unity in which one reference is closely linked to another and all may produce a picture that individual references lack. In this approach I endorse M. Grossman's reading strategies, as suggested in her article "Reading for Gender in the Damascus Document," published in *DSD* 11 (2004). Grossman singled out the *Damascus Document* as important for the Qumran covenanters, and in view of this, since "the Damascus Document establishes a specific understanding of gender norms[, r]eading the text with an eye to these constructions—the distinctions between practices and traits that are understood as 'masculine' and those that fall into the category of 'feminine'—allows us to raise questions at a number of levels."[14] Like Grossman I look at one text and like Grossman I "read the constructions of gender [in this case in 1QSa T.I.] not in isolation but in light of other texts that we know existed simultaneously with it, and (perhaps) within the same community."[15] Unlike Grossman, however, I am interested in what the text is saying specifically about women in Qumran. I am also extremely interested in the history of research associated with the reconstruction and publication of this text, and the women therein. Careful attention to this history reveals the disbelief scholars have displayed and are still displaying toward evidence of women in the received texts, and consequently how the silencing of women works to this day. Silencing processes have been one of my major projects recently, as the name of my last book, *Silencing the Queen* indicates.[16]

---

[14] M. Grossman, "Reading for Gender in the Damascus Document," *DSD* 11 (2004): 212–239, 214.

[15] Ibid., 217.

[16] T. Ilan, *Silencing the Queen: The Literary Histories of Shelamzion and other Jewish Women* (TSAJ 115; Tübingen: Mohr Siebeck, 2006).

1. The Introductory Passage

I begin with the text itself. For convenience sake, I provide the section under discussion in the Hebrew original and suggest various translations throughout the discussion:

1 וזה הסרך לכול עדת ישראל באחרית הימים בהספם] ליחד להתה[לך

2 על פי משפט בני צדוק הכוהנים ואנושי בריתם אשר סר[ו מלכת ב]דרך

3 העם, המה אנושי עצתו אשר שמרו בריתו בתוך רשעה לכפ[ר בעד האר]ץ.

4 בבואם יקהילו את כל הבאים מטף עד נשים וקראו בא[וניהם]את

5 [כ]ול חוקי הברית להבינם בכול משפ[טיה]מה פן ישגו במ[שוגותיהמ]ה

1QSa begins with the words וזה הסרך לכול עדת ישראל באחרית הימים "this is the rule for the entire congregation of Israel at the end of times." Thus, L.H. Schiffman designated his comprehensive study devoted to this text *The Eschatological Community of the Dead Sea Scrolls*. What does it mean that this text is designed to set down the law for the end of times? Is this law only good for the future, or is it applicable now, for the present covenanters? In the interest of time I do not attempt to answer this question, but note that Schiffman and Charlotte Hempel, who wrote a comprehensive article on the literary layers in this composition, suggested that the text had practical implications for the Qumran community who produced it.[17] Hempel went so far as to argue that the eschatological introduction and conclusion to the text are later additions to the whole. When removed, the text becomes no more than another legal corpus of the present day Qumranites.

For my purpose it is important to continue reading this introduction. The purpose of this composition is described with the word בה⟨א⟩ספם ("when they gather") and the editors have completed the lacuna following this word with the term ליחד (namely, "to the Yaḥad," the name the community gave itself). This restoration is probably based on lines I:26, 27 and II:2 where עצת היחד is explicitly mentioned, but even if the reference is to the עדה ("congregation") as is much more common throughout the text, the composition of this gathering is interesting. In line 4, we read: בבואם יקהילו את כל הבאים מטף עד נשים וקראו בא[וניהם]את [כ]ול חוקי הברית להבינם בכול משפ[טיה]מה פן ישגו במ[שוגותיהמ]ה "when they come [together] they shall gather all those present including children and women and will read in their ears all the laws of the covenant to instruct them in all

<hr />

[17] L.H. Schiffman, *The Eschatological Community of the Dead Sea Scrolls* (SBLMS 38; Atlanta: Scholars Press, 1989), 8–9; C. Hempel, "The Earthly Essene Nucleus of 1QSa," *DSD* 3 (1996): 253–269.

its laws, so that they not err in their errors." No one has ever doubted the reading of these words, although they clearly mention women and children present in this gathering. This is probably because these words depend heavily on a biblical verse, Deut 29:9–10: אַתֶּם נִצָּבִים הַיּוֹם כֻּלְּכֶם לִפְנֵי ה׳ אֱלֹהֵיכֶם רָאשֵׁיכֶם שִׁבְטֵיכֶם זִקְנֵיכֶם וְשֹׁטְרֵיכֶם כֹּל אִישׁ יִשְׂרָאֵל טַפְּכֶם נְשֵׁיכֶם וְגֵרְךָ אֲשֶׁר בְּקֶרֶב מַחֲנֶיךָ מֵחֹטֵב עֵצֶיךָ עַד שֹׁאֵב מֵימֶיךָ "You are all present today before the Lord your God, the heads of your tribes, the elders and officers, all the men of Israel, your children, your wives, the foreigner in the midst of your camp from your wood cutter to your water drawer." In her article on the *Damascus Document*, M. Grossman stated that the "Damascus Document show[s] familiarity with the book of Deuteronomy" and in order to demonstrate the ideology of this book, which she terms an "inclusive covenant," she cites this verse, although it is not explicitly or implicitly cited in that document. She summarizes her discussion of this verse with the words "What is found in [it] should not be romanticized as an 'egalitarian' community; it is, rather, a gender-inclusive community grounded in an androcentric ideology."[18] Her comments seem as much if not more pertinent to 1QSa. Nevertheless, with the mention of women and children into the very introduction of this composition, one should not dismiss out of hand the possibility that women and children are intended in the following sections of this text as well.

2. Education and Testimony in the Assembly

That children are included in the overall plan of this composition is very clear. The text continues with a description of the sect members' education from childhood (נעוריו):

6   וזה הסרך לכול צבאות העדה לכול האזרח בישראל מן נע[וריו]
7   [יל]מדהו בספר ההגי וכפי יומיו ישכיליהו בחוק[י] הברית ול[פי שכלו]
8   [יי]סרו במשפטיהמה. עשר שנים [י]בוא בטף ו[בן] עשרים ש[נה יעבור על]
9   הפקודים לבוא בגורל בתוך משפ[ח]תו ליחד בעד[ת] קודש ולוא י[קרב]
10 אל אשה לדעתה למשכבי זכר כי אם לפי מולאות לו עש[רי]ם שנה בדעתו [טוב]
11 ורע. ובכן תקבל להעיד עליו משפטות התורא ולהת[י]צב במשמע משפטים
12 ובמלוא בו.

Here we observe what books and what laws and ordinances a member is to study and what he must do at the age of ten. I have framed this sentence in male language, as 1QSa also does, but the possibility that

---

[18] Grossman, "Reading for Gender," 222–224.

it is gender inclusive, and includes children (טף) of either sex should not be ruled out. After all, in the *Damascus Document*, the author, certainly a member of the sect, makes the general statement regarding the language of the law that משפט העריות לזכרים הוא כתוב וכהם הנשים ("the law of incest is written for males but similarly refers to females" CD 5:9–10). Applying this principle here in 1QSa is justified not just because the text has just included women and children (of both sexes) in the gathering, but because of what comes next. In lines 9–10 we are informed that until the age of twenty, the male member (זכר) of the sect is not allowed to engage in sex with a woman. This he is then permitted. This sentence is clearly concerned with males, and it may give the impression that it reflects on the previous lines concerned with education, and on the following line, which deals with giving testimony. However, as to the latter, the text here performs a complex exercise and switches from the male who is forbidden to go near a woman (יקרב), to the female who is expected to give evidence against him (תקבל להעיד עליו).

Before going on with my reading, it is important to note how this sentence was treated before the 1990s. In Licht's edition of the text from 1965 the reading found within the text is the masculine יתקבל (in בניין התפעל meaning "he shall be accepted"). Licht notes that the manuscript reads תקבל but states that "the assumption that the reference here is to the woman who would give evidence against her husband will not solve the linguistic difficulty and will lead us to a set of strange assumptions (השערות מוזרות) about the position of women in society."[19] Twenty-four years later Schiffman wrote in a similar manner: "This sudden shift from the masculine to the feminine and its implication of women's participation in the judicial process has caused some scholars to be suspicious ... After all, the context clearly refers to males. It is difficult to understand why a wife's acceptability as a witness should be connected with that of her husband. Finally, it is unlikely that women were entrusted with assuring the faithfulness of their husbands to the sectarian way of life."[20] He suggested emending the text to the masculine יקבל.

In an article I published in 1995, I wrote: "In the final analysis, this text, taken at face value, tells more about the sect than about its attitude

---

[19] J. Licht, *The Rule Scroll: A Scroll from the Wilderness of Judaea: 1QS, 1QSa, 1QSb: Text, Introduction and Commentary* (Jerusalem: Bialik Institute, 1965), 257 (Hebrew). The translation is mine.

[20] Schiffman, *Eschatological Community*, 18–19.

to women. The text suggests that the wife turn informer on her husband's degree of compliance with the sect's laws. The Qumran sect thus favors loyalty to the sect over loyalty to one's spouse. It displays a system which values regulating the lives of its members over respecting their privacy and conjugal intimacy."[21] My comments were never read by Qumran scholars. Neither J.E. Taylor and P.R. Davies, who wrote about women's testimony in 1QSa in 1996,[22] nor D. Rothstein, who wrote about it again in 2004[23] ever refer to it. Yet both articles tend in the same direction. Davies and Taylor read the text together with the *Damascus Document* which rules against engaging in sex with menstruants (CD 5:7). They understand the testimony a wife should give against her husband as one referring to her own state of purity during the act of intercourse. This attitude is one where instead of emending the text, we limit its application. In his article, eight years later, D. Rothstein rejected the limitations set on the topic of the wife's testimony by Davies and Taylor. He wrote: "It is perfectly reasonable to demand that a wife testify on all aspects of her husband's private conduct, including less concrete offences such as her husband's pride and the like ... while a plausible case can be made for interpreting 1QSa 1:9–11 as referring to something other than testimony by the wife, there is most certainly good reason for understanding the passage to require testimony of the wife against her husband."[24]

There were other stages on the way to this conclusion, which I have skipped in the interest of space,[25] but what it demonstrates in general is the way the interpretation of this text has gone from complete disbelief to complete acceptance of its credibility. In light of this conclusion, I still think my interpretation of 1995 is the most valid, for it takes into account, beyond gender issues, the social-sectarian character of the Dead Sea sect and does not view women's testimony as an indication of an egalitarian society, but rather of a totalitarian one. I thus suggest that it is only a question of time before one will be willing to read the previous verses on

---

[21] T. Ilan, "The Attraction of Aristocratic Jewish Women to Pharisaism," *HTR* 88 (1995): 1–33, 32–33.

[22] P.R. Davies and J.E. Taylor, "On the Testimony of Women in 1QSa," *DSD* 3 (1996): 223–235.

[23] D. Rothstein, "Women's Testimony at Qumran: The Biblical and Second Temple Evidence," *RevQ* 21 (2003): 597–614.

[24] Ibid., 612–614.

[25] E.g. N.H. Richardson, "Some Notes on 1QSa," *JBL* 76 (1957): 108–122; J.M. Baumgarten, "On the Testimony of Women in *1QSa*," *JBL* 76 (1957): 266–269.

the education of children as referring to female ones as well. How could the women of the sect know whether their husbands are fulfilling the laws and obligation when they had not been educated (or should I say indoctrinated) into the sectarian ways?

3. Those Excluded from the Yaḥad Assembly

I move from here to 1QSa II:3–9:

וכול איש מנוגע באחת מכול טמאות 3

האדם אל יבוא בקהל אלה וכול איש מנוגע באלה לבלתי 4

החזיק מעמד בתוך העדה וכול מנוגע בבשרו נכאה רגלים או 5

ידים פסח או עור או חרש או אלם או מום מנוגע בבשרו 6

לראות עינים או איש זקן כושל לבלתי התחזק בתוך העדה 7

אל יבו[או]אלה להתיצב [ב]תוך עדת א[נ]ושי השם כיא מלאכי 8

קודש בעצתם 9

And every person who is inflicted with one of humankind's impurities should not join the assembly of these, and each who is inflicted with these who cannot hold himself within the congregation and each who is inflicted in this flesh, amputated in his legs or arms, lame or blind or deaf or mute or is inflicted by an infirmity in his flesh visible to the eye or an old tottering man who cannot hold himself within the congregation, should not present himself within the congregation of the people of honor because holy angels are among them (the translation follows the CD text).

This text I suggest reading for women, precisely because of their absence from it. If we would like to know who is not invited to participate in the assembly to which this entire scroll is devoted, we should look to this list. Unlike the list at the beginning of the scroll which includes women and children, this list which excludes a large number of deformed persons, mentions neither women nor children.

Lists of persons excluded from certain activities were quite common in the sectarian literature of Qumran. One is found in the *Damascus Document*. I bring here the text both from the Cairo Genizah manuscript and from one of the *Damascus Document* fragments from Qumran, because the latter complements the former. The text is followed by a translation:

CD 15

אויל ומשוגע וכל פת[י] ש[ו]גה 15

וכהה עינים לבלתי ראות וחגר או פסח או חרש ונער ז[עטו]ט אל 16

יבוא אי[ש מאלה אל תוך העדה כי מלאכי קודש] 17

4Q266 8 i

וכול היות אויל 6

[ומ]שוגע אל יבו וכול פתי ושוגה וכה עינים לבלתי ראות 7

[ו]חגר או פסח או חרש או נער זעטוט א[ל יבו] איש 8

[מ]אלה אל תוך העדה כי מלאכ[י] הקוד[ש בתוכם] 9

A fool, a mentally unstable and every dim witted who rents and the blind and the lame or limping or deaf and a small boy, none of these should come into the community because holy angels …

A similar list is also found in the *War Scroll* (1QM VII:3–6):

וכול נער זעטוט ואשה לוא יבואו למחנותם בצאתם 3

מירושלים ללכת למלחמה עד שובם. וכול פסח או עור או חגר או איש אשר מום 4
עולם בבשרו או איש מנוגע בטומאת

בשרו כול אלה לוא ילכו אתם למלחמה. כולם יהיו אנשי נדבת מלחמה ותמימי רוח 5
ובשר ועתודים ליום נקם וכול

איש אשר לוא יהיה טהור ממקורו ביום המלחמה לוא ירד אתם כיא מלאכי קודש 6
עם צבאותם יחד.

And every small child and a woman should not come to their camp when they go forth from Jerusalem to go to war, till they return. And every lame or blind or limping person or a person who has a permanent infirmity in his flesh or one who is inflicted with impurity in his flesh, all these shall not come, and not go forth with them to war. All will be tribute of war and pure of spirit and flesh, and prepared for the day of revenge. And every person who will not be pure at his source on the day of war shall not go down with them, because holy angels are in together with them are in their armies.

I have presented both these texts because both, like 1QSa, also mention the reason for the exclusion as the presence of angels in the community. This issue has been noticed and fully discussed by A. Shemesh. He has compared these lists to similar ones found in rabbinic literature, and concluded that despite different formulations, both fulfill similar functions—exclusion of persons with physical deformities from the divine presence.[26] However, as can be noted in the lists I have presented, the exclusions are not always the same. In CD we find mention of אויל ומשוגע וכל פת[י] ש[ו]גה ("a fool, a mentally unstable and every dim witted who rents") as well as נער זעטוט ("a small boy"). On this basis, Shemesh concluded that there is "a significant difference between the lists in 1QSa and CD. [T]he former's failure to mention the demented fool, the simple-minded or errant man, evidently [shows that] the author of 1QSa chose

---

[26] A. Shemesh, "'The Holy Angels are in their Council': The Exclusion of Deformed Persons from Holy Places in Qumranic and Rabbinic Literature," *DSD* 4 (1997): 179–206.

to concentrate solely on disqualifications due to physical deformities ... Having noted this it becomes readily apparent that the list[s are] ... specific ..."[27]

From our perspective, it is interesting to note that while the *War Scroll* lists women and children in its catalogue of exclusions, and the *Damascus Document* lists children, 1QSa lists neither. It should also be noted that this follows on 1QSa I:4, which, as we have observed above, included women and children in the congregation. The text is consistent. Nevertheless, for the record of the history of research on women in Qumran, I am compelled to refer to a recent article by the same A. Shemesh on the issue of women in Qumran. There Shemesh wrote: "From the context it is clear that this passage refers to the assembly of the council of the Yaḥad both for the purpose of discussing issues relevant to the congregation and the study of Torah and for communal meals. It is hard to decide why women are not mentioned in it—is it because they are allowed to participate in the council of the Yaḥad or perhaps the opposite, and the author felt no need to list them specifically since it is so obvious that they are excluded from these gatherings? The second option seems to me more likely."[28] Thus, we see that for the purpose of defining women's position as secondary and insignificant in the sect (as is the thesis in his article), Shemesh employs a different, less rigorous reading strategy than the one he employed when discussing lists of persons with deformities and impurities.

On the other hand, I regard the differences between the lists as very significant. Women and children are mentioned in the *War Scroll* where they are specifically excluded from the war camp because they do not belong to the fighting force. In this attitude the Qumran community is certainly patriarchal and non-egalitarian. In the list of the *Damascus Document*, children are mentioned but not women, because although in formula it is very similar to 1QSa, the context therein shows that we are dealing with neophytes joining the community. The sect could by default accept invalids and fools born in its midst, but did not accept new members from among such disqualified people. Children they did not accept as neophytes because these do not yet know their own minds. Women are not in this list because they were accepted as potential members.

Note also, in this context, that while the 1QSa list includes old people, the list in CD does not. Their inclusion in 1QSa could be explained with

---

[27] Ibid., 196–197.
[28] Shemesh, "Halakhic and Social Status of Women," 541. The translation is mine.

Shemesh, as resulting from the fact that they are infirm and unpleasing to the eye, as the community described therein should be.[29] In CD they are not mentioned in the list of exclusions, because apparently old people were allowed to join the sect. Similarly, Shemesh had characterized the list in 1QSa as different from the one in CD, because it does not include mentally challenged people.[30] In this way 1QSa shares a premise with the *War Scroll* list, which also does not mention fools and the mentally sick. Is this omission not significant? Indeed, it is interesting to note that this omission in 1QSa II:3–9 is compensated for in 1QSa I:19–21:

וכול איש פיתי 19

אל יבוא בגורל להתיצב לעדת ישראל לרי[ב מ]שפט ולשאת משא עדה 20

ולהתיצב במלחמה להכניע גויים רק בסרך הצבא יכתוב משפחתו 21

And every foolish man should not be included in the lot to enlist in the congregation of Israel to pass judgment and bear responsibility and enlist in the war to subdue nations. Only his family shall be recorded in the rule of the army.

Here we are informed that the fool (פתי) is excluded from serving as judge and warrior, but is to be enlisted in the army (סרך הצבא). This explains well why these people are not mentioned in the *War Scroll* list. Unlike women and children, fools and the mentally sick were welcome in the war camp.

So as not to be accused of attempting to produce an overtly "feminist" and women-friendly portrait of the Dead Sea sect, let me stress that I do not think that women's absence from the exclusions list in CD and 1QSa is an indication of the "egalitarian" character of this community. Just as I do not consider the women's right to testify against their husbands in the sect an indication of gender equality, but rather as an indication of the way the system worked, so too, I view this list as functional. In 1QSa an event is described which includes women and children, as is stated categorically in 1QSa I:4. But women and children (as in rabbinic texts) were often excluded from various cultic activities described in other sectarian texts from Qumran. This can be deduced from two further documents. In the *Temple Scroll* (11QT[a] XXXIX:7), we read in association with the middle court of the Temple: לוא תבוא בה ה אשה וילד עד יום ("A woman and child shall not enter it until the day …") and in 4Q265 3 3 we read: [אל] יאכלו נער זעטוט ואשה [בזב]ח הפסח ("A small child and a woman shall not partake in the Pesaḥ sacrifice"). The Dead Sea sect, as other groups in Jewish

---

[29] Shemesh, "'The Holy Angels are in their Council.'"
[30] Ibid., 196–197.

society during the Second Temple period, was a patriarchal society in which women were secondary participants, and excluded from various activities at random.[31]

4. Women in the Yaḥad Council

I would like to conclude this reading for gender of 1QSa with a completely new suggestion, not previously noted or raised by anyone. In 1QSa I:25–II:3 we read:

25 ואם תעודה תהיה לכול הקהל למשפט או
26 לעצת יחד או לתעודת מלחמה וקדשום שלושת ימים להיות כול הבא
27 עת[יד לע]צה אלה הנשים הנקראים לעצת היחד מבן עש.   כול
28 ח[כמי]העדה והנבונים והידעים תמימי הדרך ואנושי החיל עם
29 [שרי השב]טים וכול שופטיהם ושוטריהם ושרי האלפים ושרי[ם למאות]

Col. II

1 ולחמשים ולעשרות והלויים בתו[ך מחל]קת עבודתו, אלה
2 אנושי השם קוראי מועד הנועדים לעצת היחד בישראל
3 לפני בני צדוק הכוהנים.

I refrain from suggesting a translation for this section at this point. Instead, I discuss each section and offer my translation of it as I go along. I begin with 1QSa I:27: אלה הנשים הנקראים לעצת היחד. The words should probably be translated: "These are the women appointed to the council of the Yaḥad." But a look at the history of research on this passage quickly indicates that not everyone has read it this way. Beginning with Licht, we find the reading אלה האנשים ("these are the men") printed in his edition. Licht notes here: "(The scribe) began writing הנאשים. When he noted his mistake he incorporated the א into the ש following it. The resulting reading הנשים is suspect and should be read האנשים."[32] This is an ingenious interpretation and was wholeheartedly adopted by later scholars. So we find it in the text offered by Schiffman, who makes no comment on this reading as an emendation,[33] and so we find it in Hempel's edition, with an indication that the reading is an emendation, but with no explanation.[34]

The reason why the alternative reading has never been anticipated is because of the way most have understood the syntax of this text.

[31] In this I agree with Shemesh, "Halakhic and Social Status of Women."
[32] Licht, *The Rule Scroll*, 263. The translation is mine.
[33] Schiffman, *Eschatological Community*, 32.
[34] Hempel, "Earthly Essene Nucleus of 1QSa," 260.

The words אלה הנשים הנקראים לעצת היחד are usually seen as opening a new sentence and followed by a colon. These (אלה) refers to the people mentioned thereafter: "All the sages of the congregation and the wise and informed, those of unblemished ways and the warriors with the heads of the tribes and their judges and officers, commanders of thousands and commanders of hundreds and fifties and tens and the Levites within their ritual divisions." Obviously all are men. There is a problem with this reading, however, for in 1QSa II:1–2 we read: אלה אנושי השם קוראי מועד הנועדים לעצת היחד בישראל לפני בני צדוק הכוהנים, which, if I am translating correctly, means: "Theses are the men of honor who designate times, who gather to the council of the Yaḥad in Israel under the leadership of the Sons of Zadok the priests." If these words are to be contrasted to the words אלה הנשים, or as most would read them, אלה האנשים, they too should be followed by a colon and by a list of people who stand under this heading (sages, nobles etc). They are not. Instead, this heading is immediately followed by the list of those disqualified from the assembly, which I have discussed previously. Because of this difficulty, Hempel suggested that this last sentence is a gloss, indicating later editorial activity.[35] But this is not the only textual solution to this conundrum. It is possible that the word אלה, repeated twice in this text, does not refer forward but rather backward. A nice example of such a use of אלה הנשים contrasted with אלה האנשים is found in the early tannaitic midrash *Mek. de Rabbi Ishmael*: "כה תאמר לבית יעקב", אלו הנשים; "ותגד לבני ישראל", אלו האנשים to be translated as " 'Thus you shall say to the House of Jacob' (Exod 19:3) these are the women, 'and tell the people of Israel' (ibid.) these are the men" (*Mek. de Rabbi Ishmael*, Yitro ba-Ḥodesh 2). Although this is a rabbinic midrash, and although it refers back to a biblical verse and not to a formulation suggested by the rabbis, the similarity to the 1QSa text is striking.

If we accept this suggested reading, the words אלה אנושי השם must refer back to the "sages of the congregation and the wise and informed, those of unblemished ways and the warriors with the heads of the tribes and their judges and officers etc." If this reading is correct, we should assume that the words אלה הנשים (or האנשים) also refer back. Here we should ask ourselves: to what part of the sentence exactly do they refer? The words immediately preceding אלה הנשים are: ואם תעודה תהיה לכול הקהל למשפט או לעצת יחד או לתעודת מלחמה וקדשום שלושת ימים להיות כול הבא עת[י]ד לע[צ]ה. Schiffman translated this text with the words: "And if there shall be a

---

35 Ibid.

convocation of all the congregation for judgment or for a council of the community or for a convocation of war, they shall sanctify themselves for three days, so that everyone who comes shall be pre[pared for the coun]cil."[36] Such a translation suggests that this is a complete sentence, ending with a full stop, and the words אלה הנשים begin a new sentence. I can imagine a plausible alternative syntax. We can read the first sentence as ואמ תעודה תהיה לכול הקהל למשפט או לעצת יחד או לתעודת מלחמה וקדשום שלושת ימים or in English: "And if there shall be a convocation of all the congregation for judgment or for a council of the community or for a convocation of war, they shall sanctify themselves for three days." The next sentence would begin with the words להיות כול הבא, which could be translated as "All those who come should be." These words are followed by a lacuna which is restored above (together with Licht and later editions) as עת[יד לע]צה. I do not have an alternative emendation, but this does not mean that I cannot reject this reading. I suggest we read the second sentence as follows: להיות כול הבא עת] [צה אלה הנשים, or in English "All those who come should be [...] these are the women." The next sentence begins with the words: הנקראים לעצת היחד מבן עש[רים ...] כול ח]כמי [העדה והנבונים והידעים תמימי הדרך[translated as: "Those appointed to the Council of the Yaḥad from the age of twe[nty ...] all the sa[ges of]the congregation and the wise and informed, those of unblemished ways etc." By such a division of this entire paragraph, I suggest we read the women back into the text and assume with the introductory paragraph that women (and children) are included in the events described in this short text. In this paragraph, which describes the עצת היחד (council of the Yaḥad), we learn that it consists of two components: women and men of honor. Following this description, we are informed of those who are excluded from the council.

In this essay I hope to have exemplified my vision for the methodology of "reading for gender" in Qumran. I think M. Grossman got it right that we should discuss whole documents, and I hope I have been able to show that 1QSa lends itself nicely to a similar project. I also know that my suggestion may appear to some rather radical. I am used to finding my suggestions for reading gender and women into unlikely places scoffed at and dismissed. I understand that some readers will dismiss my readings and/or my larger exegetical method. In light of what we have learned and the strides we have made since the Qumran texts were first deciphered,

---

[36] Schiffman, *Eschatological Community*, 29–30.

it would be prudent towait patiently and see how this entire text (and particularly the last paragraph I discussed) will be understood in say fifteen years.

THE TEXTUAL HISTORY OF THE HEBREW
BIBLE IN LIGHT OF THE DEAD SEA SCROLLS

THE *HODAYOT*'S USE OF THE PSALTER: TEXT-CRITICAL CONTRIBUTIONS (BOOK 2: PSS 42-72)

JOHN ELWOLDE
United Bible Societies

The Qumran *Hodayot* make extensive use of biblical texts, in particular of the Psalms. Accordingly, Jean Carmignac, after attempting an exhaustive listing of biblical "citations in the *Hodayot*," concluded that "l'auteur est surtout nourri d'*Isaïe* et des *Psaumes*."[1] Although the *Hodayot* writers aimed at conveying ideas expressed by, or associated with, the biblical text, rather than at "quoting" that text, it is likely, nonetheless, that the wording of the source text was at least sometimes reflected in a *Hodayot* author's new composition. The aim of the present study is to identify and to analyse evidence about the form of the biblical source texts employed by the *Hodayot* author(s) (whether consciously or unconsciously) on the basis of the verbal similarities that exist between various *Hodayot* sequences and biblical ones. Potentially significant text-critical evidence emerges when, for example, a series of words that varies slightly from the Masoretic tradition (or that agrees with the Masoretic tradition when other ancient traditions diverge) appears in contexts where there are no obvious stylistic or exegetical signals for the deliberate manipulation of a biblical text. Similar studies relating to Books 1 and 3 (Pss 1–41; 73–89) have been published and the present paper employs the same analysis for Book 2 (Pss 42–72).[2]

The texts discussed in this article include the eighteen listed by Carmignac (p. 375)—Pss 42:7; 43:1; 44:14; 51:3–4/69:17; 51:6, 7, 8; 52:4; 54:3, 6; 55:23; 57:5 (twice); 64:4; 68:23, 34; 69:22; 71:9—as well as three

---

[1] J. Carmignac, "Les citations de l'Ancien Testament, et spécialement des Poèmes du Serviteur dans les Hymnes de Qumran," *RevQ* 2 (1959–1960): 357–394, 391.

[2] "The Hodayot's Use of the Psalter: Text-Critical Contributions (Book 1)," in *Psalms and Prayers: Papers Read at the [Thirteenth] Joint Meeting of the Society of Old Testament Study and Het Oudtestamentisch Werkgezelschap in Nederland en België, Apeldoorn [21–24] August 2006* (ed. B. Becking and E. Peels; OtSt 55; Leiden: Brill, 2007), 79–108; "The Hodayot's Use of the Psalter: Text-Critical Contributions (Book 3: Pss 73–89)," *DSD* 17 (2010): 159–179. A paper covering Book 4 (Pss 90–106) will be published in the proceedings of the IOSOT XX Conference (Helsinki, August 2–4, 2010).

others discussed only by Preben Wernberg-Møller[3]—Pss 51:10; 66:9; 72:19. Psalm 54:5, also presented by Wernberg-Møller, is discussed in the paper on Book 3, in connection with Ps 86:14.[4]

Ps 42:7 = 1QHᵃ VIII[XVI]:32–33

Ps 42:6–8, 12 [= 43:5]:

מַה־תִּשְׁתּוֹחֲחִי נַפְשִׁי וַתֶּהֱמִי עָלָי
הוֹחִילִי לֵאלֹהִים כִּי־עוֹד אוֹדֶנּוּ יְשׁוּעוֹת פָּנָיו:
אֱלֹהַי עָלַי נַפְשִׁי תִשְׁתּוֹחָח עַל־כֵּן אֶזְכָּרְךָ מֵאֶרֶץ יַרְדֵּן
חֶרְמוֹנִים מֵהַר מִצְעָר:
תְּהוֹם־אֶל־תְּהוֹם קוֹרֵא לְקוֹל צִנּוֹרֶיךָ
כָּל־מִשְׁבָּרֶיךָ וְגַלֶּיךָ עָלַי עָבָרוּ:
מַה־תִּשְׁתּוֹחֲחִי נַפְשִׁי וּמַה תֶּהֱמִי עָלָי...
הוֹחִילִי לֵאלֹהִים כִּי־עוֹד אוֹדֶנּוּ יְשׁוּעֹת פְּנֵי וֵאלֹהָי.

1QHᵃ VIII:31–32 [XVI:32–33]:[5] ויתעופפו עלי משברים ונפשי עלי תשתוחח לכלה.

There is no comparable expression in the rest of the Dead Sea Scrolls, but in MT note also Lam 3:18, זָכוֹר תִּזְכּוֹר וְתָשׁוֹחַ עָלַי נַפְשִׁי, and, less strikingly, Ps 44:25a: כִּי שָׁחָה לֶעָפָר נַפְשֵׁנוּ. However, within Ps 42, as Hughes indicates, the words of the *Hodayot* passage "my soul within me is bowed down" might contain an allusion to any one of vv. 6, 7, or 12, or to two, or to all three of them.[6] Hughes is the only commentator I have noticed who also

---

[3] P. Wernberg-Møller, "The Contribution of the *Hodayot* to Biblical Textual Criticism," *Text* 4 (1964): 133–175.

[4] Unbracketed references are to E.L. Sukenik's edition, bracketed ones to Martin Abegg's electronic edition of the Dead Sea Scrolls, as accessed through the Accordance software, from which the *Hodayot* texts are also taken. (Significant differences from the edition of Sukenik are noted.) Abegg's edition also includes the text of *Hodayot* MSS from Cave 4, 4QHᵃ⁻ᶠ (4Q427–433), as they appear in E. Schuller's edition in *DJD* XXIX (1999): 69–232.

[5] Note that Sukenik has ⁻⁻⁻ for the first עלי; J. Licht, *The Thanksgiving Scroll: A Scroll from the Wilderness of Judaea: Text, Introduction, Commentary and Glossary* (Jerusalem: Bialik Institute, 1957), 139, restores [פחי]; S. Holm-Nielsen, *Hodayot: Psalms from Qumran* (ATDan 2; Aarhus: Universitetsforlaget, 1960), 144, 157 n. 68, restores [גלי]ו, noting that גל "wave" is found in Ps 42:8, and that "the following expression [i.e., ונפשי עלי תשתוחח] also seems dependent upon Ps. 42."

[6] J.A. Hughes, *Scriptural Allusions and Exegesis in the Hodayot* (STDJ 59; Leiden: Brill, 2006), 160. Other sources referred to are: Licht, *Thanksgiving Scroll*; M. Mansoor, *The Thanksgiving Hymns Translated and Annotated with an Introduction* (STDJ 3; Leiden: Brill, 1961); A. Dupont-Sommer, *Le Livre des Hymnes découvert près de la mer Morte (1QH): Traduction integrale avec introduction et notes* (Sem 7; Paris: Adrien-Maisonneuve, 1957); M. Delcor, *Les Hymnes de Qumran (Hodayot): Texte hébreu, introduction, traduction, commentaire* (Autour de la Bible; Paris: Letouzey et Ané, 1962); Holm-Nielsen, *Hodayot*; M. Wallenstein, "A Striking Hymn from the Dead Sea Scrolls,"

correctly draws attention to the use of מֹשְבָּרִים "breakers" in line 31, and to its occurrence in Ps 42:8.[7] However, beyond this possible additional parallel and the shared genre of individual lament there is nothing in the verbal or conceptual context of the *Hodayot* passage to link it clearly to v. 6 (or 7 or 12). Indeed, one could even argue that the source of the *Hodayot* sequence here is not the Psalter at all but rather Lam 3:18, noted above.

If, however, we agree with commentators like Carmignac, Licht, and Dec in seeing the primary linguistic influence as coming from Ps 42:7, it is difficult to draw any text-critical conclusions from the difference between עָלַי נַפְשִׁי תִשְׁתּוֹחָח in the Psalm and ונפשי עלי תשתוחח. LXX (in all its traditions), Peshitta, *Psalterium iuxta hebraicum*, and *Tg. Ps.* support the word order of MT. Nevertheless, the absence of a preceding divine name in the *Hodayot* passage and the initial waw (ונפשי) might be seen to support the text division in LXX:[8]

σωτήριον τοῦ προσώπου μου (καὶ) ὁ θεός μου
πρὸς ἐμαυτὸν ἡ ψυχή μου ἐταράχθη·

or Peshitta:

ܠܦܘܪܩܢܐ ܕܐܦܘܗܝ ܐܠܗܝ
ܐܬܕܠܚܬ ܥܠܝ ܢܦܫܝ

BHS recommends emending MT to: יְשׁוּעַת פְּנֵי וֵאלֹהָי: עָלַי נַפְשִׁי תִשְׁתּוֹחָח (cf. 42:12 = 43:5); Briggs and Briggs prefer: יְשׁוּעוֹת פְּנֵי אֱלֹהָי "the saving acts of the presence of (Yahweh) my God."[9] Barthélemy, in his lengthy discussion of the ending of Ps 42:6 and the beginning of Ps 42:7, points out that "[le] très ancien papyrus B24" reads as MT, and may represent

---

BJRL 38 (1956): 241–265; M.A. Knibb, *The Qumran Community* (Cambridge Commentaries on Writings of the Jewish and Christian World 200 BC to AD 200 2; Cambridge: Cambridge University Press, 1987), 157–182; B.P. Kittel, *The Hymns of Qumran: Translation and Commentary* (SBLDS 50; Missoula: Scholars Press, 1981); A.M. Gazov-Ginsberg, M.M. Elizarova, and K.B. Starkova, *Teksti Kumrana* (Pamyatniki Kulturi Vostoka, 7; St. Petersburg: Tsentr Peterburgskoe Vostokobedenie, 1996), 181–258; P. Dec, "Zwoje Hymnów Dziekczynnych znad Morza Martwego [*Megillôt haHôdajôt*] 1QHᵃ [1QHᵇ/4Q427– 4Q440]" (Ph.D. diss., Papal Theological Academy Krakow, 2004); G. Roye Williams, "Parallelism in the Hodayot from Qumran" (Ph.D. diss., Annenberg Research Institute, 1991).

[7] Hughes, *Scriptural Allusions*, 160 n. 111, 171.

[8] Cf. F. Field, ed., *Origenis Hexaplorum quae supersunt: Sive Veterum interpretum graecorum in totum Vetus Testamentum fragmenta*, vol. 2: *Jobus—Malachias: Auctarium et indices* (Oxford: Clarendon, 1875; repr. Hildesheim: Olms, 1960]), 155b (http://www.archive.org/stream/origenishexaploro2origuoft#page/154/mode/2up [21 April 2010]).

[9] C.A. Briggs and E.G. Briggs, *A Critical and Exegetical Commentary on the Book of Psalms* (ICC; 2 vols.; Edinburgh: T&T Clark, 1909), 1:366, 373.

the original form of MT rather than פָּנַי וֵאלֹהָי.[10] The *Hodayot* evidence, weak as it is, thus might support the majority view, against Barthélemy.

Ps 43:1b = 1QHᵃ IV:20 [XII:21]

Ps 43:1b: מֵאִישׁ־מִרְמָה וְעַוְלָה תְפַלְּטֵנִי.

1QHᵃ IV:20 [XII:21]: ותכרת במ[שפ]ט כול אנשי מרמה וחוזי תעות לא ימצאו עוד.

The evidence against this passage being dependent on any specific biblical passage is quite strong. First, the collocation אנשי מרמה only occurs in this one text (although אנשי [ה]רמיה is found at 1QHᵃ II:16 [X:18]; 1QS IX:8, and 1QHᵃ XIV:14 [VI:25]: כול פועלי רשע ואנשי רמיה).[11] Secondly, תעות does not occur in the Bible, so its parallelism with מרמה in the *Hodayot* passage is, unfortunately, irrelevant for determining a biblical source for כול אנשי מרמה. Thirdly, the Psalter's combination of מרמה and עולה is not found anywhere in the Dead Sea Scrolls (although רמיה and עולה are found in more or less close combination at 1QS IV:23; 1QHᵃ 3 10, 15 [XXI:30, 35]; cf. Job 13:7; 27:4). Thus, one wonders why Ps 43:1 was chosen by Carmignac for this *Hodayot* passage rather than Ps 5:7, אַנְשֵׁי דָמִים וּמִרְמָה לֹא־יֶחֱצוּ יְמֵיהֶם, or Ps 55:24, אִישׁ־דָּמִים וּמִרְמָה יְתָעֵב י׳. In fact, Holm-Nielsen cites all three passages, whereas Mansoor chooses to refer only to Ps 54:24.[12] Only Delcor agrees with Carmignac in referring to Ps 43:1 alone.[13]

LXX and Peshitta have a different order of adjectives from MT in this Psalms passage (ἀπὸ ἀνθρώπου ἀδίκου καὶ δολίου ῥῦσαί με), but it can hardly be argued that the *Hodayot* passage gives support to the order of MT here.[14]

Ps 44:14 = 1QHᵃ II:9, 33–34 [X:11, 35–36]

Ps 44:14: תְּשִׂימֵנוּ חֶרְפָּה לִשְׁכֵנֵינוּ לַעַג וָקֶלֶס לִסְבִיבוֹתֵינוּ.

1QHᵃ II:9–10 [X:11–12]: ותשימני חרפה וקלס לבוגדים.

1QHᵃ II:33–34 [X:35–36] = 4QHᵇ (4Q428) 3 2–3:

וישימוני לבוז וחרפה בפי כל דורשי רמיה.

---

[10] D. Barthélemy, ed., *Critique textuelle de l'Ancien Testament*, vol. 4: *Psaumes* (OBO 50.4; Fribourg: Academic Press, 2005), 252–255.

[11] Cf. Dec, "Zwoje Hymnów," 235 n. 559.

[12] Holm-Nielsen, *Hodayot*, 83 n. 44; Mansoor, *Thanksgiving Hymns*, 126 n. 7.

[13] Delcor, *Hymnes*, 154.

[14] Pace Wernberg-Møller, "Contribution," 158.

In the Dead Sea Scrolls, the combination of שים and חרפה is found only in these two *Hodayot* passages. In the Bible, however, the construction is attested not only at Ps 44:14, but also at Ps 39:9: מִכָּל־פְּשָׁעַי הַצִּילֵנִי וְשַׂמְתִּיהָ חֶרְפָּה עַל־כָּל־יִשְׂרָאֵל. Note also 1 Sam 11:2: חֶרְפַּת נָבָל אַל־תְּשִׂימֵנִי. הָיִינוּ חֶרְפָּה לִשְׁכֵנֵינוּ לַעַג וָקֶלֶס לִסְבִיבוֹתֵינוּ, Ps 79:4, and Jer 20:8, כִּי־הָיָה דְבַר־יְ לִי לְחֶרְפָּה וּלְקֶלֶס כָּל־הַיּוֹם, are also mentioned by commentators as possible sources. Although Wernberg-Møller claims that "Our author ... adapted the Biblical phrase [at Ps 44:14] to suit the requirements of his context,"[15] Holm-Nielsen characterizes the situation as follows: "It is impossible to say where ותשימני חרפה וקלס is taken from, because the words are found in practically identical sequences in Ps. 44:14 and 79:4, and Jer. 20:8 is a third possibility."[16]

Of the two *Hodayot* passages, the first (II:9–10) can more credibly claim a link with Ps 44:14, in view of the presence in both texts of, on the one hand, וקלס, and, on the other hand, a noun preceded by -ל, introducing those before whom the speaker fears humiliation: לסביבותינו; לבוגדים (the construction is relatively common in the *Hodayot*).[17] The sequence shared between *Hodayot* and Psalter at the level of lexical identity (ותשימני חרפה), however, is too short to establish a clear direct link with Ps 44:14, and there are no further contextual clues in the *Hodayot* passage that might point to the same biblical text. If dependency on Ps 44:14 is assumed, however, the *Hodayot* text would confirm MT against the proposal of, for example, Oesterley and Briggs and Briggs to read הָיִינוּ for תְּשִׂימֵנוּ, as at Ps 79:4 (הָיִינוּ חֶרְפָּה לִשְׁכֵנֵינוּ), because of the repetition of תְּשִׂימֵנוּ in the next verse, Ps 44:15: תְּשִׂימֵנוּ מָשָׁל בַּגּוֹי),[18] and against the insertion of a -ל before חֶרְפָּה, as reflected in some Greek and Latin MSS (see the apparatus to the Göttingen edition).[19] As Wernberg-Møller

---

[15] Ibid., 148.

[16] Holm-Nielsen, *Hodayot*, 38.

[17] T. Muraoka, "Verb Complementation in Qumran Hebrew," in *The Hebrew of the Dead Sea Scrolls and Ben Sira: Proceedings of a Symposium held at Leiden University 11–14 December 1995* (ed. idem and J.F. Elwolde; STDJ 26; Leiden: Brill, 1997), 92–149, 141.

[18] W.O.E. Oesterley, *The Psalms: Translated with Text-Critical and Exegetical Notes* (London: SPCK, 1959), 246; Briggs and Briggs, *Critical and Exegetical Commentary on the Book of Psalms*, 1:376.

[19] A. Rahlfs, ed., *Psalmi cum Odis* (3rd ed.; Septuaginta: Vetus Testamentum Graecum Auctoritate Academiae Scientiarum Gottingensis 10; Göttingen: Vandenhoeck & Ruprecht, 1979), 218.

points out, there is no evidence from versions or MSS for the singular pronoun of the *Hodayot* (ותשימני) as against the plural one of MT.[20]

Ps 51:3–4 / 69:17 = 1QHᵃ I:31–32 [IX:33–34];

XIII:17 [V:34]; VII:27 [XV:30];

XVIII:14 [XXIII:15]; IV:32 [XII:33]

Ps 51:3–4:   חָנֵּנִי אֱלֹהִים כְּחַסְדֶּךָ כְּרֹב רַחֲמֶיךָ מְחֵה פְשָׁעָי: הֶרֶב כַּבְּסֵנִי מֵעֲוֹנִי וּמֵחַטָּאתִי טַהֲרֵנִי:

Ps 69:17:   עֲנֵנִי יְ׳ כִּי־טוֹב חַסְדֶּךָ כְּרֹב רַחֲמֶיךָ פְּנֵה אֵלָי:

1QHᵃ I:31–32 [IX:33–34]:   ואתה ברחמיכה וגדול חסדיכה ... טהרתה מרוב עוון

The parallel here with 1QHᵃ I:31–32 is claimed only by Wernberg-Møller.[21] The four additional *Hodayot* passages cited (by Carmignac) also include various forms of the combination רוב רחמים. A search of Abegg's electronic version reveals an additional three occurrences (or restorations) in the main *Hodayot* scroll, 1QHᵃ, and nine in other Dead Sea Scrolls. The fact that the constituent parts are so common in the *Hodayot* (רחמים is found 44 times in all *Hodayot* texts, including restorations, and רוב 39 times) indicates a strong statistical probability that their combination is a natural result of the use of the Hebrew language (in speech or in writing) by members of the Dead Sea Scrolls community. Demonstration of a direct relationship of any one *Hodayot* text with either of the Psalms passages in which the collocation also occurs would require the presence of additional elements linking that *Hodayot* text to one of those passages.

Counting against any such dependency is the fact that in none of the up to ten occurrences of רוב רחמים in all *Hodayot* texts (including 4Q material) does the prefixed ־כ, which characterizes both biblical usages, appear.[22] For Wernberg-Møller, however, Ps 51:3–4 represents a specific source of wording in 1QHᵃ I:31–32 [IX:33–34]. The additional גדול in the *Hodayot* passage (וגדול חסדיכה for MT's חַסְדֶּךָ) is seen by Wernberg-Møller as reflecting a LXX-type *Vorlage*:[23] LXX reads κατὰ τὸ μέγα ἔλεός σου, which, of course, better fits the parallel כְּרֹב רַחֲמֶיךָ. Similarly, according to Wernberg-Møller, the *Hodayot*'s חסדיכה supports a Hebrew MS that reads the plural form as against the singular חַסְדֶּךָ in all other exam-

---

[20] Wernberg-Møller, "Contribution," 148.

[21] Ibid., 168.

[22] Wernberg-Møller notes support in Hebrew MSS (see *BHS*) for a reading with ־ב rather than ־כ at Ps 51:3, i.e., ברחמיכה rather than כְּרֹב רַחֲמֶיךָ (ibid.).

[23] Ibid., 168–169.

ples of MT.[24] No light is cast, however, on the additional conjunction that appears in LXX (κατὰ τὸ μέγα ἔλεός σου καὶ κατὰ τὸ πλῆθος τῶν οἰκτιρμῶν σου) and Peshitta (see *BHS*). No other commentator agrees with Wernberg-Møller in seeing a connection between these two passages.

Of the four *Hodayot* texts listed by Carmignac, perhaps VII:27 [XV:30] has the clearest immediate claim to a biblical connection of some kind, in as much as it also employs חסד, found in both the Psalms texts:

הודעתני ובחסדיכה לאיש [   ] ברוב רחמיכה לנעוי לב.

Holm-Nielsen also cites IV:36–37 [XII:37–38]: כי נשען[תי] בחסדיכה והמון רחמיכה.[25] Note also VII:18 [XV:21]:

ואני נשענתי ברו[ב רחמיכה ובהמון] חסדכה אוחיל.

1QH[a] X:15 [XVIII:18], once restored, might also reflect the penitential thought as well as the language of Ps 51:3:

[   ] לחסדכה בגדול טובכה ורו[ב רחמיך ואני [אשתעשעה בס[ליחותיכה].

At 1QH[a] IV:32, Delcor notes a parallel with Ps 51:3, and Holm-Nielsen refers to Ps 69:17 as well.[26] Additionally, Holm-Nielsen points out "the similar רחמים רבים" in four other biblical texts.

Ps 51:6 = 1QH[a] I:6 [IX:8]; VII:28
[XV:31]; 4 10 [XXII:29]; IX[XVII]:14–15

Ps 51:6:	לְמַעַן תִּצְדַּק בְּדָבְרֶךָ תִּזְכֶּה בְשָׁפְטֶךָ.
1QH[a] I:6 [IX:8]:	וארוך אפים במשפט ואת[ה צדקתה בכל מעשיכה.
1QH[a] VII:28 [XV:31]:	ומי יצדק לפניכה בהשפטו.
1QH[a] 4 10 [XXII:29]:	ומי יזכה במשפטכה.
1QH[a] IX[XVII]:14–15:	כי לא יצדק כול במש[פ]טכה ולא יז[כה ב]רבכה.

Of the *Hodayot* texts cited by Carmignac, only frg. 4 10 [XXII:29] has an at least superficially clear correspondence with Ps 51:6, the only biblical passage in which the verbal roots שׁפט and זכה are collocated. Having said this, in the Psalms passage זכה is stated of God, whereas in the *Hodayot* the purity of any being other than God is questioned. Thus, beyond the fact of broad lexical similarity, there is no clear syntactic or

---

[24] Ibid., 169.
[25] Holm-Nielsen, *Hodayot*, 27 n. 65.
[26] Delcor, *Hymnes*, 154; Holm-Nielsen, *Hodayot*, 85 n. 81.

conceptual parallelism between the *Hodayot* and the biblical passages, and any dependency can only be of the most general kind.[27]

Ps 51:7 = 1QHᵃ IV:29–30 [XII:30–31]

Ps 51:7:   הֵן־בְּעָווֹן חוֹלָלְתִּי וּבְחֵטְא יֶחֱמַתְנִי אִמִּי.

1QHᵃ IV:29–30 [XII:30–31]:   והוא מרחם ועד שבה באשמת מעל.

It is difficult to see anything beyond a merely conceptual parallel here. For example, Hughes comments: "The all-encompassing phrase, *from the womb and unto old age*, echoes biblical language such as that found in Ps 51:5 [7]."[28] Similarly, Holm-Nielsen: "For the train of thought, cf. Ps. 51:7"; and: "The last words in line 29 and the first in line 30 are possibly inspired by Ps. 51:7."[29] Mansoor refers "the idea" to Ps 51:7 and Ps 58:4 (זֹרוּ רְשָׁעִים מֵרֶחֶם תָּעוּ מִבֶּטֶן דֹּבְרֵי כָזָב); similarly, Delcor, who compares "le contenu doctrinal" of the *Hodayot* passage with that of the Psalm.[30]

Ps 51:8 = 1QHᵃ IV:27–28 [XII:28–29];
VII:26–27 [XV:29–30]; X:4–5 [XVIII:6–7]

Ps 51:8b: הֵן־אֱמֶת חָפַצְתָּ בַטֻּחוֹת וּבְסָתֻם חָכְמָה תוֹדִיעֵנִי.

1QHᵃ IV:27–28 [XII:28–29]:   כי הודעתני ברזי פלאכה ובסוד פלאכה הגברתה.

1QHᵃ VII:26–27 [XV:29–30]:   כי השכלתני באמתכה וברזי פלאכה הודעתני.

1QHᵃ X:4–5 [XVIII:6–7]:   כי תשכילנו בנפלאות כאלה ובסוד אמ[תכה] תודיענו.

With regard to the second and third *Hodayot* passages, Licht comments that the collocation of השכיל and הודיע is frequent in the *Hodayot*.[31] Carmignac is virtually the only commentator to draw parallels between the Psalm and any of the three *Hodayot* texts.[32] The only exception is Delcor who supports Carmignac in seeing a possible "allusion" at

---

[27] Cf. ibid., 265 n. 6: "[t]he same usage, but in a different sense."

[28] Hughes, *Scriptural Allusions*, 117.

[29] Holm-Nielsen, *Hodayot*, 85 n. 74, 88.

[30] Mansoor, *Thanksgiving Hymns*, 129; Delcor, *Hymnes*, 147; see also ibid., 154.

[31] Licht, *Thanksgiving Scroll*, 128.

[32] For each passage, Dec, "Zwoje Hymnów," 236 n. 586, 253 nn. 901–904, 269 n. 1268, notes a variety of *Hodayot* and other Dead Sea Scrolls parallels but no biblical text. At VII:26, Holm-Nielsen, *Hodayot*, 138–139 n. 2, compares Ps 32:8, אַשְׂכִּילְךָ וְאוֹרְךָ בְּדֶרֶךְ־זוּ; Dan 9:22, יָצָאתִי לְהַשְׂכִּילְךָ בִינָה, and, in particular, Neh 9:20: וְרוּחֲךָ הַטּוֹבָה נָתַתָּ לְהַשְׂכִּילָם; תֵלֵךְ.

IV:27–28,[33] but it is difficult to sustain any clear parallel here in lexis or construction. If we accept MT as it stands, the -בְּ of בְּסָתֻם, refers to the location at which instruction is to take place (in the interior of a human being), whereas in the *Hodayot*, the -ב always introduces the object, or topic, of instruction. In the *Hodayot*, the object of instruction is never specified as חָכְמָה and the construction in question is always found in parallel with a clearly synonymous sequence, which is not the case in the Psalms passage.

As an indication of some textual confusion in the biblical passage, note LXX's τὰ ἄδηλα καὶ τὰ κρύφια τῆς σοφίας σου ἐδήλωσάς μοι (< [?] בְּטֻחוֹת וּסְתֻמוֹת חָכְמָתְךָ תוֹדִיעֵנִי), which might reflect a text that was closer in syntactic shape to the construction found in the *Hodayot* (albeit without the introductory -ב). Even so, there would still no lexical grounds for drawing a parallel between the *Hodayot* texts and the biblical passage. The most that might be argued is that the frequency of the construction represented by the *Hodayot* passages (with two nominal expressions in parallel and suffixed nomen rectum) adds support to a LXX-type *Vorlage* as more original than the text found in MT (for τῆς σοφίας σου note also Peshitta ܚܟܡܬܟ ܝ ܐܘܕܥܬܢܝ ܐܟܣܝܬܐ)

Ps 51:10 = 1QH^a II:5–6 [X:7–8]

Ps 51:10:   תַּשְׁמִיעֵנִי שָׂשׂוֹן וְשִׂמְחָה תָּגֵלְנָה עֲצָמוֹת דִּכִּיתָ.

1QH^a II:5 [X:7]:   ומשמיעי שמחה לאבל יג[ון]מבשר ש[לום לכול הוות]י.

In view of the different verbal forms, ומשמיעי שמחה "and those who proclaim rejoicing," as against תַּשְׁמִיעֵנִי שָׂשׂוֹן "you cause me to hear gladness," and the absence of other contextual clues, it is difficult to see any connection between these two passages. In fact, no connection is made by any commentator other than Wernberg-Møller.[34] Mansoor sees here an "allusion" to Jer 31:13, וְהָפַכְתִּי אֶבְלָם לְשָׂשׂוֹן וְנִחַמְתִּים, Est 9:22, וְהַחֹדֶשׁ אֲשֶׁר נֶהְפַּךְ לָהֶם מִיָּגוֹן לְשִׂמְחָה וּמֵאֵבֶל לְיוֹם טוֹב, and similar passages.[35] In any case, the *Hodayot* reading would not support the Peshitta variant here, ܐܣܒܥܢܝ "satisfy me with."[36]

---

[33] Delcor, *Hymnes*, 154. In lines 29–30, Holm-Nielsen, *Hodayot*, 88, also notes a possible reference to Ps 51:7.

[34] Wernberg-Møller, "Contribution," 157.

[35] Mansoor, *Thanksgiving Hymns*, 104 n. 10.

[36] Cf. Wernberg-Møller, "Contribution," 157; *BHS*.

Ps 52:4 = 1QHᵃ V:26–27 [XIII:28–29] + 4QHᶜ (4Q429) 2 8

Ps 52:4:   ‏הַוּוֹת תַּחְשֹׁב לְשׁוֹנֶךָ כְּתַעַר מְלֻטָּשׁ עֹשֵׂה רְמִיָּה.
1QHᵃ V:26–27 [XIII:28–29] + 4QHᶜ 2 8:

‏והמה הוות לבם יחשובו [ודברי] בליעל פתחו לשון שקר.

As the construction ‏לַחְשֹׁב הַוּוֹת is only attested in these two texts, a
relationship of dependency of the *Hodayot* author here on the biblical text is at least a prima facie possibility.[37] The presence of ‏לשון in
both texts and also ‏שקר (in Ps 52:5) might seem to point in the same
direction as well. However, the fact that in neither of these general lexical parallels do we find the exact wording of the Psalms text clearly
reflected, and that words and concepts expressed in one text are absent
from the other, suggests that any dependence was vague and probably unconscious or, alternatively, that there was a conscious and deliberate use of the Psalms text, not, as it were, to *quote*, but rather simply to *employ* some of its elements in a creative way. Along with a reference to the Psalms passage, Holm-Nielsen also notes 1QHᵃ IV:13–
14 [XII:14–15], ‏זמות בליעל יחשובו,[38] a parallel usage that at least raises
the possibility that ‏לַחְשֹׁב הַוּוֹת simply represents an expression of the
Hodayot author's own literary creativity, independent of any real dependence on the biblical text. Significantly, Holm-Nielsen does not indicate Ps 52:4 as a source of the *Hodayot* usage in V:26, and Wallenstein compared ‏והמה הוות לבם יחשובו with Mic 7:3, ‏וְהַגָּדוֹל דֹּבֵר הַוַּת נַפְשׁוֹ,
‏וּפִי־מִרְמָה עָלַי פָּתָחוּ דִּבְּרוּ אִתִּי לְשׁוֹן and ‏פתחו לשון שקר with Ps 109:2, ‏הוּא
‏שָׁקֶר.[39]

In any case, the *Hodayot* text is not obviously relevant to the issue
of the text division in Ps 52:3–4: see the *Psalterium Gallicanum*, which
includes ‏כָּל־הַיּוֹם from the end of v. 3 in MT at the beginning of v. 4: *Tota
die injustitiam cogitavit lingua tua*; note also the layout of *BHS*, followed
by NRSV and REB, which takes ‏לשונך as the subject not of the preceding
‏הַוּוֹת תַּחְשֹׁב, but of the following complement: ‏כְּתַעַר מְלֻטָּשׁ.[40]

---

[37] See *DCH* 2:502a; 3:327a.
[38] Holm-Nielsen, *Hodayot*, 107 n. 32; also Licht, *Thanksgiving Scroll*, 105; Dupont-
Sommer, *Livre des Hymnes*, 50 nn. 1–2.
[39] Holm-Nielsen, *Hodayot*, 124; Wallenstein, "Striking Hymn," 253 nn. 5–6.
[40] See also Briggs and Briggs, *Critical and Exegetical Commentary on the Book of
Psalms*, 2:12, 13, 15; Oesterley, *Psalms*, 275–277.

Ps 54:3 = 1QH[a] IV:18–19 [XII:19–20]

Ps 54:3: .אֱלֹהִים בְּשִׁמְךָ הוֹשִׁיעֵנִי וּבִגְבוּרָתְךָ תְדִינֵנִי

1QH[a] IV:18–19 [XII:19–20]:[41] .כי אתה אל תענה להם לשופטם בגבורתכה

In view of the fact that the limited similarity here is in large measure conceptual rather than lexical, and that both משפט/שפט and גבורה occur so often in the *Hodayot* (77 and 33 times respectively; the noun דין is found just once in the *Hodayot*, at IX[XVII]:9]), it seems most likely that the usage in this *Hodayot* passage reflects not dependence on a biblical text but rather the natural linguistic creativity of the author or indeed of the Qumran hymn writers in general. Note, for example at 4QShirShabb[d] (4Q403) 1 i 37:

[כיא הוא]אלוהים לכול מרני }דעת{ עד ושופט בגבורתו לכול רוחי בין

At 1QM (1Q33) XIII:9, ומשפטי גבורות פלאכה might reflect familiarity with this hymnic usage. Apart from Carmignac, only Delcor claims that the *Hodayot* text "se réfère probablement au" Ps 54:3 (although Delcor also draws attention to the difference between שפט and דין).[42] In any case, *BHS* notes no relevant textual variants in the biblical passage.

Ps 54:6 = 1QH[a] II:7 [X:9]

Ps 54:6: .הִנֵּה אֱלֹהִים עֹזֵר לִי אֲדֹנָי בְּסֹמְכֵי נַפְשִׁי

1QH[a] II:7 [X:9]: .ותתן מענה לשון לער[ול] שפתי ותסמוך נפשי בחזוק מותנים

The striking declaration אֲדֹנָי בְּסֹמְכֵי נַפְשִׁי is not clearly reflected in the *Hodayot* passage, where, instead, we probably have no more than an expression of the biblical concept of God's upholding of the faithful, attested not only at Ps 54:6, but also at Ps 51:14, וְרוּחַ נְדִיבָה תִסְמְכֵנִי, and perhaps also Ps 112:8, סָמוּךְ לִבּוֹ לֹא יִירָא. The idea was widely appropriated among the *Hodayot* writers and other members of the Dead Sea Scrolls community, as indicated by the following texts:

1QH[a] VII:6 [XV:9]: .אודכה אדוני כי סמכתני בעוזכה

1QH[a] XVIII:13 [XXIII:14]: .ליצר אשר סמכתה בעוזכה

1QH[a] IX[XVII]:32: .ובאמת נכון סמכתני וברוח קודשכה תשעשעני

---

[41] At 4QH[d] (4Q430) 1 7, תענה is followed by -ב rather than -ל; see E. Schuller in *DJD* XXIX [1999]: 198.

[42] Delcor, *Hymnes*, 153.

4QpIsa^d (4Q161) VIII:18:

4QH^b (4Q428) 14 3:

11QPs^a (11Q5) XIX:13:

ואל יסומכנו ב[‏ .

אותך אדוני זכרתי ונסמך לבי.

ועל חסדיכה אני נסמכתי.

Of commentators consulted other than Carmignac, only Dec links our
two passages, saying that the *Hodayot* sequence is a "parafraza" of the
one found at Ps 54:6.[43] *BHS* indicates no textual diversity.

Ps 55:23 = 1QH^a IX[XVII]:34

Ps 55:23:

1QH^a IX[XVII]:34:

הַשְׁלֵךְ עַל־יְ׳ יְהָבְךָ וְהוּא יְכַלְכְּלֶךָ.

ועד שיבה אתה תכלכלני.

Here, again, it is difficult to justify any but the broadest conceptual
dependency on biblical passages referring to God's sustaining of the
faithful. Three other passages in the Bible and three in the Dead Sea
Scrolls make reference to the same idea:

Neh 9:21:

1 Kgs 17:4:

1 Kgs 17:9:

1QS III:17:

1QH^a IX[XVII]:36:

4QShir^b (4Q511) 1 8:

וְאַרְבָּעִים שָׁנָה כִּלְכַּלְתָּם.

אֶת־הָעֹרְבִים צִוִּיתִי לְכַלְכֶּלְךָ שָׁם.

הִנֵּה צִוִּיתִי שָׁם אִשָּׁה אַלְמָנָה לְכַלְכְּלֶךָ.

והואה יכלכלם בכול חפציהם.

וכאומן בחיק תכלכל לכול מעש[י]כה.

וכול בני עולה לוא יתכלכל.

Of the Dead Sea Scrolls texts, 1QS III:17 would appear to have a stronger
claim than our *Hodayot* one to dependency on the Psalms passage. Holm-
Nielsen compares Ps 55:23 and Ruth 4:15, לְכַלְכֵּל אֶת־שֵׂיבָתֵךְ, which at
least on the linguistic level would seem to be a more likely source of our
Hodayot passage than Ps 55:23.[44] Among other commentators, only Licht
and Mansoor compare Ps 55:23.[45] *BHS* records no textual issues.

Ps 57:5 = 1QH^a V:6–7, 9–10 [XIII:8–9, 11–12]

Ps 57:5:

1QH^a V:6–7 [XIII:8–9]:

1QH^a V:9–10 [XIII:11–12]:

נַפְשִׁי בְּתוֹךְ לְבָאִם אֶשְׁכְּבָה לֹהֲטִים בְּנֵי־אָדָם

שִׁנֵּיהֶם חֲנִית וְחִצִּים וּלְשׁוֹנָם חֶרֶב חַדָּה.

ותתן [ ] בתוך לביאים מועדים לבני אשמה

אריות שוברי עצם אדירים ושותי ד[ם] גבורים.

ותסגור פי כפירים אשר כחרב שניהם ומתלעותם כחנית חדה.

---

[43] Dec, "Zwoje Hymnów," 223 n. 365.

[44] Holm-Nielsen, *Hodayot*, 164 n. 157.

[45] Licht, *Thanksgiving Scroll*, 149; Mansoor, *Thanksgiving Hymns*, 162 n. 2.

Although בתוך is followed by a word for lion only in these two passages, other parallels are rather weak: Carmignac highlights the parallelism of בני אדם and בני אשמה. There is also an overall similarity in the general structure, with the second part of each sequence (as presented above) apparently expanding on the destructive nature of the lion mentioned in the first part. In that case, what appears in MT as לְהֲטִים בְּנֵי־אָדָם "devouring the children of Adam" would correspond to מועדים לבני אשמה in the *Hodayot*: "appointed for the children of guilt." The second part of the *Hodayot* text, "lions breaking the bone(s) of the mighty and drinking the blood of warriors," might then represent a creative reworking of the second part of MT, focussing on the consequences of the characteristics of the lions as presented in MT: "their teeth (for breaking bones) are a spear and arrows and their tongue (for drinking blood), a sharp sword." If the idea of this kind of creative reworking is accepted, then it is also already evidenced in the use of בני אשמה for בני אדם, noted above.

The likelihood that the Psalms passage underlies the *Hodayot* one here is somewhat strengthened by possible echoes of the same Psalms passage later in the same *hodayah*. In fact, 1QHᵃ V:5–19 [XIII:7–21] is the only literary unit in the *Hodayot* where lions are mentioned, at lines 7, 9, 13, and 19 [9, 11, 15, 21],[46] and an argument for dependence on Ps 57:5 can be made in the first two of these three additional passages.

This is rather clear in lines 9–10[11–12] (see above), which might reflect an inaccurate recollection or a creative reworking of the second half of v. 5 (see above). Whereas Dupont-Sommer (followed by Delcor), simply says that the usage here is "inspiré de Ps., LVII, 5,"[47] Holm-Nielsen sees the parallelism of שניהם with מתלעות rather than לשון as arising from a merging, whether unconscious or creative, of the text in Ps 57:5 with that of Joel 1:6: שִׁנָּיו שֵׁנֵּי אַרְיֵה וּמְתַלְּעוֹת לָבִיא לוֹ.[48] Mansoor refers additionally to Job 4:10, וְשִׁנֵּי כְפִירִים נִתָּעוּ, for the mention of כפירים in the *Hodayot* text, although here Gazov-Ginsberg is probably right to identify Ps 58:7, מַלְתְּעוֹת כְּפִירִים נְחֹץ י׳, as the source of both the כפירים and the מתלעות in the *Hodayot* passage.[49]

---

[46] Contrast the Psalms, where there are at least eleven references, mainly in Book 1: Pss 7:3; 10:9; 17:12; 22:14, 22; 34:11; 35:17; 57:5; 58:7; 91:13; 104:21.

[47] Dupont-Sommer, *Livre des Hymnes*, 47 n. 2; Delcor, *Hymnes*, 157.

[48] Holm-Nielsen, *Hodayot*, 97.

[49] Mansoor, *Thanksgiving Hymns*, 133 n. 3; Gazov-Ginsberg, *Teksti Kumrana*, 244 n. 200.

Ps 57:5 might also lie behind the usage found in our *Hodayot* unit's third mention of lions, at line 13[15], ותצל נפש עני במעון אריות אשר שננו כחרב לשונם, which might recall in a different form וּלְשׁוֹנָם חֶרֶב חַדָּה of the Psalm. Neither Carmignac nor any other commentator consulted, however, makes this connection. Delcor is, of course, correct in seeing the exact words of the *Hodayot* text at the beginning of Ps 64:4, אֲשֶׁר שָׁנְנוּ כַחֶרֶב לְשׁוֹנָם, said not of lions but of the פֹּעֲלֵי אָוֶן at the end of v. 3.[50] Formal identity with one Psalms passage does not, however, rule out influence from another that is is merely similar, especially when the latter passage has already been cited or alluded to once and perhaps even twice in the preceding lines.

Returning to Ps 57:5, then, if dependency of this *Hodayot* text on the biblical one is accepted, there are several textual issues for which the *Hodayot* passage might be relevant.

At the beginning of the verse, in LXX the "soul" (MT נַפְשִׁי, represented in all the versions) is the object of "save": καὶ ἐρρύσατο τὴν ψυχήν μου. Because of this verb, LXX then reads, apparently, מתוך (ἐκ μέσου) instead of בתוך. Here, however, the *Hodayot* passage, if accepted as relevant, clearly supports MT.

The following word in MT is the hapax לְבָא. Here, most probably, the *Hodayot* writer saw (or heard or interpreted as) the normal לָבִיא. The *Hodayot* reading thus supports MT and LXX (ἐκ μέσου σκύμνων) against both Peshitta, ܡ ܢ ܚܠܬܐ (in other respects, Peshitta supports, or relies on, LXX here), and *Tg. Ps.* במצע שלהובין.

If the *Hodayot* is dependent on this Psalms passage, its interpretation of לְבָא as לָבִיא is, of course, confirmed by the words that follow: ... אריות, etc. Moreover, the *Hodayot* text would clearly indicate an interpretation in which the בני אדם cannot be the possessors of the destructive teeth and tongues of the second half of the biblical verse, but, rather, their victims. Note here the observation of Gazov-Ginsberg: "the author of the hymn identifies himself not with the persecuted but with the persecutors [my translation]"![51] The point is probably more accurately expressed by Licht: "the meaning of the imagery is different: in the Psalms, the lions are a symbol of the wicked, but the lions in this *hodayah* are appointed for

---

[50] Delcor, *Hymnes*, 159; also Dupont-Sommer, *Livre des Hymnes*, 47 n. 11; Mansoor, *Thanksgiving Hymns*, 134 n. 1; Licht, *Thanksgiving Scroll*, 101; Holm-Nielsen, *Hodayot*, 96 n. 32, 98.

[51] Gazov-Ginsberg, *Teksti Kumrana*, 243 n. 147.

the wicked; they are a symbol of the punishment threatened against the children of iniquity … [,] a symbol of the angels of destruction appointed for the wicked [my translation]."[52]

Nothing corresponding to MT's אֶשְׁכְּבָה, or indeed אֶשְׁכְּבָה לֹהֲטִים seems to be present in the *Hodayot*, and thus no light is cast on LXX's ἐκοιμήθην τεταραγμένος (cf. Peshitta: ܘܕܡܟܬ ܟܕ ܕܠܝܚ ܐܢܐ); the same applies to the difficult נפשי חיירא / חדיא "my soul glows" in *Tg. Ps.*[53]

Because the second *Hodayot* sequence, in lines 9–10[11–12], differs significantly from the corresponding text at the end of Ps 57:5, it can have no obvious text-critical relevance. The text of MT here, שִׁנֵּיהֶם חֲנִית וְחִצִּים וּלְשׁוֹנָם חֶרֶב חַדָּה, is reflected in the versions, with the slight possible exception of LXX's ὅπλον "weapon, armour" for חֲנִית "spear."

Note that Holm-Nielsen makes no reference to Ps 57:5 in connection with lines 6–7, preferring to see the background of the *Hodayot* usage in the biblical account of Daniel in the lions' den (Dan 6:17–24).[54] Dec does not refer to the Psalms passage in his discussion of "lions" in the Bible.[55] Delcor refers to Ps 56:5 only as one of several passages in which enemies and lions are compared.[56]

At line 9[11], Gazov-Ginsberg sees the primary provenance of the *Hodayot* usage in Dan 6:23: אֱלָהִי שְׁלַח מַלְאֲכֵהּ וּסֲגַר פֻּם אַרְיָוָתָא.[57] That Dan 6:17–24 has a primary role here is also accepted by Holm-Nielsen.[58] Curiously, Licht makes no mention of the Daniel story in his introduction to the *Hodayot* passage or in his comments on it (although he cites Dan 6:23 at line 9[11]), but appears to view the Psalm as the primary source of the lion imagery in the *hodayah*.[59] Similar comments apply as well to the treatments of Delcor and Mansoor.

---

[52] Licht, *Thanksgiving Scroll*, 99.

[53] D.M. Stec, *The Targum of Psalms: Translated, with a Critical Introduction, Apparatus, and Notes* (ArBib 16; London: T&T Clark, 2004), 115. Cf. Jastrow, 426, 451a, 501b, and the apparatus in Stec, *Targum of Psalms*, 115.

[54] Holm-Nielsen, *Hodayot*, 92 nn. 7–8, 98.

[55] Dec, "Zwoje Hymnów," 239 n. 628.

[56] Delcor, *Hymnes*, 156.

[57] Gazov-Ginsberg, *Teksti Kumrana*, 244 n. 200. See Kittel, *Hymns*, 96–97, for an overview of the literary and thematic significance of the lion imagery in our *Hodayot* unit and its background in the biblical story of Daniel.

[58] Holm-Nielsen, *Hodayot*, 97.

[59] Licht, *Thanksgiving Scroll*, 99.

Ps 64:4a = 1QHᵃ V:13 [XIII:15]

Ps 64:4a: אֲשֶׁר שָׁנְנוּ כַחֶרֶב לְשׁוֹנָם .

1QHᵃ V:13 [XIII:15]: ותצל נפש עני במעון אריות אשר שננו כחרב לשונם .

See above, on Ps 57:5. The text here is identical to Ps 64:4a in MT, for which no significant variants are found. Moreover, the words do not occur elsewhere in this form. The nearest parallel to our sequence in the Bible or Dead Sea Scrolls is שָׁנֲנוּ לְשׁוֹנָם כְּמוֹ־נָחָשׁ at Ps 140:4. The parallel with the *Hodayot* passage has found its way into modern commentaries on Psalms,[60] but it is curious that such an exact coincidence of wording is not highlighted in editions and studies of the *Hodayot*.

Ps 66:9 = 1QHᵃ II:20 [X:22]

Ps 66:9: הַשָּׂם נַפְשֵׁנוּ בַּחַיִּים וְלֹא־נָתַן לַמּוֹט רַגְלֵנוּ .

1QHᵃ II:20 [X:22]: אודכה אדוני כי שמתה נפשי בצרור החיים .

This parallel is not listed by Carmignac nor mentioned by any other commentator apart from Wernberg-Møller.[61] The combination שים נפש occurs six times more in the Bible (Judg 12:3; 1 Sam 19:5; 28:21; 1 Kgs 19:2; Isa 53:10; Job 13:14), but in only one of these is God, as in Ps 66:9, the subject: Isa 53:10, אִם־תָּשִׂים אָשָׁם נַפְשׁוֹ. In the Dead Sea Scrolls, it is attested only once elsewhere, again in the *Hodayot*, III:6 [XI:8], where, however, the subject is the author's enemies: וישימו נפש[י] כאוניה ב[מ]צולות ים. The combination in our *Hodayot* passage with חיים (בצרור החיים) makes a relationship with the Psalms text more likely (הַשָּׂם נַפְשֵׁנוּ בַּחַיִּים), even though it is clear that the dominant imagery is probably drawn from 1 Sam 25:29, וְהָיְתָה נֶפֶשׁ אֲדֹנִי צְרוּרָה בִּצְרוֹר הַחַיִּים (as noted by the great majority of commentators). Moreover, there are no other elements in the *Hodayot* text that link it obviously with the Psalm. Perhaps we could at best venture to characterize the situation as one in which the imagery of the Samuel passage has been expressed by means of the language and structure of the Psalms one.

To go beyond this statement and argue that the singular suffix in the *Hodayot* passage is of text-critical relevance to the Psalm is much less easy to justify, in view of the reworking of language and imagery that

---

[60] E.g., A.A. Anderson, *The Book of Psalms*, vol. 1: *Psalms 1–72* (The New Century Bible Commentary; Grand Rapids: Eerdmans, 1972), 461, probably via Mowinckel.

[61] Wernberg-Møller, "Contribution," 149.

has taken place more generally in the construction of this sequence in the *Hodayot*, whether consciously or unconsciously influenced by one or both of the biblical passages. This argument is, however, defended by Wernberg-Møller, who saw the *Hodayot*'s נפשי as supporting LXX's τὴν ψυχήν μου against נפשנו of MT: "The evidence of G [and VL and V] suggests that the form of the suffix [נפשי] was not merely changed ... to fit ... a new context, but was actually present in Hebrew MSS at the time of the first translation of the Psalter into Greek."[62] Wernberg-Møller's claim assumes the Greek translator faithfully represented a Hebrew text that had a singular pronoun rather than raising the possibility that the translator himself changed from plural to singular for translational or editorial reasons.

Ps 68:23 = 1QHᵃ III:6 [XI:7]

Ps 68:23:   אָשִׁיב מִמְּצֻלוֹת יָם.

1QHᵃ III:6 [XI:7]:   וישימו נפש[י] כאוניה ב[מ]צולות ים.

In the Bible and the Dead Sea Scrolls, the combination מצלות ים occurs only in these two passages and Mic 7:19, and there is nothing in the context to recommend the Psalms passage as the closer parallel over the Micah one, where, moreover, there is a prefixed -ב, as in the *Hodayot*. Indeed, Mansoor refers only to Micah, whereas Delcor and Holm-Nielsen compare both biblical verses.[63] In the Dead Sea Scrolls, the noun מצולה is found twice elsewhere in the *Hodayot* (III:14 [XI:15]; VIII:19 [XVI:20]) and six times in other texts. The collocation with ים is unremarkable and might easily reflect the *Hodayot* author's own linguistic creativity rather than any dependency on either of the biblical passages in which this combination is found. It can hardly be used as evidence in support of an LXX *Vorlage* with prefixed -ב (ἐν).[64]

---

[62] Ibid.

[63] Mansoor, *Thanksgiving Hymns*, 112 n. 4; Delcor, *Hymnes*, 100; Holm-Nielsen, *Hodayot*, 52 n. 8.

[64] Cf. L.C.L. Brenton, *The Septuagint Version of the Old Testament: With an English Translation and with Various Readings and Critical Notes* (London: Bagster and Sons, 1870; repr. Grand Rapids: Zondervan, 1971), 737: "I will bring *my people* again through the depths of the sea" (italics in the original); *Tg. Ps*: דימא במצולתיה; *BHS* צדיקיא די ישתניקו notes the LXX reading only, as well as some Hebrew MSS.

Ps 68:34 = 1QHª III:35 [XI:36]

Ps 68:34:   הֵן יִתֵּן בְּקוֹלוֹ קוֹל עֹז.
1QHª III:35 [XI:35]:   וצבא השמים יתנו ²קולם.

Curiously, this appears to be the only occurrence in the Dead Sea Scrolls
of the idiom נתן (ב)קול, although it is quite frequent in the Bible.[65] There
is no clear evidence from the *Hodayot* usage that Ps 68:34 influenced the
Hodayot author at this point and the usage at Ps 68:34 is of no particular
text-critical significance. Apart from Carmignac, the only commentator
to refer to Ps 68:34 is Delcor, although he also notes Ps 77:18, קוֹל נָתְנוּ
שְׁחָקִים.[66] To this last reference, Licht adds Job 38:7: וַיָּרִיעוּ כָּל־בְּנֵי אֱלֹהִים.[67]
Holm-Nielsen refers instead to Jer 12:8, נָתְנָה עָלַי בְּקוֹלָהּ.[68] Mansoor cites
Ps 77:18; Job 38:7, and Jer 12:8.[69]

Ps 69:22 = 1QHª IV:11 [XII:12]

Ps 69:22:   וַיִּתְּנוּ בְּבָרוּתִי רֹאשׁ וְלִצְמָאִי יַשְׁקוּנִי חֹמֶץ.
1QHª IV[XII]:11–12:   ויעצורו משקה דעת מצמאים ולצמאם ישקום חומץ.

This example is illustrative of the many cases in which even though a relationship between a *Hodayot* passage and a particular biblical text can easily be seen, the *Hodayot* version adds little to our knowledge of the development of the biblical text. In this example, the words are fairly clearly
drawn from a specific biblical passage,[70] but have been morphosyntacti-
cally adapted to a different context (even though, as Delcor notes, in both
passages the overall context is that of the persecution of the righteous).[71]
There are no significant text-critical issues relating to this Psalms passage,
and so the only *text-critical* value of the *Hodayot* text here is, broadly, to
support MT.

---

[65] See *DCH* 5:801a, b.
[66] Delcor, *Hymnes*, 134.
[67] Licht, *Thanksgiving Scroll*, 88.
[68] Holm-Nielsen, *Hodayot*, 73 n. 57.
[69] Mansoor, *Thanksgiving Hymns*, 121 n. 8.
[70] Cf. Hughes, *Scriptural Allusions*, 110: "a very clear allusion to Ps 69:21 [22]";
Delcor, *Hymnes*, 154: "certainement une allusion" to Ps 69:22; Dupont-Sommer, *Livre
des Hymnes*, 42 n. 11; Licht, *Thanksgiving Scroll*, 92; Mansoor, *Thanksgiving Hymns*, 124
n. 5.
[71] Delcor, *Hymnes*, 154.

Ps 71:9 = 1QHª 4 18 [XXII:37]

Ps 71:9: אַל־תַּשְׁלִיכֵנִי לְעֵת זִקְנָה כִּכְלוֹת כֹּחִי אַל־תַּעַזְבֵנִי.
1QHª 4 18 [XXII:37]: אל תעזובני בקצי.

There is no obvious relationship between the two passages, and the *Hodayot* text could just as easily reflect the use by the author(s) of the combination לא עזב five times elsewhere. הִשְׁלִיךְ with לֹא or אַל is not found in the Dead Sea Scrolls. I have seen no specific reference to Ps 71:9 in any commentary. Licht compares Ps 38:22, אַל־תַּעַזְבֵנִי י׳ אֱלֹהַי אַל־תִּרְחַק מִמֶּנִּי, "and similar verses."[72]

Ps 72:19 = 1QHª III:4 [XI:5]

Ps 72:19: וּבָרוּךְ שֵׁם כְּבוֹדוֹ לְעוֹלָם.
1QHª III:4 [XI:5]: בכבוד עולם.

In the Dead Sea Scrolls, כבוד עולם occurs in at least three other places:[73] 1QSb (1Q28b) III:4; 1QHª XIII:6 [V:23]; 4QInstruction^{d} (4Q418) 126 ii 8. Wernberg-Møller, who is the only commentator to note a possible biblical parallel, might be right in saying that Ps 72:19 is the best candidate, although Ps 104:31, יְהִי כְבוֹד י׳ לְעוֹלָם, would also be a possibility.[74] In any case, as Wernberg-Møller also accepts: "there is no reason to suppose that the [Qumran] hymnologist modelled his phraseology on that particular passage [i.e. Ps 72:19]."[75]

Summary and Conclusions

In the majority of cases, as expected, any specific relationship between a particular *Hodayot* passage and a verse from the Psalter is only tenuous. This applies to the following claimed relationships of dependency: Ps 42:7 = 1QHª VIII[XVI]:32–33; Ps 43:1b = 1QHª IV:20 [XII:21]; Ps 44:14 = 1QHª II:9, 33–34 [X:11, 35–36]; Ps 51:3–4/69:17 = 1QHª I:31–32 [IX:33–34]; Ps 51:6 = 1QHª 4 10 [XXII:29]; Ps 51:7 = 1QHª IV:29–30 [XII:30–31]; Ps 51:8 = 1QHª IV:27–28 [XII:28–29]; VII:26–27 [XV:

[72] Licht, *Thanksgiving Scroll*, 229.
[73] Cf. Dec, "Zwoje Hymnów," 227 n. 438.
[74] Wernberg-Møller, "Contribution," 160.
[75] Ibid., 160–161.

29–30]; X:4–5 [XVIII:6–7]; Ps 51:10 = 1QHᵃ II:5–6 [X:7–8]; Ps 54:3 = 1QHᵃ IV:18–19 [XII:19–20]; Ps 54:6 = 1QHᵃ II:7 [X:9]; Ps 55:23 = 1QHᵃ IX[XVII]:34; Ps 68:23 = 1QHᵃ III:6 [XI:7]; Ps 68:34 = 1QHᵃ III:35 [XI:36]; Ps 71:9 = 1QHᵃ 4 18 [XXII:37]; Ps 72:19 = 1QHᵃ III:4 [XI:5].

In the case of Ps 52:4 = 1QHᵃ V:26–27 [XIII:28–29], there might have been a conscious use of the Psalms text (הַוּוֹת תַּחְשֹׁב לְשׁוֹנֶךָ), as a resource for the *Hodayot* writer's linguistic creativity (והמה הוות לבם יחשובו), although this is far from certain. Somewhat similarly, in the case of Ps 66:9 = 1QHᵃ II:20 [X:22], it is possible that with שמתה נפשי בצרור החיים the *Hodayot* writer has merged the imagery and structure of the Psalms passage (הַשָּׂם נַפְשֵׁנוּ בַּחַיִּים) with that of 1 Sam 25:29 (וְהָיְתָה נֶפֶשׁ אֲדֹנִי צְרוּרָה בִּצְרוֹר הַחַיִּים).

Neither of these two possible parallels provides any defensible evidence of text-critical relevance to the Psalter. In two other parallels, Ps 64:4a (אֲשֶׁר שָׁנְנוּ כַחֶרֶב לְשׁוֹנָם) = 1QHᵃ V:13 [XIII:15] (אשר שננו כחרב לשונם), and Ps 69:22 (וְלִצְמָאִי יַשְׁקוּנִי חֹמֶץ) = 1QHᵃ IV:11 [XII:12] (ולצמאם ישקום חומץ), the similarity of the *Hodayot* sequences to the Psalms texts might be argued to support the Hebrew text that underlies MT, but they do not provide any further text-critically relevant data.

One passage, 1QHᵃ V:6–7 [XIII:8–9], ותתן [ ] בתוך לביאים מועדים לבני אשמה, remains where literary dependency on, although not quotation of, Ps 57:5, נַפְשִׁי בְּתוֹךְ לְבָאִם אֶשְׁכְּבָה לֹהֲטִים בְּנֵי־אָדָם, may be defended and where, if such dependence is accepted, the *Hodayot* text provides various elements of relevance to the textual development of the Psalter in this verse: מתוך with MT instead of ἐκ μέσου; the regular form לְבִיא instead of MT's hapax לְבָא, Peshitta's ܐܪܝܐ, and *Tg. Ps.*'s שלהובין; the absence of an equivalent for MT's לֹהֲטִים אֶשְׁכְּבָה or LXX's ἐκοιμήθην τεταραγμένος.

Almost half a century ago, Wernberg-Møller wrote: "The task of detecting the Biblical allusions in the [*Hodayot*] is an arduous and unenviable one."[76] One cannot escape from Wernberg-Møller's general pessimism about the very small yield of useful results in proportion to the time needed to isolate and to assess the relevant data. Nonetheless, the one passage with possible text-critical significance presented here, out of the twenty-one passages from Book 2 of the Psalter examined in the light of possible parallels from the *Hodayot*, represents at least no worse a result than the one out of fifty yielded by the study of Book 1.[77]

---

[76] Wernberg-Møller, "Contribution," 144.

[77] See my "The Hodayot's Use of the Psalter (Book 1)," 108: "On rare occasions, evidence from the Hodayot has a more compelling bearing on a known text-critical issue,

Whatever the end result of all this work and its utility for text-critics, it represents more generally a small part of that move away from the simple, and sometimes simplistic, division of the Dead Sea Scrolls texts and, correspondingly, their study, into biblical and non-biblical, and towards, I hope, a better evaluation of data from the so-called "non-biblical" corpus on the development of the text of the Bible, the message of which and the language in which it was expressed pervaded the consciousness of the "non-biblical" authors at every turn.[78]

---

as in the case of its apparent use of Ps. 18:5, although here the Hodayot evidence would simply support MT."

[78] See my "The Biblical Dead Sea Scrolls and Some Issues of Canon," in *Canon and Modern Bible Translation in Interconfessional Perspective* (ed. L.J. de Regt, Istanbul: Bible Society in Turkey, 2006), 1–41, 40–41. The analysis of Book 3 yielded three text-critically significant parallels out of a total of eighteen; see "The *Hodayot*'s Use of the Psalter: Book 3," 178–179; in the case of Book 4 (forthcoming), one significant parallel out of sixteen claimed parallels was identified.

HEBREW AND GREEK BIBLICAL MANUSCRIPTS:
THEIR INTERPRETATIONS AND THEIR INTERPRETERS

RUSSELL FULLER
University of San Diego

In this paper I examine the text of three verses from the end of the book of Malachi. I also examine the proposed redactional history of the end of the book of Malachi and the tendency in biblical scholarship to concentrate solely on the masoretic form of the text when attempting to reconstruct the redactional history of biblical compositions. I argue that such reconstructions must take into account all the manuscript evidence for a biblical composition, especially that of the Greek versions.

I use the short passage at the end of the book of Malachi, 3:22–24, and investigate the text according to both Hebrew and Greek witnesses. The reason I use this passage is that a recent reconstruction of the scribal production of the Bible in the Hellenistic period by Karel van der Toorn makes central use of the last three verses of the book of Malachi.[1] Van der Toorn hypothesizes the publication of an edition of all of the Minor Prophets on a single scroll by Jerusalem scribes around 250 B.C.E. He builds on observations of many scholars to hypothesize that the book of Malachi was the creation of the Jerusalem scribes at this time in order to bring the number of Minor Prophets on the scroll up to twelve.[2] Of necessity he argues that the masoretic order of the Twelve Minor Prophets, with Malachi at the end, is the original order in the collection.[3] He further builds on the work of other scholars in suggesting that Mal 3:22–24 is a postscript to the book of Malachi that was intentionally composed as such by the Jerusalem scribes. The postscript functions

---

[1] K. van der Toorn, *Scribal Culture and the Making of the Hebrew Bible* (Cambridge: Harvard University Press, 2007).

[2] Ibid., 252–253.

[3] See my edition of 4QXII^a (4Q76) in *DJD* XV (1997): 221–231, which seems to preserve the order Malachi-Jonah on the remains of a scroll of the Twelve Minor Prophets dating from ca. 150 B.C.E. See also van der Toorn, *Scribal Culture*, 253, 362–363 n. 68.

to conclude the book of Malachi and the new collection of the Twelve
Minor Prophets. Finally, in agreement with scholars such as Rudolph,[4]
he holds that Mal 3:22–24 was intended by the Jerusalem scribes to function as a postscript to the scribal edition of the prophets (Joshua through
Malachi).[5] Although he understands that the postscript/epilogue was
written by the Jerusalem scribes as one piece, he thinks that the two parts
of the epilogue allow insight into the concerns of the scribes in creating this multipurpose ending. The first section, which in the masoretic
form of the text refers to the Torah of Moses, was intended to indicate
that the collection of the prophets was not meant to take the place of
the Torah. The second section of the ending, which refers to the coming of the prophet Elijah before the great and terrible day of the Lord,
he understands as reflecting the scribes' expectation of the nearness
of that day. He claims that the ending "… suggests that the publication of the Prophets is to be situated in a time of messianic expectations."[6]

Van der Toorn's reconstruction is based on the assumption that the
masoretic form of the end of Mal 3:22–24 is the original or at least the
older form of the text and that the placement of the book of Malachi
at the end of the collection of the Twelve Minor Prophets is also origi-
nal/older than any other form the collection may have taken. The reconstruction does acknowledge the existence of variant forms of the text of
Mal 3:22–24, as is found in the Septuagint, and variations in the order of
books in other forms of the collection of the twelve such as those found
at Qumran, but these are dismissed with little or no consideration for
their implications for the reconstruction. It is my thesis that consideration of this evidence has important implications for the canonical history of the Book of the Twelve. Indeed, as a matter of course, all evidence should be considered in the reconstruction of the history of the
text.

---

[4] W. Rudolph, *Haggai, Sacharja 1–8, Sacharja 9–14, Maleachi* (KAT 13.4; Gütersloh:
Mohn, 1976), 290–291. Rudolph labels the final section of his commentary on the text of
Mal 3:22–24 as "Abschluß des Prophetenkanons."

[5] Van der Toorn cites O.H. Steck, *Abschluss der Prophetie im Alten Testament: Ein Ver-
such zur Frage der Vorgeschichte des Kanons* (Biblisch-Theologische Studien 17; Neukirchen-Vluyn: Neukirchener, 1991). See also Rudolph, *Haggai, Sacharja 1–8, Sacharja 9–
14, Maleachi*, 291.

[6] Van der Toorn, *Scribal Culture*, 254.

The Text: Textual Witnesses

Malachi 3:22–24 shows a difference in sequence in the last three verses of chapter three between the Masoretic Text and the Greek version. The Hebrew textual witnesses are unanimous in sharing the order of verses as found in the Masoretic Text.

Masoretic Text	Septuagint
22 זִכְרוּ תּוֹרַת מֹשֶׁה עַבְדִּי אֲשֶׁר צִוִּיתִי בְחֹרֵב עַל־כָּל־יִשְׂרָאֵל חֻקִּים וּמִשְׁפָּטִים:	23 καὶ ἰδοὺ ἐγὼ ἀποστέλλω ὑμῖν Ηλιαν τὸν Θεσβίτην πρὶν ἐλθεῖν ἡνέραν κυρίου τὴν μεγάλην καὶ ἐπιφανῆ
23 הִנֵּה אָנֹכִי שֹׁלֵחַ לָכֶם אֵת אֵלִיָּה הַנָּבִיא לִפְנֵי בּוֹא יוֹם יְהוָה הַגָּדוֹל וְהַנּוֹרָא:	24 ὃς ἀποκαταστήσει καδρίαν πατρὸς πρὸς υἱὸν καὶ καδρίαν ἀνθρώπου πρὸς τὸν πλησίον αὐτοῦ μὴ ἔλθω καὶ πατάχω τὴν γῆν ἄρδην
24 וְהֵשִׁיב לֵב־אָבוֹת עַל־בָּנִים וְלֵב בָּנִים עַל־אֲבוֹתָם פֶּן־אָבוֹא וְהִכֵּיתִי אֶת־הָאָרֶץ חֵרֶם	22 μνήσθητε νόμου Μωυσῆ τοῦ δούλου μου καθότι ἐνεταιλάμην αὐτῷ ἐν Ξωρηβ πρὸς πάντα τὸν Ισραηλ προστάγματα καὶ δικαιώματα

These include the oldest witness to the text of Malachi in Hebrew, the Qumran biblical manuscript 4QXII[a] (4Q76) which dates to approximately 150–125 B.C.E.[7]

4QXII[a](4Q76) IV:14–20 (frgs. 10 & 7)—Malachi 3:22–24

[עשה אמר יהו]ה צבאות 22זכרו תורת מש̇ה [ע]בדי	14	frg. 10
[אשר צויתי או]ת̇[ו ב]חורב ע̇ל כל י̇[שר]אל חקים ו[משפטים]	15	
[23]הנה אנכי שלח]לכם את אליהו הנב̇[יא]	16	
לפני̇] בוא יום יהוה הגדול וה[נ̇ו̇רא] [	17	frg. 7
24והשיב לב[ ] *vacat*	18	
אבות] על בנים ולב בנים על אבותם פן אבוא]	19	
והכיתי] את הארץ חרם *vacat* [	20	
[bottom margin]		

⁷ R.E. Fuller in *DJD* XV (1997): 221. The following transcription is adapted from ibid., 228.

The major Greek witnesses are unanimous (i.e., W [Washington papyrus, 3rd cent. C.E.], B [Vaticanus, 4th cent. C.E.], V [Venetus, 8th cent.
C.E.]) such that Ziegler reconstructed the order shown above as that of
the Old Greek in his critical edition.[8] Unfortunately, the book of Malachi
is not extant in the important manuscript 8HevXII gr which would
surely give us important information on this difference in the two textual
traditions.

The Text: Literary Criticism

Malachi 3:22–24 is variously described as integral to the book of Malachi
and thus from the writer's own hand or as secondary. Those scholars who
see this passage as secondary frequently see redactional significance in
both vv. 22 and 23–24.[9]

Objective

My objective in this paper is to use the analysis of a single biblical
text to illustrate the fact that in studies of the Hebrew Bible it is no
longer possible to make the assumption that the Masoretic Text is the
oldest form of the text or the original form of the text where there are
variant forms of the text. This is especially true because of the wealth of
textual evidence from the Judean Desert. Unfortunately, many scholars
still make this assumption. It is an assumption with a deep history that
goes back at least to the time of Jerome (ca. 347–420 C.E.) but is perhaps as
early as the time of Origen (ca. 185–254 C.E.) at least in Christian circles.
(It is possible to argue that this tendency can be traced back to the time
of the Naḥal Ḥever Greek Minor Prophets Scroll which is dated from the
late Hellenistic Period to the early Roman Period [ca. 100–50 B.C.E.?] in
Jewish circles.) Jerome defended the concept of the *Hebraica Veritas*.

---

[8] J. Ziegler, ed., *Duodecim prophetae* (2nd ed.; Septuaginta: Vetus Testamentum Graecum Auctoritate Academiae Scientiarum Gottingensis 13; Göttingen: Vandenhoeck &
Ruprecht, 1967). There are Greek witnesses which agree with the Masoretic Text in the
order of these verses, but these seem to be secondary, S^c, L' (86^{txt}), C, etc.

[9] S.B. Chapman, *The Law and the Prophets: A Study in Old Testament Canon Formation* (FAT 27; Tübingen: Mohr Siebeck, 2000), 131–146.

One Hebrew witness from Qumran exists, 4QXII[a] (4Q76) which shows agreement with the Masoretic Text in the order of the verses. The majority of scholars assume the priority of the order in the Masoretic Text.[10]

With the wealth of textual data from Qumran and elsewhere in the Judean Desert we now have a great deal of information which allows us, at least sometimes, to gauge whether or not the Greek translators were free with their *Vorlage*. In many cases where evidence now exists, it is clear that the Greek translators frequently were faithful to their Hebrew *Vorlage*. One might take as an example the well known case of the differences between the Hebrew text of Jeremiah and the Greek text of Jeremiah. While older scholarship was free to assume that the Greek translators had altered their *Vorlage*, access to the Hebrew biblical manuscripts from Qumran shows us that they seem to have been faithful to the Hebrew *Vorlage* that was the basis for their translation (4QJer[b], etc.). Likewise in the case of Hos 13:4, I have argued that the so-called expansion in the Greek version is matched in a Hebrew fragment of Hosea from cave 4 at Qumran (4QXII[c]).[11] I could give more examples, but these are sufficient to indicate that the Greek translator did not willy nilly expand or alter the text of their *Vorlage*.

The "moral" of the story, so-to-speak, is that where the Greek and Hebrew texts vary from each other we cannot simply make the assumption that the differences between the two texts are a result of changes made in the Greek text. This may have been the case on occasion, but we now possess enough examples to the contrary that scholars must be cautious.

Emanuel Tov has also demonstrated that in many cases—even where we do not have corroborating manuscript evidence—the Septuagint seems to preserve the older form of the text and was faithful to its Hebrew *Vorlage*.[12]

In the case of Mal 3:22–24, we do not have a Hebrew text which corresponds to the order of the last three verses in the Greek version, but we must not make the automatic assumption that the Greek form of

---

[10] See the discussion ibid., 138–139.

[11] R.E. Fuller, "A Critical Note on Hosea 12:10 and 13:4," *RB* 3 (1991): 343–357.

[12] E. Tov, "Some Sequence Differences Between the MT and LXX and Their Ramifications for the Literary Criticism of the Bible," *JNSL* 13 (1987): 151–160.

the text represents a deliberate change from the original form of the text, and that the original form is to be identified with the Masoretic Text.

I hypothesize instead that there is sufficient circumstantial evidence to conclude that the order of the last three verses that are preserved in the Greek version are original or at least older than the form of the text preserved in the Masoretic Text and in 4Q76 and that the change in sequence happened in the Hebrew textual tradition. I suggest a time period in which I think this intentional change occurred and I suggest a motivation on the part of the scribe who made the change.

The Time Period of the Change

Ben Sira 49:10,

> And may the bones of the twelve prophets
> sprout anew out of their place,
> for they comforted Iakob
> and they redeemed them in confidence of hope.[13]

With its reference to the twelve prophets, is normally taken as evidence that the collection of the twelve prophets was complete before the time of Ben Sira who wrote sometime between 200–180 B.C.E. It is very difficult to narrow down the time of the translation into Greek of the Minor Prophets, but since 8HevXII gr, which is understood to be a revision of the Greek translation to bring it closer to a developing Hebrew text, may be dated perhaps 100–50 B.C.E., it seems reasonable to assume that the Greek translation of the Twelve was made at least in the century prior to the copying of 8HevXII gr, that is, perhaps between 200–100 B.C.E. I would suspect closer to 200 B.C.E.

This places the Greek translation of the Minor Prophets relatively close in time to one of the oldest Hebrew copies of the Minor Prophets, 4QXII[a] (4Q76) mentioned above. This manuscript is dated to ca. 150–125 B.C.E. on the basis of the paleographic analysis of the editor. 4QXII[a] (4Q76) agrees with the Masoretic Text in the order of the last three verses of Malachi. If all of these ruminations about the date of translations and manuscripts are accurate, then the change in the order of the final three verses may be dated some time between 200–125 B.C.E., probably close to

---

[13] Translation of B.G. Wright in *A New English Translation of the Septuagint and the Other Greek Translations Traditionally Included Under that Title* (ed. A. Pietersma and B.G. Wright; Oxford: Oxford University Press, 2007).

the time of the copying of 4QXII[a] (4Q76), or roughly put, to the middle of the second century B.C.E.

THE REASON FOR THE CHANGE

Why would a scribe in Palestine in the middle of the second century B.C.E. have made such a change in the text of this small prophetic book? Another way of stating the question would be: what was happening in the middle of the second century B.C.E. that might have motivated a scribe to make such a change?[14]

The mid second century B.C.E. is the time of the transition from full Seleucid control of Palestine to the rise of the Hasmonean state. It was apparently a time of religious conflict or at least of conflict in which religion played a role, rhetorically or otherwise. Part of the religious rhetoric was that of the Day of Yahweh and eschatological expectations. Part of the conflict is described as a conflict between generations, not just in Mal 3:23, but also in compositions from the second century B.C.E. such as the book of *Jubilees*:

> *Jub.* 23:16
>
> And in this generation children will reproach their parents and their elders on account of sin, and on account of injustice, and on account of the words of their mouth, and on account of great evil which they will do, and on account of their forsaking the covenant which the Lord made between them and himself so that they might be careful and observe all of his commandments and his ordinances and all his law without turning aside to the right or left.[15]

See also the later passage *Jub.* 23:19:

> Some of these will strive with others, youths with old men and old men with youths, the poor with the rich, the lowly with the great, and the beggar with the judge concerning the law and the covenant because they have forgotten the commandments and covenant and festivals and months and Sabbaths and jubilees and all of the judgements.

---

[14] I am indebted to the excellent discussion of this period and the literary clues to the sects which left us this literature by A. Rofé, "The Onset of Sects in Postexilic Judaism: Neglected Evidence from the Septuagint, Trito-Isaiah, Ben Sira, and Malachi," in *The Social World of Formative Christianity and Judaism* (ed. J. Neusner et al.; Philadelphia: Fortress, 1988), 39–49.

[15] O.S. Wintermute, "Jubilees (Second Century B.C.): A New Translation and Introduction," in *OTP* 2:35–142, 101.

These two passages from the book of *Jubilees* describe a generational
conflict over the law and the covenant which is connected with the eschaton.[16] The final two verses in the Masoretic Text of Malachi emphasize
both the generational conflict, which the prophet Elijah is called upon to
resolve, as well as eschatological expectations, in this case for the immi-
nent Day of Yahweh and the threat of complete destruction. The passages
mentioned above from the book of *Jubilees* show the same interests. Perhaps this corresponds to the beginning of the Hasmonean revolt against
Seleucid rule. The Hasmoneans did not start out as Hellenizers.

I think there is sufficient reason to hypothesize that a scribe, perhaps
in Jerusalem, made a simple change in the copy of the text of Malachi, a
change which made the text, already critical of the temple in Jerusalem,
already eschatological in focus, even more relevant for his time and the
conflicts that were occurring and made use of the rhetoric that was being
used in those conflicts, contemporary compositions such as the book of
Jubilees.

If this hypothesis is accepted, that is, if the change in sequence did
occur in the Hebrew textual tradition, and not in the Greek textual tradition as is usually assumed, then there are some important implications
for recent scholarship outside the area of textual criticism. As mentioned
above, the reconstruction of the scribal production of the Hebrew Bible
by Karel van der Toorn assumes, as do many other scholars, that the
Masoretic Text of Mal 3 preserves the original form of the text. I have
argued that the older or original order of the last three verses of Mal 3
are more likely to be preserved in the Septuagint. There, the return of
Elijah before the Day of the Lord is mentioned first. The admonition to
remember the Torah of Moses, the servant of the Lord closes the book.
There is no doubt that these verses allude to both Josh 1 and the book
of Deuteronomy. There is also little doubt that Mal 3:22–24 is intended
to close both the book of Malachi as well as the collection of the Twelve
Minor Prophets. I agree with those scholars who have argued in addition that Mal 3:22 (MT) is intended to recall the beginning of the book

---

[16] This is a motif which has its roots in older prophetic material, see for example Mic
7:5–7:

5 Trust no friend, Rely on no intimate; Be guarded in speech With her who lies in
your bosom. 6 For son spurns father, Daughter rises up against mother, Daughter-in-law
against mother-in-law—A man's own household Are his enemies. 7 Yet I will look to the
LORD, I will wait for the God who saves me, My God will hear me. (NJPS)

This older passage however, shows no interest in any sort of eschatological event. The
passages in Malachi and in *Jubilees* may adapt this older idea and build upon it.

of Joshua and to link the Prophets with the Torah. However, this literary *inclusio* which hinges on Mal 3:22 (MT) works even better when this verse occupies the final position as it does in the Septuagint and, as I have argued, in the Hebrew *Vorlage* of the Septuagint. The change in order at the end of Mal 3 probably takes place in the middle of the second century B.C.E., shortly before our oldest copy of Malachi is made, 4Q76. It is made as part of a scribal "updating" of the text to emphasize the intensifying expectations of the Day of the Lord and the intergenerational conflicts which are alluded to in contemporary writings of this period, such as the book of *Jubilees*.

Van der Toorn's reconstruction provides us with much insight into the role of ancient scribes in the construction of the Hebrew Bible. Although it offers many insights into scribal practice and culture and the growth of the Hebrew Bible, it is ultimately incomplete. In addition to ignoring the evidence for the text which is offered by the Greek Bible, it does not take into account other evidence which might not fit well with the reconstruction. For example, although 4Q76, which uniquely seems to preserve Jonah in last position in a scroll of the Minor Prophets, this piece of evidence is simply dismissed. In addition, evidence from lists in both Jewish and Christian writers, which attest to the varying order of the Twelve Minor Prophets versus the three "major" prophets, is ignored.[17] To repeat, because recent work on the scribal production of the Bible either ignores or does not adequately take into account the current state of the field, the reconstructions are incomplete. There have been several scholarly reconstructions of the scribal production of the Hebrew Bible. Most of these reconstructions make the assumption that the masoretic manuscripts represent the original form of the Hebrew text, including the sequence of verses and the order of the "books" which became part of the collection. However without taking into account all of the textual evidence and the implications of that evidence for the growth of the collection, these reconstructions lose much of their validity.

---

[17] N.M. Sarna, "Bible," *EncJud* 4 (1971): 827–830. The order of the prophets in Hebrew editions varies only in the order of Isaiah, Jeremiah, and Ezekiel. The Minor Prophets always follow the Three in Jewish sources, see *b. B. Bat.* 14b: "Our Rabbis taught: the order of the prophets is Joshua, Judges, Samuel, Kings, Jeremiah, Ezekiel, Isaiah, and the Twelve." See also E. Tov, *Textual Criticism of the Hebrew Bible* (Minneapolis: Fortress, 1992), 3–4, and H.B. Swete, *An Introduction to the Old Testament in Greek* (Cambridge: University Press, 1914), 197–230.

Conclusion

In this brief paper I have used the difference in order of the last three verses of the book of Malachi in the Greek and Hebrew forms of the text to emphasize the necessity of examining all the information that is available for the reconstruction of the production of the Bible. I have argued that the order preserved in the Greek version of Malachi is older than the version preserved in the Masoretic Text. I have also argued that the version preserved in the Masoretic Text has its origin no later than the middle of the second century B.C.E. This is supported by 4QXII[a] (4Q76), which is dated to this time period. I have also suggested that a scribe made the simple change of moving a single verse in order to highlight the eschatological perspective in the last section of Malachi and thus to emphasize the rhetorical language being used in contemporary compositions like the book of *Jubilees*.

STUDYING THE BIBLICAL TEXT IN THE LIGHT OF HISTORICO-LITERARY CRITICISM: THE REPROACH OF THE PROPHET IN JUDG 6:7–10 AND 4QJUDGᵃ

ALEXANDER ROFÉ
The Hebrew University of Jerusalem

The aim of the present article is to illustrate how much historico-literary criticism is needed for a proper study of the biblical text, especially when the scholar must decide which is the *lectio praeferenda*. In my opinion, this direction of research has unjustifiably been neglected in the last generations. In the first place, there is widespread skepticism toward textual criticism, an attitude also evident from the exegetes' practice to note textual variants without making any comment or decision about them. In addition, there is no little mistrust concerning historico-literary criticism, the "higher criticism," and its achievements for the understanding of the history of biblical literature. And in any case, monographs and commentaries usually do not put together the results obtained by textual criticism and "higher criticism," but let them stay separate.[1] Finally, since textual criticism is considered as a kind of groundwork, while "higher criticism" is taken to be the superstructure, one does not conceive the historico-literary inquiry to be an essential first step in order to obtain the *constitutio textus*.

The task of historico-literary criticism is threefold: to identify in the biblical books sundry documents or layers of composition and redaction, to identify in these documents the various literary genres to which they

---

[1] Among present day scholars there are some who elude both higher and lower criticism. This is the case of M. Brettler who in a recent article—"The Composition of 1 Samuel 1–2," *JBL* 116 (1997): 601–612—defined 1 Sam 2:12–17 (MT) as "a midrashic explication of the sins of the sons of Eli" (p. 612). I wonder how a cultic story that ignores the laws of sacrifice of both Deut 18:3 and Lev 7:31–34 could be a "midrashic explication." Brettler describes 1 Sam 2:22–26 as a secondary addition. In his opinion, this perception finds confirmation in the reference to the "women who performed tasks at the entrance of the Tent of Meeting" (1 Sam 2:22) because they are mentioned by the Priestly Document in Exod 38:8. He did not notice that the phrase in v. 22bβ is a gloss; it is absent in 4Q51 (the so called 4QSamᵃ) and not represented by the LXX.

belong or which were incorporated in them, and to date the documents, absolutely when possible or at least relatively i.e., vis-à-vis the other biblical compositions.

I maintain here—with no pretension of innovating—that more often than not it is our decision concerning the original cast of a document and its date of composition that will determine our conclusions about primary and secondary readings. This especially applies to those texts in which the Septuagint or one of the Qumran Scrolls present variants of considerable size.

As an example of the method to be followed, I have chosen Judg 6:7–10, a pericope that has recently drawn some attention due to the publication of a hitherto unknown textual witness found at Qumran. In my opinion, one may properly evaluate this witness only by means of the historico-literary criticism, naturally integrated at times with data obtained from other realms of our discipline. The present analysis comes to supplement other, previous studies in which I upheld the need of combining the various directions of research in order to obtain valid results in the study of the Hebrew Bible.[2]

Judg 6:7–10

(7) וַיְהִי כִּי זָעֲקוּ בְּנֵי יִשְׂרָאֵל אֶל ה' עַל אֹדוֹת מִדְיָן: (8) וַיִּשְׁלַח ה' אִישׁ נָבִיא אֶל בְּנֵי יִשְׂרָאֵל וַיֹּאמֶר לָהֶם כֹּה אָמַר ה' אֱלֹהֵי יִשְׂרָאֵל אָנֹכִי הֶעֱלֵיתִי אֶתְכֶם מִמִּצְרַיִם וָאֹצִיא אֶתְכֶם מִבֵּית עֲבָדִים: (9) וָאַצִּל אֶתְכֶם מִיַּד מִצְרַיִם וּמִיַּד כָּל לֹחֲצֵיכֶם וָאֲגָרֵשׁ אוֹתָם מִפְּנֵיכֶם וָאֶתְּנָה לָכֶם אֶת אַרְצָם: (10) וָאֹמְרָה לָכֶם אֲנִי ה' אֱלֹהֵיכֶם לֹא תִירְאוּ אֶת אֱלֹהֵי הָאֱמֹרִי אֲשֶׁר אַתֶּם יוֹשְׁבִים בְּאַרְצָם וְלֹא שְׁמַעְתֶּם בְּקוֹלִי:

(7) When the Israelites invoked the Lord on account of Midian, (8) the Lord sent a man, a prophet, to the Israelites who said to them: "Thus said the Lord, the God of Israel: I brought you up from Egypt and took you out of the house of bondage. (9) I rescued you from the Egyptians and from all your oppressors; I drove them out before you and gave you their land. (10) And I said to you: 'I the Lord am your God. Do not worship the gods of the Amorites in whose land you dwell.' But you did not obey Me."[3]

---

[2] In addition to the articles mentioned in nn. 7, 11, 21, cf. A. Rofé, "Textual Criticism in the Light of Historical-Literary Criticism: Deuteronomy 31:14–15," *ErIsr* 16 (1982): 171–176 (Hebrew); idem, "Historico-Literary Aspects of the Qumran Biblical Scrolls," in *The Dead Sea Scrolls Fifty Years After Their Discovery: Proceedings of the Jerusalem Congress, July 20–25, 1997* (ed. L.H. Schiffman et al.; Jerusalem: Israel Exploration Society, 2000), 30–39.
[3] Translations from the Hebrew Bible have been adapted from the NJPS.

This short pericope, whose essence is found also in the Septuagint, is absent from a fragment of the book of Judges retrieved at Qumran, 4QJudgª, dated on paleographic grounds to the years 50–25 B.C.E.[4] The fragment preserves the text of Judg 6:2–6, 11–13, thus directly connecting the description of Midian's forays and Israel's imploration with the designation of Gideon. No trace remains here of the reproach of the man-prophet mentioned above. Thus the question is pressed upon us: does 4QJudgª present an earlier form of the text of the book of Judges or is this sequence the result of a textual accident when a copyist's eye skipped a whole paragraph that even in the ancient manuscripts could have been included between two *parašiyyot petuhot* (open sections).[5]

The choice between these two possibilities necessarily depends upon arguments that belong to the realm of higher criticism, because what determines the critic's decision is the date he attributes to the composition of the reproach of the man-prophet. If it was written at an early date, one must conclude that it belongs to an original composition, and its omission was due to error. Vice versa, if the reproach was composed by a later scribe, it will follow that due to its late date of composition, it failed to be introduced in all manuscripts, and the Qumran fragment still attests to a previous stage in the growth of the book of Judges.

The latter alternative has been upheld by Julio Trebolle Barrera who published the fragment. In his opinion:

> vv. 8–10 have been generally recognized by modern critics as a literary insertion, attributed in past times to an Elohistic source and now generally considered a piece of a late Dtr. redaction … Vv. 8–10 cannot be genuine pre-Dtr. or Dtr. material, but a later compilation of juxtaposed Dtr. formulas[6]

---

[4] J. Trebolle Barrera, "Textual Variants in 4QJudgª and the Textual and Editorial History of the Book of Judges," *RevQ* 54 (1989): 229–245; idem in *DJD* XIV (1995): 161–164.

[5] Thus in the Aleppo and Leningrad manuscripts. Even in our times editorial staffs collate copies or translations with the original in order to ascertain that no paragraph has been left out. As for 4QJudgª, Richard Hess has noted that the absent verses are found in the MT between two "open" sections; cf. R. Hess, "The Dead Sea Scrolls and Higher Criticism of the Hebrew Bible: The Case of 4QJudgª," in *The Scrolls and the Scriptures* (ed. S.E. Porter and C.A. Evans: Sheffield: Sheffield Academic Press, 1997), 122–128. Unfortunately, he deduces from this fact a hypothesis that seems to me as farfetched. The general correspondence between the Isaiah scrolls from Qumran and the MT manuscripts concerning the *parašiyyot* has been upheld by Maori. Cf. Y. Maori, "The Tradition of *Pisqaʿot* in Ancient Hebrew MSS: The Isaiah Texts and Commentaries from Qumran," *Text* 10 (1982): א-נ (Hebrew).

[6] Trebolle Barrera, "Textual Variants," 238. Thus also E. Tov, *Textual Criticism of the*

This peremptory verdict has not been backed up by a minute examination of the style and the contents of the reproach. Further on we shall
try to fill in this omission. In favor of Trebolle's thesis one must concede,
however, that in the books of the Former Prophets one comes upon two
instances of late interpolations which did not find their way into all textual witnesses. On the face of it, we have here two analogue cases which,
therefore, deserve discussion.

In Josh 20, three verses—vv. 4, 5 and most of v. 6—contradict the
substance of that Priestly chapter, stand out by their Deuteronomistic
style and are missing in the Septuagint.

(4) וְנָס אֶל אַחַת מֵהֶעָרִים הָאֵלֶּה וְעָמַד פֶּתַח שַׁעַר הָעִיר וְדִבֶּר בְּאָזְנֵי זִקְנֵי הָעִיר הַהִיא אֶת
דְּבָרָיו וְאָסְפוּ אֹתוֹ הָעִירָה אֲלֵיהֶם וְנָתְנוּ לוֹ מָקוֹם וְיָשַׁב עִמָּם: (5) וְכִי יִרְדֹּף גֹּאֵל הַדָּם אַחֲרָיו
וְלֹא יַסְגִּרוּ אֶת הָרֹצֵחַ בְּיָדוֹ כִּי בִבְלִי דַעַת הִכָּה אֶת רֵעֵהוּ וְלֹא שֹׂנֵא הוּא לוֹ מִתְּמוֹל שִׁלְשׁוֹם:
(6) וְיָשַׁב בָּעִיר הַהִיא ... עַד מוֹת הַכֹּהֵן הַגָּדוֹל אֲשֶׁר יִהְיֶה בַּיָּמִים הָהֵם אָז יָשׁוּב הָרוֹצֵחַ
וּבָא אֶל עִירוֹ וְאֶל בֵּיתוֹ אֶל הָעִיר אֲשֶׁר נָס מִשָּׁם:

(4) He shall flee to one of those cities, present himself at the entrance to
the city gate, and plead his case before the elders of that city; and they
shall admit him into the city and give him a place in which to dwell among
them. (5) Should the blood avenger pursue him, they shall not hand the
manslayer over to him, since he killed his country-man without intent and
had not been his enemy in the past. (6) He shall dwell in that city ... until
the death of the high-priest who will be in office at that time. Thereafter,
the manslayer may go back to his home in his hometown, to the town from
which he fled.

As noted by the biblicists of the nineteenth century whom I followed,[7]
this is a relatively late exegetical addition, written about the fourth century B.C.E. by an epigonic scribe who availed himself of Deuteronomistic
idiomatic expressions. In his attempt to describe the judicial procedures
for the acceptance of the manslayer in the asylum, this scribe contra-
dicted the Priestly main story of Josh 20. This addition was not copied
into the Hebrew manuscript that served as *Vorlage* for the Greek translation and therefore, the reported verses do not appear in the Septuagint.
Here we have a tangible proof of the habit of late copyists to interpolate
their texts while imitating the style of the classical documents of the Pentateuch.

Hebrew Bible (2nd ed.; Minneapolis: Fortress, 2001), 344–345. Tov erroneously attributes
the same view to Moore and Burney (cf. below, n. 15).

   [7] Cf. A. Rofé, "Joshua 20: Historico-Literary Criticism Illustrated," in *Empirical Models for Biblical Criticism* (ed. J. Tigay: Philadelphia: University of Pennsylvania Press,
1985), 131–147.

An even more pertinent analogy is extant in

1 Kgs 6:11–13

‏(11) וַיְהִי דְּבַר ה׳ אֶל שְׁלֹמֹה לֵאמֹר: (12) הַבַּיִת הַזֶּה אֲשֶׁר אַתָּה בֹנֶה אִם תֵּלֵךְ בְּחֻקֹּתַי וְאֶת‎
‏מִשְׁפָּטַי תַּעֲשֶׂה וְשָׁמַרְתָּ אֶת כָּל מִצְוֹתַי לָלֶכֶת בָּהֶם וַהֲקִמֹתִי אֶת דְּבָרִי אִתָּךְ אֲשֶׁר דִּבַּרְתִּי אֶל‎
‏דָּוִד אָבִיךָ: (13) וְשָׁכַנְתִּי בְּתוֹךְ בְּנֵי יִשְׂרָאֵל וְלֹא אֶעֱזֹב אֶת עַמִּי יִשְׂרָאֵל:‎

(11) The word of the Lord came to Solomon saying: (12) "As for this house
which you are building, if you follow My laws and observe My rules and
steadily keep all My commandments, I will fulfill for you the promise that
I gave to your father David: (13) I will abide among the children of Israel,
and I will never forsake My people Israel."

Here too there are signs of interpolation.[8] The prophecy deviates from
the context, which is entirely dedicated to the technical description of
the building of the Temple. Besides, this intrusive section is delimited by
a *Wiederaufnahme*, which is an evident sign of expansion, mostly by a
second hand. Here we note the repetition:

v. 9:	‏ויבן את הבית ויכלהו‎
v. 14:	‏⁹ויבן שלמה את הבית ויכלהו‎

Moreover, the style of this section is a mix of expressions from the
Holiness Code (cf. Lev 26:3, 14, 15) and the Priestly Document (Exod
25:8), again two major documents of the Pentateuch. Finally, the passage
in question does not obtain in the LXX. No doubt, there is enough
evidence to establish the secondary provenience of the prophecy of 1 Kgs
6:11–13 and its late insertion into the report concerning the building of
the Temple.

The similarity of Judg 6:7–10 and 1 Kgs 6:11–13 is great indeed. Both
passages present a prophetical speech uttered directly by the Lord or
through an *'îš nābî'*, a speech that expresses the theological outlook
of the author. Prophecies of this kind, which we may define as "historiographic," are present all along the biblical historical-writings. The

---

[8] Cf. the exhaustive analysis by C.F. Burney, *Notes on the Hebrew Text of the Book of
Kings* (Oxford: Clarendon, 1903; repr. New York: Ktav, 1970), 68–69.

[9] One must admit, however, that here the *Wiederaufnahme* is not a neat one, because
it is "disturbed" by vv. 9b–10. Important contributions on the *Wiederaufnahme* are:
I.L. Seeligmann, "Hebräische Erzählung und biblische Geschichtsschreibung," *TZ* 18
(1962): 305–325; M. Anbar, "La 'reprise,'" *VT* 38 (1988): 385–398.

genre is still employed by the Chronicler who scolds King Amaziah by means of an anonymous prophet, because the king has worshiped the gods of Seir (2 Chr 25:14–16). Thus, one should not be surprised if even in later times epigonic scribes introduced into the texts their own views disguised as the word of God, pronounced by Him or by His prophet.

Should we conclude, then, that all "historiographic prophecies" belong to such a late date? Not really. In 1 Sam 2:27–36 a Man of God blames Eli, Priest of Shiloh, and forecasts the rejection of his line from being priests and its substitution by another house of priests, a righteous and devoted one. Several *indicia* show that this prophecy is not that late or, at least, contains some early elements:[10] The election of the House of Eli took place in Egypt, "at (the service of [?]) the House of Pharaoh" (v. 27), not in Sinai, not in connection with Moses and Aaron. Among the duties of the priests are the carrying of the *'ēpôd* (v. 28)—a function that was put to silence by the D document in its records of the priestly duties (Deut 10:8; 18:5; 20:2–4; 21:5; 24:8). What is said about the future priest "who will walk before (= serve) my anointed evermore" (v. 35) ignores the fall of the monarchy and the rise of the priestly predominance in postexilic times. Finally, the description of Eli's descendants who will go to beg admittance to one of the priestly offices (*kĕhunnôt*) not just work (*'abôdâ*) in order "to eat a morsel of bread," ignores the distinction between priests and Levites announced by Ezekiel (44:6–24), established by the Priestly Document and enhanced by the Chronicler. It is hard indeed to assign a precise date of composition to the reproach of the Man of God to Eli. Its content, however, appears to precede the emergence of the two major schools of the seventh to fifth centuries, the Deuteronomic and Priestly. Evidently, this prophecy was written during monarchical times, not in the exilic-postexilic periods.

We may conclude that even if one establishes the secondary character and the relatively late date of composition of an anonymous prophecy, this does not determine that date in absolute terms. The age can fluctuate between the eighth and the fourth centuries, namely between the period

---

[10] Cf. C. Steuernagel, "Die Weissagung über die Eliden (1 Sam 2²⁷⁻³⁶)," in *Alttesta-mentliche Studien: FS R. Kittel* (ed. A. Alt et al.; BWAT 13; Leipzig: Hinrichs, 1913), 204–221; M. Tsevat, "Studies in the Book of Samuel, I: Interpretation of I Sam. 2:27–36—The Narrative of Kareth," *HUCA* 32 (1961): 191–216. The various opinions expressed on this passage have been reviewed by H.F. van Rooy, "Prophetic Utterances in Narrative Texts, with Reference to 1 Samuel 2:27–36," *OTE* 3 (1990): 210–215.

of composition of the Ephraimite history[11] and that of the Chronicler. The dating of the pericope in Judg 6:7–10 will be established, therefore, by an exact scrutiny of this text, not by analogy with comparable passages.

In the first place, one has to assess the function of this passage vis-à-vis its context. The reproach details the favors of the Lord to Israel in the past (vv. 8–9), specifies the duties He imposed on the people (v. 10a), and ends with mentioning the latter's disobedience (v. 10b: ולא שמעתם בקולי). In vain one looks for the ensuing divine reaction to the sin of the nation. Taking as an example Judg 10:10–16, one could expect to read about the people's repentance. This too is missing. How come? The reason lies in the function of the passage: it answers Gideon's assertions. He mentioned one favor of the Lord: the exodus from Egypt (v. 13). The pericope answers with a whole list of favors, six lines long, reaching from Egypt to the inheritance of the Land (vv. 8–9). Besides, Gideon assailed the angel saying: "If the Lord is with us, why has all this befallen us" etc. (v. 13). The reproach of the man-prophet replies that it is the sin of the people that caused "all this."[12] Therefore, the passage, even being secondary, has a clear function in the saga of Gideon. Such was not the case with 1 Kgs 6:11–13 where the speech of the Lord did not connect at all with the report of the Temple's construction. This clear difference between the two divine speeches indicates a different origin for each of them.

The next step is the analysis of style. The accumulation of recurrent idioms conveys the impression of an imitative pastiche; yet, taken one by one, the idioms are not late. The verb העלה, "bring up," concerning the Exodus, is not typical of the main, relatively late, documents of the Hexateuch: D, H and P. They usually employ הוציא, "bring out," while העלה features in passages that were attributed in the past to the Elohistic Document (E).[13] The definition of the Egyptian bondage as בית

---

[11] Cf. A. Rofé, "Ephraimite versus Deuteronomistic History," in *Storia e tradizioni di Israele: Scritti in onore di J.A. Soggin* (ed. D. Garrone and F. Israel; Brescia: Paideia, 1991), 221–235.

[12] This has been brought to my attention by Dr. Michael Segal (Hebrew University, Jerusalem). Most commentators consider the pericope as a justification of the Midianite oppression described in vv. 1–6. Thus, also Y. Amit, *The Book of Judges: The Art of Editing* (Biblical Interpretation Series 38; Leiden: Brill, 1999), 250. Nevertheless, on p. 251, she maintains that vv. 7–10 "explain why an atmosphere of disappointment was widespread among the people and why Gideon uttered such harsh things, doubting the presence of the Lord among his people and his desire to save them."

[13] J.E. Carpenter and G. Harford, *The Composition of the Hexateuch* (London: Longmans, 1902), 392.

עבדים, "house of slaves," does not belong to the original layer of the Ten Commandments, as quoted for instance in Ps 81:10–11,[14] but it appears in the "lawsuit against Israel" in Mic 6:1–5, which has the flavor of early literature (cf. in v. 4 the role of Miriam as leader of Israel). The phrase אני ה' אלהיכם, "I, the Lord, am your god" (v. 10) is indeed the hallmark of legal collections, H in particular, but when connected to לא תיראו את אלהי האמרי, "do not worship the gods of the Amorites," it sounds as a paraphrase of the two first commandments. Thus, from the stylistic point of view, the passage in question does not show signs of recent phraseology.[15]

As for the contents, several elements point towards a relatively early date. V. 9: "I rescued you from the Egyptians and from all your oppressors; I drove them out before you and gave you their land." This is not the representation of the conquest as delineated by the D-Dtr school. According to the latter, the wars of Canaan were actively fought by Israel under the Lord's guidance (Josh 1–11). Here, to the contrary, Israel is passive: upon entering the Land they were harassed by its inhabitants (cf. Judg 4:3, which states that Sisera harshly oppressed the Israelites). Then the Lord intervened to succor his people. Such a description of a passive Israel is common to Judg 6:7–10, as well as Josh 24:5–18, and the speeches of Samuel at the election of Saul (1 Sam 10:18–19a; 12:8–11). We encounter here the theological concept of what was once defined as "the late Elohistic school," which I prefer to term as Ephraimite.[16]

The Lord chased out (גרש, v. 9) the inhabitants of the Land before Israel. This is the image of the conquest extant in the older, pre-Deuteronomic documents, such as Exod 23:20–33; 33:2; 34:11 and Josh 24:12, 18. The D-Dtr school has a completely different portrayal: an annihilation under the ban, *herem*, as explicitly prescribed in Deut 7. In the latter chapter, moreover, there is a restatement of Exod 23: the Lord arrogates to

---

[14] Hos 13:4 also paraphrases the first two commandments. A paraphrase of the first commandment alone is given in Hos 12:10; Ps 50:7.

[15] Among the scholars who attribute the reproach to a pre-Deuteronomistic, Elohistic author or redactor one counts some of the leading names: Budde, Moore, Lagrange, Burney and Cooke; cf. K. Budde, *Die Bücher Richter und Samuel: Ihre Quellen und ihr Aufbau* (Giessen: Ricker, 1890), 107–108; idem, *Das Buch der Richter* (KHC 7; Freiburg: Mohr Siebeck, 1897); G.F. Moore, *A Critical and Exegetical Commentary on Judges* (ICC 7; Edinburgh: T&T Clark, 1895; repr. Edinburgh: T&T Clark, 1976); M.J. Lagrange, *Le livre de Juges* (EBib; Paris: Lecoffre, 1903); C.F. Burney, *The Book of Judges* (London: Rivingtons, 1918; repr. New York: Ktav, 1970); G.A. Cooke, *The Book of Judges* (Cambridge Bible; Cambridge: Cambridge University Press, 1918).

[16] Cf. n. 11.

himself the functions of the angel, and the ban substitutes the expulsion of the Canaanites.[17] The Dtr story of the conquest in the book of Joshua (chs. 1–11) follows suit: all inhabitants of the Land are exterminated under the ban. We note here a fundamental difference between the two schools, the Elohistic-Ephraimite on one hand and the D-Dtr on the other. Evidently, the reproach of the man-prophet in Judg 6:7–10 aligns itself with the older documents which preceded the D-Dtr school.

But the decisive proof that we are not dealing here with a redactional Deuteronomistic or post-Deuteronomistic layer comes from v. 10: "And I said to you: I the Lord am your God. Do not worship the gods of the Amorites in whose land you dwell." At first sight it looks as a repetition of trite expressions, taken from older injunctions, but it is not. When did the Lord impart this command? According to the order of events, only after the inheritance of Canaan. It is not part of the Sinai or Plains of Moab legislation. And indeed, the precept does not run "the gods of the Amorites in whose land *you are going to dwell,*" rather, "the gods of the Amorites *in whose land you dwell.*" According to this wording, the command was intimated *in the Land* after the settlement.[18] It was not given to Moses, nor contained in the Torah.

Such a concept cannot be late, because late biblical authors, in the latter half of the Persian period, already attributed all divine laws to the Mosaic legislation. The concept cannot be Deuteronomistic either, because the D document in Deuteronomy considers the laws as part and parcel of Moses' speeches. Thus, Judg 6:7–10, as it precedes the emergence of those proto-canonical tenets, most plausibly belongs to an older document.

In search for additional tracks of this old concept of divine legislation given to Israel in the Land, we come upon the reproach of the angel of the Lord at Bokim in Judg 2:1–5.[19] There, at vv. 1b–3 one reads:

(1b) וָאֹמַר אַעֲלֶה אֶתְכֶם מִמִּצְרַיִם וָאָבִיא אֶתְכֶם אֶל הָאָרֶץ אֲשֶׁר נִשְׁבַּעְתִּי לַאֲבֹתֵיכֶם וָאֹמַר
לֹא אָפֵר בְּרִיתִי אִתְּכֶם לְעוֹלָם: (2) וְאַתֶּם לֹא תִכְרְתוּ בְרִית לְיוֹשְׁבֵי הָאָרֶץ הַזֹּאת ... וְלֹא
שְׁמַעְתֶּם בְּקֹלִי מַה זֹּאת עֲשִׂיתֶם: (3) וְגַם אָמַרְתִּי לֹא אֲגָרֵשׁ אוֹתָם מִפְּנֵיכֶם וְהָיוּ לָכֶם לְצִדִּים
וֵאלֹהֵיהֶם יִהְיוּ לָכֶם לְמוֹקֵשׁ:

---

[17] Cf. A. Rofé, *The Belief in Angels in the Bible and in Early Israel* (Jerusalem: Makor, 1979), 280–298 (Hebrew), and the bibliography quoted there. Pride of place should be given to D. Neumark, *The Philosophy of the Bible* (Cincinnati: Ark Publication, 1918), passim and especially p. 73.

[18] To my knowledge, the first to note this point was G. Schmitt, *Der Landtag von Sichem* (AzTh 1/15; Stuttgart: Calwer Verlag, 1964), 43–45.

[19] For the text-reconstruction and a study of this pericope cf. Rofé, *Belief in Angels,* 256–271.

(1b) I brought you up from Egypt and I took you into the land which I had promised on oath to your fathers and I said "I will never break My covenant with you. (2) And you must make no covenant with the inhabitants of this land …" But you have not obeyed Me; what have you done! (3) Therefore, I have resolved: "I will not drive them out before you; they shall become hunters[20] against you and their gods will become your traps."

One faces here an author distinct from the one of Judg 6:7–10. In the first place, because the story contains an etiology explaining the sanctity of the place: an angel of the Lord appeared there and therefore the people built an altar on the spot. No such *hieros logos* is extant in Judg 6:7–10. Accordingly, the messenger of the Lord differs: an angel here, a man-prophet there. It looks as if the author of Judg 6:7–10 transferred the role of the angel to the prophet! And yet, some common elements are extant: Judges 2:3 too does not mention the ban (*herem*), but rather the expulsion (*gērēš*) of the Amorites by the Lord; here too, the making of the covenant with the relative imposition of commands on Israel are recorded after the entrance to the Land. The latter point is confirmed by the very diction of the commands: "you must make no covenant with the inhabitants of *this* land." Judges 2:1–5 corroborates Judg 6:7–10 concerning the place and time of the Lord's covenant with Israel.

However, the fundamental text that tells the giving of the Lord's laws to Israel in the Land is Josh 24. There, at vv. 25–26, one reads:

(25) וַיִּכְרֹת יְהוֹשֻׁעַ בְּרִית לָעָם בַּיּוֹם הַהוּא וַיָּשֶׂם לוֹ חֹק וּמִשְׁפָּט בִּשְׁכֶם: (26) וַיִּכְתֹּב יְהוֹשֻׁעַ אֶת הַדְּבָרִים הָאֵלֶּה בְּסֵפֶר תּוֹרַת אֱלֹהִים וַיִּקַּח אֶבֶן גְּדוֹלָה וַיְקִימֶהָ שָּׁם תַּחַת הָאַלָּה אֲשֶׁר בְּמִקְדַּשׁ ה':

(25) Joshua made a covenant for the people on that day and set them law and rule at Shechem. (26) And Joshua wrote these words in a book of Torah of God. He took a great stone and set it up at the foot of the oak, which is in the sanctuary of the Lord.

The text is explicit: Joshua made a covenant with the tribes of Israel—there is no reference to an earlier covenant made by Moses—he set them "law and rule" at Shechem—same formulation as in Exod 15:25 referring to Moses in Marah—and wrote in a (or: the) book of Torah of God. What did Joshua write? If not the "law and rule" mentioned above, then what is meant is all the event of the making of the covenant, inclusive of the preface and the negotiation with the people. In any case, the prescription of "law and rule" to Israel and the writing in a/the book of

---

[20] Read *ṣadim* or *ṣōdim*.

Torah single out Josh 24 as against the whole concept first proclaimed by Deuteronomy (and then accepted by Jews and Christians until the beginning of historical criticism) to the effect that Moses, the single legislator to Israel, was the author of the Torah.[21]

We have here a segment of a pre-Deuteronomistic literary layer, which I elsewhere defined as "Ephraimite." According to this layer, the laws were delivered to Israel in the Land. Coherently, this composition, while scolding Israel for his sins, does not make appeal to the book of Torah, but to his duty of faithfulness and obedience towards the Lord (cf. Judg 10:11–16; 1 Sam 8:7–8; 10:18–19a). In the same way, "the law of kingship" mentioned in this work (1 Sam 10:25), not to be confused with "the practice of the king" (1 Sam 8:9–18), originates with old Samuel, not in the Mosaic Torah.

In this state of affairs, how should one explain the absence of Judg 6:7–10 from 4QJudg[a]? It is just an omission due to *parablepsis*, i.e., the copyist's eye skipped a whole paragraph. The omission, however, was favored by the contents of the pericope in question. Although not being a late addition from the end of biblical times, nevertheless an addition it is, a relatively ancient one, aiming to reply to Gideon's complaint "why has all this befallen us" (Judg 6:13). Its quality as appendix is evident also from the way it connects to the preceding section:

Judg 6:6–7

(6) וַיִּדַּל יִשְׂרָאֵל מְאֹד מִפְּנֵי מִדְיָן וַיִּזְעֲקוּ בְנֵי יִשְׂרָאֵל אֶל ה': (7) וַיְהִי כִּי זָעֲקוּ בְנֵי יִשְׂרָאֵל אֶל ה' עַל אֹדוֹת מִדְיָן:

(6) Israel was reduced to utter misery because of the Midianites and the Israelites cried to the Lord. (7) When the Israelites cried to the Lord on account of Midian[22]

---

[21] Cf. S.D. Sperling, "Joshua 24 Re-examined," *HUCA* 58 (1987): 119–136; C. Brekelmans, "Joshua XXIV: Its Place and Function," in *Congress Volume Leuven* (ed. J.A. Emerton; VTSup 43, Leiden: Brill, 1991), 1–9; A. Rofé, "The Assembly at Shechem (Joshua 24, 1–28.31): The Text, Literature and History," in *Proceedings of the Twelfth World Congress of Jewish Studies, Jerusalem, July 29—August 5, 1997*, Division A: *The Bible and its World* (ed. R. Margolin: Jerusalem: World Union of Jewish Studies, 1999), 17–25 (Hebrew).

[22] V. 7a (to the *atnaḥ*) is lacking in the LXX[B]. It was probably omitted due to *homoioteleuton*; cf. J. Schreiner, *Septuaginta-Massora des Buches der Richter* (AnBib 7; Rome: Pontifical Biblical Institute, 1957), 47.

Elsewhere I defined this kind of connection as a "related expansion."[23] It occurs when a new author attaches his contribution to an existing report, quoting the last words of the latter and then going on with his own appendage. Let me emphasize that all the passages identified so far as related expansions are extant in the various textual witnesses, a fact that demonstrates the relative antiquity of this technique. To conclude: it is because of its character as addition, even an ancient one, that the absence of the passage examined here, was not noted by one (or: some) of the copyists once it had been omitted by a banal error of *parablepsis*. The passage was not essential to the continuity of the narrative.

One cannot avoid the question, how much the conjecture and the reconstruction here suggested are credible. Three phases have been proposed: (a) a given text; (b) its secondary amplification; (c) its undergoing a textual mishap that restored the text to its original shape in one of the textual witnesses. I will answer this question with the example of a similar case in Jer 39. Vv. 4–13 are not represented in the LXX. One cannot expound here the literary and textual history of that chapter.[24] Suffice it to say, that the case of Jer 39 is even more convincing, because there the textual accident (phase c) did not obliterate all the results of the preceding literary activity (phase b).

A general conclusion emerges. The biblical books have a long history of composition, hundreds of years long. Our textual witnesses, such as the Masoretic Text, the Samaritan Pentateuch, the Septuagint and the Qumran Scrolls, when compared with one another, can reveal the textual vicissitudes that occurred at the end of that long history. They can also disclose the last literary operations performed in these books, between the end of the Persian and the beginning of the Hellenistic periods. But by their very date, they cannot tell us much about the preceding literary history, when the large historiographical works, the Ephraimite and the Deuteronomistic, were composed, between the eighth and the fifth centuries B.C.E. The fortunes of this works should be conjectured

---

[23] Cf. A. Rofé, *The Book of Balaam: Numbers 22:2–24:25* (Jerusalem: Simor, 1979) (Hebrew). The passages listed there as "related expansion" are Num 22:22 (to v. 20); Josh 4:1 (to 3:17); 1 Sam 15:20 (to v. 19); 18:6 (to 17:57); 23:15 (to v. 14). To my examples Y. Zakovitch added one more; cf. his review in *Kiryat Sefer* 54 (1979): 785–789. At p. 788 he pointed out as "related expansion" 1 Sam 5:2 (to v. 1). Fourteen years later, Frank Polak renamed this phenomenon as "linkage"; cf. F. Polak, *Biblical Narrative: Aspects of Art and Design* (2nd ed.; Jerusalem: Bialik Institute, 1999), 79–80 (Hebrew).

[24] Cf. the outstanding discussion of R. Goldstein, "Life of a Prophet: The Traditions about Jeremiah" (Ph.D. diss., The Hebrew University of Jerusalem, 2006), esp. 170–180 (Hebrew).

with the means of historico-literary criticism. Plausibly, processes that occurred to biblical books at the time of their creation were utterly different, perhaps even opposed, to the processes inherent to the later textual transmission.

ANCIENT SEMITIC LANGUAGES
AND THE DEAD SEA SCROLLS

THE DEAD SEA SCROLLS AND THEIR CONTRIBUTION TO THE STUDY OF HEBREW AND ARAMAIC

Steven E. Fassberg
The Hebrew University of Jerusalem

A. Hebrew

On the eve of the discovery of the Dead Sea Scrolls in 1947, the study of pre-medieval Hebrew and Aramaic looked considerably different from what it would look like just a few years after the publication of the first manuscripts. In this paper I trace in broad strokes the impact of the Dead Sea Scrolls on the study of Hebrew and Aramaic, as well as their influence on the question of language contact between Hebrew and Aramaic at the close of the Second Temple period.[1] I begin with the pre-Dead Sea Scrolls era, move on to the years immediately following the publication of the first Scrolls, and then on to subsequent scholarship. I conclude with an evaluation of the contribution of the Scrolls to current linguistic research.

I. *Pre-1947 Research into Hebrew*

Research into Hebrew before 1947 tended to concentrate on three topics:

1. Biblical Hebrew as reflected in the Tiberian tradition of vocalization. This was by far the most widely-studied field of Hebrew.
2. Other traditions of Biblical Hebrew, namely, those reflected in the Babylonian and Palestinian vocalization systems, the Samaritan Pentateuch, and the Hebrew traditions underlying the Greek and Latin transcriptions of Hebrew found in the Septuagint, the

---

[1] Neither the earlier (4th century) Wadi el-Daliyeh documents nor the contemporaneous Nabatean documents from the Judean Desert are included in this survey.

Hexapla, and the writings of St. Jerome.[2] These traditions received far less attention than the Tiberian tradition.

3. Tannaitic Hebrew. A quiet revolution was taking place in Palestine as scholars began to shift their focus from the printed editions to manuscripts and the living oral traditions.[3] This led to a gradual but dramatic change in the grammatical description of the language of the Tannaim.

II. *Post 1947—Present Research into Hebrew*

The publication of the first partial descriptions of the Hebrew Dead Sea Scrolls in 1948 by Eliezer Lipa Sukenik in מגילות גנוזות in Jerusalem,[4] and by Millar Burrows[5] and John Trever[6] in their articles in the American periodicals *Journal of Biblical Literature* and the *Bulletin of the American Schools of Oriental Research*, caught the immediate attention of scholars, which intensified with the full publication by Burrows in 1950 of 1QIsaᵃ (the Great Isaiah Scroll) and 1QpHab (*Pesher Habakkuk*), and in 1951 of 1QS (the *Manual of Discipline*).[7] Articles soon followed both in Israel and abroad, in which the most striking linguistic peculiarities were

---

[2] See, e.g., P. Kahle, *Masoreten des Ostens: Die ältesten punktierten Handschriften des Alten Testaments und der Targume* (Leipzig: Hinrichs, 1913); idem, *Masoreten des Westens* (2 vols.; Stuttgart: Kohlhammer, 1927–1930); Z. Ben-Ḥayyim, "Samaritan Hebrew," *Leš* 12 (1943–1944): 45–60, 113–126 (Hebrew); G. Lisowsky, *Die Transkription der hebräischen Eigennamen des Pentateuch in der Septuaginta* (Basel: Theologische Fakultät der Universität Basel, 1940); E.A. Speiser, "The Pronunciation of Hebrew According to the Translations in the Hexapla," *JQR* 16 (1925–1926): 343–382; 23 (1932–1933): 233–265; 24 (1933–1934): 9–46; E. Brønno, *Studien über hebräische Morphologie und Vokalismus auf Grundlage der Mercatischen Fragmente der zweiten Kolumne der Hexapla des Origenes* (Abhandlungen über die Kunde des Morgenlandes 28; Leipzig: Brockhaus, 1943); A. Sperber, "Hebrew Based upon Greek and Latin Transliterations," *HUCA* 12–13 (1937–1938): 103–274.

[3] See, e.g., articles of Henoch Yalon in the volumes he edited, קונטרסים לעניני הלשון העברית, vols. 1–2 (Jerusalem: n.p., 1937–1939) (Hebrew), and עניני לשון (Jerusalem: Mosad ha-Rav Kook, 1942) (Hebrew); E. Porath, *Mishnaic Hebrew as Vocalised in the Early Manuscripts of the Babylonian Jews* (Jerusalem: Bialik Institute, 1938) (Hebrew).

[4] E.L. Sukenik, מגילות גנוזות מתוך גניזה קדומה שנמצאה במדבר יהודה: סקירה ראשונה (Jerusalem: Bialik Institute, 1948).

[5] M. Burrows, "Variant Readings in the Isaiah Manuscript," *BASOR* 111 (1948): 16–24, 113 (1948): 24–32; idem, "Orthography, Morphology, and Syntax of the St. Mark's Isaiah Manuscript," *JBL* 68 (1949): 195–212.

[6] J.C. Trevor, "Preliminary Observations on the Jerusalem Scrolls," *BASOR* 111 (1948): 3–16.

[7] M. Burrows, *The Dead Sea Scrolls of St. Mark's Monastery* (2 vols.; New Haven: American Schools of Oriental Research, 1950–1951).

noted, viz., extreme plene orthography, weakening of gutturals, length-
ened pronominal forms, pausal-looking forms in context, frequency of
lengthened imperfects (the cohortative), and presence of Aramaic-like
forms.

The most significant initial linguistic contributions were undoubtedly
those of Henoch Yalon, whose studies were not well known in Europe and
North America, because he published in Hebrew periodicals in Palestine.[8] Yalon went beyond pointing out the surprising forms that deviated
from the Tiberian Masoretic norm. In an impressive display of erudi-
tion, he gathered parallel phenomena from other sources: Classical Biblical Hebrew, Late Biblical Hebrew, various biblical traditions (not only
Tiberian, but also Babylonian, Samaritan, and Greek and Latin transcriptions), Tannaitic Hebrew, Paytanic Hebrew, the medieval Hebrew reading
traditions (Sephardic, Babylonian, Yemenite), works of Hebrew medieval
grammarians, and Aramaic. His approach stood in sharp contrast with
that found in several other early articles, which tended to focus on the differences between the text of 1QIsa[a] and the Masoretic Text and similar
readings in the Septuagint and the Targum. Yalon's illuminating comparison to other Hebrew sources determined the path for all future linguistic
investigations.

During the first decade of the study of the Dead Sea Scrolls, Yalon,
and others who followed his lead, showed that the language of the Scrolls
supplied missing pieces in the history of ancient Hebrew.[9] As argued by
paleographers and now confirmed by carbon-14 dating, the Scrolls fit-
ted in chronologically between Classical Biblical Hebrew and Tannaitic
Hebrew;[10] linguists demonstrated that they were contiguous to Late Biblical Hebrew, the Samaritan oral and written traditions of the Pentateuch,
as well as the original language underlying the medieval exemplars of

---

[8] H. Yalon, *Studies in the Dead Sea Scrolls: Philological Essays (1949–1952)* (Jerusalem:
Shrine of the Book, 1967) (Hebrew). See also additional notes on the language of the
Scrolls in his collected papers, *Studies in the Hebrew Language* (Jerusalem: Bialik Institute,
1971), 478–481 (Hebrew).

[9] E.g., M.H. Goshen-Gottstein, *Text and Language in Bible and Qumran* (Jerusalem:
Orient, 1960); Z. Ben-Ḥayyim, *Studies in the Traditions of the Hebrew Language* (Madrid:
Instituto Arias Montano, 1954), 77–92; idem, "Traditions in the Hebrew Language, with
Special Reference to the Dead Sea Scrolls," *ScrHier* 4 (1958): 200–214.

[10] See the seminal article of F.M. Cross, "The Development of the Jewish Scripts," in
The Bible and the Ancient Near East: Essays in Honor of W.F. Albright (ed. G.E. Wright;
Garden City: Doubleday, 1961), 133–202. For a summary of paleographic research, see
B. Webster in *DJD* XXXIX (2002): 352–362. On carbon-14 dating, see idem in *DJD*
XXXIX (2002): 362–368.

Ben-Sira and the *Damascus Document* from the Cairo Genizah. Though a linear development between Classical Biblical Hebrew, the Dead Sea Scrolls, and Tannaitic Hebrew could not be shown, these corpora do, nonetheless, share isoglosses that prove their geographical and chronological proximity.

Eduard Yechezkel Kutscher's 1959 book on the language and linguistic background of the Dead Sea Scrolls was a tour de force and arguably the most important book written on Hebrew linguistics in the 20th century.[11] Kutscher presented a comprehensive analysis of 1QIsaᵃ and other Dead Sea Scrolls in the light of Classical Biblical Hebrew, Late Biblical Hebrew, Tannaitic Hebrew, Greek and Latin transcriptions, Aramaic dialects, and Northwest Semitic in general. He composed a detailed linguistic profile of the language and concluded that 1QIsaᵃ was a popular version of the book of Isaiah, whose language reflected "the linguistic situation prevailing in Palestine during the last centuries B.C.E."[12] Or to be more precise, "the linguistic anomalies of I Isaᵃ reflect the Hebrew and Aramaic currently spoken in Palestine towards the end of the Second Commonwealth."[13] He argued that the language of the Scrolls was literary with occasional vernacular features that had penetrated the text. He thought that the scribes of the Scrolls attempted to imitate Late Biblical Hebrew as much as possible and their language "should be considered as the last offshoot of Late Biblical Hebrew."[14]

I think it is accurate to say that Kutscher's view of the language of the Dead Sea Scrolls as essentially literary prevails even today, though it is not shared by all. Already in 1954 both Shelomo Morag and Ze'ev Ben-Ḥayyim emphasized the vernacular in the Scrolls. Morag, in discussing the origin of the lengthened independent pronouns הואה and היאה,[15] concluded that they were authentic living forms of a previously unknown Hebrew dialect, and Ben-Ḥayyim explained several curious orthographic practices in the Dead Sea Scrolls as reflecting a pronunciation that was similar to that found in the oral tradition of Samaritan Hebrew, and which reflected the pronunciation of Hebrew during the

---

[11] E.Y. Kutscher, *The Language and Linguistic Background of the Isaiah Scroll* (Jerusalem: Magnes, 1959). An English translation appeared under almost the same title, *The Language and Linguistic Background of the Isaiah Scroll (1QIsaᵃ)* (Leiden: Brill 1974).

[12] Kutscher, *Isaiah Scroll*, IX (Hebrew edition).

[13] Kutscher, *Isaiah Scroll*, 3 (English edition).

[14] E.Y. Kutscher, "The Dead Sea Scrolls, Hebrew Language," *EncJud* 16:1584.

[15] S. Morag, "The Independent Pronouns of the Third Person Masculine and Feminine in the Dead Sea Scrolls," *ErIsr* 3 (1954): 166–169 (Hebrew).

period when Aramaic was the lingua franca in Palestine.[16] Elisha Qimron has continued this approach and for the past twenty years has argued
forcefully in his 1976 and 1986 grammars and in many articles that the
Hebrew in the Scrolls reflects a previously unknown Hebrew dialect.[17]

The linguistic picture that emerged from the first published Dead Sea
Scrolls in the 1950's differed significantly from the language of documents from Wadi Murabbaʿat (legal contracts as well as letters, including those written by Shimʿon Bar Kosiba) and the *Copper Scroll* (3Q15),
which Józef T. Milik prepared for publication in the early 1960's in *DJD*
II and *DJD* III.[18] These documents clearly demonstrated that the language of 1QIsaᵃ and that of the other scrolls (e.g., 1QS, 1QH) was not
the only language-type attested in the Judean Desert. The Bar Kosiba letters, from a slightly later period than the Qumran material, were written
in what was clearly a variety of Tannaitic Hebrew and showed unequivo-
cal signs of being a vernacular text. Milik designated the language of the
Copper Scroll "dialecte mishnique" on the basis of its similarity to Tannaitic Hebrew, in particular, its use of the relative particle ‏ש‎- as opposed
to the biblical ‏אשׁר‎, and the m.pl. nominal morpheme -*n* as against the
biblical -*m*.[19]

4QMMT (*Miqṣat Maʿaśeh ha-Torah*, originally designated 4QMish),
which was published officially by Qimron and John Strugnell only in
1994 in *DJD* X, though it circulated earlier, added further to the evidence
of linguistic heterogeneity. Qimron and Strugnell summarized the language of 4QMMT as "most closely reflects the Hebrew spoken at Qumran. Its vocabulary resembles that of MH more than that of BH: its grammar resembles BH's more than MH's. ... Its similarity to MH results from
the fact that both MMT and MH reflect spoken forms of Hebrew current
in the Second Temple period."[20]

---

[16] Ben-Ḥayyim, *Studies*, 77–92.

[17] E. Qimron, "A Grammar of the Hebrew Language of the Dead Sea Scrolls" (Ph.D.
diss., The Hebrew University of Jerusalem, 1976) (Hebrew); idem, *The Hebrew of the Dead
Sea Scrolls* (HSS 29; Atlanta: Scholars Press, 1986); idem, "Observations on the History of
Early Hebrew (1000 B.C.E. – 200 C.E.) in the Light of the Dead Sea Documents," in *The
Dead Sea Scrolls: Forty Years of Research* (ed. D. Dimant and U. Rappaport; Leiden: Brill,
1992), 349–361; idem "The Nature of DSS Hebrew and Its Relation to BH and MH," in
*Diggers at the Well: Proceedings of a Third International Symposium on the Hebrew of the
Dead Sea Scrolls and Ben Sira* (ed. T. Muraoka and J.F. Elwolde; STDJ 36; Leiden: Brill,
2000), 232–244.

[18] J.T. Milik in *DJD* II (1961): 67–180 and *DJD* III (1962): 201–302.

[19] J.T. Milik in *DJD* II (1961): 222.

[20] E. Qimron and J. Strugnell in *DJD* X (1994): 108.

Following their lead, Morag sought to analyze all the Hebrew material from Qumran typologically and concluded that the evidence points to three different language varieties.[21] According to Morag, most Scrolls were written in "General Qumran Hebrew," 4QMMT in "Qumran Mishnaic," and as for the difficult language of 3Q15, he chose the neutral term "Copper Scroll Hebrew."

Today, now that almost all the manuscripts have been published, and with the perspective of sixty years of research, it is clear that the Dead Sea Scrolls have left an indelible mark on Hebrew linguistic research:

1. They have demonstrated beyond doubt that the written Hebrew of the Second Temple period was not monolithic. The literary remains attested in the late books of the Hebrew Bible, Ben-Sira, the Samaritan Pentateuch, and the Dead Sea Scrolls, betray varying features and constellations of Classical Biblical Hebrew, Late Biblical Hebrew, Tannaitic Hebrew, and Aramaic. The existence of different dialects in ancient Palestine cannot be denied, though it is not certain that all the differences in language between the corpora are dialectal and not due to genre and literary conventions.

2. The Scrolls have focused scholarly discussion on the question of spoken versus written language during the Second Temple period. After six decades of research, however, the linguistic nature of the Dead Sea Scrolls is still contested: some argue that the Scrolls reveal a literary Hebrew with occasional vernacular forms; others believe that the language *in toto* reflects a vernacular. All agree that vernacular forms have penetrated the literary texts found at Qumran; the disagreement lies in the extent of the phenomenon. It should be stressed that it is only the Bar Kosiba letters from Wadi Murabba'at and Naḥal Ḥever, though from a later period, that provide certain colloquial evidence, and no less important is the fact that the vernacular of Bar Kosiba differs considerably from the vernacular elements in the Dead Sea Scrolls.

3. The verbal system attested in the language of the Scrolls has, I think, been one of the unnoticed catalyzing factors in the renewed investigation into the debate over the temporal vs. aspectual nature of the Classical Biblical Hebrew verbal system. Though Hans Reichenbach's 1947 book on relative tense has also played an important role,

---

[21] S. Morag, "Qumran Hebrew: Some Typological Observations," *VT* 38 (1988): 148–164.

the evidence for the breakdown of the classical system attested in Late Biblical Hebrew and paralleled in the Dead Sea Scrolls (e.g., the less frequent and non-classical use of *waw*-consecutive forms), together with the fact that the Tannaitic verbal system is temporal, has led to a reassessment of the Classical Biblical Hebrew system on the part of some scholars, who argue that the Classical system was in fact temporal from the start.[22]

B. Aramaic

Research into pre-medieval Aramaic before the discovery of the Aramaic Dead Sea Scrolls dealt with

1. The small corpus of Old Aramaic inscriptions.
2. Tiberian Biblical Aramaic.
3. The Elephantine papyri.[23]
4. Targumic Aramaic, both that of *Targum Onqelos*, on the one hand, and that of the so-called Jerusalem Targumim, on the other hand, i.e., *Targum Pseudo-Jonathan* (*Tg. Yer I*), and the *Fragment Targum* (*Tg. Yer II*).
5. Nabatean and Palmyrene.

The publication of Aramaic Qumran fragments in 1955 by Dominique Barthélemy, Józef Milik, Maurice Baillet, and Michel Testuz, and of the first lengthy Aramaic manuscript in 1956, 1QapGen (the *Genesis Apocryphon*) by Nahman Avigad and Yigael Yadin, ushered in a new era in Aramaic studies since it provided scholars for the first time with documents of early Palestinian provenance.[24] Two years later in 1958, Kutscher described the language of 1QapGen in an article that has had

---

[22] H. Reichenbach, *Elements of Symbolic Logic* (New York: Free Press, 1947). For a survey of the different views of the Biblical Hebrew verbal system, see K.M. Penner, "Verb Form Semantics in Qumran Hebrew Texts: Hebrew Tense, Aspect, and Modality between the Bible and the Mishnah" (Ph.D. diss., McMaster University, 2006).

[23] A.E. Cowley, *Aramaic Papyri of the Fifth Century B.C.* (Oxford: Clarendon, 1923).

[24] D. Barthélemy and J.T. Milik in *DJD* I (1955): 134–135, 150–152, 147–148; J.T. Milik, "Le Testament de Lévi en araméen: Fragment de la grotte 4 de Qumrân," *RB* 62 (1955): 398–406; M. Baillet, "Fragments araméens de Qumran 2: Description de la Jérusalem nouvelle," *RB* 62 (1955): 222–245; M. Testuz, "Deux fragments inédits des manuscrits

a significant impact on Aramaic dialectology.[25] Kutscher stressed the importance of the Palestinian background of the document and examined its linguistic profile in the light of later Palestinian Aramaic corpora and other Aramaic corpora in general. Among other things, he showed the influence of Biblical Aramaic on the language of 1QapGen, and also pointed out affinities with later Palestinian Aramaic dialects (Galilean Aramaic, Christian Palestinian Aramaic, and Samaritan Aramaic) as well as with *Targum Onqelos*, whose origin had been disputed (Palestinian or Babylonian?). Kutscher demonstrated by means of salient features in 1QapGen that *Targum Onqelos* was roughly contemporaneous and also originally composed in Palestine, though this view has come under attack in the past two decades by Edward M. Cook and Christa Müller-Kessler.[26]

Kutscher's comparative Palestinian approach to the language of the Aramaic Dead Sea Scrolls has continued to guide research in Qumran Aramaic to this day. It views the Aramaic of the Dead Sea Scrolls as the harbinger of later Palestinian Aramaic. Abraham Tal has demonstrated the value of this approach in a series of articles that lay out a linear development of certain grammatical features from the Dead Sea Scrolls up until the Western Neo-Aramaic dialect of Ma'lula. The features he examined include the suffixed *nun* on verbal and non-verbal forms, demonstrative pronouns, and infinitival forms.[27]

The Aramaic documents from the Dead Sea published before 1960 were literary works. In the beginning of the 1960's, however, Aramaic

---

de la Mer Morte," *Sem* 5 (1955): 37–38, 38; N. Avigad and Y. Yadin, *A Genesis Apocryphon: A Scroll from the Wilderness of Judaea: Description and Contents of the Scrolls, Facsimiles, Transcription and Translation of Columns II, XIX–XXII* (Jerusalem: Magnes, 1956).

[25] E.Y. Kutscher, "The Language of the Genesis Apocryphon: A Preliminary Study," *ScrHier* 4 (1958): 1–35.

[26] E.M. Cook, "A New Perspective on the Language of Onqelos and Jonathan," in *The Aramaic Bible: Targums in Their Historical Context* (ed. D.R.G. Beattie and M.J. McNamara; JSOT 166; Sheffield: JSOT Press, 1994), 142–156. In the same volume, S.A. Kaufman ("Dating the Language of the Palestinian Targums," 118–141, 123–124) attacks Abraham Tal's analysis of the language of *Targum Jonathan* as also being of Palestinian origin. See A. Tal (Rosenthal), *The Language of the Targum of the Former Prophets and Its Position within the Aramaic Dialects* (Tel-Aviv: Tel-Aviv University, 1975) (Hebrew). See also C. Müller-Kessler, "The Earliest Evidence for Targum Onqelos from Babylonia and the Question of Its Dialect and Origin," *Journal for the Aramaic Bible* 3 (2001): 181–198.

[27] A. Tal, "Layers in the Jewish Aramaic of Palestine: The Appended Nun as a Criterion," *Leš* 43 (1979): 165–184 (Hebrew); idem, "Studies in Palestinian Aramaic: The Demonstrative Pronouns," *Leš* 44 (1980): 43–65 (Hebrew); idem "The Forms of the Infinitive in Jewish Aramaic," in *Hebrew Language Studies Presented to Professor Zeev Ben-Hayyim* (ed. M. Bar-Asher et al.; Jerusalem: Magnes, 1983), 201–218 (Hebrew).

legal documents (marriage and divorce contracts, deeds of sale, IOU's) and letters from two other sites in the Judean Desert (Wadi Murabba'at and Naḥal Ḥever) were made accessible, the most famous being the Aramaic letters of Bar Kosiba.[28] As was the case with the Hebrew letters of Bar Kosiba, here, too, the language revealed itself to be markedly different from the literary Aramaic Dead Sea Scrolls, as well as from the legal documents, which by nature are conservative. Kutscher was the first to publish a comprehensive analysis of the Aramaic Bar Kosiba letters from Naḥal Ḥever.[29] As he did with the language of 1QapGen, Kutscher stressed the importance of the letters as genuine documents of Palestinian Aramaic (as opposed to *Tg. Yer I and II*) and showed their affinities with Christian Palestinian Aramaic and *Targum Onqelos*. A more recent treatment of the letters can be found in *The Documents from the Bar Kokhba Period in the Cave of Letters*.[30]

A decade went by and the Aramaic of the Dead Sea Scrolls took a new turn. The publication of 11QtgJob (*Job Targum*) in 1971 by Johannes van der Ploeg and Adam van der Woude[31] presented scholars with a slightly different type of Aramaic from that of 1QapGen, which was reflected in orthography, morphology, syntax, and lexicon. Various explanations were advanced, some attributing the differences to genre, others to chronology, degree of archaizing, or even provenance. On the basis of word order and dissimilation of gemination by insertion of *nun*, Takamitsu Muraoka went so far as to argue that it represented an Eastern type of Aramaic and thus was not native to Palestine.[32] This idea dovetailed with the argument that there was a library at Qumran containing works from elsewhere.

---

[28] Milik in *DJD* II (1962): 67–171; Y. Yadin, "Expedition D," *IEJ* 11 (1961): 36–52; E.Y. Kutscher, "The Language of the Hebrew and Aramaic Letters of Bar Kosiba and His Contemporaries: 1. The Aramaic Letters," *Leš* 25 (1960–1961): 117–133 (Hebrew).

[29] Ibid.

[30] Y. Yadin et al., eds., *The Documents from the Bar Kokhba Period in the Cave of Letters: Hebrew, Aramaic and Nabatean-Aramaic Papyri* (JDS; Jerusalem: Israel Exploration Society, 2002). The language of the letters is also included in U. Schattner-Rieser, *L'araméen des manuscrits de la mer Morte, 1. Grammaire* (Instruments pour l'étude des langues de l'Orient ancient 5; Lausanne: Zèbre, 2004).

[31] J.P.M. van der Ploeg and A.S. van der Woude with the collaboration of B. Jongeling, *Le targum de Job de la grotte XI de Qumrân* (Leiden: Brill, 1971). See also M. Sokoloff, *The Targum to Job from Qumran Cave XI* (Ramat-Gan: Bar-Ilan University, 1974).

[32] T. Muraoka, "The Aramaic of the Old Targum of Job from Qumran Cave XI," *JJS* 25 (1974): 425–442.

Subsequently published manuscripts and fragments from Qumran have not changed the general picture of the Aramaic of the Dead Sea Scrolls. The contribution of the Aramaic Dead Sea Scrolls to the study of Aramaic is no less striking than was the contribution of the Hebrew Dead Sea Scrolls to the study of Hebrew. I consider the following to be noteworthy and of lasting importance:

1. The Aramaic reflected in the literary documents does not reflect spoken speech. This was not the initial view of some scholars who claimed early on to have found the spoken language of Jesus. As is true for Hebrew, the Aramaic of the Scrolls is a written language that occasionally reveals colloquialisms. Jonas Greenfield argued that "Qumran Aramaic is also Standard Literary Aramaic but written on Palestinian soil."[33]

2. The concept of "Standard Literary Aramaic," a term coined by Greenfield, helps to explain the strong influence of the Biblical Aramaic of Daniel on the language of the Aramaic Qumran documents.[34]

3. Based on a comparison with the *Genesis Apocryphon*, the dating and Palestinian provenance of *Targum Onqelos* is widely, though not universally, accepted.

4. The evidence from Qumran, along with an increase in material from all periods of Aramaic, has led to a replacement of the old periodization of Aramaic (Old, Middle, and Late Aramaic) proposed by Franz Rosenthal into a more detailed chronological division (Old, Official, Middle, Late, and Modern) suggested by Joseph A. Fitzmyer, in which the Aramaic Dead Sea Scrolls together with other documents from the Judean Desert, Nabatean, Palmyrene, Hatran, Edessan, *Targum Onqelos* and *Targum Jonathan to the Former Prophets*, and the Aramaic words found in Josephus and the New Testament, all belong to Middle Aramaic (200 B.C.E.–200 C.E.), a period in which clear local differences distinguish the Aramaic corpora.[35]

---

[33] J.C. Greenfield, "Standard Literary Aramaic," in *Actes du premier congrès international de linguistique sémitique et chamito-sémitique, Paris 16–19 juillet 1969* (ed. A. Caquot and D. Cohen; The Hague: Mouton, 1974), 280–289, 286; repr. in *'Al Kanfei Yonah: Collected Studies of Jonas C. Greenfield on Semitic Philology* (ed. S.M. Paul, M.E. Stone, and A. Pinnick; 2 vols.; Jerusalem: Magnes, 2001), 1:111–120, 117.

[34] See, e.g., H.H. Rowley, "Notes on the Aramaic of the *Genesis Apocryphon*," in *Hebrew and Semitic Studies Presented to G.R. Driver* (ed. D.W. Thomas and W.D. McHardy; Oxford: Clarendon, 1963), 116–129.

[35] F. Rosenthal, *Die aramaistische Forschung seit Th. Nöldeke's Veröffentlichungen* (Lei-

C. Hebrew and Aramaic Language Contact

Finally, I turn to the prevailing views on the linguistic situation in Palestine at the end of the Second Temple period current before the discovery of the Dead Sea Scrolls. The topic aroused considerable interest among scholars of Christianity and Judaism. In the case of the former, there was a strong desire to identify the language or languages that Jesus spoke. At the time, the only way to attempt to recover his language was through the investigation of the Semitisms in the Greek New Testament. For many, Aramaic rather than Hebrew, seemed to be their source. See, e.g., Gustaf Dalman's influential *Die Worte Jesu* from 1898, in which he argued that Jesus spoke Aramaic.[36] Of the dialects known in Dalman's time and available for comparison, he considered the closest to the language of Jesus to be those of *Targum Onqelos* and the Jerusalem Talmud.[37]

For scholars of Judaism, on the other hand, the language question was important for determining whether or not Hebrew was still spoken at the end of the Second Temple period and in the Tannaitic period. The evidence was thought to lie in the late books of the Hebrew Bible and especially in the Mishna. During the 19th century, Abraham Geiger had argued that the Rabbis during the Tannaitic period spoke Aramaic but wrote a Hebrew that had no basis in the spoken reality, a *Gelehrtensprache*.[38] Other scholars followed him, arguing for the primacy of Aramaic and the artificiality of Hebrew. In 1908 Moshe Hirsch Segal took Geiger and those who adopted his view to task in a seminal article in which he downplayed the effect of Aramaic on Tannaitic Hebrew and demonstrated that features of Tannaitic Hebrew could only be explained if they came from a living language.[39]

---

den: Brill, 1939); J.A. Fitzmyer, "Phases of the Aramaic Language," in *A Wandering Aramean: Collected Aramaic Essays* (Missoula: Scholars Press, 1979), 57–84. Fitzmyer first proposed this classification in *The Genesis Apocryphon of Qumran Cave I: A Commentary* (BibOr 18; Rome: Biblical Institute, 1966), 19–20 n. 60.

[36] G.H. Dalman, *Die Worte Jesu mit Berücksichtigung des nachkanonischen jüdischen Schrifttums und der aramäischen Sprache* (Leipzig: Hinrichs, 1898). See also the revised English and German editions: The *Words of Jesus Considered in the Light of Post-Biblical Jewish Writings and the Aramaic Language* (trans. D.M. Kay; Edinburgh: T&T Clark, 1909); *Die Worte Jesu mit Berücksichtigung des nachkanonischen jüdischen Schrifttums und der aramäischen Sprache* (2nd ed.; Leipzig: Hinrichs, 1930).

[37] Dalman, *Words of Jesus*, 88.

[38] A. Geiger, *Lehr- und Lesebuch zur Sprache der Mischnah* (Breslau: Leukart, 1845), 1.

[39] M.H. Segal, "Mišnaic Hebrew and its Relation to Biblical Hebrew and to Aramaic,"

Today, the existence of Hebrew documents and of Aramaic documents at Qumran and elsewhere in the Judean Desert, as well as the Hebraisms in the Aramaic documents and the Aramaisms in the Hebrew documents, prove conclusively that speakers in Palestine before and after the turn of the Common Era were bilingual.[40] Moreover, the similarity between the Bar Kosiba letters and the language of the Tannaim reinforces the view that Tannaitic Hebrew was a living and developing language. This was recognized immediately by Milik in 1961 when he published the Hebrew letters of Bar Kosiba: "La thèse de savants comme Segal, Ben Iehuda et Klausner, d'après lesquels l'hébreu mishnique a été une langue parlée par la population de la Judéa aux époques perse et greco-romaine, n'est pas plus un hypothèse, elle est un fait établi. Plusieurs actes de Murabba'ât son rédigés en mishnique."[41]

Nonetheless, one gets the impression that some scholars today still seem to find it difficult to accept the notion that Tannaitic Hebrew, in addition to Aramaic, was a natural vernacular for large numbers of Jews. See, e.g., Fitzmyer: "but pockets of Palestinian Jews also used Hebrew, even though its use was not widespread";[42] or Klaus Beyer: "If one bears in mind the fact that Greek too was used in the larger cities, it is difficult to see where Hebrew could have been still spoken in Jesus'

JQR (Old Series) 20 (1908): 647–737. See also M.H. Segal, *A Grammar of Mishnaic Hebrew* (Oxford: Clarendon, 1927) and the expanded Hebrew version, דקדוק לשון המשנה (Tel-Aviv: Dvir, 1936).

[40] For a recent and thorough investigation of Hebraisms in the Aramaic Dead Sea Scrolls, see C. Stadel, *Hebraismen in den aramäischen Texten vom Toten Meer* (Schriften der Hochschule für Jüdische Studien Heidelberg 11; Heidelberg: Winter, 2008). Greek papyri, inscriptions, and literary works also point to a trilingual situation among some speakers.

[41] Milik in *DJD* II (1961): 70. See also C. Rabin, "If mishnaic hebrew was a spoken language in the first century C.E., we are entitled to assume that it must have been spoken, in some form or other, for some centuries previously" ("Hebrew and Aramaic in the First Century," in *The Jewish People in the First Century: Historical Geography, Political History, Social, Cultural and Religious Life and Institutions* [ed. S. Safri and M. Stern; 2 vols.; CRINT 1; Assen: Van Gorcum, 1976], 2:1007–1039, 1025).

[42] J.A. Fitzmyer, "The Languages of Palestine in the First Century A.D.," *CBQ* 32 (1970): 501–531, 531; repr. in *Wandering Aramean*, 29–56, 46. Cf., e.g., "In all likelihood Hebrew was used in the villages of Judea during this period, Aramaic was used in the Jewish urban areas and in the Galilee, while Greek was used in the Hellenistic cities throughout the land and along the coast" (J.C. Greenfield, "The Languages of Palestine, 200 B.C.E.–200 C.E.," in *Jewish Languages: Theme and Variations: Proceedings of Regional Conferences of the Association for Jewish Studies Held at the University of Michigan and New York University in March–April 1975* [ed. H.H. Paper; Cambridge: Association for Jewish Studies, 1978], 143–154, 149; repr. in *'Al Kanfei Yonah*, 376–387, 382).

time ... Hebrew had not been spoken in Palestine since 400 B. C."[43] The desire of others to attribute the use of Hebrew at Qumran mainly to reasons of holiness, or the use of Hebrew by Bar Kosiba primarily to reasons of nationalism ignore the demonstrated vitality of Tannaitic Hebrew during this period.[44] A more nuanced position is that of Hanan Eshel, who believes that the use of Aramaic in Mur 42 stems from the author's difficulty to express himself in Hebrew.[45] Those familiar with research into the field of Tannaitic Hebrew and into the dialectal varieties it evidences will surely take strong exception to what appears to be a lingering prejudice from a bygone era.[46]

---

[43] K. Beyer, *The Aramaic Language* (Göttingen: Vandenhoeck & Ruprecht), 40–43. Cook writes in response: "Beyer's position on Hebrew (that it died c. 400 BCE) is a futile attempt to turn back the clock" (E.M. Cook, "Qumran Aramaic and Aramaic Dialectology," in *Studies in Qumran Aramaic* [ed. T. Muraoka; AbrNSupp 3; Louvain: Peeters, 1992], 1–21, 21).

[44] See, e.g., S. Schwartz, "Language, Power, and Identity in Ancient Palestine," *Past and Present* 148 (1995): 3–47. Holiness and nationalism no doubt contributed to the choice of Hebrew, but they were surely not the factors that enabled the writing of a colloquial type Hebrew that differed from the more prestigious biblical language. For bibliography on the choice of Hebrew at Qumran and during the period of Bar Kosiba, see H. Eshel, "Hebrew in Economic Documents from the Judean Desert," *Leš* 63 (2001): 41–52 (Hebrew).

[45] Eshel, "Economic Documents," 41. In the same vein he points out P.Yadin 3:12–15: "It was written in Greek because of no means having been found to write it in Hebrew." See H. Lapin, "Palm Fronds and Citrons: Notes on Two Letters from Bar Kosiba's Administration," *HUCA* 64 (1993): 111–135, 114–115. In a more recent treatment of the papyrus by Hannah M. Cotton, however, the difficulty of the Greek reading and its interpretation is stressed and discussed. She dismisses the older interpretation of the lines and suggests that Soumaios is not Simeon Bar Kosiba, but rather a Nabatean, and for this reason he has difficulties writing in the Jewish Aramaic (as opposed to Nabatean) script. At any rate, Eshel's interpretation of the papyrus is far from certain. See H.M. Cotton, "The Bar Kokhba Revolt and the Documents from the Judaean Desert: Nabataean Participation in the Revolt (*P.Yadin* 52)," in *The Bar Kokhba War Reconsidered: New Perspectives on the Second Jewish Revolt Against Rome* (ed. P. Schäfer; TSAJ 100; Tübingen: Mohr Siebeck, 2003), 133–152. As indicated above, I prefer to see the use of Aramaic in Hebrew documents (and Hebrew in Aramaic documents) as proof of the widespread and natural use of the two related languages.

[46] See, e.g., M. Bar-Asher, "The Study of Mishnaic Hebrew Grammar Based on Written Sources: Achievements, Problems, and Tasks," *ScrHier* 37 (1998): 9–42; idem, *L'hébreu mishnique: études linguistiques* (Orbis Supplementa 11; Leuven: Peeters, 1999), 3–45.

TWO ISSUES IN QUMRAN HEBREW:
SYNCHRONIC AND DIACHRONIC PERSPECTIVES[*]

MOSHE BAR-ASHER
Hebrew Language Academy and
The Hebrew University of Jerusalem

INTRODUCTORY COMMENTS

§ 1 The study undertaken here is designed to situate the Hebrew of the Dead Sea Scrolls[1] in the historical context of written Hebrew, which stretches more than 1300 years:[2] beginning with Biblical Hebrew, through the Qumran scrolls, and ending with the language of the Tannaim. Throughout this time, a spoken language stood behind this written heritage. The intent here is not to embark upon a general study, or to arrive at general conclusions regarding the relationships between these three strata of classical Hebrew. General conclusions require comprehensive examinations upon which to build, and what is necessary is this type of examination of many grammatical and lexical issues. I would like to offer here studies of just two linguistic issues, which provide insights into the diachronic developments that encompassed these three strata. It is clear, however, that every linguistic fact that can be examined through diachronic lenses will add to the general picture of the language.[3]

---

[*] My learned friends Devorah Dimant, David Talshir, Mordechai Mishor, and Steven Fassberg read this article, brought a few bibliographic items to my attention, and added important comments. I thank them all for their help.

[1] Obviously, I mean here the scrolls that were actually composed in the time of Qumran—roughly the beginning of the second century B.C.E. through the second half of the first century C.E. The scrolls from Qumran that were copied from earlier texts without any significant changes, such as the second Isaiah scroll from Cave 1, are not representative of Qumran Hebrew.

[2] In other words, from archaic biblical poetry of the eleventh or tenth century B.C.E. through literature of the Tannaim, redacted in the third century C.E.

[3] There have been many studies of linguistic issues—whether grammatical or lexical—which have focused on the three major strata of classical Hebrew: Biblical, Qumran (together with Ben Sira), and Mishnaic. I will mention only a few of these studies: first and foremost is Kutscher's book on the Great Isaiah Scroll (Y. Kutscher, הלשון והרקע הלשוני של מגילת ישעיהו השלמה ממגילות מדבר יהודה [Jerusalem: Magnes, 1959]); H. Yalon, מגילות

Before turning to the data themselves, I would like to make two further introductory comments.

§ 2 First: it goes without saying that the Hebrew reflected in the Qumran texts should be described, on its own terms, as an independent entity. Scholarship should first establish its lexicon[4] and describe the grammar of the various texts within Qumran Hebrew (QH).[5] More than a few scholars have disputed the claim that QH is nothing more than a repository of Hebrew words and forms drawn from disparate sources, and that in this repository biblical Hebrew occupies pride of place, and Aramaic forms are found in abundance. S. Morag and E. Qimron, each in his own way, see in QH an independent entity, i.e., an independent dialect and not merely artificial or literary forms.[6] But clearly even this approach does not deny the necessity to study QH in its diachronic context, in a sequence beginning with biblical Hebrew and ending with Mishnaic Hebrew.

§ 3 Second: there is an important methodological difficulty in this type of study. On the one hand the dates of the Qumran texts are relatively

---

מדבר יהודה: דברי לשון (Jerusalem: Shrine of the Book, 1967) also should be mentioned. Of course, the important works by M. Kister and E. Qimron belong here, too (see below, nn. 4–5). I, too, have tried my hand in this field (cf. "A Few Remarks on Mishnaic Hebrew and Aramaic in Qumran Hebrew," in *Diggers at the Well: Proceedings of a Third International Symposium on the Hebrew of the Dead Sea Scrolls and Ben Sira* [ed. T. Muraoka and J.F. Elwolde; STDJ 36; Leiden: Brill, 2000], 12–19, and "על כמה לשונות בעברית של קומראן," *Leš* 64 [2002]: 7–31). Further literature is listed in Muraoka and Elwolde, *Diggers at the Well*, 275–307; see further the list at the end of that book, 309–310 (which are not paginated). I should also mention that whenever I speak of the Hebrew of Qumran or the Hebrew of the Dead Sea Scrolls, I refer to what S. Morag called "General Qumran Hebrew" (= GQH; S. Morag, "לשונן של מגילות מדבר יהודה: קווי מבנה ומהותם," in הברית העברית העולמית: הכנס העברי המדעי השישי באירופה (לונדון תשמ"ד) [Jerusalem, 1988], 11–19, 11–12; idem, "Qumran Hebrew: Some Typological Observations," *VT* 38 [1988]: 149–164, 149).

[4] In addition to the sources mentioned in the previous note, Kister's articles on the lexicon in QH and the Hebrew of Ben Sira belong here (M. Kister, "Some Observations on Vocabulary and Style in the Dead Sea Scrolls," in *Diggers at the Well*, 137–165, and his other studies listed in Muraoka and Elwolde, *Diggers at the Well*, 289).

[5] Here E. Qimron's books should be mentioned ("דקדוק הלשון העברית של מגילות מדבר יהודה" [Ph.D. diss., The Hebrew University of Jerusalem, 1976] and *The Hebrew of the Dead Sea Scrolls* [HSS 29; Atlanta: Scholars Press, 1986]) and his many articles (see Muraoka and Elwolde, *Diggers at the Well*, 296–297). Qimron is currently working on an expanded and improved edition of his grammar of QH.

[6] See Morag, "Qumran Hebrew," and E. Qimron, "Observations on the History of Early Hebrew (1000 B.C.E. – 200 C.E.) in the Light of the Dead Sea Documents," in *The Dead Sea Scrolls: Forty Years of Research* (ed. D. Dimant and U. Rappaport; STDJ 10; Leiden: Brill, 1992), 349–361, and idem, "The Nature of DSS Hebrew and its Relation to BH and MH," in *Diggers at the Well*, 232–244; against this see J. Blau, "A Conservative View of the Language of the Dead Sea Scrolls," in *Diggers at the Well*, 20–25.

well-known to us: they date from a period of roughly three hundred years, from the beginning of the second century B.C.E. until the second half of the first century C.E. Additionally, the texts come to us directly, without the intervention of scribes' tampering hands.

On the other hand, the Bible, which was completed—or, better, which crystallized—apparently around 200 B.C.E., and which includes texts written centuries earlier, reached us in copies dating only from the second half of the first millennium C.E. (the time of the Masoretes). In other words, a tremendous amount of time separates the dates of the biblical books' compositions from the dates of their earliest textual witnesses.[7] Additionally, Tannaitic literature, which was edited between the end of the second- and beginning of the third-century C.E., was transmitted orally for many generations prior to being written, and the earliest manuscripts date no earlier than the eighth century; the best manuscripts we have are partly from the end of the first millennium and primarily from the beginning of the second millennium. So in some senses, QH is earlier not only than Mishnaic Hebrew, but than biblical Hebrew, as well.

Fortunately, however, we do not have to operate with only these texts in a vacuum. The historical study of Hebrew in the nineteenth- and especially the twentieth-centuries has shown that the Masoretes, in Tiberias, elsewhere in Palestine, and in Babylonia, transmitted a linguistic system whose basic features match the late biblical period, around 200 B.C.E., and that only very few later influences made their way into the Masoretic text. The reliable manuscripts of rabbinic literature, too, reflect a Hebrew which preserves the basic nature it possessed centuries earlier when it was a spoken dialect. It should be emphasized that with regard to both the Bible and the Mishnah, the consonantal texts of the best witnesses—without the vocalizations—clearly reflect authentic representations of the original languages, or at least the languages spoken when these texts were finally edited.

It is therefore clear that we can trace phenomena diachronically, in the accepted chronological order: Bible, Dead Sea Scrolls, Mishnaic Hebrew. And it is understood that any phenomenon in the Hebrew of Qumran that is investigated in the context of this sequence needs to be checked carefully to ensure that the proper historical sequence is used.

I now turn to the two phenomena to be discussed here, one nominal form and one verbal form.

---

[7] Obviously this is probably less acute with regard to the biblical books that were copied at Qumran.

מָבוֹא/מָבוֹי (מְבוֹאִי)

§ 4 The noun מָבוֹא occurs twenty-five times in the Bible. It can be said
that it has two[8] basic meanings:[9]

a. A verbal noun of the *qal*, which denotes the action done by one who
   is בָּא, in either of the two meanings of בָּא: one who arrives at a place,
   or one who enters a place. In other words, in this meaning מָבוֹא is
   the equivalent of the verbal noun—known from QH itself, and from
   MH—בִּיאָה.[10] This meaning is found in verses such as וְיָבוֹאוּ אֵלֶיךָ
   כִּמְבוֹא-עָם וְיֵשְׁבוּ לְפָנֶיךָ "they will come to you as a people comes and sit
   before you" (Ezek 33:31), and בָּאוּ בִשְׁעָרֶיךָ כִּמְבוֹאֵי עִיר מְבֻקָּעָה "when
   he enters your gates, as men enter a breached city" (Ezek 26:10).

b. A noun denoting the place[11] through which one enters into a different place. In other words, in this meaning, מָבוֹא is an equivalent of
   the nouns פֶּתַח and שַׁעַר. This is the meaning in verses such as מָבוֹא
   הַשְּׁלִישִׁי אֲשֶׁר בְּבֵית ה' "the third entrance of the House of the Lord"
   (Jer 38:14) and עֹמֵד עַל-עַמּוּדוֹ בַּמָּבוֹא "standing by his pillar at the
   entrance" (2 Chr 23:13). This meaning should also be seen, in the
   derived meaning "port" < "place of entry into the sea," in הַיֹּשֶׁבֶת עַל-
   מְבוֹאֹת יָם "who dwell at the gateway of the sea" (Ezek 27:3). Another

---

[8] Here I follow Ben-Yehudah's dictionary s.v. (E. Ben-Yehuda, מלון הלשון העברית הישנה
והחדשה [17 vols.; Berlin-Schöneberg: Langenscheidt, 1908–1959], 6:2767–2768), except
that I am presenting the meanings in reverse order: what is given there as meaning 2 is
cited here as meaning 1, and what is given there as meaning 1 is here meaning 2.

[9] There are some who detect more than two meanings in the biblical attestations, since
they divide the two meanings into various sub-areas (with no adequate justification). This
is, for example, the view of *HALOT*; there one will find four meanings.

[10] In its only appearance in BH (וְהִנֵּה מִצָּפוֹן לְשַׁעַר הַמִּזְבֵּחַ סֵמֶל הַקִּנְאָה הַזֶּה בַּבִּאָה), "and,
behold, north of the gate of the altar was the infuriating image [סמל הקנאה] in the
entrance" [Ezek 8:5]), the noun בִּיאָה has the second meaning of מָבוֹא: a noun meaning
"opening, entranceway." In Qumran, on the other hand, the word functions as a verbal
noun, as in לתחלת ביאתם לארץ "for the beginning of their entry into the Land" (4Q379 12
5; ed. C. Newsom in *DJD* XII [1996]: 270; although the editor reads בואתם, the text should
be read ביאתם). This verbal noun בִּיאָה also appears a few times in 4Q324, which was
published by S. Talmon, J. Ben-Dov, and U. Glessmer in *DJD* XXI (2001). For example,
in 4Q324 1 1, 4, 7 (104–105) we read: ביאת [אלישיב] "the coming of Eliashib," ביאת אמר
"the coming of the '*mr*," ביאת ח[זיר] "the coming of *ḥ*[*zyr*]." The issue of the verbal noun
in MH does not need to be discussed at length here. It is found in general use, such as
ביאת המקדש (*m. Naz.* 7:4); הקיש ביאתן בימי עזרא לביאתן בימי יהושע (*y. Qidd.* 51c), and in
specialized usages: ביאת השמש "sunset" (found in expressions like ביאת שמשו "his sunset"
[*b. Ber.* 2a]), and sexual relations, such as ולא חלק בין ביאה לביאה (*m. Yebam.* 6:1).

[11] This fits with the many other nouns of the pattern מִקְטָל which denote places, such
as מוֹשָׁב, מָדוֹר, מִקְדָּשׁ, מִגְדָל, and מִקְטָל.

sub-meaning apparently derived from this one is מָבוֹא in the sense of "the place of entry (= setting) of the sun"—i.e., the West[12]—in the expressions אַחֲרֵי דֶּרֶךְ מְבוֹא הַשֶּׁמֶשׁ "beyond the western road" (Deut 11:30), שֶׁמֶשׁ יָדַע מְבוֹאוֹ "the sun knows its setting" (Ps 104:19), מִמִּזְרַח- שֶׁמֶשׁ וְעַד-מְבוֹאוֹ "from where the sun rises to where it sets" (Mal 1:11), and more.[13]

§5 By Mishnaic, or, more precisely, Tannaitic Hebrew changes had befallen the word מָבוֹא with in both morphology and meaning. There were two morphological changes:

a. מְבוֹי < מָבוֹא: Very often, instead of some roots containing a medial *wāw* and a final *'ālep*, in MH we find forms with medial *wāw* and final *yôd*. Although most forms, both nominal and verbal, from the root בו"א appear in manuscripts (and in printed editions) as derived from בו"א, rather than the secondary root בו"י—like בִּיאָה, מֵבִיא, הֵבִיא, לָבוֹא, יָבוֹא, בָּאתִי, תְּבוּאָה, הֲבָאָה; and more—a few forms do appear as derived from בו"י. Besides the noun מְבוֹי, the third person fem. sg. perfect in the *qal* appears as בָּאת,[14] which is the form

---

[12] A. Even-Shoshan, ed., *A New Concordance of the Bible* (2nd ed.; Jerusalem: Qiryat Sefer, 1988), s.v., was not correct when he defined מָבוֹא as sunset. In all the contexts in which מְבוֹא appears in the construct attached to the sun, it denotes the place, and not the act, of setting. Even if historically מְבוֹא השמש once meant sunset, its meaning changed to the *place* of sunset, as noted in *HALOT* s.v.: "descent, setting … esp[ecially] of the sun > the west."

[13] It is possible that the expression מבוא השמש is "the place into which the sun enters": not the entrance itself, but the entire area beyond the entrance. If this is true, we have two sub-meanings: מָבוֹא "entrance" and מָבוֹא "area into which one enters through the entrance."

[14] For example, of the eighteen occurrences of the third person fem. sg. *qal* perfect, 17 are vocalized in MS K as בָּאת (e.g., *m. Yebam.* 15:1[2]). The only exceptional occurrence of בָּאה, as if from the root בו"א, is in *m. Neg* 5:1 (ספק שהיא היא, ספק שאחרת באה תחתיה). In MS Parma de Rossi 497 (Parma B), too, only בָּאת appears (e.g., *m. Nid.* 8:3; *m. Yad.* 3:1[2]). But in the passage in *m. Neg.* 5:1, Parma B also reads בָּאה. G. Haneman, תורת הצורות של לשון המשנה על פי מסורת כתב-יד פרמה (דה-רוסי 138) (Tel Aviv: Tel Aviv University, 1980), 396 already noted that Parma de Rossi 138 (Parma A) always reads באת, again excepting the passage in *m. Nega'im*, where Parma A, too, reads באה. According to Haneman, the *tāw* with which the following word begins ("באה תחתיה") explains this exception as "nothing but a mistaken division of the continuous phonetic string in which the taws were caught." In other words, באת תחתיה was analyzed as באה תחתיה mistakenly. Another possibility is that the form is not a perfect at all, but a participle; syntactically there is no obstacle to this interpretation.

expected from a final *yôd* root, and not the form בָּאָה,[15] as expected
from a final *'ālep* root.[16]

I want to emphasize that the form מָבוֹי, known to us from printed
editions, is found already in reliable texts; this is the form in the
"Eastern" sources of the Mishnah, such as Parma B,[17] MS Antonin
(A),[18] and the Mishnah with Babylonian vocalization.[19] However,
reliable "Western" texts show two other realizations: (a) מָבוֹיִ
(*māḇōyi*)—in which the diphthong has been broken up, *oy* > *oyi*;[20]
(b) מָבוֹאִי (*māḇōy* > *māḇōyi* > *māḇō'i*)—with an *'ālep* in place of the
yôd.[21]

b. In biblical Hebrew two different plural forms appear: מְבוֹאִים as well
as מְבוֹאוֹת. Both, however, appear only in the construct: כִּמְבוֹאֵי עִיר "at
the entrances of the city" (Ezek 26:10); מְבוֹאֹת יָם "gateways of the sea"
(Ezek 27:3). In rabbinic literature, on the other hand, only the plural
ending וֹת– is attested, and the form is written מבואות in the absolute.
It should be noted that all the reliable witnesses vocalize the form
מָבוֹאוֹת (with the קמץ preserved!): MS K reads וּבְמָבוֹאוֹת אפילים (*m.
Ter.* 11:10) and וּבְמָבוֹאוֹת אֲפוּלִים[22] (*m. Pesaḥ.* 4:4), and Parma A and
MS Paris 328–329, too, read מָבוֹאוֹת (twice). This was also the read-
ing of the Babylonian tradition—וּבמָאבוֹאוֹת, with a plene spelling

---

[15] On the other hand, it is worth emphasizing that the scribe who wrote the last pages
of MS K (K2), in the single example within his corpus, reads בָּאָה and not בָּאת: מעשה באשה
אחת שבאה לפני אבא (*m. Yad.* 3:1).

[16] In other verbs and nouns from roots which were originally final *'ālep*, we also find
III-*yôd* forms alongside III-*'ālep* forms. For example, we have מָשָׁא, נָשָׂאתִי, and נִישׂוֹאִין on the
one hand, but נָשׂוּי, מָשׂוּי/מָשׂוֹי, and נָשָׂאת/נִשֵּׂאת (*nip'al* third person fem. sg. perfect forms)
on the other hand. We even find suppletion within a single paradigm: מְצָאתִי alongside
מְצִינוּ.

[17] For example, בַּמָּבוֹי ... הַמָּבוֹי (*m. Nid.* 7:1, Parma B).

[18] For example, במבוי ... המבוי (ibid., A).

[19] This is the form cited by Y. Yeivin, מסורת הלשון העברית המשתקפת בניקוד הבבלי
(Jerusalem: Hebrew Language Academy, 1985), 1023.

[20] In MS K there are thirteen attestations of מָבוֹיִ (e.g., *m. 'Erub.* 1:2) or מָבוֹיִ (e.g., *m.
'Erub.* 1:1), but we also find מָבוֹי (*m. 'Erub.* 1:2) and מָבוֹיִ (*m. Nid.* 7:2) with the diphthong
intact. In Parma A, too, the form מָבוֹי predominates (e.g., *m. Šabb.* 16:1). According to
Haneman, תורת הצורות, 20–21, the dot under the *yôd* is not a *ḥîreq*, but a *mappîq*; in other
words, the form in front of us is *māḇōy*, not *māḇōyi*. On the other hand, the existence of
the form מָבוֹאִי in MS K, as we cite below, supports the understanding of מָבוֹיִ/מָבוֹיִ in this
MS as a form with the diphthong broken up, *māḇōyi*; in מָבוֹאִי the glide /y/ was replaced
by the glottal stop /-/. Further on this issue, cf. my book פרקים במסורת לשון חכמים של יהודי
איטליה ('Edah ve-Lashon 6; Jerusalem: Magnes, 1980), 43–45.

[21] There are eight example of מָבוֹאִי in MS K (e.g., *m. 'Erub.* 5:2 [2×]; 6:8; 9:3).

[22] The letter between the פ and the ל in this word is certainly a *wāw*, not a *yôd*.

with *ʾālep*, or without it, וּבְמְבוֹאוֹת[23]—and so, too, in a Yemenite
manuscript of *m. Terumot* (11:1).[24] The vocalization מְבוֹאוֹת (in the
two mishnayot just mentioned) is found in the editions printed in
Amsterdam in 1646, Venice in 1737, Mantua in 1777, and Livorno
in 1929. This was also the vocalization adopted by H. Yalon, as well
as by H.N. Bialik (in *m. Terumot*).

§ 6 The (only?)[25] meaning of מְבוֹאִי (מָבוֹי, מָבוֹי) in MH (and in the language
of the Amoraim) is "a type of street … between two rows of houses."[26]
It is surprising that whoever wrote the entry for מָבוֹי in Ben-Yehudah's
Thesaurus began the entry, "כמו מָבוֹא," intending, apparently, to equate
MH מָבוֹי with BH מָבוֹא. They are clearly not the same, however: in MH
there is something of an expansion of the meaning of the term, and also
some specialization: מָבוֹי cannot denote the entranceway into a house or
a city, but only a small street which serves as the conduit into courtyards
and to a large street.[27] It should be emphasized that מְבוֹי, which means
most basically "small street,"[28] is not only found in the rabbinic laws of
ʿErubin, but in other contexts as well. For example, it appears in the laws of
ritual purity, as in the case השרץ שנמצא במבוי מטמא למפרע, עד שיאמר בדקתי
את המבוי ולא היה בו שרץ "a [ritually impure] creeping animal which was

---

[23] The vocalization of מְפוֹל-pattern nouns with the preservation of the קמץ in the plural
is found also for the noun מָשׁוֹט: מְשׁוֹטוֹת (*m. Makš.* 5:7)—so in MSS K, Parma B, Antonin,
and the Babylonian vocalization (Yeivin, מסורת הלשון העברית, 1025), as well as MS Paris.

[24] The evidence from the Babylonian vocalization and the Yemenite tradition is cited
by Yeivin (מסורת הלשון העברית, 1023); he also cited the form בִּמְבוֹיֵי in a Yemenite
manuscript of the *piyyutim* of R.S. Shabazi.

[25] See below, n. 28.

[26] Cf. Ben-Yehudah's *Thesaurus*, s.v., 2678 ("כעין רחוב … בין שתי שורות בתים"). A
similar definition can be found in H.Y. Kosowsky, *Thesaurus Mishnae* (2nd ed.; Jerusalem:
Massada, 1959), s.v. ("רחוב צר שלפני שורות חצרות הפתוחות לה. והוא פתוח לרחובה של עיר—
שהמבוי פתוח אליו").

[27] Compare Kosowsky's definition, cited in the previous note.

[28] It must be said that in one mishnah, at least, it is difficult to understand מבוי as a type
of street: in the opening mishnah of ʿErubin, the rule is given that מבוי שהוא גבוה מעשרים
אמה ימעט "a *mābōy* which is taller that twenty cubits, he shall reduce [it]." It is not, of
course, possible that the rule is enjoining the reduction of the street itself by using a לחי
and a קורה; instead, only the opening into the entranceway is being reduced. Perhaps מבוי
here means the gate (opening) of the street, like the second meaning of the BH lexeme,
as discussed above—in other words, an *opening* into the street whose top is more than 20
cubits (אמות) to drive needs to be made shorter. I wonder if this may not be an example
of an early mishnah in which the word is used in its meaning as in BH, as we often find
that early mishnayot utilized typically biblical elements (J.N. Epstein and E.Z. Melamed,
מבואות לספרות התנאים [Jerusalem: Magnes, 1957], 27; cf. recently my article, "רושמי לשון
המקרא במשנה," in מחקרים בתלמוד ובמדרש: ספר זיכרון לתרצה ליפשיץ [eds. M. Bar-Asher,
J. Levinson, and B. Lifschitz; Jerusalem, Bialik Institute, 2005], § 4).

found in a small street (מבוי) defiles retroactively, [as far back as] until one says, 'I checked the small street (מבוי) and there was no creeping animal there'" (*m. Nid.* 7:2). In other words, this is a legitimate general feature of MH,

§7 I now turn to the data in QH, and to the conclusions that can be drawn from them. There are now sixteen attestations of the noun in the texts from Qumran, and another three in restored passages in fragmentary texts.[29] I begin by commenting on the word's morphology at Qumran, and then move on to its meaning.

§8 a. The singular form appears eleven times. It is almost always written מבוא, i.e., its biblical form. In the absolute we find דלתי מגן לאין מבוא (*Hodayot*: 1QHᵃ VI:27–28).[30] The rest of the attestations are in the construct. Two examples are במבוא מועדים לימי חודש (*Community Rule*: 1QS X:3)[31] and מבוא אור (*Hodayot*: 1QHᵃ XII:4).[32]

Once, however, we find the spelling פתחי מבואי ושערי מוצא משמיעים מבואי כבוד המלך: (*Songs of the Sabbath Sacrifice*: 4Q405 23 i 9).[33] It would appear that the common spelling in the Scrolls—מבוא—is an imitation of the biblical form, but that the spelling מבואי[34] in the *Songs of the Sabbath Sacrifice* points towards the form known to us from rabbinic literature. This, then, provides us with evidence that the "rabbinic" form—מָבוֹי/מָבוֹי/מָבוֹאי—was already in use in the living language in Palestine centuries earlier than its attestation in the Mishnah. To put it another way, the common writing with the biblical form reveals a literary conservatism whereas the single exceptional spelling provides us with crucial insight into the living language.[35]

---

[29] There is one example in the *War Scroll* (1QM XIV:13; cf. Y. Yadin, מגילת מלחמת בני אור בבני חושך [2nd ed.; Jerusalem: Bialik Institute, 1957], 342), עם מ[בו]א יומם ולילה, and two examples in the *Songs of the Sabbath Sacrifice*: [אולמי מב]ואי[(11Q17 IV:4; cf. F. García-Martinez and E.J.C. Tigchelaar in *DJD* XXIII [1998]: 275) and סם במב]וא (4Q402 1 1; cf. C. Newson in *DJD* XI [1998]: 223).

[30] See J. Licht, מגילת ההודיות ממגילות מדבר יהודה (Jerusalem: Bialik Institute, 1957), 117.

[31] J. Licht, מגילת הסרכים ממגילות מדבר יהודה (Jerusalem: Bialik Institute, 1965), 209.

[32] Licht, מגילת ההודיות, 172. Once we find the word written defectively, מבא "עם] מבא אור לממשל[תו" (*Hodayot*: 4Q427 8 ii 11; cf. E. Schuller in *DJD* XXIX [1999]: 110).

[33] See Newson in *DJD* XI (1998): 335.

[34] Prof. E. Qimron accepts the reading מבואי, but suggests considering also the reading מבואו, in which the final vowel of *mābō'*, following the quiescence of the 'ālep, is realized not as a long vowel /ō/, but as a doubly long vowel /ō:/! For a different explanation of מבואי proposed by Qimron, see his "A Review Article of *Songs of the Sabbath Sacrifices: A Critical Edition* by Carol Newsom," *HTR* 79 (1986): 349–371, 353–354.

[35] In other places where the graphemic string מבואי is found, the plural construct form מְבוֹאֵי seems to be meant, e.g., מבואי מלך (*Songs of the Sabbath Sacrifice*: 4Q405 14–15 4;

b. It should be noted that the only plural form so far attested at Qumran is מבואים. Here, too, it appears in the construct, מבואי,[36] and with suffixed pronouns: הרחוקים מפתחיה הנדחים ממבואיה (11QPs[a] XVIII:5–6),[37] and אולמי מבואיהם (*Songs of the Sabbath Sacrifice*: 4Q405 14–15 4).[38]

§9 The main uses of מבוא at Qumran are as follows:

a. A verbal noun with the meaning "coming" (arriving at a certain place or entrance into a certain place): for example, עם מבוא אור ממעו[נתו] (*Hodayot*: 1QH[a] XII:4), meaning "with the coming (= arrival) of the light from its resting spot" (i.e., the morning);[39] דלתי מגן לאין מבוא (*Hodayot*: 1QH[a] VI:27–28), in which the word means "entrance" (the action of the enterer), meaning דלתי מגן "which does not allow entrance."

The word מבוא also means "arrival" in the sense of "beginning," as in במבוא מועדים לימי חודש (*Community Rule*: 1QS X:3), meaning the beginning of the festivals ("תחילתם של המועדים," as indicated by Licht[40]). The same is true for the line מבוא יום ולילה (*Community Rule*: 1QS X:10[41]); as Licht insightfully noted, "מבוא ... the beginning of a period of time."[42] There are other examples of the same.

b. A noun meaning "gate, opening," as in אולמי מבואיהם (*Songs of the Sabbath Sacrifice*: 4Q405 14–15 4), which the editor, C. Newsom, perceptively translated, "the vestibules of their entryways,"[43] and

---

cf. Newsom in *DJD* XI [1998]: 330), and במבואי אלי דעת (*Songs of the Sabbath Sacrifice*: 4Q405 23 i 8).

[36] See the examples cited in the previous note.

[37] See J.A. Sanders in *DJD* IV (1965): 39.

[38] See Newsom in *DJD* XI (1998): 330.

[39] Licht, מגילת ההודיות, 172.

[40] Licht, מגילת הסרכים, 209. Others, too, have translated correctly; cf. e.g., P. Wernberg-Møller, *The Manual of Discipline: Translated and Annotated with an Introduction* (STDJ 1; Leiden: Brill, 1957), 36, who translates "At the entering of the times," which is approximately the translation of J. Carmignac and P. Guilbert, *Les textes des Qumran traduits et annotés*, vol. 1: *La Règle de la Communauté, La Règle de la Guerre, Les Hymnes* (Paris: Letouzey et Ane, 1961), 66, as well: "A l'entrée des saisons."

[41] Licht, מגילת הסרכים, 215.

[42] This is how it is translated by Wernberg-Møller, *Manual of Discipline*, 37, as well: "the entering of day and night"; Carmignac and Guilbert, *Les textes des Qumran*, 70, translate, "l'arrivée du jour et de la nuit."

[43] See above, n. 38. It might be noted that the expression אולמי מבואיהם can be well explained as an inverted construct phrase, equivalent to מבואי אולמיהם. This is a phenomenon well-known in QH, as was shown already years ago by Yalon (מגילות מדבר יהודה, 85), but which I cannot elaborate here.

פתחי מבואי ושערי מוצא משמיעים כבוד המלך (*Songs of the Sabbath Sacrifice*: 4Q405 23 i 9), in which the first four words were translated by the editor, "the portals of entrance and the gates of exit."

§ 10 In essence, the two meanings of מבוא in QH are the same as those in BH: a verbal noun, "coming," meaning both "arrival" and "entrance," and a noun meaning "gate, entryway." There are, however, two differences between BH and QH that should be stressed.

a. The first meaning, "coming," also serves with units of time to mean "the beginning." The expression מבוא מועדים is parallel to ראשי מועדים in the same text (*Community Rule*: 1QS X:4–5), and equivalent to the biblical phrase (י)ראש(י) חדשים; מבוא and ראש are, in other words, synonyms meaning "beginning."

b. The expression מבוא יום in QH means, therefore, "beginning of the day," as opposed to מבוא השמש in BH, which originally meant "the coming of the sun" into the west, and later on denoted "the west" itself.

Grammatically, however, מבוא is used in QH exactly as it is used in MH. The one exceptional form מבואי in the *Songs of the Sabbath Sacrifice* proves that this form, previously known only from later rabbinic litera-ture, already existed at this early stage. In other words, this establishes that the transition to a form based on a final-*yôd* root (מָבוֹא > מָבוֹי > מְבוֹי/מָבוֹאי), known from Tannaitic literature, occurred in Second Tem-ple times, long before the destruction in 70 c.e., and centuries prior to the redaction of the Mishnah.

§ 11 The following table summarizes the data in the three levels of the language:

Morphology

Biblical Hebrew	מָבוֹא	מְבוֹאִים/מְבוֹאוֹת[44]
Qumran Hebrew	מבוא/מבואי[45]	מבואים[46]
Mishnaic Hebrew	מָבוֹאי > מָבוֹי > מָבוֹי	מְבוֹאוֹת[47]

---

[44] These two forms are attested only in the construct, ־מְבוֹאֵי and ־מְבוֹאוֹת, as mentioned above (see also below, n. 49). The form מוֹבָאֶיךָ (2 Sam 3:25) seems to be a singular form, analogous to מוֹצָאֲךָ, and there is no reason to take it as a plural; the LXX, for example, translates these words with singular nouns of its own: τὴν ἔξοδόν σου καὶ τὴν εἴσοδόν σου "your exiting and entering."

[45] As already discussed, מבוא is an imitation of the biblical form, whereas מבואי reflects the form known in the then-current living language.

Semantics

Biblical Hebrew	1. Verbal noun, "coming" ("arriving," "entering")
	2. Noun meaning "opening, entryway"; the phrase מְבוֹא שֶׁמֶשׁ means "west"
Qumran Hebrew	1. Verbal noun, "coming" ("arriving," "entering"); with periods of time: "beginning"
	2. Noun meaning "opening, entryway"
Mishnaic Hebrew	"Small street between two rows of houses" (the biblical meaning "opening" may be attested in one mishnah[48])

§ 12 To summarize, the morphological change (III-'ālep > III-yôd) took place already during Second Temple times, as the one attestation of מבואי in the *Songs of the Sabbath Sacrifice* shows, although scribes continue to write מבוא in its biblically-attested form. The semantics of the word remain constant through the Bible and Qumran, however, with two differences: (a) the phrase מבוא שמש is attested only in BH, and מבוא יום in QH means morning, not evening; (b) מְבוֹא in QH also means "beginning" (of a period of time). In MH, on the other hand, מָבוֹי is not used with the meanings it possesses in BH and QH, even in the tractates *Middot* and *Tamid*, which deal with the Temple. Its meaning was specialized, as described, to just a small narrow street between two rows of houses.

(הֶעֱשִׂיא הֶעֱשָׂה AND עָשָׂה)

§ 13 As is known, the verbal root עש״י meaning "to do, to make," appears in the Bible only in the *qal*[49] and *nip'al binyanim*, and the contrast

---

[46] The form is attested only in the construct (מבואי-) and with suffix pronouns (מבואיהם). The pl. construct alone is not enough, of course, to allow us to reconstruct the absolute form with certainty, since there are nouns with plurals ending in ת- whose construct form nevertheless shows the ending י-. Cf. the excellent article by S. Sharvit, "שמות כפולי צורה בריבוי בלשון התנאים," *Meḥqarim ba-Lašon* 4 (1990): 335–373, on nouns with two plural endings.

[47] The קמץ is preserved in all reliable witnesses, as detailed above (§ 5b).

[48] See n. 28, above.

[49] In *HALOT*, עש״י "to do" is listed as עש״י I, and in the entry are given a number of examples of the verb in the *qal* which are in fact derived from other roots, such as בְּעֶשּׂוֹת (Ezek 23:21), which is from עש״י II "to squeeze, crush." Actually, though, בְּעֶשּׂוֹת may be explained as a development of an original בְּעֲשּׂוֹת (*pi'el*), as is indicated in *HALOT* later on (compare לְעֲשֵּׂר* > לְעֵשֵּׂר). *HALOT* also lists עש״י III (cognate with Arabic غشّي "to cover") and עש״י IV (cognate with Arabic غشر "to come, turn, outstretch"); see ibid.

between them is active/passive,[50] as is the contrast between *qal* and *nipʿal*
for many verbs. Other forms in other *binyanim* differ either in meaning or
etymology. For example, עֻשּׂוּ (Ezek 23:3, 8) means "press, crush."[51] There
are no attestations of the root, with the meaning "to do," in the causative,
whether *hipʿil* or *piʿel*. In other words, there is no verb comparable to
Modern Hebrew הִפְעִיל "to cause one to do" (from *qal* פָּעַל "to do")[52] or
הֶעֱסִיק from *qal* עָסַק.

§ 14 It is worth broadening the scope of this point. There are other
words that have meanings similar to עָשָׂה, such as בָּרָא, יָצַר, עָבַד, פָּעַל, and
יָגַע. It is true that some of these have more specific or limited meanings,
such as the exertion implied by יָגַע and the intensive activity implied by
many occurrences of עָבַד, but they are all squarely in the same semantic
field as עָשָׂה.

The verbs פָּעַל and יָצַר also do not have causative forms attested, either
hipʿil or *piʿel*.[53] The verb בָּרָא, too, appears only in the *qal* and the *nipʿal*,
and the one example of the *hipʿil* (1 Sam 2:29) means "to feed, to fatten,"
and is irrelevant to this discussion.

§ 15 The words יָגַע and עָבַד, on the other hand, do have corresponding causative *hipʿil* forms. The two verbs appear together in two verses
in Isa 43: לֹא הֶעֱבַדְתִּיךָ בְּמִנְחָה וְלֹא הוֹגַעְתִּיךָ בִּלְבוֹנָה "I have not burdened you
with meal offerings, nor wearied you with incense" (v. 23) and הֶעֱבַדְתַּנִי
בְּחַטֹּאותֶיךָ הוֹגַעְתַּנִי בַּעֲוֹנֹתֶיךָ "you have burdened me with your sins, you have
wearied me with your iniquities" (v. 24).[54] It is easy to see that in these
verses the verbs carry additional semantic baggage beyond simply "cause
to work": in הוֹגִיעַ there is the additional sense of "to cause fatigue, exertion, and exhaustion,"[55] and the same is true for the other two attestations
of הוֹגִיעַ in BH: הוֹגַעְתֶּם ה' בְּדִבְרֵיכֶם וַאֲמַרְתֶּם בַּמֶּה הוֹגָעְנוּ "you have wearied the
Lord with your talk, but you ask, 'With what have we wearied [Him]?'"
(Mal 2:17).[56]

---

[50] No examples of the *nipʿal* with a reflexive meaning are found.

[51] See n. 52 above. The form עֻשֵּׂיתִי (Ps 139:15), which looks like a *puʿal*, is not
necessarily related to the *piʿel* form עֻשּׂוּ cited in the text. Note that the Targum of Psalms
translates at this place, אתעבדית ("I was made"), and it is possible that this is a *qal* passive
form—namely the passive of עָשָׂה "to do"—rather than a *puʿal*, as mentioned by *HALOT*.

[52] I mean the root פע"ל in the *qal* and the *hipʿil*.

[53] The form יוֹצַר (Isa 54:11) is best explained as a *qal* passive form, rather than a *puʿal*.

[54] The Targum translates הוגעתיך with אתקיפית עלך "I overpowered you" and הוגעתני
with אתקיפתא קדמי "you became strong in front of me."

[55] Compare the Targum's translations (cited in the previous and following notes).

[56] Here the Targum translates (אלהיתן) אהליתן "you have tired (s.o. out)" and אהלינא
(אלהינא) "we have tired (s.o. out)."

§ 16 In the two verses from Isa 43 just cited, הֶעֱבִיד, too, carries additional semantic weight: it indicates forced labor, even actual servitude.[57] This is also seen in other biblical texts, such as Jer 17:4, וְהַעֲבַדְתִּיךָ אֶת-אֹיְבֶיךָ, which the Targum translates ותשתעבדון לבעלי דדביכון. In other verses, however, this semantic component seems to be absent from העביד, and all that remains is the causation; if the text does indicate that the labor is forced and difficult, this is weight not carried by the verb, but by other words in the sentence, as in וַיַּעֲבִדוּ מִצְרַיִם אֶת-בְּנֵי יִשְׂרָאֵל בְּפָרֶךְ "the Egyptians forced the Israelites to work ruthlessly" (Exod 1:13). וַיַּעֲבִדוּ in this sentence means only "caused that others might work (ע״בד)," and the servitude is indicated by the prepositional phrase בפרך. And in fact, here Tg. Onq. does not translate with שַׁעֲבֵּד, but with אַפְלַח: ואפלחו מצראי ית. So, too, the Targum of Ezek 29:18, נְבוּכַדְרֶאצַּר מֶלֶךְ-בָּבֶל בני ישראל בקשיו הֶעֱבִיד אֶת-חֵילוֹ עֲבֹדָה גְדוֹלָה אֶל-צֹר "King Nebuchadrezzar of Babylonia has made his army expend vast labor on Tyre": נבוכדרצר מלכא דבבל אפלח ית משרייתה פולחן רב על צור. The difficulty of the work is indicated by the internal direct object פולחן רב = עבודה גדולה.

§ 17 To sum up, in BH, הוֹגִיעַ means "to cause to work with fatigue or exhaustion"; הֶעֱבִיד sometimes means simply "to cause to work," and on other occasions denotes "to enslave, to force (someone) to labor."

§ 18 I must stress, though, that nowhere in the Bible do we find any expression of causing another to perform the will of God, fulfill His teaching, or obey His commandments. We do find the opposite: alongside חָטָא we have the word הֶחֱטִיא, and the two even appear in tandem: אֲשֶׁר חָטָא וַאֲשֶׁר הֶחֱטִיא אֶת-יִשְׂרָאֵל "(the sins) he committed and led others to commit" (1 Kgs 14:16; 15:30). The opposite, positive, expression, however, is not attested in the Bible. One may cite the verse mentioned above (§ 15), לֹא הֶעֱבַדְתִּיךָ בְּמִנְחָה (Isa 43:23), as an exception, but from the context it is clear that the meaning here is, "I did not weary you through the bringing of a meal offering," and not "I caused you to bring a meal offering to the Temple."

§ 19 In contrast, the use of the hipʿil and piʿel of עש״י are attested in MH to denote "to cause to do." In some of the cases, there is nothing more than causation involved; in others, there is an element of force implied. Among the many examples are some in which the context reveals that

---

[57] Again, compare the Targum: אסגיתי "I have multiplied" and אסגיתא "you have multiplied."

the agent is causing another to do the will of God or fulfill His laws. Here are some examples:[58]

a. מעשה בחזקיה מלך יהודה שהעשה את הצבור לעשות פסח שני "Once Heze-kiah, king of Judah, caused the community to do (העשה) the Second Paschal Lamb (pesaḥ)" (t. Pesaḥ 8:4).[59] Here the king is causing the people to perform a commandment, the paschal lamb, and it would appear that some element of force was involved, as well. Immediately thereafter the text continues, לא מפני שהעשי את הצבור לעשות פסח שני ... אף מפני שהעשי את הצבור לעשות פסח שני "not because he forced the community to do the second pesaḥ ... but because he forced the community to do the second pesaḥ" (t. Pesaḥ 8:5).[60] The same incident finds echoes in the Yerušalmi: חזקיה העשי לציבור לעשות פסח שני "Hezekiah forced the community to do the second pesaḥ" (y. Ned. 9:6 [39d]) and עישה יחזקיהו לציבור לעשות פסח שיני "Hezekiah forced the community to do a second pesaḥ" (y. Sanh. 1:2 [18d]). It is mentioned in the Bavli, as well: מפני שהעשיא את ישראל לעשות פסח שני[61] (b. Sanh. 12a).

b. The expression גט מעושה/מעושה/מעוסה is well known (m. Giṭ. 9:8).[62]

c. There are also contexts in which הֶעֱשָׂה (הֶעֱשִׂיא) is spoken of as a positive: כל המעשה[63] את חבירו לדבר מצוה מעלה עליו הכתוב כאילו עשאה

---

[58] The texts quoted here (from rabbinic literature, piyyut, and other sources) are from the databases of the Historical Dictionary of the Hebrew Language Project of the Academy of the Hebrew Language.

[59] Alongside the reading שהעישה of MS Vienna, we find also שעישה in MS Erfurt and שהעסיא (as if from a III-ʾalep root) in MS London. A confused form appears already in the editio princeps: שמעישה, which appears to be a mistaken development from Erfurt's שעישה with the addition of a מ, or of a plene spelling of MS Vienna's שהעישה, with the confusion of a ה with a מ. These data and those cited in the following note are quoted, of course, from S. Lieberman, ed., The Tosefta According to Codex Vienna, with Variants from Codices Erfurt, London, Genizah Mss and Editio Princeps (Venice 1521), vol. 2: The Order of Moʿed (New York: Jewish Theological Seminary of America, 1962) (Hebrew).

[60] MS London has שהעשיא ... שהעסיא, and MS Erfurt has שהעשי ... שעישה.

[61] The Vilna edition reads שהשיא, which is derived from שהעשיא with the loss of the ʿayin.

[62] In later Hebrew, the same expression appears with forms of the binyan נתפעל: נתעשה (found a number of times in ספר הישר by Joshua b. Judah, in the translation by Jacob b. Šimʿon, in the eleventh century; this according to the databases [Maʾagarim] mentioned above, n. 58).

[63] Of course, the orthographies מעשה and מעשין (participles), and יעשה and יעשו (futures) could be either piʿel (מְעַשֶּׂה, מְעַשִּׂין, יְעַשֶּׂה, and יְעַשּׂוּ) or hipʿil (מַעֲשֶׂה, מַעֲשִׂין, יַעֲשֶׂה, and יַעֲשׂוּ), but for good reasons, they are taken to be piʿel forms by the reading traditions of the Sephardim and the Yemenites. It is possible that the hipʿil forms—the participles מַעֲשֶׂה and מַעֲשִׂין/ם—were rejected because they were identical to the singular and plural forms of the

"whoever causes his fellow to perform a commandment, Scripture counts it as if he performed it himself" (*b. Sanh.* 99b).

d. Also to be mentioned in this discussion is the well-known expression, גדול המעשה יותר מן העושה (*b. B. Bat.* 9a)[64] whose meaning is clear: even more important than performing the commandments oneself is causing another to perform them.[65] Many similar examples can be cited in *piyyutim*.

§ 20 It has recently become clear that the idea of הֶעֱשָׂה (הֶעֱשִׂיא) with regard to Torah and religious obligations, which is found in Tannaitic literature and later, already held sway in the intellectual world and language of Qumran. Thus we find in 4Q470, in speaking of the righteousness of Zedekiah: לעשות ולהעשות את כל התורה "to do and to cause (others) to do[66] the entire Torah" (1 4).[67] The orthography להעשות could represent the infinitive of the *nip'al* or the *hip'il*, but the context makes it certain that it is the *hip'il* that was intended.[68]

It is true that syntactically the use of להעשות here in QH differs from its use in MH—here we find להעשות את התורה, and in MH we have העשיא את הפסח—but the aspect of causation is common to both.

§ 21 To summarize: When we speak of "doing" and its causation in biblical Hebrew, we find the pair יגע and הוגיע, which denote doing accompanied by fatigue or exhaustion, and we find the pair עָבַד and הֶעֱבִיד, the latter of which on occasion denotes simply "to cause to do" (as in הֶעֱבִיד

---

noun מַעֲשֶׂה, and the future forms יַעֲשֶׂה and יַעֲשׂוּ were rejected because they were identical to the *qal* forms. Only the participial and future forms with final *'āleps* (מעשיא/מעשי) and (יעשיא/יעשי) could be preserved; we in fact find the form למעשיאיהם in Yannai (קדושתות) שופט דן את הדין והשוטר' מעשי' (דב, כי אתנן הם Devarim, לשבתות השנה) and in *Pesiq. Rab.* 33: את הדין [מעשיא/מעשין].

[64] This phrase expresses clearly the opposite of the חָטָא/הֶחֱטִיא contrast found in the Bible and discussed above, although the syntax of this line differs from that one.

[65] The forms העשיא/העסיא/העסי and מעשיאיהם (see n. 63 above) are not the only evidence for a shift from III-*yôd* עש"י to III-*'ālep* עש"א. For this, see M. Bar-Asher, "לתצורת הבינוני של גזרת ל"י בנפעל בלשון חז"ל בלשונות עברית," 33–35 (1992): 39–51, 43, § 16.

[66] The same combination of words, in reverse order, appears in a *piyyut* of Yannai: (אשרי נאמן Shemot, קדושתות לשבתות השנה) לשמוע ולראות להעשות ולעשות.

[67] This fragment was published by E. Larson, L.H. Schiffman, and J. Strugnell in *DJD* XIX (1995): 237.

[68] So, too, the editors (*DJD* XIX [1995]: 239). In 4Q440 3 i 21 (published by E. Schuller in *DJD* XXIX [1999]: 252), we find כולנו להשותנו כיא]. This form of the verb could represent the *nip'al* infinitive (לְהֵעָשׂוֹתֵנוּ) or the *hip'il* infinitive (לְהַעֲשׂוֹתֵנוּ). The editor preferred the first (judging from her translation ibid., 253), the fragmentary state of the text does not allow for certainty in either direction, and so no edifices can be constructed on this basis.

אֶת־חֵילוֹ),[69] but on occasion denotes "to force to work hard, to enslave" (as in וְהַעֲבַדְתִּיךָ אֶת־אֹיְבֶיךָ).[70] If we focus specifically on doing, or causing another to do God's commandments or Torah, we find that the concept is not attested in the Bible at all, although its negative counterpart חָטָא and הֶחֱטִיא—is well attested: חָטָא is the basic word, and הֶחֱטִיא denotes the causation of a sin of one party by another. As opposed to the biblical state of affairs, in Qumran we find both the idea and the language of עָשָׂה and הֶעֱשָׂה; this is true also for Tannaitic literature and all later literature, as well, where we find עָשָׂה and הֶעֱשָׂה/עִישָׂה.[71] Again, here are the results summarized in tabular form:

	Basic action	Causative
Biblical Hebrew	עָשָׂה	_[72]
Qumran Hebrew	עָשָׂה	הֶעֱשָׂה
Mishnaic Hebrew (and later)	עָשָׂה	הֶעֱשָׂה/הֶעֱשִׂיא/עִישָׂה

Concluding Comments

§ 22 As I indicated at the outset, I would not venture general conclusions at this point regarding the diachronic relationship between the three layers of Hebrew discussed here—Biblical, Qumran,[73] and Mishnaic (specifically Tannaitic); I prefer to suffice with what arises from the two issues studied here. In conclusion, I would like to emphasize a number of aspects:

§ 23 (a) We have empirical evidence that the word מָבוֹא turned into מָבוֹי during Second Temple times already, and the only form attested in rabbinic literature (מָבוֹאי > מָבוֹי > מָבוֹי) is already glimpsed in the Dead Sea Scrolls, but only once. In the remainder of the cases, the scribes hewed closely to the biblical orthography.

---

[69] Cf. above, §§ 15–16.

[70] Cf. there.

[71] Other examples from *piyyut* of the pairing of עשה with העשה are found elsewhere in Yannai: [עושי]הם כמעשיאיהם (כל השומע, 4); קדושתות, Devarim, ושכר עושה ומעשה שיויתה) (אם לא חוקותי, Vayyikra, קדושתות, 6); see also the citation above, n. 66.

[72] Cf. what I wrote above (§§ 15, 18) regarding לא העבדתיך במנחה.

[73] Clearly, when one wishes to speak of the Hebrew used in the period between the Bible and the Mishnah, one ought to include the Hebrew of Ben Sira alongside that of the Dead Sea Scrolls, and attention should also be paid to Hebraisms which are visible to us in translations, such as the LXX. But this is not the place to elaborate.

Also with regard to עָשָׂה and הֶעֱשָׂה (or הֶעֱשִׂיא or עִשָּׂה), the Qumran text reveals that what was is seen in Tannaitic literature, and into the Amoraic period and *piyyut*, was in fact already a feature of the Hebrew in use in Hasmonean times. Furthermore, it is not only the linguistic fact, but the idea itself—that one who causes another to fulfill the Torah or commandments is listed alongside one who fulfills them him/herself— which was already formulated in the time of the Qumran sect. This idea has no expression in the Bible.

We see, then, that in both issues studied here, the data from Qumran show that aspects of Tannaitic Hebrew are actually far older than we would have otherwise known.

§ 24 (b) In contrast, when it comes to the semantics of מְבוֹא/מְבוֹי, we find that the dividing line is drawn sharply between biblical and Qumran Hebrew on the one hand, and Mishnaic Hebrew on the other. In the former, מְבוֹא (מבוא) is a verbal noun ("coming" and "onset [of time]") and a noun meaning "entrance, opening," whereas in MH the meaning of מְבוֹי (and מְבוֹאִי/מְבוֹי) has become restricted to "a narrow street ... between two rows of houses." If there is even one attestation of the older meaning of מבוי in the Mishnah, it is a borrowing from the language of the Bible.[74]

§ 25 (c) This is how diachronic analysis must proceed: every lexeme and every grammatical feature has its own history. Sometimes important thematic developments underlie a word's development, as when the idea of causing another to fulfill a commandment comes to take its place alongside one's own fulfillment of the commandments, giving prominence to the term הֶעֱשָׂה (הֶעֱשִׂיא). The real significance of this painstaking method, following each feature through all the stages of its history, is not only in the details thus uncovered, however; it also allows us to contextualize every stage within a diachronic framework stretching over many generations. It is especially important to realize that the transitions take place at different times for different features;[75] regarding one issue, Qumran may line up with biblical Hebrew and against later Mishnaic Hebrew, while in other cases Qumran and Mishnaic Hebrew are set off from biblical Hebrew.

§ 26 (d) Additionally, each of the two later layers of the language may go in one of two directions:

---

[74] Cf. n. 28 above.

[75] For a penetrating study of the idea of a "transition language" in general, and in the history of Hebrew in particular, see M. Mishor, "מן העבודה בתולדות המילים," *Lešonénu la-'Am* 39 (1988): 186–199.

a. They may reveal the changes that have taken place in the language, by utilizing forms from the living language of the time. In our context, the uses of מבוא/מבוי and העשה in Qumran and Mishnaic Hebrew are examples of this.

b. They may utilize forms borrowed from the Bible: both the scribes of Qumran (to a great extent) and those of rabbinic literature (to a lesser extent) mimic biblical forms in their own texts. Here we have seen the examples of the biblicizing spelling מבוא at Qumran and, less certainly, the use of מבוי with the meaning "entryway" in the first mishnah of ʿErubin.

Often distinguishing between these two is difficult work for the researcher, but accuracy in describing the language depends on success in puzzling out these details.

THE LEXEMES תרומה AND מנה IN THE POETIC TEXTS OF QUMRAN: ANALYSIS OF A SEMANTIC DEVELOPMENT

FRANCESCO ZANELLA
University of Siegen, ThWQ Project

0.0. INTRODUCTION

In the poetic texts of Qumranic Hebrew (QH) the lexemes תרומה and מנה occur with semantic values that are unknown in Biblical Hebrew (BH). In QH תרומה can refer both to an "offering of a prayer" and to a "contribution of knowledge," while מנה denotes a "selected prayer." The new semantic values of the lexemes תרומה and מנה do not substitute any biblical lexeme, and could therefore lexicalise new concepts. As I shall demonstrate, these new notions consist in a positive connotation of speech and speech acts, which clearly results from the new syntagmatic and paradigmatic structures of תרומה and מנה in QH. Interestingly enough, the innovative usages of תרומה and מנה only apply to texts which current scholarship understands as "sectarian" and could therefore reflect particular aspects of an explicitly Qumranic ideology.

The present paper aims at investigating the main syntagmatic and paradigmatic aspects of the semantic shift of both lexemes from BH to QH, thereby providing an explanation of its possible conceptual grounds.

0.1. *Poetic Texts of Qumran*

As far as a possible definition of the "poetic texts" of Qumran is concerned, I refer to both lists of "Poetic and Liturgical Texts" and "Sapiential Texts" identified by Armin Lange and Ulrike Mittmann-Richert.[1] Furthermore, since my specific focus is of a linguistic kind, I would also include among this group passages from other kinds of texts (e.g., rules) which are qualified by "poetic" content, context, and vocabulary.[2]

---

[1] A. Lange and U. Mittman-Richert in *DJD* XXXIX (2002): 115–164.
[2] An exhaustive list of or Qumranic works reflecting a "poetic language" is available in

0.2. *Prayer and Sacrifice in Qumran: A Debated Issue*

The new usages of the lexemes תרומה and מנה in QH are linked to the debated issue of the relationship between prayer and sacrifice in Qumran. As far as this subject is concerned, one may refer to at least two opposing positions.

0.2.1. *Prayer as a Substitution of Sacrifice*

The first perspective consists in understanding prayer as a substitution for the sacrificial system. This thesis is well supported by Georg Klinzing.[3] In his monograph, Klinzing exhaustively analyses the issue of the new trends of liturgy and cult in the Qumranic community: the *Yaḥad* was without Temple and, therefore, without the possibility of regularly practicing a sacrificial cult.[4] The *Yaḥad*, thus, found a symbolic solution to this problem: it redefined itself as "Temple" and its prayers as sacrifices. Furthermore, Klinzing argues "daß das gesamte Leben der Gemeinde in den Kultus einbezogen wurde. Nicht nur der hochgeschätzte Lobpreis, der ganze 'untadelige Wandel' (1QS 9,5) der Gemeinde und ihre Leiden im Exil (1QS 8,3) treten an die Stelle des Opfers, und werden unter kultischem Aspekt gesehen."[5] This perspective is also supported by more recent papers, for instance, that of Esther G. Chazon who argues that in Qumran prayer "provided an alternative means of worship as well as an instrument for the atonement of sin. The sectarian documents regularly refer to prayer in sacrificial terms, equating it with sacrifice metaphorically as well as functionally."[6]

I. Zatelli, "The Study of Ancient Hebrew Lexicon: Application of the Concepts of Lexical Field and Functional Language," *Kleine Untersuchungen zur Sprache des Alten Testaments und seiner Umwelt* 5 (2004): 129–159, 141.

[3] G. Klinzing, *Die Umdeutung des Kultus in der Qumrangemeinde und im Neuen Testament* (Göttingen: Vandenhoeck & Ruprecht, 1971).

[4] Ibid., 40–41, Klinzing argues: "nach dem Willen Gottes mußte jetzt an die Stelle des blutigen Opfers etwas anderes treten. Ohne Opfer sollte das göttliche Wohlgefallen erworben werden." Furthermore, Klinzing points out that "es gibt eine Reihe von Stellen, die zeigen, daß man sich wirklich mit diesen Fragen beschäftigte. ... Was konnte an die Stelle des gottwohlgefälligen Opfers treten? Auf welche Weise konnte im Exil Sühne erlangt werden?" (ibid., 93).

[5] Ibid., 105.

[6] E.G. Chazon, "An Introduction to Prayer at Qumran," in *Prayer from Alexander to Constantine* (ed. M. Kilyz et al.; London: Routledge, 1997), 9–13, here 9–10.

0.2.2. *Prayer as a Mere Expression of Righteousness*

According to the second position, one should not understand the relationship between prayer and sacrifice in terms of substitution or equivalence. Russell Arnold, for instance, argues that in Qumran "the essential comparison is made between the wicked and the righteous, not prayer and sacrifice," even admitting that "Qumran texts do use sacrificial language in connection with prayer."[7] Prayer, concludes Arnold, "should be understood, ultimately, not as means of communicating with the divine nor as a way of filling the void left because of the community's alienation from the sacrificial cult, but, rather, as a communal act of righteousness."[8] A similar position is also supported by Paul Heger who also notices that speech acts (Heger refers to the lexeme שׂפה) are closer to teaching than to praising.[9] In my opinion, this perspective does not provide a sufficient account of the completely new usage of the sacrificial vocabulary of the Bible, which Klinzing extensively analyses.

0.2.3. *Is a Third Way Possible?*

A convincing hypothesis is brilliantly discussed by Eileen M. Schuller and consists in slightly changing the focus of the problem.[10] The substitution of prayer to sacrifice might have been plausible, argues Schuller, but one should understand it as a "present expediency rather than a theological rejection."[11] From a theological point of view, Schuller also notices that many eschatological hopes conveyed by the Qumran texts actually refer to the restoration of the Temple of Jerusalem, i.e., of the sacrificial cult. Thus, according to Schuller, "it seems that the recitation of prayers is not to replace, indeed cannot replace, ultimately the sacrificial system ordained by God for all eternity in the Torah; only in the present 'time of Belial' did it need to take on that role."[12] A similar perspective is suggested

---

[7] R.C.D. Arnold, "Qumran Prayer as an Act of Righteousness," *JQR* 95 (2005): 509–529, here 511.

[8] Ibid., 512.

[9] P. Heger, "Did Prayer Replace Sacrifice at Qumran?" *RevQ* 22 (2005): 213–233, esp. 232.

[10] E.M. Schuller, "Worship, Temple and Prayer in the Dead Sea Scrolls," in *Judaism in Late Antiquity*, part 5: *The Judaism of Qumran: A Systemic Reading of the Dead Sea Scrolls*, vol. 1: *Theory of Israel* (ed. A. Avery-Peck, J. Neusner, and B. Chilton; HO 56; Leiden: Brill, 2001), 125–143.

[11] Ibid., 131.

[12] Ibid.

by Daniel K. Falk who argues that "both prayer as sacrifice and prayer as response to exile can be found. The two are not mutually exclusive, but it does not seem possible to distinguish roughly between praise as metaphorical sacrifice and petitionary prayer—including confession of sins—as deriving from an exile ideology."[13]

However one chooses to understand it, the relationship between prayer and sacrifice in Qumran cannot be analysed separately from an exhaustive semantic investigation aimed at showing how the language itself expresses it.

1.0. The Lexemes תרומה and מנה in BH

1.1. תרומה: *Cultic Contribution, Tax*

In BH תרומה is a lexical item typical of sacrificial vocabulary. The lexeme often denotes a cultic contribution. Exodus 35:24 represents a good example of this generic usage of תרומה: כָּל־מֵרִים תְּרוּמַת כֶּסֶף וּנְחֹשֶׁת הֵבִיאוּ אֵת תְּרוּמַת יְהוָה וְכֹל אֲשֶׁר נִמְצָא אִתּוֹ עֲצֵי שִׁטִּים לְכָל־מְלֶאכֶת הָעֲבֹדָה הֵבִיא. In this context, תרומה lexicalises the giving of goods for the construction of a common cultic building. Besides this general use, in the cultic texts of BH the lexeme תרומה can denote a specific tax to be paid in order to atone for the census (see e.g., Exod 30:14).

The poetic-sapiential texts of BH (cf. Prov 29:4) point to an interesting secular use of the lexeme תרומה, which might refer to a generic kind of taxation, namely to an important instrument that should be properly used by the rulers of a nation.

1.2. מנה: *Portion of the Sacrificed Animal, Gift of Food*

In the biblical texts, the lexeme מנה is partially linked to the sacrificial lexicon. The word in fact denotes the gift of portions of the sacrificed animal, which are not necessarily intended for the priests. This usage might be exemplified by the passage in 1 Sam 1:4: וַיִּזְבַּח אֶלְקָנָה וְנָתַן לִפְנִנָּה אִשְׁתּוֹ וּלְכָל־בָּנֶיהָ וּבְנוֹתֶיהָ מָנוֹת. As we can see, the recipients of the מנה are not members of the priestly group. Interestingly, in the cultic texts

---

[13] D.K. Falk, "Prayer in the Qumran Texts," in *The Cambridge History of Judaism*, vol. 3: *The Early Roman Period* (ed. W. Horbury, W.D. Davies, and J. Sturdy; Cambridge: Cambridge University Press, 1999), 852–876, here 875–876.

as well, the recipient of the מנה is not necessarily a priest.[14] In this regard Exod 29:26 and Lev 7:33 act as useful pieces of evidence. In the former verse, the recipient of the מנה is Moses. The latter verse is more problematic, since the recipient of the מנה actually belongs to the בני אהרן. An analysis of the context of the verse, however, shows that the recipient of the מנה is entitled to receive it not because of his family, but, rather, because he happens to be the one performing the sacrifice.

As far as the lexeme מנה is concerned, traces of a semantic shift can be found in Late Biblical Hebrew (cf. Esth 9:19, 22; Neh 8:10, 12), where the lexeme refers to the gift of food dishes served at a banquet. A further new usage of מנה is found in Ben Sira (26:3), where it occurs with reference to a "deserved portion," i.e., "good fate, destiny." In this case the lexeme מנה is used to connote a good wife (אשה טובה).

1.3. Syntagmatic and Paradigmatic Relations of the Lexemes תרומה and מנה in BH

In BH the lexemes תרומה and מנה are qualified by well defined syntagmatic and paradigmatic relations, which I exhaustively analysed in my doctoral thesis.[15] On the one hand, תרומה shows syntagmatic and paradigmatic relations with the sacrificial lexicon which the following lexemes can exemplify: משאת ("cultic contribution"), נדבה ("spontaneous gift to God"), קורבן ("offering to God"), עלה ("burnt offering"), מעשר ("tithe"). On the other hand, מנה frequently occurs in a syntagmatic relationship with the verb זבח "to sacrifice" and with lexemes referring to specific parts of the sacrificed animals which are offered as a present and then eaten.

In the next part of this paper I aim to demonstrate that the semantic coordinates of these two lexemes patently vary in QH.

---

[14] In this regard I would not agree with J. Conrad ("מָנָה," ThWAT 4:979–980) as he writes that "in priesterschriftlichen Texten bezeichnet manah den Anteil der Priester am (Schlacht-)Opfer (Ex 29,26; Lev 7,33 …)."

[15] For a revised version thereof see F. Zanella, The Lexical Field of the Substantives of "Gift" in Ancient Hebrew (SSN 54; Leiden: Brill, forthcoming).

2.0. The Lexemes מנה and תרומה in QH

2.1. תרומה: *Distribution*

In QH almost one third of the 26 occurrences of the lexeme תרומה can be found in poetic-sectarian compositions. This distribution is at variance with BH, where the poetic occurrences of תרומה are only five out of a total of 76. As I shall demonstrate, this innovative poetic *milieu* is likely to affect the semantic structures of תרומה. Noteworthy is that the cultic Qumran texts still reflect the main context of usage of the lexeme in QH and that תרומה maintains its typical reference to a cultic contribution. In this section of the paper I focus only on the new usages of the lexeme, thereby analysing the main syntagmatic and paradigmatic relations of תרומה, "offering of a prayer" and "contribution of knowledge."

2.1.1. תרומה *"Offering of a Prayer"*

The use of the תרומה with reference to an "offering of a prayer" occurs five times (1QS IX:4–5; X:6, 14; 4QS[b] [4Q256] XIX:4, 4QShir[b] [4Q511] 63–64 ii 4).

2.1.1.1. 1QS X:14
The passage in 1QS X:14 is a good example of the syntagmatic relations reflected by the new usage of תרומה.

ואברכנו תרומת מוצא שפתי

> and I will bless him (with) the תרומה of that, which comes out from my lips[16]

תרומה is here used outside of its typical sacrificial context and occurs within a new syntagmatic *milieu*, where the references to the semantic domain of speech acts play a key role. The lexeme, in fact, can function (a) as the (prepositional) object of the verb ברך, and (b) as the nomen regens of the genitival syntagm תרומת מוצא שפתי ("the תרומה of that, which comes out from my lips"), which metonymically refers to an act of speech, namely to an utterance.

2.1.1.2. 1QS X:6
One may find similar syntagmatic structures in 1QS X:6 (par. 4QS[b] [4Q256] XIX:4).

---

[16] Unless otherwise noted, all translations are mine.

{oo} תרומת שפתים הברכנו כחוק חרות לעד

(with) the תרומה of lips I will bless Him, as a statute forever engraved

Once again, תרומה functions as the nomen regens of the genitival syntagm תרומת שפתים ("תרומה of lips"). The lexeme שפתים ("lips") metonymically refers to an utterance. This syntagm should be understood as a subjective genitive, referring to an offering (of a prayer as well as of a blessing) performed by the lips.[17] The lexeme also functions as the (prepositional) object of the verb ברך.

2.1.1.3. 1QS IX:4–5

The passage in 1QS IX:4–5 represents an interesting syntagmatic case.

לכפר על אשמת פשע ומעל חטאת ולרצון לארץ מבשר עולות ומחלבי זבח ותרומת
שפתים למשפט כניחוח צדק

in order to atone for the guilt of transgression and the rebellion of sin, becoming an acceptable (sacrifice) for the land through the flesh of the burnt offerings, and the fat parts of the sacrifices, and the תרומה of the lips becoming justice, just like a sweet savour of righteousness

In this passage תרומה clearly occurs within a specific sacrificial context which the following lexical items highlight: כפר ("to atone"), מנחה ("vegetable offering"), עלה ("burnt offering"), זבח ("sacrifice"), and בשר ("flesh"). In spite of this typical sacrificial context, I take the position that the lexeme תרומה is actually used here with its new semantic value. In fact, the genitival syntagm תרומת שפתים ("תרומה of lips") attests to the reference to an "offering of a prayer." The mention of justice and righteousness, which one would not expect to find in a sacrificial context, is also consistent with this.

2.1.1.4. 4QShir[b] (4Q511) 63–64 ii 4

The occurrence of תרומה in 4QShir[b] (4Q511) 63–64 ii 3–4 provides a slightly different contextual *milieu*.

ברישית כול מחשבת לבב דעת ותרומת מזל שפתי צדק

at the beginning of every purpose of the mind *is* knowledge, and (at the beginning) of a תרומה of an utterance *are* lips of righteousness

תרומה occurs here within a context of thanksgiving, blessing, and praise to God. Once again, the lexeme functions as a nomen regens in a genitival relation with a lexical item referring to a speaking act (מזל, "utterance").

---

[17] See in BH, the genitival syntagm תרומת ידכם ("the תרומה of your hand," Deut 12:6, 11) which refers to the contribution offered by the hands of the sender.

The lexeme שפתים ("lips") also occurs in the passage.

To conclude, תרומה "offering of a prayer" reflects the following syntag-matic relations.

a. תרומה always occurs as a nomen regens, and is always used in a genitival relationship with the lexeme שפתים ("lips") and with other lexical items referring to speech acts. These genitival syntagms are so consistent and recurrent that it is possible to understand them as fixed pairs. In these cases, I would tend to analyse the genitival syntagm as a single semantic unit, since there cannot be a clear-cut division between the meaning of a lexeme and the meaning of the genitival syntagms in which it repeatedly occurs.

b. In three occurrences (1QS X:6, 14; 4QS^b [4Q256] XIX:4) תרומה functions as the (prepositional) object of the verb ברך ("to bless").

In light of these data one could argue that תרומה denotes a specific act of praise and blessing. From a syntagmatic point of view, the main difference between BH and QH clearly consists in using a typical lexical item of the sacrificial lexicon within a new context qualified by constant references to speech acts.

2.1.2. תרומה "Contribution of Knowledge"

The use of תרומה with reference to a "contribution of knowledge" involves three poetic occurrences (4QShirShabb^a [4Q400] 2 7; 4QShirShabb^d [4Q403] 1 ii 26; 4QShirShabb^f [4Q405] 23 ii 12). The syntagmatic struc-tures of these verses are different from those of תרומה "offering of a prayer." Such differences, as I contend, would attest to a further new usage of the lexeme. תרומה would here occur with a cognitive *nuance* reflect-ing recurrent syntagmatic and paradigmatic relations with lexemes of the semantic domain of knowledge.

2.1.2.1. 4QShirShabb^a (4Q400) 2 7
The passage in 4QShirShabb^a (4Q400) 2 7 represents a good example of the syntagmatic relations qualifying תרומה "contribution of knowledge."

מה] תרומת לשון עפרנו בדעת אל[ים

> [what] is the תרומה of the tongues of our dust (compared) with the knowl-edge of the g[ods?

תרומה here functions as the nomen regens in the genitival syntagm תרומת לשון ("the תרומה of the tongue"). The cognitive *nuance* clearly results from the paradigmatic opposition between the syntagms תרומת לשון עפרנו ("the

תרומה of the tongues of our dust") and דעת אלים ("the knowledge of the g[ods"). In the poetic texts of Qumran the lexeme דעת denotes a "true knowledge (of spiritual realities)."[18] In light of this specific value given to דעת, the genitival syntagm תרומת לשון עפרנו ("the תרומה of our tongues of dust") would then refer to a human, i.e., *typically rough*, kind of knowledge. Thus, the syntagm תרומת לשון, subjective genitive, would denote the contribution of knowledge performed by human utterances.

2.1.2.2. 4QShirShabb[d] (4Q403) 1 ii 26

One may find a similar syntagmatic context in the passage from 4QShir-Shabb[d] (4Q403) 1 ii 26:

לאל אלים מלך הטהור ותרומת לשוֹנֵיהֹם [∘∘ שבע רזי דעת

> to the God of gods, King of splendour, and the תרומה of their tongues [seven mysteries of knowledge

The verse is rather fragmentary. Nonetheless, one can identify the following syntagmatic data.

a. תרומה functions as the nomen regens of the genitival syntagm תרומת לשוניהם ("the תרומה of their tongues"). The third person masc. pl. pronominal suffix refers to the previously mentioned "chiefs of the congregation of the King in the assembly."

b. The syntagm תרומת לשוניהם occurs in syntagmatic and paradigmatic relation to the lexeme דעת.

In light of these syntagmatic data one may assume that the genitival syntagm תרומת לשוניהם is used with reference to knowledge. What kind of knowledge could it denote, if compared with the perfection of the דעת? According to lines 27–29 these tongues *of knowledge* are supposed to "grow strong sevenfold" (תגבר שבעה). The aim (or the result?) of this growth could be expressed by line 35, which refers to "those who cause knowledge (דעת) to shine among all the gods of light." Thus, the kind of knowledge referred to by the syntagm תרומת לשוניהם is supposed to grow, perhaps in order to reach the perfect level of knowledge which the substantive דעת lexicalises. In this framework, thus, one may conclude that the syntagm תרומת לשוניהם denotes a *perfectible* kind of knowledge.

---

[18] M.P. Sciumbata, "Il campo lessicale dei sostantivi di 'conoscenza' in ebraico antico" (Ph.D. diss., Università degli Studi di Firenze, 1996), 106–108.

2.1.2.3. 4QShirShabb[f] (4Q405) 23 ii 12

The passage in 4QShirShabb[f] (4Q405) 23 ii 12 is the most problematic in the group.

כבודו vacat בראשי תרומות לשוני דעת[ו]ברכו לאלוהי דעת בכול מעשי כבודו

> (of) His glory vacat in the chiefs of the תרומות of the tongues of knowledge [and] they bless the God of knowledge together with all the works of his glory

Florentino García Martínez and Eibert J.C. Tigchelaar interpret the syntagm בראשי תרומות לשוני דעת as a nominative clause,[19] thereby interrupting the genitival chain and interpreting תרומות as an absolute state. In light of the data resulting from the analysis of the previous occurrences, however, one would expect תרומות to be in the construct state, and the syntagm תרומות לשוני דעת to be a subjective genitive. At present, however, I do not see any plausible alternative to García Martínez's and Tigchelaar's translation. Apart from the problematic rendering of this text, one may observe that תרומה once again occurs in a syntagmatic relationship with the lexeme לשון as well as, in the following lines, with lexical items belonging to the semantic domain of knowledge, such as דעת, בינה ("comprehension"), and שכל ("understanding").

To conclude, תרומה "contribution of knowledge" reflects the following syntagmatic relations.

a. תרומה always[20] functions as the nomen regens of the genitival syntagm תרומת לשון. As in the case of תרומת שפתים, one should understand תרומת לשון as a subjective genitive, referring to a contribution (of knowledge) performed by a speech act. The relationship between תרומה and לשון is so close and recurrent that I would tend to analyse both lexemes as a fixed pair, as I did for the lexemes תרומה and שפתים.

b. תרומה "contribution of knowledge" always occurs in syntagmatic and paradigmatic relations with lexical items belonging to the semantic domain of knowledge (e.g., דעת and בינה). In some occurrences there is enough evidence to argue that the whole syntagm תרומת לשון refers to a human and perfectible kind of knowledge.

---

[19] See F. García Martínez and E.J.C. Tigchelaar, eds., *The Dead Sea Scrolls Study Edition* (2 vols., Leiden: Brill, 1997–1998), 2:837.
[20] In the case of 4QShirShabb[f] (4Q405) 23 ii 12 this is debatable.

2.2. מנה: *Distribution*

In QH seven out of nine occurrences of מנה belong to sectarian poetic compositions. This distribution is rather surprising, when compared with BH, where מנה never occurs in poetic texts. The usage of מנה within a poetic *milieu* actually affects the semantic value of the lexeme which occurs with the reference (unknown to BH) to a "selected prayer."

2.2.1. מנה *"Selected Prayer"*

This new use of מנה is found in six[21] poetic occurrences (1QS X:8; 4QS^d [4Q258] IX:7; 4QShirShabb^d [4Q403] 1 i 40; 1 ii 20; 4QPoetic Text A [4Q446] 1 4; 4QBarkhi Nafshi^a [4Q434] 7b 2).

2.2.1.1. 1QS X:8

The passage in 1QS X:8 (par. 4QS^d [4Q258] IX:7) represents a good example of the semantic coordinates qualifying the usage of מנה with reference to a "selected prayer."

> ובכול היותי חוק חרות בלשוני לפרי תהלה ומנת שפתי {אשא} [...]

and for my whole life, engraved statute on my tongue, as fruit of praise, and I will lift the מנה of my lips

The usage of the lexeme מנה is qualified by syntagmatic relations to lexemes referring to speech and prayer, thereby providing interesting analogies with the usage of תרומה "offering of a prayer." In fact, (a) מנה occurs in a syntagmatic relationship with the lexemes לשון and שפתים, which metonymically refer to an act of speech; (b) מנה functions as the nomen regens of the genitive מנת שפתי. Furthermore, the passage highlights a parallelism between the genitival syntagms פרי תהלה ("the fruit of prayer") and מנת שפתים. Both syntagms refer to the same subject, i.e., a praise. The former (פרי תהלה) makes explicit reference to it, and the latter (מנת שפתים) metaphorical. Thus, the lexeme תהלה describes the concrete effects of the speech act (שפתים), whereas the lexeme פרי ("fruit") helps us to understand the reference of the lexeme מנה which would then denote the *best part*, the *selected part* of a prayer.[22]

---

[21] I excluded 4QpapPrFêtes (4Q509) 280 1, since the text is highly fragmentary: [א֯א
[מנה. The scroll consists in fragments of texts probably referring to festivals.

[22] Moreover, as Klinzing notices (*Umdeutung*, 96) the lexeme פרי ("fruit") is itself a sacrificial term used outside of its specific technical context and transposed onto the context of prayer. Klinzing furthermore interprets the form מנת in 1QS X:8 as a

2.2.1.2. 4QShirShabb^d (4Q403) 1 i 40

The passage in 4QShirShabb^d (4Q403) 1 i 39–40 patently confirms the syntagmatic relations between מנה and the semantic domains of speech and prayer, which here also involve singing and rejoicing.

זמרו לאלוהי עז במנת רוח רוש ל[מזמו]ר בשמחת אלוהים

> let us sing praise to the God of Might with a מנה of choicest spirit to [a son]g of divine joy

Three data are worth mentioning: (a) the lexeme מנה functions as the prepositional object of the verb זמר ("to sing praise"); (b) it occurs as the nomen regens of the genitival syntagm מנת רוח רוש ("a מנה of choicest spirit"); (c) it once again occurs together with lexical items referring to a selection (or the result of a selection—cf. פרי "fruit" in 1QS X:8), namely the lexeme רוש ("head, top, *choicest*").

2.2.1.3. 4QPoetic Text A (4Q446) 1 4

[וכלשוני מנות הודו]ת ∞[

> and in my tongue *are* מנות of thanksgiving

מנה functions here as the nomen regens of the genitival syntagm מנות הודות ("מנות of praise, thanksgiving"). The lexeme is also used in close syntagmatic relationship with the lexeme לשון.

2.2.1.4. 4QShirShabb^d (4Q403) 1 ii 20

The passage in 4QShirShabb^d (4Q403) 1 ii 20 represents an interesting occurrence.

ורוממוהו ראשי נשיאים במנה פלאיו

> and exalt him, o chief princes with a מנה, his wonder

מנה functions as the prepositional object of the verb רום (*po'lel*, "to exalt"). Moreover, the passage shows that מנה can also occur *in the absolute state* with reference to an act of praise. This fact is extremely relevant semantically, since it shows that מנה can also *independently* lexicalise a speech act of praise. I would like to suggest that מנה here reaches a

---

"Schreibfehler für מנחת" (*Umdeutung*, 96). In my view, the occurrence in the passage of the lexeme מנחה can be refuted in light of syntagmatic and paradigmatic pieces of evidence: the occurrence of sacrificial terms *together with* lexemes belonging to the semantic domains of speech acts does not apply to the use of מנחה (neither in BH nor in QH), whereas it constitutes a recurring feature of the use of מנה in QH. To conclude, it is in light of the lexical context of 1QS X:8–9 that one should here *paradigmatically* argue for the occurrence of the substantive מנה instead of מנחה.

deeper level of lexicalisation than תרומה, since its new meaning is not necessarily expressed by genitival syntagms. Unfortunately, the available textual evidence is too exiguous to argue that, and this explanation must remain hypothetical.

To conclude, מנה "selected prayer" reflects the following syntagmatic relations.

a. מנה always occurs in close syntagmatic and paradigmatic relations with lexical items of the semantic domains of speech and prayer.

b. These relations are often rendered by genitival syntagms, where מנה functions as a nomen regens, such as מנת שפתים ("the מנה of my lips"), מנת רוח ("מנה of spirit"), and מנות הודות ("מנות of praise, thanksgiving"). One should understand these syntagms as objective genitives referring to "selected portions, i.e., offerings, of speech acts" aimed at praising God. These syntagmatic relations are so close and recurrent that, just like in the case of the lexeme תרומה, the study of the meaning of the lexeme מנה cannot be separated from the investigation of these relations.

c. Interestingly, מנה happens to occur in the absolute state. I consider this specific case proof that the semantic range of the lexeme מנה itself includes the reference to speech acts, which does not need to be explicitly expressed through a genitival relationship.

3.0. A New Connotation of Speech in QH

The data resulting from the semantic analysis of תרומה and מנה in QH show that both lexemes can occur outside of their specific biblical contexts. In QH both substantives are in fact transposed onto a new poetic context which consists in recurrent syntagmatic and paradigmatic relations with the semantic domains of speech acts (mostly prayer, praise and blessing) and knowledge. One should also notice (a) that the new usages of both words do not actually substitute any previous biblical lexeme, and (b) that they specifically apply to sectarian writings. This begs the question of whether these new meanings actually result from extra-linguistic factors (i.e., whether they reflect new concepts such as beliefs, feelings, and perceptions) which one should understand as typical of the Qumran community.

In this regard, one should also notice that the semantic domain of speech, at least as far as the occurrences of מנה and תרומה are concerned, always reflects a positive connotation. Lips (שפתים) and tongue (לשון)

are understood and described as positive instruments aimed at exalting
God. Moreover, the act of praising God and His nature often coincides
with reaching a deeper level of knowledge and results from a process of
acknowledgment and comprehension. Within this specific framework it
became clear that comparing the connotation of the semantic domain
of speech in BH and QH could be useful to detect the presence of new
concepts. A difference in the connotation of this semantic domain could
in fact reflect a process of conceptual shift, of which the new meanings
of the lexemes תרומה and מנה would just be a part. In light of the data
resulting from the analysis of תרומה and מנה, my expectation was to
understand the positive connotation of speech as a typical feature of QH.
Working from this premise, I analysed the occurrences of the lexemes
שפתים and לשון in both *corpora*, and the result I could find would actually
confirm my preliminary assumption. In the last part of the paper I
compare some data concerning the connotation of the lexemes לשון and
שפתים in BH and QH.[23]

3.1. *Speech in BH and QH*

In both BH and QH three kinds of connotations qualifying the usage of
the lexemes לשון and שפתים can be identified, namely a "neutral connotation," a "negative connotation," and a "positive connotation." The connotation is neutral if the lexemes merely refer to specific parts of the
mouth, to geographical entities or to concrete objects. The connotation
is negative if the lexemes are used together with lexical items referring
to falsehood, evil, destruction, lie, and the like. The connotation is positive if the words are used together with lexical items belonging to the
semantic domains of praise, prayer, wisdom, knowledge, and the like. As
I shall demonstrate, the connotation of these lexemes changes remarkably between BH and QH.

3.1.1. לשון
3.1.1.1. BH
In BH לשון is frequently used with neutral and with negative connotations; each kind of connotation involves 43 % of the occurrences of the

---

[23] Obviously this is not supposed to be an exhaustive study of the whole semantic
domain of "speech" in both BH and QH; rather, this is an attempt to see how the usage
the lexemes לשון and שפתים may reflect the perception of this concept.

lexeme. In the first case לשון can refer to the part of the mouth, to a language, to geographical entities (e.g., headland), and to concrete objects (e.g., flames and blades). In its negative connotation, לשון denotes an aspect of the human nature[24] linked to exuberance and exaggeration (see e.g., לשון מדברת גדולה, Ps 12:4), which can easily become perversity (תהפוכות, Prov 10:31) and cause calamities (הות, Prov 17:4; cf. also Ps 52:14). The tongue is a means of communication between human beings and an instrument of interrelation between man and God. It often provokes mischief, evil, deceitfulness (תרמית, Zeph 3:13; cf. also Ps 52:6; Jer 9:7), blasphemy, and falsehood (שקר, Prov 6:17; 12:9; 21:6; 26:28; Jer 9:2; Ps 102:9; cf. also Prov 25:23).[25]

Only 14% of the occurrences of לשון in BH (mostly in the Psalms) reflect a positive connotation: in these passages the lexeme is used with specific reference to an act of prayer. In this context, the tongue becomes "the pen of a ready writer" (Ps 45:2; cf. also Pss 66:17; 71:24; 119:172), who aims at declaring and singing God's righteousness (Pss 35:28; 51:16). Such themes will have a predominant role in the usage of the lexeme in QH.

3.1.1.2. QH

The connotation of לשון in QH clearly shows an inverted trend. Half of the occurrences of לשון in QH are qualified by a positive connotation, showing an increase of 36%. In these passages the lexeme denotes a part of the human body and nature concretely linked to the act of praising, blessing, and exalting God. In such occurrences לשון is frequently used in syntagmatic relationship with the lexeme שפתים. Thus, lips and tongue generate a fountain of words (מקור, 1QH[a] XXIII:10; 4QShir[b] [4Q511] 63 iii 1 etc.) which are more pleasing than wine (4QNarrative and Poetic Composition[b] [4Q372] 3 5).[26] Each word "forms the foundation of joyous songs" (1QH[a] XIX:4–5). In this positive context, the tongue shall be pure (טוהר, e.g., 4QMyst[b] [4Q300] 3 i 2; דכי, 4QEschatological Work B [4Q472] 2 3) and purged from any kind of abomination (שקוצים, 1QS X:22). "Human rebellion" and "impure and crafty design" shall not

---

[24] See also B. Kedar-Kopfstein ("לָשׁוֹן," ThWAT 4:601): "bei diesen und ähnlichen Versen geht aus dem Textzusammenhang deutlich hervor, daß לשון nicht einen einmaligen Aussageakt darstellt, sondern eine, allerdings sich in der Rede realisierende, Wesenart."

[25] An exhaustive list of this kind of connotation is available ibid., 603–605.

[26] The *Hodayot* are numbered according to M. Abegg in *Poetic and Liturgical Texts* (ed. D.W. Parry and E. Tov, The Dead Sea Scrolls Reader 5; Leiden: Brill, 2005).

belong to the praise to God (1QS X:24). The necessary prerequisite of praise is the recognition of God's power, nature, and glory (1QHᵃ IV:17 etc.). In this regard, praising sometimes results in an experience of pure knowledge which can be demonstrated as follows: the tongue shall sing and *at the same time* the mind (לב) shall understand "the secret of the origin of the work of all men" (4QShirᵇ [4Q511] 63 iii 1) as well as the mysteries of knowledge (רזי דעת, 4QShirShabbᵈ [4Q403] 1 ii 27). Furthermore, God has engraved "a measuring line (קו) [to] declare to the human vessel his lack of understanding" on the tongue of the man (1QHᵃ XXIII:11). With "purposeful speech" (במעני לשון, 4QpPsᵃ [4Q171] 1–10 iv 27) the tongue shall be ready to utter holy words (דברי קודש, 4QBarkhi Nafshiᶜ [4Q436] 1a+b i 7), and its level of understanding will grow in strength (תגבר, see 4QShirShabbᵈ [4Q403] 1 ii 27–32; 4QShirShabbᶠ [4Q405] 11 4–5).

3.1.2. שפה

3.1.2.1. BH

Half of the occurrences of שפה in BH are qualified by a neutral connotation: the lexeme explicitly refers to "the fleshy edge of the mouth,"[27] to natural and geographical entities, and to objects (hems, edges). In BH the usage of the lexeme שפה more frequently reflects a negative connotation (31% of the occurrences) than a positive connotation (19% of the occurrences). Thus, if negatively connoted, the lips represent an instrument of lying (שקר, Prov 10:18; 12:22; 17:7b; Ps 31:19), deceitfulness (מרמה, Ps 17:1), and flattery (חלקה, Ps 12:3, 4). Lips can cause trouble (און, Prov 17:4), if they are the lips of a fool (Prov 18:6; Qoh 10:12; cf. also Prov 10:8, 10), as well as transgression (פשע, Prov 12:13) and perversion (לזות, Prov 4:24), if they are unclean and impure (טמא, Isa 6:5). Positively connoted, the lips are used "to keep knowledge" (דעת, Prov 5:2; Mal 2:7) and wisdom (חכמה, Prov 10:13). Moreover, the opening of lips (מפתח שפתי, Prov 8:6) shall consist in utterances of truth (אמת, Prov 8:7) and right things (מישרים, Prov 8:6). In the Psalms the lexeme is often used with reference to the act of praising God (see. e.g., Pss 51:17; 63:4; 71:23).

3.1.2.2. QH

In comparison to BH, the proportion between negative and positive connotations in QH is patently inverted. In fact, the usage of the lexeme

---

[27] B. Keder-Kopfstein, "שָׂפָה," *ThWAT* 7:841. For the English translation see *TDOT* 14:176.

שפה in the Dead Sea Scrolls is largely qualified by a positive connotation which shows an increase of 26%. If positively connoted, the lips are shown to have great new features: by the power of the lips the wicked ones can be killed (1QSb [1Q28b] V:24), and with this very power God generates all the eternal spirits (4QShirShabb[d] [4Q403] 1 i 35). In light of these new positive features the texts repeatedly state that "foolish things and wicked lying [and de]ceptions and falsehoods" shall no longer be found on the lips (4QS[f] [4Q260] V:3; cf. also 4QShir[b] [4Q511] 18 ii 5), but, rather discipline (מוסר, 4QSapiential-Didactic Work A [4Q412] 1 5), fidelity (אמונה, 4QInstruction[d] [4Q418] 148 ii 8), and righteousness (צדק, 4Qcrypt A Words of the Maskil to All Sons of Dawn [4Q298] 1–2 i 3). The utterances of the lips constitute a direct link between man and God through praise, thereby "forming the foundation of joyous songs" (1QH[a] XIX:5). In this regard, the praise requires mighty lips (שפתי עוז, 4QH[a] [4Q427] 7 i 16), because it has to be like a spring, like a fountain (מקור, 4QInstruction[d] [4Q418] 81+81a 1; 4QShir[b] [4Q511] 63 iii 1), and like the music of a flute (חליל שפתי, 1QS X:9), so that he who praises God can do it properly. Finally, it should be noticed that if the lexeme שפה refers to a prayer, it may also occur together with lexical items of the sacrificial vocabulary.

3.1.3. Conclusions

The analysis of the connotation of the lexemes לשון and שפה in BH and QH highlights a remarkable difference between the two corpora. Thus, in BH the usage of both lexemes frequently reflect a negative connotation, whereas QH attests to a positive connotation. The increase in the positively connoted occurrences in QH is clearly remarkable for both lexemes. As far as לשון is concerned, this increase directly corresponds to a significant decrease in the negatively connoted occurrences, which is also noticeable for the lexeme שפה, even if it is in a smaller scale.

What kind of interpretation could be drawn in the light of these quantitative data? How are they linked to the new semantic values of the lexemes תרומה and מנה? I consider these results as evidence that (a) in Qumran an innovative and positive concept of speech is found, and that (b) this positive perspective on speech is likely to be linked to the special cultic and liturgical situation of the *Yaḥad*.

Thus, these results highlight a shift from a negative perspective on the concept of speech to a positive one. In fact, according to the Qumran texts, speech is no longer (or mostly not) linked to perversion, falsehood, and mischief. Speech acts, rather, consist in praising and exalting the true nature of God, which must be at first fully comprehended. The act of praising, therefore, originates from a cognitive (perhaps mystical?) process that brings the speaker/petitioner to a deeper level of knowledge.[28] Within this framework, at least in the Qumranic "sectarian" texts such a mixture of praise and true knowledge would become the preferred way to communicate with God. It may also assume the form of an "oral sacrifice" which one perhaps should understand as a substitution of the animal sacrifices to be offered in Jerusalem. This reference to the sacrifice is highlighted by the explicit usage of the biblical sacrificial vocabulary which is actually transposed onto these new conceptual coordinates and adapted to them.

I argue that that this whole framework is deeply consistent with the new usages of the lexemes תרומה and מנה in QH. Actually, it represents the conceptual prerequisite of their two new semantic values. In their new meanings, in fact, both lexemes patently lexicalise these innovative relations between praise, true knowledge, and "oral sacrifice."

---

[28] The close relation between prayer and knowledge is clearly highlighted by S.C. Reif, "Prayer in Ben Sira, Qumran and Second Temple Judaism: A Comparative Overview" in *Ben Sira's God: Proceedings of the International Ben Sira Conference, Durham—Ushaw College 2001* (ed. R. Egger-Wenzel; BZAW 321; Berlin: de Gruyter, 2002), 321–341, 330: "the Scribe is expected to develop intellectually, to understand God's mysteries, and to express himself intelligently and ethically. He should at the same time, however, appreciate that all this is intended as a religious exercise. He should also therefore humbly and enthusiastically seek and praise God, pray for the forgiveness of his sins, and take pride in mastering (and teaching?) the Torah."

ARAMAIC TEXTS FROM QUMRAN
IN LIGHT OF NEW EPIGRAPHICAL FINDS[1]

ESTHER ESHEL

Bar Ilan University

A. INTRODUCTION

Four Aramaic manuscripts from Qumran Cave 4 correspond to the third part of the Ethiopic Book of Enoch, *1 En.* 72–82, which is titled "The Book of the Revolution of the Luminaries of Heaven." Since none of these manuscripts preserve parts of the other Enochic books, it was suggested that these scrolls circulated independently from the other Enochic works, and that these four scrolls represent four different copies of a single composition. Those scrolls document the "synchronistic calendar," which is believed to be the earliest known full synchronization of the movements of the moon and the sun during the 364 day year. In his monumental work on the Aramaic fragments of *1 Enoch* published in 1971, J. Milik presented an edition of these manuscripts,[2] to which E.J.C. Tigchelaar and F. García Martínez later added some unpublished fragments.[3]

B. 4QENASTR^d AR (4Q211)

In what follows, I would like to shed some light on one of these scrolls, 4QEnastr^d ar (4Q211), based upon two new ostraca found in Mareshah, which also shed light on the cultural connections between Babylon and southern Syria during the Persian and Hellenistic periods. The *Astronomical Book of Enoch* is dated to around the middle of the third century

---

[1] I would like to thank my colleague, Jonathan Ben-Dov, for his helpful remarks and for sharing with me the relevant parts of his book prior to its publication, *Head of All Years: Astronomy and Calendars at Qumran in their Ancient Context* (STDJ 78; Leiden: Brill, 2008).

[2] J.T. Milik, *The Books of Enoch: Aramaic Fragments of Qumrân Cave 4* (Oxford: Clarendon, 1976), 273–297.

[3] E.J.C. Tigchelaar and F. García Martínez in *DJD* XXXVI (2000): 95–171.

B.C.E.[4] 4Q211 stems from the second part of the *Astronomical Book of Enoch*, corresponding to *1 En.* 76–78, and also contains the conclusion of the work, which is lost in the Ethiopic Enoch. 4Q211 was dated to the second half of the first century B.C.E., based on paleographic grounds. It reads as follows:[5]

4QEnastr[d] *ar (4Q211) 1 ii*

2 דן מן משחתה[ה○]

3 מעשר תשיע ח[ד

4 תשיע חד וכוכ[בין] נזחו ב[תרע] שמיא קד[מא⁶ ובאדין] נפקו

5 ביומא קדמיא [חד] מעשר[בשתי]ת חד ותנינא חד מן חמשת

6 עשר בשתית ח[ד ו]תלתיא ח[ד מ]ן תלתין בשתית חד *vacat*

2 this [...] from its measure [...]
3 a tenth (part) of a ninth (part) [... a tenth (part)]
4 of a ninth (part). And the sta[rs] move through the fi[rst gate] of heaven; [and then] they come forth.
5 On first days, [one] tenth [by] one [six]th; on second (days), one fif-
6 teenth by o[ne] sixth; on third (days), o[ne] thirtieth by one sixth [...]

4Q211, was described by Milik as a manuscript which "is preserved practically only in a single fragment, a horizontal strip containing from six to two lines of the text, which comes from three successive columns placed towards the end of the scroll. Column i contains a description of winter; so it should be placed after the existing conclusion of the Astronomical Book in the Ethiopic Enoch, where we have the description of the two first seasons only, spring (En. 82: 15–17) and summer (82: 18–20)," while the Aramaic original probably included all four seasons.[7] As noted by J. Ben-Dov, the context of the specific passage included in frg. 1 ii quoted above, are the "temporal hours," which resemble calculations documented in some Neo-Assyrian texts.[8] Thus, scholars are in agreement as to the scientific knowledge of the author of the so-called "synchronistic calendar," being "an offshoot of a Mesopotamian

---

[4] The earliest manuscript of the *Astronomical Book of Enoch* (4QEnastr[a]) was dated by Milik to the beginning of the second century B.C.E., see Tigchelaar and García Martínez in *DJD* XXXVI (2000): 106.

[5] Milik, *Books of Enoch*, 296–297.

[6] Milik, ibid., 296 reconstructs: [ב]תרעי] שמיא קד[מיא]. The reconstruction of [ב]תרע] שמיא קד[מא] was suggested by Ben-Dov, *Head of All Years*, 194 n. 194.

[7] Milik, *Books of Enoch*, 274.

[8] J. Ben-Dov, "Astronomy and Calendars at Qumran: Sources and Trends" (Ph.D. diss., The Hebrew University of Jerusalem, 2005), 162 (Hebrew). As for the question of the placement of this passage in *1 Enoch*, see his discussion ibid., 22, 157–162.

intellectual tradition, reflected in the astronomical series Mul.Apin,"[9] which is dated to the seventh century B.C.E. As has been shown, "the Aramaic fragments describe the movements of the sun and the moon through the various gates, thus suggesting not only solutions to the temporal gaps but also to the gaps in space."[10]

In 4Q211 1 ii 2, we find the phrase מן משחתה. The word משחה was interpreted as "measurement" and translated as "from its measurements."[11] This noun is known in other Aramaic texts from Qumran.[12] The closest in context, albeit fragmentary, is the *Aramaic Levi Document*, which mentions both שמיא and משחה (1QLevi[a] [1Q21] 37 2–3). Milik connected frg. 37 with the *Testament of Levi*, chs. 2–3, where the description of heaven is included, thus suggesting that frg. 37 might be identified as one of Levi's visions.[13] Nevertheless, no reference to measurements is included in these chapters of the *Testament of Levi*. A reference to the measurements of heaven can be found in Isa 40:12 ושמים בזרת תכן וכל בשלש עפר הארץ, which was translated in the Targum as: ומשחת שמיא כאלו בזרתא מתקנין ועפרא דארעא כאילו במכילא איתכל, "and the length of the heavens as if with the span established, the dust of the earth as if measures in a measure …" Thus, we might tentatively conclude, based on Isaiah, that both *Aramaic Levi Document* 37 and 4Q211 refer to the measurements of the heavens, or are somehow connected with it.

4Q211 1 ii 4 mentions that וכוכ[בין] נזחו ב[תרעו] שמיא קד[מא] "the sta[rs] move through the fi[rst gate] of heaven," and in lines 5–6 of the same column, a series of days is mentioned, followed by numerical figures, most of which are fractions. Various interpretations were suggested to these lines,[14] concluding, that "it clearly forms part of the

---

[9] J. Ben-Dov, "The Initial Stages of Lunar Theory at Qumran," *JSJ* 54 (2003): 125–138, 127, with references to earlier discussions.

[10] Ibid., 129.

[11] Milik, *Books of Enoch*, 297; see M. Sokoloff, *A Dictionary of Jewish Palestinian Aramaic of the Byzantine Period* (2nd ed.; Ramat Gan: Bar Ilan University Press, 2002), 333–334. משחה translates the biblical מדה in both *Tg. Neof.* and *Tg. Onq.*

[12] E.g. in 2QNJ ar (2Q24) 1 4 [פרזיתא] [כול משחת [נ]י[זי]אח[וכדן], "… And so he showed me the measurement of all [the blocks"; M. Baillet in *DJD* III/1 (1962): 85.

[13] J.T. Milik in *DJD* I (1955): 90; see J.C. Greenfield, M.E. Stone, and E. Eshel, *The Aramaic Levi Document: Edition, Translation, Commentary* (SVTP 19; Leiden: Brill, 2004), 230–231.

[14] Milik, *Books of Enoch*, 297; O. Neugebauer, *Ethiopic Astronomy and Computus* (Sitzungsberichte der Österreichischen Akademie der Wissenschaften, philosophisch-historische Klasse 347; Wien: Verlag der Österreichischen Akademie der Wissenschaften, 1979), 169; M. Albani, *Astronomie und Schöpfungsglaube: Untersuchungen zum astronomischen Henochbuch* (WMANT 68; Neukirchen-Vluyn: Neukirchener Verlag, 1994), 61–66.

Mul.Apin-type astronomical teaching."[15] In what follows, I would like to discuss the usage of the verb נזח in two additional astronomical texts, the first is a newly discovered ostracon, found in Mareshah, and the second is the so-called "Birth of Noah" text (4Q535), where, based on the occurrence of נזה, I would like to suggest a new interpretation of this text. But first some introductory words are necessary with regard to the two ostraca discovered in Mareshah.

C. The Mareshah Ostraca

Mareshah (or Marisa), is located in the Shephela, 30 km north-east of Ashkelon. The site was partly excavated in the 1900s by Bliss and Macalister and by Peters and Tiersch.[16] More recent excavations were conducted by A. Kloner.[17] Mareshah is mentioned in the Bible, where its earliest reference appears among the cities of Judah (Josh 15:44). After the destruction of the First Temple, Mareshah, together with all of southern Judah, became Edomite territory. In the Hellenistic period Mareshah replaced Lachish as the capital of Idumea, and during that period a Sidonian community settled in Mareshah.

Between 1989 and 1999 seventy-two sherds inscribed with Semitic script were found in Mareshah by Kloner. The majority can be dated from the fourth to the second centuries B.C.E., based on their paleography. The first assemblage to be published in the near future includes a Hebrew ostracon dated to the seventh century B.C.E.; 64 Persian and Hellenistic inscriptions written in Aramaic language and script; two fragments of a Persian inscription written in Phoenician script; two Edomite inscriptions dated to the Hellenistic period and written in Aramaic script; and three inscriptions in Jewish script dated to the first or second centuries C.E.[18] Important additions to this assemblage are fragments of four

---

[15] Ben-Dov, *Head of All Years*, 195.

[16] F.J. Bliss and R.A.S. Macalister, *Excavations in Palestine during the Years 1898–1900* (London: Committee of the Palestine Exploration Fund, 1902); J.P. Peters and H. Tiersch, *Painted Tombs in the Necropolis of Marissa* (London: Palestine Exploration Fund, 1905).

[17] A. Kloner, "Mareshah (Marisa)," *NEAEHL* 3:948–957. For the first in a series of final reports on the excavations at Mareshah during the 1980s and 1990s, see A. Kloner, *Maresha Excavations Final Report I: Subterranean Complexes 21, 44, 70* (IAA Reports 17; Jerusalem: Israel Antiquities Authority, 2003).

[18] E. Eshel, "Chapter 2: Inscriptions in Hebrew, Aramaic, and Phoenician Script," in A. Kloner, E. Eshel, and C. Korzakova, *Maresha Excavations Final Report III* (IAA Reports; Jerusalem: Israel Antiquities Authority, forthcoming).

bowls bearing scribal exercises, some of which are inscribed on both the recto and the verso. All together there are 16 inscriptions of which seven, written on two bowls, were recently published.[19] In later excavations carried out in the last two years by Kloner, more than one hundred and fifty inscribed sherds and ostraca written in Semitic scripts were discovered. I would like to express my gratitude to A. Kloner for granting me the responsibility to publish all Semitic inscriptions found in Mareshah. On the basis of paleographic considerations, it is possible to date most of these inscriptions to the Persian and Hellenistic periods. Included in this corpus is a group of twenty-five Aramaic ostraca with inscriptions of various types, all sharing the formula הן ... הן, "If X then Y," but sometimes either the protasis or the apodosis is missing, or is not included. The first published Mareshah text of this kind includes a quotation from an otherwise unknown wisdom text, copied as a scribal exercise on a bowl.[20]

Among the new finds are two ostraca with the formula "If X then Y," which might help us interpret 4Q211. Based on paleographical grounds, these inscriptions should be dated to the second century B.C.E. From their content they seem to be related to the Akkadian commentaries on the omen series.[21]

Ostracon no. 1 was written on a body sherd of a jar which measures 73 × 83 mm. This ostracon includes seven written lines. Above the first line remains of ink are visible, which might show that the original inscription included at least another written line. It reads as follows:

Ostracon No. 1 from Mareshah

oooo	1
מחשא הן מן אלהין נזח	2
נזחהה *vacat*	3
ונזך חזוא הן מן אלהין	4
והן חזהי	5
אין(?) נגפת בלליתא	6
ושתקו והן אותוקא]	7

---

[19] E. Eshel, E. Puech, and A. Kloner, "Aramaic Scribal Exercises of the Hellenistic Period from Mareshah: Bowls A and B," *BASOR* 345 (2007): 39–62.

[20] Eshel, Puech, and Kloner, "Aramaic Scribal Exercises," 41–47.

[21] Wayne Horowitz, Shaul Shaked, and myself are now preparing these two ostraca for publication.

Translation

1 [...]
2 A comet (is seen) it is from the gods, it moves
3 its movement
4 And [or: should] a comet in sight (= is seen), it is from the gods,
5 and indeed, you see it!
6 If you are hurt by Lilith [or: if you meet Lilith],
7 and (by) ŠTQW, and if (you are hurt by) ʾWTWQʾ [...]

The subjects of the first readable four lines are two objects, מחשא and נזך,
which are moving or seen. Concerning these two objects it is said: הן מן
אלהין "it is from the gods." The key to the interpretation of this passage
is provided by the word נזך which occurs twice in the second ostracon
found in Mareshsah (written as נזוך).

The noun נזך is known from 11QtgJob, where it translates the word
חנית of Job 39:23. As noted by J. Greenfield and S. Shaked, "the word
NZK is of Iranian origin, and has been known to be of that origin, as
it exists as a widely used loan-word in both Syriac *naizkā* and Arabic
nayzak [and *nayzaq*]."[22] The same term, *naizkā*, is used in the Peshitta to
Job 39:23 mentioned above. The Syriac *naizkā* means not only "lance,
spear, javelin," translating the biblical words: כידון,[23] חנית,[24] and צנה,[25]
but can also be used with an astronomical connotation for "shooting
stars," or "meteors,"[26] and can thus refer to a comet, such as Halley's
comet. We therefore suggest interpreting the Aramaic word נזך in the
two Mareshah ostraca as related to an astrological object, i.e. to Halley's
comet, which is shaped like a spear when seen in the sky. Ancient sources
even feature descriptions of the appearance of Halley's comet as a spear.[27]
The historical significance assigned to Halley's comet in antiquity will be
discussed below.[28]

---

[22] J.C. Greenfield and S. Shaked, "Three Iranian Words in the Targum of Job from
Qumran," in J.C. Greenfield, *ʿAl Kanfei Yonah: Collected Studies of Jonas C. Greenfield on
Semitic Philology* (ed. S.M. Paul, M.E. Stone, and A. Pinnick; 2 vols.; Jerusalem: Magnes,
2001), 1:344–352, 349.

[23] Josh 8:18; Job 39:23; 41:21; Jer 6:23; 50:42.

[24] Ps 46:10; Nah 3:3.

[25] Ezek 23:24; 38:4; 39:9; see further Jdt 11:2.

[26] C. Brockelman, *Lexicon Syriacum* (Halle: Niemeyer, 1928), 427; R. Payne-Smith,
Thesaurus Syriacus (Oxford: Clarendon, 1879–1901), 2360; J. Payne-Smith, ed., *A Com-
pedious Syriac Dictionary founded upon the Thesaurus Syriacus of R. Payne Smith* (Oxford:
Clarendon, 1903), 338.

[27] Cf. e.g. *Midrash ha-Gadol* to Numbers, and *Sib. Or.* 3:672–679, 796–800; 5:155–166;
206–213.

[28] For a general study, see H. Hunger et al., *Halley's Comet in History* (ed. F.R. Stephen-
son and C.B.F. Walker; London: British Museum Publications, 1985).

Next, lines 1–2 of the first Mareshah ostracon read: גזח נזחהא. The basic meaning of the root נזח is "to move."[29] The phrase נזחהא is to be compared with the internal (or: cognate) object known from Biblical Hebrew, where it is defined as "an abstract noun of action, identical with, or analogous to the action expressed by the verb."[30] It can be found used together with intransitive verbs.[31] Thus, we might translate the phrase נזח נזחהא as "it moves its movement." In lines 3–4 of this ostracon we might encounter a word-play of נזך with *kāp* and נזח with *ḥêt*.

Since נזח appears in an astrological context in the Mareshah ostracon, it can be compared to two Qumran Aramaic texts of similar character. The first text is 4Q211 1 ii which was mentioned above, and which reads: וכוכ[בין] נזחו ב[תרע] שמיא קד[מא ובאדין] נפקו, "And the sta[rs] *move* through the fi[rst gate] of heaven; [and then] they come forth" (line 4).

The verb נזח is also mentioned in 4Q535, the so-called "Birth of Noah" text. This composition was preserved in three copies (4Q534–536).[32] The first two copies include fragmentary descriptions of a certain features of a human body which include different sorts of marks and moles, as well as the weight of a newborn. The subject of this text is a figure entitled "the elect of God," whose name did not survive in the Qumran fragments. Various identifications of this figure were suggested, among them the Messiah, Noah, Melchizedek, and the eschatological high priest.[33] I am inclined to agree with the identification of this figure as Noah. In this text one finds a few mentions of the figure's מולדה "birth," which probably refers to his horoscope; and more specifically, we read in a broken context זמן מולדה "his time of birth."[34] It is possible to attribute predictive value to

---

[29] See J.C. Greenfield and M. Sokoloff, "The Contribution of Qumran Aramaic to the Aramaic Vocabulary," in *'Al Kanfei Yonah*, 1:472–492, 477, who connected it to the Jewish Babylonian Aramaic נ/נזה, which appears in Magic bowls and means "to move." Cf. M. Sokoloff: *A Dictionary of Jewish Babylonian Aramaic of the Talmudic and Geonic Periods* (Ramat Gan: Bar Ilan University Press, 2002), 739.

[30] Joüon § 125q.

[31] Cf. e.g. Ezek 18:21 חיה יחיה, "he will live life."

[32] É. Puech in *DJD* XXXI (2001): 117–170.

[33] For a summary of the various suggested identifications, pointing to the possibility of being a prototype of the Merkavah mystic, see J.R. Davila, "4QMess ar (4Q534) and Merkavah Mysticism," *DSD* 5 (1998): 367–381.

[34] Puech in *DJD* XXXI (2001): 156 (4Q535 2 1); see F. Schmidt, "Ancient Jewish Astrology: An Attempt to Interpret 4QCryptique (4Q186)," in *Biblical Perspectives: Early Use and Interpretation of the Bible in Light of the Dead Sea Scrolls: Proceedings of the First International Symposium of the Orion Center for the Study of the Dead Sea Scrolls and*

the references to marks and moles on his body, but it is equally possible that they are being used as identity markers.[35] In one of those fragments we read as follows:

4Q535 *frg. 3 (par. 4Q536 frg. 1)*[36]

upper margin

עד (די) (ל)הו]ה מתילד והוין מרמש כחדה] 1
והוא בשעה חמ]ש בליליא מתילד ונפק של]ם 2
תקל תקלין תלת מאה וחמ]שין (וחד) 3
יו]מיא דמך עד מפלג ית] י]ומיא ש] 4
ביממא עד משלם ש]נין תמנה 5
נזחה לה מנה] ו]לב]תר שניא תמנא 6

lower margin

1 [... until] is born and they shall be together from the evening [...]
2 and he at the fif]th[hour is born at night and comes out who[le ...]
3 [... at a]weight of three hundred and fi[fty-(one)] shekels [...]
4 [... in the d]ays, he sleeps until half his days are done [...]
5 [...] in the daytime until the completion of [eight yea]rs [...]
6 [...] shall be moved from him; [and] af[t]er e[ight year]s.[37]

The editor of this text, É. Puech, explains the word נזחה in line 6 as a fem. participle of נזח originating from Hebrew זוח I, and translates it as "*shall be moved from him.*"[38] As we have seen, 4Q211 1 ii 4, reads: וכוכ]בין נזחו ב]תרע [שמיא קד]מא, "And the sta[rs] move through the fi[rst gate] of heaven."

Based on this parallel I would like to suggest connecting נזח with the movement of the stars, thus tentatively reconstructing the text of 4Q535 as something like "[and a star] shall [not] move from him." This would connect this phrase to some astrological prediction related to the figures' future, based on his horoscope.

To come back to line 4 of the first Mareshah ostracon, its second, hitherto unknown object is מחשא. Of it the ostracon says נזח נזחהא, "it moves its movement." One possible interpretation would be to relate this word to

Associated Literature, 12–14 May, 1996 (ed. M.E. Stone and E.G. Chazon; STDJ 28; Leiden: Brill, 1998), 189–205, 196 n. 26.
[35] For a study of horoscope texts found in Qumran, see K. von Stuckrad, *Frömmigkeit und Wissenschaft: Astrologie in Tanach, Qumran und frührabbinischer Literatur* (Europäische Hochschulschriften XXIII/572; Frankfurt am Main: Lang, 1996;), 117–132.
[36] Puech in *DJD* XXXI (2001): 157–159.
[37] D.W. Parry and E. Tov, eds., *The Dead Sea Scrolls Reader* (6 vols.; Leiden: Brill, 2004–2005), 3:377.
[38] Puech in *DJD* XXXI (2001): 159; see *HALOT* 1:266.

מחוש, "pain, sickness,"[39] which can go well with הן מן אלהין, but less so with נזח נזחהא. This would be best translated as two separate sentences: "[...] the pain (or: sickness) is from the gods. It moves its movement." The subject of the movement is not mentioned. Nevertheless, since both מחשא and נזך are said to be "from the gods," since I interpret נזך as a comet, and since as mentioned above, the verb נזח is also found in 4Q211 in connection with מחשא and the stars, one might be tempted to interpret מחשא as a heavenly phenomenon as well. A possible interpretation of מחשא is a metathesis of the Akkadian *mišhu* A, meaning "a luminous phenomenon in the sky, usually produced by stars or a meteor."[40]

The word חזוא in line 4 can be found in an astronomical context in 4QEnastr[b] ar (4Q209) 26 5–6, which parallels *1 En.* 78:17 (according to the Ethiopic version).

4QEnastr[b] ar (4Q209) 26 5–6[41]

5 [... בלליא מן]קצת דמי חזוא דן כדמות אנש] [וביממא מן] קצת (?)
6 [... נהור]ה בלחודהי ...

5 in the night, for] part (of the time), this appearance looks as if it was the image of a man; and by day for [part(?) (of the time)
6 [...] her [light] only ...

From line 6 on of the Mareshah ostracon the text of the ostracon seems to move to a new subject, i.e. to demons, as we are told: "If you are hurt by Lilith," or: "if you meet Lilith." The female demon Lilith, here ליליתא, is mentioned once in the Bible, in Isa 34:14, but is known since the third millennium B.C.E. in Mesopotamia and later also in Syria. The name Lilith appears in the Aramaic magical texts and in the scriptures of Mandaean literature of southern Mesopotamia.[42]

The last line of the ostracon mentions שתקו והן אותוקא "and (by) ŠTQW, and if (you meet) ʾWTWQʾ"—which, like Lilith, seem to be two additional demons. Starting with אותוקא, this noun should be compared with the Akkadian evil demon *utukku(m)*.[43] The second noun שתקו seems to

---

[39] Sokoloff, *Dictionary of Jewish Palestinian Aramaic*, 299.

[40] *CAD* 10/2:120–121.

[41] J.T. Milik in *DJD* XXXVI (2000): 163–164. This verse was interpreted by Ben-Dov as part of Version II of "Moon I" type (*1 En.* 78:10–14, 17), describing the light of the moon at night and day during one lunar moth, as well as its distance from the sun (not from the gates of heaven); see Ben-Dov, "Astronomy and Calendars," 87–90 (Hebrew), [10–11] (English).

[42] M. Hutter, "LILITH לילית," *DDD* (2nd ed.; Leiden: Brill, 1999), 973–976.

[43] J. Black, A George, and N. Postgate, eds., *A Concise Dictionary of Akkadian* (2nd ed.; Wiesbaden: Harrassowitz, 2000), 430.

be related to the root שתק, meaning "to be silent," which is used in Aramaic in both *pa'el* "to silence" and *itpa'el* "to be silent."[44] In the Mareshah ostracon we might explain it with regard to a demon whose power is to make people deaf-mute, or paralyzed. The term can be compared with the name שתיקא mentioned on an amulet found in the Cairo Genizah.[45]

Moving on to the second ostracon found in Mareshah, only four lines have survived from this text, the last of which preserves only the head of a *lāmed*. Since no remains can be seen above the first line, it might have been the first line of this ostracon, or else a continuation of now lost text (see below). In what remained, the right margin can be seen, but the left end of the lines is missing, thus the width of the ostracon cannot be reconstructed. The ostracon measures 65 × 30 mm. It reads as follows:

Ostracon No. 2 from Mareshah:

1 מנדת יתקטירת ד∘[
2 והן נזוך והן רוחא]
3 זי נזוך בחזוא מללתא די[ן
4 .[ל]ל[

Translation

1. period comes to an end (or: a payment will be recieved) *d*∘[. . .]
2. and if a comet, if the spirit [. . .]
3. that a comet in appearance, MLLT' *dy*[. . .]
4. [. . .]*l*[. . .]

This ostracon refers to both celestial bodies (נזוך) as well as to demons (מללתא, רוחא). The first line can be read in various ways, and might have been the beginning of the texts or a continuation of now lost text. It starts with מנדת יתקטירת. This enigmatic phrase can be interpreted in various ways:

a. We can interpret מנדת from the Akkadian *middatu*, which means "measure" of either capacity or length, area, and time.[46] If we interpret it as "measure of time,"[47] and understand יתקטירת as related to the Akkadian verb *qatû* in the *quttû* form (4c), meaning "to go to the end of a period of time," here in line 1 it means something like "a period comes to an end."[48]

---

[44] Sokoloff, *Dictionary of Jewish Palestinian Aramaic*, 569.

[45] T.-S. AS 142.12 line 36; see P. Schäfer and S. Shaked, *Magische Texte aus der Kairoer Geniza*, vol. 1 (TSAJ 42; Tübingen: Mohr Siebeck, 1994), 85.

[46] CAD 10/2:46–47.

[47] Ibid., 47.

[48] CAD 13:181.

b. Another possibility is to interpret יתקטירת as a form of the root קטר in the context of an incantation. The use of the noun קטרא in Aramaic magic bowls where it designates a "knot, tying," (cf. "Further, I adjure, invoke ... all mysteries of sorcerers ... knots [קטרין], blows, spells ..."[49]) could argue as much for this interpretation as their use of the verb קטר in the *pa'el* ("to tie," e.g.: "Thoroughly bound, sealed, tied [קטורי יטרין] and charmed [may you be] by the Name [(namely, of God)]"[50]), and in *itpa'el* (e.g. "[...] the sons and daughters of Shelta, may they be tied and [ליתקטרון] bound by an evil, strong and clasping binding"[51]). This meaning probably goes back, as noted by Sokoloff,[52] to Akkadian *kiṣiru* "knot, made for magic purposes," (e.g. "you tie seven and seven knots and you recite an incantation over every [knot] you tie"[53]). In this interpretation, the meaning of מנדת remains unclear.

c. Another possible interpretation of מנדת יתקטרת is in the context of payment. The word מנדת/מנדה or its emphatic form מנדתא, meaning "payment, duty," can be frequently found in the Elephantine papyri,[54] as one of their economic loan-words,[55] originating from the Akkadian term *maddattu* (*mandattu*), which has various meanings, among them "tribute," or "rent (for field etc.), additional fee."[56]

The term קתרא (which is the parallel of קטרא), meaning a "tie, receipt" is found in an Aramaic receipt from the Bar Kokhba period, P.Yadin 43.[57] In this papyrus, the term is used for the partial payment of a lease. If this third interpretation is accepted, the term מנדת יתקטירת might be translated as: "[...] a payment will be received." As in omen-lists (see

---

[49] J. Naveh and S. Shaked, *Magic Spells and Formulae: Aramaic Incantations of Late Antiquity* (Jerusalem: Magnes, 1993), 124–125, Bowl 19:5–6.

[50] Ibid., 113, Bowl 14:1.

[51] Ibid., 139–140, Bowl 26:4.

[52] Sokoloff, *Dictionary of Jewish Babylonian Aramaic*, 1012.

[53] *CAD* 8:437; see R.C. Thompson, *Assyrian Medical Texts from the Originals in the British Museum* (New York: AMS Press, 1982), no. 104:14.

[54] *DNWSI* 2:656; see also B. Porten and J.A. Lund, *Aramaic Documents from Egypt: A Key-Word-in-Context Concordance* (Winona Lake: Eisenbrauns, 2002), 222–223.

[55] See T. Muraoka and B. Porten, *A Grammar of Egyptian Aramaic* (Leiden: Brill, 1998), 377 (no. 22), 380.

[56] *CAD* 10/1:13–16.

[57] Reading in line 7: קתרא דנן יהוא קים, "This 'tie' shall be valid"; see Y. Yadin et al., eds., *The Documents from the Bar Kokhba Period in the Cave of Letters: Hebrew, Aramaic and Nabataean-Aramaic Papyri* (JDS; Jerusalem: Israel Exploration Society, 2002), 152–155, and the discussion of this term on pp. 373–379.

below), we would have in this case in the second Mareshah ostracon an apodosis of an unpreserved protasis. The whole sentence could be reconstructed as: "[If X is seen or happened], then a payment will be received."

Line 2 of the ostracon mentions together with גזון, i.e. Halley's Comet, also רוחא "the spirit," which is either anonymous, or named in the missing part of the line. In line 3 we read מללתא. This word either means "evil speech,"[58] or is a name of a demon.[59] Of these two options the second seems to fit our context better. This demon can be found in the Aramaic incantation text from Nippur which reads: "... with them are repressed all evil spirits and impious amulets spirits and Liliths male and female ... and counter-charms and MLLT' (מללתא)."[60] It can also be found in a Mandaic golden amulet, which reads: "... and sealed against the seven speaking ones (מללאתא)—male and female—who are sent against men and women" (lines 17–21);[61] as well as in an Aramaic incantation bowl, which reads "... the evil sorcerers, the plaguing demons, the commanding demons and the speaking ones (מללתא) came against me" (lines 5–6).[62]

If we are to conclude what we have learnt from the two ostraca discussed here, they include short and enigmatic sentences, formed as "if X," sometimes followed by the sentence הן מן אלהין probably to be translated as "it is from the gods." These short sentences refer to either astronomical objects, the most popular is גז(ו)ן, "a comet" or "Halley's comet," or another "luminous phenomenon produced by the stars or a meteor," if we accept such an interpretation for מחשא. A general reference to the zodiac cycle might also be found in the second ostracon, if we accept the interpretation of the phrase: מנדת יתקטירת as "a period comes to an end."

---

[58] For example, ומללתא דאיסתרתא, "and the speech of the (female) goddesses," in the Babylonian-Aramaic Bursippa Bowl 1:5; as well as in the construct state: ומן מללת לישנא, "and from the (evil) speech of the (slandering) tongue" (line 10); see C. Müller-Kessler, "Aramäische Koine: Ein Beschwörungsformular aus Mesopotamien," BaghM 29 (1998): 342–344. Thanks are due to Christa Müller-Kessler for her notes and references concerning this word.

[59] Sokoloff, Dictionary of Jewish Babylonian Aramaic, 682.

[60] J.A. Montgomery, Aramaic Incantation Texts from Nippur (Philadelphia: The University Museum, 1913), 141–144, no. 6:9.

[61] BM 135791 obverse; see C. Müller-Kessler, "A Mandaic Gold Amulet in the British Museum," BASOR 311 (1998): 83–88, 84.

[62] BM 135563; see C. Müller-Kessler and T. Kwasman, "A Unique Talmudic Aramaic Incantation Bowl," JAOS 120 (2000): 159–165, 162–163.

As an integral part of these astrological objects we can find references to various demons: לליתא ,שתוקו ,אותוקא, and מללתא as well as to רוחא "the spirit" whose name might have been lost.

The most significant term found in this inscription is נזך or נזוך. A detailed description of a comet—maybe Halley's comet, is found in Pliny the Elder, *Nat.* 2.89–94.[63]

> "Javelin-stars" quiver like a dart; these are very terrible portent. To this class belongs the comet about which Titus Imperator Caesar in his 5th consulship wrote an account in his famous poem, that being its latest appearance down to the present day. The same stars when shorter and sloping to a point have been called "Daggers"; these are the palest of all in color, and have a glean like the flash of a sword ...[64]
>
> (Pliny the Elder, *Nat.* 2.89)

D. Halley's Comet in Jewish Texts of the Hellenistic and Early Roman Periods

An appearance of Halley's comet was understood as an important turning point in various Jewish texts of the Hellenistic and Early Roman periods, of which the most significant ones are:

1. In *Sib. Or.* 3, as part of the prophecies on the Nations, among them Gog and Magog,[65] we hear of a reference to the appearance of Halley's comet. It reads as follows:

> [333] All your land will be desolated and your cities desolate ruins.
> [334] But in the west a star will shine which they *will*[66] call "*Comētēs*,"

---

[63] Pliny, *Natural History* (trans. H. Rackham et al.; 10 vols.; LCL; Cambridge: Harvard University Press, 1938–1962), 1:230–239.

[64] Ibid., 232–233. For the study of Halley's comet and its appearances through history, suggesting that the appearance of Halley's comet in 540 B.C.E. fits the description of Isa 14:12–15 and refers to the end of Nabonidus, see D.V. Etz, "Is Isaiah XIV 12–15 a Reference to Comet Halley?" *VT* 36 (1986): 289–301.

[65] J.J. Collins, *The Sibylline Oracles of Egyptian Judaism* (SBLDS 13; Missoula: Scholars Press, 1974), 26–27; see idem, "Sibylline Oracles (Second Century B.C.—Seventh Century A.D.): A New Translation and Introduction," in *OTP* 1:317–472, 369 n. j2. For another reference to such astral event, see *Sib. Or.* 8:190–193: "[190] All the stars will fall directly into the sea [191] all in turn, and men will call a shining comet [192] 'the star,' a sign of much impending toil, [193] war, and slaughter."

[66] A. Wolters, "Halley's Comet at the Turning Point in Jewish History," *CBQ* 55 (1993): 687–697, 691, added "will," because he assumed it was a future event from the vantage point of the composition.

[335]   a sign to mortals of sward, famine, and death,
[336]   destruction of the leaders and of great illustrious men.[67]

The author of this text is usually identified as a Jew living in Egypt, and the quoted verses are defined as the most ancient part of this book, dated to the middle of the second century B.C.E.[68] A. Wolters suggested a connection between this reference in the *Sibylline Oracle* and the appearance of Halley's comet in 164 B.C.E., and the various crucial events of that year, among them the sudden death of Antiochus IV and the purification of the Jerusalem Temple, by Judah the Maccabee.[69] As evidence for the appearance of Halley's comet in 164 B.C.E. Walters refers to some cuneiform tablets.[70]

2. As noted by Wayne Horowitz, there is evidence in some Babylonian tablets of yet another comet (not Halley's), which appeared in the ancient Near Eastern sky a year later, in 163 B.C.E. This comet was seen also in Judaea. Horowitz suggested that this astronomical event fortified the Jewish believe in their victory during the Hasmonean Revolt.

3. A comet was said to have been seen in Judea in 66 C.E., at the outbreak of the First Jewish Revolt, as described by Josephus: "So it was when a star, resembling a sword, stood over the city, and a comet (κομήτης) which continued for a year" (Josephus, *J.W.* 6.289).[71] H. Newman suggests that this event actually refers to two stars, seen one after the other. The first star Newman identifies with a comet seen by Chinese astronomers in the summer of 65 C.E., while for Newman the second is Halley's comet which was seen at the beginning of year 66 C.E.[72]

4. Newman suggested that a fourth appearance of the Halley's comet occurred before the outbreak of the Bar Kokhba Revolt, in the year

---

[67] Collins, "Sibylline Oracles," 369.

[68] Ibid., 356.

[69] Wolters, "Halley's Comet," 687–697.

[70] See W. Horowitz, "Halley's Comet and Judaean Revolts Revisited," *CBQ* 58 (1996): 456–459, who adds two more Babylonian astronomical diaries which refer to this event. See further D. Gera, "Antiochus IV in Life and Death: Evidence from the Babylonian Astronomical Diaries," *JAOS* 117 (1997): 240–253.

[71] *Josephus* (trans. H.S.J. Thackeray et al.; 10 vols.; LCL; Cambridge: Harvard University Press, 1926–1965), 2:460–461; see Horowitz, "Halley's Comet," 458–459.

[72] H. Newman, "The Star of Bar Kokhba," in *New Studies on the Bar Kokhba Revolt* (ed. H. Eshel and B. Zissu; Ramat Gan: Bar Ilan University Press, 2001), 95 (Hebrew).

129/130 C.E.[73] A hint to such event can be found, according to New-man, in *Sib. Or.* 5, written after 117 C.E. when Hadrian became Roman Emperor. It reads as follows:

[155] But when after the fourth year a great star shines
[156] which alone will destroy the whole earth, because of
[157] the honor which they first gave to Poseidon of the sea,
[158] a great star will come from heaven to the wondrous sea
[159] and will burn the deep sea and Babylon itself
[160] and the land of Italy, because of which many
[161] holy faithful Hebrews and a true people perished.[74]

Thus, Newman argued that the appearance of a comet or comets before the Bar Kokhba Revolt was understood by the Jews as a sign for the coming redemption, as we have seen in the First Revolt. Newman also found later references to these events in some Medieval *Midrashim*.[75]

As argued above, such mention of celestial objects and demons, phrased in "if X" formula, initially brings to mind the omen lists known from the Ancient Near East. Nevertheless, omen lists are usually built in protasis formula: "if something is seen," followed by an apodosis: "then something (good or bad) will happen." But in the Mareshah ostraca the apodosis is missing. Ostracon no. 1 seems to preserve seven complete lines, though we might be missing additional lines, which preceded the extant text, but did not survive. With regard to ostracon no. 2, it is clear that the end of its lines are missing, so that one cannot be sure whether the original ostracon included the apodosis or not. Therefore, in what is preserved it cannot be defined as a regular omen text, but as a text related to this *genre*.

E. The Mareshah Ostraca and Mesopotamian Commentaries to Omen Texts

As suggested by W. Horowitz, the fragments found at Mareshah are rem-iniscent of Mesopotamian commentaries to omen texts which typically quote a full omen (protasis and apodosis), or passages from an omen, and then offer exegesis to a difficult word or words. Many examples from the series *Enūma Anu Enlil* are available in astronomical reports from the

---

[73] Newman, "The Star of Bar Kokhba," 97.
[74] Collins, "Sibylline Oracles," 397.
[75] Newman, "The Star of Bar Kokhba," 96–97.

seventh century to the Assyrian kings Esarhaddon and Assurbanipal,[76] but late-Babylonian examples also survive in tablets of *Enūma Anu Enlil* and its commentaries. More directly relevant to the Mareshah fragments may be another type of astrological text that preserves short comments on astronomical observations and/or phenomena drawn from *Enūma Anu Enlil*, but without quoting the omens themselves. These are collected in the *Enūma Anu Enlil* series in what is today known as Assumed Tablet 50.[77] This tablet is known from Neo-Assyrian sources, but parallels are available from the late-Babylonian period as well.[78] In this tablet, short astrological comments are added as a sort of exegesis to the main entry which comes before. A good example can be found in the entry for Scorpio, where it is explained that observations of Scorpio (the constellation "The Scorpion") can be correlated with the price of sesame:

> The star which stands after it is Scorpio, (the goddess) Išhara—For the price of sesame, favora[ble].

The ostraca from Mareshah may have been making use of the same type of learned exegesis in their astrological materials related to comets, especially if we accept the interpretation of מנדת יתקטירת in line 1 of Ostracon no. 2 as: "[If X is seen or happened], then a payment will be received."

Bearing in mind that the majority of Mareshah's inhabitants were Edomites, it is interesting to note, that I. Eph'al has shown that the Jews were not the only nation returning from their exile in Babylon, but that some Arameans also returned to Nirab. The cuneiform tablet discovered in Tell Tawilan, a village not far from Petra, proves that some Edomites might have been familiar with Mesopotamian culture, since they had returned from Babylon to Edom in the Persian period, bringing cuneiform tablets with them.[79] We therefore conclude that finding texts

---

[76] H. Hunger, *Astrological Reports to Assyrian Kings* (SAA 8, Helsinki: Helsinki University Press), 1992.

[77] E. Reiner and D. Pingree, *Babylonian Planetary Omens*, part 2: *Enūma Anu Enlil Tablets 50–51* (BMes 2.2; Malibu: Undena Publications, 1981), 28–51.

[78] E.g. BM 55502 from Hellenistic Babylon; see W. Horowitz and J. Oelsner, "The 30 Star-Catalogue HS 1897 and the Late Parallel BM 55502," *AfO* 44–45 (1997–1998): 176–185.

[79] For the cuneiform tablet discovered in Tell Tawilan, a village not far from Petra, see: S. Dalley, "Appendix A: The Cuneiform Tablet from Tell Tawilan," *Levant* 16 (1984): 19–22. According to the editor, it is a contract "concerning a sale of livestock, in which the sellers were Samsa-yadi and Samsa-idri, and the buyer was Qusušama' son of Qusu-yada." As noted by the editor, the sellers have Aramaic names "with a possible parallel for the writing of the Sun god name Samsa (with which they are compounded) from Neirab

that resemble Mesopotamian commentaries on omen series at Mareshah, the first of which are found in alphabetic script, is of significance and that they might shed light on the cultural connections between Babylon and southern Syria during the Persian and Hellenistic periods.

F. The Knowledge of Astronomy in Southern Syria in the Hellenistic Period

As for the existence of the knowledge of astronomy in southern Syria in the Hellenistic period, one should mention three astronomical compositions known from Qumran:

a. As noted above, the *Astronomical Book of Enoch* is preserved in four Aramaic manuscripts in Qumran. I argued that its synchronistic 364-day-calendar was dependant on the seventh century B.C.E. cuneiform composition of MUL.APIN.[80]

b. 4QZodiology and Brontology ar (4Q318) includes two types of texts: A *selenodromion* and a *brontologion*. The *selenodromion* indicates the movement of the moon through the various zodiacal signs in the sky during the twelve months of the year. Based on the surviving text the editors suggest that the original text began with the month of Nisan, and that it was based on a year of 360 days. Thus they argued that, "This 360-day calendar has its origin in Mesopotamia ... This calendar is used in traditional Mesopotamian astronomical works from the late second millennium BCE and the first half of the first millennium BCE, such as the astrolabes and MUL.APIN."[81] The second text of 4Q318 is a *brontologion*. It includes two distinct types of brontological texts: the first part is "a table in which the days of the twelve synodic months?—in each of which the new moon occurs in one of twelve synodic months— are correlated with the sign in which the moon is on that day," and

---

tablets" (19), while the buyer and his father have Edomite names. This document proves that the Edomites were familiar with the Mesopotamian culture, since some Edomites had returned from Babylon to Edom; see I. Eph'al, "The Western Minorities in Babylonia in the 6th–5th Centuries BC," *Or* 47 (1978): 74–90.

[80] For further dependence of Qumran texts recording lunar phases (4Q320, 321, 321a) on the Akkadian MUL.APIN and *Enūma Anu Enlil*, see J. Ben-Dov, "*Dwq* and Lunar Phases in Qumran Calendars: New Mesopotamian Evidence," *Meghillot* 3 (2005): 3–28 (Hebrew).

[81] J.C. Greenfield and M. Sokoloff in *DJD* XXXVI (2000): 264.

the second is "A set of predictions based on thunder occurring in each zodiac sign."[82] E.g. "[If in Taurus] it thunders (there will be) *msbt* against [... and] affliction for the province, and a sword [in the cou]rt of the king, and in the province ..." (4Q318 VIII:6–7).[83] Regarding the latter part of 4Q318 they argued that, "This goes back to a well attested section in the Akkadian omens series *Enūma Anu Enlil.*" But based on a comparison with a Greek parallel (Supp. gr. 1191), D. Pingree has suggested that the *brontologion* of 4Q318 is "a version of either the Akkadian original or one of its Greek descendants."[84]

c. 4QPhysiognomy ar (4Q561).[85] As shown recently by M. Popović, this text includes only physiognomic teachings (and not astrology).[86] Since this text also includes some non-scientific material, which is written in narrative style, Holst and Høgenhaven suggested that the scientific section was part of a larger apocalyptic composition,[87] while Popović argued that 4Q561 was an independent scientific composition. As for the practical application of 4Q186, it might have been used "as a diagnostic tool during a physiognomic inquiry." Such diagnosis "was believed to determine people's horoscopes and the nature of their zodiacal signs and spirits."[88]

Nevertheless, as we suggested earlier, the two Mareshah ostraca are not only dealing with astrology and astronomy, but also with demonology. Thus, we suggest the following interpretation: The first ostracon mentions sighting a comet, which comes from the Gods. It then mentions some demons, among them Lilith. It thus combines astrology and astronomy with demonology. This combination is even more evident in the sec

---

[82] Ibid., 270–271.

[83] Ibid., 263–264.

[84] See the discussion of D. Pingree in *DJD* XXXVI (2000): 270–274.

[85] M. Geller, "New Documents from the Dead Sea: Babylonian Science in Aramaic," in *Boundaries of the Ancient Near Eastern World: A Tribute to Cyrus Gordon* (ed. M. Lubetski, C. Gottlieb, and S. Keller; JSOTSup 273; Sheffield: Sheffield Academic Press, 1998), 227–229. A somewhat related text is 4Q186, which in cryptographic Hebrew has many similarities with 4Q561. See Schmidt, "Ancient Jewish Astrology," 189–205; Stuckrad, *Frömmigkeit und Wissenschaft*, 117–132.

[86] M. Popović, *Reading the Human Body: Physiognomics and Astrology in the Dead Sea Scrolls and Hellenistic-Early Roman Period Judaism* (STDJ 67; Leiden: Brill, 2007), 54–55.

[87] S. Holst and J. Høgenhaven, "Physiognomy and Eschatology: Some More Fragments of 4Q561," *JJS* 57 (2006): 26–43.

[88] Popović, *Reading the Human Body*, 57.

ond ostracon, where we have astrology or astronomy, combined together with demonology. One might speculate that another unpreserved part might have followed presenting a solution to the problem of being hurt by a demon. The solution may have involved sympathetic magic.

Such a combination of the various fields of ancient knowledge, such as astrology, demonology, magic or medicine can be traced in various ancient texts, among them in some Qumran scrolls such as 4Q186 mentioned above.[89]

4Q186 also mentions a specific אבן צונם "granite stone," which might have associated certain stones with zodiacal signs and spirits, "used for purposes of magico-medicinal treatment, or as preventative, apotropaic elements."[90] This text might have been used, as suggested by M. Popović, for both "preventive measure, which regulates membership of the group and prevented wrong people and their zodiacal spirits from entering and threatening the community, as well as a diagnostic tool, similar to the magico-medical context, to determine the kind of treatment and cure for community members attacked by zodiacal spirits of a less harmful nature."[91] As indicated by 4Q186, the nature of someone's zodiacal spirits is modified according to the position of the zodiacal sign at the moment of birth, which also brings to mind the "Birth of Noah" text mentioned above.

Another such combination is known from the *Testament of Solomon*. This text, as described by C.C. McCown, "is a collection of astrological, demonological, and magical lore, brought together without any attempt at consistency ... [the producer of the text] is a compiler rather than an author."[92] A major part of the text combines astrology and demonology, when demons and human beings are said to reside in a star, or a sign of the zodiac. The most detailed relevant descriptions are those in ch. 18, which lists the names of "heavenly bodies" who are demons, the harm they cause to humans, and the means for driving them away and curing people. As noted by P. Alexander, this catalogue combines demonology

---

[89] Popović argued, that the word, "spirit" (רוח) is used in 4Q186 "to refer to spirits that are related to the zodiacal signs," that is, "the spirits mentioned in the text are zodiacal spirits; one for each of the zodiacal signs" (ibid., 195). This meaning of רוח might also be applied to Ostracon no. 2 from Mareshah, interpreting רוחא as also referring to the Zodiacal spirit.

[90] Popović, *Reading the Human Body*, 237.

[91] Ibid., 239.

[92] C.C. McCown, *The Testament of Solomon* (Leipzig: Hinrichs, 1922), 43.

with astrology.[93] An interesting connection between demons and astrology is found later in ch. 20, with respect to the demon Ornias. In a description of how demons ascend into heaven it says: "But we who are demons are exhausted from not having a way station from which to ascend or on which to rest; so we fall down like leaves from the trees and the men who are watching think that stars are falling from heaven. That is not true …" (*T. Sol.* 20:16–17).[94]

The second century C.E. physician Galen, in his *On the Temperament and Forces of Simple Drugs* ridicules a man names Pampilus for claiming to use thirty-six sacred herbs of the demons (= horoscopes) and decans from a hermetic text, and also for his use of incantations and spells when gathering these herbs. This criticism shows that at least some people believed in existing connections between astrology, demonology, and medicine in an intricate and meaningful way.[95]

CONCLUSIONS

We have examined some enigmatic texts found in Qumran, all sharing knowledge of the various fields of astronomy, astrology and demonology. We were able to suggest better translations for two Aramaic terms which are documented in 4Q211, by introducing evidence from two ostraca of about the same date, but of different origin. The two ostraca are from pagan Mareshah, which was populated by various ethnic groups, such as Edomites and Sidonites. These ostraca were based on Babylonian knowledge of astrology and demonology, as were some Qumran texts. We were able to draw some parallels in terminology, such as the usage of the noun מחשא to be interpreted as referring to a luminous phenomenon

---

[93] P.S. Alexander, "Contextualizing the Demonology of the Testament of Solomon," in *Die Dämonen—Demons: Die Dämonologie der israelitisch-jüdischen und frühchristlichen Literatur im Kontext ihrer Umwelt—The Demonology of Israelite-Jewish and Early Christian Literature in Context of their Environment* (ed. A. Lange, H. Lichtenberger, and K.F.D. Römheld; Tübingen: Mohr Siebeck, 2003), 613–635, 632.

[94] Translation according to D.C. Duling, "Testament of Solomon (First to Third Century A.D.): A New Translation and Introduction," in *OTP* 1:935–987, 983.

[95] *De simplicium medicamentorum temperamentis ac facultatibus* 6 pr, in *Claudii Galeni Opera Omnia* (ed. C.G. Kühn; 20 vols.; Leipzig: Cnobloch, 1821–1833; repr. Hildesheim: Olms, 1964–1965), 11:796–798. See T.S. Barton, *Power of Knowledge: Astrology, Physiognomics, and Medicine under the Roman Empire* (Ann Arbor: University of Michigan Press, 1994), 53–54, 196 n. 127. We would like to thank M. Popović for drawing our attention to this text.

made by stars or meteors. This in turn, might help us to interpret משחתה found in 4Q211 as referring to the same phenomenon. Further, I suggest, based on the usage of the verb נוח to describe the movement of the Halley's Comet in the Mareshah ostraca, that this word is used in the same way in the "Birth of Noah" text, thus probably referring to the horoscope of the "Elect of God."

Finally, we have looked at the broad context of these texts and compared them with other contemporaneous texts that combine knowledge of astrology, astronomy and demonology, trying to draw some conclusions as to the cultural connections between Babylon and southern Syria during the Persian and Hellenistic periods.

FOUR DIMENSIONS OF LINGUISTIC VARIATION: ARAMAIC DIALECTS IN AND AROUND QUMRAN[*]

AARON KOLLER
Yeshiva University

1. INTRODUCTION

A significant contribution of the Qumran Aramaic texts to the study of Aramaic has been the clarification it forced in our ideas of Aramaic dialectology. This has found expression, for example, in the shift they provoked from a tri-partite division of the history of Aramaic to a history consisting of five parts.[1] This paper argues that this revision did not go far enough, however, and that the new data provided by the Aramaic texts from Qumran and elsewhere in the Judean Desert cannot be accommodated by simply refining our old models of Aramaic dialectology. Instead, we need to replace them with new multi-dimensional models to account for the variability now evident in our corpora.

One comment must be made before proceeding. Nearly everything said below has been said by others, and the intention is to articulate a realization which, it seems, has been implicit in much recent work.

Both the older tripartite model and the newer five-part model rely heavily on chronological divisions to make sense of the history of Aramaic. In addition, geography plays an important role in all descriptions of the Aramaic dialects, and the division between Western and Eastern dialects is a particularly well-studied subject. If we suffice with the two dimensions of chronology and geography, we ought then to be able to conclude that texts composed in the same area at the same time will look similar linguistically; yet this is not the case. We need not admit that chaos reigned, however: by discussing some aspects of the Aramaic language situation in Roman-era Palestine, roughly 200 B.C.E. to 200 C.E.,

---

[*] This paper owes much of its present form to insightful comments by Elitzur Avraham Bar-Asher on an earlier draft. At a later stage, Prof. Steven Fassberg graciously read the paper and supplied both criticisms and encouragement.

[1] For details and references, see S.E. Fassberg's contribution to this volume.

it may be possible to show that a dialectological model which includes
more dimensions of variation can accommodate the data more fully.

2. Languages in Palestine: Hebrew,
Aramaic, Greek, Latin, Arabic, Arabian

As is well known, Palestine in the last two centuries B.C.E. and the first
two centuries C.E. was awash in a dizzying array of languages. Fitzmyer's
survey of the languages involved focused on four: Hebrew, Aramaic,
Greek, and Latin.[2] The choice of languages may not have been altogether
justified, but this is not the place to re-open this issue.[3] Instead, I wish

---

[2] J.A. Fitzmyer, "The Languages of Palestine in the First Century A.D.," *CBQ* 32
(1970): 501–531; repr. in J.A. Fitzmyer, *A Wandering Aramean: Collected Aramaic Essays*
(Missoula: Scholars Press, 1979), 29–56. See also J.A. Lund, "The Languages of Jesus,"
Mishkan 17–18 (1992–1993): 139–155; B. Spolsky, "Triglossia and Literacy in Jewish
Palestine of the First Century," *International Journal of Sociology and Language* 42 (1983):
95–109; J. Myhill, *Language in Jewish Society: Towards a New Understanding* (Multilingual Matters Series 128; Clevedon: Multilingual Matters, 2004), 109–111.

[3] The role of Latin is not of the same type as the other three; see the recent study of
W. Eck, "The Language of Power: Latin in the Inscriptions of Iudaea/Syria Palaestina," in
*Semitic Papyrology in Context: A Climate of Creativity: Papers from a New York University
Conference Marking the Retirement of Baruch E. Levine* (ed. L.H. Schiffman; Culture and
History of the Ancient Near East 14; Leiden: Brill, 2003), 123–144, concluding that it
was used exclusively by people who were "the representatives of (the ruling) power," and
even they only used it "when representing Rome." Still, the Latin loanwords in Mishnaic
Hebrew show that it had a real effect on the speakers of Hebrew in Israel, and there
have been excellent recent studies of Latin bilingualism more generally which should
illuminate these issues; see especially the masterful work of J.N. Adams, *Bilingualism
and the Latin Language* (Cambridge: Cambridge University Press, 2003). On the other
hand, two languages which are discussed far less in this context, but which probably
belong in the discussion, are Arabic and the North Arabian dialects. Texts in both
are found relatively nearby to Jerusalem and Qumran. The Arabian dialects are being
spoken and written just 30 to 100 km away from Jerusalem and Qumran. Dozens of
texts in Thamudic scripts B, C, and D have been found in the Negev (cf. N. Tsafrir,
"New Thamudic Inscriptions from the Negev," *Mus* 109 [1996]: 137–167) and many
more just over the Jordan River; indeed, the longest texts ever found in Thamudic
E come from the Madaba region south of Amman; D.F. Graf and M.J. Zettler, "The
Arabian 'Thamudic E' Inscription from Uraynibah West," *BASOR* 335 (2004): 53–89.
We also know that writers of Safaitic texts had good reason to keep tabs on what
happened in Palestine: see the texts discussed in M.C.A. MacDonald, "Herodian Echoes
in the Syrian Desert," in *Trade, Contact, and the Movement of Peoples in the Eastern
Mediterranean: Studies in Honour of J. Basil Hennessy* (ed. S. Bourke and J-P. Descœudres;
Mediterranean Archaeology Supplements 3; Sydney: MeditArch, 1995), 285–290, and
discussed in D.F. Graf, "Language and Lifestyle as Boundary Markers: The North Arabian
Epigraphic Evidence," *Mediterranean Archeology* 16 (2003): 27–56, 40. We also have long

to focus on another issue: can one really speak of "the Hebrew" or "the Aramaic" of Roman Palestine?

3. Varieties of Hebrew and of Aramaic

The simple answer is no: it is well known that neither Hebrew nor Aramaic of Roman-era Palestine were monolithic. While this is a dialectological given regarding spoken languages, this diversity is more striking when encountered in the written record, especially since a few centuries earlier the literary dialects we call Standard Biblical Hebrew and Imperial Aramaic were so dominant, even if the homogeneity of each of these is not as great as it sometimes appears.[4]

My focus will be on the Aramaic side, but let me survey the Hebrew situation briefly first. Proto-Mishnaic Hebrew must have been spoken somewhere, and the *Copper Scroll* and MMT reflect its close kin. Qumran Hebrew is of course very different, and the question of whether it was a spoken dialect or not need not detain us here. The Bar Kosiba letters are different again, and the Hebrew documents from the time of the Great Revolt, such as Mur 29 and 30, show still more dialectal differences,[5] such as the preservation of the ה of the definite article even after

---

first-century texts in what appears to be classical Arabic from both ʿEn ʿAvdat in the Negev and Uraynibah, 35 km east of the Dead Sea; cf. A. Negev, with a contribution by J. Naveh and S. Shaked, "Obodas the God," *IEJ* 36 (1986): 56–60, and the much improved reading of D. Testen, "On the Arabic of the ʿEn ʿAvdat Inscription," *JNES* 55 (1996): 281–292. Of course, Arabs had been living in the Negev for centuries: see, for example, the onomastic evidence in I. Ephʿal and J. Naveh, *Aramaic Ostraca of the Fourth Century BC from Idumaea* (Jerusalem: Magnes, 1996); cf. the discussions in A. Kloner and I. Stern, "Idumea in the Late Persian Period (Fourth Century B.C.E.)," in *Judah and the Judeans in the Fourth Century B.C.E.* (ed. O. Lipschits, G.N. Knoppers, and R. Albertz; Winona Lake: Eisenbrauns, 2007), 139–144, and E. Eshel, "The Onomasticon of Mareshah in the Persian and Hellenistic Periods," in *Judah and the Judeans in the Fourth Century B.C.E.*, 145–156, as well as D.F. Graf, "The Origin of the Nabataeans," *ARAM* 2 (1990): 45–75, 50.

[4] For studies emphasizing the heterogeneity in these corpora, see especially I. Young, *Diversity in Pre-exilic Hebrew* (FAT 5; Tübingen: Mohr Siebeck, 1993) for biblical Hebrew, and M.L. Folmer, *The Aramaic Language in the Achaemenid Period: A Study in Linguistic Variation* (Leuven: Peeters, 1995) for Imperial Aramaic.

[5] H. Cotton, "Survival, Adaptation and Extinction: Nabataean and Jewish Aramaic versus Greek in the Legal Documents from the Cave of Letters in Nahal Hever," in *Sprache und Kultur in der kaiserzeitlichen Provinz Arabia* (ed. L. Schumacher and O. Stoll; Mainzer Althistorische Studien 4; Mainz: St. Katherinen, 2003), 1–11, 8.

the prepositions -בְּ, -כְּ, and -לְ.[6] With the exception of Proto-Mishnaic Hebrew, whose home territory is unknown, the other three dialects are attested within 20 km of each other. This proximity of *findspots*, when taken together with the linguistic diversity among the texts, makes a point which recurs often: where texts are found is irrelevant and potentially misleading.

Turning now to Aramaic, we can begin up north with the Galilean Aramaic dialect. In the south there was the Judean Aramaic dialect seen in the Yadin papyri, as well as the literary dialects of texts such as the *Aramaic Levi Document* and the *Targumim Onqelos* and *Jonathan*, the different dialect of the *Job Targum* from Qumran, the again different dialect of the *Genesis Apocryphon* (more on which below), and Nabatean—again, found within 20 km of each other. Somewhat more distantly, Wajsberg has shown in admirable detail that the language of the early Palestinian rabbis quoted in later Babylonian sources is not Babylonian and not Galilean, and does not precisely match any other known dialect, either.[7]

4. MULTIPLE DIMENSIONS OF VARIABILITY

What do we do with this variability? Within models which utilize only the axes of chronology and geography, this situation will appear chaotic; multi-dimensional models, on the other hand, will be driven by data just such as these. There are probably around half a dozen dimensions required in a model that can account for all the Middle Aramaic data from Palestine, but three will be explored here. The discussion will begin with two examples of the impact geography can have, in order to illustrate its impact beyond the division into Eastern and Western dialects. The

---

[6] Cf. especially D. Talshir, "העברית במאה השנייה לספירה: לשון האפיגרפיה בהשוואה ללשון עיונים בלשון חכמים: תקצירי ההרצאות לסדנה על הנושא דקדוק לשון חכמים ומילונה," in התנאים, (Jerusalem: Hebrew University Academy for Advanced Research, 1996), 42–49, and also E. Qimron, "Observation on the History of Early Hebrew (1000 B.C.E. – 200 C.E.) in the Light of the Dead Sea Documents," in *The Dead Sea Scrolls: Forty Years of Research* (ed. D. Dimant and U. Rappaport; STDJ 10; Leiden: Brill, 1992), 349–361; M. Mishor, "מייחודי הלשון של התעודות מזמן המרד הגדול," *Leš* 63 (2000–2001): 327–332; J.F. Elwolde, "3Q15: Its Linguistic Affiliation, With Lexicographical Comments," in *Copper Scroll Studies* (ed. G.J. Brooke and P.R. Davies; JSPSup 40; Sheffield: Sheffield Academic Press, 2002), 108–121, and J. Lübbe, "The Copper Scroll and Language Issues," in *Copper Scroll Studies*, 155–162.

[7] E. Wajsberg, "הלשון הארמית של היצירה הארץ-ישראלית בתלמוד הבבלי," *Leš* 66 (2004): 243–282; 67 (2005): 301–326; 68 (2006): 31–61.

discussion will then turn to one syntactic phenomenon which may be a function of a text's genre, and finally a brief comment on the role of linguistic ideologies in dialectology will be offered.

a. *Geography*

Geographical variability exists, but in many cases we ignore it and make the "simplifying assumption" of geographic homogeneity.[8] Geography imposes a sense of order when it divides dialects, but geography also blurs neat *Stammbaum* pictures when wave effects spread through dialects which dwell in close proximity but are not closely related.[9] No pretense is being made of offering an exhaustive analysis for the examples below. Instead, they are meant to serve as illustrative examples; full descriptions and explanations of each would require a more robust presentation than is allowable here.

i. *Waves: Non-Metathesis*

One of the distinctive morphological features of some of the Middle Aramaic Palestinian dialects is the non-metathesis in the infixed -t-stem forms of initial-coronal roots.[10] Metathesis in such contexts is the rule in Hebrew and in most earlier and later dialects of Aramaic,[11] but the situation in Roman Palestine seems to have been exceptional.[12] The Yadin papyri and the Bar Kosiba letters show a "consistent lack of the expected

---

[8] See recently R.C. Steiner, "Variation, Simplifying Assumptions, and the History of Spirantization in Aramaic and Hebrew," in *Sha'arei Lashon: Studies in Hebrew, Aramaic and Jewish Languages Presented to Moshe Bar-Asher*, vol. 1: *Biblical Hebrew, Masorah, and Medieval Hebrew* (ed. A. Maman, S.E. Fassberg, and Y. Breuer; Jerusalem: Bialik Institute, 2007), *52–*65.

[9] This is of course well known when *language* contact is studied, but is more difficult to ascertain, and therefore less often studied, when what is in contact is not distinct languages but different dialects of the same language.

[10] For a generative phonological account of the metathesis (setting aside all philological discussions), see E. Aïm, "Aramaic & Hebrew Metathesis," *Proceedings of the Israel Association for Theoretical Linguistics* 20 (2004), available online at http://linguistics.huji. ac.il/IATL/20/Aim.pdf.

[11] Exceptional unmetathesized forms may not be unique to the Roman period; cf. יתשמע in Sefire I A 29, and possibly also יִתְזֵן and the like in BA. See the discussion in E. Qimron, *Biblical Aramaic* (2nd ed.; The Biblical Encyclopedia Library 10; Jerusalem: Bialik Institute, 2002), 48–49.

[12] For most of this data, see M.L. Folmer, "Metathesis in Jewish Aramaic: A So-Called 'Pan-Semitic Feature' Reconsidered," in *Hamlet on a Hill: Semitic and Greek Studies Presented to Professor T. Muraoka on the Occasion of his Sixty-Fifth Birthday* (ed.

sibilant metathesis," with forms like אתזבן (P.Yadin 7:16), מתזנן (P.Yadin 10:14), התשדר (P.Yadin 53:3), and יתשכח (P.Yadin 54:10).[13] Nabatean also shows this lack of metathesis,[14] but the forms in the *Genesis Apocryphon* do conform to the metathesis rule.[15]

This last point is a red herring, though: since the *Genesis Apocryphon* was not written at Qumran, all the dialects known to have been used in the area around the Judean Desert (Yadin papyri, Bar Kosiba letters, and Nabatean) share this feature. Especially significant is that similar Hebrew forms from this period are attested, as well, in 1QIsa^a and the Qumran *Hodayot*.[16] Since this list of dialects crosses all genealogical diagrams of the dialects' ancestry, this suggests that the non-metathesis spread through these neighboring dialects areally, crossing genealogical lines in doing so.

ii. Stammbaum *Issues: Mareshah Bowls and the Aramaic Written in Idumea*

Geography can create different results when a dialect lives alone for an extended period of time. Some recent additions to our Aramaic mix are the texts on bowls from Mareshah, published by Eshel, Kloner, and Puech, which are dated by the editors to around 200 B.C.E. and understood by them to be scribal practice texts.[17] Although the editors

---

M.F.J. Baasten and W.T. van Peursen; OLA 118; Leuven: Peeters, 2003), 233–243, esp. 241. See also her comments in M.L. Folmer, "The Spelling of the Aramaic Bar Kosiba Letters Compared to Contemporary Documents," *Dutch Studies* 5.1–2 (2003): 59–74, 70.

[13] And התשכו (P.Yadin 54:6), which is suspected of being an error for התשכחו. The quotation is from B. Levine and A. Yardeni, in Y. Yadin et al., eds., *The Documents from the Bar Kokhba Period in the Cave of Letters: Hebrew, Aramaic, and Nabatean-Aramaic Papyri* (JDS; Jerusalem: Israel Exploration Society, 2002), 23. On the "preservation" of the initial ה, see below, at n. 18. The non-metathesis is not entirely consistent if the uncertain reading תשדרן is correct in P.Yadin 55:4, 6; see the epigraphic notes in *The Documents from the Bar Kokhba Period*, 315.

[14] See M. Morgenstern, "The History of the Aramaic Dialects in the Light of Discoveries from the Judaean Desert: The Case of Nabataean," *ErIsr* 26 (1999): 134*–142*, 139*.

[15] The *Genesis Apocryphon* has משתני (II:2), אשתני (II:11), אשתבשון (V:16), אשתעי (XIX:18), and אזדמנו (XXI:25); see J.A. Fitzmyer, *The Genesis Apocryphon of Qumran Cave 1 (1Q20): A Commentary* (3rd ed.; BibOr 18/B; Rome: Pontifical Biblical Institute, 2004), 280.

[16] E.Y. Kutscher, *The Language and Linguistic Background of the Isaiah Scroll* (Jerusalem: Magnes, 1959), 266 (Hebrew).

[17] E. Eshel, É. Puech, and A. Kloner, "Aramaic Scribal Exercises of the Hellenistic Period from Maresha: Bowls A and B," *BASOR* 345 (2007): 39–62. See also E. Eshel, "Two

do not comment on the language of the texts, there are a number of very striking details. This is not the place for a full discussion, but two features will be singled out, one notably progressive, and the other archaic.[18]

On the progressive side, the texts show the word for "wood, tree" as אע, with the dissimilation of the earlier double ע. This is the same form

---

Aramaic Ostraca from Mareshah," in *A Time for Change: Judah and Its Neighbours in the Persian and Early Hellenistic Periods* (ed. Y. Levin; Library of Second Temple Studies 65; London: T&T Clark, 2007), 171–178.

[18] The texts also show *hap'el* forms with the ⟨h⟩ (/h/?) preserved, at least word-initially, although it was being lost already in the Hermopolis papyri centuries earlier. For the claim that the shift of the *hap'el* to *ap'el* was long complete, see, e.g., S.A. Kaufman, review of S. Segert, *Altaramäische Grammatik*," *BO* 34 (1977): 94–95, based on the sporadic writings in biblical Aramaic; also D.M. Gropp, "The Language of the Samaria Papyri: A Preliminary Study," *Maarav* 5–6 (1990): 169–187, 176–177, and Qimron, *Biblical Aramaic*, 36 (§ 3.1.1.2). Both the Hermopolis papyri (T. Muraoka and B. Porten, *A Grammar of Egyptian Aramaic* [Leiden: Brill, 1998], 113–116) and the Aramaic incantation in cuneiform (M.J. Geller, "Philology versus Linguistics and Aramaic Phonology," *BSOAS* 69 [2006]: 79–90, 86) show a mixture of the two. Even the particularly stubborn Nabatean scribes cannot preserve more than a handful of *hap'els*, and those only in the perfect (Morgenstern, "History of the Aramaic Dialects," 138*–139*). For differing explanations of the shift, see S. Kaufman, "Aramaic," *ABD* 4:177 ("weakening of the *Hap'el* [*hktb/yhktb*] to *ap'el* [*'ktb/yktb*]") and I.A. Yun, "A Case of Linguistic Transtition: The Nerab Inscriptions," *JSS* 51 (2006): 19–43, 37 (syncopation of intervocalic ה in the prefixed conjugation followed by analogical pressure on the suffixed conjugation), and the idiosyncratic presentation in Muraoka and Porten, *Grammar of Egyptian Aramaic*, 113–114. In the *Genesis Apocryphon* the ⟨h⟩ is entirely gone, but the scribe of 11QtgJob preserved it in word-initial position. To accommodate the data from Nabatean and 11QtgJob, E.M. Cook, "Qumran Aramaic and Aramaic Dialectology," in *Studies in Qumran Aramaic* (ed. T. Muraoka; AbrNSup 3; Leuven: Peeters, 1992), 1–21, 14 simply rules that these are "unrepresentative archaisms in the whole spectrum of Middle Aramaic, which uniformly has gone over to the ʾAph'el [sic!]." This data suggests, however, that the transition was not as uniform as portrayed (M. Sokoloff, "Qumran Aramaic in Relation to the Aramaic Dialects," in *The Dead Sea Scrolls Fifty Years After Their Discovery: Proceedings of the Jerusalem Congress, July 20–25, 1997* [ed. L.H. Schiffman et al.; Jerusalem: Israel Exploration Society, 2000], 746–754, 753). Further complicating the picture are the forms התשכו (התשכחו*?) and התשדר in the Bar Kosiba letters (also above, at n. 13). These have been explained as Hebraisms by E.Y. Kutscher, "The Language of the Hebrew and Aramaic Letters of Bar Kosiba and His Contemporaries: 1. The Aramaic Letters," *Leš* 25 (1961): 117–133, 122 and this view has remained the conventional wisdom (cf. E.M. Cook, "The Aramaic of the Dead Sea Scrolls," in *The Dead Sea Scrolls after Fifty Years: A Comprehensive Assessment* [ed. P.W. Flint and J.C. VanderKam; 2 vols.; Leiden: Brill, 1998–1999], 1:359–378, 374), although in light of the 11QtgJob examples, perhaps this should be re-examined; especially noteworthy in this regard is that the Aramaic within the Mishnah uniformly preserves the ה. Furthermore, in the recently published legal document from Beit ʿAmar, the form התקבלת appears; attention was drawn to this by M. Bar-Asher, "On the Language of the Document from Beit ʿAmar," *Cathedra* 132 (2009): 25–32, 26 n. 8 (Hebrew). A full study of the Aramaic within the Mishnah is needed.

as appears in the *Genesis Apocryphon*,[19] but a more progressive form than the עץ that appears in the *Prayer of Nabonidus* (4Q242 1–3 8) and other Qumran Aramaic texts.[20]

On the other hand, the word חזר "to return" appears, with a ז for **d*. Lest this be explained as a Hebraism, it may be added that the relative pronoun appears as זי, not די, and I have found no examples in these texts of graphic ד for etymological **d* in actual lexemes.[21] The phonological shift of **/ḏ/ → /d/* is supposed to have been complete by late Imperial times.[22] Because scribes are trained to mask phonological changes in their written texts,[23] we expect most examples of **/ḏ/* to be written with ז in Imperial Aramaic, which is what we in fact find. What is surprising is that the scribes at Mareshah, working two to three centuries later, are actually more stubborn than the Imperial Aramaic scribes.[24]

---

[19] It appears in XIV:11, but there U. Schattner-Rieser, *Textes araméens de la Mer Morte: Édition bilingue, vocalisée et commentée* (Langues et cultures anciennes 5; Brussels: Safran, 2005), 68 reads עא. I do not know if this is just a typographical error or a different reading. See Fitzmyer, *Genesis Apocryphon*, 168.

[20] See J.A. Fitzmyer, "The Aramaic and Hebrew Fragments of Tobit from Qumran Cave 4," *CBQ* 57 (1995): 655–675, 673.

[21] The single counter-example is a PN בעלדכר (mentioned as an example of the use of בעל in PNs in Eshel, "The Onomasticon of Mareshah," 147), but PNs are obviously subject to different rules than normal language. This is because if etymological **/ḏ/* was actually pronounced [d] at this time, the scribes would have to memorize a list of words in which they said [d] but were to write ⟨z⟩. (This should not surprise writers of English or French.) When it came to a PN, however, the scribe would presumably write what he heard. For a very similar example, compare the PN קוסדכר attested in the Wādī Dāliyeh papyri (WDSP 9:1), in a corpus which is otherwise distinguished by its rigorous use of ⟨z⟩ for etymological **/ḏ/* (on the name see recently F.M. Cross, "Personal Names in the Samaria Papyri," *BASOR* 344 [2006]: 75–90, 84).

[22] See U. Schattner-Rieser, *L'araméen des manuscrits de la mer Morte, I. Grammaire* (Instruments pour l'étude des langues de l'Orient ancien 5; Lausanne: Zèbre, 2004), 36. Schattner-Rieser also points out (65) that in 4QEn^g ar (4Q212) 1 iii 25 the scribe first wrote זי and then corrected the ז to a ד. Might this point to a scribe who was trained in a place like Mareshah, where he was taught to write ⟨zi⟩, and then moved to a place like Qumran where he had to be re-taught to write ⟨di⟩?

[23] See especially R.C. Steiner, "Papyrus Amherst 63: A New Source for the Language, Literature, Religion, and History of the Aramaeans," in *Studia Aramaica: New Sources and New Approaches* (ed. M.J. Geller, J.C. Greenfield, and M.P. Weitzman; JSSSup 4; Oxford: Oxford University Press, 1995), 199–207.

[24] Something similar is true for the Samaria Papyri, and Gropp notes: "In spite of being chronologically later [than Egyptian Imperial Aramaic texts], the language of the Samaria Papyri is even more consistently conservative." Note the comment of D.M. Gropp to this effect in *DJD* XXVIII (2001): 4, and see Gropp's fuller study: "The Language of the Samaria Papyri," 169–185.

Remaining in the same geographic area, but glancing backwards chronologically, we find that almost all of the texts we have from the Negev show this same pattern. The fourth-century ostraca published by Eph'al and Naveh, for example, also use זי consistently, although there is one other example of *ḏ written ד.[25] In the fourth-century Arad ostraca, too, the relative pronoun is זי.[26] On the other hand, the fourth-century texts have the Imperial Aramaic form for the word "wood," עק.

What does this show? If in fact the Negev should be treated as a scribal monolith (an open question at this point), the shift of */ḏ/ → ⟨d⟩ took place apparently at some point after the third century, whereas the writing of */ḏ/ shifted from ⟨עק⟩ to ⟨אע⟩ rather quickly—between the fourth and third centuries.[27] By strict chronological guidelines, the Mareshah bowls apparently should be classified as Middle Aramaic. But clearly this is too broad a brush with which to paint our picture: the scribes in the Negev did not follow the same rules as the scribes in Qumran or Syria, and there is no reason to have expected that they would.[28]

b. Genre

In response to the claim that Qumran Aramaic represented a vernacular dialect, J.C. Greenfield argued that it was a late representative of the literary dialect he termed Standard Literary Aramaic. This dialectal claim has now been buttressed with detailed morphological and syntactic data

---

[25] Eph'al and Naveh, *Aramaic Ostraca*; the exception is the word דכר "ram" (no. 46). Here, too, the initial ה in the *hap'el* is still preserved, even intervocalically in prefix-conjugation forms. עק appears in nos. 25 and 167; *hap'el* forms are הנעל (passim in the corpus), המטא (no. 26), הקבלת (no. 199), הקים (no. 199), and מה]ף[(no. 199). The last form is restored מה[ז]ף[by Michael Sokoloff in his review of Eph'al-Naveh, *IEJ* 47 (1997): 283–286, 284 n. 5. Similar—but less certain—patterns can be seen in the texts published by A. Lemaire: *Nouvelles inscriptions araméennes d'Idumée au Musée d'Israël* (Transeuphratène suppl. 3; Paris: Gabalda, 1996), and *Nouvelles inscriptions araméennes d'Idumée*, vol. 2: *Collections Moussaïeff, Jesselsohn, Welch et divers* (Transeuphratène suppl. 9; Paris: Gabalda, 2002).

[26] J. Naveh *apud* Y. Aharoni, *Arad Inscriptions* (Jerusalem: Israel Exploration Society, 1981), 168 (inscription no. 41).

[27] One may wonder whether the scribes in the Negev ever learned to write עע, or whether the phonological dissimilation was immediately reflected in their scribal practices.

[28] It is worth emphasizing that this is presumably a matter of scribal training rather than dialectology, although without more data, it is difficult to be certain.

by Fassberg.[29] The full significance of this claim is not limited to the detailed analysis of Qumran Aramaic, but makes an important claim about the language used in a written text. If Greenfield is correct, one must ask what would prompt a writer to utilize a standard literary dialect, as opposed to a vernacular, in writing a particular text. But this also opens the door to ask whether there was only one standard literary dialect of Aramaic: perhaps different types of texts would be composed in differing literary dialects. Were there different registers of Aramaic appropriate for different genres of texts?

One isogloss which does seem to illustrate the significance of genre is the syntax of direct objects.[30] There are three constructions attested in Aramaic: pronominal suffixes, a synthetic construction with the direct object marked with the particle ית(א), and a similar construction with the object marked with the preposition -ל. Pronominal suffixes are attested in Old Aramaic already, but those same texts also show the particle ית(א); notably, the texts from Tel Dan and Bukān both show this construction. On the other hand, this particle is not attested in the (eastern?) Faḥariya inscription, and is later almost certainly missing from (eastern?) Imperial Aramaic, as well.[31]

---

[29] See J.C. Greenfield, "Standard Literary Aramaic," in *Actes du premier congrès international de linguistique sémitique et chamito-sémitique, Paris 16–19 juillet 1969* (ed. A. Caquot and D. Cohen; The Hague: Mouton, 1974), 281–289; repr. in *'Al Kanfei Yonah: Collected Studies of Jonas C. Greenfield on Semitic Philology* (ed. S.M. Paul, M.E. Stone, and A. Pinnick; 2 vols.; Jerusalem: Magnes, 2001), 1:111–120; S.E. Fassberg, "Salient Features of the Verbal System in the Aramaic Dead Sea Scrolls," *Aramaica Qumranica: The Aix-en-Provence Colloquium on the Aramaic Dead Sea Scrolls* (ed. D. Stökl Ben Ezra and K. Berthelot; STDJ; Leiden: Brill, forthcoming).

[30] Most of the data is collected by A. Rubin, *Studies in Semitic Grammaticalization* (HSS 57; Winona Lake: Eisenbrauns, 2005), 91–127 (esp. 94–105 and 115–121), but the little analysis he provides is idiosyncratic, and this is most likely not an example of grammaticalization. Earlier important studies (not superseded by Rubin's) are Kutscher, "Language of the Hebrew and Aramaic Letters," 129–133, esp. 131 n. 59א, and A. Tal, "The Dialects of Jewish Palestinian Aramaic and the Palestinian Targum of the Pentateuch," *Sef* 46 (1986): 441–448; see also Cook, "Qumran Aramaic and Aramaic Dialectology," 4. There is still much more to be said about the history and distribution of this syntactic feature in the various dialects.

[31] The western distribution makes a possible connection with Hebrew את tempting, and it seems likely that this is a feature whose early history will include a description of areal spread.

In Middle Aramaic, it is found only a handful of times in all of the Qumran Aramaic texts (never in the *Genesis Apocryphon*),[32] but often in Nabatean and consistently in epigraphic Judean Aramaic, as represented by the Bar Kosiba letters and the texts from Wadi Murabba'at and Naḥal Ḥever. It is also standard in later epigraphic Judean Aramaic, such as the synagogue inscriptions of Ein Gedi and Jericho, and in CPA, as well as the fragments of Palestinian Targumim.[33]

Eastern dialects, on the other hand, mark the direct object with a -ל: this is found occasionally in Imperial Aramaic, and is standard in Mandaic and Syriac and in certain syntactic environments in JBA,[34] as well as the *Genesis Apocryphon* and other Qumran Aramaic texts,[35] as well as the non-translational parts of *Targum Onqelos* and *Jonathan*.[36] The third syntax, suffixed objects, falls out of favor in most Middle Aramaic dialects but is often used in Nabatean and Qumran Aramaic, and turns out to be the norm in Galilean JPA.[37]

---

[32] It appears, for example, in the chronograph that is 4Q559 (3 3 ם[ר]עמ ית אולד, and probably five more times in the same text); for the possible implications, see M.O. Wise, "To Know the Times and the Seasons: A Study of the Aramaic Chronograph 4Q559," *JSP* 15 (1997): 3–51, 22 and below.

[33] E.Y. Kutscher, *Studies in Galilean Aramaic* (trans. M. Sokoloff; Ramat-Gan: Bar-Ilan University, 1976), 4 n. 14.

[34] M. Morgenstern, "העברית ואחיותיה," "המושא הישיר בארמית הבבלית 4–5 (2005): 167–187. The particle ית appears in JBA only in the more archaic and/or literary dialect; cf. M. Sokoloff: *A Dictionary of Jewish Babylonian Aramaic of the Talmudic and Geonic Periods* (Ramat Gan: Bar Ilan University Press, 2002), 44; esp. with the comments of E. Wajsberg, "ארמית דיאלקטית במילון החדש לארמית הבבלית היהודית," in *Sha'arei Lashon: Studies in Hebrew, Aramaic and Jewish Languages Presented to Moshe Bar-Asher*, vol. 2: *Rabbinic Hebrew and Aramaic* (ed. A. Maman, S.E. Fassberg, and Y. Breuer; Jerusalem: Bialik Institute, 2007), 393–407, 397.

[35] See for example the comments of Fitzmyer, "The Aramaic and Hebrew Fragments of Tobit," 666 with n. 40, regarding the consistent use of -ל rather than ית in 4QTob[a–d] ar (4Q196–199).

[36] It should be mentioned that this is attested in BH as well: cf. 1 Sam 23:10; 2 Sam 3:30; Job 5:2, and Amos 1:6 according to R. Gordis, "Studies in the Book of Amos," *PAAJR* 46/47 (1979/1980): 201–264, 207. P.K. McCarter, *II Samuel* (AB 9; Garden City: Doubleday, 1984), 110 claims that these are influenced by Aramaic, but since the Aramaic picture is far from uniform, this is not a helpful suggestion.

[37] For Nabatean Arabic influence has sometimes been suspected, but (a) the syntax is native to earlier Aramaic, (b) this would leave Qumran and Galilean Aramaics unexplained, and (c) early Arabic does show -ل prefixes marking direct objects. (For this last point, see S. Hopkins, *Studies in the Grammar of Early Arabic Based Upon Papyri Datable to Before 300 A.H./912 A.D.* [Oxford: Oxford University Press, 1984], 209–210.)

	Synthetic 1: ית	Synthetic 2: -ל	Pronominal suff.
Old Aramaic	Frequent (note Dan and Bukān), but not Faḥariya		Frequent
Imperial Aramaic	No	Yes	
Middle Aramaic	Tg. Onq. and Ps.-J. only translating BH את Epigraphic Judean Aramaic (Bar Kosiba letters, Wadi Murabbaʿat, Naḥal Ḥever [and later inscriptions of Ein Gedi and Jericho]) Nabatean Sporadically in Qumran Aramaic	Tg. Onq. and Ps.-J. in non-translational passages 1QapGen ar and other QA texts	Nabatean
Late Aramaic	JBA in "literary or archaic passages"	Mandaic, Syriac, JBA	Galilean JPA

There is clearly much to say about this distribution, but here the focus here is on the Qumran texts, and especially on the *Genesis Apocryphon.* Setting aside the Targumim as a geographic wild-card, we note that the *Genesis Apocryphon* lines up with the *Eastern* Late Aramaic dialects. If we insist on geography as our sole organizing criterion, we would be forced to conclude that the *Apocryphon* is eastern. Although this possibility should not be ruled out a priori, it seems unlikely.[38]

A better possibility, it seems, is to consider the fact that the *Genesis Apocryphon* and the Targumim, which alone among the Middle Aramaic dialects share the use of the -ל, are also related by genre. Certainly this would not be a simplistic question of "formal" as opposed to "colloquial" registers,[39] but the economical explanation is to divide up these texts

---

[38] Dialectological discussions of Middle Aramaic texts of unknown provenance are particularly complicated because many of the isoglosses characteristic of later Eastern Aramaic texts are difficult to date. For example, the Uruk incantation has imperfects with initial *yod*, for example, but seems to have plurals in -*ē*. For discussions of the former, see S.A. Kaufman, *The Akkadian Influences on Aramaic* (AS 19; Chicago: University of Chicago Press, 1974), 124–126, whose theory has since been confirmed by the Faḥariya inscription (and the summary in A. Rubin, "On the Third Person Preformative *n*-/*l*- in Aramaic, and an Ethiopic Parallel," *Ancient Near Eastern Studies* 44 [2007]: 1–28).

[39] See also M.O. Wise, *Thunder in Gemini: And Other Essays on the History, Language and Literature of Second Temple Palestine* (JSPSup 15; Sheffield: JSOT Press, 1994), 107 n. 16. Interestingly, Cook, "Qumran Aramaic and Aramaic Dialectology," 3–14 n. 13 notes that although Beyer claimed that the shift of intervocalic *yod* > *aleph* was supposedly a phenomenon of the vernacular Judean Aramaic, it is not found in the Bar Kosiba letters.

by genre: epigraphic texts (Nabatean, Bar Kosiba, Naḥal Ḥever, Wadi Murabbaʿat) which use ית vs. literary or biblically-oriented texts (Targumim, *Genesis Apocryphon*) which use -ל.[40] Neither is necessarily "colloquial," and neither can be assumed to clearly reflect the spoken dialect. It may be a question of register (one more self-consciously literary, and the other more prosaic), or simply a matter of genre: different grammatical structures would be used for different types of literary products in different literary genres.

c. Ideological

The final variable I would like to mention here is ideology. For lack of space, I will forego a specific example, and just note that there is ample evidence not only that Aramaic speakers in Roman Palestine paid attention to what language they and others were speaking, but that they made language choices in part based on ideologies and value-judgments—like all speakers in multilingual societies throughout human history. This linguistic consciousness is occasionally articulated in Qumran and *Jubilees*, but is covertly expressed in a number of ways.

Little has been done in studying the ideological values of the different Aramaic dialects, although the use of Nabatean and Judean Aramaic dialects in such close proximity provides excellent raw material for the study of at least one example. Another example is the use of Standard (Jewish) Literary Aramaic studied now by Fassberg. If he is correct, this is an ideologically charged dialect whose use is meant in part to connect the work being written to earlier works such as the book of Daniel.[41]

The ideological power and uses of Hebrew has been studied more. One of the striking examples is the use of Hebrew by the rebels of the Great Revolt as well as Bar Kosiba's revolt.[42] There have also been a few attempts

---

[40] For 4Q559, Wise plausibly suggested that the use of ית indicates that it was a private text, made for independent study, and not a literary composition. Note that elsewhere, Wise insists that there are no autographs among the Qumran corpus (*Thunder in Gemini*, 121–122 n. 58), which would necessitate at least a modification of the idea that any text would be simply a scholar's independent notes, so to speak.

[41] Fassberg, "Salient Features of the Verbal System in the Aramaic Dead Sea Scrolls."

[42] H.M. Cotton, "The Languages of the Legal and Administrative Documents from the Judaean Desert," *ZPE* 125 (1999): 219–231; H. Eshel, "Documents of the First Jewish Revolt from the Judean Desert," in *The First Jewish Revolt: Archaeology, History, and Ideology* (ed. A.M. Berlin and J.A. Overman, London: Routledge, 2002), 157–163; H.M. Cotton, "Language Gaps in Roman Palestine and the Roman Near East," in *Medien*

at reading the ideology of Qumran Hebrew, but these have not yet been entirely convincing, I think.[43] According to Seth Schwartz, the composition of the Mishnah in Hebrew was also an ideological statement.[44] Although some have expressed reservations, I think the suggestion has much to commend it, if it can be appropriately nuanced. Moshe Bar-Asher has pointed to the lack of foreign loanwords in rabbinic prayers, as opposed to rabbinic texts, and explained this as an ideologically-driven decision;[45] I would add that this shows an impressive level of linguistic sophistication on the part of the formulators of the prayers.[46]

5. CONCLUSIONS AND DIRECTIONS FORWARD

Before concluding it is worth stressing a point that has long been known and has recently been emphasized by Schattner-Rieser: the heterogeneity

---

im antiken Palästina: Materielle Kommunikation und Medialität als Thema der Palästi-naarchäologie (ed. C. Frevel; FAT 2/10; Tübingen: Mohr Siebeck, 2005), 151–169.

[43] W.M. Schniedewind, "Qumran Hebrew as an Antilanguage," *JBL* 118 (1999): 235–252; S. Weitzman, "Why Did the Qumran Community Write in Hebrew?" *JAOS* 119 (1999): 35–45; W.M. Schniedewind, "Linguistic Ideology in Qumran Hebrew," in *Diggers at the Well: Proceedings of a Third International Symposium on the Hebrew of the Dead Sea Scrolls and Ben Sira* (ed. T. Muraoka and J.F. Elwolde; STDJ 36; Leiden: Brill, 2000), 245–255.

[44] S. Schwartz, "Language, Power and Identity in Ancient Palestine," *Past & Present* 148 (1995): 3–47; idem, "Hebrew and Imperialism in Jewish Palestine," in *Ancient Judaism in its Hellenistic Context* (ed. C. Bakhos, JSJSup 95; Leiden: Brill, 2005), 53–84. Compare also I. Gluska, "הנאמנות הלשונית' של דוברי העברית בתקופת הבית השני," *Balšanut 'Ivrit* 41–42 (1997): 33–43.

[45] M. Bar-Asher, "Les Formules de Bénédiction forgées par les Sages (Étude Prélimi-naire)," *REJ* 166 (2007): 441–461, esp. 446–448.

[46] All this is worth stressing because in both the Gospel of John (5:2; 19:13, 17, 20; 20:16) and in Acts the word *Hebraisti* seems to be used for Aramaic. Some explain that this shows "the apparent perception of ancient Palestinian Jews that Hebrew and Aramaic were essentially the same language" (J.M. Watt, "The Current Landscape of Diglossia Studies: The Diglossic Continuum in First-Century Palestine," in *Diglossia and Other Topics in New Testament Linguistics* [ed. S.E. Porter; JSNTSup 193; Studies in New Testament Greek 6; Sheffield: Sheffield Academic Press, 2000], 18–36, 32–33; so, too, Fitzmyer, "The Languages of Palestine in the First Century A.D.," 43). If this is correct, it is strikingly different from the situation in the Jewish texts just analyzed. A case can be made, however, that the authors of John and Acts do mean to refer to Hebrew, not Aramaic at all. But if *Hebraisti* really does refer to Aramaic, what does this say about the culture out of which the Gospel of John and Acts emerged? I leave these questions to others to sort out. It should suffice to emphasize that if John or Paul equates Hebrew with Aramaic, he is living in a different world than the Jews of Roman-era Palestine.

of the Aramaic texts found at Qumran.[47] It is not just 11QtgJob and the *Genesis Apocryphon* that are exceptional, as there are clearly different groups of texts among the smaller ones, as well. Schattner-Rieser has suggested that some of the texts date from the Persian period, some from Hellenistic times, and some from later on,[48] and this is probably true, but as I have been arguing throughout, chronology need not be our sole explanatory model. Geography, genre, and ideological affiliation may also dictate language choices.

It must be admitted that this makes life more difficult. A final example regarding the *Genesis Apocryphon* may make these difficulties clear. One of the linchpins of Kutscher's theory of *Onqelos'* origins was that the language of the consonantal text of *Onqelos* matched that of the *Genesis Apocryphon*, and so was Palestinian in origin. But two objections ought to be raised to this line of argumentation. First, the place of origin of the *Genesis Apocryphon* is unknown. Second, there may be other explanations for the features shared by these texts, such as that of genre discussed above, which may supersede considerations of time and place. I do not wish to contest the point that the Targumim have their roots in Eretz Israel of the first century, but I do wish to question the assumption that shared features must be explained on the basis of geography and chronology alone. One could easily think of other reasons the *Genesis Apocryphon* and the Targumim may share a linguistic heritage, whatever the origins of each. The Roman Period was linguistically fluid, politically and socially tempestuous, and culturally rich, and all sorts of interesting things happen in environments like that.

---

[47] Contrast, for example, Cook, "Qumran Aramaic and Aramaic Dialectology," 7–8.

[48] Schattner-Rieser, *L'araméen*, 25 divides the corpus into Hellenistic texts (parts of 4QEn ar, 4QLevi ar, 4QVisions of Amram ar, 4QPrNab ar), more recent texts (11QtgJob, 1QapGen ar), and Persian period texts (parts of 4QEn ar, 4Q550 [formerly called "Proto-Esther"], 4QPrNab ar [!]).

THE LINGUISTIC HERITAGE OF QUMRAN ARAMAIC

CHRISTA MÜLLER-KESSLER
Friedrich-Schiller-Universität Jena

This article[1] continues my study, "The Earliest Evidence for Targum

---

[1] Abbreviations and Sigla employed: < BTA = has BTA influence; ! = new reading; AL = Aramaic London bowls in the Samir Dehays Collection; ALD = *Aramaic Levi Document*; AMB A, B = J. Naveh and S. Shaked, *Amulets and Magic Bowls: Aramaic Incantations of Late Antiquity* (Jerusalem: Magnes, 1985); Amulet A–B, Paul Ghetty Museum = R. Kotansky, "Two Inscribed Jewish Amulets from Syria," *IEJ* 41 (1991): 267–281; AO = Antiquité Orientale, Louvre; APM = Allard Pierson Museum in K.A.D. Smelik, "An Aramaic Incantation Bowl in the Allard Pierson Museum," *BO* 35 (1978): 175–177; BM = British Museum; BS = Bowl Syriac; BTA = Babylonian Talmudic Aramaic; CBS = Collection of Babylonian Section, Philadelphia in J.A. Montgomery, *Aramaic Incantation Texts from Nippur* (Publications of the Babylonian Section 3; Philadelphia: University Museum, 1913); C. Müller-Kessler, *Die Zauberschalentexte in der Hilprecht-Sammlung, Jena, und weitere Nippur-Texte anderer Sammlungen* (Texte und Materialien der Frau Professor Hilprecht Collection of Babylonian Antiquities im Eigentum der Friedrich-Schiller-Universität Jena 7; Wiesbaden: Harrassowitz, 2005); CPA = Christian Palestinian Aramaic; GA = Galilean Aramaic; Geller A–D = M.J. Geller, "Four Aramaic Incantation Bowls," in *The Bible World: Essays in Honor of Cyrus H. Gordon* (ed. G. Rendsburg; New York: Ktav, 1980), 47–60; Gordon A–F = C.H. Gordon, "Aramaic Magical Bowls in the Istanbul and Baghdad Museums," *ArOr* 6 (1934): 319–334, pls. 10–15; Gordon G = C.H. Gordon, "An Aramaic Exorcism," *ArOr* 6 (1934): 466–474; Gordon H = C.H. Gordon, "Aramaic and Mandaic Magical Bowls," *ArOr* 9 (1937): 84–106, pls. 2–13; Hermitage bowl = A.J. Borisov, "Epigrafičeskie zametki," *Epigrafika Vostoka* 19 (1969): 3–13; HS = Hilprecht-Collection in Müller-Kessler, *Zauberschalentexte*; HSM = Havard Semitic Museum; IM = Iraqi Museum; JDA = Documentary Jewish Aramaic (Naḥal Ḥever, Murabbaʿat, and others); JTS = Jewish Theological Seminar; KS = Koine Syriac; M = Mandaic; Moriah bowl = C.H. Gordon, "Magic Bowls in the Moriah Collection," *Or* 53 (1984): 220–241; Moussaieff = D. Levene, *A Corpus of Magic Bowls* (London: Kegan, 2003); Moussaieff 1 = S. Shaked, "'Peace be Upon You, exalted Angels': on Hekhalot, Liturgy and Incantation Bowls," *JSQ* 2 (1995): 197–219; Moussaieff 164 = D. Levene, "'If You Appear as a Pig': Another Incantation Bowl (Moussaieff 164)," *JSS* 52 (2007): 59–70; Moussaieff amulet = M.J. Geller, "More Magic Spells and Formulae," *BSOAS* 60 (1997): 327–335, pls. 1–4; MSF A, B = J. Naveh and S. Shaked, *Magic Spells and Formulae: Aramaic Incantations of Late Antiquity* (Jerusalem: Magnes, 1993); QA = Qumran Aramaic; S = Syriac; SA = Samaritan Aramaic; SD = Samir Dehays Collection in D. Levene and S. Bhayro, "'Bring to the Gates ... upon a Good Smell and upon Good Fragrances': An Aramaic Incantation Bowl for Success in Business," *AfO* 51 (2005–2006): 242–246; SLAT = Standard Literary Aramaic in Babylonian Talmud; SLBA = Standard Literary Babylonian Aramaic in magic bowls; TA = Targum Aramaic; TJPA = Targum Jewish Palestinian Aramaic; VA = Vorderasiatisches Museum; WA = Western Aramaic;

Onqelos from Babylonia and the Question of Its Dialect and Origin."[2]
In this article I argued that the language of the two official Targums,
Onqelos and *Jonathan*, is based on a linguistic import from Palestine.
This language transfer occurred at the latest after the destruction of
the Second Temple, but before the devastation of Nehardea. I discussed
the theory of Edward Cook, who claimed that Syriac and both official
Targums share certain morphemes found in Palmyrene and Qumran
Aramaic.[3] He classified them as Central Aramaic, following an earlier
suggestion of Daniel Boyarin.[4] Cook selected the following linguistic
features for his arguments: 1. The independent personal pronoun of the
third plural masculine; 2. The independent personal pronoun of the
second singular masculine and the first plural; 3. The demonstrative
pronouns of nearness; 4. The suffixes of the third singular masculine on
plural nouns and verbs and the third singular feminine; 5. The suffix of
the masculine plural on participles of the verbs lamed-*yod* (III-*y*).[5]

For the inflection of the imperfect, Cook considered a different set of
problems and postulated a double series for the imperfect, one indicative
with *y*-prefix and one jussive with *l*-prefix.[6] This, however, raises the
question of how the *l*-prefix can occur in certain Aramaic dialects and

---

Wiseman bowl in Müller-Kessler, *Zauberschalentexte*, 11d. Certain bowl texts that do
not belong to large public collections are cited by its publication or accepted standard
abbreviations, e.g., Geller A or Gordon H.

QA texts are quoted according to their official Qumran editions. In case of diverging
reading this is specifically noted. The TA, SLAT and Geonic examples can be taken from
the references dictionaries and grammars and are only indicated in case of important
divergence. The data of the Aramaic bowls in SLBA is more extensively cited, since there
exist no comprehensive study or overview to date. Preference is given to quoting the collection number of the text material as many text editions carry reading mistakes or list the
data under incorrect grammatical categories, e.g. Levene, *Corpus*, see C. Müller-Kessler,
"Of Jesus, Darius, Marduk ...: Aramaic Magic Bowls in the Moussaieff Collection," *JAOS*
125 (2005): 49–70.

[2] *Journal for the Aramaic Bible* 3 (2001): 181–198. The journal is a forerunner of
Aramaic Studies, Sheffield Academic Press, now Brill, Leiden.

[3] See E.M. Cook, "A New Perspective on the Language of Onqelos and Jonathan," in
The Aramaic Bible: Targums in their Historical Context (ed. D.R.G. Beattie and M.J. McNa-
mara; JSOTSup 166; Sheffield: Sheffield Academic Press, 1994), 142–156, esp. 150–155.
It continues his article on the position of Qumran Aramaic, see idem, "Qumran Aramaic
and Aramaic Dialectology," in *Studies in Qumran Aramaic* (ed. T. Muraoka; AbrNSup 3;
Leuven: Peeters, 1992), 1–21.

[4] See D. Boyarin, "An Inquiry into the Formation of the Middle Aramaic Dialects,"
in *Bono Homini Donum: Essays in Historical Linguistics in Memory of J. Alexander Kerns*
(ed. Y. Arbeitman and A.J. Bombard; Amsterdam: Benjamins, 1981), 613–649.

[5] See Cook, "New Perspective," 150–153.

[6] See ibid., 152.

periods, such as in Tell Fekheriye, at an early stage but not in the Aramaic dockets and endorsements (seventh to sixth centuries B.C.E.) from Upper and Lower Mesopotamia. The feature is not at home in Imperial Aramaic of the West (Egypt) and the East (Mesopotamia, Iran, including the recently published few texts from Baktria and unpublished Ostraca from Babylon). l- is attested, however, in Biblical Aramaic (only for הוי) and in a number of Qumran Aramaic texts (*Book of Giants*, *1 Enoch* [various sources], *Targum of Job*), the private documents from Wadi Murabba'at (only for הוי) but not in the *Genesis Apocryphon*, and other Judean desert documents. The usage of the l-prefix did not live on in Western Aramaic at all. It is considered an Eastern Aramaic feature that merged later with n- as a positional variant. It is also not a morpheme in SLBA, comprising TA, SLAT, Aramaic in magic bowls, and the Geonic *responsa*. While one could still argue that on account of the y-prefix *Tg. Onq.* and *Tg. Jon.* were translated in Palestine and later redacted in Babylonia, this cannot be said of the magical bowl texts and Geonic *responsa* that share between them more features (graphical conventions, morphemes, syntagms, lexemes) with Targumic Aramaic than with any of the Western Aramaic dialect, despite some minor variations.

Cook only dealt with grammatical phenomena, as the lexical affinities were not an issue in his article. I claimed, however, that the background of the eastern Targum Aramaic dialect is probably the "Rabbinic" literary language as found in the Aramaic of Qumran. This is the dialect that had been transferred to Babylonia at the latest after the Revolt of the Jews against the Romans. It forms a mutual group with Syriac, based on common lexemes.[7] This dialect stands in contrast to Western Aramaic (Christian, Jewish Palestinian and Samaritan Aramaic) and the true Eastern Babylonian Aramaic dialects (Babylonian Talmudic Aramaic, *koiné* Babylonian Aramaic, Mandaic). The Hebrew loanwords in Targum Aramaic have to be exempted from the lexical comparison as they are not relevant for Syriac. These loans are often not identical to the ones attested in the surviving text corpus of Qumran Aramaic.[8] The documentary language type from the Judean desert also continued in Babylonia but only in the style of transmission of text formulae in the Babylonian Talmud.

---

[7] A. Tal, *The Language of the Targum of the Former Prophets and its Position within the Aramaic Dialects* (Tel Aviv: Tel-Aviv University Press, 1975), XI (Hebrew), dealt with this relationship.

[8] See now C. Stadel, *Hebraismen in den aramäischen Texten vom Toten Meer* (Schriften der Hochschule für Jüdische Studien Heidelberg 11; Heidelberg: Winter, 2008).

In his monumental work on the Aramaic texts from the Dead Sea, Klaus Beyer defined the term Babylonian Documentary Aramaic (siglum **u** in grammar and glossary) as a continuation of Hasmonean. It is attested in the legal language of the divorce writ, the *Fast Scroll*, etc., and is closer related to the texts from Qumran than to Babylonian Targumic (siglum **bt**). It shows the following features: אנתי "you f."; -יכי "your f."; די "who"; דנ and הדין "this"; עשר "ten"; בת "daughter of"; -תי suffix 1 sg. with verbs III-*y*; -יין suffix 2 sg.f. on verbs III-*y*.[9] The diverse terms used by Beyer for the Aramaic dialects before and after the turn of the Common Era in Palestine and Babylonia are more than confusing. The Jews did not stop using certain literary dialects and later created new ones according to period and geographical surrounding. These dialects were either transferred to Babylonia[10] or underwent further developments within the Western Aramaic dialects of Palestine (CPA, GA, SA, TJPA = Beyer **gt**).

The Aramaic as found in the Qumran texts, in Nabatean, partially in JDA, and later in SLBA that includes the official Targums (*Tg. Onq.*, *Tg. Jon.*), SLAT (Babylonian Talmud), most of the magic literature on bowls, and writings of the Geonim is rather fixed and continues the SLA type from Imperial Aramaic onwards with incorporated loans from Hebrew and certain innovations (see below, §12). That this SLA type had been under the influence of the linguistic geography where it was in use is not surprising, since such loans are to be expected. For example, the first appearance of the *nota accusativi* is in Nabatean and Qumran Aramaic. This makes the final redaction of the Aramaic part of the book of Daniel rather late, where it occurs only once. It is does not occur in the Idumea ostraca.[11] The full development of the usage of תי can be better observed in SLBA (see below, §8) than in good Western Aramaic dialects such as CPA that restricts its use to pronominal suffixes. The western amulet texts from Palestine and Syria in Aramaic script, however, display similar usage.

---

[9] See K. Beyer, *Die aramäischen Texte vom Toten Meer: samt den Inschriften aus Palästina, dem Testament Levis aus der Kairoer Genisa, der Fastenrolle und den alten talmudischen Zitaten: Aramaistische Einleitung, Text, Übersetzung, Deutung, Grammatik/Wörterbuch, deutsch-aramäische Wortliste, Register* (2 vols. and Ergänzungsband; Göttingen: Vandenhoeck & Ruprecht, 1984/1994/2004), 1:40.

[10] Also Beyer is of the opinion that this dialect (**bt**) continues as import in Babylonia, see K. Beyer, *The Aramaic Language* (Göttingen: Vandenhoeck & Ruprecht, 1986), 20.

[11] This particle is not attested in the Idumea texts.

It stands to reason that the Qumran Aramaic text witnesses do not show a homogenous language type as the SLBA texts do.

The only intermediary text between Qumran, JDA, and SLBA in Babylonia is the *ALD* from the Cairo Genizah. Another potential witness would be the lead roll incantation from the Moussaieff collection, but it is unprovenanced.[12] It cannot be denied that the *ALD* shows common features with *Tg. Onq.* and *Tg. Jon.*, as some authors have rightly pointed out, but the language is not so advanced as the latter. The forerunner of the *ALD* points to a compilation soon after the transfer of SLA from Palestine to Babylonia, at the latest after the revolt against the Romans (135 B.C.E.). The arguments are the following: the historical -ה prefix for *haf'el* and once for *itpa'el* are partially in use; non-assimilated spellings are still extant להנסקה (7:3); מהנסק (8:3); the long imperfect of הוי occurs; the conjunction ארי is employed; the demonstrative pronouns דנה, דן, and אילן occur outside fixed idioms; historical spellings such as in the conjunctions די "that" and כדי "when" (frequent) are extant;[13] √חמי (התחמיון) is plausible as a root in SLBA too, e.g., מיתחמי "is appearing" (Moussaieff 112:6); it preserves the nouns אע "wood, tree," עאן "flock," and the verb רחע "to wash" (frequently attested)[14] that are not in use in Late Aramaic on account of total dissimilation ע > א (see below, § 11.1); Hebrew lexemes are found: הרה "to conceive," כבוד "honour," and כותל "wall" etc.[15]

The innovations that make the *ALD* from the Cairo Genizah an eastern text source are the following: plene spellings: צוארה "his neck" (8:4); pl. emph. ירכאתא "haunches" (8:4); the perfect suffix -תי with the verb group III-*y* (e.g., הויתי 11:10; חזיתי 7:4; 12:9; קראתי 11:8; קריתי 13:1; שריתי 13:1); the nominal ending -אה for adjectives, ordinals, and gentilics: טומאה "unclean" (6:1, 3); the use of the lexemes נחשירותא "chase" < Iranian and נצפתא "conflict" might point to a close lexical affinity of Targum Aramaic with Classical Syriac, but need not be the result of Syriac influence,[16]

---

[12] This intermediary text has not been incorporated as such by Beyer, *Die aramäischen Texte*, vol. 2.

[13] J.C. Greenfield, M.E. Stone, and E. Eshel, *The Aramaic Levi Document: Edition, Translation, Commentary* (SVTP 19; Leiden: Brill, 2004), 240, have listed it as an "adverb," although it is a conjunction.

[14] The intermediary forms of רחק "to wash, rinse" and of מחק "to smite" are still unattested.

[15] See S.E. Fassberg, "Hebraisms in the Aramaic Documents from Qumran," in *Studies in Qumran Aramaic*, 48–69. קטר "to smoke" is not just limited to Hebrew as indicated by Greenfield, Stone, and Eshel, *Aramaic Levi Document*, 240, but it also occurs in QA and in Eastern Aramaic (TA, BTA, M).

[16] This was proposed by Greenfield, Stone, and Eshel, *Aramaic Levi Document*, 23.

since both share many lexemes.[17] The same is true for גישפא, a term for "a special sort of fine flour," which is now attested for QA and in the preceding Idumea ostraca. The *ALD* also shows eastern overtones that appear in *Tg Onq* and *Tg Jon.*, such as the plural of the emphatic state ending י- /-ē/ and infinitive forms of the derived stems קיטולי and אקטולי. But other Babylonian features are not found in this Targum yet.

By describing a written dialect and its graphic features, one can obtain a certain idea of its geographical affinity. Since we are dealing with a literary language type that was in use as a "Kunstsprache" or "scholarly language," however, spellings tend to be rather conservative.[18] The following selected features are intended to demonstrate the close relationship of QA and the Aramaic attested in the documents from the Judean Desert with their linguistic heir in Babylonia, i.e., SLBA. The various linguistic features that are in use in these texts hardly deviate from each other. Among the SLBA bowl texts there exists a certain conformity, as can be demonstrated in the tables below.

1. Graphic Features

1.1. *Final* hê

The most striking graphical trait is that final /ā/ is frequently marked by *hê* instead of *'ālep* in SLBA. Spellings may vary from text to text or even in one and the same text.[19] It is not only limited to the emphatic state as Beyer claimed,[20] but can also be found in other morphemes. Often it depends on the provenance of the text source. *'Ālep* in this position is the rule in the Eastern Aramaic dialects such as Syriac and Mandaic, and is also predominant in BTA.

---

[17] See Müller-Kessler, "Earliest Evidence," 184.

[18] See G. Dalman, *Grammatik des jüdisch-palästinischen Aramäisch* (Leipzig: Hinrich, 1905), 13, who understood TA as a "Kunstsprache" and belongs to the group of scholars who favour a Western origin.

[19] One cannot simply generalize this spelling convention as done by Beyer, *Aramaic Language*, 33.

[20] See Beyer, *Die aramäischen Texte*, 1:47.

1.1.1. Pronouns

אנה "I" (AMB B6:6; CBS 16020:1); הנה "this" (MSF B18:1).

1.1.2. Emphatic State

אסיה "the healer" (Moussaieff amulet obv. 4'); ארעה "the earth" (HSM 2036:1; Moussaieff amulet obv. 6'); בישאתה! "evil" (Geller A4, 5); בליליה "at night" (HS 3016:6); בני אינשה "the human beings" (Moussaieff 123:8); דברה "the desert" (CBS 16020:2); חרצה "the loin" (BM 139524:9);[21] חשוכה "the darkness" (BM 139524:4, 7); יומה "the day" (Moussaieff amulet rev. 3'); ליליאתה! "Liliths" (Geller A5, 13); מלאכה "the angel" (Moussaieff amulet obv. 5'); מומתה! "the oath" (Geller A17); צילמה "the picture" (MSF B18:1); קמיעה "the amulet" (Geller A2); רבה "great" (Geller A4, 15, 17; BM 139524:3; Moussaieff amulet obv. 3', 4', 15'); רבתה "great" (CBS 16020:8); שלניתה "the plunderess" (CBS 16020:2); שמה "the name" (Geller A4, 15, 17); שמתה "the ban" (IM 56544: inner circle c); and many other examples.

1.1.3. Perfect pe'al of Verbs III-y

הוה "he was" (Geller A4;[22] CBS 9010:2).

1.1.4. Active/Passive Participles Singular Feminine or Masculine of Verbs III-y

מיתדמיה "is appearing (itpe'el sg.m./f.)" (MSF B18:2; B25:2); דנסבה "who takes (sg.f.)" (Moussaieff 155:11); מחיה "(Lilith) plagues (sg.f.)" (HS 3034:2); אפיכה "overturned (sg.f.)" (HSM 2036:1); etc.

---

[21] The meaning of this common Aramaic and Hebrew term for "loin, hip" eluded the editor: "חרצא: The meaning is supplied from context, since although the Mishnaic Hebrew passive participle חורץ "decreed, decided," is common, an Aramaic noun חרצא seems to be unattested." See Geller, "Four Aramaic Incantation Bowls," esp. 56 n. 9. This Aramaic word, however, changes in Aramaic between /r/ and /l/ on account of phonetic conditions depending on the dialect, and is well attested since Biblical Aramaic onwards in the standard dictionaries, see HALOT 5:1880; J. Levy, Chaldäisches Wörterbuch über die Targumim (2nd ed.; Leipzig: Baumgärtner, 1867–1868), 284b; Jastrow 505b.

[22] Occurs in periphrastic tense עליכן וגזרית אשבעית בישאתה! רוחי על שליט דהוה "who ruled over evil spirits. I adjured and decreed upon you" and not "which rules over all evil spirits. I adjure and I decree against you" as Geller, "Four Aramaic Incantation Bowls," 49.

1.2. *Graphic* ש *for* *⟨ś⟩ *instead of* ס

This orthographic trait prevails in Aramaic square script texts in QA, JDA, and SLBA, and even in good BTA texts.[23]

1.2.1. *Etymological Cases*

QA, JDA show always ש for *⟨ś⟩ instead of ס. This feature also continues in SLBA: בשר "flesh" (AMB B13:10 < BTA); בישריה "his flesh" (AMB B7:8 [KBA]); ישראל "Israel" (Moussaieff 50:6; 101:10; 164:4 < BTA) but יסראל with supralinear correction (Moussaieff 164:6 < BTA); שמלהון "their left hand side" (CBS 2916:10); שעריהון "their hairs" (APM 9163:2); const. שר "prince of" (Moussaieff 103:9) but סרא "the prince" (Moussaieff 103:10; amulet obv. 2').

1.2.2. *Non-Etymological Cases*

QA, JDA: שלעין "Selas" (XḤev/Se 10 3).—SLBA: לשצטמא "to shackle" (Moussaieff 101:1); משצטמת˙ "you (sg.m.) are shackled" (AMB B12b:3). All are variant spellings of a *saf'el* סצטם;[24] שרפוהי "his Seraphs" (Moussaieff 123:4).

1.3. *Non-Spelling of Final* yod *in Nouns of Roots III-y*

QA: מומה "an oath" (4Q560 1 ii 5); מומתה "the oath" (4Q197 5 12 [Tob 9:4]*); JDA: מומא frequent—SLBA: מומתה˙ (Geller A17; frequent in TA).

2. PHONETIC FEATURES

To describe phonetic features in a written standard dialect or language is a speculative endeavour. Nevertheless, historical spellings such as graphemes for gutturals are extant in QA, JDA, and SLBA. It should be pointed out that in good SLBA texts one does not find any mixing of these

---

[23] See for this graphical trait already Beyer, *Die aramäischen Texte*, 1:46–47, 51.

[24] See for more examples of this particular verb in magical context in C. Müller-Kessler, "SSṬM, ŚSṬM, ŚSṬM, SSṬM or ŠSTM: A Technical Term for Shackling Demons: Contributions to the Babylonian Aramaic Dictionary," *Ancient Near Eastern Studies* 37 (2000): 224–228. It is also to be noted in a collated reading: מיססטם˙ instead of מיסטנין (Moussaieff 121:3) as in Levene, *Corpus*, 81.

graphemes. This absence has already been observed for *Tg. Onq.* and *Tg. Jon.* as well as for the Geonic *responsa*. It is a graphical trait comparable to QA and JDA text material where the orthography appears in the etymological form. How can any loss of gutturals in an established and fixed literary language be proved anyway? It does not come as a surprise that Babylonian scribes could still handle this literary language and write it without major scribal slips. One must presume that during their training, word lists were probably used, although none have been preserved, from which the scribes drew their spelling skills, since one is dealing here with a written language where spellings were fixed. It speaks for a good scribal practice that was later transferred to Babylonia. A comparable situation existed for many centuries in Europe in the form of "Gelehrtenlatein."

2.1. *Retaining Gutturals*

2.1.1. *Retaining ʾālep, hê, and ʿayin*

Gutturals are retained in QA and JDA. This is also the case in reliable text sources in SLBA,[25] especially when *ʾālep* occurs as a second radical in a root.

QA: *afʿel* pass. participle pl.m. מבאשין "ill" (4QapocrLevi[b]? ar [4Q541] 7 5*).—SLBA: pass. participle pl.m. מבאשין "ill" (AMB B6:7); it is also attested in the impf. דתבאשון' ית פגרהא "that you (pl.m.) will make her body ill" (Moussaieff amulet obv. 13ʾ).

Biradical nouns in QA, JDA retain the augmented *hê* in the plural.[26]— The same is to be noted for SLBA: אבהתנא "our fathers" (MSF B19:8); pl. abs. אמהן "maids" (SD 34:4); שמהתא "the names" (AMB B2:7). How conservative spellings in Geonic and SLAT can be is demonstrated by the word for "thigh" עטמיה "his bones" *b. Giṭ* 69b [Geonic source]; *Sword*

---

[25] There is no confusion of gutturals to be found in the SLBA bowl texts as claimed by Levene, *Corpus*, 6. When it occurs, it is limited to KBA texts (Moussaieff 102; CBS 2945 + 2923; 2972; BM 91771; 91776; K 2080) or BTA texts (BM 135563; Moussaieff 145); BS (AO 17.284; IsIAO 5206); KS (AMB B10; MSF B26; IM 60960) or text formulas drawn from Mandaic (e.g. AMB B13) that are so far in the minority. Even there the spelling conforms to the expected orthography. This is comparable to the diversity of language layers in the Aramaic part of the Babylonian Talmud. The magical bowl texts in Aramaic square script cannot be taken as a homogenous dialect. Studies like H. Juusola, *Linguistic Peculiarities in the Aramaic Magic Bowl Texts* (StudOr 86; Helsinki: Finnish Oriental Society, 1999), introduced more confusion than describing the actual dialect diversity in the magical text corpus on account of the lack of a methodological approach.

[26] For relevant examples, see Beyer, *Die aramäischen Texte*, vols. 1 and 2.

of Moses 40:14; in a SLBA bowl it appears already without ע: טמין‭ ‬‏ "bones" (Gordon H10). In QA and JDA this lexeme is not attested.[27]

2.1.2. *'Ālep is Unstable in the Verb Group I* א.

It is reduced to a vowel when closing a syllable since the earliest Aramaic attestations. Sometimes even the vowel letter in first syllable is not expressed in the script.—SLBA: √אבד: תיבדון "you (pl.m.) shall perish" (Moussaieff 131:4) but תיאבדון (Moussaieff 123:8); √אזל: תיזלין‭ ‬‏ "you (sg.f.) shall go" (MSF B25:11);[28] √אסי: תיתסי "you (sg.m.) may be healed" (Moussaieff 103:2); √אסר: למיסר "to bind" (Moussaieff 101:1); √אתי: תיתי "(the flame) will come" (AMB B9:4); לא יתון "they shall not come" (MSF B25:4); לא תיתון "you (pl.m.) shall not come" (Moussaieff 101:7).

2.2. *Non-Apocope of Final Consonant*

Despite a few examples extant in text editions, one has to point out that all these are based on misreadings and are in need of be being corrected: שקילנא‭ ‬‏ "I take" (CBS 9010:1).[29] The old reading שקינא would be a case of syncope or assimilation but not of apocope. Only the Syriac variants of this formula show a syncopated form.

2.2.1. *Non-Assimilation of Initial* nûn *to a Pharyngeal*

QA: הנחתה "to bring down" (11QtgJob XXXI:3).—SLBA: אנחתנא "we brought down" (CBS 9013:9; 2976:9* < BTA).

2.2.2. *Non-Assimilation of* nûn *to* tāw

QA: אנתתה "wife" (1QapGen XX:23); JDA: אנתתי "my wife" (Mur 19 16).— SLBA: אנתתיה‭ ‬‏ "his wife" (BM 91755:9; Geller B6); אינתתיה (HS 3016:1; Moussaieff 149:7); אינתיה (Moussaieff 142:6); אינתה (HS 3001:1, 5); cf. אנתי "my wife" (Mur 19 3, 14),[30] but there are already cases of assim-

---

[27] The statement by Beyer, *Die aramäischen Texte*, 1:419 is perplexing, since he does not indicate in which of the dialects an apheresis of ʿ*ayin* occurs in עטמא.

[28] According to C. Müller-Kessler, "Die Beschwörung gegen die Glaukom-Dämonin: Eine Neubearbeitung der aramäischen Zauberschale aus dem Smithsonian Institute, Washington, D.C. (MSF B25)," *WO* 37 (2007): 78–89; esp. 79.

[29] See J.N. Epstein, "Gloses babylo-araméennes," *REJ* 73 (1921): 27–58; esp. 37.

[30] Is obviously a mistake for the independent personal pronoun 2 sg.f.

ilation as in the independent pronoun of the second person in certain bowls with eastern overtones: אית֯ה "the wife" (Moussaieff 101:6);[31] איתתיה (CBS 2963:3; 9013:4, 10, 16); איתתה "his wife" (Moussaieff 121:2); איתתא "the wife" (BM 91716:2; 91720:17; 91758:11).

2.3. Assimilation of Final nûn in the Preposition מן to the Following Consonant

A Western Aramaic trait inherited from Hebrew is the assimilation of final *nûn* in the preposition מן to the following consonant. In Biblical Aramaic it is attested in Ezra 6:8, 14; Dan 4:22, 30 and in QA it occurs in *Targum of Job, ALD*, rarely in JDA.[32] Further it is attested in a number of cases in *Tg. Neof.*, and it is most frequent in the Eastern Targumim[33] and in the SLBA bowl texts: מאחורה "from behind" (MSF B22:3); מיאחי "from Ahay" (Moussaieff 123:8); מארבע כנפי ארעה "from the four corners of the earth" (Gordon D14); מיאמי "from Immay" (Moussaieff 123:8); מיאתר "from a place," מימדינה "from a town" (SD 34:12); מיבנוהי "from his sons" (Moussaieff 123:9); מיביתיה "from his house" (Moussaieff 123:9); מיחלביהין֯ "from their (f.) milk" (Moussaieff 155:11); מכל "from each" (MSF B22:4; CBS 16020:0); מיכסותהון "from their garment" (CBS 8694:6); מילבושהון "from their clothes" (CBS 8694:6); מילות "with" (CBS 2963:3); מילעילא "from above" (Gordon D14); מיעיבר "from beyond" (CBS 2976:8; 16020:9); מיעיבדתיה֯ "from his deed(s)" (Wiseman bowl 6); מילרע "below" (Gordon D14); מיעיל "above" (CBS 8694:6); מיפום שבע זבין "from the mouth of seven rivers" (Moussaieff 164:11 < BTA); מישמיה "from his name" (Wiseman bowl 5); מישעותיה֯ "from his story" (Wiseman bowl 6); מיתחות כורסי יקריה "from below the throne of his honour" (Hekhalot bowl line 11' [German private collection]) but אישתא נפקא מן תחות כורסי יקריה "fire went out below the throne of his honour" line 10'.[34]

---

[31] See Müller-Kessler, "Of Jesus, Darius," 225.

[32] See Beyer, *Die aramäischen Texte*, 1:626; Ergänzungsband: 375; 2:432. In Mandaic it never occurs, in contrast to Beyer's listing.

[33] See Dalman, *Grammatik*, 227.

[34] C. Müller-Kessler, "Eine ungewöhnliche Hekhalot-Zauberschale" (paper presented at the XXVIII. DOT, Bamberg 1 April 2001).

3. Independent Personal Pronoun

3.1. הוא "*he*"

Striking is the phenomenon that the spellings of the independent personal pronouns in QA, and also JDA correspond to later SLBA. The historical spelling of הוא in QA and JDA appears again in SLBA bowls, Geonic Aramaic, as well as in standard phrases in the Babylonian Talmud. The common eastern variant is הו without ʾālep (KBA, M except for BTA איהו). הוא is rarely employed in SLBA as an independent pronoun, but it functions as a copula or object pronoun. A few examples are והוא הוה במותב רבי יהושוע בר פרחיא "and he was in the presence (lit. at the seat) of R. Joshua bar Perahiya" (Moussaieff 50:1);[35] הוא גדיה וחילקיה "he, his lot, and his part" (Moussaieff 163:2).[36]

3.2. היא "*she*"

The same as for the masculine pronoun can be said of the feminine. In QA and JDA היא is the regular form. This feminine variant is hardly ever attested. Only one example can be noted in a KBA bowl text היא תיפרוסינון "she (Dilbat) will spread them (the mysteries)" (CBS 2972:4).[37] In the unpublished variant CBS 2937 + 2977 only the first letter *hê* is legible. In the function as a copula it occurs in הדא היא עיזקתא "this is the seal-ring" (Istanbul uncatalogued line 1).[38]

3.3. אנתה "*you (sg.m.)*"

QA: אנתה frequent; JDA: not attested.—Recently more examples of this non-assimilated variant have surfaced in SLBA: אסירת וחתימת אנתה שידה

---

[35] According to the Syriac parallels it should be the deictic pronoun of distance.

[36] Levene, *Corpus*, 143, lists quite a number of attestations, but most of them are not the independent personal pronoun "he." M112:13 and M117:1 are Hebrew forms in a Hebrew sentence, M155:4, 8, 10; M163:23, 25, 26, 27 are participles of the auxiliary verb הוי "to be" used in the periphrastic tense, M102:12 reads הוה "was," and M102:13 is the demonstrative pronoun ההוא "that." This leaves only the following passages in Levene's glossary: M50:1; M102:4, 11 and M163:2 with the independent personal pronoun.

[37] היא occurs in unclear context in BM 91719:10, see J.B. Segal, *Catalogue of the Aramaic and Mandaic Incantation Bowls in the British Museum* (London: British Museum Press, 2000), 53.

[38] In H.V. Hilprecht, *In the Temple of Bêl at Nippur* (Philadelphia: Department of Archaeology, 1904), photo after p. 446.

ב בישה "you are bound and sealed, you, evil Šeda" (23AL:9 unpublished); variant: אנתא מגלגלג סרה רבה דעלמה "you MGLGLG, the great prince of the world" (SD 34:7–8); by analogy it is also employed for the second feminine singular to stress the object after the perfect: דשבקית ופטרית אנתה לילית "since I forsook and let go, you, Lilith" (HS 3019:4–5). The assimilated form את, however, is frequently attested (Exod 15:11 = HS 3030:6; Wiseman bowl 3; AMB B13:6[1] < BTA influence)[39] of Late Aramaic in general with the exception of Mandaic 'n't.[40]

3.4. אנתי "you (sg.f.)"

QA, JDA: אנתי frequent.—SLBA: אנתי (BM 91767:2; CBS 16020:2; Moussaieff 103:7; Moussaieff 156:7, 9, 10; frequent). However, an apocopated variant occurs in אסירת וחתימית אנת הי ליליתא "bound and sealed are you, you, Lilith" (Moussaieff 164:1 < BTA). Late Aramaic dialects tend to assimilated forms אתי (CPA, SA, GA) or apocopated forms אנת (BM 91763:2) or 'n't (M) for both genders. Syriac, however, shows the same orthographical spelling but with assimilated pronunciation.

3.5. אנה "I"

The spelling of the first singular plural is often attested with final *hê* as in QA, JDA and Western Aramaic (JPA).—SLBA: אמר אנה "I said" (8AL:3 unpublished).

3.6. א(י)נון "they (m.)"

QA אנון and in JDA א(י)נון are already spelled without initial *hê* and defectively.—SLBA: in Babylonia the pronoun mostly occurs in plene spelling: אינון (MSF B15:3; BM 91767:6; Moussaieff 155:10) but in defective spelling אנון (CBS 2976:16; BM 91742:8) as well.

---

[39] The text should not be emended to ⟨א⟩את as suggested by the editors, since it makes better sense to emphasize the subject with the pronoun before the imperatives את! מריא אתא גיס קריב עליהון "you, lord, come, meet (and) come upon them"; see C. Müller-Kessler, "More on Puzzling Words and Spellings in Aramaic Incantation Bowls and Related Texts," *BSOAS* (in print) for the new interpretation. Cf. also in אתון אסורו! חליצו וחריזו על "you, bind and harness and gird against" (CBS 16018:13).

[40] Magic bowl texts hardly ever contain a second singular masculine, since mostly female demons are addressed in the singular or plural feminine.

3.6.1. *Syntactical Usage of Independent Pronouns*

In QA and JDA the independent pronouns show similar syntactical usage as in the SLBA bowls in Babylonia. It can be well demonstrated by the example of the third person plural masculine אינון.[41]

3.6.1.1. Independent Pronouns as Object Pronouns

Object pronoun יקרא אינון "he will call/name them" (31AL:8 unpublished); as object suffix and pronoun: אכרויזינון אינון עלכי "he proclaimed them against you (sg.f.)" (Moussaieff 1:15); in use in TA as well בלת אנון (Exod 15:12 *Tg. Onq.* = 3 N 130:4).[42]

3.6.1.2. Independent Pronouns for the Usage as Copula

Copula: בניהון אנון "(who) are their children" (CBS 2976:16); אינון מלאכין "they are angels" (CBS 8694:4); דכארמין אינון בחיזוא דליליא "who are vineyards in the vision of the night" (7AL:10 unpublished).

3.6.1.3. Independent Pronouns to Stress the Subject

To stress the subject: וPN דין בר PN וPN דא בת PN אינון ובניהון "and this PN bar PN and this PN bat PN, they and their sons" (Gordon D5–6; similar Gordon B3–4).

3.6.1.4. Independent Pronouns before the Imperfect

To stress the subject before the imperfect: אינון יתברון "they shall break" (Moussaieff 155:7); אינון יבטלון וישמתון "they shall annul and ban" (CBS 9009:9); אינון יתון ויפקון "they shall go and go out" (CBS 16009:5–6); ייבשון ויבטלון דמה "they shall dry and remove her blood" (Moussaieff 155:10).

3.6.1.5. Independent Pronouns to Form the Active Participle Present

To form the active participle present: די מפקדין אינון "because they command" (Moussaieff 156:4).

3.7. אינין *"they (f.)"*

QA: אינין—SLBA: אינין (8AL:11 unpubl.; BM 136204:7).

---

[41] For examples in QA, see Beyer, *Die aramäischen Texte*, 1:563 and 2:385.

[42] See Müller-Kessler, "Earliest Evidence," 179.

3.8. אנתון *"you (pl.m.)"*

QA and JDA has still אנתון, while SLBA shows only assimilated spellings אתון (BM 91767:10; CBS 16018:13; Wiseman bowl 7, 8).

3.9. אנתין *"you (pl.f.)"*

For QA and JDA exist no attestations. The long variant אנתין does not occur in a magic bowl, since the text has the assimilated variant אתין (Hermitage bowl 3:3).[43]

3.10. אנחנא *"we"*

The long form אנחנא is attested in QA and JDA (1QapGen XIX:12; 1QEnGiants[c] 19 3 etc.)—It is in use in SLBA texts,[44] among them the magic bowls (Moussaieff 142:5; CBS 8693:14). All the non standard Late Aramaic dialects tend to shortened variants אנה, אנן (BTA, CPA, GA, SA), in M *'nyn.*[45]

One can conclude that the standard forms of the independent personal pronouns were transferred to Babylonia and are retained in Eastern Aramaic only in the artificial language of SLBA.

4. Pronominal Suffixes

The pronominal suffixes conform in QA, JDA and in SLBA to the same spelling.

4.1. והי- *"his"*

QA: אברוהי "his (body) members" (4Q561 III:4); שנוהי "his teeth" (4Q561 III:3); JDA: not attested.—SLBA: עלוהי "against him" (CBS 2976:15); קדמוהי "before him" (CBS 2976:11; 16059:13; Moussaieff 164:5 < BTA); שרפוהי "his Seraphs" (Moussaieff 123:4).

---

[43] Old reading in M. Sokoloff, *A Dictionary of Jewish Babylonian Aramaic of the Talmudic and Geonic Periods* (Ramat Gan: Bar Ilan University Press, 2002), 147a.

[44] See ibid., 144b.

[45] אנן is listed under bZauberschalen in Beyer, *Die aramäischen Texte*, 2:350. This is not the case, since only the long form אנחנא is attested except for one KBA text (BM 91776:a5), where a short form אנחן is to be noted.

4.2. הא- *"her"*

QA: הא- is frequent in the *Genesis Apocryphon* and the *ALD*, while other QA and JDA texts show only ה-.—SLBA: הא- is sometimes attested: ספוותהא "her lips" (Num 30:7 *Tg. Onq.*); לא תעיקון להא "do not cause her distress" (Moussaieff amulet rev. 13');[46] לא תשלטון בהא "do not take hold of her" (Moussaieff amulet rev. 14'); פגרהא "her body" (Moussaieff amulet obv. 13').

4.3. יכי- *"your (sg.f.)"*

QA, JDA:[47] יכי-; יכ-.—SLBA: יתיכי "you" (CBS 2922:3; Moussaieff 1:15; 156:10); ליכי "to you" (Moussaieff 103:6, 7); לכי "to you" (CBS 9013:7); ספר תירוככי "your letter of separation" (CBS 2976:14); עליכי (CBS 9013: 13; BM 91767:2, 7); עלכי "against you" (CBS 2976:15; Moussaieff 1:15).

5. Demonstrative Pronouns

Another striking similarity is to be noted for the demonstrative pronouns that are retained in the non-augmented stage in SLBA. One cannot just speak of archaic forms like Epstein[48] and Sokoloff[49] when a certain literary language style did not cease. Other SLA lexemes were retained as well and are not specifically indicated in the JBA Dictionary of Sokoloff as archaic.[50]

---

[46] This text without a collection number appears on a lead amulet strip written in ink and was published by Geller, "More Magic Spells and Formulae," 331–335. It displays rather conservative spellings. Although the object has no provenance it has the eastern filiation type with בת instead of -ברתה ד as in Palestinian amulets.

[47] The singular masculine form ך- in use for the feminine in XḤev/Se 12:1, 6, 7 is obviously caused by analogy.

[48] See J.N. Epstein, *A Grammar of Babylonian Aramaic* (Jerusalem: Magnes, 1960), 23–24 (Hebrew).

[49] See Sokoloff, *Dictionary of Jewish Babylonian Aramaic*, 14.

[50] The article by G.W. Nebe on deictic pronouns is more in the style of "Wörterbuch-Philologie." The pronouns are not drawn from primary text studies. Therefore many unchecked readings based on unattested spellings are found in his "Zu den Bausteinen der deiktischen Pronomina im babylonisch-talmudisch-Aramäischen," in *Der Odem des Menschen ist eine Leuchte des Herrn* (ed. R. Reichman; Schriften der Hochschule für Jüdische Studien Heidelberg 9; Heidelberg: Winter, 2006), 251–272.

5.1. דין, דן *"this"*

QA: דן frequently attested; JDA: not attested.—SLBA: this plene spelled form דין of the masculine singular demonstrative pronoun of nearness occurs more or less in fixed expressions that were already in use in QA. Only one example so far occurs outside a fixed expression: דין איסורה "this (magical) bond" (MSF B18:2); דין יומא מכל יומא "this day of all days" (CBS 16020:0); מן יומא דין ושעהsic דא ולעלם "from this day and this hour for ever" (Moussaieff 101:7); מן יומא דין ולעלם "from this day and for ever" (MSF B19:9; B18:2 similar); דין קמיעה "this amulet" (Moussaieff 155:9); דין רזא "this mystery" (MSF B19:1).

5.2. דה, דא *"this"*

QA: דא (frequent); JDA: דא (Babatha archive); דה (Murabbaʿat).—SLBA: an exception is the spelling ושעתא דה "and this hour" (HSM 2036:4). The more frequent spelling is דא: מומתא דא "this oath" (Moussaieff 101:5); PN PN בת דא "this PN bat PN" (Gordon D6); מן יומא דין ושיעה דא וילעולם "from this day and this hour till forever" (Moussaieff 107:9).

5.3. דנין, דנן *"this"*

QA: not attested; JDA: דנן is typical for the Engedi documents מן יומא דנן עד עלם (Mur 47 7); דנן כתבה "this document" (P.Yadin 47:6).—SLBA: רזא דנן "this mystery" (AMB B6:1); PN דנן בר PN "this PN bar PN" (Gordon D5–6); mostly in fixed expressions: מן יומא דנן ושעתא דה וילעלם "from this day and this hour for ever" (HSM 2036:4); מין יומא דנין ולעלם "from this day for ever" (MSF B25:4, 7; similar דנן Moussaieff 121:5; 123:9; 138:12; 142:8; AMB B8:II6; BM 91742:6); קביילו קובלא! דנן "receive this counter-charm"[51] (Moussaieff 155:12).

5.4. דנה *"this"*

QA: frequent; JDA: frequent.—SLBA: not attested.[52]

---

[51] The reading should better be קובלא and not קיבלא as often found in various editions, since it is the verbal noun paʿʿel of √קבל. Cf. Mandaic *qwblʾ*, however, in Syriac it is *qyblʾ*.

[52] The only attestations known so far is a misreading by Montgomery (*Aramaic Incantation Texts from Nippur*, 165) in a magic bowl AIT 10:1 (CBS 16014), where the text shows הנא.

5.5. אילין "these"

QA and JDA have only defectively spelled forms אלין, אלין.—SLBA: here the spelling may vary and occurs without initial hê in the historical form: דאזלין ˈ אילין "these who go" (APM 9163:4); אילין אסירין "these bonds" (AMB B2:8; BM 91713:8; 91758:9); אתותא אילין ˈ "these signs" (MSF B15:8); אילין שמהתא "these names" (BM 91745:3); כולהון אילין "all these" (BM 91723:2); שמהתא אילין דמתקרן "these names who are called" (BM 91742:6); אילין (BM 91751:10; 91767:6).

6. Noun Patterns

The noun pattern qaṭōl/ūl for the directions of the wind was borrowed from Hebrew into QA and JDA. Its usage continued in WA and it is also extant in SLBA.

6.1. Colour Terms

The noun pattern for colours are borrowed from Hebrew into QA, and later WA: אכום "black" 4QEn[d] 2 i 26; ירוק "green" 11QtgJob XXXII:7 and JDA: שמוקא "red."—SLBA: ירוק "green, yellow"; סמוקתא "red" Deut 19:2 Tg. Onq.; the eastern pattern quṭṭāl, however, is also attested.

6.2. Directions of the Wind

The noun pattern for the directions of the wind צפונא "north" and דרומא "south" are the regular forms in QA and WA. The other set, as known from Syriac, Mandaic גרביא "north" and תימן "south"—probably the original Aramaic ones—only occur in 1 Enoch. They are also extant in later SLBA.

QA: דרומא 1QapGen XVII:12; צפונא 1QapGen XVI:10; JDA: דרומא P.Yadin 11:6; צפונא P.Yadin 7:6.—SLBA: common in Tg. Onq. and Tg. Jon. and in the magic bowls: דרומא (VA 2422:10; BM 91707:13); צפונא (VA 2422:10; similar BM 91707:13).

7. Prepositions and Conjunctions

7.1. אם "if" < Hebrew

QA: אם frequent; JDA: not attested.—SLBA: ואם לא אתי [sic] עליכון מיא מיפום שבע זבין "and if I did not bring water upon you (pl.m.) from the mouth of seven rivers" (Moussaieff 164:11 < BTA); אם תיהויין ראשהא ושליטא "if you (sg.f.) will be head and have power" (Moussaieff 103:6); ואם לא תיזחון ותיפקון מן ביתיה "and if you (pl.m.) do not go out and leave from his house" (Moussaieff 164:12 < BTA).

7.2. אף "also"

QA and JDA: אף.—SLBA: אף. If *Tg. Onq.* and *Tg. Jon.* would have been composed in Palestine, the conjunction would have been spelled אוף as in CPA, GA and SA.

7.3. ארי "since"

QA: While this conjunction occurs in QA, it is not attested in JDA.—SLBA: In TA it is the conjunction of cause. For the SLBA bowl texts including the Geonic *responsa* there are no examples. This conjunction ארי derives from the interjection ארו. It is not in use in Western Aramaic.

7.4. בדיל "on account of"

QA: The preposition בדיל is already attested in the *Genesis Apocryphon* but not in JDA.—Later it is extant in WA (CPA [*lbdyl*], SA, JPA) as well as in TA, Geonic, and in the SLBA bowl texts: בדיל שמיה רבה "because of his great name" (Moussaieff 155:5–6). It is the eastern preposition מטול that is only attested in 11QtgJob in the non-assimilated variant מן טלל.

7.5. בדיל ד- "because"

The conjunction בדיל די occurs a few times in QA but is not attested in JDA.—TA, Geonic: The use of בדיל די continues there as well. It appears once in an unclear passage of a KBA bowl text (CBS 2972:4).

7.6. ‫כמה ד-‬ "how"

The conjunction ‫כמה ד-‬ is loaned from Hebrew and is extant in QA but not in JDA. It is extant in the eastern Targums (TA) and the SLBA bowl language. There are also passages found in the Babylonian Talmud and later in the Geonic literature that make use of this "Western" conjunction. SLBA bowl attestations are: ‫כמה דעינין לכון‬ "as you (pl.m.) have eyes" (AMB B6:4); ‫כמא דאיתמחי שימה‬ "as his name is blotted out" (AMB B9:12); ‫כמא דשתין שידי גיטי כיתבין לנשיהון‬ "as the sixty Šedas write their *Geṭ*-document for their wives" (HS 3026:7); ‫כמה דשני שידא קדמאה‬ "as the first Šeda changed (his path)" (Moussaieff 155:12); ‫כמה דפרישו⸢ מן‬ ... "as they parted from ..." (Moussaieff 156:11); ‫כמה דאיתברו כרבין⸢ תקיפין‬ "as powerful Cherubin were broken" (Moussaieff 156:10) etc.

8. DIRECT OBJECT MARKERS

In QA and JDA the direct object is very often not marked, very rarely introduced by the marker borrowed from Hebrew, known as *nota accusativi* ‫ית‬, randomly by ‫-ל‬. The option with the direct object suffix[53] is given preference. A case as described by T. Muraoka is the verb ‫חוי‬ "to show" which can either take a direct object (object suffix) or an indirect object. This is not correct.[54] The option for verbs in Aramaic is that they might merge between transitive or intransitive usage. Different text sources (4QEnastr[b] 26 6; 4QEnGiants[b] 2 ii+6–12 13; 4QVisions of Amram[f] 1 ii–2 14 with ‫-ל‬ and 11QtgJob XXXVI:9*; XXXVIII:4[55] with object suffix or not marked) may show variation in usage.

In SLBA one finds a different situation. Here ‫ית‬ is the predominant feature to introduce the direct object. It occurs more often than ‫-ל‬ as accusative marker or the object suffixes. An Aramaic origin of this morpheme can clearly be ruled out, although many studies still claim that

---

[53] An object suffix cannot be termed a proleptic suffix as by T. Muraoka, "The Verbal Rection in Qumran Aramaic," in *Studies in Qumran Aramaic*, 99–118; esp. 101.

[54] Muraoka, "Verbal Rection," 103, is vague on the matter of direct and indirect objects, whereas the glossary in Beyer, *Die aramäischen Texte*, is far more reliable, since it especially lists prepositional objects and gives detailed information on verbs with direct and indirect objects. A preposition in Semitic languages can always give a verb a different meaning.

[55] The syntagm ‫יחוא להון עבדיה[ו]ן‬ (11QtgJob XXXVI:9) has to be understood "he will inform them (concerning) their deeds" with accusative.

the Hebrew *Vorlage* is responsible for its usage in *Tg. Onq.* and *Tg. Jon.*[56] This position can no longer be maintained on account of its frequent occurrence in SLBA in general. This particle makes it appearances from Nabatean and Qumran Aramaic onwards and cannot be considered archaic but an innovation at that period. It stands out in the dialect geography of Babylonia as an alien morpheme and can only be taken as an artificial linguistic institution that developed into regular usage. Only in instances when the *Vorlage* is dependent on a Jewish text, even magic bowls inscribed in Syriac script, do texts employ ית as well.[57] This particle ית takes only singular suffixes and never plural ones.[58]

Since vague ideas still persist in Aramaic studies concerning the linguistic details in the magic bowl material, it should be pointed out that good SLBA bowl texts do not make use of object suffixes, but consistently introduce the accusative by ית and not by -ל. In some glossaries of magic bowl publications (e.g., MSF; Levene, *Corpus*) one finds incorrect attributions. There the preposition -ל is declared as an "acc. particle."[59] This misinformation is caused by the fact that the editors do not distinguish between transitive and intransitive verbs.[60] -ל, however, is employed in this magic text group as a preposition,[61] or can denote with pronominal suffixes possession.[62] Also in the passage ולא תיקרבון ליהון "do not go near them" (Gordon G8) -ל shows the function of a dative particle,[63]

---

[56] See among the supporters of this view Muraoka, "Verbal Rection," 101.

[57] The particle is attested in only two texts: *npqwn ytky* "they shall drive you out" (VA 3383:6). The other example occurs in a number of variants in the same text *dmqbl y'th* (CBS 2943:7) *dmqbyl y'th* (BM 91712:6); corrupted variant *y'h* (Finnish National Museum VK 5738:3:6); *y'twh* not with *Seyāmē*, but dot on *hê* (AMB B1:6).

[58] According to Naveh and Shaked, *Amulets*, 128, יתיכי is a plural suffix, although יכי- is the expected suffix of 2 singular feminine in SLBA.

[59] It had been listed as such in the glossary of Naveh and Shaked, *Magic*, 260 that was later taken over by Levene, *Corpus*, 146, in the glossary, but in M102:5, 6, 7, 8, 11 (KBA), משיילנה ליה "I ask him" M145:9 (BTA), and M163:16, 19 (< S) -ל is introducing a direct object.

[60] In Levene, *Corpus*, 146: M50:2; M59:8, 12; M101:7; M103:13; M103:1, 6; M119:1, 6; M123:5; M138:8; M142:7; M145:10; M156:7.

[61] See ibid.: M142:10; M156:1, 3, 9.

[62] See ibid.: M59:8; M102:23; M103:7; M119:7; M121:2; M163:5, 7, 13, 24.

[63] Also in *wlmytlyh dgbryn* "and for the coming to him of men" (SD 34:3) *l-* cannot be a dative particle as explained by Levene and Bhayro, "'Bring to the Gates,'" 245, since an intransitive verb אתי "to come" cannot govern a direct or indirect object. According to the syntax it has to be here a proper name or noun "possession" < *m' 'yt lyh* "what he has" as it stands parallel to *tyhwy lyh l* PN *br* PN *wl'ysqwpt bytyh wlšrywt ydyh d* PN ... *wlmytlyh* "(healing) shall be for PN bar PN and for the threshold of his house and for the loosening of PN ... and for what he has/owns/PN" (SD 34:1–3).

since the text employs ית in other passages to introduce the direct object. In a case where -ל introduces the direct object, it is mostly before proper names with the verb עוק√ in the *af'el*: דימעיקן ליה ל PN "who distresses PN" (Gordon H13), דלא ,(AMB B3:3) PN ומעיק לה ל PN "and distresses PN" תיעיקין' ליה ל PN "so that you do not distress PN" (MSF B25:6)[64] but דלא תעיקון להא "so that you do not distress her" (Moussaieff amulet rev. 13').[65] All the other examples derive from texts that are composed in an eastern style dialect, e.g., BTA or KBA, or have eastern linguistic overtones.[66] One more example occurs in a set of variant texts with identical clients מומנא ומשבענא ליכי "I adjure and put an oath upon you (sg.f.)" (Moussaieff 103:7; 119:7; MS 2053/209:7; MS 2053/253:7). All text variants show what is probably an eastern form with a reduced -ל < על, as partially attested in BTA and Mandaic.[67] The *af'el* of שבע always governs either ית or על.[68]

8.1. *Direct Object without Marker*

There are hardly any cases in SLBA texts to be noted where the direct object follows without a marker, e.g., יבטלון חרשי "they shall annul sorcery" (Gordon C1–2); לבטלא שידא "to annul Šeda" (Gordon B8); דקטיל גברא מילות איתתיה "who kills a man with his wife" (CBS 2963:2–3), and more examples in the same text.

8.2. *Direct Object with Object Suffixes*

The direct object can also be indicated by object suffixes. This more historical Semitic way of expressing the direct object occurs infrequently in QA and JDA and later continues in TA. That TA (*Tg. Onq.* and *Tg. Jon.*) gives preference to object suffixes is another argument to deny any

---

[64] According to Müller-Kessler, "Glaukom-Dämonin," 79.

[65] לא דבקת לטורא קדישא "you did not reach the Holy Mountain" (1QapGen XIX:8) has to be a second person and not a first singular with object suffix, since דבק requires a direct object. The first person needs to be expressed in the following style *דבקת לה לטורא.

[66] In the SLBA bowl texts this construction is only attested with the verb עוק√. It is noteworthy that the *af'el* of עוק√ in WA is attested either as intransitive in CPA, JPA or transitive in JPA (before PN without marker; ית and -ל with pronominal suffixes or without in *Tg. Neof.*).

[67] See T. Nöldeke, *Mandäische Grammatik* (Halle: Buchhandlung des Waisenhauses, 1875), 193, 353–357.

[68] -ל occurs in משבע'נה' לך (Papyrus of Oxyrhynchus 11:2), see M.J. Geller, "An Aramaic Incantation from Oxyrhynchos," *ZPE* 58 (1985): 96–98.

Palestine origin, since in WA object suffixes are rarely employed, whereas *Tg. Onq.* and *Tg. Jon.* show plenty of examples. Not all can be adduced to a Hebrew *Vorlage* in *Tg. Onq.* and *Tg. Jon.*, since the translators were writing in a good Standard Aramaic. Attestations in SLBA bowls are very rare: אכריזינון אינון "he proclaimed them" (Moussaieff 1:15); ילבשונה "they will clothe her" (CBS 8694:6); יכסונה "they will cover her" (CBS 8694:6); לא תרתתינה ולא תשרגזינה¹ "do not make (sg.f.) her quiver and do no enrage her" (Moussaieff 156:13); לא תריתותיה¹ "do not cause him to quiver" (MSF B25:7).[69] Both bowl texts show Babylonian Aramaic overtones in other morphemes and syntagms as well.[70]

8.3. *Direct Object with* nota accusativi ית

One way to mark a direct object is the *nota accusativi*. Beginning with Nabatean and Qumran Aramaic, this Hebrew morpheme came into regular use in the dialect geography of Western Aramaic. Not all scholars are convinced of the Hebrew origin of this particle. The issue why, however, cannot be addressed in this study.[71] ית can be suffixed by a pronominal suffix or be followed by a noun, personal or place name.

QA: תעל ית עבידתי "you (sg.m.) will introduce my deeds" (4Q550c 1 i 7); שבחו ית דכרון מרכון "praise the memory of your (pl.m.) Lord" (1Qap-Gen X:8); אלהא בר[ך] ית א[יו]ב "God praised Job" (11QtgJob XXXVIII:9); JDA: אח[לף ליך ית ש]טרא "[I shall] change your do[cument]" (Mur 21 19). Compare a similar construction with two objects (indirect, direct) after the verb *yhb* in succeeding CPA: *ldn dyhb yth lrwḥ qdyšt' bgwkwn* "the one who gives him to the Holy Spirit among you (pl.m.)" (1 Thess 4:8 O). One would have expected *yth* after *lrwḥ qdyšt'*; other examples are: *yhb yty [lḥ]rbn* "he handed me over to destruction" (Lam 1:13

---

[69] Corrected in Müller-Kessler, "Glaukom-Dämonin," 79.

[70] A similar distribution of expressing the direct object with a suffix can be found in three text variants of *Toldot Jeshu*: ולא אשכחוניה על צליבא G; ולא אשכחוהי על צליבא H; אשכח יתיה על צליבא B. All various direct object indications are possible in eastern Jewish text sources, see W.F. Smelik, "The Aramaic Dialect(s) of the Toldot Yeshu Fragments," *Aramaic Studies* 7 (2009): 39–73, esp. 47–48.

[71] Beyer, *Die aramäischen Texte*, 1:601, as well as Stadel, *Hebraismen*, 65, took it as Canaanite. Fassberg, "Hebraisms," obviously did not consider it a Hebraism in QA, since he did not treat it in his article. M. Morgenstern, "The History of the Aramaic Dialects in the Light of Discoveries from the Judaean Desert: The Case of Nabataean," *EI* 26 (1999): 134–142, however, doubted it and considered ית a non-Aramaic particle. The latter contribution is not found in Beyer, *Die aramäischen Texte*, 2:413, and Stadel, *Hebraismen*.

O); *yhb yth l'r:ysyn* "he gave it (the land) to the tenants" (Matt 21:33 C1); *yhb yth l'ymh* "he gave him to his mother" (Luke 7:15 P^g).[72]— SLBA:[73] לאבדא ית סדום "to annihilate Sodom" (BM 91763:6–7); יסון ית PN "they may heal PN" (31AL:9 unpublished); דמזע ומרתית ית כל הדמי "who moves and makes quiver all body members of the human beings" (Gordon H3); דימחבלא ית בני אינישה "who destroys human beings" (Gordon H9); PN יחבקון ית "they shall embrace PN" (CBS 8694:4); דאוליד ית חוה "who begot Hawa" (CBS 8694:5); PN לטיטו ית "they cursed PN" (BM 91751:9); אנחתנא ית מאי דשמיע להון "I brought down what they had heard" (CBS 9013:9 < BTA); סבו ית רוחא בישתא "take the evil spirit" (Moussaieff 155:12); אפילו ית חיליה "drop his power" (BM 91767:8); PN סטטימו ית "they shackled PN" (BM 91745:6); רוחא בישתא פגעת ית PN "the evil spirit met/plagued PN" (33AL:9); לא תיקטול ית הדין PN "do not kill this PN" (CBS 2963:4); לא תיקטלין ית בנה ובנתה "do not kill her sons and her daughters" (CBS 16022:9); דרחיק ית מרכבתיה "who removed his chariot" (CBS 16017:2); דמרתית ית גיסא "who makes quiver the side" (Gordon H3/4); דימרתית ית איברא דסמולא "who makes quiver the left hand limb" (Gordon H9); מרתתן ית כל הדמי קומתה דיבני אינישא "they make quiver all body parts of the human beings" (Gordon H6); אשבית ית¹ רוחין בישין "I adjured[74] evil spirits" (Moussaieff amulet obv. 20'–21'); שגישת ית רעיונוהי "she disturbed his thoughts" (Gordon H7); דימשגיש ית גיסא דימינא "who disturbs the right hand side" (Gordon H4); PN לנטרא ולשיזבא ית "to protect and save PN" (Moriah bowl 2:5); שליפו ית רוחיה "they removed his

---

[72] CPA passages cited according to the standard edition by C. Müller-Kessler and M. Sokoloff, *A Corpus of Christian Palestinian Aramaic* (5 vols.; Groningen: Styx, 1997–1999).

[73] The usage of ית is similar in the WA dialects: בכל אתר דיתחזון¹ ית קמיעה דן "in each place wherever you see this amulet" (AMB A3:13–15) not "in every place where the amulet will be see (דיתחזה)" as Naveh and Shaked, *Amulets*, 50. Two other obscure interpretations are suggested by Beyer, *Die aramäischen Texte*, Ergänzungsband: 261: "wo dieses Amulet in Erscheinung tritt," but in the glossary (ibid., 346): "man sieht"! How can an accusative object follow a passive verb as in Naveh and Shaked, *Amulets*, 54, or even indicate the subject of a passive according to Beyer, *Die aramäischen Texte*, 2:413? אסי ית PN "heal PN" (MSF A31:4); נטר ית PN "protect PN" (MSF A31:7); תאסון ית PN "you shall heal PN" (Amulet B:1–2); אסו ית PN "heal PN" (Amulet B:1–2); שזוב ופלט ית PN "save and protect PN" (Amulet A:1).

[74] The addition in אשבעת ית[כון] רוחין בישין (Moussaieff amulet obv. 20'–21') by Geller, "Magic Spells," 331, is not possible, since the text requires a pronominal suffix third plural masculine אשבעת ית[הון] and not a second plural. Also the construction with ית plus a pronominal suffix referring to the following direct object is not possible in Aramaic. It should read אשבעת ית רוחין בישין. Only the object marker ל- may be repeated again before the direct object with a pronominal suffix, or with a prepositional object introduced by על, מן, and ב-.

spirit" (BM 91767:9); דימשנקא ית רעיוני ליבא "who tortures the thoughts of the heart" (Gordon H4).

8.4. ית *with Pronominal Suffixes*

QA: יפלגון יתה "they will split him" (11QtgJob XXXV:9).—SLBA: לאלפא יתי "to teach me" *ALD* 5:8; אסי ונטר יתיה "heal and protect him" (31AL:1/2 unpublished); אסרית יתכון "I bound you (pl.m.)" (CBS 16087:7); מבטילנא יתהון "I annul them" (MSF B19:7); איבטיל יתכון "I shall annul you (pl.m.)" (Moussaieff 164:11 < BTA); בלומו יתיה "muzzle him" (BM 91770:2) (SLBA); אדריכו יותיה "they overtook him" (AMB B12a:6); חבילו יתה "de-stroy her" (BM 91713:10); לחבלא יתכון "to destroy you (pl.m.)" (CBS 9010:8; Moussaieff 50:4); למיחנק יותיה "to strangle him" (AMB B12a:7); ירחמון יתיכי "they shall excommunicate you (sg.f.)" (Moussaieff 156:10); חתמית יתכון "I sealed you (pl.m.)" (CBS 16087:7); קניא דשב גובי דשב נשי חרשתא דכבין' יתיה "canes of seven nodes of seven sorcerous women that pain him" (Moussaieff 164:11 < BTA);[75] לא תיכבשון יתיה "do not subdue him" (MSF B25:8–9); לא תלושין יתה "do not knead her" (22AL:16 unpub-lished); אימחי יתכון "I shall smite you (pl.m.)" (Moussaieff 164:11 < BTA); לא תנזקון יתהון "do not harm them" (MSF B19:8); תפק יתיה "you shall bring him out" (BM 117870:4); לאפקא יתכון "to bring you (pl.m.) out" (CBS 9010:8; Moussaieff 50:5); איסאיב' יתכון "I shall defile you (pl.m.)" (Moussaieff 164:10 < BTA); לסיעא יתיה "to help him" (BM 127396:3); עני יתיה "he answered him" (MS 1927/2:1); פטרנא יתכון "I release you (pl.m.)" (Moussaieff 50:6); קליא יתהון "(she) roasts them" (Moussaieff 155:11); כולהון קטל יתהון סדרוס "Sidrus killed all of them" (AMB Ba12:1–2); למיקטל יותיה "to kill him" (AMB B12a:7); אנה רחימנא יתכון "I love you (pl.m.)" (AMB B6:3); לרחקא יתיכי "to distance you (sg.f.)" (Mous-saieff 1:15); משבענא יתכון "I beswear you (pl.m.)" (AMB B6:8); שדרית יתיכי "I sent you (sg.f.)" (HS 3034:3); שדרית יתהון' "I sent them (pl.m.)" (APM 9163:3); כד שמע יתיה "when he heard him" (CBS 2963:7, 8/9 < BTA); ישמתון יתיכי "they shall ban you (sg.f.)" (Moussaieff 156:10); יתברון יתיכי "they shall break you (sg.f.)" (Moussaieff 156:10).[76]

---

[75] Reading and interpretation of דשב נשי חרשתא רכבין יתיה "... of the seven sorcerous women are *riding*" in Levene, "'If You Appear as a Pig,'" 62 cannot be correct as a transitive verb is required before יתיה. A solution with the verb רכב could be דשב נשי חרשתא רכבין יתיה "... of seven sorcerous women overriding him" (Moussaieff 164:11).

[76] For WA see the following examples: [ל]מקטול יתה "[to] kill him" (AMB A15:17); ולמסיה יתה ולמנטרה יתה "and to heal and to protect him" (MSF A19:7); דיעקור יתיך "that he shall uproot you (sg.f.)" (MSF A19:12–13), but before a PN: את אסי ל PN "you, heal PN"

8.5. *With -ל*

Another possibility to introduce the direct object is to employ the preposition -ל. An exception is found in a text formula that shows both accusative markers -ל and ית: קטליה ליברה short for קטל ליה* "he killed her son" (AMB B12a:5) which was probably influenced by the western amulet *Vorlage* קטל לברה (AMB A15:11), לא איקטול ליבנין "I shall not kill the children" (AMB B12b:12) but with ית in למיקטל יותיה "to kill him" (AMB B12a:7).

9. VERB INFLECTION

9.1. תא-, תה- *Suffix Perfect of 2 Singular Masculine*

The perfect suffix of the second singular is תא-, תה- in QA but it is not attested in JDA.—SLBA: only in TA one finds תא-, but for the magic bowl it is not extant so far, since mostly only feminine singular demons are addressed in the second person.

9.2. אה- *Suffix Perfect 3 Plural Feminine or Imperative 3 Plural Feminine with the Verbs III-y.*

QA, JDA: not attested.—SLBA: איתמסיא "(heights) be dissolved" (HS 3046:4), in another variant איתמסיאה (Moussaieff 50:4).

9.3. -י *Prefix of the Imperfect 3 Singular and Plural Masculine*

This common imperfect prefix -י in Aramaic is also in use in SLBA despite the common eastern -ל/-נ ones in the surrounding dialects (BTA, Mandaic, Syriac) from Hatra onwards. Even the individual magic bowl texts discriminate here between -י and -ל/-נ prefix. Only in cases when the magical frame is composed in another dialect does the prefix differ between frame and magical formula.[77] The unique text source that could

---

(MSF A19:31); אסרנה יאתיך "I bind you (sg.f.)"; אשבעת יתכון "I adjured you" (Silver Amulet lines 9, 25 in R. Kotansky, J. Naveh, and S. Shaked, "A Greek-Aramaic Silver Amulet from Egypt in the Ashmolean Museum," *Mus* 105 [1992]: 5–25).

[77] This is the weakness of the study on the linguistic peculiarities by Juusola, *Linguistic Peculiarities*, 174–181, on this matter. It makes his methodological approach question-

have thrown light on the question of continuity of the prefix -י in the east is the Aramaic Uruk incantation in cuneiform. This text, however, is lacking any evidence of imperfect forms.[78]

9.4. ין- *Affix of the Imperfect 2 Singular Feminine*

QA: *תעבדין "you shall do" (1QapGen XIX:20); תמללין "you shall speak" (1QapGen II:7); JDA: תהוין "you (sg.f.) will be" (Naḥal Ḥever documents frequent); תמרין (Mur 19 10).—SLBA: לא תיזלין "do not go" (Moussaieff 156:9); 'תבאשין "you shall make ill" (Moussaieff amulet obv. 13'); לא תידמין "do not you appear (*itpeʿel*)" (HS 3008:3–4); תיהויין "you shall be" (Moussaieff 103:6); לא תיחדרין "you shall not return" (CBS 9013:16); לא תחוחין "you shall not be friendly" (CBS 16020:9); לא תיחזין "do not appear" (Moussaieff 156:9); 'תפצין "you shall deliver" (Moussaieff amulet obv. 8'); לא תיקמין "do not stand" (Moussaieff 156:13); לא תישלטין "do not rule" (Moussaieff 156:12).

9.5. *Imperfect Affix of 2 Feminine Singular*

The imperfect affix of the 2 singular feminine -יין only occurs in JDA. SLBA shows it as well.

9.6. י- *Affix Imperative 2 Singular Feminine*

This consistent SLA ending is attested beginning with Imperial Aramaic. QA: בועי "rejoice" (4Q196 18 2 [Tob 13:13]); JDA: not attested.—SLBA: אפילי: √נפל "let fall" (BM 91767:8); גבולי "form" (BM 91767:4); ⟨י⟩גלח "shave" (HS 3034:5); 'חתומי "seal" (CBS 2952:1; 2976:15); לחושי "enchant" (CBS 2952:1); נפוחי "blow" (BM 91767:4); עקורי "uproot" (HS 3026:7); עירוקי "flee" (HS 3034:5); פוקי: √נפק "go out" (CBS 2976:9); צותי "hear" (CBS 2976:4, 9); קבילי "receive" (CBS 2976:14); קטולי "kill" (BM 91767:5); 'קטורי "knot" (CBS 2952:1); שלופי "draw out" (BM 91767:9); שמעי "hear" (CBS 16020:5); תיבי: √יתב "sit" (BM 91767:4).

---

able, since he takes every text on a magic bowl as a complete unit. Most of the magical bowl texts, however, are imbedded in doxological frames that differ in dialect or even language (Hebrew) from the magic formula.

[78] Other indicative features as demonstrative pronouns, conjunctions, and infinitives of the derived stems are lacking as well.

9.7. *Infinitives of the Derived Stems*

Infinitive patterns of the derived stems can define a dialect group in Aramaic. The following patterns (*qattālā* and [*h*]*aqtālā*) are transmitted from Tell Fekheriye through Imperial Aramaic up until the Geonic time and can be taken as the basic infinitive type of "Hocharamäisch." The other two types are typical for Western Aramaic (*maqattālā, maqtālā*) since the Hermopolis papyri and Aḥiqar frame or for another Aramaic literary dialect type (*maqattālū, maqtālū*) since the Aḥiqar proverbs onwards.[79]

9.7.1. *paʿel: qattālā*

QA: לחבלא "to destroy" (11QtgJob XXIV:5); מללא "to speak" (11QtgJob XIV:3*); JDA: only with מ-prefix מקטלה:למזבנה "to sell" (XḤev/Se 47 8); למקנה "to acquire" (XḤev/Se 47 8); מקטלו:למזבנו (XḤev/Se 7 17).—SLBA: לאבדא "to destroy" (BM 91763:6); לבטלא "to annul" (Gordon B8); לחבלא "to destroy" (Moussaieff 50:4); לחתומה < *לחתמה "to seal" (HS 3003:1); לחתמא (BM 91720:12); לנטורה < *לנטרה "to protect" (HS 3003:1); לסיעא "to help" (BM 127396:3); לפרנסא "to sustain" (BM 127396:3); לרחקא "to remove" (Moussaieff 1:15; 101:2).

9.7.2. *(h)afʿel: (h)aqtālā*

QA: הנחתה "to bring down" (11QtgJob XXXI:3); להנפקה "to bring out" (11QtgJob XXXI:5); להסבעה "to satisfy" (11QtgJob XXXI:4); להיתיה "to bring" (11QtgJob IV:1);[80] JDA: הקטלה:להעמקה "to deepen" (XḤev/Se 47 7) but מקטלה in למזבנה "to sell" (XḤev/Se 47 8); למעמקה (P.Yadin 81:6); but למנעלו "to bring in" (P.Yadin 7:26).—SLBA: לאזהא' "to drive out" (MSF B20:3); לאפקא "to bring out" (MSF B20:3; Moussaieff 50:5; 101:2) and plenty of other examples.

---

[79] See J.C. Greenfield, "The Infinitive in the Aramaic Documents from the Judean Desert," in *Studies in Hebrew and Other Semitic Languages Presented to Chaim Rabin* (ed. M.H. Goshen-Gottstein et al.; Jersualem: Academon, 1990), 77–81 (Hebrew); M. Folmer, *The Aramaic Language in the Achaemenid* Period (OLA 68; Leuven: Peeters, 1995), 191–198.

[80] The reading suggested by Beyer, *Die aramäischen Texte*, 1:285, is correct.

10. Syntagms

10.1. *Absolute State*

SLBA retains the absolute state even in cases where it went out of use in Central Babylonian Aramaic (BTA, KBA, M), where it was only employed with exceptions, although it is required according to the Standard Aramaic rules, e.g., after cardinals, after כל and in distributive expressions.

10.1.1. *The Absolute State is Observed when Denoting Indetermination*

QA, JDA: observed.—SLBA: mostly observed אשבית ית‎! רוחין בישין "I adjured evil spirits" (Moussaieff amulet obv. 20'–21'); עבדת לחרשין דינחשה "I practised sorcery of bronze" (HS 3003:4); שביבין דנור וזיו "sparks of fire and splendour" (Moussaieff 155:8); מחשכא עינין ומפחא נפש "(she) darkens eyes and blows out breath" (Gordon B7); רוח טמאה "unclean spirit" (Moussaieff 1:7).

10.1.2. *After כל*

QA, JDA: observed.—SLBA: כל חיזונין סניין כל מינין בישין "all hateful visions, all evil bad sorts" (HSM 3027:3); כל אינש "everyone" (Moussaieff 103:6); בכל גוגין כל‎! עובדין בישין "all evil practices" (Moussaieff amulet obv. 10'); כל ובכל דימון "with all colours and with all apparitions" (HS 3034:4–5); כל אתר "each place" (HS 3003:8); כל דמו "each apparition" (HS 3008:4); כל עררין ואיסרין "all ... and bonds" (HS 3019:1); כל פגעין בישין "all evil plagues" (HS 3001:1–2).

10.1.3. *After Cardinals*

QA, JDA: observed.—SLBA: שבע זבין "seven rivers" (Moussaieff 164:11 < BTA); שבעה חתמין "seven seals" (MSF B14:5); שבעין איסרין "seventy bonds" (Gordon E2); שבעא ניקבין "seven holes" (Moussaieff 1:11); שיתין וארבע פרצופין "sixty-six kings" (Moussaieff 155:10); ושיתא מלאכין "sixty-four faces" (Moussaieff 1:11); תלתא שורין "three walls" (MSF B14:5); תריעשר בנין "twelve sons" (HS 3003:2).

10.1.4. *Distributive*

In distributive expressions the absolute state is the rule.

QA, JDA: observed.—SLBA: בצימחו! צִימְחוּ! גוני! בגוני "by each colour, by each shining" (APM 9163:3).

10.1.5. *Genitive of Material*

QA, JDA: observed.—SLBA: דברזל "of iron" (Wiseman bowl 9); שביבין דנור וזיו "sparks of fire and splendour" (Moussaieff 155:8).

10.1.6. *Proper Nouns*

Proper nouns are used in the absolute state.

QA, JDA: observed.—SLBA: גיהנם "Gehenna" (BM 91763:4, 8); שאול "underworld" (CBS 2916:12); תיביל "Tebel" (Moussaieff 155:5).

10.1.7. *Enumerations*

QA, DJA: observed.—SLBA: בנין ויבנן "sons and daughters" (CBS 2976:8; 11); יד ודרע "hand and arm" (HS 3008:6–7). Often accounts start off with forms in the absolute, but then continue in the emphatic state: ומיפגעין בישין מן מרכבתא בישתא ומיחרשי בישי "and from evil afflictions, from evil chariots and from evil sorcery" (Moussaieff 121:3–4).

10.1.8. *Adverbial expressions*

QA, DJA: observed.—SLBA: ולא בימם ולא בלילי "and neither by daytime nor by night" (Moussaieff 155:6); לא בימם ולא בלילה (CBS 3997:5); בין בימם! בין בלילי "between daytime and nighttime" (Moussaieff amulet rev. 15'–16'); לא בכל רמש וצפר "neither every evening nor morning" (CBS 3997:5); לעלמין "for ever" (Moussaieff 155:8).

10.2. *Genitive Construction*

As in QA and JDA the original Semitic genitive construction is still productive in SLBA in contrast to its neighbouring dialects (BTA, KBA, M). It is noteworthy that this construction often occurs in fixed expressions, e.g., ברחמי שמיא, but there are plenty of other examples where it is still extant. This is a further proof for retaining old syntactical constructions in SLBA from an earlier period. The genitive constructions with בת, בר, and בית have to be taken as compound nouns.

SLBA attestations: אלף אלפין "thousand of thousands" (Moussaieff 164:4 < BTA; both in the absolute as in WA); איסרי עלמא "(magical) bonds of the world" (Geller D3); איסקופת ביתה "the threshold of his house" (HS 3046:2); איסור¹ נחשא ופרזלא "a bond of bronze and iron" (CBS 16087:7); במותב רבי "by the seat of Rabbi" (CBS 9010:2; HS 3046:1; frequent); במרי שמיה¹ ובמרי ארעה "by the lord of heaven and by the lord earth" (MSF B19:7); ברחמי שמיא "by the mercy of heaven" (BM 139524:3) is a frequently occurring phrase; בהיכל נורא וברדא "in a palace of fire and hail" (Moussaieff 155:8); הדמי קומתיה "limbs of his body" (BM 91763:18); לכיף ימא "to the shore of the sea" (BM 91767:13); לסוף תלתין יומין "at the end of thirty days" (BM 91767:5); מחת רוחתא בישתא "the smiting of the evil spirits" (Moussaieff 156:4); מיצרי ביתיה "the boundaries of his house" (BM 136204:7); מלאך מותא "the angel of death" (BM 91767:2); נורי גיהנם "fires of Gehenna" (BM 91763:4); קל גברא "a voice of a man" (BM 91745:6); ריבוꜟ ᵗᶤᶜ ריבון "myriad of myriads" (Moussaieff 164:5; both in the absolute as in WA); רוח מלאכה רבתי "the great spirit of the angel" (BM 139524:9);[81] שכינת אל "dwelling of El (Hebrew ?)" (MSF B22:3); תרעי גיהנם "gates of Gehenna" (BM 91763:8); etc.

10.3. Postposition of כל

One of the noteworthy syntagms is to stress a noun by repeating כל after a noun with a pronominal suffix in postposition. This postposition is known from Biblical Hebrew וכל בית ישראל כלה (Ezek 11:15), but is more widely attested in post Biblical Hebrew כל העולם כולו (p. Demai I,21d).[82] Later it was loaned into JDA in fixed expressions כל אנוש כלה "everybody." Thus the postposition of כל occurs frequently in the Naḥal Ḥever documents:[83] בכל אתר כלה (Babatha document 1:30*). Later one

---

[81] The translation of the genitive construction רוח מלאכה רבתי with a following adjective was misunderstood by Geller, "Four Aramaic Incantation Bowls," 56 and translated as "the spirit—the great Angel of Death." Also Segal, Catalogue, 65, did not understand this construction. According to a common rule in Semitic languages a fixed genitive construction cannot be split up by adjectives. Adjectives referring to the regens must follow after the rectum.

[82] See J.C. Greenfield and E. Qimron, "The Genesis Apocryphon Col. XII," in Studies in Qumran Aramaic, 70–77, esp. 75.

[83] See Y. Yadin et al., eds., The Documents form the Bar Kokhba Period in the Cave of Letters: Hebrew, Aramaic and Nabatean-Aramaic Papyri (JDS; Jerusalem: Israel Exploration Society, 2002), glossary.

finds examples in the *Tosefta to Ezekiel* מכל עלמא כוליה (Ezek 1:1) and in the *Zohar* כל הני רוחין כולהון (Genesis I,45a [ed. Margoliot]). It cannot be traced in Western Aramaic (CPA, GA, SA).[84] This construction can also be observed in SLBA bowl texts: כל רוחין כלהין‎ (MSF B25:6);[85] כל מזיקי כלהון (MSF B25:6); כל גיברי כולהון (AMB B5:8); כל גיברין כולהון (28AL:12 unpublished) but not in the Babylonian Aramaic dialects (BTA, KBA, M). Thus postposition of כל must be considered a Rabbinic linguistic import to Babylonia.

Other examples of postposition of כל in SLBA bowl texts are: מן מיביתיה כוליה "from his whole house" (Moussaieff 101:10); ביתה כוליה (Moussaieff 123:9).

10.4. *Periphrastic Tense*

דהוא כביש שידין "who has suppressed Šedas" (BM 136204:6); דהוא קיים שלמא עלך "that peace has existed for you (sg.m.)" (BM 91745:11); דהוא יתיב על כורסיה "who has been sitting on the throne" (Moussaieff 155:4–5); דהוא שרי בהיכל נורא וברדא "who has been dwelling in a palace of fire and ice" (Moussaieff 155:8).

11. LEXEMES

Many of the lexemes in use since the early Aramaic inscriptions are still extant in QA and continue in Geonic Aramaic, but are not attested otherwise in Late Aramaic, including SLBA. This can be explained by lack of sufficient text material.

11.1. אע *"wood, tree"*

The most interesting lexeme is the word for "wood, tree." It goes back to proto-Semitic *ʕḍ. In the earliest source of its attestation, which is a cuneiform letter of the King of Tyros (735/732) to the Assyrian King of Assarhadon, it is transcribed as *e-qu*.[86] Again it occurs in the Ara-

---

[84] If something is not attested and is not in use it does need to be mentioned in grammatical treatments. Therefore the remark "eine Konstruktion mit doppeltem כול wird in den Grammatiken nicht erwähnt" by Stadel, *Hebraismen*, 24 n. 130 is obsolete.

[85] Corrected in Müller-Kessler, "Glaukom-Dämonin," 79.

[86] 2686:8, 14 in H.W.F. Saggs, ed., *The Nimrud Letters, 1952* (The Cuneiform Texts from Nimrud 5; London: British School of Archaeology in Iraq, 2001), 154. For this

maic Uruk incantation in cuneiform as *iq* (AO 6489:12). In the Idumea ostraca it is spelled עקן (25:2; 167:2), in QA עעין (*ALD* 7:5*), אעא (1Qap-Gen XIV:11). As אע it is attested in *Tg. Onq.* and *Tg. Jon.* and later in Geonic Aramaic. In Western Aramaic it occurs only in the SA Targum and in the Talmud Yerushalmi. This Aramaic lexeme could only survive in Late Aramaic dialects where guttural loss was prevelant. אא was at first dissimilated to /ʔʔ/, finally reduced to two vowels */aʔa/, and then length-ened to */ā/. In Late Aramaic, however, אא was completely replaced by other lexemes as, e.g., אילן "tree" and קיס "wood." A comparable situation also exists for the lexemes עאן "flock" and רחע "to wash" that went out of use on account of dissimilation of ע in initial and final position.[87]

11.2. עבע, אבע "*to hurry*"

There has been a lot of discussion of the root of לעובע "in a hurry" (1QapGen XX:9). It has been demonstrated that it cannot derive from < √בעע,[88] but only from √עבע. The verb lives on in TA in a dissimilated variant √אבע.[89] It is a root only in use in SLA.

11.3. לחח "*to be moist*"

The Hebrew root √לחח "to be moist" occurs in the form of a demon name in לחלחיא דכרא and in the feminine form חלחלית נקבתא (4Q560 1 i 3). It is a reduplication, as in other geminate roots, with metathesis: דרדקיא "little boys," דרדקיתא "little girls" (here with dissimilation /r/ < /d/). This partly preserved incantation text also shows other Hebrew loanwords פשע "crime," עוין "offence" (4Q560 1 i 4).

It is striking that many lexemes containing the phoneme ע, going back to Protosemitic /ḏ/, are only typical for SLA and do not occur in other dialects of Late Aramaic.

---

interpretation see the oral communication by K. Deller in Beyer, *Die aramäischen Texte*, 2:353.

[87] On the question of /ʕ/ based on Protosemitic /ḏ/ in Aramaic lexemes, see J.C. Green-field, "Studies in Aramaic Lexicography I," *JAOS* 82 (1962): 290–299.

[88] Found in M.G. Abegg with J.E. Bowley and E.M. Cook, *The Dead Sea Scrolls Concordance*, vol. 1: *The Non-Biblical Texts from Qumran* (Leiden: Brill, 2003), 801.

[89] See J.C. Greenfield and M. Sokoloff, "The Contribution of Qumran Aramaic to the Aramaic Vocabulary," in *Studies in Qumran Aramaic*, 78–98, esp. 83.

12. Innovations

There exist quite a number of linguistic innovations that are to be noted in the SLBA texts in general. They occur in TA, SLAT, bowl Aramaic, and Geonic. Only a few of the most frequent attested features were picked out here to show how far the eastern texts in SLBA are more developed, and therefore differ from, the QA and JDA dialect types. It is noteworthy that none of the listed characteristics can be traced in any of the pure Western Aramaic dialects (CPA, GA, JPAT, SA), except for לא, certain pronouns and adverbs augmentated by -ה, and the short imperfect of הוי. This clearly places *Tg. Onq.* and *Tg. Jon.* within the dialectal geography of SLBA and makes it feasible that the official Targums originate from the Rabbinic schools in Babylonia. Place of composition is often not identical to place of discovery, e.g., the eastern text sources in the Cairo Genizah.

12.1. *Intervocalic Shift of Labials*

A phonetic feature only to be found in the dialect geography of Babylonia is the intervocalic shift of labials. This shift /m/ < /w/ is frequently attested in the *ištaf'al* of √ידע: אישתמודע in *Tg. Onq.* and *Tg. Jon.* It occurs so far in a KBA bowl text לישתמודע (Moussaieff 102:8) but has not been attested yet in SLBA bowl texts. Such forms are only feasible in the phonetic realm of Babylonia and are not characteristic for WA.

12.2. *Demonstrative Pronouns Augmented by -ה*

The demonstrative pronouns of nearness and distance are augmented by the emphazising element -ה: הדין, הדא, הלין; only for the deictic pronouns of distance ההוא, ההיא, and הליך. One finds hardly any attestations in SLBA. This augmentation is an innovation in Late Aramaic dialects in general, in the west as well as in the east, starting in the first century C.E.[90]

QA: not in use; JDA: first evidence occurs the Judean desert documents.—SLBA: frequent usage, e.g., הדא (HS 3046:2, 5; Moussaieff 101:5); הדין (CBS 8693:5; Moussaieff 112:7).

---

[90] This feature is not suitable for comparing QA and Palmyrene with Targumic Aramaic as proposed by Cook, "New Perspective," 150.

12.3. *Affix* -אה

The affix of ordinals, gentilics, adjectives, and sometimes nouns III-*y* is -י /-āy/ for the masculine forms in QA, JDA, and WA but -אה in SLBA. This linguistic isogloss is restricted to SLA of Babylonia that makes the text source of the *ALD* from the Cairo Genizah (Cambridge T.-S. 16, fol. 94, Bodleian Heb. c. 27) an eastern text witness and not a western. The three attested forms of טומאה "uncleaniness," טומאה (*ALD* 6:1), [sic]אה (*ALD* 6:3), and 'טומאה (*ALD* 6:5) point to an eastern origin of the text. The old reading שור יהודה קדמאה "Judah was the first to jump up" (*ALD* 2:1) is corrected now to קדמא, since there is a clear space after *'ālep* before [משבק.[ל.

12.4. *Plural Emphatic Ending on Masculine Nouns* -י

The short form of the emphatic state on the masculine noun plural is not attested in QA and JDA.—SLBA (TA, SLAT, bowls, and Geonic) and the other Eastern Aramaic dialects obviously use this borrowed morpheme from Akkadian. It might also be a shortened form of *-ē* < **-ayyā*. This plural ending predominates over the former Aramaic ending -אי. The latter is restricted to certain phrases, e.g., שמיא וארעא! וטוריא "heaven and earth and mountains" (CBS 9010:6) and certain words, e.g., plurale tanta שמיא, מיא, חייא.[91]

12.5. *Šafʿel in Aramaic*

It should be pointed out that in QA and JDA, attestations of *šafʿel* and its passive-reflexive stem *ištafʿal* are limited to the loaned verbs from Akkadian in their frozen forms as שיזב, שוצי, and שכלל.[92] The same is true for the preceding and contemporary Aramaic dialects as in Imperial Aramaic, Biblical Aramaic, Nabatean, and Palmyrenean. Only in the

---

[91] How Beyer, *Die aramäischen Texte*, 2:19, comes to the conclusion that the emphatic state plural masculine is represented by *-ayyā* cannot be based on his own study of these texts, since it is not the case. It is repeated again in Juusola, *Linguistic Peculiarities*, 146 since the dissertation on the dialect of Nedarim by S.F. Rybak, "The Aramaic Dialect of Nedarim" (Ph.D. diss., Yeshiva University, 1980), although Rybak on p. 115 really said concerning -אי "Evidence of the written plural emphatic -אי ending, if indeed it was once typical of Nedarim, would be difficult to find."

[92] For the etymology and attestations, see S.A. Kaufman, *The Akkadian Influences on Aramaic* (AS 19; Chicago: University of Chicago Press, 1974), 127–128, and the glossaries in Beyer, *Die aramäischen Texte*, vol. 1, Ergänzungsband, and vol. 2.

Late Aramaic dialects was the *šafᶜel* productive as stem for Aramaic verbs, but it is far more often used in WA than in the EA.[93] In SLBA (TA, SLAT, bowls, and Geonic), one notes a higher distribution than in BTA and Mandaic, e.g., לשצטמא "to shackle" (Moussaieff 101:1) and משצטמת "you (sg.m.) are shackled!" (AMB B12b:3) are in fact *safᶜels* (see above, § 1.2.2); לא תשרגזינה "you (sg.f.) shall not incense her" (Moussaieff 156:13); לישתמודע "he shall inform" (Moussaieff 102:8 in KBA); for TA the following other verbs can be added: שלהב "to enflame," שלחף "to exchange," שעמם "to confuse," שרגג "to entice."[94]

12.6. Suffix of the 1 Singular תי- on Verbs III-y

The suffix of the first person singular in SLBA (TA, SLAT, bowls, and Geonic) on the verbs III-*y* is תי-. It can be taken as an innovation in Babylonia and is obviously a loan from Hebrew, although doubted by Cook and considered curious by Kutscher.[95] What stays unanswered is the fact why this Hebrew morpheme occurs only with this verb class III-*y*: איתיתי "I brought" (Moussaieff 50:4); בריתי "I created" (BM 91707:3); עשיתי "I made" (Moussaieff 50:7) etc. The latter verb can be taken for a clear Hebraism in this text.

12.7. Affix of the 2 Feminine Plural

The affix of the second feminine plural imperfect in SLBA is ן- but its attestation is rare: תישרן "you shall dwell" (BM 91767:3); תירמן "you shall cast" (BM 91767:7).

12.8. Plural Masculine Ending on Participles ן- with Verbs III-y

The plural masculine ending on the participles of the verbs III-*y* ן- is considered by Cook a contraction of איין -: ואתן "and they come" (SD 34:12);

---

[93] The question is where to list the *šafᶜel* stem in the dictionaries. I am of the opinion that only the ones loaned from Akkadian should be listed alphabetically, all the others should be added under the individual root as the stem is regularly in use in the Late Aramaic dialects.

[94] For more examples in Aramaic and Hebrew, see also C. Rabin, "The Nature and Origin of the Šafᶜel in Hebrew and Aramaic," *EI* 9 (1969): 148–158.

[95] See Cook, "New Perspective," 152–153 and E.Y. Kutscher, "Aramaic," *EncJud* 1:259–287; esp. 268. It is not the only morphological feature that was borrowed from Hebrew into SL(B)A as mentioned above (among them noun patterns for colours and directions of the wind; the *nota accusativi* ית etc.)

ממנן[96] ;(123:4 קרני לון מרכבתיה "rays accompany his chariot" (Moussaieff
"they are counted" (Moussaieff 155:10;[97] BM 91767:6); מתחזן "they appear" (Moussaieff 50:2); מסגן "they move about" (Gordon B2); סגן "they
hate" (BM 91767:8); קרן "they are called" (HS 3005:8; Moussaieff 101:13);
שרן "they dwell" (BM 91767:10; CBS 9009:12) etc.

12.9. Short Imperfect

QA and JDA still show the long imperfect of הוי.—SLBA: in this dialect
group the short imperfect form is the rule as in WA יהי (HS 3022:5;
Moussaieff 155:1; AMB B5:1 etc.); תיהון (Moussaieff 164:12 < BTA).

12.10. Negation of the Jussive

אל is still extant in Qumran, but merges in Late Aramaic in general with
לא.

CONCLUSION

In light of the presented linguistic features (graphemes, phonemes, morphemes, and syntagms) it is now obvious that *Tg. Onq.* and *Tg. Jon.*
belong to the dialect geography of Babylonia in the style of a traditional
"Gelehrtensprache." Although Targumic Aramaic still preserves features
of Qumran Aramaic, it is already far more developed than the latter.
Therefore its placement within the group of Middle Aramaic has to be
reconsidered. The occurring Eastern features cannot be simply adduced
to redactional corrections after the transfer of *Tg. Onq.* and *Tg. Jon.* to
Babylonia by a rabbinic group of the Academies of Nehardea, and later
Sura and Pumbeditha. That true eastern features surface in Targum Aramaic of Babylonia is quite natural. Thus it is not only eastern Targum
Aramaic that shows these specific traits but also SLBA in magic bowl
texts, the Aramaic parts of the Babylonian Talmud, and even later the
Aramaic of Geonic *responsa*. Standard Literary Aramaic of Babylonia can
be taken as the true heir of Qumran Aramaic. Qumran Aramaic, however, was never a unified Aramaic dialect, but represents diverse literary
dialects from text sources of obscure backgrounds. With such a small

---

[96] Levene, *Corpus*, 84, did not understand the word לון and took it for a proper noun.
[97] Levene, ibid., 111, 148, corrected מגן to מגין.

Aramaic text basis, surviving mostly in fragmentary states, it is impossible to establish where the *Vorlagen* or originals were composed and compiled, despite convincing arguments by experts of Qumran text criticism. Therefore the diversity in the linguistic elements of Qumran Aramaic presents a non-homogenous language style that differs from text to text.

The linguistic succession of Qumran Aramaic is expected in the Western Aramaic dialect group of Christian Palestinian, Galilean, and Samaritan Aramaic, not in the eastern literary Aramaic group. Also, the Judean legal documents do not seem to have been written in a linguistic style that continued in Western Aramaic, as can be seen from the contrasting infinitives patterns, *maqattālū*, *maqtālū* in Murabbaʿat, Syriac, and through Syriac influence partially in the later period in CPA. *maqattālā*, *maqtālā* is found in Naḥal Ḥever and later in Western Aramaic except for CPA and *qattālā*, *aqtālā* etc., is extant in the Standard Aramaic Literary group (SLBA).[98] Infinitive patterns are the salient indicators of dialect affinities and continuity in Aramaic and should be recognized as an argument for defining dialect relations and the continuation of language traits.

Table 1. Graphic Features

Linguistic features	Qumran Aramaic	Judean Documents	TA, SLAT Geonic Aramaic	SLBA in bowls[99]
ה- for final /ā/	ה- partially in use	ה- partially in use	ה- partially in use	ה- partially in use
ש ⟨ś⟩ for ס	partially in use	partially in use	partially in use	partially in use
non spelling of final root radical י	מומה, emph. מומתה "oath"	מומא	מומתה	מומתה

---

[98] The usage of infinitives in CPA is not popular. One even finds Hebrew absolute infinitive forms without prefix in the *peʿal*, despite its translation from the Greek *Vorlage*. Most of the infinitives are employed as verbal nouns and not in classical infinitive constructions as in the other Aramaic dialects.

[99] A number of features were already discussed by T. Harviainen, *Diglossia in Jewish Eastern Aramaic* (StudOr 55; Helsinki: Finnish Oriental Society, 1983), 97–113. Since Havaianen's article more texts came to our attention that change the view of some morphemes.

Table 2. Phonetic Features

Linguistic features	Qumran Aramaic	Judean Documents	TA, SLAT Geonic Aramaic	SLBA in bowls
Preservation of gutturals	always	always	nearly always	nearly always
Non apocope of consonants	always	always	nearly always	always
nûn not assimilated in pronouns, nouns	always	always	assimilated; not in Geonic	partially
nûn assimilated in מן "from"	מ-	מ-	-(י)מ (regularly)	-(י)מ (often)

Table 3. Independent Personal Pronoun

Linguistic features	Qumran Aramaic	Judean Documents	TA, SLAT Geonic Aramaic	SLBA in bowls
הוא "he"	הוא	הוא	הוא	הוא
היא "she"	היא	היא	היא	היא
אנתה "you (sg.m.)"	אנתה	אנתה	–	אנתא, אנתה
אנת "you (sg.m.)"	–	אנת	אנת	אנת
את "you (sg.m.)"	–	את	את	את
אנתי "you (sg.f.)"	אנתי	א(נ)ת(י)	– (את); אנתי Geonic	אנתי
אנה "I"	אנה	אנה	אנא, אנה	אנא, אנה
א(י)נון "they; them (m.)"	אנון	א(י)נון	א(י)נון	א(י)נון
א(י)נין "they; them (f.)"	א(י)נין	אינין	אינין	אינין
אנתון "you (pl.m.)"	אנתון	not attested	–	אנתון
אתון "you (pl.m.)"	–	–	אתון	אתון
אנתין "you (pl.f.)"	אנתן	not attested	not attested	only אתין!
אנחנא "we"	אנחנא	אנחנא	אנחנא	אנחנא

Table 4. Pronominal Suffixes

Linguistic features	Qumran Aramaic	Judean Documents	TA, SLAT Geonic Aramaic	SLBA in bowls
והי- "his"	והי-	והי-	והי-	והי-
הא-; ה- "her"	ה-; הא-	ה-; הא-	ה-; הא-	ה-; הא-
יכי- "your (sg.f.)"	(י)כי-	(י)כי-	(י)כי-	(י)כי-

Table 5. Demonstrative Pronouns

Linguistic features	Qumran Aramaic	Judean Documents	TA, SLAT Geonic Aramaic	SLBA in bowls
דן "this"	דן	דן	דין	דין
דנן "this"	–	דנן	דנן	דנ(י)ן
דנה "this"	דנה, דנא	דנה, דנא	דנה	דנה
דא "this (f.)"	דא	דא	דא	דא
אלן "these"	אלן, אלן	אלין	אילין, אלין	אילין
אלך "those"	not attested	אלך	אליך	not attested

Table 6. Noun Patterns

Linguistic features	Qumran Aramaic	Judean Documents	TA, SLAT Geonic Aramaic	SLBA in bowls
qatōl for colours	אכום "black" 4QEn^d 2 i 26 ירוק "green" 11QtgJob XXXIX:8	שקומא "red"	ירוק "green, yellow" סמוקתא "red" Deut 19:2 *Tg. Onq.*	ירוק
qatōl for the directions of the wind	דרומא "south" צפונא "north" קדום "east"	דרומא צפונא –	דרומא not attested –	דרומא צפונא –

Table 7. Prepositions and Conjunctions

Linguistic features	Qumran Aramaic	Judean Documents	TA, SLAT Geonic Aramaic	SLBA in bowls
אם "if"	אם	not attested	–	אם
אף "also"	אף	not attested	אף	אף
ארי "since"	ארו 11QtgJob XXVIII:23	–	ארי	–
בדיל "because of"	בדיל בדילה 11QtgJob XLII:10	not attested	בדיל	בדיל
בדיל די "since"	בדיל די 11QtgJob XXXVII:17*	בדיל די	בדיל ד-	בדיל ד-
כדי "when"	כדי	כדי	כד	כד
כמה די	כמה/א די	not attested	כמה/א די	כמה/א די

Table 8. Direct Object Marker

Linguistic features	Qumran Aramaic	Judean Documents	TA, SLAT Geonic Aramaic	SLBA in bowls
Not marked	often	often	rarely	rarely
Object suffixes	preference	preference	preference	rarely
Nota accusativi	ית	ית	ית	ית
ית + pronominal suffixes	יתה 11QtgJob XL:30	יתה etc.	יתיה etc.	יתיה etc.
-ל object marker	-ל rarely employed	-ל rarely employed	-ל rarely employed	-ל rarely employed

Table 9. Verb Inflection

Linguistic features	Qumran Aramaic	Judean Documents	TA, SLAT Geonic Aramaic	SLBA in bowls
Suffix perfect 2 sg.m.	תה-, תא-	not attested	תא-	not attested
Suffix perfect 3 pl.f. III-*y*	אה-	not attested	אה-	אה-
Prefix imperfect 3 m.	י-	י-	י-	י-
Affix imperfect 2 sg.f.	ין-	ין-	ין-	ין-
Affix imperfect 2 sg.f. III-*y*	not attested	יין-	יין-	יין-
Affix imperative 2 sg.f.	י-	not attested	י-	י-
Infinitive patterns				
pa"el קטלה	*pa"el* קטלה	*pa"el* מקטלה מקטלו	*pa"el* קטלא	*pa"el* קטלא
af'el הקטלה	*af'el* הקטלה	*af'el* הקטלה מקטלה	*af'el* אקטלא	*af'el* אקטלא

Table 10. Syntagms

Linguistic features	Qumran Aramaic	Judean Documents	TA, SLAT Geonic Aramaic	SLBA in bowls
Absolute state	observed	observed	observed	observed
	a) general	a) general	a) general	a) general
	b) attributive	b) attributive	b) attributive	b) attributive
	c) after כל	c) after כל	c) after כל	c) after כל
	d) after cardinals	d) after cardinals	d) after cardinals	d) after cardinals
	e) distributive	e) distributive	e) distributive	e) distributive
	f) genitive of material	f) genitive of material	f) genitive of material	f) genitive of material
	g) proper nouns	g) proper nouns	g) proper nouns	g) proper nouns
	h) enumeration	h) enumeration	h) enumeration	h) enumeration
	i) adverbs	i) adverbs	i) adverbs	i) adverbs
Postposition of כל	attested	not attested	attested	attested
Construct state	preference	preference	preference	preference

Table 11. Lexemes

Linguistic features	Qumran Aramaic	Judean Documents	TA, SLAT Geonic Aramaic	SLBA in bowls
אימה "fright"	אימה 11QtgJob XXXIX:20 אימתכן 1QapGen XI:17	not attested; later in SA Targum; JPA	אימתה Exod 15:16 *Tg. Onq.*	not attested
אע "wood, tree"	אעא 1QapGen XIV:11 עעין *ALD* 7:5*	אעי *Fast Scroll*; later in SA Targum, JPA Targum	אעא e.g., Lev 14:4 *Tg. Onq. Shimmush de-Tefillin* 488:1	not attested
√חזי "to see"	√חזי	√חזי	√חזי	√חזי
√יכל < Hebrew "to be able"[100]	√יכל	√יכל	√יכל	not attested
לחח < Hebrew "to be moist"	*לחח	not attested	not attested	not attested
√נטל < Hebrew "to lift"	√נטל	not attested	√נטל	*√נטל[101]
√נשי "to take"	√נשי	not attested	נסי√ ,נשי√	not attested[102]
עאן "flock"	עאן	not attested	עאן	not attested
√עבע "to hurry"	עבע√ מבע *af'el* 11QtgJob XX:5	not attested	אבע√ *af'el* TA; אבע√ *af'el* ייבע Letter of R. Šarrira Gaon 122:1	not attested
√רחע "to wash"	√רחע "to wash"	not attested	√רחע "to wash" *ALD* 7:2, 3; 8:2, 4	not attested

---

[100] It is a definite loan from Hebrew since Qumran Aramaic onwards, as the Aramaic root √כהל came out of use after Imperial Aramaic and did not merge with √יכל. The reading in 4QEnGiants[b] ar (4Q530) 5 2 is doubtful. As for many other lexemes their occurrence depends on the text genre.

[101] The reading of תינטלון (Moussaieff 123:8) is incorrect, since the text shows clearly תיבטלון; see Müller-Kessler, "Of Jesus, Darius," 229.

[102] Is not extant in the Babylonian Aramaic dialects (BTA, KBA, M).

Table 12. Innovations

Linguistic features	Qumran Aramaic	Judean Documents	TA, SLAT Geonic Aramaic	SLBA in bowls
אישתמודע *ištafʿal* √ידע‎ /m/ < /w/	not in use	not in use	אישתמודע Tg. Onq., Tg. Jon.	אישתמודע
augmented by ה- הדין "this (m.)"	not in use	not attested	הדין	הדין
הדא "this (f.)"	not in use	הדא	הדא	הדא
הלין "these"	not in use	not in use	הלין	הלין
אה- suffix	not in use	not in use	אה- suffix קדמאה טומאה	אה- suffix קדמאה טומאה
י- plural emph. on m. nouns	not in use	not in use	י-; rarely אי-	י-; rarely אי-
šafʿel	only in borrowed Akkadian verbs	only in borrowed Akkadian verbs	*šafʿel* with Aramaic roots	*šafʿel* with Aramaic roots
תי- suffix perfect 1 sg. on verbs III-*y*	not in use	not in use	תי-	תי-
ן- affix 2 sg. f. on verbs III-*y*	not in use	not in use	ן-	ן-
ן- plur. m. of participles on verbs III-*y*	יין-	ין-	ן-	ן-
Short imperfect √הוי "to be"	(long imperfect)	(long imperfect) but תהון Mur 21 15	short imperfect	short imperfect
Negation particle for jussive	אל	לא	לא	לא

THE HEBREW BIBLE AND OTHER
SECOND TEMPLE JEWISH LITERATURE
IN LIGHT OF THE DEAD SEA SCROLLS

LEVITICUS IN THE LIGHT OF THE DEAD SEA SCROLLS: ATONEMENT AND PURIFICATION FROM SIN[*]

MILA GINSBURSKAYA
University of Birmingham

INTRODUCTION

In D. Lodge's novel *Small World*, a well-known satire on academic life, a young scholar jokingly tells a publisher that the topic of his dissertation is T.S. Eliot's influence on Shakespeare. However absurd this inverse perspective may sound, it definitely appeals to the publisher who immediately offers the young man a contract. Although reading the Bible in the light of the Dead Sea Scrolls may similarly come across as paradoxical, this is exactly what I am going to propose in the present paper. As I hope to demonstrate, certain concepts in the Scrolls, rather than being a later development, seem to spell out what remained implicit or understated in the Hebrew Bible and can therefore be taken as an important witness to biblical thought. Obviously, the earlier we date the scrolls and the later we date the final redaction of the biblical texts, the more the likelihood of the ideological/theological continuity increases, although it is not necessary to accept the minimalist position in order to benefit from the approach being advanced here.[1]

The focus of my present investigation is the concept of atonement for sin and how it relates to the ideas of purification and divine forgiveness. I examine texts that involve cultic and non-cultic atonement, both in the Hebrew Bible and in the Qumran corpus, with reference to terminology and underlying concepts.[2]

---

[*] I am grateful to James Aitken, Philip Jenson, Jutta Jokiranta, and Siam Bhayro who read this paper at different stages of its development and shared with me their insightful comments.

[1] Late dating was advocated, e.g., by P.R. Davies, *In Search of 'Ancient Israel'* (JSOTSup 148; Sheffield: JSOT Press, 1992) and N.P. Lemche, "The Old Testament: A Hellenistic Book?" in *Did Moses Speak Attic?* (ed. L.L. Grabbe; JSOTSup 317; Sheffield: Sheffield Academic Press, 2001), 287–318. For further discussion and criticism of this view see W.M. Schniedewind, *How the Bible Became a Book: The Textualization of Ancient Israel* (Cambridge: Cambridge University Press, 2004).

[2] I use the word "atonement" or "expiation" to render the Hebrew כִּפֶּר.

I. Atonement, Forgiveness, and Purification
in Leviticus and the *Temple Scroll*

The verb כִּפֶּר in Leviticus and other cultic texts of the Hebrew Bible refers specifically to sacrificial rituals in the context of atonement for major physical impurities (e.g., those resulting from leprosy or abnormal genital discharges) and in the context of the expiation of sin/transgression.[3] In this section I limit my discussion to the latter, which in due course I will compare with atoning sacrifices for physical impurities.

There are two types of atoning sacrifices for sins in Leviticus and Numbers: individual sacrifices performed throughout the year (Lev 4–5; 19:21–22; Num 5:6–9; 15:22–29) and the collective non-specific sacrifices of the Day of Atonement, which coincide with the overall purgation of the sanctuary. Although these rituals have many elements in common, the language describing the outcome of the sacrificial procedures varies. Thus, the outcome of the individual atoning rites is described in terms of forgiveness, while Lev 16 uses the terminology of purification. Compare:

וכפר עליו הכהן (לפני יי) ונסלח לו	כי ביום הזה יכפר עליכם **לטהר** אתכם מכל חטאתיכם לפני יי **תטהרו**
And the priest shall perform the act of atonement for him, and he shall be **forgiven**[4]	for on this day shall atonement be made for you, to **cleanse** you; from all your sins you shall be **clean** before the LORD
(Lev 4:20, 26, 31, 35; 5:10, 13, 16,* 18,* 26;* 19:22;*5 Num 15:28)	(Lev 16:30)

---

[3] There is a discussion as to what types of transgressions required sacrificial remedy. According to I. Knohl, *The Sanctuary of Silence: The Priestly Torah and the Holiness School* (Minneapolis: Fortress, 1995), 139–140, 175–186 and passim, it concerned only cultic transgressions. Cf. M. Douglas, *Leviticus as Literature* (Oxford: Oxford University Press, 1999), 132. While I agree with Knohl that initially this might have been the case, it appears that by the time the final redaction of Leviticus and Numbers took place, the scope of atoning sacrifices was widened to include *any* transgression of God's commandments (Num 15:22).

[4] Biblical translations are based on the RSV. Qumran texts and translations are based on: E. Tov, ed., *The Dead Sea Scrolls Electronic Reference Library* (rev. ed.; Leiden: Brill, 2006) and F. García Martínez and E.J.C. Tigchelaar, *The Dead Sea Scrolls Study Edition* (2 vols.; Leiden: Brill, 1997–1998).

[5] Instances indicated with an asterisk are those requiring אשם. See n. 8 below.

What shall we conclude about this terminological inconsistency? Does it indicate that purification is not envisioned in the individual atoning rites or that forgiveness is not envisioned on Yom Kippur? This is suggested, for example, by R.E. Gane, who develops a theory of a two-stage purification, according to which individual sacrifices throughout the year procure forgiveness, while the Day of Atonement rituals bring about purification "beyond forgiveness."[6]

Gane's reading presupposes that Leviticus, with pharmaceutical precision, lays down in exact words the recipes for carrying out the rituals, so that a change of a word would signal a change of a concept. Meanwhile, as Klingbeil rightly noted, "in the ancient texts the author's intention was not always to provide a minutely detailed account to be used in a court case setup, but rather to artistically interconnect information, give subtle clues."[7] We therefore need to look not only at linguistic but also at structural parallels between the rituals performed in similar contexts and use imagination, logic, and conceptual thinking to decipher these abbreviated accounts. Below I argue that structural and conceptual similarities between various atoning rituals requiring the חטאת offering suggest the unity of their goal, which could be identified as purification.[8]

I.1. חטאת as Purification Offering

Milgrom contended that חטאת was a purification offering par excellence.[9] He argued, however, that חטאת purified *only* the sanctuary—never the offerer. His argument is based on texts where the purpose of כִּפֶּר (+ sanctuary/altar as a direct object) is elucidated by the verbs חִטֵּא (e.g.,

---

[6] R.E. Gane, *Cult and Character: Purification Offerings, Day of Atonement and Theodicy* (Winona Lake: Eisenbrauns, 2005), esp. 233–241, 267–284.

[7] G.A. Klingbeil, "Altars, Ritual and Theology—Preliminary Thoughts on the Importance of Cult and Ritual for a Theology of the Hebrew Scripture," *VT* 54 (2004): 495–515, 507.

[8] In addition to חטאת, there is another atoning offering, אשם. The difficulty in distinguishing between the two has been acknowledged by many scholars. See, e.g., J. Milgrom, *Cult and Conscience: The Asham and the Priestly Doctrine of Repentance* (SJLA 18; Leiden: Brill, 1976), 1 and passim; B.A. Levine, *In The Presence of the Lord: A Study of Cult and Some Cultic Terms in Ancient Israel* (Leiden: Brill, 1974), 91–114. According to Milgrom, only חטאת has the function of purification (see discussion below). I am personally inclined to believe that אשם, required in certain cases of graver offences, constitutes a subtype of חטאת, with similar functions. In this paper, however, I limit my discussion to the instances with חטאת, whose scope of application is wider.

[9] J. Milgrom, "Israel's Sanctuary: The Priestly 'Picture of Dorian Gray,'" *RB* 83 (1976): 390–399.

Exod 29:36; Lev 8:15; Ezek 43:20) and טִהַר (e.g., Lev 16:18–19; Ezek 43:26) and on the observation that כִּפֶּר never takes a human person as a direct object.[10] He thus construes that the act of purgation "is not carried out on the offerer but only on his behalf."[11] This conclusion is, however, in tension with Lev 16:30, which speaks of the purification of the people.

My suggested solution to the problem was prompted by Milgrom's own ingenious comparison of the priestly doctrine of defilement with The Picture of Dorian Gray: "On the analogy of Oscar Wilde's novel, the priestly writers would claim: sin may not leave its mark on the face of the sinner, but it is certain to mark the face of the sanctuary."[12] The portrait acted as a kind of mirror—reflecting the inner condition of its owner/subject. Exactly the same principle seems to underlie the biblical concept of the defilement of the sanctuary and the land: it reflects the measure of impurity among the people of Israel, functioning as a kind of a "spiritual barometer" (another of Milgrom's metaphors) which evaluates the state of divine-human affairs.[13] If this model is correct, then it would also be logical to assume that the purification of the sanctuary would coincide with the purification of the people achieved by means of the same atoning offerings.[14] Indeed Lev 16:30 is generally believed to refer back to vv. 15–16, describing the purification of the sanctuary by the sacrifice of the חטאת-goat "for the Lord" on behalf of the people.[15]

---

[10] כִּפֶּר with people or individuals always requires indirect prepositions (עַל, ל, בעד), while both direct (כִּפֶּר + אֶת) and indirect (כִּפֶּר + בעד, ל, עַל) constructions are possible with inanimate objects. See the summaries in B. Janowski, Sühne als Heilsgeschehen: Studien zur Sühnetheologie der Priesterschrift und zur Wurzel KPR im Alten Orient und im Alten Testament (WMANT 55; Neukirchen-Vluyn: Neukirchener Verlag, 1982), 186–189 and J. Sklar, Sin, Impurity, Sacrifice, Atonement: The Priestly Conceptions (Hebrew Bible Monographs 2; Sheffield: Sheffield Phoenix Press, 2005), 188–189. In cultic texts, the sanctuary or the people are the usual objects of כִּפֶּר; in non-cultic these are "people" or "sins." It could be argued that in the construction כִּפֶּר + direct object the notion of cleansing is more enhanced. Thus, e.g., Levine, In The Presence of the Lord, 56–66 and J. Milgrom, Leviticus 1–16: A New Translation with Introduction and Commentary (AB 3; New York: Doubleday, 1991), 1079–1084.

[11] Milgrom, "Israel's Sanctuary," 391. Cf. N. Kiuchi, The Purification Offering in the Priestly Literature: Its Meaning and Function (JSOTSup 56; Sheffield: JSOT Press, 1987), 87–109; Gane, Cult and Character, 106–143.

[12] Milgrom, "Israel's Sanctuary," 398.

[13] Ibid.

[14] Kiuchi also arrives at this conclusion, Purification Offering, 61–65 and idem, Leviticus (Apollos Old Testament Commentary 3; Nottingham: Apollos, 2007), 310.

[15] Another possibility is that the verse refers to the scapegoat ritual. Milgrom, Leviticus, 1056, considers the two options as alternatives, while Gane, Cult and Character, esp. 106–143, 242–266; B.J. Schwartz, "The Bearing of Sin in the Priestly Literature," in Pomegranates and Golden Bells: Studies in Biblical, Jewish, and Near Eastern Ritual,

Notably, commenting on Lev 16:30, Milgrom himself is compelled to admit that "as the sanctuary is polluted by the people's impurities, their elimination, in effect, also purifies the people."[16]

I.2. *Purification and Forgiveness in Individual Atoning Rituals*

This principle of the Day of Atonement rituals can be extended to the individual atoning sacrifices performed throughout the year, as they have many elements in common. They share the same offering (חטאת), the same locus (sanctuary), a similar sequence of actions (sacrificial slaughter; sprinkling and/or smearing of blood on parts of the sanctuary, etc.) and the same actors (the offerer, on whose behalf the ritual is carried out, the priest who performs it, and God behind the scenes). A double purification of offerer and sanctuary could thus be perceived as the outcome of all חטאת-rituals in the context of atonement.

Although the concluding formula for the individual atoning rituals in the context of sin involves the notion of forgiveness, structurally these rituals are identical with those atoning for major physical impurities, which, just as the rites of the Day of Atonement, are concluded with טהר:[17]

Atonement for sins	Atonement for physical impurities
וכפר עליו הכהן ונסלח לו	וכפר עליו הכהן וטהר
(Lev 4:20, 26, 31, 35; 5:10, 13, 16,* 18,* 26;* 19:22;* Num 15:28)	Lev 12:8; 14:20

Giving more weight to such structural and conceptual similarities, I would assume that here also purification is envisaged as the ultimate outcome of the rituals of atonement for sin. I consider the reasons for the variation in terminology below.

Law, And Literature in Honor of Jacob Milgrom (ed. D.P. Wright, D.N. Freedman, and A. Hurvitz; Winona Lake: Eisenbrauns, 1995), 17–18, and Kiuchi, *Leviticus*, 303–305 attempt to reconcile them. Most scholars nonetheless believe that the Azazel-goat ritual has an independent history and was at some stage incorporated into the Day of Atonement rituals. For a comprehensive review of existing theories and an alternative proposition see A. Pinker, "A Goat to Go to Azazel," *Journal of Hebrew Scriptures* 7 (2007): 2–25.

[16] Milgrom, *Leviticus*, 1056.

[17] Notably Lev 16:16 suggests that the same offering purifies the sanctuary from both physical and sin-impurities.

I.3. *Forgiveness and Purification on the Day of Atonement*

Terminology notwithstanding, most interpretations of Leviticus have maintained that the Day of Atonement does provide forgiveness from all sorts of moral faults.[18] This interpretation is supported by the evidence of the *Temple Scroll* which "corrects" the "omission" of Lev 16 (11QT[a] XXVI:3–10).[19] There the description of the sacrifice of the חטאת-goat "for the Lord," with which atonement is made on behalf of the people, is concluded with the following statement:

9 … (for it is) the sin offering for the assembly; and he shall atone with it for all the people of the assembly,	9 … חטאת הקהל הוא ויכפר בו על כול עם הקהל
10 and they shall be **forgiven**.	10 ונסלח להמה

The terminology of purification that characterizes Lev 16:30 is replaced in 11QT[a] XXVI:9–10 with the terminology of forgiveness, reiterated also in 11QT[a] XXVII:2, concluding the exposition on the Day of Atonement.[20] Although the word "sins" (חטאים) is also absent from this passage, which constitutes yet another terminological discrepancy with Lev 16:30,[21] it is almost certain that sins and not physical impurities are envisioned here, as the notion of forgiveness suggests. The *Temple Scroll* thus harmonizes the Day of Atonement with levitical accounts of the individual atoning sacrifices throughout the year. While Gane considers this harmonization to be a later development,[22] it seems more likely that, by evoking the notion of forgiveness, the *Temple Scroll* spells out what remained implicit

---

[18] Thus, e.g., S.A. Geller, "Blood Cult: Toward a Literary Theology of the Priestly Work of the Pentateuch," *Proof* 12 (1992): 107–110; A. Schenker, *Versöhnung und Sühne: Wege gewaltfreier Konfliktlösung im Alten Testament: mit einem Ausblick auf das Neue Testament* (BibB 15; Freiburg: Schweizerisches Katholisches Bibelwerk, 1981), 112–116. See more bibliography and discussion in Gane, *Cult and Character*, 233–235. In Jenson's words, "purification of the sanctuary and the offerer is … the way in which the forgiveness of sins is expressed": P. Jenson, *Graded Holiness: A Key to the Priestly Conception of the World* (JSOTSup 106; Sheffield: Sheffield Academic Press, 1992), 159.

[19] On the structural analysis of the *Temple Scroll* passages on the Day of Atonement see D. Volgger, "The Day of Atonement according to the Temple Scroll," *Bib* 87 (2006): 251–260.

[20] The forgiveness formula in 11QT[a] XXVI describing the outcome of the ritual is attached immediately to the description of the sacrifice of the goat "for the Lord," which reinforces the possibility of Lev 16:30 relating back to Lev 16:15–20 rather than to the scapegoat ritual (Lev 20–22).

[21] I am grateful to George Brooke for drawing my attention to this detail.

[22] Gane, *Cult and Character*, 233–235.

in Lev 16, which focused primarily on the theme of purgation.[23] This is even more plausible if we accept the early dating of the scroll.[24]

I.4. *Conceptual Considerations*

If the interchange of the terminology does not indicate the change of a concept, how then shall we relate the notions of forgiveness and purification? Are they completely synonymous? And if not, what is the difference?

If we consider that the concept of impurity indicates deviation from the original state of purity and integrity, it is logical and natural that the restoration of a person to his/her original state would be conceived in terms of purification, which is achieved by *means* of atonement. On the other hand, since sin/transgression is an offence against God, the process of purification in this case cannot take place without God's forgiveness, the element notably absent from atonement for physical impurities. The whole process can be visualized with the help of the diagram (see Plate 1 on p. 270).[25]

I would agree with Gane that forgiveness is a prerequisite for purification, but suggest that every atoning ritual entails both. In fact, the two notions are linked inseparably, and it is precisely because of their relation that they can be used alternatively in different texts. Depending on the context and the goals of the author/editor, one of the notions may be emphasized, thus coming into the foreground, while the other remains

---

[23] Regarding the reworking of the Pentateuch in the *Temple Scroll*, see, e.g., L.H. Schiffman, "The Case of the Day of Atonement," in *Biblical Perspectives: Early Use and Interpretation of the Bible in Light of the Dead Sea Scrolls, Proceedings of the First International Symposium of the Orion Centre for the Study of the Dead Sea Scrolls and Associated Literature, 12–14 May, 1996* (ed. M.E. Stone and E.G. Chazon; STDJ 28; Leiden: Brill, 1998), 181–188 and G.J. Brooke, "The Temple Scroll: A Law Unto Itself?" in *Law and Religion: Essays on the Place of the Law in Israel and Early Christianity* (ed. B. Lindars; Cambridge: Clarke, 1988), 34–43, and esp. 41 on the Day of Atonement.

[24] The earliest dating (fifth to second centuries B.C.E.) was proposed by H. Stegemann, "The Literary Composition of the Temple Scroll and Its Status at Qumran," in *Temple Scroll Studies: Papers Presented at the International Symposium on the Temple Scroll, Manchester, December 1987* (ed. G.J. Brooke; JSPSup 7; Sheffield: JSOT Press, 1989), 123–148. Most scholars however seem to uphold Yadin's placement of the scroll within the Hasmonean period: Y. Yadin, *The Temple Scroll* (4 vols.; Jerusalem: Israel Exploration Society, 1983) 1:386–390. See the review of opinions in M.O. Wise, *A Critical Study of the Temple Scroll from Qumran Cave 11* (SAOC 49; Chicago: The Oriental Institute, 1990), 26–31, 189–194.

[25] I do not discuss here steps 1–3 given the limited scope of this paper. On suffering sin's consequences leading to realization of sin see, e.g., Sklar, *Sin, Impurity*, 39–43.

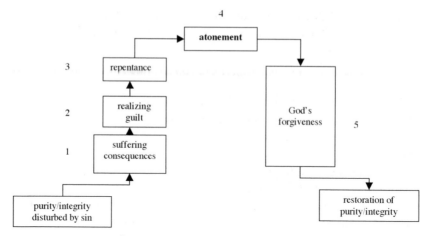

Plate 1. Structural Relationship between
Atonement, Forgiveness and Purification

in the background.[26] In the minds of people sharing the same ideological/theological milieu, however, one would have inextricably evoked the other.

In cultic texts, atonement, with all its complex elements, is presented as a means for achieving forgiveness and purification. It may be taken in a wider sense, however, encompassing also the outcome.[27] It is therefore possible—and indeed it happens in non-cultic texts—that the terminology of atonement may also be used interchangeably with the terminology of forgiveness and purification.

II. Atonement, Forgiveness, and Purification in Non-Cultic Texts (Hebrew Bible and Dead Sea Scrolls)

II.1. *Hebrew Bible*

In non-cultic texts of the Hebrew Bible, particularly in the Psalms, we observe the synonymous alternation of the verbs כִּפֶּר, טהר and סלח. For example, Ps 65:4 uses the terminology of atonement:

---

[26] See the discussion in J. Goldingay, *Theological Diversity and Authority of the Old Testament* (Grand Rapids: Eerdmans, 1987), 29–58.

[27] Indeed one of the possible derivations of the Hebrew כִּפֶּר is from the Akkadian verb *kuppuru* [D stem of *kapāru* II], "to wipe clean." This cognate notwithstanding, the concept of cultic (and non-cultic) atonement in the Hebrew Bible is more complex and cannot be reduced solely to the notion of cleansing.

When our transgressions prevail over us, thou **atone**[28] for them.

דִּבְרֵי עֲוֹנֹת גָּבְרוּ מֶנִּי פְּשָׁעֵינוּ אַתָּה תְכַפְּרֵם:

Ps 51:4 prefers the language of purification:

Wash me thoroughly from my iniquity, and **cleanse** me from my sin!

הֶרֶבה כַּבְּסֵנִי מֵעֲוֹנִי וּמֵחַטָּאתִי טַהֲרֵנִי:

And Jer 31:34 employs the terminology of forgiveness:

for I will **forgive** their iniquity, and I will remember their sin no more.

כִּי אֶסְלַח לַעֲוֹנָם וּלְחַטָּאתָם לֹא אֶזְכָּר־עוֹד:

It is clear from the context that in all these examples the different terms are used to convey the same idea: removal of the stain of transgression from a person and restoration of his/her relationship with God.

In Jer 33:8 the terms טהר and סלח appear in parallel (or complementary) clauses:

I will **cleanse** them from all the guilt of their sin against me,
and I will **forgive** all the guilt of their sin and rebellion against me.

וְטִהַרְתִּים מִכָּל־עֲוֹנָם אֲשֶׁר חָטְאוּ־לִי
וְסָלַחְתִּי לְכָול־עֲוֹנוֹתֵיהֶם אֲשֶׁר חָטְאוּ־לִי וַאֲשֶׁר פָּשְׁעוּ בִי:

In Jer 18:23 the parallelism is between כִּפֵּר and מחה חטא (another expression used in the Bible to convey the notion of forgiveness):[29]

Yet, thou, O LORD, knowest all their plotting to slay me.
Atone[30] not for their iniquity, nor **blot out their sin** from thy sight.

וְאַתָּה יְהוָה יָדַעְתָּ אֶת־כָּל־עֲצָתָם עָלַי לַמָּוֶת
אַל־תְּכַפֵּר עַל־עֲוֹנָם וְחַטָּאתָם מִלְּפָנֶיךָ אַל־תֶּמְחִי:

The three terms alternate freely, which highlights their conceptual interrelation. If we possessed only non-cultic texts, however, it would be difficult to distinguish between them. It is the cultic texts presenting forgiveness/purification as an *outcome* of the process of atonement that enable us to establish the structural and consequential relationship between these notions.

---

[28] RSV: "forgive."

[29] Cf. other texts which use the terminology of נשא עָוֹן (e.g., Ps 85:3) and מחה/פֶּשַׁע/חטא עָוֹן (e.g., Ps 51:3, 11; Isa 43:25; 44:22). On these constructions see Schwartz "The Bearing of Sin," 8–21. In Ezek 37:23 we find הושעתי + טהר—the notion of salvation/deliverance, which approximates one of the possible meanings of כִּפֵּר. In Isa 6:5 כִּפֵּר is paired with סר עֲוֹנֶךָ.

[30] RSV: "forgive."

II.2. *Dead Sea Scrolls*

The interplay of the terminology of atonement, purification, and forgiveness becomes a common feature in many predominantly non-cultic
Qumran texts, in contrast to the Hebrew Bible where the phenomenon is
limited to the few examples listed above. Moreover, while in the Hebrew
Bible Jer 33:8 is the only verse that simultaneously employs the two technical terms also used in cultic texts (טהר and סלח), in the Scrolls we often
encounter interchangeable terminological pairs, with the third notion
usually being conveyed by a synonym or otherwise suggested by the
immediate context. Below I review passages containing the terminological pairs of טהר + כִּפֶּר, כִּפֶּר + סלח, טהר + סלח.

כִּפֶּר *and* טהר

In the following passages כִּפֶּר and טהר appear in adjacent clauses; the
third technical term סלח is absent, but the notion of God's forgiveness is
conveyed through other terms, such as חסד or רחמים. Thus, for example,
in 1QS XI:14–15 God in his mercy/compassion reinstates fellowship
with a repentant sinner, atoning for and purifying him from bodily
uncleanness and from defilement of sins:

> he will draw me near in his mercies, and by kindnesses set in motion [14]
> my judgment; he will judge me in the righteousness of his truth, and in his
> plentiful goodness always **atone** for all my sins; in his righteousness he will
> **cleanse** me from the uncleanness of the human being [15] and from the
> sin of the sons of man.

> ברחמיו הגישני ובחסדיו יביא [14] משפטי בצדקת אמתו שפטני וברוב טובו יכפר בעד
> כול עוונותי ובצדקתו **יטהרני** מנדת [15] אנוש וחטאת בני אדם.

The terminology of atonement and purification following the evocation
of God's compassion features also in 1QH[a] XII:37:

> For I leaned [37] on your kindness and the abundance of your compas-
> sion. For you **atone** iniquity and cle[anse] man of his guilt through your
> righteousness.

> נשען[ת]י [37] בחסדיכה והמון רחמיכה כי **תכפר** עוון **ולטה[ר**]אנוש מאשמה
> בצדקתכה.

In 1QH[a] IV:11–12 "purify/purified" seems to be a plausible reconstruction,[31] as the notions of God's compassion/mercy and the removal of sins

---

[31] Thus, e.g., García Martínez and Tigchelaar, *The Dead Sea Scrolls Study Edition*,

are likewise present. If the reconstruction is correct, the notions of bearing away sin and of atonement here seem to explain how purification from sin is achieved. Also, in the examples quoted above, purification seems to be presented as an outcome of the atoning act. This supports my suggested sequential relationship between the elements of forgiveness, atonement and purification.

כִּפֶּר and סלח

כִּפֶּר in conjunction with סלח appears in 1QS II:8, where the community curses "all men of the lot of Belial":

> May God not be merciful when you entreat him. May he not **forgive** by **atoning** for your sins.

ולוא יחונכה אל בקוראכה ולוא יסלח לכפר עוווניך.

The passage containing this curse is followed by a proclamation of the impossibility of purification for those who do not return to God (III:4–6). Thus, in spite of the absence of the term טהר, the theme of purification is evoked by the immediate context.

Sometimes a specific technical term may be replaced by a synonymous phrase. Thus, for example, in CD 2:4–5 (= 4Q266 2 ii 4–5) the notion of forgiveness is communicated with the phrase רוב סליחות, rather than with the verb סלח:

> patience with him and **abundance of pardon**, [5] to **atone** for those who repent from sin.

ארך אפים עמו ורוב סליחות [5] לכפר בעד כל שבי פשע.

Compare CD 3:17–18, where the notion of divine forgiveness is conveyed by the expression וישא לפשעם, while the theme of purification is evoked through the language of defilement:

> And although they had wallowed in the sin of humanity and in impure ways and said, "Surely this is our business," God in His mysterious ways **atoned** for their iniquity and **bore away** their transgression.

והם התגוללו בפשע אנוש ובדרכי נדה
ויאמרֹו כי לנו היא ואל ברזי פלאו כפר בעד עונם וישא לפשעם

1:148–149; M. Mansoor, *The Thanksgiving Hymns Translated and Annotated with an Introduction* (STDJ 3; Leiden: Brill, 1961), 188; J. Licht, *The Thanksgiving Scroll: A Scroll from the Wilderness of Judaea: Text, Introduction, Commentary and Glossary* (Jerusalem: Bialik Institute, 1957), 207.

סלח *and* טהר

The combination of סלח with טהר is particularly characteristic for the
Hodayot and the Psalms scroll 11QPsᵃ. Thus in 11Q5 XIX:13–14 (= 11Q6
4–5 14–15) we read:

> **Forgive** my sin, O LORD, [14] and **cleanse me** from my iniquity[32]

סלחה ‎חטאתי [14] **וטהרני** מעווני

Apart from סלח, the terms סליחות, רוב סליחות, נחמה and רחמים are employed in the *Hodayot* in combination with טהר to refer to God who in
his compassion purifies man from the defilement of sin (1QHᵃ IX:31–32;
XIV:8–9; XV:29–30; XIX:9–11, 30–32).

III. Between Cultic and Non-Cultic: The Witness of Dead Sea Scrolls

We have established the close association between the concepts of atonement, forgiveness, and purification, which allows for the interplay of terminology. This feature is particularly characteristic of non-cultic texts,
but can also occur in cultic texts. I have suggested that terminology alone
is not a sufficient criterion for interpretation, and we need to broaden the
scope of our analysis and consider the underlying concepts to try to pen-
etrate the logic of ritual.

This discussion has implications for the ongoing debate on whether
cultic and non-cultic texts represent conflicting or compatible/comple-
mentary ideologies.[33] In light of my analysis, I am inclined to support
the second option. Of course, there are differences in the way these texts
address the idea of atonement and its related issues, but these differences
appear to be due more to the peculiarities and specific concerns of each
particular genre, rather than to a contradiction between them. If we look
at Leviticus through the lens of the approach fostered by M. Douglas,
we see that, by using the language of rituals (often obscure to a modern thinker), it conveys essentially the same message about the cosmic

---

[32] Cf. 11Q5 XXIV:11–12.

[33] For a useful review of this question, see J. Klawans, *Purity, Sacrifice, and the Temple: Symbolism and Supersessionism in the Study of the Ancient Judaism* (Oxford: Oxford University Press, 2006), 75–100. Cf. J. Barton, "The Prophets and the Cult," in *Temple and Worship in Biblical Israel* (ed. J. Day; Library of Hebrew Bible/Old Testament Series 422; London: T&T Clark, 2005), 111–122.

order and the relationship between humans and their creator as do the non-cultic texts.[34] In fact, the latter can be perceived as deciphering what remained obscure in Leviticus. Rather than dismissing the sacrificial cult, the prophets (alongside the poets and sages) unravel its meaning, denying it the automatic effect and emphasizing the role of God, to whom belongs the last word. Notably, in CD 11:18–21, the instruction concerning the purity of sacrifices is supported by Prov 15:8: "The sacrifice of the wicked is an abomination; but the prayer of the righteous is like a pleasing offering."[35] The quotation serves to emphasize the point that an unrighteous sacrifice is ineffective and the way the sacrifice is performed reflects the inner disposition of the worshiper.

Another apparent contradiction arises from the observation that in cultic texts the acts of sacrificial atonement are performed by a priest, while God as the real agent of the desired purification/forgiveness is only hinted at by the impersonal passive of נסלח.[36] In the non-cultic texts, on the other hand, God is often a grammatical subject of כִּפֶּר (as well as of טהר and סלח). The difference between the two, however, is like the difference between the metonymic "the violin played" and "the musician played the violin": the latter uncovers the moving force behind the act. This becomes particularly visible in the Dead Sea Scrolls where humans and God may alternatively appear as the subject of כִּפֶּר in the passages expressing essentially the same idea.[37] Thus, for example, in 1QHᵃ IV:11–12 God is said to atone for אשמות and מעל, while in 1QS IX:4 the same function is attributed to the men gathered in the community.

Similarly it can be argued that no conceptual change is signalled by the variation of the grammatical *object* of כִּפֶּר and its prepositions. Whether the text speaks of "atonement/cleansing of the sanctuary," "atonement for people" or "atonement for sins," the benefiting party are always people restored in their integrity and fellowship with God.[38] This possibility can be exemplified with the help of another analogy, this time from

---

[34] Douglas, *Leviticus as Literature*, 12–40.

[35] Cf. Sir 38:10–11.

[36] Although, cf. Lev 17:11.

[37] On syntagmatic relationships of כִּפֶּר in the Dead Sea Scrolls see, e.g., B. Janowski and H. Lichtenberger, "Enderwartung und Reinheitsidee: Zur eschatologischen Deutung von Reinheit und Sühne in der Qumrangemeinde," *JJS* 34 (1983): 31–62 and P. Garnet, *Salvation and Atonement in the Qumran Scrolls* (WUNT 2/3; Tübingen: Mohr Siebeck, 1977), 124–135.

[38] Note the unusual mixture of cultic and non-cultic features in CD 14:18–19: the Messiah (probably acting as a High Priest) performs atonement by means of חטאת (cultic); עוון + כִּפֶּר as a direct object (non-cultic).

the domestic sphere. Whether we say "wipe a table" or "wipe the dust from the table," the result is the same, and the benefiting party are the inhabitants of the house. Regardless of the grammatical interchange of the subject and the object of atonement, the respective roles of God and humans in the process need to be clearly distinguished. While the final stroke, with which the stain of defilement is removed, belongs to God, it is for humans to fulfil the necessary conditions upon which the atoning process can be completed.

The evidence of the Dead Sea Scrolls seems to undermine the attempt to explain the differences between cultic and non-cultic texts by assuming that the former were written by professionals (i.e. priests who knew the ritual cultic system from the inside) and the latter by lay people who comprehended the rituals from the outside. The Qumran collection comprises compositions of both types, sometimes coexisting within the same document (e.g., the *Damascus Document*). While the exact provenance and dating of these texts continues to be debated, it is generally accepted that they originated within the same movement (perhaps at different stages of its development) led by priests. If this assumption is correct, then the contraposition of the insiders/professionals to the outsiders/laity becomes redundant. If the priests were the leaders of the community/communities and also in charge of the scribal activities, it is most likely that both types of text were produced or at least approved by them, which also suggests that they perceived no ideological discontinuity/dichotomy between the cultic and prophetic-poetic trends.

In this regard, the *Community Rule* is a particularly expressive example. There the presentation of repentance, righteous living and prayer as an acceptable sacrifice and a means of atonement, found in prophetic, poetic, and sapiential writings, is established within a cultic framework.[39] The language of the sacrificial cult is employed to emphasize the parallel: ריח ניחוח ("a pleasant aroma": 1QS III:11; VIII:9; IX:5); אז ירצה בכפורי ניחוח לפני אל ("Then indeed will he be accepted by God, offering the sweet aroma of atoning sacrifice": III:11); מתנדבים/נדבה ("volunteers"/"freewill offering": V:1, 10, 22; IX:5; etc.),[40] with the emphasis on the atoning function of the community (III:4, 8, 11; V:6; VIII:6, 10; IX:3–5). The authors/compilers drew upon a variety of biblical texts, both cul-

---

[39] Cf., e.g., Ps 51:19; Prov 16:6; Sir 3:3; 35:3; cf. Isa 57:15; 66:2; Ezek 9:3–6; Job 22:30; 36:15.

[40] D. Dimant, "The Volunteers in the *Rule of the Community*: A Biblical Notion in Sectarian Garb," *RevQ* 23 (2008): 233–245.

tic and non-cultic, combining them in a creative manner in order to pro-
mote their case that the community provided an adequate alternative to
the sacrificial system of worship assuring an ongoing relationship with
God.[41]

Summary

I have explored the concept of atonement and the related ideas of purification and divine forgiveness as presented in both cultic and non-cultic
texts of the Hebrew Bible and the Dead Sea Scrolls. It has been suggested
that, where the Bible allows for ambiguity, the evidence from Qumran
tips the balance in favour of a certain understanding, spelling out what
remains vague in the biblical texts. Thus the connection between the
ideas of atonement, forgiveness, and purification from sin is particularly
enhanced in the Dead Sea Scrolls. On the other hand, the synthesis of cultic and non-cultic trends in the Dead Sea Scrolls also supports the view
that there is no ideological discontinuity between these two types of writings. It can be argued, therefore, that the Dead Sea Scrolls are an important witness to biblical thought, especially where the results obtained on
the basis of internal biblical evidence match their interpretation.

---

[41] On the analogy between the community/communities behind 1QS and some other
Qumran texts and the Temple worship see, e.g., B. Gärtner, *The Temple and the Community in Qumran and the New Testament: A Comparative Study in The Temple Symbolism
of the Qumran Texts and the New Testament.* (SNTSMS 1; Cambridge: Cambridge University Press, 1965); F. García Martínez, "The Problem of Purity: The Qumran Solution,"
in idem and J. Trebolle Barrera, *The People of the Dead Sea Scrolls: Their Writings, Beliefs
and Practices* (trans. W.G.E. Watson; Leiden: Brill, 1995), 139–157; G.J. Brooke, "The Ten
Temples in the Dead Sea Scrolls," in *Temple and Worship in Biblical Israel,* 417–434.

ADJUSTING THE APOCALYPSE: HOW THE *APOCRYPHON OF JEREMIAH C* UPDATES THE BOOK OF DANIEL[1]

BENNIE H. REYNOLDS III

The University of North Carolina at Chapel Hill

The techniques by which writers of Hellenistic Jewish literature interpreted, rewrote, reworked, and referred to authoritative literature have been the focus of considerable study since the discovery of the Dead Sea Scrolls.[2] Most of these techniques are not new.[3] But because texts such as *Jubilees*, the *Pesharim*, and the *Temple Scroll* can typically be dated with more confidence than, for example, the redactional layers of the Pentateuch, texts from the Hellenistic Period sometimes provide a more secure data set for understanding the Judaism(s) of their time. In this paper I attempt to highlight how one Hellenistic work attempted to update an earlier Hellenistic work whose apocalyptic prophecy had not come to fruition.[4] I argue that the writer of the *Apocryphon of Jeremiah C*

---

[1] Portions of this paper were presented at the Qumran section of the SBL Annual Meeting in San Diego (2007). I am especially thankful for comments offered by Hanan Eshel, Moshe Bernstein, and Armin Lange both in San Diego and in Vienna and from Daniel Stökl Ben Ezra in Vienna.

[2] The literature is vast. For the purposes of this essay, I mention only some of the most recent book-length works on the subject. See S. White Crawford, *Rewriting Scripture in Second Temple Times* (Studies in the Dead Sea Scrolls and Related Literature; Grand Rapids: Eerdmans, 2008). D.K. Falk, *The Parabiblical Texts: Strategies for Extending the Scriptures in the Dead Sea Scrolls* (Library of Second Temple Studies 63; London: T&T Clark, 2007). E.G. Chazon, D. Dimant, and R.A. Clements, eds., *Reworking the Bible: Apocryphal and Related Texts at Qumran: Proceedings of a Joint Symposium by the Orion Center for the Study of the Dead Sea Scrolls and Associated Literature and the Hebrew University Institute for Advanced Studies Research Group on Qumran, 15–17 January, 2002* (STDJ 58; Leiden: Brill, 2005). Most of these works are dependant, to one extent or another, on the now-classic study by M.A. Fishbane, *Biblical Interpretation in Ancient Israel* (Oxford: Clarendon, 1985).

[3] It is sufficient in this context to mention a single work and refer the reader to the excellent bibliographic essay that concludes the book: B.M. Levinson, *Legal Revision and Religious Renewal in Ancient Israel* (Cambridge: Cambridge University Press, 2008), esp., 95–182.

[4] In light of this particular context, this study holds significance not only for understanding the Dead Sea Scrolls or Hellenistic Judaism, but the study of apocalypticism in religion more generally. The process by which end-times prophecies are made and

(hereafter *Apocryphon)* realized that prophecies from Dan 9–12 had failed and attempted to update them. I argue that this update can be precisely dated to the reign of the Hasmonean king John Hyrcanus. Thus, this study not only treats the literary strategies of the *Apocryphon*, but provides important insight in to the reception history of the book of Daniel a mere generation after it was set in its current form. After giving a general introduction to the text and dealing with the issue of date of composition, I analyze motif-historical and linguistic connections between Daniel and the *Apocryphon.*

Introduction to the *Apocryphon of Jeremiah C*

The *Apocryphon of Jeremiah C* is a non-symbolic apocalypse that consists primarily of an extended *ex eventu* prophecy.[5] Based on surviving manuscripts, it appears that the prophecy begins during the period of the Judges or the early monarchy (Samuel, son of Elqanah is mentioned in 4Q389 5 3). The prophecy details events from the Babylonian exile, the Persian period, and the Hellenistic period. These events culminate in a final apocalyptic battle (cf. 4Q387 4 4; 4Q385a 17 ii 1–9). After the battle the righteous are gathered into the foliage of the tee of life—presumably to enjoy eternal life (4Q385a 17 ii 2–3).

---

then rewritten and updated can be found in modern religions. The ancient and modern works shed light on each other and allow for a sharper image of religious apocalypticism. A modern example of the phenomenon is found in the sequence of booklets published by NASA rocket scientist: E. Whisenant, *88 Reasons Why the Rapture Will Be in 1988* (Nashville: World Bible Society, 1988). Idem and G. Brewer, *The Final Shout Rapture Report: 1989* (Nashville: World Bible Society, 1989). For a classic treatment of rewriting apocalyptic prophecies in the modern world, see L. Festinger, H. Riecken, and S. Schachter, eds., *When Prophecy Fails: A Social and Psychological Study of a Modern Group that Predicted the Destruction of the World* (Minneapolis: University of Minnesota Press, 1958).

[5] For the term non-symbolic apocalypse, see A. Lange and U. Mittmann-Richert in *DJD* XXXIX (2002): 120–121. My dissertation deals at length with language of ancient Jewish apocalypses and the issue of symbolic vs. non-symbol representation techniques, B. Reynolds, "Between Realism and Symbolism: The Use of Symbolic and Non-Symbolic Language in Ancient Jewish Apocalypses 333–63 BCE" (Ph.D. diss., The University of North Carolina at Chapel Hill, 2009). Dimant prefers to view the *Apocryphon* as an apocalypse. D. Dimant in *DJD* XXX (2001): 100. Werman holds that it is not and that it militates against an apocalyptic worldview. C. Werman, "Epochs and End-Time: The 490-Year Scheme in Second Temple Literature," *DSD* 13 (2006): 229–255, 242.

There is still no consensus on the exact make-up of the *Apocryphon*. John Strugnell first grouped the manuscripts 4Q383–4Q391 and described them as "*un écrit pseudo-jérémien*."[6] He later remarked that the work contained "a notable pseudo-Ezekiel section."[7] Devorah Dimant, the editor of the *editio princeps*, initially argued for the existence of a third literary work within 4Q383–4Q391, which she characterized as "pseudo-Moses."[8] She has since abandoned that thesis and settled on the two works that Strugnell initially indicated.[9] Monica Brady has argued that the manuscripts 3Q383–391 compose a single literary work and Cana Werman has defended Dimant's original tripartite division of the manuscripts.[10] Hanan Eshel has argued that 4Q390 should not be treated as part of the larger work—though he does not agree with Werman's characterization of it as "pseudo-Moses."[11] Like Werman and Eshel, I do not treat 4Q390 as part of the *Apocryphon*.

Date of Composition

The date of the *Apocryphon* is crucial for this investigation. The content of the text indicates its relationship to the book of Daniel, but its date of composition locates the hermeneutics of the *Apocryphon* in a particular historical context. The *terminus ante quem* for the *Apocryphon* is

---

[6] See M. Baillet et al., "Le travail d'édition des fragments manuscrits de Qumrân," *RB* 63 (1956): 49–67, 65.

[7] J. Strugnell, "The Angelic Liturgy at Qumrân—4QSerek Šîrôt 'Ôlat Haššabāt," in *Congress Volume, Oxford 1959* (VTSup 7; Leiden: Brill, 1960), 318–345 (344).

[8] D. Dimant, "New Light from Qumran on the Jewish Pseudepigrapha—4Q390," in *The Madrid Qumran Congress: Proceedings of the International Congress on the Dead Sea Scrolls, Madrid 18–21 March, 1991* (ed. J. Trebolle Barrera and L. Vegas Montaner; 2 vols.; STDJ 11.1–2; Leiden: Brill, 1992), 2:405–448.

[9] D. Dimant in *DJD* XXX (2001): 7–88; 91–260. Eventually Strugnell came to believe that all manuscripts belonged to one work, "An Apocryphon of Ezekiel, first designated as *Pseudo-Ezekiel* and later as *Second*-Ezekiel." Dimant, "New Light from Qumran on the Jewish Pseudepigrapha—4Q390," 406.

[10] M. Brady, "Prophetic Traditions at Qumran: A Study of 4Q383–391" (Ph.D. diss., University of Notre Dame, 2000). In a more recent article, Brady pushes further by arguing that the manuscripts 4Q383–391 all make use of the same type of biblical interpretation. M. Brady, "Biblical Interpretation in the 'Pseudo-Ezekiel' Fragments (4Q383–391) from Cave Four," in *Interpretation at Qumran* (ed. M. Henze; Studies in the Dead Sea Scrolls and Related Literature; Grand Rapids: Eerdmans, 2005), 88–109. Werman, "Epochs and End-Time," 229–255.

[11] H. Eshel, "4Q390, the 490-Year Prophecy, and the Calendrical History of the Second Temple Period," in *Enoch and Qumran Origins: New Light on a Forgotten Connection* (ed. G. Boccaccini; Grand Rapids: Eerdmans, 2005), 102–110. See also H. Eshel, *The Dead Sea Scrolls and the Hasmonean State* (Grand Rapids: Eerdmans, 2008), 22–27, 131.

established by the paleographic date of the earliest manuscripts: the second half of the first century B.C.E.[12] The *terminus post quem* is established at 164 by the *Apocryphon*'s use of material from Dan 9–12 and by its apparent knowledge of the Hellenistic religious reforms and the Maccabean revolt. But it is possible to be more precise about the date of the *Apocryphon*. 4Q385a 5a–b 7–8 = 4Q387 3 4–5 describes "Three priests who will not walk in the ways [of the] former [priests] (who) by the name of the God of Israel were called." Before the three priests arise, the action of the highly fragmentary text is characterized by descriptions of 1) the altar, 2) those felled by the sword and 3) an act of defiling. During the time of the three priests the text describes 1) the downfall of those who have colluded with foreigners and 2) severe internal strife over religious issues in the Jewish state.

For Dimant there are two possible interpretations of the three priests. "The priests referred to here could be High Priests (Jason [174–171 BCE], Menelaus [171–167 BCE], Alcimus [162–161 BCE]), or the Hasmonean priestly kings (Simeon [142–134 BCE], John Hyrcanus [134–104 BCE], Alexander Jannaeus [103–76 BCE])."[13] Dimant's second possibility is more attractive than the first. I think she is correct that the three priests under discussion are probably Maccabees, but I propose a different combination than Dimant: Jonathan, Simon, and John Hyrcanus. Why these three? In what follows, I indicate why Dimant's initial suggestion of Hellenizing high priests (Jason, Menelaus, Alcimus) is unlikely and then I argue for my combination of Maccabean high priests.

While one imagines that Jason, Menelaus, and Alcimus would, in a certain sense, fit into the category of those "who will not walk in the ways of the former priests of Israel," there are problems with such an association. First, and most importantly, the three priests in the *Apocryphon* arise *after* the desecration of the Jerusalem temple. Jason and Menelaus were both active before and during the time of the Hellenistic religious reforms.[14] The combination of Jason, Menelaus, and Alcimus would seem to be ruled out. Second, unlike the Maccabean high priests who were criticized by prominent Jewish groups for being illegitimate holders of the office, Jason had the correct priestly credentials—even if he acquired the

---

[12] Dimant in *DJD* XXX (2001): 115.
[13] Ibid., 193.
[14] Cf. 2 Macc 4:7–5:20.

office through intrigue.[15] He was the brother of the high priest Onias III. If the phrase, "will not walk in the ways of the former priests of Israel," has anything to do with correct family lineage, it cannot be applied to a group that includes Jason. Third, the text reports that, "in their days will be brought down the pride of those who violate the covenant as well as the servants of the foreigner" (4Q385a 5a–b 8–9 = 4Q387 3 6). Such a scenario is hardly characteristic of the terms of Jason, Menelaus, and Alcimus. Indeed, *they* are the leaders of those who "violate the covenant" and are "servants of the foreigner" in the second century B.C.E. Below I argue that "those who violate the covenant" (מרישיעי ברית) must be understood as Seleucid sympathizers. If I am correct, what second century Jew could be described as more sympathetic to Seleucid concerns than Menelaus? In summary, Jason, Menelaus, and Alcimus are unlikely to be the *Apocryphon's* three priests "who will not walk in the ways" since they 1) appear after the Hellenistic religious reforms, 2) are not all illegitimate holders of the office, and 3) are Seleucid sympathizers.

The three priests "who will not walk in the ways" are better identified as Maccabees. I disagree, however, with one figure on Dimant's list of Hasmoneans (Simon, John Hyrcanus, Alexander Jannaeus).[16] In what follows, I explain why. The most important reason why the list must end with John Hyrcanus and not Alexander Jannaeus is that the *Apocryphon* describes three priests, not four. There is no doubt that Jonathan held the office of high priest and that he was the first Maccabee to do so. According to 1 Macc 10:21, "Jonathan put on the sacred vestments in the seventh month of the one hundred sixtieth year, at the festival of booths" (NRSV). Jonathan was followed by Simon and John Hyrcanus. Alexander Jannaeus would be the fourth (or fifth) Maccabean high priest—at least one too many.[17] Thus, Jannaeus cannot be included in the group since the

---

[15] See for example the story about John Hyrcanus and the Pharisees related by Josephus, *A.J.* 13.288–300. Cf. J. VanderKam, *An Introduction to Early Judaism* (Grand Rapids: Eerdmans, 2001), 27–30.

[16] The connection of the three priests "who will not walk in the ways" is strengthened by a few several words that appear in the following line (על שם אלהי ישראל יקראו). As Dimant astutely notes, a compelling parallel is found in 1QpHab VIII:8–9—a passage almost universally agreed to be describing one of two Hasmonean rulers (either Jonathan or Simon): הכוהן הרשע אשר נקרא על שם האמת בתחלת עומדו "the wicked priest, who was called by the name 'truth' (i.e., had a good reputation) at the beginning of his service." See Dimant in *DJD* XXX (2001): 193.

[17] This presumes that Aristobulus I (104–103 B.C.E.) is not counted. Given his attenuated reign, it seems reasonable not to count him. Should he be counted, however, Alexander Jannaeus would be the fifth Maccabee to wear the priestly vestments.

writer of the *Apocryphon* only knew of the first three Maccabean priests.
Dimant seems to think that if the priests are Maccabees, they should
be drawn from the group of Maccabees who also held the title "king."
The text makes no mention of any such qualification and Dimant places
no such requirement on her first set of suggestions (Jason, Menelaus,
Alcimus). Why, if the referents are Maccabees, must they also hold the
title of מלך to be included on her list?[18] The identification of the three
priests proves crucial for dating the text. The text is an *ex eventu* prophecy.
Since it only knows of three Maccabean high priests, it makes the most
sense to identify them with the *first* three Maccabean high priests. The
three priests "who will not walk in the ways" must be Jonathan, Simon,
and John Hyrcanus. If my thesis about the three priests is correct, then
the text must have been written after 134 but before 104 B.C.E. i.e., during
the reign of Hyrcanus.[19] This time frame is crucial to contextualizing the
linguistic and motif-historical connections between the *Apocryphon* and
the book of Daniel. In the next section, I begin analysis of these issues.

Analysis

I am not the first to notice similarities between the book of Daniel and the
Apocryphon. Most of the linguistic parallels analyzed below are noted by
Devorah Dimant in the *editio princeps*.[20] Neither am I the first to notice
motif-historical connections between the two works. Cana Werman has
analyzed the 490 year motif in the *Apocryphon* and argues that the text
is a reaction to the apocalyptic worldview in the book of Daniel.[21] In
what follows, I build on some of the ground-work that has already been
done and attempt to highlight some connections that have not yet been
made. There is not sufficient space to discuss *each* of the sometimes
verbatim linguistic parallels in this paper. I have chosen to highlight three
expressions that seem to be part of a re-narration of events found in Dan

---

[18] Dimant in *DJD* XXX (2001): 193.
[19] Dimant lists several slightly earlier dates—based on the inclusion of 4Q390. Nevertheless she also arrives at a second-century date, which is, as she notes, "suggested by the
affinities it displays to various second-century BCE writings (Epistle of Jeremiah, Book of
Baruch, *Animal Apocalypse, Jubilees*, and *Damascus Document*)." Moreover, Dimant has
pointed out, the Romans are mentioned nowhere in the text while the Seleucids and the
Ptolemies both play significant roles. See Dimant in *DJD* XXX (2001): 116.
[20] See ibid., 91–234.
[21] Werman, "Epochs and End-Time," 229–255.

11:31–35, 12:1–3. I begin, however, with a look at the 490-year motif in the *Apocryphon*. As Werman has already shown, it establishes that the relationship between the *Apocryphon* and the book of Daniel is not only linguistic, but almost certainly the result of an intentional re-framing of Daniel. Werman and I disagree on the question of *how* the *Apocryphon* does this.

Motif-Historical Comparison

Before analyzing the linguistic similarities between the *Apocryphon* and Daniel, it is useful to highlight a motif that both texts employ: 490 years of punishment. The 490 year motif helps to set the stage for my arguments that the linguistic similarities between Daniel and the *Apocryphon* attest to a more programmatic relationship. What is the 490 year motif? In Jer 25:11–12 and 29:10, the prophet declares that there will be seventy years of destruction and Babylonian dominion. Dan 9 updates Jeremiah's 70-year prophecies in the Hellenistic period by reinterpreting the number 70 as a reference to weeks, not years.[22] In other words, Jeremiah did not forecast 70 years of destruction, but 490 (70 × 7). The *Apocryphon* uses the same 490 year period, but divides it in a different way. In other words, the writer of the *Apocryphon* apparently realized that the chronology and history in Daniel's prophecy was problematic, just as the writer of Daniel perceived Jeremiah's 70-year prophecy to be problematic. It is especially intriguing that Daniel is updated by a pseudonymous prophecy of Jeremiah, since Daniel derives its 490 year scheme from the book of Jeremiah in the first place. Perhaps it is not by chance.

Daniel divides the 490 years of punishment into three periods: 7 weeks (49 years) for the Babylonian Exile, 62 weeks (434 years) from the rebuilding of Jerusalem until the assassination of Onias III and the rise of Antiochus IV Epiphanes, and 1 week (7 years) divided into two stages: 1) the desecration of the temple by Antiochus and his Jewish supporters and 2) the end of the desecration.[23] The problem, as one imagines the writer

---

[22] See J.J. Collins, *Daniel: A Commentary on the Book of Daniel* (Hermeneia; Minneapolis: Fortress, 1993), 347–349.

[23] H. Eshel agrees with J. Montgomery that the first period refers to the period between 586 and 538 B.C.E. If so, this would mean that the first period of Daniel's prophecy is historically accurate. Eshel, "4Q390, the 490-Year Prophecy, and the Calendrical History of the Second Temple Period," 103. See S.R. Driver, *The Book of Daniel: With Introduction and Notes* (The Cambridge Bible for Schools and Colleges; Cambridge: Cambridge University Press, 1900), 137. J. Montgomery, *A Critical and Exegetical Commentary on*

of the *Apocryphon* understood, is that most calculations of the 490-year scheme conclude a considerable distance from the death of Antiochus IV and the end of the Hellenistic religious reforms—especially if the 62 week period ends with the assassination of Onias III (cf. Dan 9:26). In other words, if one begins their calculation in 586 B.C.E., an end-date of somewhere around 100 B.C.E. is unavoidable. The latter date does not square with the events Daniel describes on the cusp of the eschaton.

Apocryphon of Jeremiah C divides the 490 years not into weeks, but Jubilees, i.e., 49 year periods. The text does not appear to enumerate events in terms of specific Jubilee periods in the way that 4Q390 does, e.g., "In the seventh jubilee of the devastation of the land, they will forget statute, festival, and Sabbath, and covenant" (4Q390 1 7–8). The text does, however, use formulaic language to describe the transitions from one imperial power to the next during the period of 490 years. For example, expressions such as "in those days shall arise a king of the nations, a blasphemer" (4Q387 2 ii 7–8 = 4Q385a 4 4–6; 4Q388a 7 2–3 = 4Q389 8 i–ii 9) and "the kingdom of Israel shall perish" (4Q387 2 ii 7 = 4Q385a 4 4–5; cf. 4Q388a 7 3–5 = 4Q389 8 i–ii 10–11 = 4Q387 2 iii 1–2) are used on multiple occasions. The historical progression of the text indicates that the similar expressions in the *Apocryphon* do not refer to the same persons and events.

Werman's analysis of the 490 year motif in the *Apocryphon* leads her to conclude that the *Apocryphon* was written in reaction to Daniel—apparently soon after the book of Daniel was completed—and challenged Daniel's apocalyptic worldview. While Werman is undoubtedly correct that the *Apocryphon* responds to Daniel and adapts the basic chronology at work in Dan 9, I disagree with her about *how* it responds. Werman holds that the *Apocryphon* responds to Daniel by eschewing its apocalyptic worldview. She writes:

> Whereas in Daniel no explanation is supplied for the deaths incurred during the persecution, and one must await resurrection (Dan. 12:2–3) to establish their cause, as far as can be determined, the *Apocryphon*

---

the Book of Daniel (ICC; Edinburgh: T&T Clark, 1927), 391. See also K. Koch, *Das Buch Daniel* (EdF 144; Darmstadt: Wissenschaftliche Buchgesellschaft, 1980), 150. But John Collins has noted that Montgomery had to acknowledge that "the dating is then not from the issue of the word," but later (Collins, *Daniel*, 355). Collins is skeptical of reading the dates as anything but schematic since it is nearly impossible to interpret them literally and still arrive at a date towards the end of the reign of Antiochus IV—especially if the 62 week period must end at the time of the assassination of Onias III.

of Jeremiah views these deaths as justified. Its author validates reality, and therefore seeks redemption neither in upper regions nor in cosmic revolutions.[24]

I suggest, however, that the apparent Deuteronomic theology (i.e., retributive justice in this lifetime) found in the *Apocryphon* relates specifically to its condemnation of priests (cf. 4Q387 2 iii 6–7 = 4Q388a 7 6–7; 4Q385a 5a–b 6–7 = 4Q387 3 4–5)—not necessarily all of Israel. Moreover, the text does appear to include the idea of a final, eschatological battle after which the righteous are gathered into the foliage of the tree of life (4Q385a 17 ii 2–3). The tree of life (עֵץ הַחִיִּים) motif unambiguously points to the concepts of resurrection and eternal life.[25] Moreover, Deuteronomic thought is not missing from the book of Daniel itself (cf. the prayer in Dan 9). In other words, "deuteronomic" and "apocalyptic" cannot be treated as mutually exlusive categories in the thought of Hellenistic Jewish writers. Morever, the way in which the *Apocryphon* reworks a portion of the prophecy in Dan 11 indicates a different relationship to the 490 year motif. In the next section, I highlight linguistic connections between the two texts. These shared expressions and their literary contexts indicate that the *Apocryphon* must have been written to correct Daniel—not oppose it.

Linguistic Comparisons

Three adjectival descriptions from *Apocryphon of Jeremiah C* have significant parallels in Dan 10–12. Two of the expressions are found in the overlapping fragments 4Q385a 5a–b and 4Q387 3 and parallel terms used in Dan 11: הנופלים בחרב and מרישיעי ברית. A third expression, from 4Q388a 7 9, has a parallel in Dan 12: [ם]המצדקי. Below I provide a combined translation of the portion of the text in which these expressions are found. The narrative probably describes the rise of Antiochus IV, his campaign against Egypt in 170 B.C.E., the rise of the Hellenizing high priests (i.e., Jason, Menelaus) and the Hellenistic religious reforms. It presumes the Maccabean revolt (as well as resistance by other groups), the advent of the Hasmonean state, and internal struggles during the Hasmonean period.[26]

---

[24] Werman, "Epochs and End-Time," 242.

[25] Cf. Dimant in *DJD* XXX (2001): 158–159. I provide a lengthier treatment of the tree of life motif in my Ph.D. dissertation, "Between Symbolism and Realism," 317–320.

[26] These lines of text are taken from the complete combined text and translation found in my dissertation, "Between Symbolism and Realism," 333–334. In the edition above

57 [Jacob. In] those[days] will arise a king of the nations, a blasphemer, and a doer *Of evils* and [

58 *And in his days* [I will invalidate (i.e., remove)] Israel from *(being) a people. In* his days I will break the kingdom of

59 Egypt [   ] and Egypt *and Israel I will break and hand over* to the sword

60 And I will [dev]astate the [la]nd and (from it) will *I remove humanity* and I will abandon

61 *the land* into the hands of the angels of Mastemot, and I will hide [my face]

62 [from Is]rael. And this will be a sign for them: On the day that I abandon the land *in d[esolation],*

63 then the priests of Jerusalem will [return] *to serving other gods and [to ac]t*

64 according to the abominations of the [nations].

65 three who will rul[e

66 [and] the holy of holie[s]

67 and th[ose] who lead to righteousness

68] God[

69]a number of priests[

70] others [

71]*the altar[*

72 those felled by the sword

73] *it defiled* [

74] three priests *who will not walk in the ways*

75 [of the] first/former [priests] (who) by the name of the God of *Israel were called.*

76 And in their days will be brought down the pride of those who act wickedly (against the) *covenant as well as servants of the foreigner.*

77 And in th[at] generation, Israel will be rent asunder, each m[a]n warring with his neighbor

---

lines 57–67 correspond to 4Q388a 7 3–10 = 4Q387 2 iii 1–7 = 4Q389 8 i–ii 9–11 and lines 68–76 correspond to 4Q385a 5a–b 1–8 = 4Q387 3 1–6. Overlaps are italicized. Since in some cases as many as three manuscripts overlap, there is no distinction between which manuscript preserves which letters of the overlapping word(s).

78 over the Torah (or, "teaching") and over the covenant and I will cast
   a hunger over the l[an]d, but not

79 for bread, and a thirst, but n[ot] for water, [ra]ther, to [hear my
   word]

A significant portion of the narrative above may mirror Dan 11:30–35.
Dan 11:30–35 details Antiochus' failed attack on Egypt (foiled by the
Romans) and his subsequent campaign into Jerusalem. The brief passage
is worth quoting in its entirety:

> The ships of the *Kittim* shall come against him and he shall lose heart and
> retreat. He shall rage against the holy covenant and he shall take action and
> returning he shall pay heed to those who forsake the holy covenant (עזבי
> ברית קודש). His forces shall occupy and profane the temple and the fortress.
> They shall do away with the regular offering and set up the abomination
> of desolation. Now those who have violated the covenant (מרשיעי ברית) he
> shall seduce with flattery, but the people who know their God shall stand
> strong and take action. The wise among the people (משכילי עם) shall give
> understanding to many. They shall fall by sword (ונכשלו בחרב) and flame
> and (shall suffer) captivity and plunder for some days. When they stumble,
> they shall receive a little help, but many shall join them insincerely. Some
> of the wise shall stumble, so that they might be refined, and purified, and
> whitened until the time of the end, for it is yet the appointed time.
>
> (NRSV)

The first important expression is found in line 72: נופלים בחרב "those
felled by the sword." Flusser notes that the "sword of God" motif has wide
currency as an eschatological motif within ancient Jewish apocalypses,
but "those felled by the sword" in the *Apocryphon* do not fit within this
context.[27] The time frame in which the individuals fall by the sword is
not the final apocalyptic battle, but apparently the time of Antiochus'
religious reforms and the Maccabean revolt. It is apparently not the
enemies of God that fall by the sword, but the faithful. This scenario finds
a parallel in the book of Daniel.[28]

---

[27] The motif appears in Daniel, *1 Enoch*, *Sib. Or. 3*, the *Oracle of Hystaspes*, and
1QM. See D. Flusser, *Judaism of the Second Temple Period*, vol. 1: *Qumran and Apocalypticism* (Grand Rapids: Eerdmans, 2007), 150–151.

[28] There is no lack of individuals falling by the sword in the Hebrew Bible. Cf. Num
14:3, 43; 2 Sam 1:12; 3:29; 2 Kgs 19:7; 2 Chr 32:21; Ps 78:64; Is 3:25; 13:15; 31:8; 37:7; Jer
19:7; 20:4; 44:12; Lam 2:21; Ezek 5:12; 6:12; 11:10; 17:21; 23:25; 24:21; 25:13; 30:5, 6, 17;
32:22–24; 33:27; 39:23; Hos 7:16; 14:1; Amos 7:17. What sets Daniel apart is that it, like
the *Apocryphon*, uses the term while addressing the Hellenistic religious reforms.

The book of Daniel reports that the משכילים will "fall by the sword" (ונכשלו בחרב): "The wise among the people will give understanding to many; for some days, however, they shall fall by the sword and flame, and suffer captivity and plunder" (Dan 11:33). The group that "falls by the sword" is also referred to as מצדיקי הרבים in 12:3 (see below). The *Apocryphon* uses nearly the same description (המצדקי[ם]) for the group in the midst of the religious reforms—not just at the eschaton. Alone the expression might tell an interpreter little, but when coupled with the expressions מרישיעי ברית and עבדי נאכר, which find even more compelling parallels in Dan 11, the book of Daniel emerges as a likely source of this portion of the *Apocryphon*.

The מרישיעי ברית "Those who act wickedly (against the) covenant" and עבדי נאכר "servants of the foreigner" (lines 74–76) appear to be synonymous in the *Apocryphon*. Both adjectival descriptions portray Jews by characteristic actions. The expression מרישיעי ברית and another similar expression, עזבי ברית, are used in at least two other roughly contemporary texts—though not with the same orthography: Daniel and 1QM.[29]

In Dan 11, עזבי ברית "those who forsake the holy covenant" and מרשיעי ברית "those who have violated the covenant" are synonymous. In both cases they refer to Jewish (priestly) officials who were hellenizers. In other words, these figures are sympathetic to the vision of οἰκουμένη pursued by Alexander the Great and developed in Syro-Palestine by Antiochus IV. "Those who have violated the covenant" (מרשיעי ברית) is almost certainly a reference to the high priest Menelaus and his party (though it could probably be as well applied to the former high priest Jason). According to 2 Macc 5:15, Menelaus not only allowed Antiochus' desecration of the temple, but personally guided Antiochus through the temple. He is described as καὶ τῶν νόμων καὶ τῆς πατρίδος προδότην γεγονότα "a traitor both to the laws and to his country" (2 Macc 5:15). Martin Hengel points to an account in the Tosefta, that while legendary, nevertheless expresses how in his words, "The extreme Hellenists under Menelaus had lost any interest in sacrifice according to the law."[30]

---

[29] The first *yod* is unanticipated. Dimant speculates that the first *yod* placed after the *reš* may stand for the *i*-sound of *reš* which was pronounced as the *i*-sound of the following *šin*. Based on extant vocalizations of III-guttural *hipʿil* participles, however, I suggest that it is more likely a scribal error—an ancient typo.

[30] M. Hengel, *Judaism and Hellenism: Studies in their Encounter in Palestine during the Early Hellenistic Period* (trans. J. Bowden; Philadelphia: Fortress, 1981), 283.

> And when the gentiles went into the sanctuary, she came along and stamped on the altar, screaming at it, "Wolf, wolf! You have wiped out [devoured] the fortune of Israel and did not then stand up for them in the time of their trouble."[31]   (t. Sukkah 4:28)

Hengel comments about the passage, "The uselessness of the *tamid* offering could not be expressed more vividly. The age of this legend is shown by the fact that it was later transferred to Titus."[32] Indeed, the thesis of Hengel's famous *Judaism and Hellenism* is that Menelaus and his Tobiad supporters were the authors of the edict of persecution. While I disagree with Hengel that, "One cannot speak of a deliberate policy of Hellenization on the part of the Seleucids or Antiochus IV," there seems little doubt that the political ambitions of Jews such as Menelaus played a major role in the development and implementation of the Hellenistic religious reforms. Regardless of who was the driving force behind the Hellenistic religious reforms, and we err in attempting to isolate only one, Menelaus' role would have easily won him and his supporters the titles מרישיעי ברית "violators of the covenant" and עבדי נאכר "servants of the foreigner." Other evidence points in the same direction.

In 1QM I:1–2 the expression מרשיעי ברית is used to describe Jews who collaborate with foreign powers against the faithful:

> The first attack of the Sons of Light shall be undertaken against the forces of the Sons of Darkness, the army of Belial the troops of Edom, Moab, the sons of Ammon, and [   ] Philistia and the troops of the Kittim of Asshur. Supporting them are those who have violated the covenant (מרשיעי ברית).[33]

David Flusser has shown that Dan 11 and the specific term מרשיעי ברית was taken up by the writer of 1QM and used to describe those who collaborate with Greek imperialists—though in a later historical setting. Flusser finds that 1QM appropriates the term to name Seleucid sympathizers in the time of Alexander Jannaeus—preferring to see in the "violators of the covenant" a reflection of the invasion of Demetrius II (Eucaerus) in 89 B.C.E. with Jewish help. In any case, he holds that the historical situation must be in Hasmonean times and must predate the fall of Seleucid Syria in 83 B.C.E., since the text includes the Kittim of Ashur in the battle.[34]

---

[31] Trans. J. Neusner, *The Tosefta: Second Division, Moed (The Order of the Appointed Times)* (New York: Ktav, 1981).

[32] Hengel, *Judaism and Hellenism*, 283.

[33] Trans. M. Wise, M. Abegg, and E. Cook in *Texts Concerned with Religious Law* (ed. D.W. Parry and E. Tov; The Dead Sea Scrolls Reader 1; Leiden: Brill, 2004), 209.

[34] Flusser, *Judaism of the Second Temple Period*, 1:154–155.

I suggest, like Flusser did about 1QM, that *Apocryphon of Jeremiah C* attempts to update the eschatological prophecy in Dan 11 (as well as the 490 year prophecy) slightly earlier.[35]

A final expression that finds an important parallel in the book of Daniel is located in line 67. A group is described as [ם]יקדצמה "th[ose] who lead to righteousness." The group appears on the scene after Jerusalem priests begin to "serve other gods" during the Hellenistic period (lines 63–64). The text perhaps even includes a veiled reference to Jason, Menelaus, and Alcimus as "three who will rule" (line 65). "Those who lead to righteousness" are active in the wake of the Hellenistic religious reforms and, ostensibly, attempt to resist the reforms.

Dimant suggests a parallel with Dan 12:3: "Those who are wise shall shine like the brightness of the sky, and those who lead many to righteousness (מצדיקי הרבים), like the stars forever and ever." In Dan 12:3, the משכלים and the מצדיקי הרבים are probably synonyms. Both expressions describe groups present during the Hellenistic religious reforms who will be rewarded for their faithfulness at the end of days. They are not groups that emerge after the death of Antiochus IV or with the advent of the eschaton. The eschaton is merely the time of their reward. (I.e., While their location in Dan 12:3 might appear suggest a context later in time than the events described in Dan 11:31–35, it does not. "Those who lead many to righteousness" are almost certainly the same as the "wise" from Dan 11—some of whom "fell by the sword"). Since the context of line 67 appears to be the reign of Antiochus IV and his religious reforms, this fragment provides a group-specific term shared by the *Apocryphon* and Dan 12. It is notable that this term is not found elsewhere in Hellenistic Hebrew. The *Apocryphon* shares expressions with Daniel that are, with one exception, not widespread.

Few would disagree that the *Apocryphon*, like Dan 11, narrates the Hellenistic religious reforms and their immediate aftermath. I hope to have shown, however, that the *Apocryphon* not only narrates the same or similar events, but appropriates specific vocabulary found in Dan 11–12. In other words, the *Apocryphon* does not merely narrative the same events as the book of Daniel, it narrates events *from* the book of Daniel. Below is a chart of the similarities I have highlighted.

---

[35] Another related expression is found in CD 20:26–27. Cf. also CD 4–5; *Pss. Sol.* 2:8–13; 8:9–13.

Book of Daniel	Apocryphon of Jeremiah C
490 year scheme (9:24)	490 year scheme (4Q387 2 i–ii 1–5)
ונכשלו בחרב And they will fall by the sword (11:34)	הנופלים בחרב those felled by the sword (line 72 = 4Q385a 5a–b 5 = 4Q387 3 2)
מרשיעי ברית those who have violated the covenant (11:32)	מרישיעי ברית those who have violated covenant (line 74 = 4Q385a 5a–b 9 = 4Q387 3 6)
מצדיקי הרבים those who lead many to righteousness (12:3)	המצדק[ים] th[ose] who lead to righteousness (line 67 = 4Q388a 7 10)

CONCLUSIONS

In this paper I focused on three issues that illuminate the relationship of the *Apocryphon* to the book of Daniel. First, I argued that based on content, the *Apocryphon* should be dated precisely to the period of the reign of John Hyrcanus, 134–104 B.C.E. This date places the *Apocryphon* only 30–60 years after the completion of the book of Daniel. Since it postdates the book of Daniel, similarities in motif and language point to the *Apocryphon*'s potential dependence on the book of Daniel. This dependence is made problematic by the fact that the *Apocryphon* uses a chronological motif that is, ostensibly, already exhausted in the book of Daniel. In other words, while it is noteworthy in and of itself that the *Apocryphon* and Daniel share some relatively rare terms, the fact that they use those terms to narrate the same events indicates that the *Apocryphon* is not simply aware of Daniel or influenced by Daniel, but is making a literary argument by means of Daniel. For Werman, the *Apocryphon* attempts to neutralize Daniel's apocalyptic message and place the deity's justice back in the here-and-now. The text strikes me as a more likely example of rewriting/reworking in which the prophecies from the book of Daniel are updated and corrected for application in a new day. That new day must be the reign of John Hyrcanus. While the writer of the *Apocryphon* must have realized that the book of Daniel did not correctly apply the 490-year scheme, he nevertheless believed in the ultimate truth of the concept. By using the language that Daniel used to narrate the history that Daniel narrated, the writer breathes new life into Daniel's prophecies and specifically the 490 year scheme and gives them a fresh chance at coming to fruition. So the writer of the *Apocryphon* was not an opponent of Daniel, but a proponent of Daniel. He believed in the ultimate truth of Daniel's prophecy and attempted to situate it at a time when its potential could exist in a nearly, but not yet realized state once more.

There are more linguistic parallels between the book of Daniel and the *Apocryphon of Jeremiah C* than I have had space to discuss in this paper. These additional expressions include, for example, מלך הצפון "king of the north" as a description for Seleucid kings. I hope to have demonstrated, however, that the *Apocryphon* shares not only random linguistic similarities and a common chronological motif with the book of Daniel, but that it actually appropriates elements from Daniel's narrative prophecy in order to adjust the advent of the eschaton. The *Apocryphon* continues to narrate the *ex eventu* prophecies from Dan 9–12 past the time frame found in the book of Daniel and through the first three Maccabean high priests (Jonathan, Simon, John Hyrcanus) to the time of its own writer. The writer of the *Apocryphon* understood that the end of the world did not occur just after Antiochus IV died. In spite of this major problem with Daniel's prophecy, the writer of the *Apocryphon* apparently did not dismiss Daniel's prophecy as totally failed or finished. Instead, the writer carried on some of Daniel's narrative prophecy and updated it approximately sixty years later. The new prediction found in the *Apocryphon* fits much closer to the date at which one arrives when subtracting 490 from 586 or even 597 (the sort of date one might have expected the book of Daniel to arrive at in the first place). The *Apocryphon* thus attempts to show that Daniel was not ultimately wrong, but perhaps mistaken in its calculations.

IDENTIFYING BIBLICAL
INTERPRETATION IN PARABIBLICAL TEXTS

MICHAEL SEGAL

The Hebrew University of Jerusalem

REWRITTEN BIBLE AND PARABIBLICAL TEXTS:
BRIEF METHODOLOGICAL REFLECTIONS

(1) The discovery of the Dead Sea Scrolls sixty years ago and their subsequent publication have led to a renewed interest in and evaluation of biblical interpretation in the Second Temple period. Previously unknown genres of interpretation, such as the *pesharim*, were found alongside compositions already known from ancient translations. "New" works that generically resemble other Jewish compositions of the Second Temple period, such as those classified as Rewritten Bible or parabiblical, were uncovered and the Qumran corpus has highlighted the prevalence and significance of these texts within Jewish literature in Antiquity.[1] The attributes "rewritten" and "para-" texts both indicate some level of relationship to a base-text that has been expanded, changed, reworked,

---

[1] The term "Rewritten Bible" was first used by G. Vermes, *Scripture and Tradition in Judaism: Haggadic Studies* (StPB 4; Leiden: Brill, 1961), 95. Subsequent studies that have analyzed the nature and extent of this phenomenon in Jewish literature of the Second Temple period include G.W.E. Nickelsburg, "The Bible Rewritten and Expanded," in *Jewish Writings of the Second Temple Period: Apocrypha, Pseudepigrapha, Qumran Sectarian Writings, Philo, Josephus* (ed. M. Stone; CRINT 2.2; Assen: Van Gorcum, 1984), 89–156; D.J. Harrington, "The Bible Rewritten," in *Early Judaism and Its Modern Interpreters* (ed. R.A. Kraft and G.W.E. Nickelsburg; Atlanta: Scholars Press, 1986), 239–247; P.S. Alexander, "Retelling the Old Testament," in *It is Written: Scripture Citing Scripture: Essays in Honour of Barnabas Lindars* (ed. D.A. Carson and H.G.M. Williamson; Cambridge: Cambridge University Press, 1988), 99–121; E. Tov, "Rewritten Bible Compositions and Biblical Manuscripts, with Special Attention to the Samaritan Pentateuch," *DSD* 5 (1998): 334–354; S. White Crawford, "The 'Rewritten' Bible at Qumran: A Look at Three Texts," *ErIsr* 26 (1999): 1–8; G.J. Brooke, "Rewritten Bible," *Encyclopedia of the Dead Sea Scrolls* (ed. L.H. Schiffman and J.C. VanderKam; 2 vols.; Oxford: Oxford University Press, 2000), 2:777–781; M. Segal, "Between Bible and Rewritten Bible," in *Biblical Interpretation at Qumran* (ed. M. Henze; Studies in the Dead Sea Scrolls and Related Literature; Grand Rapids: Eerdmans, 2005), 10–28; M.J. Bernstein, "'Rewritten Bible': A Generic Category which has Outlived its Usefulness?" *Text* 22 (2005): 169–196.

or interpreted. Some scholars have objected to the use of these terms, because the descriptions assume the existence of a biblical text that was rewritten or reworked. According to their argument, since there was no one fixed text for each of the biblical books in the late Second Temple period, the term Bible itself is inaccurate and anachronistic, and therefore the derivative term Rewritten Bible is misplaced and misleading.[2]

Contrary to this objection, however, the claim that the fluid nature of biblical texts throughout the Second Temple period invalidates the notion of authoritative compositions during this time seems to me to be exaggerated. Although we cannot speak of *the one and only* text of Genesis or Exodus from this era, the differences between the various textual witnesses all fall within a relatively narrow range. Even in the most radical of cases for which we have textual evidence of multiple literary editions of the same biblical book, such as Esther or Daniel,[3] there is no question in the mind of a reader that they indeed reflect the same composition.[4] This is even more pronounced in those books where the various witnesses exhibit some degree of textual fluidity and variation, but essentially point to the same literary edition. The presence of textual variation does not negate the presence of identifiable, authoritative compositions. One should avoid confusing the notions of authoritative works (or "canonicity" with all of its accompanying problems) on the hand, and

---

[2] See e.g., the discussions of H. Najman, *Seconding Sinai: The Development of Mosaic Discourse in Second Temple Judaism* (JSJSup 77; Leiden: Brill, 2003), 7–9; J.G. Campbell, "'Rewritten Bible' and 'Parabiblical Texts': A Terminological and Ideological Critique," in *New Directions in Qumran Studies: Proceedings of the Bristol Colloquium on the Dead Sea Scrolls, 8–10 September 2003* (ed. idem, W.J. Lyons, and L.K. Pietersen; London: T&T Clark, 2005), 43–68; R.A. Kraft, "Para-mania: Beside, Before and Beyond Bible Studies," *JBL* 126 (2007): 5–27; A.K. Petersen, "Rewritten Bible as a Borderline Phenomenon: Genre, Textual Strategy, or Canonical Anachronism?" in *Flores Florentino: Dead Sea Scrolls and Other Early Jewish Studies in Honour of Florentino García Martínez* (ed. A. Hilhorst, É. Puech, and E. Tigchelaar; JSJSup 122; Leiden: Brill, 2007), 285–306.

[3] For a description of the unique character of these witnesses, see most recently E. Tov, "Three Strange Books of the LXX: 1 Kings, Esther, and Daniel Compared with Similar Rewritten Compositions from Qumran and Elsewhere," in *Die Septuaginta: Texte, Kontexte, Lebenswelten* (ed. M. Karrer and W. Kraus; WUNT 219; Tübingen: Mohr Siebeck, 2008), 369–393; repr. in *Hebrew Bible, Greek Bible, and Qumran: Collected Essays* (TSAJ 121; Tübingen: Mohr Siebeck, 2008), 283–305.

[4] I proposed a similar argument a number of years ago with specific reference to the so-called Reworked Pentateuch texts from Cave 4; see M. Segal, "4QReworked Pentateuch or 4QPentateuch?" in *The Dead Sea Scrolls Fifty Years After Their Discovery: Proceedings of the Jerusalem Congress, July 20–25, 1997* (ed. L.H. Schiffman et al.; Jerusalem: Israel Exploration Society, 2000), 391–399; idem, "Between Bible and Rewritten Bible."

an authoritative text on the other. The concept of Bible can exist even without one, specific established version of the text.

(2) I would like to express a different reservation about using the term "rewritten" Bible, which is perhaps solved by employing the term "parabiblical."[5] Classic examples of parabiblical texts include the book of *Jubilees*, the *Genesis Apocryphon* from Cave 1, and the *Temple Scroll*. In each of these instances, the rewritten composition can be compared to the known versions of the biblical text, and from this synoptic perspective, the relationship between the source text and the rewritten text can be described. The differences between the "original" and the rewritten versions can be compared in order to determine in what ways and for what reasons the latter has revised the former. From this perspective, the rewritten version is an immediate descendant of the biblical source-text, sometimes following it closely, and at other times at more of a distance. However, this theoretical description assumes that the rewritten biblical texts currently in our possession are *direct* rewritings of a biblical text, each working off of a specific biblical text. However, I suggest that this assumption is methodologically problematic. As has been demonstrated by various scholars, and as I myself attempted to show in the case of *Jubilees*,[6] compositions that we describe as Rewritten Bible, do not rely on the Bible alone for their source material.[7] Works such as *Jubilees* are

---

[5] As noted by S.D. Fraade, "Rewritten Bible and Rabbinic Midrash as Commentary," in *Current Trends in the Study of Midrash* (ed. C. Bakhos; JSJSup 106; Leiden: Brill, 2006), 59–78, at 60–61 n. 5, this term appears to have been proposed first by H.L. Ginsberg, review of J.A. Fitzmyer, *The Genesis Apocryphon of Qumran Cave I: A Commentary*, TS 28 (1967): 574–577, at 574, in reference to the *Genesis Apocryphon*. The label "parabiblical" has gained popularity of late, and was chosen as the name of the four volumes of *DJD* (XIII, XIX, XXII, XXX), which present texts related to the Bible. See also e.g., G.J. Brooke, "Parabiblical Prophetic Narratives," in *The Dead Sea Scrolls after Fifty Years: A Comprehensive Assessment* (ed. P.W. Flint and J.C. VanderKam; 2 vols.; Leiden: Brill, 1998–1999), 1:271–301. For further use of this term and a discussion of the importance of this literature before Qumran, see A. Lange, "The Parabiblical Literature of the Qumran Library and the Canonical History of the Hebrew Bible," in *Emanuel: Studies in Hebrew Bible, Septuagint and Dead Sea Scrolls in Honor of Emanuel Tov* (ed. S.M. Paul et al.; VTSup 94; Leiden: Brill, 2003), 305–321. In the *Encyclopedia of the Dead Sea Scrolls* 2:636, the entry "Parabiblical Literature" consists of a reference to Brooke, "Rewritten Bible."

[6] M. Segal, *The Book of Jubilees: Rewritten Bible, Redaction, Ideology and Theology* (JSJSup 117; Leiden: Brill, 2007).

[7] E.g., for the *Genesis Apocryphon*, see most recently M.J. Bernstein, "Divine Titles and Epithets and the Sources of the Genesis Apocryphon," *JBL* 128 (2009): 291–310. For the *Temple Scroll*, see Y. Yadin, *The Temple Scroll* (3 vols.; Jerusalem: Israel Exploration Society, 1983), 1:386 ("or at least its main sections"), 390; A.M. Wilson and L. Wills,

based not only on the texts of the various biblical books, but also upon other earlier, extant rewritten biblical texts. In fact, the process of rewriting and reuse is perhaps the most fundamental of literary activities in ancient Israelite and Jewish culture. In that sense, the term Rewritten Bible is misleading, since it seemingly refers to the process of composition of the new work, but in reality refers to the nature of the later work vis-à-vis a biblical book. It implies that the biblical book is being rewritten, and not that the final product is a rewritten form of the biblical book. This problem is obviated by the use of the term "parabiblical," which does not posit any direct implications as to the process by which the text was created, but merely indicates that the text reflects some degree of relationship with the Bible itself.

(3) While many of these parabiblical works are assumed to interpret the Bible, and therefore can be classified as exegesis, some scholars have called for a reconsideration of the interpretive nature of these compositions. They suggest instead that the texts reflect the crystallization of alternative, "pre-canonical" traditions, parallel to those that were recorded in the Bible. According to this claim, the perspective of source and interpretation is the result of certain canonical conceptions (or misconceptions), according to which the books that eventually became those that made up the Bible are perceived as "sources," and all other related books are immediately assumed to be interpreting them. Theoretically, in any of these instances, the so-called parabiblical text might reflect not interpretation or reuse, but rather an independent crystallization of the motifs and themes also found in the biblical text.[8] This possibility is bolstered if one assumes that both biblical and parabiblical texts are themselves each based upon sources, as noted above. Why assume that composition A is based upon composition B, when they both might be based upon common building-blocks? Are there any criteria by which one can determine whether a certain work is "pre-canonical," reflecting an alternate literary development, or "post-canonical," reflecting interpretation of an authoritative textual composition?

"Literary Sources of the *Temple Scroll*," *HTR* 75 (1982): 275–288; M.O. Wise, *A Critical Study of the Temple Scroll from Qumran Cave 11* (SAOC 49; Chicago: Oriental Institute of the University of Chicago, 1990); S. White Crawford, *The Temple Scroll and Related Texts* (Companion to the Qumran Scrolls 2; Sheffield: Sheffield Academic Press, 2000), 22–24.
    [8] See Kraft, "Para-mania."

A Rabbinic "Postcursor" of Earlier Traditions

In the context of this brief article, I limit my remarks to one example, which I suggest demonstrates the contribution of rabbinic interpretation to this question. The recognition that many of the phenomena found implicitly in rewritten biblical texts of the Second Temple period correspond to common, later midrashic principles, often expressed explicitly in rabbinic literature, demonstrates the interpretive nature of the former.[9] Although one must always be careful methodologically of retrojecting later assumptions into earlier texts, the presence of similar approaches and techniques in both of these bodies of literature offers the basis for a fruitful comparison of the two. The texts under discussion here stand along a continuum of intensive Jewish interpretive activity from inner-biblical interpretation through the rabbinic period. While there were clearly developments along the way, both in specific interpretations and in the development of new genres, many of the same underlying interpretive principles can be identified throughout these works. A discussion of all of the various modes and methods of rabbinic interpretation is far beyond the scope of this discussion, and I have chosen to analyze here one extended example of this phenomenon. I suggest that this instance illustrates the much broader trend of rewritten biblical compositions serving as forerunners of subsequent modes of biblical interpretation.

The specific example concerns the biblical narrative in Gen 12, which records Abram and Sarai's descent to Egypt due to famine in the Land of Canaan. The events of this story are retold in both the *Genesis Apocryphon* and in *Jubilees*, each adding details, with numerous parallels between them. For example, it is unclear from the biblical story how much time the protagonists spent in the Land before they went to Egypt, or for how long they remained in Egypt before returning. Both the *Genesis Apocryphon* and *Jubilees* relate to these questions, and offer identical chronological details, although each uses a different literary strategy to present these data. In *Jubilees*, the dates are part of the larger heptadic chronological framework of the entire book, which begins with the creation of the world, and by which every event in the biblical period is dated, including these specific events. In the *Genesis Apocryphon*, the dating of these specific events is somewhat anomalous, since at least in

---

[9] See also the insightful discussion of Fraade, "Rewritten Bible and Rabbinic Midrash," who identifies some of the formal and non-formal elements of "Rewritten Bible" within rabbinic midrashim.

the preserved portions of the scroll, there is no attempt to systematically date the many events in the biblical narrative, akin to what is found in *Jubilees*. The *Genesis Apocryphon*'s chronology of the events surrounding Abram and Sarai's descent to, sojourn in, and departure from Egypt can be pieced together from a number of lines in columns XIX–XXII:[10]

(a) 1QapGen ar XIX:9–10[11]

והוית אזל לדרומא [ו]את[ית] עד די דבקת לחברון ול[ה ז]מנא אתב[נ]יאת חברון
ויתבת/ [תמ]ן [תרתין שנ]ין   *vacat*   והוה כפנא בארעא דא כולא ושמעת די ע[בו]ר
איתי במצרין

And I kept going southward [and] wen[t] until I reached Hebron. At [that time] Hebron was bu[i]lt, and *I dwelt/ [the]re [for two ye]ars.   vacat* Now there was a famine in all this land, and I heard that [there was] gr[ai]n in Egypt.

(b) 1QapGen ar XIX:23–24

ולסוף חמש שניא אלן

[אתו] לי תלתת גברין מן רברבי מצרי[ן   ] די פרע[ו] צע[ן] על מל[י] ועל אנתתי

And at the end of those five years,/ three men from the nobles of Egyp[t came] to me [   ] of Pharaoh Zoan concerning [my] words and concerning my wife.

(c) 1QapGen ar XXII:27–29

בתר פתגמיא אלן אתחזי{ו} אלהא לאברם בחזוא ואמר לה הא הא עשר שנין/ שלמא מן יום
די נפקתה מן חרן תרתין עבדתה תנה ושבע במצרין וחדא/ מן די תבת מן מצרין

After these events God appeared to Abram in a vision and said to him, "Look, *ten years have elapsed since the day that you departed from Haran. You passed two here, seven in Egypt, and one since you returned from Egypt.*"

The relevant periods added to the biblical text are as follows: two years in Hebron on the way down to Egypt, five years in Egypt before Sarai was taken by Pharaoh, followed by two more years until they left Egypt. I suggest that some of this new data is the result of a broader exegetical phenomenon in this section of the *Genesis Apocryphon*, namely the harmonization or assimilation of two parallel pentateuchal stories: Abram

---

[10] All of the readings and translations here are those of J.A. Fitzmyer, *The Genesis Apocryphon of Qumran Cave 1 (1Q20): A Commentary* (3rd ed.; BibOr 18/B; Rome: Pontifical Biblical Institute, 2004), unless noted otherwise.

[11] In truth, this first source does not contribute to the chronological discussion, since the relevant information is reconstructed, based upon 1QapGen ar XXII:27–29. As will be demonstrated in the discussion below, however, this source does provide important evidence for the harmonization of the rewritten story in Gen 12 with the subsequent story of national enslavement and emancipation.

and Sarai in Egypt from Gen 12 and the much longer narrative describing the descent of Jacob's family to Egypt, the subsequent subjugation of the Israelites, and the eventual Exodus and return to the Promised Land.[12] The parallel between the personal patriarchal pericope and the national narrative was later recognized explicitly in rabbinic literature, most clearly expounded in *Gen. Rab.* 40 in the name of R. Phineas, a fourth century C.E. Amora living in Israel, who provided a long list of parallels between Abram and Sarai's descent to Egypt due to famine and their eventual departure in Gen 12, and the later enslavement and exodus of the Israelites from the end of Genesis through the book of Exodus:[13]

> AND HE DEALT WELL WITH ABRAM, etc. (Gen 12:16). It is written, *And Pharaoh gave men charge concerning him*, etc. (ibid. 20). R. Phinehas commented in R. Hoshaya's name: The Holy One, blessed be He, said to our father Abraham, "Go forth and tread out a path for thy children." For you find that everything written in connection with Abraham is written in connection with his children.

> In connection with Abraham it is written, *And there was a famine in the land* (ibid. 10); while in connection with Israel it is written, *For these two years hath the famine been in the land* (Gen 45:6).

> Abraham: *And Abram went down into Egypt*; Israel: *And our fathers went down into Egypt* (Num 20:15).

> Abraham: *To sojourn there*; Israel: *To sojourn in the land are we come* (Gen 47:4).

> Abraham: *For the famine was sore in the land*; Israel: *And the famine was sore in the land* (Gen 43:1).

---

[12] The relationship between these stories in the Bible itself has been noted by many scholars. See e.g., U. Cassuto, *A Commentary on the Book of Genesis* (trans. I. Abrahams; 2 vols.; Jerusalem: Magnes, 1961–1964), 334–337; A. Shinan and Y. Zakovitch, *Abram and Sarai in Egypt: Gen. 10:10–20 in the Bible, the Old Versions and the Ancient Jewish Literature* (Research Projects of the Institute of Jewish Studies Monograph Series 2; Jerusalem: Hebrew University, 1983), 139–140 (Hebrew). For the phenomenon of assimilation or harmonization between biblical narratives, see Y. Zakovitch, "Assimilation in Biblical Narratives," in *Empirical Models for Biblical Criticism* (ed. J. Tigay; Philadelphia: University of Pennsylvania Press, 1985), 175–196; M.J. Bernstein, "Re-arrangement, Anticipation and Harmonization as Exegetical Features in the Genesis Apocryphon," *DSD* 3 (1996): 37–57.

[13] English translation taken from *Midrash Rabbah: Translated into English with Notes, Glossary and Indices* (ed. H. Freedman and M. Simon; 10 vols.; London: Soncino, 1961), 1:330–331. For the Hebrew text, see J. Theodor and C. Albeck, eds., *Midrash Bereshit Rabbah* (Jerusalem: Wahrmann, 1965), 385–386.

Abraham: *And it came to pass, when he was come near to enter into Egypt*; Israel: *And when Pharaoh drew nigh*—(Exod 14:10).

Abraham: *And they will kill me, but thee they will keep alive*; Israel: *Every son that is born ye shall cast into the river, and every daughter ye shall save alive* (Exod 1:22).

Abraham: *Say, I pray thee, that thou art my sister, that it may be well with me*; Israel: *And God dealt well with the midwives* (ibid. 20).

Abraham: *And it came to pass, that, when Abram was come into Egypt*; Israel: *Now these are the names of the sons of Israel, who came in Egypt* (ibid. 1).

Abraham: *And Abram was very rich in cattle, in silver, and in gold* (Gen 13:2); Israel: *And He brought them forth with silver and gold* (Ps 105:37).

Abraham: *And Pharaoh gave men charge concerning him, and they sent him away*; Israel: *And the Egyptians were urgent upon the people, to send them out* (Exod 13:33).

Abraham: *And he went on his journeys* (Gen 13:3); Israel: *These are the journeys of the children of Israel* (Num 33:1).

This midrashic source lists numerous similarities between the two stories (including the historiographical Psalm 105). While some of the correspondences are more convincing than others, the general thrust of the argument does appear to be valid. The parallels between the two include:

1. Abram and Jacob/Israel descended to Egypt due to famine in Canaan;
2. Sarai and the Israelites were taken/enslaved by Pharaoh;
3. God afflicted Pharaoh and the Egyptians with plagues;
4. Abraham and the Israelites departed with great wealth;
5. Abraham and Israel returned to Canaan.

I suggest that the exegetical principle made explicit in R. Phineas' formulation, "For you find that everything written in connection with Abraham is written in connection with his children," serves as the motivation for a number of details in the *Genesis Apocryphon*, including the division into the periods of two and five years at the time of the descent into Egypt. Note the following additions or changes in the *Genesis Apocryphon*'s rewritten version of Gen 12:[14]

---

[14] The interpretive thrust outlined here is one among many found in the *Genesis Apocryphon*'s rewritten story of Abram and Sarai in Egypt, and is not intended to be an exhaustive analysis of the biblical interpretation that finds expression in that section.

(i) Genesis 12:10 records that there was a famine in the Land, and that Abram travelled to Egypt to wait it out. There is no explanation in the biblical text as to why he specifically chose Egypt as his destination, but this information is provided in 1QapGen ar XIX:10: "Now there was a famine in all this land, and I heard that [there was] gr[ai]n in Egypt." This explanation is not the creation of this author, but rather is based directly upon Gen 42:2: ויאמר הנה שמעתי כי יש שבר במצרים, "and [Jacob] said, 'Now I hear that there are rations to be had in Egypt'" (cf. the Targumim to Gen 42:2 for the similar formulation in Aramaic). Bernstein adduces this case as "the simplest and least conscious type of harmonization ... the translation or adaptation of a biblical text is affected linguistically by another passage which is analogous to it or with which it shares common elements."[15] At the same time, he allows for the possibility that the association between the stories was performed intentionally,[16] a possibility that is bolstered by the other parallels suggested here.

(ii) In Gen 12:17, the victims of the afflictions are listed in brief as Pharaoh and his household. There is no description of any attempt to mitigate or cure the maladies that plagued them. In contrast, 1QapGen ar XX:18–21 offers an expanded version, according to which Pharaoh enlisted the assistance of his magicians and wise men in an attempt to ward off their deleterious effects:

> So he sent for (19) all the [wi]se [men] of Egypt, all the magicians, together with all the physicians of Egypt, (to see) whether they would be able to cure him of this plague, and the men of (20) his house. But none of the physicians, magicians or any of the wise men were able to rise up and cure him, for that spirit afflicted all of them (too) (21) and they fled.

The general motif here can be described as the competition between a successful, victorious Israelite/Jewish courtier and the unsuccessful Gentile wise men, and is also found in biblical texts such as Gen 41:8–45; Exod 7:11, 22; 8:3; 9:11; Dan 2:2–12; 4:3–6, 15; 5:7–8, 11–12.[17] The formulation in the *Genesis Apocryphon* combines elements from the Daniel narratives, particularly the inclusion of magicians (אשפיא) amongst the wise men (cf. Dan 2:10, 27; 4:4; 5:7, 11, 15). The strongest inspiration,

---

[15] Bernstein, "Re-arrangement," 48; Fitzmyer, *Genesis Apocryphon*, 182 accepts Bernstein's suggestion of unconscious harmonization.

[16] Shinan and Zakovitch, *Abram and Sarai*, 7.

[17] See Fitzmyer, *Genesis Apocryphon*, 206.

however, appears to once again be the influence of the Exodus story upon the "mini"-Exodus in the time of Abram, especially Exod 9:11 in which the חרטמים were unable to withstand the effects of the plague of boils.

(iii) According to Gen 12, after Abram reached Canaan, he first traveled to Shechem (v. 6), and then to Bethel (v. 8). His subsequent stops along the way to Egypt are not mentioned explicitly, and instead the Hebrew text reads: ויסע אברהם הלוך ונסוע הנגבה "Abraham journeyed by stage toward the Negeb" (v. 9). The rewritten story in the *Genesis Apocryphon* (and *Jub.* 13:10) adds another detail—Abram dwelled in Hebron prior to arriving in Egypt. Where were Jacob and his clan living prior to their migration to Egypt during the famine? According to Gen 37:14, when Jacob sent Joseph to inquire about his brothers, leading to his eventual sale, he sent him from the valley of Hebron. Between this story and the beginning of the famine at the end of Gen 41, there is no mention of any change of location of Jacob's family. In *Jub.* 44:1 (parallel to Gen 46:1), it is added explicitly that when Jacob left Canaan for Egypt, he departed from Hebron.[18] The addition of Abram's two-year sojourn in Hebron serves to foreshadow the later departure from Hebron to Egypt two generations later.

(iv) Seven years passed from the point in time that Abram and Sarai reached Hebron, which was built at that time (1QapGen ar XIX:9), until she was taken by Pharaoh Zoan. This period is based upon the explicit biblical notice that Hebron was built seven years prior to Zoan (Num 13:22). The connection to the pentateuchal verse is made explicit in *Jub.* 13:12,[19] though the division into two periods of time, two years (in

---

[18] For the sake of precision, it should be noted that the Geʿez manuscripts of *Jubilees* read *Kārān* (= Haran), but all translators of *Jubilees* since Dillmann (A. Dillmann, "Das Buch der Jubiläen oder die kleine Genesis (II)," *Jahrbücher der biblischen Wissenschaft* 3 [1851]: 1–96, 72 n. 74) agree that this reading is a corruption of Hebron, which could have occurred in Hebrew, Greek, or Ethiopic; see R.H. Charles, *The Book of Jubilees or the Little Genesis: Translated from the Editor's Ethiopic Text* (London: Black, 1902), 238; J.C. VanderKam, *The Book of Jubilees* (2 vols.; CSCO 510–511; Scriptores Aethiopici 87–88; Leuven: Peeters, 1989), 2:288.

[19] The dependence of the *Genesis Apocryphon* upon Num 13:22 has been noted by many scholars, including N. Avigad and Y. Yadin, *A Genesis Apocryphon: A Scroll from the Wilderness of Judea: Description and Contents of the Scroll, Facsimiles, Transcription and Translation of Columns II, XIX–XXII* (Jerusalem: Magnes, 1956), 24–25; Fitzmyer, *Genesis Apocryphon*, 181; Shinan and Zakovitch, *Abram and Sarai*, 61; Bernstein, "Rearrangement," 45. It was of course recognized earlier in the history of *Jubilees* scholarship, e.g., by Charles, *Book of Jubilees*, 98–99.

Hebron) and five years (prior to Sarai's abduction), does not have any specific source in the context of Gen 12 or in Num 13. An important parallel to this division of time can be found later in Genesis, within the seven years of famine that led to the descent of the Israelites to Egypt. According to Gen 45:6, Joseph revealed his identity to his brothers and invited Jacob and his family to come to Egypt after two years of famine, with five years left to go: "It is now two years that there has been famine in the land; and there are still five years to come, in which there shall be no yield from tilling" (NJPS). If the Pentateuch describes a two-year period during which Jacob's family was still in Canaan, followed by five-year period in which they were in Egypt to benefit from its food resources, prior to their eventual subjugation at the hands of Pharaoh, the rewritten story draws a parallel by adding a two-year sojourn in Canaan, followed by five years in Egypt during the famine, after which Sarai was abducted by the Egyptian monarch.

I suggest that these four details in the *Genesis Apocryphon* should be viewed as conscious attempts to assimilate the two stories, with the specific interpretive goal of transforming the story of Abraham into a precursor of the national story of Israel. While these motifs are presented implicitly in the *Genesis Apocryphon*, they match the general interpretive thrust found explicitly in the later rabbinic text, about which there is no argument as to its interpretive nature. This example is but one of many in which one can demonstrate implicit interpretation in earlier rewritten compositions that matches later explicit interpretation, primarily in rabbinic and medieval Jewish commentaries. This shared mode of reading the biblical text corroborates the suggestion that these earlier texts do indeed reflect interpretive compositions, and not merely the canonical assumptions of modern scholars. While there is certainly much to be gained by reflecting on and rethinking our various scholarly assumptions, in this instance our conclusions match this common conception.

APPENDIX: 490 YEARS IN *JUBILEES*

As can be discerned from the details above, the rewritten version of the story in the *Genesis Apocryphon* shares details with that in *Jubilees*, including the division of two and five years, and the addition of Hebron. It is possible to suggest that this idea is further developed in the chronological framework of *Jubilees*, although the following suggestion is less certain than the analysis above (and hence is relegated to an appendix). As is well-known, the book of *Jubilees* dates all of the events from the creation of the world until the entry into Canaan according to a system of jubilees, weeks and years. The narrative culminates in "the jubilee of jubilees," the fiftieth 49-year period in history, during which time Israel was freed from their servitude in Egypt and returned to their ancestral land, Canaan. As noted by VanderKam, these two aspects parallel the two primary elements of the jubilee law in Lev 25, according to which all slaves are freed and all property is returned to its rightful inheritor. The chronological framework of *Jubilees* thus transforms the social law in Leviticus, which refers to the individual, into a blueprint for the nation's fortunes.[20]

Jubilees is not the only composition in the Second Temple period to employ a system of jubilees and weeks in order to date the events of history, but it is the only one to attempt to implement this system in such a systematic and detailed fashion. In many of the other compositions, the period of 490 years is of significance, whether it be 10 jubilees (as in 4QapocrJer C[b] [4Q387] 2 ii 3–4);[21] or seventy weeks of years (as in Dan 9:24–27), a length of time that appears to be absent from *Jubilees'* reckoning. In these other compositions, 490 years often represents a complete period in history, at the end of which the world returns to its original, peaceful state, and therefore, marking the beginning and end of such a period is of great significance for these authors. While there is no doubt that the fifty-jubilee scheme reflects the primary periodization in the book of *Jubilees*, it is possible that there are is also a hint of the recognition of a ten-jubilee period in the chronological framework of the book. Since the chronology in *Jubilees* continues until the end of the fiftieth jubilee, then the final ten-jubilee period at the end of this cycle would commence at the beginning of the forty-first jubilee (forty-first to fiftieth). What events are dated to the beginning of the forty-first jubilee? In the following table, the events surrounding these years are presented in detail:

---

[20] J.C. VanderKam, "Studies in the Chronology of the Book of Jubilees," in *From Revelation to Canon: Studies in the Hebrew Bible and Second Temple Literature* (JSJSup 62; Leiden: Brill, 2000), 522–544 at 532–540; trans. of "Das chronologische Konzept des Jubiläenbuches," *ZAW* 107 (1995): 80–100.

[21] *DJD* XXX (2001): 179.

Jubilees	Event	Jubilee	Week	Year	Year from Creation
13:8	Abram builds an altar in Bethel	40	7	1	1954
13:10	Abram dwells in Hebron for two years				1954–1956
13:11	Abram travels to Egypt	40	7	3	1956
13:11	Five year period before Sarai is taken				1956–1960
13:16	Abram returns to the same location in Canaan	41	1	3	1963
48:1	The Exodus	50	2	2	2410
50:4	Israelites return to Canaan	50	7	7	2450

According to the data in the chronological framework, the periods of two and five years described above fall out in the final week of the fortieth jubilee (13:10, 11). It can therefore be deduced that in the first year of the forty-first jubilee, Sarai was taken by force to Pharaoh. Precisely at the beginning of this final ten-jubilee period, after Abram and Sarai departed from Canaan and went to Egypt, Sarai was subjugated to Pharaoh. The end of this ten-jubilee period describes the conclusion of the parallel events but on a national scale, when Israel was released from this servitude and returned to Canaan. Perhaps by demarcating the ten-jubilee period, the author responsible for the chronological framework indicated the inherent connection between the *Urzeit* and *Endzeit* of this period. The story of Abram and Sarai here too perhaps serves as a portent of future events on a national scale.

At the same time, however, it must be noted that although the dates fall exactly as described here, there is no explicit emphasis on the ten-jubilee period or of the specific date in question, and it is only implicitly derived from the chronological information contained in the rewritten narrative. While implicit interpretation is characteristic of some of the dates added to the rewritten biblical stories in *Jubilees*,[22] the absence of any notice of the beginning of the forty-first jubilee is highly suspect if the emphasis is supposed to be upon a ten-jubilee period. Furthermore, there does not seem to be another instance in the book in which the ten jubilee periods play a similar role (i.e, between jubilees 1–10, 11–20, 21–30, and 31–40). Therefore, despite the potential support that

---

[22] See for example my discussion of the interpretation of the 120-year period of Gen 6:3 in *Jubilees* in Segal, *Book of Jubilees*, 119–125.

the chronological framework in *Jubilees* offers for the continuation of this interpretive trajectory, there is an equally strong possibility that the numbers here have aligned as a matter of chance,[23] and not due to an elaborate chronological scheme

---

[23] In a future study I hope to address the issue of the literary relationship between the *Genesis Apocryphon* and *Jubilees* in this passage, with special reference to their common chronology. If the five-year delay has its origins in the *Genesis Apocryphon* and was subsequently adopted by *Jubilees* (a proposition that I will further develop there), then the specific timing of Sarai's subjugation would possibly be the result of the adoption and inclusion of the *Genesis Apocryphon*'s chronological data within *Jubilees*, and not part of an elaborate ten-jubilee construct.

MIRIAM MISBEHAVING?
THE FIGURE OF MIRIAM IN 4Q377 IN LIGHT
OF ANCIENT JEWISH LITERATURE

HANNA TERVANOTKO

University of Helsinki and University of Vienna

4QApocryphal Pentateuch B (4Q377) is one of three texts from the Qumran library that mentions the figure of Miriam.[1] According to the editors of 4Q377, James C. VanderKam and Monica Brady, the text preserves at least one line that deals with Miriam's opposition to Moses in Num 12.[2] They also propose that 4Q377 2 i 10 might attest to Num 12.[3] Because the suggested connection between 4Q377 2 i 9–10 and Num 12 has not yet been studied in detail, this is the task of the present article. After a critical analysis of lines 9 and 10, this study takes into consideration other re-narrations of Num 12: Demetrius (the Chronographer); Philo, *Leg.* 1.76; 2.66–67; 3.103; *m. Soṭah* 1:7, 9; and *Sipre Num* 99. Their style of rephrasing the Pentateuchal narration is analyzed and I ask if they can illuminate the reconstruction of 4Q377. I also consider the reception of the figure of Miriam in the re-narrations of Num 12 in general and in 4Q377 in particular.

---

[1] J.C. VanderKam and M. Brady in *DJD* XXVIII (2001): 205–218. Miriam is also referred to in the *Visions of Amram* (4Q543 1 i 6 = 4Q545 1 i 5; 4Q546 12 4; 4Q547 9 10; 4Q549 2 i 8), see É. Puech in *DJD* XXXI (2001): 283–405, and in 4QRP^c (4Q365) 6 ii 1–7, see E. Tov and S. White in *DJD* XIII (1994): 255–318. For a general presentation of Miriam in the Dead Sea Scrolls see H. Tervanotko, "The Hope of the Enemy has Perished: The Figure of Miriam in the Qumran Library," in *From Qumran to Aleppo: A Discussion with Emanuel Tov about the Textual History of Jewish Scriptures in Honor of his 65th Birthday* (ed. A. Lange, M. Weigold, and J. Zsengellér; FRLANT 230; Göttingen: Vandenhoeck & Ruprecht, 2009), 156–175; S. White Crawford, "Traditions about Miriam in the Qumran Scrolls," *Studies in Jewish Civilization* 14 (2003): 33–44; eadem, "Miriam," *Encyclopedia of the Dead Sea Scrolls* (ed. L.H. Schiffman and J.C. VanderKam; 2 vols.; Oxford: Oxford University Press, 2000), 1:566–567.

[2] VanderKam and Brady in *DJD* XXVIII (2001): 212.

[3] Ibid.

1. Introduction to the Manuscript 4Q377

The preserved text of 4Q377 does not directly quote the Pentateuch, but reworks it by using it as related stories. 4Q377 demonstrates an interest in the wilderness period, and it contains references to Exodus, Numbers, and Deuteronomy. The figure of Moses plays a prominent role throughout the narration. Prior to the *DJD* edition published in 2001, this text was known as "4QApocryphon of Moses C" due to the centrality of Moses.[4] The previous title also indicates that 4Q377 was assigned to a collection of texts (4Q374–375) that were already thought to belong together.[5]

In the *DJD* edition, the text of 4Q377 was given a new title, "4QApocryphal Pentateuch B." The new title does not merely highlight the key figure of the text but its wider content.[6] The text is interpreted by the editors as a pentateuchal re-narration. In the same way that its first title carried generic implications, the new title indicates that it displays similarities with at least one other text: "4QApocryphal Pentateuch A" (4Q368), also published by VanderKam and Brady.[7] The two texts exhibit common elements. The figure of Moses plays a prominent role in them and they both use the Pentateuch in their narrations.[8] Despite these similarities it is difficult to say how the connection between 4Q368 and 4Q377 should be interpreted. The texts do not overlap. VanderKam and Brady argue that their portrayal of Moses is different.[9] Given these hesitations, 4Q377 is treated as an independent text in this study.[10]

---

[4] D.K. Falk, "Moses, Texts of," *Encyclopedia of the Dead Sea Scrolls* 1:577–581, uses the title "Apocryphon of Moses C"; cf. G.J. Brooke, "Rewritten Bible," *Encyclopedia of the Dead Sea Scrolls* 2:771–781; É. Puech, "Le fragment 2 de 4Q377, Pentateuch Apocryphe B: L'exaltation de Moïse," *RevQ* 21 (2004): 469–475.

[5] Collections or circles of texts; see E. Tov, *Hebrew Bible, Greek Bible, and Qumran: Collected Essays* (TSAJ 121; Tübingen: Mohr Siebeck, 2008), 432.

[6] See n. 1; the *DJD* edition (mainly frg. 2 ii) has been revised by Puech, "Le fragment 2 de 4Q377," 469–475; cf. Falk, "Moses, Texts of," 1:581.

[7] J.C. VanderKam and M. Brady in *DJD* XXVIII (2001): 131–149.

[8] VanderKam and Brady in *DJD* XXVIII (2001): 207: "It is understandable that 4Q368 and 4Q377 have been associated with each other by being named 4QApocryphon Pentateuch A–B, even though the two do not overlap. Both clearly reflect and rework materials from various parts of the Pentateuch, especially Exod (the Sinai sections), Num and Deut."

[9] Ibid., 207–208: "4Q368 portrays Moses and God conversing whereas in 4Q377 Moses is depicted as a man."

[10] All text editions of the Dead Sea Scrolls do not assign 4Q368 and 4Q377 into the same literary groups. For instance, *The Dead Sea Scrolls Reader* groups 4Q368 within the category of "Re-written Bible," whereas, 4Q377 is "an un-classified document." This

4Q377 has a first century B.C.E. paleographic date.[11] This text was found in the collection of the Qumran library, but it does not contain any of the characteristics that are usually recognized as the "sectarian" features.[12] Free use of the tetragrammaton in this text (4Q377 2 ii 3, 4), also suggests a non-Essene origin.[13] Hence, this study presumes that the text originates from wider Hellenistic Judaism.

2. 4Q377 FRAGMENT 2

Five fragments are assigned to 4Q377. Fragment 2 is the largest of them. Column i of this fragment contains 11 lines, but only six of them preserve whole words. VanderKam and Brady identify the following structure in the text of 4Q377 2 i: Lines 4–5 contain the list of spies of Num 13.[14] Line 6 refers to the rearguard and the minimal age of military service of Num 1.[15] Line 7 is *vacat* and line 8 may allude the blessing of Levi in Deut 33:8.[16] As mentioned earlier, the editors maintain that line 9, and possibly line 10, might re-narrate the encounter between Miriam and Moses (and Aaron?) in Num 12.[17]

---

differing grouping reflects the un-determined status of some pentateuchal re-narrations and fluidity of the current terminology. See E. Tov and D.W. Parry, eds., *The Dead Sea Scrolls Reader* (6 vols.; Leiden: Brill, 2004–2005), 3:116–122, 596–599.

[11] VanderKam and Brady in *DJD* XXVIII (2001): 205–206; B. Webster in *DJD* XXXIX (2002): 351–446, 372; A. Lange, "Pre-Maccabean Literature from the Qumran Library and the Hebrew Bible," *DSD* 13 (2006): 277–305.

[12] For the sectarian features see D. Dimant, "Sectarian and Non-Sectarian Texts from Qumran: The Pertinence and Usage of Taxonomy," *RevQ* 93 (2009): 7–18; C. Newsom, "Sectually Explicit Literature from Qumran," in *The Hebrew Bible and Its Interpreters* (ed. W. Propp, B. Halpern, and D.N. Freedman; Winona Lake: Eisenbrauns, 1990), 167–187. J.C. VanderKam and P.W. Flint, *The Meaning of the Dead Sea Scrolls: Their Significance For Understanding the Bible, Judaism, Jesus, and Christianity* (New York: HarperCollins, 2002), 255–273 deal with Essene belief system and theology. A. Lange, "Kriterien essenischer Texte," in *Qumran kontrovers: Beiträge zu den Textfunden vom Toten Meer* (ed. J. Frey and H. Stegemann; Paderborn: Bonifatius, 2003), 59–69.

[13] Falk, "Moses, Texts of," 1:581.

[14] "From the tribe of Benjamin, Palti son of Raphu" (Num 13:9 NRSV).

[15] "Take a census of the whole congregation of Israelites, in their clans, by ancestral houses, according to the number of names, every male individually; from twenty years old and upwards, everyone in Israel able to go to war" (Num 1:2–3 NRSV).

[16] "And of Levi he said: Give to Levi your Thummim, and your Urim to your loyal one, whom you tested at Massah, with whom you contended at the waters of Meribah" (Deut 33:8 NRSV). The connection is based on term "pious man" (איש חסיד) that appears in both.

[17] See the introduction of this article; VanderKam and Brady in *DJD* XXVIII (2001): 207.

4Q377 2 i:[18]

3 [ ] this
4 [to the tri]be of Benjamin, Raphia
5 [ ] *ymry* to the tribe of Gad Elyo
6 [ ] the rearguard from twenty years of age
7 [ ] *vacat*
8 [ ] one of the pious ones and he lifted his voice
9 [and] he returned [his] an[ger and]Miriam [shut her]self from his eye(s) *vacat* years of
10 [ ] against us and lead to us because

2.1. *4Q377 2 i 9*

Based on the remaining words and reconstructions of the text of 4Q377 2 i, it seems that this text deals mainly with Numbers. Nevertheless, because of the fragmentary nature of this manuscript, it is possible that parts of the text that are not preserved refer to other parts of the Pentateuch. Hence, this study is not strictly limited to comparisons with Exodus and Numbers, but it takes into consideration broader pentateuchal material.

One of the words that is legible in frg. 2 is "Miriam" in line 9. As 4Q377 uses pentateuchal material, the appearance of the name could imply that lines 9 and 10 rework a pentateuchal passage that mentions Miriam: Exod 15:20–21; Num 12:1–15; 20:1; 26:59; or Deut 24:9. But Miriam is not the only character mentioned in this text. The name of Moses appears several times in 4Q377.[19] Even more lines allude to Moses without specifically naming him.[20] The frequent use of his name implies that Miriam cannot be the protagonist of the text. Its main interest lies in Moses. Therefore, the passage to which 4Q377 2 i 9 refers should be found within texts where these two figures, Miriam and Moses, are presented together. This limitation of texts narrows down the possible references, because the

---

[18] Translation by VanderKam and Brady, ibid., 212. I follow their translation in this article. Puech, "Le fragment 2 de 4Q377," 469–475, has proposed some alternative readings regarding line 10. His suggestions will be taken into consideration while analyzing 4Q377 2 i 10.

[19] 4Q377 2 ii 2, 5, 10.

[20] For instance, 4Q377 2 ii 11: "When he was sanctified, and like a messenger he would speak from his mouth, for who of fles[h] is like him." VanderKam and Brady in *DJD* XXVIII (2001): 214, 216.

two appear in interaction in only three passages of the Pentateuch: Exod 15:20–21; Num 12:1–15; and Deut 24:9.

4Q377 2 i 9 is fragmentary like the rest of the text. The first word in line 9 (שיב) is certain, as is the following one (חרון). Before the manuscript breaks, we can see traces of the next letter, which the editors suggest to be *’ālep*. In the Pentateuch the word "anger" (חרון) appears in the wilderness passages (Exod 15:7; 32:12; Num 25:4; 32:14; Deut 13:18). In these passages it is used in connection with another word describing anger, אף.[21] These terms that indicate fury do not point to just any type of anger, but exclusively the rage of God. Sentences that mention "great anger" (חרון אף) of God and refer to the Deity in third person in the Pentateuch use the tetragrammaton.[22] Interestingly, this terminology is also used in the Dead Sea Scrolls to describe God's anger (CD 9:4, 6; 10:9 = 4Q270 6 iv 19; 4Q169 1–2 11; 4Q375 1 i 3; 4Q504 1–2 iii 11; v 5; 11Q11 IV:5; 11QT[a] LV:11). In the Dead Sea Scrolls, however, their use is not restricted to the Deity. The two terms can likewise point to people e.g., the Kittim (1QpHab III:12), and members of community (4QD[e] [4Q270] 6 iii 18). Moreover, appearances of חרון and אף in the Dead Sea Scrolls do not require the context of wilderness.

The subject of line 9 is not known. Based on the use of terms אף and חרון in the Pentateuch, the tetragrammaton, which is used elsewhere in 4Q377 (2 ii 3, 5), could possibly be inserted here. From the next word only the last letter, *rêš*, survives. The editors suggest, on the basis of Num 12:14, that the word could be reconstructed "to shut, to close" (אתסגר).[23] This verb is often connected to dealing with צרעת "leprosy" in the Pentateuch and it appears in Lev 13–14 where the treatment of this illness is discussed.[24] The *nip'al* form appears only once with מן

---

[21] In Exod 15:7 the word אף follows only in the next verse, Exod 15:8.

[22] See the entries אף and חרון in *HALOT* 1:76, 351–352. Exod 15:7; 32:12; Num 25:4; 32:14; Deut 13:18 refer to the Divine in second person and the tetragrammaton does not occur in these passages.

[23] VanderKam and Brady in *DJD* XXVIII (2001): 207. "Let her be shut out (תסגר) of the camp for seven days, and after that she may be brought in again" (Num 12:14 NRSV). "So Miriam was shut out (תסגר) of the camp for seven days" (Num 12:15 NRSV). For the appearances of the verb סגר in the Qumran library see CD 1:17 (= 4Q266 2 i 21); 3:10; 6:12, 13; 7:13; 8:1 (= 4Q266 3 iii 23); 13:6; 19:13; 1QM XI:2, 13; 1QH[a] XI:19; XIII:11, 16; 1Q27 1 i 5; 4Q269 7 6 (= 4Q272 1 i 11); 4Q273 4 ii 2); 4Q271 5 ii 21; 4Q299 8 9; 4Q381 45 a+b 3; 4Q390 1 9; 2 i 4; 4Q418 126 ii 7; 201 2; 4Q422 II:5; III:9; 4Q512 67 2; 11QT[a] XXXIV:5; XLIX:2.

[24] In Lev 13:4, 5, 11, 21, 26, 31, 33, 50, 54; 14:38, 46 the verb סגר appears in *hip'il* meaning "to separate" or "to barricade" (a house). The exact nature of צרעת that is usually translated as "leprosy" remains unsolved. D. Wright and R. Jones, "Leprosy," *ABD* 4:277–282.

(preposition) with the meaning: "to be shut out" (Num 12:14). As only one letter of this word is preserved, this reconstruction is uncertain. The words indicating the "great anger" (חרון אף) can be found in two different passages where Miriam appears: Num 12:9[25] and Exod 15:7–8.[26] The first of these is a more direct reference to Miriam, whereas the latter verses belong to the Song of Moses. The third passage that mentions Miriam in the Pentateuch is Deut 24:8. It does not share any common vocabulary with 4Q377.

The style of narration of 4Q377 is not evident. God speaks in some lines. For instance, in 4Q377 1 i 6 the deity states: "I will judge between a man and his friend, between a father and his son, between a man and his sojourner." Meanwhile, text of frg. 2 often points to an outside narrator that reports the events in third person singular: "he lifted his voice" (2 i 8); "he turned his anger" (2 i 9). As we have seen, in 4Q377 2 i 10 the narration appears in the first person plural form: "us and lead it against us." The following column addresses the audience directly (2 ii 3): "Hear, congregation of YHWH, and pay attention all assembly." This might indicate again a speaker that addresses the Israelites.[27] In spite of this, the tense and the narrator of the text cannot be determined with certainty. It is possible that the narrator or the speaker changes in this text.

The text of 4Q377 is a narrative dealing with Moses' and Israel's experiences. This style should be compared with the passages where Miriam appears next. Regarding the pentateuchal Miriam passages, Exod 15:20–21 is best characterized as a victory song.[28] Deut 24:8–9 appears in the context of rules and laws given to the people. The legal setting of that text is likewise indicated by the verbs "to keep, to watch over" (שמר), "to do" (עשה), "to command" (צוה) and by its references to priests who monitor correct conduct. Moreover, its use of the pedagogic "remember"-formula (זכור) implies that audiences are reminded to bear in mind Miriam's destiny and the commandments set in Lev 13–14 for צרעת. Finally, Num-

---

[25] "And the anger of the Lord (חרון אף) was kindled against them, and he departed" (Num 12:9 NRSV).

[26] "You sent out your fury (חרונך)" (Exod 15:7 NRSV). "At the blast of your nostrils (אפיך) the waters piled up" (Exod 15:8 NRSV). In the latter examples the term אף points to nostrils and not to anger.

[27] VanderKam and Brady in *DJD* XXVIII (2001): 207.

[28] For example D. O'Donnel Setel, "Exodus," in *Women's Bible Commentary: Expanded Edition with Apocrypha* (ed. C. Newsom and S. Ridge, Louisville: Westminster John Knox, 1998), 35; M. Noth, *Exodus: A Commentary* (OTL; London: SCM Press, 1962), 120–123.

bers can be described as a narrative concerning Israel's forty years "in the wilderness."[29] As 4Q377 also reflects the "Sinai sections" and its style is somewhat similar, Num 12 corresponds the content of line 9 the best. Based on these observations I think that VanderKam and Brady are right in suggesting that 4Q377 2 i 9 uses material of Num 12:1–15.

2.2. 4Q377 2 i 10

Of line 10 only four words are legible. Puech reads this line differently from the *DJD* edition: "us and lead it against us because" (אלינו ונהגה עלינו כיא).[30] The key term of this line is the verb "to lead, to guide, to shepherd" (נהג), with which both readings agree. The verb appears in third person singular feminine or in third person singular masculine together with a suffix ("she will lead it"/"he will lead it"). If this is a continuation of the previous line, then to whom could this verb apply?

The verb appears in the Hebrew Bible about 30 times.[31] Roughly one fourth of the appearances are found in the Pentateuch, where leading (נהג) refers both to people (individuals) and God. Genesis 31:18, 20 deal with the family of Jacob and Isaac. Exodus 3:1 and 10:13 apply to Moses who shepherds his father-in-law's flock in 3:1 and brings to locust in Egypt in 10:13. The rest of the references of נהג are used for the deity. In Exod 14:25 God fights with the Israelites against the Egyptians, and in Deut 4:27; 28:37 a divine message is proclaimed that Israel will be brought among foreign people.[32] Apart from 4Q377 2 i 10, נהג appears in the re-narrations on Gen 31: 4QTNaph (4Q215) 1–3 8 and 4QpapJub^h (4Q223–224) 2 i 51 (*Jub.* 35:10).

Because of the manuscript deterioration it is difficult to determine the identity of the narrator in line 10. It is logical to think that the first person plural "us" indicates that the narrator is not an external third person, but that the speaker locates him/herself in the text. As the verb "to lead" does

---

[29] K. Doob Sakenfeld, "Numbers," in *Women's Bible Commentary*, 49.

[30] Puech, "Le fragment 2 de 4Q377," 475. English translation by the present author. For the *DJD* edition, see § 2. The most concrete difference between the readings offered by VanderKam and Brady and Puech is that the latter reads preposition "against us" connected with the verb. VanderKam and Brady read the verb without the negative preposition על ("lead to us").

[31] Gen 31:18, 26; Exod 3:1; 10:13; Deut 4:27; 28:37; 1 Sam 23:5; 30:20, 22; 2 Sam 6:3; 2 Kgs 4:24; 9:20; 1 Chr 13:7; 20:1; 2 Chr 25:11; Job 24:3; Pss 48:15; 78:26, 52; 80:1; Qoh 2:3; Cant 8:2; Isa 11:6; 20:4; 40:10; 49:10; 60:11; 63:14; Nah 2:8.

[32] Notably, this verb is not used for Aaron or Miriam in the Hebrew Bible or in the Dead Sea Scrolls.

not apply to Aaron or Miriam in the Pentateuch, it is unlikely, yet not impossible, that one of them appears here. Whereas Miriam appears in 4Q377 2 i 9, nothing indicates Aaron's presence in this passage. Moses and God are more central characters in this text, and therefore the leading should refer to one of them. When the verb "to lead" (נהג) is used for Moses in the Pentateuch, it never applies to leading of people. Moses brings (i.e., leads) locusts or shepherds lambs, but he is not described as a shepherd for people in the Pentateuch. Since 4Q377 clearly applies to leading people ("lead us"), it seems more plausible that 4Q377 2 i 10 does not indicate Moses' leading, but that of God.

Moses might be present in the passage and talk about leading. The line could find distant parallels in passages of Deuteronomy where Moses addresses people about God leading (נהג) them among foreign nations (4:27; 28:37).[33] These passages do not narrate God's leading as something positive, but rather as a scattering of the people among foreign nations that should be viewed as a punishment. This view supports Puech's reconstruction of the line.[34] Moreover, the context of the wilderness and various challenges that the Israelites met there could likewise motivate Puech's reading "against us."

In light of these arguments I suggest that the line 10 of 4Q377 does not seem to continue dealing with Num 12 and Miriam. Rather, it introduces new material into the text. This characteristic is in line with the structure of 4Q377 2 i where each line refers to different pentateuchal passage. Line 10 might return to the dialogue between Moses and the Divine.

3. NUMBERS 12 REPHRASED?

I have concluded that 4Q377 2 i 9 probably contains a reference to Num 12. This allusion concerns the figure of Miriam. The remaining content of this reference remains uncertain. A look at other Jewish texts dating to the Greco-Roman era where Num 12 is rephrased might help us to interpret this line. How was Num 12 re-narrated elsewhere? What is emphasized in the re-narrations? Do they share any common features?[35]

---

[33] God's leading of Israel is compared with a shepherd that leads his flock, for instance, in Pss 78:52; 80:1; and Isa 40:10.

[34] Puech, "Le fragment 2 de 4Q377," 475.

[35] Deuteronomy 24, which I have already mentioned while discussing the terminology of 4Q377 2 i 9, refers to the same tradition. As the relation between Num 12 and Deut 24, and especially their dates are not yet defined I have decided to not to go into more details

3.1. Demetrius (the Chronographer)

"And for this reason also, Aaron and Miriam said at Hazeroth that Moses had married an Ethiopian woman."[36]

Demetrius was a third century B.C.E. writer who lived in Ptolemaic Egypt. His writings are preserved only in citations by other writers.[37] Demetrius' goal was to write Jewish historiography to an educated audience, and his particular interest laid in explaining difficulties and filling out the gaps that the writing of history had left.[38] His reference to Num 12 (frg. 3:3) first provides a detailed survey of Moses' and Zipporah's genealogies. Demetrius concludes his study by stating that Zipporah was Abraham's descendent by his second wife, Keturah.[39] This assumption has some implications. First, it challenges the argument phrased by Aaron and Miriam in Num 12:1, i.e., that Moses married a foreign woman. Demetrius argues that this wife was Zipporah, not another second wife.[40] Second, as Zipporah was of Abrahamic origin, she was not considered a foreigner. Third, Demetrius' mention of Aaron implies the writer considered Aaron to take part in this dispute. Finally, given Demetrius' general aim to clarify passages, his attention to Num 12 indicates that this passage required further explanation. Related to this final point isthe sentence "it was for this reason that Aaron and Miriam said that Moses had married an Ethiopian woman" (frg. 3:3), which is a sign of his task and suggests that Num 12 needed clarification. This re-narration that focuses

---

here. G. von Rad leaves the relation of the texts open (*Deuteronomy: A Commentary* [OTL; London: SCM Press, 1964], 151). R. Burns, *Has the Lord indeed Spoken only Through Moses: A Study of the Biblical Portait of Miriam* (SBLDS 84; Atlanta: Scholars Press, 1987), 101–105 assumes that Num 12 is behind Deut 24. I will deal with this question more in detail in my forthcoming dissertation.

[36] Eusebius, *Praep. ev.* 9.29.3. Translation according to J. Hanson, "Demetrius the Chronographer (Third Century B.C.): A New Translation and Introduction," in *OTP* 2:843–854, 853.

[37] Eusebius, *Praep. ev.* 9. Demetrius likely wrote during the time of Philopator (ca. 221–205 B.C.E.). M. Hengel, "The Interpenetration of Judaism and Hellenism in the Pre-Maccabean Period," in *The Cambridge History of Judaism*, vol. 2: *The Hellenistic Age* (ed. W.D. Davies and L. Finkelstein; Cambridge: Cambridge University Press, 1989), 200.

[38] J.J. Collins, *Between Athens and Jerusalem: Jewish Identity in the Hellenistic Diaspora* (The Biblical Resource Series; Grand Rapids: Eerdmans, 2000), 33. For Demetrius' genealogies, see frgs. 2:1–19; 3:2–3.

[39] Frg. 3:2–3.

[40] On Moses' marriages, see T. Rajak, "Moses in Ethiopia: Legend and Literature," *JJS* 29 (1978): 111–122.

on Zipporah's lineage, implies that Moses' intermarriage was not received at ease. It required more details in the community where Demetrius wrote.[41]

3.2. *Philo of Alexandria,* Legum Allegoriae

Philo of *Alexandria* mentions the *Miriam* figure six times in his works.[42] Half of the references are found in *Legum allegoriae*, where Philo offers allegorical interpretations of Gen 1–3. True to his method, the characters of the text are understood to represent different parts of soul and Philo draws moral lessons and instructions of how one should behave from them.

Philo refers to Num 12 altogether three times in *Legum allegoriae*. In the first of them (1.76) he builds a connection between the four rivers surrounding paradise and the four Greek cardinal virtues (temperance, prudence, courage, and justice). While discussing prudence (φρόνη-σις), Philo explains that prudence is recognized in speech, but also in deeds and in actions. He uses the figure of Miriam as an example of an imprudent figure. According to Philo, Moses bids God to heal Miriam in Num 12 in order that she would not be occupied with evil things. In the second reference (2.66–67) Philo discusses Gen 3 together with nudity and shame. Miriam serves as an example also in this context. This time she symbolizes shamelessness (ἀναισχυντία) and sense-perception (αἴσθησις) because of her speaking against Moses.[43] Miriam's connection with shamelessness is repeated in 3.103 where Philo discusses some Israelites' instruction. He claims that Moses got his formation from God whereas Miriam was taught by the outward sense. Numbers 12 serves to justify this idea.

What characterizes Philo's interpretation of Num 12 is that he emphasizes that Miriam spoke against Moses (*Leg.* 2.66–67) and rose against him (*Leg.* 3.103). Philo does not attest how the speaking against or rising up against took place. He does not explicate the motives that caused a conflict between the figures. Philo's portrayal of Miriam in *Legum allegoriae* displays a rather negative reception of her. Miriam is treated as

---

[41] Hanson, "Demetrius the Chronographer," in *OTP* 2:844, argues Demetrius worked in Egypt, maybe Alexandria.

[42] *Leg.* 1.76; 2.66; 3.103; *Agr.* 80; 81; *Contempl.* 87. In *Mos.* 2.256 Philo refers to Moses' sister.

[43] D. Sly, *Philo's Perception of Women* (BJS 209; Atlanta: Scholars Press, 1990), 119–123.

an allegorical representation of the less virtuous part of the soul, and Num 12 motivates this use. Philosophy that seeks to combine gender and human soul is typical for Philo and similar schemes can be found in other passages where he deals with female figures.[44] Usually in Philo's thinking the female figures represent the inferior part of the soul, the sense perception (αἴσθησις), whereas male represent the rational (νοῦς).[45]

Philo was certainly aware of Moses' intermarriage because he reports Moses marrying "the most beautiful daughter" of a priest in Arabia.[46] He also mentions Moses' Ethiopian wife in *Leg.* 2.67, where he argues that their marriage was arranged by the Deity. Philo was also known for his opposition to intermarriage. This is reflected, for instance, in *Spec.* 3.29, where he claims that the prohibition for exogamy came from Moses himself. Hence, Philo's dealing with Moses' marriage and intermarriage displays controversy and revels that Num 12 was somehow difficult for him. When referring to Num 12 he decides to mention only Miriam and presents her as a symbol for irrational behavior. Philo completely overlooks Moses' intermarriage or other possible motives of the conflict.

3.3. Early Rabbinic Texts

Some early (i.e., Tannaitic, ca. 200 C.E.) rabbinic commentaries picked up on Num 12 too. Similarly to the styles of Philo's *Legum allegoriae* and Demetrius, their attention is focused on a specific theme of Num 12. M. *Soṭah* 1:7, 9 refer to Num 12 in a passage that deals with judging: "By that same measure by which a man metes out [to others], they mete out to him: Miriam waited for Moses, since it is said, *And his sister afar off* (Exod 2:4), therefore Israel waited on her seven days in the wilderness, since it is said, *And the people did not travel on until Miriam was brought in again* (Num 12:15)."[47]

M. *Soṭah* bears witness to an early interpretation of Num 12 where Miriam is punished and then closed off the camp. Nevertheless, the Israelites do not continue their journey until Miriam is brought back.

---

[44] Ibid.; J.R. Wegner, "The Image of Woman in Philo," *SBLSP* 21 (1982): 551–559; eadem, "Philo's Portrayal of Women—Hebraic or Hellenic?" in *Women Like This: New Perspectives on Jewish Women in the Greco-Roman World* (ed. A.J. Levine; Atlanta: Scholars Press, 1991), 41–66.

[45] Ibid.

[46] *Mos.* 1.59.

[47] J. Neusner, *The Mishnah: A New Translation* (Rensselaer: Yale University Press, 1988), 449.

According to *m. Soṭah* the Israelites waited for Miriam because she merited being waited for. This interpretation derives from Exod 2:4 where Moses is hidden in a basket and his anonymous sister follows it. At least from the second century B.C.E. on, a stream of Judaism thought that this unnamed sister was Miriam.[48] *M. Soṭah* connects the two passages, Exod 2:4 and Num 12:15, together. It was because of Miriam's earlier waiting that she merited to be waited for.

Another early rabbinic commentary interprets Num 12 differently. In *Sipre Num* 99 Zipporah tells Miriam that since Moses spoke with God, he is abstaining from their marital life.[49] After this exchange between the two women, Miriam discusses the matter with Aaron. Then *Sipre Num* adds the verse "Miriam and Aaron criticized Moses for the Cushite wife" (Num 12:1 NRSV). *Sipre Num* is similar to Demetrius in that it understands that Zipporah, whom Moses married in Exod 2:21, was the Cushite wife of Num 12:1. This reading appears in other rabbinic texts.[50] *Sipre Num* does not present Miriam or Aaron as critics for Moses' foreign wife. Rather, this text presents Miriam as an ally for Zipporah, who simply discusses Moses' marriage.

One motif of this midrash seems to lie in advocating the prominence of marital life. Some streams of Judaism highlighted the idea that since God spoke with Moses, he became a celibate. Moses abstained from his marital life in order to preserve his state of ritual purity.[51] *Sipre Num* that emphasizes the importance of marital life might originate in the same discussion. Miriam and Aaron did not criticize Moses for marrying a foreign wife, but for not having marital life with her. The interpretations preserved in *m. Soṭah* and *Sipre Num* remind one of those of the other early texts. The rabbinic commentaries raise one matter of Num 12 and focus on it. They seem to understand that the conflict between the

---

[48] This line of interpretation is notably present at least, for instance, in *Jub.* 47:4 and Ezek. Trag. 18.

[49] D. Börner-Klein, *Tannaitische Midrashim*, vol. 3: *Der Midrasch Sifre zu Numeri* (Stuttgart: Kohlhammer, 1997), 165–166.

[50] *Sipre Zuṭa* 81–82, 203–204. See also the Pentateuch Targumim. *Tg. Neof.*: "And Miriam and Aaron spoke against Moses concerning the Cushite woman that he had married; and behold, the Cushite woman was Zipporah, the wife of Moses; except that as the Cushite woman is different in her body from every other creature, so was Zipporah, the wife of Moses, handsome in form and beautiful in appearance and different in good works from all the women of that generation." M. McNamara, *Targum Neofiti 1: Numbers* (ArBib 4; Edinburgh; T&T Clark, 1995), 76.

[51] For instance, Pentateuch Targumim emphasize that Moses kept distance to his Cushite wife in Num 12:1.

figures that originated in Num 12:1 and in the question regarding Moses'
marriage. The rabbinic commentaries do not present Miriam as a critic
for Moses' marriage with a foreign wife. Rather Miriam appears as an
advocate for marriage.[52] Therefore her function in this story is positive.

4. The Cushite Wife or the Prophecy?

Numbers 12 depicts two separate clashes between Moses and Miriam. In
Num 12:1 Miriam criticizes Moses because of his Cushite wife, and in
Num 12:2 Miriam asks whether God spoke only through Moses. In the
re-narrations of Num 12, Moses' marriage receives quite some attention,
whereas the dispute regarding Moses' exclusive prophecy in contrast to
the communication of Miriam and Aaron with the Divine is not given
much attention.[53] This result is not a surprise. Intermarriage was widely
debated in the post-exilic Judaism, and towards the second century B.C.E.,
the attitudes concerning exogamy became stricter.

Various pentateuchal re-narrations of the Greco-Roman era display
uneasiness in their reports of Moses' marriage. Some texts remain silent
regarding Moses' marriage. For instance, the book of *Jubilees* argues
against mixed marriages (25:1–3, 7–11; 30:7–17; 33:18–20) but does not
mention Moses' wife while reporting his stay in Midian. Similarly, the
first century C.E. *L.A.B.* avoids the question of Moses' marriage in its
re-narration of the Pentateuch. This is peculiar because generally the
L.A.B. tends to expand passages that portray female figures.[54] Moreover,
L.A.B. generally describes intermarriage as something negative (18:13;
30:1; 44:7; 45:7).

The attitude against intermarriage is also expressed in various texts
that belonged to the Qumran library. 1QapGen outlines the endogamous
marriages of Noah's sons (VI:6–9). 4QMMT[a] describes how one should
make a difference from everything done by the gentiles (4Q394 3–7).
11QT[a] considers intermarriage between Jewish men and foreign women
as a serious threat to the community strictly forbids it (11Q19 LVII:

---

[52] D. Steinmetz, "A Portrait of Miriam in Rabbinic Midrash," *Proof* 8 (1988): 35–65.

[53] For a more detailed analysis of Num 12 renarrations, see H. Tervanotko, "Miriam's
Mistake: Numbers 12 Renarrated," in *Embroidered Garments: Priests and Gender in
Biblical Israel* (ed. D. Rooke; Hebrew Bible Monographs 25; Sheffield: Sheffield Phoenix
Press, 2009), 131–150.

[54] P. van der Horst, "Portraits of Biblical Women in Pseudo-Philo's Liber Antiquitatum
Biblicarum," *JSP* 5 (1989): 29–46.

15–17). The only exception for this prohibition is that 11QT^a appears to allow in the recapitulation of Deut 21:10–14. While allowing a warrior to marry a beautiful captive woman 11QT^a LXIII:10–15 introduces extraordinary restrictions to the religious and cultic dimensions of this exceptional case of intermarriage.[55] In the framework of marriage a particular interest is given to the nuptials of the Levite family. In the *Visions of Amram* the figure of Miriam marries her uncle (4Q545 1 i 5–7), and Amram himself marries his aunt (4Q544 1 7–9). In the *Testament of Qahat*, the head of the family warns his offspring of mixing with other nations (4Q542 1 i 4–10).

Within the texts remaining from the Qumran library there is no reference to the marriage of Moses. This may be a coincidence of history.[56] Nevertheless, a number of texts reflect that the preserved majority of the Jewish texts dating to the Greco-Roman era were at unease with the theme of Moses' intermarriage.[57] Hence, it is also possible that Moses' marriage was not narrated in the Dead Sea Scrolls. Given the length and the style of 4Q377 2 i 9, and in particular the preserved name "Miriam," it is plausible that this line that alludes to Num 12 did not deal with Moses' marriage either. It should refer to a passage that dealt with Miriam more closely.

5. Conclusions

Based on the literary genre and the legible vocabulary of 4Q377, this study supports the view of VanderKam and Brady who have argued that 4Q377 2 i 9 uses Num 12. On the same grounds, 4Q377 2 i 10 does not seem to allude Num 12, but to another, unidentified, pentateuchal passage that perhaps refers to obstacles that God brought for the Israelites during their time in the wilderness.

---

[55] L.H. Schiffman, "Laws Pertaining Women in Temple Scroll," in *The Dead Sea Scrolls: Forty Years of Research* (ed. D. Dimant and U. Rappaport; STDJ 10; Leiden: Brill, 1992), 210–228; A. Lange, "Your Daughters Do Not Give to Their Sons and Their Daughters Do Not Take for Your Sons (Ezra 9,12): Intermarriage in Ezra 9–10 and in the Pre-Maccabean Dead Sea Scrolls," *BN* 137 (2008): 17–39; 139 (2008): 79–98.

[56] J.E. Bowley, "Moses in the Dead Sea Scrolls: Living in the Shadow of God's Anointed," in *The Bible at Qumran: Text, Shape, and Interpretation* (ed. P. Flint; Studies in the Dead Sea Scrolls and Related Literature; Grand Rapids: Eerdmans, 2001), 159–181, 171.

[57] In contrast, Moses' marriage was a popular topic in wider literature dating to the Greco-Roman era, e.g., Artapanus.

The allusion of 4Q377 to Num 12 contains only one line. The length of the allusion has implications. While 4Q377 2 i refers to several pentateuchal passages, it does not single out any of them. None of them is highlighted above the others. Moreover, such short references and a lack of details or of indications where the pentateuchal passages change, have some consequences. This style suggests that the re-narration did not quote its hypotext in detail. Rather it had a loose connection with the text it reworked (the Pentateuch). Moreover, the brevity of the references implies that this text was written for the use of audiences who could relate to it even by a subtle hint. This must have meant people who knew the base text, the Pentateuch well.

This type of narration that focuses merely on one theme of the passage was common in the literature of the Greco-Roman era. Demetrius, Philo's *Legum allegoriae*, m. *Soṭah* and *Sipre Num* are all examples of this style. Their re-narrations of Num 12 are equally short and require familiarity with the base text. They reveal an interest in Moses' marriage. Demetrius demonstrates that Zipporah was not a foreigner by providing a genealogy. Philo's *Legum allegoriae* argues that Moses' marriage was set by the divine and presents the figure of Miriam as a representation of an irrational behavior. *M. Soṭah* explicates that Miriam was worth to wait for because of her deeds in Moses' infancy. Moreover, according to *Sipre Num*, Aaron's and Miriam'a talking in Num 12:1 did not concern Moses' exogamy, but rather the state of his marital life. Other pentateuchal re-narrations, that do not narrate Num 12, but that date to the same era, deal with Moses' marriage similarly. Usually this topic is avoided. Moses' intermarriage is not re-narrated in the preserved Dead Sea Scrolls. Unfortunately 4Q277 2 i is too fragmentary to make conclusions regarding its contents. Nevertheless, on the basis of the remaining vocabulary and general silence around Moses' marriage in the Dead Sea Scrolls, I suggest that this topic was not dealt in 4Q377.

Regarding the reception of the figure of Miriam in 4Q377, this text demonstrates that the tradition of Num 12 was preserved in the Dead Sea Scrolls and known by the community who used 4Q377. Moreover, the style of 4Q377 reveals that Miriam must have been a known character by the time the text was written. People were expected to relate to the tradition of Num 12 only by a subtle reference.

QUMRAN MESSIANISM,
MELCHIZEDEK, AND THE SON OF MAN

PIERPAOLO BERTALOTTO

The problem of defining the historical relationship between the Qumran Community and the Essenes of the classical and Judeo-Hellenistic sources has been at the center of the debate on the Dead Sea Scrolls since they were first discovered. It has become even more vigorous after the formulation of the so-called "Groningen Hypothesis"[1] and, especially, after Gabriele Boccaccini's proposal to trace back to Enochic Judaism the ideological roots of the Qumran sectarian literature.[2] The analysis of those texts presenting superhuman eschatological protagonists, such as the Enochic Son of Man of the *Book of Parables* and the Qumranic Melchizedek of 11QMelch (11Q13), can certainly provide new and interesting elements to the discussion.

1. Messianic Figures in the Sectarian Literature

The eschatological and apocalyptic orientation of the Qumranic ideology is an issue on which contemporary scholarship generally agrees.[3] Within such a theological framework, however, expectations centered on one or more positive eschatological protagonists appear to be of secondary

---

[1] F. García Martínez and A.S. van der Woude, "A 'Groningen' Hypothesis of Qumran Origins and Early History," *RevQ* 14 (1990): 521–541.

[2] G. Boccaccini, *Beyond the Essene Hypothesis: The Parting of the Ways between Qumran and Enochic Judaism* (Grand Rapids: Eerdmans, 1998). See also the contributions from the Second Enoch Seminar in G. Boccaccini, ed., *Enoch and Qumran Origins: New Light on a Forgotten Connection* (Grand Rapids: Eerdmans, 2005), for an overall picture of the scholar reactions to Boccaccini's theory.

[3] See for example F. García Martínez, *Qumran and Apocalyptic: Studies on the Aramaic Texts from Qumran* (STDJ 9; Leiden: Brill, 1992); J.J. Collins, *Apocalypticism in the Dead Sea Scrolls* (London: Routledge, 1997); Boccaccini, *Enoch and Qumran Origins*; J. Frey and M. Becker, eds., *Apokalyptik und Qumran* (Einblicke 10; Paderborn: Bonifatius, 2007).

relevance.[4] Often the few texts in which such characters are referred to[5] provide very little information about them. This fact significantly reduces our possibilities of reconstructing a coherent and detailed picture of Qumran messianism as a whole. The majority of scholars, however, maintain that the Qumranians expected two distinct Messiahs, one with royal attributions and the other with some priestly features.[6] Possibly a third prophetic figure was part of the messianic expectations in Qumran, perhaps characterized as a sort of eschatological pair of the historical Teacher of Righteousness.[7] Such ideas, however, stand on hypothetical foundations, mainly as a result of the difficulty in the relative dating of the composition of those texts that can with some certainty be acknowledged as the product of the sect that occupied the site of Qumran.[8] Paleography can definitely aid in formulating a hypothesis about the latest stage of the redactional development of each text, the only one that is actually

---

[4] C.A. Evans, "The Messiah in the Dead Sea Scrolls," in *Israel's Messiah in the Bible and the Dead Sea Scrolls* (ed. R.S. Hess and M.D. Carroll R.; Grand Rapids: Eerdmans, 2004), 85–101, 86.

[5] In a recent article in which he presents contemporary agreement about Qumran messianism, Craig Evans lists thirteen sectarian texts containing "messianic material": CD, 1QS, 1QSa, 1QSb, 1QM, 4QpIsa[a] (4Q161), 4QFlor (4Q174), 4QTest (4Q175), 4QCommGen A (4Q252), 4QSefer ha-Milḥamah (4Q285), 4QapocrMoses[b]? (4Q376), 4QNarrative A (4Q458), 4QMessianic Apocalypse (4Q521). He treats all these texts as sectarian (see Evans, "Messiah," 88). Xeravits adds 4QapocrDan ar (4Q246), 4QExod/Conq. Trad. (4Q374), 4QapocrPent. B (4Q377), 4QPrayer of Enosh (4Q369), 4Qapocr-Levi[b]? ar (4Q541), 4QVisions of Amram[a–f] (4Q543–548), 4QpapVision[b] ar (4Q558), and 11QMelch (11Q13). With the exception of the latter, all these texts, along with 4QNarrative A (4Q458) and 4QMessianic Apocalypse (4Q521), also mentioned by Evans, are considered non-sectarian: see G.G. Xeravits, *King, Priest, Prophet: Positive Eschatological Protagonists of the Qumran Library* (STDJ 47; Leiden: Brill, 2003), 10.

[6] Evans, "Messiah," 94.

[7] In 1QS IX:11 "the prophet" is mentioned together with "the Messiahs of Aaron and Israel," while 4QTest (4Q175) clearly deals with the eschatological actions performed by all three characters. Xeravits thinks that in 4QMessianic Apocalypse (4Q521) the announced Messiah is an eschatological pair of Elijah. See Xeravits, *King*, 217–219. See also P.W. Flint, "The Prophet David at Qumran," in *Biblical Interpretation at Qumran* (ed. M. Henze; Studies in the Dead Sea Scrolls and Related Literature; Grand Rapids: Eerdmans, 2005), 158–167, J.C. Poirier, "The Endtime Return of Elijah and Moses at Qumran," *DSD* 10 (2003): 221–242, H. Witczyk, "La missione di Elia nella tradizione dell'AT, nella letteratura intertestamentaria e negli scritti di Qumran," *ColT* 69 (1999): 25–36.

[8] See J.J. Collins, "Asking for the Meaning of a Fragmentary Qumran Text: The Referential Background of 4QAaron A [4Q540, 4Q541]," in *Texts and Contexts: Biblical Texts in Their Textual and Situational Contexts* (ed. T. Fornberg and D. Hellholm; Oslo: Scandinavian University Press, 1995), 579–590, 586.

available.[9] The presence among the Dead Sea Scrolls of texts copied in the last part of the life of the community, regardless of the precise moment in which they were originally composed, confirms the continuity of interest in those literary creations and, therefore, in the ideas embedded in them.

In spite of the difficulties in delineating a consistent and detailed general picture, and leaving out the character of Melchizedek, two features about Qumran messianism seem rather certain: 1. all the expected positive eschatological protagonists are human; 2. the royal, priestly and prophetic attributions are never concentrated into the same figure.

More than the *Rule of the Community* and the *Damascus Document*, where the presence of such a dualistic scheme of the Messianic expectation is more evident but the Messiahs of Aaron and of Israel are nothing but names, the *War Rule* deserves special attention in our analysis. In its detailed description of the eschatological war against the Kittim and their allies, it mentions a character called the Prince of the Congregation. This figure has been interpreted as a human messianic protagonist, identifiable with the Davidic Messiah already announced in some more ancient sectarian texts such as 4QpIsa[a] (4Q161) and 4QFlor (4Q174). He does not play a very important or active role, however, in 1QM. More visibility is granted in the *War Rule* to the eschatological High Priest.

4QSefer ha-Milḥamah (4Q285),[10] on the other hand, which according to Milik and other scholars[11] belongs to the last part of the *War Rule*, seems to attest a redactional phase of the same text in which the Prince of the Congregation was explicitly identified with the Branch of David, i.e. a royal and Davidic Messiah, and in which he was depicted as a main actor in the eschatological war.[12] The paleography of the fragment is early or middle Herodian. Bilhah Nitzan dates it between 50 and 20

---

[9] On this base, Gerbern Oegema has recently returned on the idea of the "development" of messianic ideas in Qumran, affirming that in the Herodian period the diarchic messianism of the hasmonean period was replaced by the expectation of just one royal and Davidic protagonist: see G.S. Oegema, "Messianic Expectations in the Qumran Writings: Theses on Their Development," in *Qumran-Messianism: Studies on the Messianic Expectations in the Dead Sea Scrolls* (ed. J.H. Charlesworth, H. Lichtenberger, and G.S. Oegema; Tübingen: Mohr Siebeck, 1998), 53–82, 55.

[10] *Editio princeps*: P. Alexander and G. Vermes in *DJD* XXXVI (2000): 228–246.

[11] J.T. Milik, "Milkî-ṣedeq et Milkî-rešaʿ dans les anciens écrits juifs et chrétiens," *JJS* 23 (1972): 95–144, 143; Collins, "Asking," 59.

[12] P.S. Alexander, "A Reconstruction and Reading of 4Q285 (4QSefer ha-Milḥamah)," *RevQ* 19 (1999–2000): 333–348, 348.

B.C.E.[13] Fragment 7 is particularly interesting for the topic of this study, as it describes a scene in which the royal-Davidic Messiah, possibly in conjunction with his priestly counterpart, is involved in the judgment and in the condemnation of the king of the Kittim.[14] In line 3 the verb נשפטו is used, a *nipʿal* form of the root שׁפט, followed by the preposition את. This way of expressing the active meaning of the verb is very unusual, assuming that the subjects of the verb were the two messiahs.[15] Philip Alexander proposes reading the *nipʿal* form as "inceptive," citing Jer 2:35 as a scriptural parallel for such a use.[16] 1 Samuel 12:7 (אִשָּׁפְטָה אִתְּכֶם לִפְנֵי יְהוָה), however, probably represents a closer and more profitable example on this issue. 1 Samuel 12 accounts for Samuel's discourse before the people after the proclamation of Saul as the anointed king of Israel. In his speech, the prophet accuses Israel for her numerous rebellions against God, the last of which was the request to choose a human king besides YHWH. In this scene, God seems to play the role of the judge, while Samuel and the people stand for the two parties in an ideal trial. The newly chosen king-messiah is also mentioned as being present. Fragment 7 of 4Q285 probably preserves the ends of the lines of the original manuscript. Hence, any insertion of the text must be placed at the beginning of line 4, which presently preserves twenty-one letter-spaces. If we add the expression המלך כתיים לפני יהוה, which parallels the syntactical construction attested in 1 Sam 12:7, we would then have 21 more letter-spaces in the line. The explicit mention of the King of the Kittim would also justify the third-person pronominal suffix in the following verbal form המיתו, which, in all probability, referred to the same royal figure. We also propose to insert the expression ושפטו יהוה, attested in this form in 2 Sam 18:19, which, from a syntactical point of view, would mirror the next expression with the subject following the verb. By doing this we would reach 51 letter-spaces for this line, perfectly within the range 50–55 letter-spaces per-line proposed by Alexander and

---

[13] B. Nitzan, "Benedictions and Instructions for the Eschatological Community (11Q-Ber; 4Q285)," *RevQ* 16 (1993): 77–90, 79. Ibba dates the fragment to the end of the 1st cent. B.C.E.: G. Ibba, *Il "rotolo della Guerra": Edizione critica* (Quaderni di Henoch; Torino: Zamorani, 1998), 55. See also the abovementioned *editio princeps*.

[14] Alexander, "Reconstruction," 345.

[15] Abegg links the plural form of the verb with the "judiciary body" of twelve people referred to in CD 10:4–10; 13:2–12: See M.G. Abegg, "Messianic Hope and 4Q285: A Reassessment," *JBL* 113 (1994): 81–91, 88.

[16] Alexander, "Reconstruction," 345.

Abegg.[17] This reconstruction, hypothetical though perfectly reasonable on the basis of the hints preserved in the text and the parallels found in 1 and 2 Samuel, would depict a scene in which the two messiahs participate in the judgment as the accusers of the King of the Kittim while God acts as the one who pronounces the sentence of condemnation.[18] The Prince of the Congregation would then kill him (המיתו), as the "branch" of Isa 11:5 does with the wicked (יָמִית רָשָׁע),[19] in execution of God's verdict. The high priest too plays a role in this phase, probably commanding the cleansing of the land from the impurity caused by the corpses of the Kittim.[20] Fragment 10, which according to Alexander's reconstruction preserves parts of col. VI and, therefore, would follow frg. 7,[21] probably describes an atonement performed by the high priest, finalized to purify the land from the pollution caused by the corpses of the slain. The atonement would also grant pardon to those who had fallen into the temptation of hoarding booty during the burial of the corpses.[22] The idea that the priestly messiah would atone at the end of the days is also attested elsewhere in the Dead Sea Scrolls.[23]

The two- or threefold messianic expectation, though certainly not central to the ideological identity of the community, is well attested in the Qumran sectarian literature from the time of the composition of the *Damascus Document* and 1QS until around the end of the first century B.C.E., when texts like 4Q161, 4Q174, 4Q252, 4Q285, and 1QM

---

[17] See n. 14 above.

[18] All the modern commentators maintain that in this passage the judge is the Davidic Messiah, with no distinction between the one who pronounces the sentence and the one who executes it. Corrado Martone, for instance, mentions 1QSb (1Q28b) V:20–29 and 4QpIsa[a] (4Q161) 8–10 (III) in which Isa 11 is quoted and interpreted as referring to the triumphant Prince-Messiah: see C. Martone, "Un testo qumranico che narra la morte del Messia? A proposito del recente dibattito su 4Q285," *RivB* 42 (1994): 329–336, 330, 335. In 1QSb, however, Isa 11:4a, in which the root שפט is used, is integrated because of the presence of a lacuna in the scroll and, therefore, we cannot be sure that it was actually there. Furthermore, in both cases, and in Isaiah too, this root is never used in a "judicial" context, i.e., it never seems to express the sense of emitting a sentence in a trial, even less an eschatological trial against the leader of the evil army.

[19] Isaiah 11:5–6 is interpreted exactly in reference to the "Branch of David" in 4QpIsa[a] (4Q161) 8–10 16–17: see Abegg, "Messianic Hope," 88.

[20] Ibid., 82.

[21] Alexander, "Reconstruction," 343.

[22] Nitzan, "Benedictions," 89. In Nitzan's article, frg. 10 corresponds to frgs. 2 + 7.

[23] CD 14:19 par. 4QD[a] (4Q266) 10 i 12–13. See Xeravits, *King*, 215; J.M. Baumgarten, "Messianic Forgiveness of Sin in CD 14:19 (4Q266 10 I 12–13)," in *The Provo International Conference on the Dead Sea Scrolls: Technological Innovations, New Texts, and Reformulated Issues* (ed. D.W. Parry and E. Ulrich; STDJ 30; Leiden: Brill, 1999), 537–544.

were still copied as a proof of their persisting authority in the Qumran understanding of Messianism. In this context, 11QMelch represents an intriguing exception.

2. 11QMELCH (11Q13): INTRODUCTION AND TEXT

The manuscript presently consists of fifteen fragments and allows the partial reconstruction of three columns of text. Only the second of these columns, however, preserves a sufficiently continuous text. It can be classified as a sectarian thematic *pesher*.[24] Its first editor proposed to date the manuscript within the first half of the first century C.E.[25] He especially underlined the closed form of the ס which would push the dating up to the end of the proposed period. Fred Horton strongly emphasizes these "late" features of the *Handschrift*. He underlines the similarity of כ, ס, ק, and ת with those in 4QDeutʲ (4Q37) the latter dated around 50 C.E.[26] Paul Kobelski, on the other hand, prefers an earlier dating (ca. 50–25 B.C.E.), noting the appearance of a similar ע and כ in a Hasmonean manuscript.[27] Józef Milik classifies the writing as a "late hasmonean or early herodian book hand" basing his claim on the observation of the uneven dimensions of the letters and the archaic form of some of them. He dates it to the period 75–50 B.C.E., which is also supported by Émile Puech, who maintains that the apparent inconsistency of the paleographical data depends on the merging of a formal and a semi-cursive hand.[28] The majority of the evidence, however, seems to support the hypothesis of van der Woude and Horton more than Milik's and Puech's. The latter, for instance, notes that the most common form of the א is "en v renversé: avec le simple trait droit … mais le trait droit peut avoir un *apex*." This is actually characteristic of a mature Herodian

---

[24] *Editio princeps*: F. García Martínez, E.J.C. Tigchelaar, and A.S. van der Woude in *DJD* XXIII (1997): 221–242.

[25] A.S. van der Woude, "Melchisedek als himmlische Erlösergestalt in den neugefundenen eschatologischen Midraschim aus Qumran Höhle XI," *OtSt* 14 (1965): 354–373, 356–357.

[26] F.L. Horton, *The Melchizedek Tradition: A Critical Examination of the Sources to the Fifth Century A.D. and in the Epistle to the Hebrews* (Cambridge: Cambridge University Press, 1976), 73.

[27] P.J. Kobelski, *Melchizedek and Melchireša'* (CBQMS 10; Washington: The Catholic Biblical Association of America, 1981), 3.

[28] Milik, "Milkî-ṣedeq," 97; É. Puech, "Notes sur le manuscrit de 11Q Melkîsédeq," *RevQ* 12 (1987): 483–513, 507–508.

formal script, especially close to the one 4QDan[b] (ca. 20–50 C.E.). The ל looks rather late too.[29] On the other hand, the ה looks a little earlier, but again hardly earlier than early Herodian, as claimed by Puech. The same observation is also valid for the י. The semi-cursive appearance of some letters, which convinced Puech to propose a higher paleographical dating of 11QMelch is altogether scarcely recognizable. On the contrary, all the hints already identified by van der Woude and Horton, which point towards the first half of the first century C.E., seem evident. Hence, with all the caution needed when drawing conclusions based on paleographic considerations, it seems reasonable to state that manuscript 11QMelch was copied a little after the other manuscripts we have dealt with so far, i.e. not before the first half of the first century C.E. Obviously, this fact does not prove *per se* that the text was composed in that period.[30] Further evidence in support of this hypothesis will be provided in the following paragraphs.

3. MELCHIZEDEK AS AN אלוהים

The main protagonist of the literary composition of which 11QMelch is the only witness is called Melchizedek. The appellative of אלוהים is given to him by means of a citation from Ps 82:1 in 11QMelch II:10.

In 11QMelch II:10b–11 the expression ועליו אמ[ר introduces a new quotation from Ps 7:8–9 and can be interpreted as referring to the אל of Ps 82:1. The main character of Ps 7 is אל in the Qumranic text and יהוה in the MT, probably the Most High God in the exegesis of the Qumranians. Therefore it can be argued that each quotation was introduced to expose the roles of אלוהים and אל respectively in the final judgment. No contradiction exists between Melchizedek's judicial task, which according to the majority of the interpreters derives from his identification with the אלוהים of Ps 82:1 in line 10, and his acting as the performer of the divine vengeance in line 13,[31] because in this last passage the "judgments" are God's own (Hebrew: אל, not אלוהים).

---

[29] F.M. Cross, "The Development of the Jewish Scripts," in *The Bible and the Ancient Near East: Essays in Honor of W.F. Albright* (ed. G.E. Wright; Garden City: Doubleday, 1961), 133–202, 138, 175.

[30] Both Milik and Puech propose to date the composition of this text in the second half of the 2nd century B.C.E., on the basis of literary considerations. See Milik, "Milkî-ṣedeq," 129; Puech, "Notes sur le manuscrit de 11Q Melkîsédeq," 509–510.

[31] P.A. Rainbow, "Melchizedek as a Messiah at Qumran," *BBR* 7 (1997): 179–194, 183.

This fact leads to the conclusion that also within the quotation from Ps 82:1 the author assigns the role of judge to אל and not to אלוהים. This hypothesis is also confirmed, as we mentioned, by the following citation from Ps 7:8–9. Accepting this, the possibility that the אלוהים of the Psalm was actually intended to be Melchizedek no longer represents a problem for the internal consistency of the text.

4. Melchizedek and Dan 7:13–14

The similitude between the scene described by Ps 82:1, according to the sectarian interpretation, and the one in Dan 7:13–14 and 22 is worthwhile to analyze. In the Daniel passage, the "one like a son of man" *stands before* the "ancient of days" and is not involved in the judgment, which is instead exclusively reserved to the Most High. Moreover, the following lines 11QMelch fit quite well within the idea of the dominion given to Melchizedek, which is also granted to the Danielic character. He is the one who is expected to lead the other אלוהים in the struggle against Belial and his lot. Accepting the integration of his name at the beginning of line 25, Melchizedek was also associated with the reigning אלוהים of Isa 52:7, whose power, like that of the protagonist of Ps 110:2, is linked to Zion.[32] It thus appears probable that the invention of this Qumranic eschatological protagonist was ideologically rooted in a complex of highly developed interpretations of Daniel's vision. The connection of the cited scriptural passages, on the basis of the attribution of the appellative אלוהים to Melchizedek is very impressive, as is the fact that, even without any explicit citations, the Danielic background of such speculations is perfectly perceivable.

Less clear is how and why this growth of interest in that particular Danielic passage suddenly broke out at Qumran. No other sectarian text has been identified, which contains exegetical cues to Dan 7:13–14. This has even led some scholars to the conclusion that the Qumranians were really not at all concerned with the problem of understanding who the mysterious Danielic figure called "one like a son of man" was or would be. Collins, however, suggests that the character called "Son of God"

---

[32] See A. Aschim, "Melchizedek and Jesus: 11QMelchizedek and the Epistle to the Hebrews," in *The Jewish Roots of Christological Monotheism: Papers from the St. Andrews Conference on the Historical Origins of the Worship of Jesus* (ed. C.C. Newman, J.R. Davila, and G.S. Lewis; JSJSup 63; Leiden: Brill, 1999), 129–147, 136.

in 4QapocrDan ar (4Q246) could represent the result of a messianic interpretation of the Danielic vision.[33] The paleographic dating of the fragment shifts us to the last third of the first century B.C.E., i.e. a little before 11QMelch. Although attested only in the Qumran Library, it seems preferable to consider it as a non-sectarian composition.[34] The fact that it was copied at Qumran indicates that there was a persistent interest in it, at a very late stage of the life of the community. The opinions of the scholars concerning the identification of the one who "will be called Son of God" and "Son of the Most High" ranges between those who propose to see in this figure a pagan leader or an Antichrist,[35] and those who prefer a Davidic interpretation, whether messianic or not.[36] The negative understanding was first formulated by Józef Milik who argued that the so called "Son of God" could be a Syrian King.[37] It has been recently reaffirmed by the editor of the text and maintained, with slight differences, by some other scholars.[38] Many others, however, think differently.[39] The main problem with the negative interpretation is the

---

[33] J.J. Collins, "The Background of the 'Son of God' Text," *BBR* 7 (1997): 37–50. See also J. Zimmermann, "Observations on 4Q246—The 'Son of God,'" in *Qumran-Messianism*, 175–190.

[34] É. Puech, "Some Remarks on 4Q246 and 4Q521 and Qumran Messianism," in *The Provo International Conference on the Dead Sea Scrolls*, 545–565, 546.

[35] For this interpretation see E.M. Cook, "4Q246," *BBR* 5 (1995): 43–66.

[36] See for example Collins, "Background"; C.A. Evans, "Are the 'Son' Texts at Qumran Messianic? Reflections on 4Q369 and Related Scrolls," in *Qumran-Messianism*, 135–153; J.A. Fitzmyer, "The Aramaic 'Son of God' Text From Qumran Cave 4 (4Q246)," in *The Dead Sea Scrolls and the Christian Origins* (Studies in the Dead Sea Scrolls and Related Literature; Grand Rapids: Eerdmans, 2000), 41–62; F.M. Cross, "The Structure of the Apocalypse of 'Son of God' (4Q246)," in *Emanuel: Studies in Hebrew Bible, Septuagint and Dead Sea Scrolls in Honor of Emanuel Tov* (ed. S.M. Paul et al.; VTSup 94; Leiden: Brill, 2003), 151–158.

[37] See J.T. Milik, "Les modèles araméens du livre d'Esther dans la grotte 4 de Qumrân," *RevQ* 15 (1992): 321–399.

[38] See Cook, "4Q246"; K. Berger, *Jesus and the Dead Sea Scrolls: The Truth under Lock and Key?* (Lousville: Westminster John Knox, 1995), 77–79, A. Steudel, "The Eternal Reign of the People of God: Collective Expectations in Qumran Texts (4Q246 and 1QM)," *RevQ* 17 (1996): 507–525, Puech, "Remarks."

[39] J.J. Collins, "The 'Son of God' Text From Qumran," in *From Jesus to John: Essays on Jesus and New Testament Christology in Honour of M. de Jonge* (ed. M. de Boer; JSNTSup 84; Sheffield: JSOT Press, 1993), 65–82; F.M. Cross, *The Ancient Library of Qumran* (3rd ed.; Sheffield: Sheffield Academic Press, 1995), 189–191; J.J. Collins, *The Scepter and the Star: The Messiahs of the Dead Sea Scrolls and Other Ancient Literature* (ABRL; New York: Doubleday, 1995), 154–172; J. Zimmermann, *Messianische Texte aus Qumran: Königliche, priesterliche und prophetische Messiasvorstellungen in den Schriftfunden von Qumran* (WUNT 2/104; Tübingen: Mohr Siebeck, 1998), 162; Fitzmyer, "Son of God"; Xeravits, *King*, 188–189.

absence of a sufficiently precise correspondence in the pagan literature
for the cited passage in 4Q246. This passage presents the main character
as the Son of the Most High. For the Hellenistic kings, not even a single
coin appears on which one of them is referred to with the exact title of
Son of the Most High. The closest parallel for the entire passage remains
Luke 1:32. Even if we accept that neither Luke nor his sources knew
4Q246, it seems highly improbable that the author of the third Gospel
would have decided to assign these titles to Jesus if he knew that they
had already been given to some pagan king. On the contrary, Ps 2 and
2 Sam 7 probably represent the scriptural basis on which such a titular
use depends.[40]

Another very interesting interpretative option for the figure in 4Q246
has been suggested by Florentino García Martínez, who argues that the
character is the same Melchizedek, elsewhere called Michael and the
Prince of Light, mentioned in the previously analyzed Qumranic texts.[41]
No clear evidence in the text, however, can be found supporting the
hypothesis that a heavenly nature was attributed to the character in
4Q246, apart from the very ambiguous title of Son of God, which can be
better understood as a messianic and Davidic title. Rather, it is possible
that this text, because of its close connection with Daniel, and possibly
representing a very early attempt to interpret Dan 7:13–14, inspired the
author of 11QMelch. The figure of Melchizedek in 11QMelch, however,
is depicted differently from the protagonist of 4Q246. Hence, if one tentatively considers both the texts as attestations of exegesis of Dan 7:13–
14, the divergences in the respective conclusions need to be explained.
What must be noticed is that 4Q246 is probably a non-sectarian document while 11QMelch is certainly sectarian. This fact means that even
if the composition of the former served the purpose of explaining the
meaning of Daniel's vision, or was so understood by the sectarians, it
did not produce a growing interest in that scriptural passage during the
whole life of the community, at least until the end of the first century
B.C.E.[42] On the contrary, what can be inferred from the late date of the

---

[40] For a detailed argumentation against the negative interpretation, especially that of
Cook, see Collins, "Background."

[41] F. García Martínez, "The Eschatological Figure of 4Q246," in *Qumran and Apocalyptic*, 162–179.

[42] See the *editio princeps*: É. Puech in *DJD* XXII (1996): 165–184. The editor proposes
to date the fragment to 25 B.C.E. (ibid., 166), which means that the later attested copy of
this text could be easily a little earlier than 11QMelch.

copy discovered in Qumran Cave 4 is that the ideas expressed in that pre-sectarian composition regarding Daniel's "one like a son of man," were maintained by the sect during most of its history. According to this view, the character would be a human Davidic king-Messiah who fit perfectly within the diarchic scheme of Qumran messianism attested elsewhere.

5. 11QMELCH (11Q13) AND QUMRAN MESSIANISM

For many reasons, the eschatology of 11QMelch appears incompatible with the rather consistent eschatology attested in the other sectarian messianic texts. Melchizedek seems to take on himself the characteristics of the kingly, priestly, and prophetic Messiahs. The scene of judgment against the King of the Kittim in 4Q285 is similar to the one in 11QMelch except that, in the former, two human figures act as the accusers of the enemy, while, in the latter, Melchizedek appears alone in this role. Melchizedek is also the one who executes the verdict against the leader of the enemies like the branch of David does in 4Q285, but in 11QMelch the negative hero is not the human King of the Kittim anymore. He has been replaced by Belial, his heavenly counterpart. Moreover, Melchizedek presides over the eschatological Yom Kippur and thus atones like the priestly messiah was expected to do. The eschatological phase in which Melchizedek acts as the main protagonist is concluded by the instauration of his own reign, not of that of a human king-Messiah. In 11QMelch no room is left for any eschatological battle between human fighters. It probably represents then the latest and, to a certain extent, unexpected development of the messianic speculations of the Qumranites for two main reasons: 1. It renews deeply the eschatology of the group—the Qumranians probably changed their mind once by abandoning most of their traditions on messianic figures rather than twice, first upsetting their messianic expectations in 11QMelch and then returning to the point of departure in 4Q285 or in one of the other mentioned texts. 2. Both 1QM and 4Q285 make reference to the participation of the angelic hosts to the eschatological war as second leads, besides the human armies, while in 11QMelch no human fighter appears at all. The historical reasons that catalyzed this sudden and unexpected development must then be sought outside the boundaries of the community.

6. MELCHIZEDEK AND THE SON OF MAN

A closer comparison of the Son of Man of the Enochic *Book of Parables* with the Melchizedek of 11QMelch could supply new elements for the discussion. The absence of the second section of *1 Enoch* from among the Enochic fragments of the Qumran caves was interpreted by Milik as definitive evidence for its Christian origin and relatively late composition. In his opinion, the date of composition of the *Parables* could then be fixed to the third century c.e.[43] Milik's theory was questioned since its very first presentation and currently many scholars of Second Temple Judaism agree on the Jewish provenance of the *Parables* and on its dating around the turn of the era. Both the Enochic Son of Man and the Qumranic Melchizedek are described as heavenly beings, and are connected with the אלוהים. The shaping of the figure of the Son of Man probably depends on a messianic and superhuman interpretation of Ps 45, a biblical text which attributes the epithet of אלוהים to the Davidic king. Behind *1 En.* 46:1 and *1 En.* 20 probably stood a Hebrew source that contained a list of the seven archangels referred to as אלוהים. Furthermore, all four epithets attributed to the main protagonist of the *Parables*, i.e. Son of Man, Chosen One, Righteous One, and Messiah,[44] depend on the description of the protagonist of Ps 45. In Ps 45:3 this main character is presented as the "most handsome" among the "sons of men," which probably meant to the author of the *Parables* that he was a "son of man." Moreover, he is also anointed because of his righteousness beyond his companions (Ps 45:8), hence being a Messiah, a Chosen One, and a Righteous One. The king of Ps 45 is also adored, according to the text attested in the LXX (44:12),[45] by the daughters of Tyre, while the rich of the people supplicate him. Similarly, the Son of Man is worshiped and supplicated for mercy by the rich and the powerful of the earth at the time of his man-

---

[43] J.T. Milik, *The Books of Enoch: Aramaic Fragments of Qumrân Cave 4* (Oxford: Clarendon, 1976), 95.

[44] On the connection of these four epithets to one and the same character see especially J.C. VanderKam, "Righteous One, Messiah, Chosen One, and Son of Man in 1 Enoch 37–71," in *The Messiah: Developments in Earliest Judaism and Christianity* (ed. J.H. Charlesworth; Minneapolis: Fortress, 1992), 169–191.

[45] We are not stating here that the author of the *Parables* knew and used the LXX but only that the text of the Psalms he had available probably resembled more the one attested in the LXX than that of the MT. Peter Flint has observed this phenomenon in his study of the Psalms scrolls from Qumran, though not specifically with regard to the verse examined here. See P.W. Flint, *The Dead Sea Psalms Scrolls and the Book of Psalms* (STDJ 17; Leiden: Brill, 1997).

ifestation. Therefore, even apart from some philological hints suggesting that the Semitic original of *1 En.* 46:1 compared the Son of Man with an אלוהים, evidence for dependence of this figure on the protagonist of Ps 45 leads to the conclusion that his nature was thought as linked to that of the אלוהים, while the Qumranic figure is an אלוהים himself (11QMelch II:10, 25).[46]

Moreover, both the protagonists have relevant royal functions, such as that of leading the heavenly army in the eschatological punishment for Melchizedek and evaluating and pronouncing the sentence of condemnation against the wicked while sitting on the throne of God for the Son of Man.[47]

Another very interesting parallel between the two figures is the common revelatory nature. The Son of Man was expected to reveal Heavenly Wisdom to his followers according to *1 En.* 46:3. On the other hand, in 11QMelch, the title of *Anointed of the Spirit* seems to be given to Melchizedek in line 18.

The expression "Anointed of the Spirit" occurs in CD 2:12 as an appellative of the prophets. In 11QMelch it is used in the *pesher* on Isa 52:7 (II:15–19) as the interpretative counterpart of the Isaianic "herald of good news who announces peace." The "mountains" of the scriptural passage, on which this herald would stand, represent, in the author's understanding, the prophets. It is thus clear that this title confers a prophetic role to the one who carries it.

As acknowledged by many scholars, Isa 61:1–2 stands in the background of the entire sectarian text of 11QMelch.[48] Melchizedek is clearly identified in it as the one who has to proclaim the liberation of the captives (II:4–6) and to perform the vengeance of God (II:13). It seems therefore probable that the title "Anointed of the Spirit" was borrowed from this same prophetic passage. Considering that the one who is anointed and who receives the Spirit in Isa 61:1 is the same performer of the other tasks, it seems highly probable that this unity was kept in the Qumranic interpretation.[49] Moreover, having introduced this new title, the author

---

[46] P. Bertalotto, "The Enochic Son of Man, Ps 45, and the Book of the Watchers," *JSP* 19 (2010): 195–216.

[47] See *1 En.* 41:9; 45:3; 49:5; 61:8; 62:2.

[48] See M.P. Miller, "The Function of Isa 61:1–2 in 11QMelchizedek," *JBL* 88 (1969): 467–469.

[49] On this hypothesis see J.A. Sanders, "From Isaiah 61 to Luke 4," in *Christianity, Judaism and Other Greco-Roman Cults: Studies for M. Smith at Sixty*, vol. 1: *New Testament* (ed. J. Neusner; SJLA 12; Leiden Brill, 1975), 75–106, 75, P. Sacchi, *Gesù e la sua gente* (Cinisello Balsamo: San Paolo, 2003), 70.

of 11QMelch does not go further in explaining who this character actually is. He simply adds that Daniel spoke about him. Unfortunately, the Danielic quotation is not preserved because the fragment is corrupted. An interesting integration at this point would be Dan 9:24

והמבאר הו[אה] מש֗יח הרו[ח] כאשר אמר דנ[יאל עליו לחתם חזון ונביא ומבשר]

And the messenger is the anointed of the spirit about whom Daniel spoke
Dan 9:24 [to seal up vision and prophecy. And the messenger]

As an eschatological prophet, the *Anointed of the Spirit* was probably expected to be the one who would complete the prophecy. Standing "on the prophets," (II:16–18) he would be the last one to speak in God's name, to *reveal* something on his behalf.

Moreover, the suggested Danielic passage also mentions all the other events in which Melchizedek was supposed to act as the main protagonist according to 11QMelch, besides the completion of the prophecy. He would finish transgression and make an end of sins ("to free them from [the debt] of all their iniquities"; II:8); he would make reconciliation for iniquity ("atonement will be made for all the sons of [God] and for the men of the lot of Melchizedek"; II:7); he would bring in everlasting righteousness ("Melchizedek will carry out the vengeance of God's judgments"; II:13).[50] The "seventy weeks" find their corollary in the ten jubilees of line 7.[51]

In conclusion, the character of Melchizedek in 11QMelch shares three important characteristics with the Son of Man in the *Book of Parables*: 1. he is linked with the angelic appellative of אלוהים; 2. he represents an interpretative development of the "one like a son of man" of Dan 7:13–14; 3. assuming his identification with the Anointed of the Spirit, he is expected to perform some revelatory tasks.

At the same time, these two figures also show some relevant differences. Melchizedek, with regard to his prophetic role, is connected with Moses, while the Son of Man is associated with Enoch, whether actually identified with him, as suggested by VanderKam, or simply compared

---

[50] On the identification of Melchizedek and the Anointed of the Spirit and on the proposed integration of line 18, see P. Bertalotto, "L'uomo Gesù e la salvezza del suo popolo: osservazioni lessicali a partire da Mt 1, 21e 11QMelchisedek II, 17–19," in *Atti del XXXIV incontro internazionale di studiosi dell'antichità cristiana (5–7 Maggio 2005)* (SEAug 96; Rome: Institutum Patristicum Augustinianum, 2006), 305–316.

[51] Ten Jubilees corresponded, in the Second Temple period, to four hundred and ninety years, i.e. seventy weeks of years. See M. Barker, "The Time Is Fulfilled: Jesus and Jubilee," *SJT* 52 (2002): 22–32, 23.

to him because of the common righteousness, as suggested by Collins.[52] Both Enoch and Moses are accounted as revealers, the first figure revealing the Torah, the second, wisdom, which he had received during his journey in the heavens.

Another element of opposition is that the Enochic Messiah was expected to act as an eschatological judge rather than as an executor (1 En. 61:8–9; 62:11). Melchizedek, on the other hand, through the association with the אלוהים of Ps 82:1, is depicted as standing in the assembly of the principal God (אל), while the latter alone actually pronounces the sentence of condemnation. Finally, some priestly functions are attributed to the Qumranic protagonist, as his guidance of the eschatological expiation (II:7) indicates. This feature probably derived from the pre-sectarian tradition. The biblical character called Melchizedek, in fact, was a priest (Gen 14; Ps 110:4) and also in the Songs of Sabbath Sacrifice, accepting the integration of his name in 4QShirShabb[b] (4Q401) 11 3 and 22 3,[53] he is referred to as a כוהן, probably the high priest of the heavenly temple.

All these elements lead to some interesting conclusions regarding the relationship between Melchizedek in 11QMelch and the Son of Man in the Parables. Probably the former was created by the sectarians against the background of the latter, with the purpose of harmonizing the new messianic figure with some other well received non-sectarian ideas. This hypothesis explains the sudden and isolated explosion of interest in the interpretation of Dan 7:13–14, noticed in 11QMelch. It also clarifies the highly complex formulation of 11QMelch, which cannot be justified simply on the basis of the other few and generic traditional passages about the heavenly character of Melchizedek, or on a direct exegetical approach to Dan 7:13–14. The interpretative connection of Melchizedek with the אלוהים of Ps 82:1 represents the stronger evidence of the strict relationship which links the two messianic heavenly figures.

---

[52] Some elements in the text of the Parables, such as the shift from the first to the third person in the narration between 1 En. 70:1–2 and 70:3–71:17, and the evident reduplication of ending, point towards the non-originality of this section. On this see especially J.J. Collins, "The Heavenly Representative," in Ideal Figures in Ancient Judaism: Profiles and Paradigms (ed. idem and G.W.E. Nickelsburg; SBLSCS 12; Chico: Scholars Press, 1980), 111–133, 122–123 and, against this hypothesis VanderKam, "Righteous One," 177–179.

[53] See J.H. Charlesworth and C.A. Newsom, eds., The Dead Sea Scrolls: Hebrew, Aramaic, and Greek Texts with English Translations, vol. 4b: Angelic Liturgy: Songs of the Sabbath Sacrifice (The Princeton Theological Seminary Dead Sea Scrolls Project; Tübingen: Mohr Siebeck, 1999), 7. Against this integration is, among the others, M.J. Davidson, Angels at Qumran: A Comparative Study of 1 Enoch 1–36, 72–108 and Sectarian Writings from Qumran (JSPSup 11; Sheffield: JSOT Press, 1992), 253–254.

THE DEAD SEA SCROLLS AND THE SON OF MAN IN DANIEL, *1 ENOCH*, AND THE NEW TESTAMENT GOSPELS: AN ASSESSMENT OF 11QMELCH (11Q13)

J. Harold Ellens
University of Michigan

The Dead Sea Scrolls do not use the term "Son of Man." Nevertheless, two factors indicate that the concept is worth exploring in the scrolls. First, there is some reason to believe that a Son-of-Man-like-figure is present in 11QMelch (11Q13). Presumably, such a figure would have roots in the prophecy of Ezekiel, in the book of Daniel (7–10), in the *Similitudes (Parables)* of *1 Enoch* (37–71), and in Gen 14:17; Pss 2; 8; and 110.[1] These texts form the mainstream of the Jewish Son of Man tradition. Second, the figure in 11QMelch may be associated with the royal and priestly messiahs in the *War Scroll* and in the *Hodayot (Thanksgiving Hymns).*

This paper explores the possibility that 11QMelch contains or implies a figure like those in the Son of Man tradition of the Hebrew Bible and *1 Enoch*. It also examines whether the figure in 11QMelch is associated with the messiahs of the *Hodayot* and the *War Scroll*. Since those are suffering messiahs, this paper examines the possible presence of a Son-of-Man-like-figure (a virtual Son of Man?) in the Dead Sea Scrolls. If such a figure is present, this would seem to be the first instance in Second Temple Judaism in which a suffering servant (Isa 53) is associated with the promised Messiah (Isa 61:1–4). It would also be the first time in

---

[1] K. Koch asserts unequivocally that 11QMelch "clearly refers to Daniel. The subject of its preserved fragments is the tenth jubilee as the age of redemption, during which Isa 52:7's promise of Jerusalem's final salvation and the realization of the God's kingdom will be fulfilled. On this theme the commentary identifies the messenger of the good news (*m^e baśśer*) of the prophecy with 'the Messiah of the spirit ([ח]הרוח) about whom Daniel spoke.' ... however the determination 'of the spirit' is lacking here. Is the 'annointed ruler' (Dan 9:24), who arises seven 'weeks' after the 'going forth of the word' being referred to in 11Q13, or is this the Messiah who will be cut off after 69 'weeks'? Or, alternatively, does this scroll know a variant version of Daniel?" Koch thinks that this indicates that 11QMelch is not dependent upon the *Damasus Document*. K. Koch, "Stages in the Canonization of the Book of Daniel," in *The Book of Daniel: Composition and Reception* (ed. J.J. Collins and P.W. Flint; 2 vols.; Leiden: Brill, 2002), 2:421–446, 430.

Jewish tradition and literature that a suffering Messiah is associated with a Son of Man figure, as in the NT gospels.[2]

11QMELCH: A DIGEST

Thirteen (or fifteen) fragments[3] of a first century B.C.E. document[4] featuring the mysterious figure Melchizedek were found in cave 11 at Qumran and first translated by Adam van der Woude in 1965.[5] The text proclaims liberty to the captives, after the theme of Isa 61:1. This suggests that it is a midrash (or a thematic pesher) on that passage, with an eschatological tone.[6] It promises a general restoration of freedom: from prison, debt, and loss of property. This redemption is to be realized at the *eschaton*, in this case the tenth Jubilee of the 490 years of the Week of Weeks (Dan 9:24–27). It is to be accomplished by Melchizedek, a deliverer who is sent from heaven. Vermes suggests that this Melchizedek has characteristics of the archangel, Michael, and is referred to as the leader or director of the "sons of heaven" and the "gods of justice." The Melchizedek of 11QMelch is, on occasion, referred to as *El* and *Elohim*, along the lines of such usage

---

[2] I. Knohl declares that when the Royal Messiah was killed in Jerusalem in 4 B.C.E. and his body, with that of his colleague, the Priestly Messiah, was left in the street for three days, his disciples searched the Hebrew Bible to discover messianic passages that would account for this crisis. They concluded that after humiliation and death the messianic figures had ascended into heaven, as prophesied by biblical passages that they now understood in a new way. "Thus, for the first time in the history of Judaism, a conception emerged of 'catastrophic' messianism in which the humiliation, rejection, and death of the Messiah were regarded as an inseparable part of the redemptive process." I. Knohl, *The Messiah Before Jesus: The Suffering Servant of the Dead Sea Scrolls* (Berkeley: University of California Press, 2000), 3; cf. ibid., 39–45.

[3] P. Bertalotto says there are fifteen in his unpublished research paper, "The Superhuman Melchizedek: A Qumranic Response to the Enochic Son of Man" (University of Michigan, 2009). A. Steudel says there are fourteen fragments. Cf. A. Steudel, "Melchizedek," *Encyclopedia of the Dead Sea Scrolls* (ed. L.H. Schiffman and J.C. VanderKam; 2 vols.; Oxford: Oxford University Press, 2000), 1:535–537.

[4] Koch, "Stages in the Canonization," 430 thinks it is possible that 11QMelch is a second century B.C.E. document. J.F. Hobbins suggests the same possibility in his chapter in the same volume ("Resurrection in Daniel and Other Writings at Qumran," in *The Book of Daniel: Composition and Reception*, 2:395–420, 400 n. 8). G. Vermes, *The Complete Dead Sea Scrolls in English* (New York: Allen Lane/Penguin, 1997), 500, declares without apology that it is from the first century B.C.E.

[5] A.S. van der Woude, "Melchisedek als himmlische Erlösergestalt in den neugefundenen eschatologischen Midraschim aus Qumran Höhle XI," *OtSt* 14 (1965): 354–373.

[6] Vermes, *The Complete Dead Sea Scrolls*, 500, refers to it as a *midrash* and Bertalotto, "The Superhuman Melchizedek," calls it a *pesher*.

of these terms in Job 1:6, and in the *Songs of the Sabbath Sacrifice*. Vermes suggests that the names have here their secondary meaning of judge rather than deity.

> Here Melchizedek is portrayed as presiding over the final Judgement and condemnation of his demonic counterpart, Belial/Satan, the Prince of Darkness, elsewhere also called Melkiresha'. The great act of deliverance is expected to occur on the Day of Atonement at the end of the tenth Jubilee cycle.[7]

Vermes' trajectory of thought regarding Melchizedek being the Archangel Michael seems to accord with John J. Collins' claim that the "one like unto a Son of Man" in Dan 7:13 is Michael and not a human figure. His argument is based upon the notion that the Son of Man figure in Daniel is the symbolic head of the Israelite nation, just as the beasts in Dan 7–10 are symbolic figures representing the empires which are to be destroyed. He suggests that each of the symbolic national figures is the "angel of its nation," which role Michael fills for Israel.[8]

Collins' line of thought is ill advised. While Michael is referred to in Dan 12:1 as a salvific prince who stands for the children of Israel, there is no connection drawn between him in that context and the Son of Man in Dan 7:13. Secondly, the beasts are not referred to as angels of their nations but only as kings or emperors. Thirdly, if the symbolic figures for the evil nations are beasts, sub-human in their abuses and degradation, and only *worthy of destruction*; why would one not count on the symbolic figure representing "The People of the Holy Ones of the Most High" (Dan 7:27) to be a human, *worthy of exaltation*, even to the heavenly realm. Such a view takes the text seriously as it stands.[9] The Son of Man

---

[7] Vermes, *The Complete Dead Sea Scrolls*, 500.

[8] J.J. Collins, *Daniel: A Commentary on the Book of Daniel* (Hermeneia; Minneapolis: Fortress, 1993). Cf. also J.J. Collins and P.W. Flint, eds., *The Book of Daniel: Composition and Reception* (2 vols.; Leiden: Brill, 2002). In this latter work, Koch, "Stages in the Canonization," 430, asserts that 11QMelch definitely refers to the book of Daniel, and hence has implications related to the Son of Man passage in Dan 7, as well as to the associated "week of weeks," the celebrated 490 years of the prophecy. Bertalotto, "The Superhuman Melchizedek," 9–10, attempts to establish an angelmorphic character for Melchizedek in 11QMelch but succeeds only in persuading the reader that Collins' argument is specious.

[9] In her comprehensive, erudite, and articulate study of salvific figures in the *Damascus Document* and the Dead Sea Scrolls, L. Guglielmo suggests that the Son of Man figures in Second Temple Judaism are clearly human figures in their basic characteristics, but are sometimes spoken of as though they have angelic qualities. They are accorded heavenly status, they are said to associate intimately with the angelic hosts of heaven, they have assigned positions of authority among the angels (Dan 7–11; *1 En.* 37–71), and the like.

in Dan 7–10 is God's agent to run earthly operations from his position
in the divine headquarters. His field-forces are humans carrying out his
delegated responsibilities on earth. There is no justification for Collins
to accord angelic status, character, or identity to Daniel's Son of Man.
Comparably, there is no justification for Vermes to accord angelic identity
to Melchizedek.

Vermes emphasizes that 11QMelch illuminates our understanding of
references to Melchizedek as a priest with an eternal priesthood as we
find them in the Epistle to the Hebrews (Heb 5:6, 10; 6:20; 7:1), the NT
analogue being Jesus Christ. He points out that 11QMelch also enlightens
us regarding the traditions of Melchizedek (Gen 14:18; Ps 110:4) and
the Son of Man as eschatological judge or prosecutor in Second Temple
Judaism (cf. Dan 7–10 where God is the judge but the Son of Man carries
out his judgment; and 1 En. 37–71 where the Son of Man is identified
as judge and carries out the judgment). Vermes points out that there
seems to be a correlation between the figure of Melchizedek in this
Qumran document (11QMelch) and the development of the specific type
of messianic concept that we find in the Synoptic Gospels and elsewhere
in NT Christianity.[10]

In the thirteen fragments of this tractate (11QMelch), Melchizedek is a
heavenly agent who manages a divine economy in which the restoration
of freedom and prosperity includes forgiveness "of all the iniquities" and
"wrong-doings" of those who were deprived and oppressed. He "will
assign them to the Sons of Heaven." They will share the "inheritance"
and the "portion" of Melchizedek. The Day of Atonement will atone for
all the "Sons of Heaven" who are of the "lot of Melchizedek ... for this
is the moment of the year of Grace of Melchizedek" (II:8). A sound
translation of Isa 61:2 reads similarly, "to proclaim the timeliness of the
Lord's acceptance" [of needy humanity] (trans. J.H.E.).

There follows quite naturally in 11QMelch a description of Melchizedek as *El* or *Elohim*, meaning the Judge, who, because of his *exousia*
(strength, power, authority [cf. John 5:27–47]), will "judge the holy ones

---

She argues that they may, therefore, be spoken of metaphorically as having angelic qualities. This does not warrant our calling them angelmorphic beings or angels, as J.J. Collins
names the Son of Man in Dan 7:13 (see Collins, *Daniel*, 305–306). See L. Guglielmo, "Historical Allusions and Salvific Figures in the Admonitions of the Damascus Document: An
Intertextual and Historical Interpretation Carried Out on the Basis of a Physical Reconstruction of 4Q266" (Ph.D. diss., University of Naples Frederico II, 2007).

[10] Vermes, *The Complete Dead Sea Scrolls*, 500. Vermes suggests, as a source of this
idea, the work of van der Woude, "Melchisedek als himmlische Erlösergestalt."

of God" (cf. Dan 7:22, 25, 27; *1 En.* 69–71). Here the document footnotes its claim, so to speak, by citing Ps 82:1 and 2 and Ps 7:7–8 regarding the judgment performed by *Elohim.* Moreover, Melchizedek's (*Elohim-*Judge) judgment also executes *Yahweh's* vengeance against Belial and the spirits who rebelliously follow him. From their control, Melchizedek, as Eschatological Judge or Prosecutor, will snatch away all the deprived and oppressed people, and restore their liberty and prosperity as the Sons of Heaven. All the *Elohim* of Justice will join Melchizedek in this destruction of Belial and his host. There follows a doxology about what the prophets called repeatedly The Great Day of the Lord, or The Day of Judgment and Salvation.

> This is the day of [Peace/Salvation] concerning which [God] spoke [through Isa]iah the prophet, who said, [*How*] *beautiful upon the mountains are the feet of the messenger who proclaims peace, who brings good news, who proclaims salvation, who says to Zion: Your* ELOHIM [*reigns*] (Isa. lii, 7).[11]   (11QMelch II:15–16)

Here the author of the tractate is formally citing Dan 9:25, Lev 25:9, and Isa 61:1–3 as the scriptural prophecies which he quite obviously and quite consciously has in mind. Moreover, he declares that the *Elohim* in "Your *Elohim*/Lord reigns!" is Melchizedek, who saves the deprived and oppressed from the control of Belial. This short tractate makes clear that its lead figure, Melchizedek, is a man from heaven who is appointed by Yahweh to exercise the role of the eschatological judge and prosecutor. In this role he is accorded the power and authority to put down evil powers, to deliver the righteous or redeemed from the evil powers, and to gather together into the heavenly kingdom all those who are forgiven and thus redeemed; and so are known as the Sons of Heaven or the Sons of Light.

SON OF MAN IN SECOND TEMPLE APOCALYPTIC JUDAISM

It is a source of considerable scholarly astonishment that, as noted above, there is no Son of Man named as such at Qumran. That is, the title, Son of Man, is not employed in the rich and extensive literature of the Qumran Essene Sect. Other references like those in 11QMelch, however, seem to offer evidence of a figure and a concept, even a messianic concept, in the

---

[11] Vermes, *The Complete Dead Sea Scrolls*, 501.

Dead Sea Scrolls, that is notably similar to the Son of Man material in the Hebrew Bible, in Second Temple Literature, and in the NT Gospels. All these references depict an exalted human figure, given a heavenly *locus*, accorded the role of Eschatological Judge and/or Prosecutor, and possessing a redemptive- or salvific-outcome function. The presence in 11QMelch of this complex construct or depiction suggests a significant interface between the messianic images in the Dead Sea Scrolls, and those regarding the Son of Man in the minds of apocalyptic Jews of the first two centuries B.C.E., as well as in the minds of the gospel writers and of Jesus himself. Subsequently Jesus, the literary character in the gospels, identified himself or was identified by others, with those Son of Man images in the gospel dramas.

Heinz E. Tödt found, in the *Rule of the Community* (1QS IV:25; IX:11), references to the actions of a messianic figure like the one in the Son of Man sayings of Matt 19:28 and Mark 14:61–62.[12] Tödt simply noted that the only setting in the gospels in which the same notion of a messianic human moving toward an apotheosis as Eschatological Judge arises is in the Son of Man *logia*. Tödt points out that in Mark 14:61–62, the titles Son of Man and Messiah are joined. Caiaphas asks Jesus, "Are you the Messiah, the Son of the Blessed"? Jesus' reply is direct, "I am; and you will see the Son of Man sitting at the right hand of power, and coming with the clouds of heaven." At Qumran and in Mark the messianic man is divinely appointed to function as Judge in the eschaton. His identity and function is that of discerning the righteous from the condemned unrighteous, abolishing the latter, and assembling the former into the heavenly kingdom.

The Qumran reference with which Tödt joins this Markan narrative concerns the hope for the endurance of the righteous, "until the prophet comes, and the Messiahs of Aaron and Israel" (1QS IX:11).[13] Tödt claims that this hope for multiple messiahs is refined by Jesus' day into a unified messianic hope. In the form of the Enochic Essenism that became the Jesus Movement, this unified hope centered itself in the messianic Son of Man, as it had in the Royal Messiah at Qumran.[14] In the literary drama of the gospels Jesus announces that this Son of Man is the figure who is

---

[12] H.E. Tödt, *The Son of Man in the Synoptic Tradition* (trans. D.M. Barton; Philadelphia: Westminster, 1965), 91; see also 37.

[13] F. Garcia Martinez, *The Dead Sea Scrolls Translated: The Qumran Texts in English* (trans. W.G.E. Watson; 2nd ed., Leiden: Brill, 1996), 13–14.

[14] Cf. again the *Hodayot* and the *War Scroll*.

to suffer at the hands of evil men and die, in direct correspondence with the Qumran expectation regarding the Royal Messiah.

Thus Tödt sees a relationship of concepts between such references as those to the Royal Messiah of Qumran, the apocalyptic Jewish notion of the Son of Man in Ezekiel and Daniel, and the Jesus character of the Synoptic Gospel narratives. This relationship of concepts should, of course, apply as well to Melchizedek as Eschatological Judge (*Elohim*) in 11QMelch. All these figures are Eschatological Judges and/or Prosecutors, and one might add Enoch from the *Parables* of *1 En.* 37–71. Both the Royal Messiah of Qumran, depicted in the *Hodayot* and in the *War Scroll*, and the Synoptic Jesus character are suffering and dying messiahs. While the Qumran Community does not refer to the Eschatological Judge nor to the suffering Messiah as the Son of Man, in both types of references the Dead Sea Scrolls clearly have in mind the same messianic figure as the one for which *1 Enoch* and the Jesus Movement employed that title, Son of Man, the latter claiming that Jesus named himself by that title.

George W.E. Nickelsburg develops at length the relationship between Dan 7 and the *Parables of Enoch* (*1 En.* 37–71), with particular emphasis upon the judicial role of the messianic figure.[15] While he distinguishes between the judicial role of Michael in Dan 10 and 12 and the non-judicial role of the one like a Son of Man in Dan 7, he nonetheless points out: "The heavenly enthronement of the one like a Son of Man will involve Israel's earthly supremacy over all the nations." This supremacy is reminiscent of the messianic destiny of Israel in Isa 61:5–6. Nickelsburg points out that it is this supremacy of the messianic figure or people which one finds in 1QM (1Q33) XVII:8, as well. Here we read that God will exalt "the dominion of Israel over all flesh." This is apparently an extension of the earthly effects of the work of "The People of the Holy Ones of the Most High" (Dan 7:27), carried out in the name and *exousia* of the "one like unto a Son of Man."

In Dan 7 the one like the Son of Man is exalted to heavenly status. It is not clear, despite Nickelsburg's remark to the contrary, that the Son of Man is actually enthroned in heaven in Dan 7–10, but he is accorded a heavenly status next to the Most High God. Both he and his minions on earth, "The People of the Holy Ones of the Most High," are exalted over all kingdoms and powers on earth. Thus the one like unto the

---

[15] G.W.E. Nickelsburg, "Son of Man," *ABD* 6:138.

Son of Man becomes the heavenly epitome of "The People of the Holy Ones of the Most High" who are on earth. Conversely, *they* become the earthly epitome of the exalted and heavenly Son of Man. It is interesting that in Daniel the Son of Man never descends to earth, but through his "field forces" on earth, who are accorded the dominion and power that his authority and power incarnates, accomplish his task of destroying evil powers and empires, thereby establishing the reign of the heavenly kingdom in all the earth. Those field forces prosecute the divine judgment which the Son of Man has the power, authority, and responsibility to work out on earth. Daniel's Son of Man is not enthroned but he exercises eschatological judgment through "The People of the Holy Ones of the Most High."

In *1 En.* 69:26–29, the Son of Man *combines* the role of enthronement and judgment, as does the Son of Man in the Synoptic Gospels. The Enochic scene is straight-forward. The hosts of heaven witness the exaltation, enthronement, and judgment carried out by the Son of Man, subsequently designated as Enoch, himself. Nickelsburg invites us to hear clearly the strains of the overture played in the *Parables of Enoch* and which became the theme of the sonata developed in the gospels.

> And there was great joy amongst them,
> And they blessed and glorified and extolled,
> Because the name of that Son of Man had been revealed to them
> And he sat on the throne of his glory,
> And the command of the judgment was given unto the Son of Man
> And he caused the sinners to pass away and be destroyed from off the
>   face of the earth,
> (*or,* he shall never pass away or perish from the face of the earth)
>
> And those who have led the world astray
> Shall be bound with chains,
> And their ruinous assembly shall be imprisoned
> And their works shall vanish from the face of the earth.
> And from henceforth there shall be nothing corruptible
> For that Son of Man has appeared,
> And has seated himself on the throne of his glory,
> And all evil shall pass away from before his face,
> And the word of that Son of Man shall go forth.   (*1 En.* 69:27–29)

Nickelsburg clearly intimates in his superb article the mutuality of language and concept of this great variety of literatures of Second Temple Judaism associated with the Son of Man as exalted heavenly figure and eschatological judge. One can hardly miss the correlative, if not the literarily genealogical relationship between these documents. The implication of Nickelsburg's work is that Tödt's references to the messianic expectation and eschatological judgment at Qumran in the *Rule of the Community* is a correlate of the Son of Man ideology in the *Parables of Enoch*. Thus, while the Dead Sea Scrolls do not name or title a Son of Man, they present the same messianic theology of eschatological judgment which is presented more concretely in the *Parables*, where it is given the name, title, and messianic character of the Son of Man. Thus, it certainly seems that it is precisely this figure who is the Son of Man throughout *1 En.* 37–71 and the messianic suffering servant-Son of Man in the Jesus story, that is the suffering servant-Royal Messiah at Qumran, and the judge and savior in 11QMelch.

The Son of Man and the Suffering Servant at Qumran

Israel Knohl has pursued at considerably greater length than Tödt and Nickelsburg his argument for a significant messianic figure(s) in the Dead Sea Scrolls, associated in nature and role with eschatological judgment.[16] Knohl is also at pains to draw out the implication of his citations from the scrolls in relationship to the nature and role of the Son of Man in the gospel narratives. Knohl finds a suffering servant messiah in the text of two or three Dead Sea Scrolls, attested by four or five separate copies.[17] Unfortunately, these scrolls are in damaged condition, though the entire manuscript seems to be preserved, nonetheless, in various parts. If proven to be correct, Knohl's claim seems even more useful than that of Tödt, and somewhat more effectively confirmed by the textual textual data.

Knohl cites 4QH^e (4Q431); 4QH^a (4Q427) 7; 1QH^a XXVI and 4QM^a (4Q491) 11 i. The first three manuscripts belong to the first version of the *Thanksgiving Hymns*, or *Hodayot*. The fourth citation, 4Q491, is from the *War Scroll* and is a second version of the hymns.[18] The main evidence for the first version is found in two rather substantial fragments of 4QH^e. The relevant text in the first fragment speaks of the messianic figure as beloved of the king who, from the context, seems clearly to be God. This messianic figure, whom God loves, is described as dwelling among the holy ones, though rejected by humanity. The first term, regarding his

---

[16] Knohl, *The Messiah Before Jesus*, 5–51, 66–71, 75–86.
[17] Ibid.
[18] Ibid., 75–86.

exaltation by the king, certainly rings with the sounds of Pss 2; 8; and 110; the second, depicting heavenly transcendence, echoes the strains of Dan 7–10; and the third, introducing suffering and rejection, seems reminiscent of Isa 53. If these references seem a bit tenuous, they are confirmed by the second fragment which speaks of the messianic figure being despised and enduring evil.

The fragmentary nature of 4QH^e is, of course, troublesome. We are fortunate to be able to reconstruct virtually the entire document by comparative analysis of all other manuscripts in version one where "parallel expressions are sometimes preserved in a more complete form."[19] Parallels also exist in version two for most of the relevant citations. For example, 1QH^a speaks of the messianic figure expressing "gentleness to the poor" but being "oppressed" (1QH^a III[16]). Similar confirmation is evident for the expressions of divine exaltation of the messianic figure, his assignment to dwell with the angels and the holy ones, his glory, and his role as judge. Knohl reconstructs this section of the first version of the first hymn as follows.

> I shall be reckoned with the angels, my dwelling is in the holy council.
> Who ... has been despised like me and who has been rejected of men
>   like me?
> And who compares to me in enduring evil?
> No teaching compares to my teaching
> For I sit ... in heaven.
> Who is like me among the angels?
> Who would cut off my words?
> And who could measure the flow of my lips?
> Who can associate with me, thus compare with my judgment?
> I am the beloved of the king, a companion of the holy ones ...
> And to my glory none can compare ...[20]

The second version of Hymn 1 has very similar language, as one would expect. Here again we have the messianic figure on an eternal heavenly throne of power. Three times over he is declared to be assigned to the angelic council. None can compare with his glory except the sons of

---

[19] Ibid., 76.

[20] Ibid., 76–77. Cf. also E. Schuller in *DJD* XXIX (1999): 199–208; and E. Eshel, "The Identification of the 'Speaker' of the Self Glorification Hymn," in *The Provo International Conference on the Dead Sea Scrolls: Technological Innovations, New Texts, and Reformulated Issues* (ed. D.W. Parry and E. Ulrich; STDJ 30; Leiden: Brill, 1999), 619–635; eadem in *DJD* XXIX (1999): 427–428; eadem, "4Q471b: A Self-Glorification Hymn," *RevQ* 17 (1996): 175–203. Cf. García Martinez, *The Dead Sea Scrolls Translated*, 317–361 for 1QH^a, 362–428 for 4QH^a (4Q427), 369–370 for 4QH^e (4Q431), and 115–120 for 4QM^a (4Q491).

the king. No one has been so exalted. He sits in heaven and none can accompany him to this unique majestic place. The holy council is his dwelling place. He has been despised, has borne incomparable afflictions, endured incomparable evil, and he has been glorified. No one is like him, no teaching like his teaching. No one can associate with him or compare with his exercise of judgment.

Hymn 2, version 1, is preserved in 4QHᵃ (4Q427) 7 i 13–ii 14, but this hymn is an exaltation of God and celebration of his redemptive exaltation of redeemed humans. "Proclaim and say: Great is God who acts wonderfully, for he casts down the haughty spirit so that there is no remnant and lifts up the poor from the dust to the eternal height and to the clouds he magnifies him in stature, and he is with the heavenly beings in the assembly of the community ..."[21] The second version of Hymn 2 is preserved in a mere fragment, 4QMᵃ (4Q491) 11 i 13–16 but refers to the exaltation of God's Messiah to the heavenly realm with the angels, and to his being accorded heavenly power.

Of course, as suggested above, it is difficult to miss the specific correspondence between the language of suffering, exaltation, and judgment associated with the Messiah in these messianic hymns and the language of the Son of Man *logia* of the Synoptic Gospels. Indeed, references to this messianic figure fit all three of Bultmann's categories of Synoptic Gospels' Son of Man *logia*, but Knohl is particularly interested in category two, the suffering Messiah.[22] It is also obvious how dependent both literary sources, Knohl's Qumran references and the gospel *logia*, are upon Pss 8:4–6; 110:1, Isa 53:1–12, Dan 7:13–14, 26–27, and *1 En.* 37–71 (particularly ch. 69). The latter is surprising, since *1 En.* 37–71, as an identifiable text, seems to be totally absent from the Qumran library.

What is very suggestive about the associations made in this discussion thus far is the degree to which the messianic figure referred to in Daniel, in the *Parables of Enoch*, and in the gospels of the NT is like the Messiah of Qumran (the *Hodayot*, *War Scroll*, and *Rule of the Community*), though at Qumran he is never accorded the title of Son of Man. Thus the important point here lies in the relationship between that evidence which strongly

---

[21] Knohl, *The Messiah Before Jesus*, 80.
[22] Cf. R. Bultmann, *The Gospel of John: A Commentary* (trans. G.R. Beasley-Murray; Oxford: Blackwell, 1971); idem, *Theology of the New Testament* (trans. K. Grobel; 2 vols., New York: Scribner, 1951), 1:30.

relates the suffering messianic figure at Qumran with the similar suffering
messianic figure of the Synoptic Gospels known as the Son of Man,
though the community of Qumran did not employ that title.

In this regard two issues are of importance. First, there is, as we have
already noted, a remarkable correspondence of language, concept, and
content between the suffering servant passages from Qumran, to which
Knohl calls our attention, and the language of the Son of Man *logia* in
the gospels, which depict the suffering and dying Messiah. Second, there
is a notable correspondence between the ultimate heavenly exaltation
and enthronement as judge of this figure who appears on earth as the
suffering servant in the passages at Qumran, including 11QMelch and
the comparable Son of Man *logia* in the Synoptic Gospels.

We apparently have a suffering servant Messiah in the *Hodayot* and
the *War Scroll* at Qumran, who is set in the context of the messianic figure of the *Rule of the Community* and who is the impending apocalyptic Eschatological Judge. The comparative chronology of the two sets of
texts, Qumran narrative (150 B.C.E.–50 C.E.) and gospel *logia* (80–100
C.E.), is also interesting, particularly if viewed in the framework Boccaccini developed in his study of the relationship between sectarian and
extra-sectarian Essenism.[23]

WHO IS THE SUFFERING MESSIAH AT QUMRAN?

The identity of the messianic figure in the Qumran Hymns might be, as
John J. Collins argues, not the Teacher of Righteousness nor a composite
figure representing the righteous community, nor, to use Daniel's term,
"The People of the Holy Ones of the Most High," but an individual author
whose identity until now remains a mystery.[24] Knohl argues on the basis
of a constellation of references in the Oracle of Hystapes, the book of
Revelation, the *Assumption of Moses*, and Roman history that the two
messianic leaders killed in the streets of Jerusalem in 4 B.C.E. by the
Romans under Caesar Augustus were the Royal and the Priestly Messiahs
whom the Qumran Community had celebrated; and that one of these was

---

[23] G. Boccaccini, *Beyond the Essene Hypothesis: The Parting of the Ways Between
Qumran and Enochic Judaism* (Grand Rapids: Eerdmans, 1998).

[24] J.J. Collins, *Apocalypticism in the Dead Sea Scrolls* (New York: Doubleday, 1997),
147.

the speaker in the messianic hymns. Since the speaker refers to being exalted to a throne, Knohl concludes it was the Royal Messiah who gave us the hymns.

> As the two messianic leaders were killed in 4 BCE, they surely were active in the period previous to that year—that is, during the reign of King Herod (37–4 BCE). ... all four copies of the messianic hymns were written precisely at that period. One can, therefore assume that one of the two Messiahs killed in 4 BCE was the hero of the messianic hymns from Qumran. ... The hero of the hymns did not have any priestly attributes; on the other hand, he spoke of sitting on a "throne of power" and mentioned a crown. From this we may deduce he was the royal Messiah.[25]

The historical record indicates that by order of the authorities, the two slain religious figures were left unburied in the city streets for three days, after which they disappeared, leading their disciples to believe that they had risen to life and ascended to heaven, as the hero in the hymns promised. As the messianic figure in the hymns had appropriated to himself the character and role of the suffering servant of Isa 53:4–8, so also had he appropriated to himself the exaltation of Isa 52:13, "Behold, my servant shall prosper, he shall be exalted and lifted up, and shall be very high." At the time of the murder of the Royal Messiah, his disciples took the abusive neglect of his body in the streets as a reason to appropriate to him also Isa 53:9 and 12, "They made his grave with the wicked ... he was numbered with the transgressors ..."[26] It was a short leap in the minds of the disciples of the Qumran messiahs from this Isaianic notion to fashioning an association between the disappearance of the corpse and resurrection and ascension to heavenly enthronement, which the author of the hymns had anticipated and promised; and Isa 52 proposes and so permits.

Knohl sees the outcome of this historic event in Roman history to have been of great significance and relevance to the Qumran community and their literature.

> Thus after the Messiah's death his believers created a "catastrophic" ideology. The rejection of the Messiah, his humiliation, and his death were thought to have been foretold in the Scriptures and to be necessary stages in the process of redemption. The disciples (of the Qumran Messiahs) believed that the humiliated and pierced Messiah had been resurrected after three days and that he was due to reappear on earth as redeemer,

---

[25] Knohl, *The Messiah Before Jesus*, 42.

[26] Ibid., 44. Do we hear at this point a memory of the transgressor, Jezebel, who was cast into the street dead, for the dogs to eat, as in 1 Kgs 21:23, and 2 Kgs 9:36–37?

victor, and judge. Daniel prophesied that the fourth beast would be destroyed and the kingdom would be given to the "son of man," whom Daniel
described as sitting on a heavenly throne and as coming in the clouds of
heaven. The disciples and followers of the Qumranic Messiah believed that
he had been resurrected after three days and had risen to heaven in a
cloud. He now sat in heaven as he had described himself in his vision—
on a "throne of power in the angelic council." Eventually he would return,
descending from above with the clouds of heaven, surrounded by angels.
The time would then have come for the overthrow of the fourth beast—
Rome—and *the Messiah would thus fulfill Daniel's vision of the "son of
man."*[27]

Knohl points out that this is the first time in Israelite history that the
notion of catastrophic messianism is introduced in which "the humiliation, rejection, and death of the Messiah were regarded as an inseparable
part of the redemptive process" and of his inevitable exaltation, enthronement, and ultimate apotheosis as divine judge.[28]

WHY IS THE SUFFERING SERVANT AND MESSIANIC JUDGE NOT THE SON OF MAN AT QUMRAN?

The enigma here lies in one question. The Qumran community had
a model of the suffering and dying Messiah which lay close in time,
concept, geography, and socio-political setting, to the Son of Man *logia* of
the Synoptic Gospels. Moreover, that community also depended heavily
upon the Enochic tradition, as did the Jesus movement; both of which
attached to the suffering servant and dying messiah images the notions
of the exalted heavenly man and Son of Man as eschatological judge.
This multifaceted Son of Man figure was exceedingly prominent under
that name in the Enochic tradition, which both of these communities
shared. Qumran expectations were shaped by the Daniel narrative about
heavenly exaltation of the Son of Man in a way similar to the shaping of
the expectations of the Jesus Movement. So why do the Qumran texts
not employ the Enochic term, Son of Man, to refer to their messianic
eschatological judge, or to their suffering, dying, exalted, and enthroned

---

[27] Ibid., 45–46 (italics J.H.E.). It should be noted that Knohl goes beyond the narrative
in Daniel here, in that the latter has no Son of Man who "would return, descending from
above with the clouds of heaven, surrounded by angels." That language is of much later
derivation and from far different sources.

[28] Ibid., 3. See n. 2 above.

Messiah, in the manner in which the Synoptic Gospels refer to him? Is it possible, even likely, that the gospel writers identified Jesus with the Qumran model of the suffering, dying, exalted, and judging messiah, and had good reason to integrate these characteristics into their model of Jesus' self-concept as Son of Man?

In his erudite and incisive chapter on the "Schism Between Qumran and Enochic Judaism," Boccaccini emphasizes that there are two types of documents in the Dead Sea Scrolls: those which were common to Essenes both within and outside of Qumran and those which were unique to Qumran.[29] The former are pre-sectarian or extra-sectarian and remained normative for the urban Essenes, while the latter are sectarian in character and chronology, and exclusive to Qumran. Thus, prior to the cloistering of the Qumran Essenes, the *Halakhic Letter*, the *Dream Visions*, *Jubilees*, the *Temple Scroll*, the *Proto-Epistle of Enoch*, and the *Damascus Document* were theologically determinative in the thought of all Essene communities. The *Damascus Document* states that God calls his righteous people to separate themselves from the world and declares, surprisingly, that God has not elected all of Israel, but only a remnant, to salvation.[30]

However, like the other documents listed, the *Damascus Document* provides for a certain degree of free will exercised by humans and sub-divine heavenly beings. Thus, the strict supralapsarian determinism of the subsequent sectarian documents at Qumran was not standard in Essenism before and outside of Qumran. That Qumranic doctrine of determinism, Boccaccini argues, made no room for any freedom of will on the part of humans or "fallen angels." The latter were seen as the source of evil in the world. Moreover, the *Parables of Enoch*, which elaborate the Danielic tradition of the exalted Son of Man, since it was not present at Qumran, must have been an addition to the Essene literature outside of Qumran, namely, among the urban Essenes. It must have been produced after the cloistering of the sectarian community of Qumran, or known at Qumran but overtly rejected by the community for theological reasons. This is a critical fact in the argument because the *Parables* clearly speak against the Qumranic notion of supralapsarian determinism, as do other facets of 1 *Enoch*.

---

[29] Boccaccini, *Beyond the Essene Hypothesis*, 119–162.
[30] Ibid., 123.

The Epistle of Enoch does not simply lack specific Qumranic elements,
… it has specific anti-Qumranic elements. The most obvious is I En 98:4.
The passage explicitly condemns those who state that since human beings
are victims of a corrupted universe, they are not responsible for the sins
they commit, and they blame others (God or the evil angels) for having
exported "sin" into the world. "I have sworn unto you, sinners: In the same
manner that a mountain has never turned into a servant, nor shall a hill
(ever) become a maidservant or a woman; likewise, neither has sin been
exported into the world. It is the people who have themselves invented it.
And those who commit it shall come under a great curse" (98:4).[31]

In the sectarian documents unique to Qumran, evil is transcendent and
supralapsarian in both source and remedy: a state of affairs preset by
God from the beginning, by election of some to righteousness and others
to damnation. In the urban Essene movement salvation from evil is
accomplished by a divine salvific intervention. A Son of Man like the
one in Dan 7:9–14 and in *1 En.* 37–39 and 70–71 would be an adequate
redemptive resource, especially the latter when he descends as judge
to separate the righteous from the unrighteous. Boccaccini points out
that the cosmic tragedy, induced by fallen angels (Sons of God who
cavorted with the daughters of men) requires more than a human or
angelic savior, since such a judge or redeemer, in order to subdue the evil
powers, must have power superior to that of those angels who brought
evil into the world. The exaltation of the Son of Man to the heavenly
enthronement, in the Enochic tradition outside Qumran, places the Son
of Man above the angels in power and glory. Thus, in extra-Qumran
Enochic literature, the Son of Man is empowered by God to bring the
ultimate resolution to life, history, and evil, at his advent as eschatological
judge.

The most distinctive quality of this extra-Qumranic Essene model,
however, lies in the fact that humans can contribute to their legitimate
inclusion in the community of the elect by willfully conducting their lives
as the righteous ones, "The People of the Holy Ones of the Most High."
There is no possibility of such human action in will or deed at Qumran.
All is preset from eternity. Among the Essenes outside Qumran there is
a distinction made, Boccaccini declares, between the evil in the world
that has a transcendent source, namely, the fallen angels, and human
sin, which is life willfully lived in complicity with this cosmic evil. One

---

[31] Ibid., 134.

can willfully choose a righteous life, "the boundaries between the chosen and the wicked remain permeable. The door to salvation, which the Damascus Document kept open only for a limited period of time and the sectarian [Qumran] documents barred from the beginning for those who have not been chosen by God, will be open until the very last moment," according to the Essenes outside Qumran.[32]

In the Qumranic model God has preset the destiny of the elect and the reprobate. There is no room for one's volitional choice to live in complicity with evil or in identification with the righteousness of God and the people of "The People of the Holy Ones of the Most High." One has only one's preset destiny. To discern whether one's destiny is that of the elect or damned, one is invited to separate himself from the world and undertake to live the life of righteousness in the cloistered community. If a person discovers that living the community's discipline is possible for him, he can know that he is one of God's elect. If he cannot live by that discipline he has no recourse but to accept his supralapsarian reprobate status in the eternal scheme of things.

Both the elect and the damned are assigned their destiny to the glory of God. The judgment of God took place before creation and so before time. The judgment was to assign the status of the righteous and the unrighteous. The consequences of that judgment at the end of history will separate "The People of the Holy Ones of the Most High" from the unrighteous, exterminating the latter and gathering the former into the heavenly kingdom. Thus there is no theological place at Qumran for a Son of Man, as redemptive messianic figure or as messianic eschatological judge. God is the only judge and he made the final judgment by a supralapsarian act at the time that he decided to create the world and humanity in it. Both salvation and judgment, therefore, are already past. They will not come at the end of time. There is no role for the Son of Man at Qumran.

> The Qumran community did not become less apocalyptic, if we consider its roots and worldview; but it certainly became less Enochic the further it parted from the parallel development of mainstream Enochic Judaism since the first century BCE. Therefore, the decreasing influence of Enochic literature on the sectarian texts is by no means surprising; it is the logical consequence of the schism between Qumran and Enochic Judaism.[33]

---

[32] Ibid., 137–138; see also 147–148.
[33] Ibid., 149.

WHY THEN THE SUFFERING MESSIAH AT QUMRAN?

In his "Sherlock Holmes" style narrative, Knohl offers an intriguing ratio-
nale for the presence, nonetheless, of both the suffering messiah (*Hodayot*
and *War Scroll*) and the eschatological judge and savior (11QMelch) at
Qumran. He asserts that the messianic figure who produced the messianic hymns that were found among the scrolls at Qumran, was pro-
moting a notion at Qumran that ran counter to the orthodox doctrine
of the community. His idea of a suffering messianic figure, who would
facilitate the enhancement and endurance of the community of the righteous, was an attempt to recover something of the pre-sectarian quality of historic Enochic doctrine while associating the messianic figure
with Pss 2; 8; and 110, on the one hand, and Dan 7 and Isa 53, on the
other.

Knohl speculates that this doctrine was unconventional and unac-
ceptable at Qumran, indeed, a heretical theology, causing the condition of the edition of his manuscripts of the hymns as we have them.
Knohl claims that normal aging, environmental conditions, or decay
were not the cause of these manuscripts being in fragments when they
were discovered in the clay jars. Other manuscripts were discovered in
fragments in the caves at Qumran because their clay containers had
been menaced, damaged, or destroyed. The main manuscript of this
edition of the Hymns was found in its jar, undisturbed, but carefully
and intentionally torn into rather large pieces and then stored in the
container.[34] Knohl judges that this tells us an important story, namely,
that this edition of the manuscripts was suppressed at Qumran, and
thus it was torn into pieces with rather careful intentionality, but preserved by a devotee of the heretical author and thus, carefully and sur-
reptitiously placed in the clay jars and in the caves, along with the rest
of the library. This scenario, despite its speculative quality, is possible.
Whether one can declare that it is probable requires further evidence

---

[34] Unfortunately, it has not been possible for me to examine the actual manuscripts and
fragments themselves, but only the available photographs. On the face of it there seems
to be some cogency to Knohl's claim regarding the state of the manuscripts as a result of
their being intentionally torn—as well as intentionally preserved. However, in a personal
conversation with J.H. Charlesworth during the first Enoch Seminar: The International
Conference on Second Temple Judaism, 19–23 June 2001, that notable Dead Sea Scrolls
scholar stated that he believes it is likely that the fragmentary character of the remains
of these hymnic manuscripts is a result of the same process of deterioration from age,
exposure, and vermin which characterizes that of other Dead Sea Scrolls.

confirming that there was the type of heretical movement at Qumran that Knohl proposes as the key to his argument.

If this speculative theory be true to fact, in a repressed text of the Dead Sea Scrolls library three key factors conspire to form a single historical *datum* that is eminently relevant to the redemptive eschatological figure in 11QMelch, and to Jesus' self concept, as he was fashioned into the Son of Man character in the gospels. First, we have at Qumran a messianic figure who speaks of his role as that of proclaiming the kingdom of God, Bultmann's first category of Son of Man *logia* in the gospels. Second, Qumran presents a messianic figure who is suffering, dying, and then exalted by God to the status of a heavenly figure, Bultmann's second category. Finally, the *Hodoyot* and the *War Scroll*, present a Messiah who takes up the role of eschatological judge and savior (implementer of the Day of Judgment and Salvation; or Day of the Lord, of the Tanak), Bultmann's third category and the key notion in 11QMelch. Thus we have at Qumran a *virtual* Son of Man, like the *actual* Son of Man in the Jesus Movement of a century later, and of the gospel narratives of a century and a half later.

Of course, in articulating this messianic figure at Qumran it was impossible for that heretical Royal Messiah to employ the standard Enochic term for him, namely, Son of Man, which was employed by the related but later community of Enochic Judaism that became Christianity. At Qumran that term had neither credence, nor coinage, and would have made the heresy both extremely obvious and unnecessarily offensive. It would have amounted to really "sticking it into the face of the authorities" of the esoteric supralapsarian Qumran community. If Knohl's argument holds water, Jesus, the literary character who traverses the pages of the Synoptic Gospels, internalized as the second phase of his personal identity development, an Essene concept of a suffering and dying Messiah (Matt 12:40; 17:12, 22; Mark 8:27–37).

This concept had already existed for some time in what Knohl intimates was a heretical form of Qumran Essenism, and which Jesus, as literary character, is depicted as having identified with the Son of Man of 1 *Enoch*, Daniel, and Ezekiel. It is an intriguing coincidence that the death of the Qumran Messiahs took place in the very year of Jesus birth, namely, 4 B.C.E. Were the gospel writers aware of this and did they, therefore, make some association, conscious or unconscious, between the Jesus character in the gospels and the messianic characters of Qumran? We can have absolutely no way of knowing that, but certainly that association was clearly made.

BACK TO 11QMELCH: SUMMARY

Time and space prevents us from exploring in detail the Son of Man
tradition from Ezekiel, Daniel, and *1 Enoch*, each of which has a different
perspective. Let me simply summarize them. Ezekiel is addressed by God
as Son of Man 93 times in his prophecy. That prophecy is structured on
the seven-point rubrics for priestly ordination as stated in Lev 8–9.[35] In
Ezekiel, Son of Man means "mortal" or "mere mortal." Ezekiel's Son of
Man is a man who proclaims the advent of the heavenly kingdom and
the restoration of the world. Daniel's Son of Man is a man who is exalted
to heaven and presented to the Ancient of Days, that is, to God. He is
accorded dominion and power (*exousia*) to carry out God's judgment of
destroying evil powers and bringing in the heavenly kingdom. He does
this through his field forces on earth, "The People of the Holy Ones of
the Most High," while he remains in heaven. The Son of Man in *1 Enoch*
is Enoch himself, caught up into heaven by a whirlwind and shown the
places of the righteous and unrighteous, and then appointed to carry out
divine judgment on the living and the dead. He consummates history by
the administration of God's Day of Judgment and Salvation, bringing in
the heavenly kingdom on earth and in heaven.

Clearly, the Jesus character in the Synoptic Gospels starts as an Ezekiel
Son of Man. As his pilgrimage runs into difficulty in Mark 8, with
the failure of the first mission, Jesus begins to envision himself as the
messianic suffering servant of the *Hodayot* and *War Scroll*, Qumran's
virtual Son of Man. His journey runs into increasingly heavy weather
as the collision course with the authorities becomes clearer and more
inevitable. Then he begins to envision himself as the Son of Man of
Dan 7–10, exalted by God to a heavenly status in which he, nonetheless,
accomplishes the mission of putting down the evil powers by means of his
followers on earth. When he finally stands in judgment before Caiaphas
and Pilate, and the jig is up, so to speak, the Jesus character in the Synoptic
Gospels' story raises the ante one more time. He declares that he will
return from heaven as the Eschatological Judge and Prosecutor, on the
clouds of heaven, with all the holy angels, in the power and glory of God
himself. This is the Son of Man of *1 Enoch* and of 11QMelch.

---

[35] M.A. Sweeney, "Ezekiel: Zadokite Priest and Visionary Prophet of the Exile," in
idem, *Form and Intertextuality in Prophetic and Apocalyptic Literature* (FAT 45; Tübingen:
Mohr Siebeck, 2005), 125–143. Cf. also M.S. Odell, "You Are What You Eat: Ezekiel and
the Scroll," *JBL* 117 (1998): 229–248.

It is of great interest and importance that in the Gospel of John we have a quite different scenario than in the Synoptic Gospels. In John Jesus is from the outset the heavenly man and Son of Man (John 1:1–3), who descends to earth (John 1:14) to become the savior (John 3:13–18) of the whole world. In the Fourth Gospel the judgment was also supralapsarian, as at Qumran, but of an opposite sort. In that judgment God judged that he would save the whole world. So in John there is no second coming, no final judgment, no end of history, no *eschaton*, and no *parousia*. Indeed, there is no eschatological judge. Jesus is the savior. Whenever in John it is suggested that the Son of Man is, by definition, the eschatological judge, Jesus is at great pains to insist that he will not exercise his *exousia* as Judge or Prosecutor, but will exercise only the role of savior (John 5:27–47; 8:15 etc.).

Significantly, in John 3:13, Jesus aggressively sets himself apart from the Enochic Son of Man, Judge and Prosecutor, by declaring that "no man ascends into heaven but he who descended from heaven, even the Son of Man, who is heavenly." *1 Enoch* claims that Enoch ascended into heaven and returns from there, having been enthroned in heaven and appointed to be the Eschatological Judge. Jesus is declaring in John 3:13 that Enoch cannot have been the true Son of Man, since he was not a heavenly man who first descended from heaven and after finishing his work on earth returned to heaven. On the other hand, Jesus is the epitome of that proper model, therefore, Jesus is the true Son of Man. This true Son of Man foregoes his role as judge and prosecutor, since they are now irrelevant, and engages instead in the role of savior of the world. There follows the reference to the Son of Man being lifted up as Moses' serpent in the wilderness.

The picture in 11QMelch has similarities in that it is focused primarily upon the role of Melchizedek as a heavenly figure, an agent of divine action in the world as the eschatological judge and prosecutor, as well as a savior or redeemer. Here there is no indication of an Ezekiel-like Son of Man, namely, an earthly human who is called to proclaim the reign of God on earth, as in the Synoptics before Mark 8:13. As in John we have in 11QMelch, instead, echoes of a *heavenly man*, the Son of Man in Dan 7–10. Melchizedek is, moreover, not just an agent to prosecute the cause of the heavenly kingdom on earth. He is an *Elohim*, a divinely appointed judge and prosecutor, whose task is very like that of Enoch in the *Parables* (*1 En.* 37–71, especially chs. 69–71).

Melchizedek is the eschatological judge, but in this process his prominent role, repeatedly emphasized, is that of securing the deliverance and salvation (liberty and prosperity) of "The People of the Holy Ones of the Most High," that is, the Sons of Light or the Sons of Heaven. It is not difficult to see, therefore, that the author of Heb 5 styles him as a priest of the Most High God, as in Abraham's experience (Gen 14:18; cf. also Ps 110:4), and hence a type of Jesus, as the savior of the world, the eternal anchor of hope grounded in the heavenly world.

It is clear, therefore, that at Qumran we have a *virtual* Son of Man in the *Hodayot* and the *War Scroll*, in the *Rule of the Community*, and in the form of a messianic figure who is also the suffering servant. Moreover, it is clear that in 11QMelch we have a figure with key elements of the Son of Man tradition of apocalyptic Judaism, namely, the authority and power of eschatological judge and the function of rescuer or savior of the people of God.[36] Of course, the suffering messiah and the eschatological judge both stand in contrast with the mainstream of Qumran's supralapsarian determinist theology. The documents we have cited from the Qumran library suggest that a heretical movement existed within the community that envisioned the possibility of hope and salvation beyond the scope of the predestined elect. This enticed them, perhaps, to contemplate and militate for a theology of a salvation that required a savior-messiah who would, perforce, suffer for being at cross purposes with the orthodox determinists, but who would in the end be exalted of God and appointed as the eschatological judge of the living and the dead. Knohl would seem, therefore, to be correct in suggesting that in this repeated combination of judge and savior in the Dead Sea Scrolls, associated significantly with messianic suffering, we have the first time in Jewish tradition an occasion in which Isa 53 and 61 are conjoined, a coalescence that became the key to the identity of Jesus as Son of Man in the gospels.

---

[36] G.W.E. Nickelsburg notes that in 11QMelch we have a priestly and royal figure, such as are mentioned in Gen 14:18–20 (the Abraham encounter with Melchizedek), and Ps 110 (symbolic references to the man exalted and enthroned by God). See G.W.E. Nickelsburg, *Ancient Judaism and Christian Origins: Diversity, Continuity, and Transformation* (Minneapolis: Fortress, 2003), 101; idem, *Jewish Literature between the Bible and the Mishnah* (2nd ed.; Minneapolis: Fortress, 2005), 132. The implication of this perspective is a strong relationship between 11QMelch and the passages regarding the suffering messiahs in the *War Scroll* and *Hodayot* narratives (the Royal and Priestly Messiahs), who Knohl suggests, were killed in Jerusalem in 4 B.C.E. and thought by their disciples to have ascended into heaven, as the Royal Messiah had promised in his hymns.

We do not have a Son of Man in the Dead Sea Scrolls, but we have a *virtual* Son of Man: suffering messiah and savior, exalted to heavenly status as the eschatological judge in the *Hodayot*, the *War Scroll*, and in 11QMelch. In John 3:13–18 and 5:27–47, as well as in Dan 7–10 and *1 En.* 37–71, this combination of characteristics and functions is noted as the essential and defining identity of the Son of Man of Second Temple Judaism.

ANCIENT JEWISH LITERATURE IN
GREEK AND THE DEAD SEA SCROLLS

THE DEAD SEA SCROLLS AND THE GRECO-ROMAN WORLD: EXAMINING THE ESSENES' VIEW OF SACRIFICE IN RELATION TO THE SCROLLS

JAMAL-DOMINIQUE HOPKINS
Interdenominational Theological Center, Atlanta, Ga.

A. INTRODUCTION

Hellenistic Judaism was diverse in thought, practice, and social organization. One issue that exemplifies its complexity is animal sacrifice. This study examines one group's view of sacrifice, namely the Essenes. As described by the early Jewish writers, Philo and Josephus, the Essenes were one of four Jewish sectarian groups that held to certain priestly ideals.[1] On the basis of the descriptions given in Philo's *Quod omnis probus liber sit* 75 and Josephus' *Jewish Antiquities* 18.19, the Essene's views on the religious cult seem to be congruent with the ideology of the community related to the Dead Sea Scrolls. Due to space limitations, this study focuses on the Essene group as described by Josephus. I perform a textual analysis of *Ant.* 18.19 in order to understand its overall context. Subsequently, I will argue for the possible connection of the Essenes with the larger movement associated with the Dead Sea Scrolls (the DSS movement hereafter). If, in fact, this latter connection can be made, then insight concerning the cultic ideology of the entire DSS movement (which includes the later Qumran community) can be determined. Here, as will be demonstrated below, there are no less than two streams of thought concerning the cultic ideology. With this in mind, Josephus' description also needs to be investigated alongside the texts of the DSS movement, most notably the sectarian texts of the Dead Sea Scrolls.

---

[1] Philo's most notable description of the Essenes is found in *Prob.* 75–87.

B. Josephus' Description of the Essene View of Sacrifice

1. Introduction

Jewish Antiquities 18.19 is attested variously in six MSS.[2] It has been problematic for translators due to the variant readings. Textual differences exist in at least two different textual traditions. The {Lat.} and {E} versions render *Ant.* 18.19 as follows:

> εἰς δὲ τὸ ἱερὸν ἀναθήματα στέλλοντες θυσίας [οὐκ] ἐπιτελοῦσιν διαφο-
> ρότητι ἁγνειῶν, ἃς νομίζοιεν, καὶ δι' αὐτὸ εἰργόμενοι τοῦ κοινοῦ τεμε-
> νίσματος ἐφ' αὐτῶν τὰς θυσίας ἐπιτελοῦσιν.[3]

The {A}, {M}, {W}, and {Zon.} witnesses render the same passage in the following way:

> εἰς δὲ τὸ ἱερὸν ἀναθήματα στέλλοντες θυσίας ἐπιτελοῦσιν διαφορότητι
> ἁγνειῶν, ἃς νομίζοιεν, καὶ δι' αὐτὸ εἰργόμενοι τοῦ κοινοῦ τεμενίσματος
> ἐφ' αὐτῶν τὰς θυσίας ἐπιτελοῦσιν.[4]

It is because of the textual variant above that scholars remain unresolved about whether or not the Essenes participated in sacrifice. Different solutions have been put forth, and these differences have resulted in variant views regarding both the identity and the cultic ideology of the DSS movements. Compounded together with these issues, and also in relation to the scrolls, is the lack of insight regarding the time or period for which Josephus' account is relevant. Josephus could be referring to at least one of four scenarios:

1. The above citation reflects the ideology of the entire Essene movement, which remained unchanged.
2. It reflects the ideology of the entire movement during a particular stage.

---

[2] *Ant.* 18.19 is found in the following MSS: {A} Codex bibliothecae Ambrosianae F 128, dating from the 11th century; {M} Codex Medicaeus bibliothecae Laurentianae plut. 69, codex 10, dating from the 14th to 15th centuries; {W} Codex Vaticanus Gr. no. 984, dating 1354 C.E. (the 12th century); {E} The Epitome Antiquitatum, noted by H.S.J. Thackeray as being used by Zonaras. Thackeray also contended that Niese conjectured that this version was made in the 10th or 11th century; {Lat.} Uersio Latina, the Latin version of Cassiodorus from the 5th or 6th century (which is also the oldest extant MS for 18:19) and {Zon.} The Chronicon of Zonaras, from the 12th century.

[3] See S.A. Naber, ed., *Flavii Josephi Opera Omnia: Post Immanuelem Bekkerum* (6 vols.; Leipzig: Teubner, 1888–1896), 4:139, who gives this reading.

[4] This is the reading given by B. Niese, ed., *Flavii Josephi Opera* (7 vols.; Berlin: Weidmann, 1885–1895), 4:143, which is followed by the LCL.

3. It reflects the ideology of at least one of the movement's group (i.e. an offshoot group that emerged from the larger parent movement), which remained unchanged.

4. It reflects the ideology of at least one of the movement's groups during a particular stage.

Further examination of the aforementioned passage could reveal that Josephus' account reflects two multiple streams of thought that reveal the ideology of at least two groups within the larger DSS movement.[5] Irrespective of the scenario, however, the same ideology or ideologies would need to be reflected somewhere in the scrolls, particularly if the movement (and its various groups) related to the scrolls can be identified as Essene.

Concerning the textual variant the main issue surrounds the more original reading of the first clause of *Ant.* 18.19. As noted above, the {A}, {M}, {W}, and {Zon.} Greek MS witnesses render *Ant.* 18.19 in the following way, without the negation (οὐκ):

> εἰς δὲ τὸ ἱερὸν ἀναθήματα στέλλοντες θυσίας ἐπιτελοῦσιν διαφορότητι ἁγνειῶν, ἅς νομίζοιεν, καὶ δι' αὐτὸ εἰργόμενοι τοῦ κοινοῦ τεμενίσματος ἐφ' αὑτῶν τὰς θυσίας ἐπιτελοῦσιν.

> They send votive gifts to the temple but perform sacrifices with different purifications, which they suppose, for this reason they were excluded from the public precinct of the temple thus they perform sacrifices by themselves.[6]

The {Lat.} and {E} versions negate the second line of the first clause, εἰς δὲ τὸ ἱερὸν ἀναθήματα στέλλοντες θυσίας [οὐκ] ἐπιτελοῦσιν διαφορότητι ἁγνειῶν. Difficulty in translating the first clause of this passage is also heightened in view of θυσίας ἐπιτελοῦσιν also occurring in the last line of this passage (ἐφ' αὑτῶν τὰς θυσίας ἐπιτελοῦσιν). In view of the textual issue concerning οὐκ, which subsequently has affected the translation, meaning and overall understanding of this passage, four particular issues will be examined in this section: (1) should this passage be read with or without the negation (οὐκ)? (2) How should

---

[5] As discussed below, these two streams of thought likely reflect the cultic ideology of the larger DSS movement and the later Qumran community (a distinct offshoot group from the larger parent movement that resettled at Qumran). Due to their observance of the 364-day calendar, the former group appears to have offered certain non-calendar binding sacrifices, or alternatively, sacrifices for non-temple associated festivals.

[6] My translation.

the term ἀναθήματα in the first line be understood? (3) How should εἰργόμενοι be translated, grammatically? and (4) how should the statement ἐφ᾽ αὐτῶν τὰς θυσίας ἐπιτελοῦσιν be read, particularly in view of the translation of θυσίας ἐπιτελοῦσιν in the first part of this passage?

Before discussing these issues, it is important to note that the Essenes are described as sending ἀναθήματα to the temple. This suggests that like in Philo (*Prob.* 75) and what we know about the entire DSS movement, Josephus' Essenes revered the temple and cult in principle. As Albert Baumgarten perceptively notes, the Essenes' reverence for the temple and cult is also indicated by the fact that according to Josephus, Judah the Essene was teaching in the temple and John the Essene was appointed at a meeting in the temple.[7]

Ἀναθήματα is typically rendered as "votive offerings."[8] John Strugnell, followed by Joseph Baumgarten, rightly noted that ἀναθήματα is non-sacrificial.[9] According to A. Baumgarten, this term can be interpreted in a number of ways. Following John Nolland,[10] A. Baumgarten contends that it could include the temple tax that all Jews were required to pay.[11] Alternatively, he suggests that sending ἀναθήματα could have meant voluntary sacrifices, which both Jews and non-Jews were free to send.[12] Despite how ἀναθήματα is interpreted, as is discussed below, sending it to the temple suggests that for some reason these particular Essenes were not able to bring it themselves, further implying that they were

---

[7] See A. Baumgarten, "Josephus on Essene Sacrifice," *JJS* 45 (1995): 169–183, 175 and n. 27. Also see J. Nolland, "A Misleading Statement of the Essene Attitude to the Temple," *RevQ* 9 (1977–1978): 555–562, 557–558, who similarly notes the point that the Essenes revered the temple. The presence of Essenes in Jerusalem and at the temple reflects the notion that in view of the *Damascus Document* (particularly CD 3:21b–4:2a; 9:14a; 11:17b–18a; 14:19b [= 4Q266 10 i 13]; 16:13–17a and 4Q266 11 1–8a) the larger DSS movement participated in some sacrifices. This similarity speaks to the probable link between the Essenes and the DSS movement.

[8] See LSJ s.v.

[9] See J. Strugnell, "Flavius Josephus and the Essenes: *Antiquities* XVIII.18–22," *JBL* 7 (1958): 106–115, 114 n. 36 and J.M. Baumgarten, "The Essenes and the Temple: A Reppraisal," in *Studies in Qumran Law* (SJLA 24; Leiden: Brill, 1977), 57–74, 68.

[10] See Nolland, "Misleading Statement," 557–558.

[11] For a discussion of the half-shekel offering see J. Liver, "The Half-Shekel Offering in Biblical and Post-Biblical Literature," *HTR* 56 (1963): 173–198; J. Magness, "Temple Tax, Clothing, and the Anti-Hellenizing Attitude of the Sectarians," in *The Archaeology of Qumran and the Dead Sea Scrolls* (Studies in the Dead Sea Scrolls and Related Literature; Grand Rapids: Eerdmans, 2002), 188–209, 188–193 and 206–209.

[12] See A. Baumgarten, "Josephus," 174–175.

not present around the temple. But what was the reason(s) for their position? Due to the variant reading of this passage (the {Lat.} and {E} against the others), *Ant.* 18.19 becomes ambiguous at this point.[13] Certain possibilities will be probed in order to determine this.

2. *Accepting or Rejecting the Reading of* οὐκ *in the Text*

The {Lat.} version of *Ant.* 18.19 is at least five to six centuries older than the extant Greek MSS where οὐκ is absent. Nolland rightly favored the former ({Lat.} followed by {E}); he accurately stressed its importance on the basis of being the oldest extant witness.[14] The {Lat.} version is a fifth or sixth century MS made by the order of Cassiodorus. Outside of his version of *Ant.* (particularly 18.19), all of the extant MSS of this passage are known in Greek.[15] Presumably, {Lat.}, which is followed by {E}, derived from an earlier Greek source;[16] however, whether or not the reading favored in {Lat.} predated the source from the extant Greek MSS where οὐκ is absent is uncertain.

Marie-Joseph Lagrange (working before the discovery of the scrolls) favored the tradition behind the Greek MSS. He reasoned that οὐκ was inserted into the {Lat.} because of Philo and Eusebius' influence: "La négation a été ajoutée dans le latin d'après l'idée accréditée par Philon et surtout par Eusèbe que les Esséniens ne faisaient pas d'immolations."[17] Lagrange drops the οὐκ in his translation:

> Ils envoient des objects consacrés au Temple et s'acquittent des sacrifices avec des purifications supérieures, à ce qu'ils pensent, et se tenant à l'écart pour dela même de l'enceinte du Temple commune (à tous) ils s'acquittent entre eux des (dits) sacrifices.[18]

---

[13] As opposed to the larger DSS movement, the Qumran community chose to refrain from visiting the temple. This is attested throughout *MMT*, the *Rule of Community*, and 4QFlor (4Q174) (= 4QMidrEschat^a; cf. A. Steudel, *Der Midrasch zur Eschatologie aus der Qumrangemeinde [4QMidrEschat^{a.b}]: Materielle Rekonstruktion, Textbestand, Gattung und traditionsgeschichtliche Einordnung des durch 4Q174 ["Florilegium"] und 4Q177 ["Catena A"] repräsentierten Werkes aus den Qumranfunden* [STDJ 13; Leiden: Brill, 1994]).

[14] Nolland "Misleading Statement," 558.

[15] Although it is non-extant, a fourth century Latin version of the *Jewish Antiquities* was attributed to Hegesippus.

[16] This is against Black, who thinks that the οὐκ was imported into the texts from a misunderstood Latin translation. See below for this discussion.

[17] M.-J. Lagrange, *Le Judaïsme avant Jésus-Christ* (Paris: Gabalda, 1931), 317.

[18] Ibid., 316.

He also asserted that the Essenes wanted to sacrifice; yet their "raffinements de purifications" prevented them, unless they risked contamination; here Lagrange described the absence of οὐκ as naturally harmonizing better with Josephus' further statement, ἐφ' αὑτῶν τὰς θυσίας ἐπιτελοῦσιν.[19]

Lagrange is correct to note that the Essenes wanted to prevent risk of impurity. This forward thinking action adheres with the group decision to separate themselves (εἰργόμενοι as middle) from the sanctuary. Lagrange also rightly observes that the group's "raffinements de purifications" prevented them from sacrificing. His suggestion that they sacrificed in the temple from which they withdrew, however, is untenable; this, surely, would have incurred impurity. The rejection of offering sacrifice by the Qumran group is particularly evident during the latter stages of its development.[20]

Joseph Thomas (also writing before the discovery of the scrolls, and principally arguing against Lagrange) rejected the evidence of the majority of the Greek MSS in favor of the {Lat.} and the {E} tradition, which favored οὐκ. He contended that even though the {Lat.} and {E} predated the Greek MSS, argument for accepting or rejecting οὐκ should not be based on textual tradition. Rather, he suggested that the meaning of *Ant.* 18.19 should be based on internal criteria.[21] David Wallace (who also accepted οὐκ) followed Thomas' assertions. He reasserted four of Thomas' reasons (based on internal evidence, which this study also accepts) why οὐκ should be retained:[22]

1. He claimed that the first clause, indicating that the Essenes sent their offerings to the Temple, could be justified by their avoidance of it, "The Essenes avoided going into the Temple, but sent their offerings

---

[19] See ibid., 316 n. 5.

[20] Lagrange's assertions are problematic on a number of grounds. Firstly, he assumes that the Greek MSS reading of this passage is to be accepted over the older {Lat.} and {E}. Secondly, assuming that there is a link between the Essenes and the DSS movement, the type of sacrifice discussed in *Ant.* 18.19 is not spelled out. On the basis of this, Lagrange likely assumes that various sacrifices are referred to. This position is against the ideology of the larger DSS movement, which participated in some sacrifice while adopting a more idealized and eschatological view of the sacrificial cult.

[21] See J. Thomas, *Le mouvement baptiste en Palestine et Syrie* (Gembloux: Duclot, 1935), 12 n. 3, for his discussion concerning the criteria of determining the more original reading of *Ant.* 18.19.

[22] See D. Wallace, "The Essenes and Temple Sacrifice," *TZ* 13 (1957): 335–338.

instead."[23] As discussed below, this assumption rests on construing εἰργόμενοι in the second clause as grammatically middle.

2. In order for the first clause to make sense, στέλλοντες and ἐπιτελοῦσιν must be in opposition to one another. Wallace suggests here that the passage without οὐκ would be meaningless, particularly if the passage reads "they send ἀναθήματα to the temple but they offer θυσίας." On the basis of this, Wallace is correct to asks, "if it was their habit to go to the temple to sacrifice, why would they also send it?"[24]

3. He suggested that στέλλοντες was an adversative participle which required the negation, particularly on the basis of his belief that "a participial form when used in preference to a finite verb indicates subordination which is either causal, temporal, or adversative."[25] Moreover, he also contended that δέ was to be read as an adversative in conjunction with οὐκ.

4. He contended that there was a natural antithesis between ἀναθήματα and θυσίας, and he argued that the omission of οὐκ would make this clause meaningless. Wallace further contended that the anarthrous use of θυσίας suggests a negation. Also, he noted θυσίας as being included in the generic use of the word ἀναθήματα.

Thomas' first two assumptions (put forth here by Wallace) correctly rely on the verb εἰργόμενοι as being grammatically middle, "they separated themselves." Ralph Marcus, followed by Strugnell[26] and Frank Cross[27] (all of whom argued their case after the discovery of the scrolls), on the other hand, noted that εἰργόμενοι is always passive in Josephus.[28] Apart from Marcus, they (along with Louis Feldman and J. Baumgarten, who later adopted this interpretation)[29] based their view on reading the first clause of *Ant.* 18.19 without οὐκ, "they send ἀναθήματα to the temple but θυσίας ἐπιτελοῦσιν with different purification." Moreover, these scholars

---

[23] Ibid., 335.

[24] Ibid.

[25] Ibid.

[26] See Strugnell, "Flavius Josephus," 114, also his n. 34.

[27] See F.M. Cross, *The Ancient Library of Qumran And Modern Biblical Studies: The Haskell Lectures 1956–1957* (London: Duckworth, 1958), 76 n. 119.

[28] See R. Marcus, "Pharisees, Essenes, and Gnostics," *JBL* 73 (1954): 157–161, 158, and also his n. 2 there. Also see this discussion below.

[29] See Flavius Josephus, *The Jewish Antiquities, Books 18–19* (trans. L.H. Feldman; LCL 433; Cambridge: Harvard University Press, 1965), 16–17 n. a, and J. Baumgarten "The Essenes and the Temple," 63.

also seem to take the last part of this passage, ἐφ᾽ αὐτῶν τὰς θυσίας ἐπιτελοῦσιν, as reinforcing the same directive (they offer sacrifice).[30] These scholars assume this reading in view of the discovered animal bones found at Qumran, which they took as representing a sacrificing Essene community.

Strugnell, Cross, Feldman, and J. Baumgarten assume that the Essenes and the DSS movement are the same. Moreover, they place them both at Qumran.[31] These scholars also claim that the Essenes (particularly at Qumran) offered sacrifice. These claims are untenable on a number of grounds. Firstly, they fail to recognize that there may have been at least two or more groups (from the larger DSS movement) of Essenes which reflected at least two streams of thought. Although the larger DSS movement may have participated in some sacrifices,[32] no sacrifices were offered at Qumran;[33] the animal bones found at Qumran are not from sacrifice, but rather from a kind of ritual meal.[34] Despite the peculiar way the animal bones were buried, no altar was found. It is likely that at least one group (the group related to Qumran) ceased offering sacrifice close to their Qumran occupation.[35] Secondly, they contradict themselves in

---

[30] See below where the meaning of this line is discussed.

[31] Although this connection is probable, only a branch of this movement (i.e. the Qumran community) resided at Qumran. The above scholars make the assumption that the Essenes, the DSS movement, and Khirbet Qumran are all connected without qualifying their claim.

[32] As previously noted (n. 7 above), this position may also be evident in Josephus' description concerning Judah the Essene and John the Essene. See below for Josephus' references.

[33] The situation at Qumran more reflects the ideology and stance of the later Qumran community, which although separated from the larger DSS movement, remained part of this movement in view of their Essene makeup.

[34] F.E. Zeuner, highlighted by R. de Vaux, examined 39 bone deposits from the entire site. Both concluded that the remains of some bones were charred. This indication led them to believe that they were either roasted or boiled off, thus leading to the conclusion that they were the remains of a religious meal. See R. de Vaux, *Archaeology and the Dead Sea Scrolls* (The Schweich Lectures of the British Academy 1959; London: Oxford University Press, 1973), 12 and especially 14, and F.E. Zeuner, "Notes on Qumran," *PEQ* 92 (1960): 27–36, 30. Also see J. Magness, "Communal Meals and Sacred Space at Qumran," in *Shaping Community: The Art and Archaeology of Monasticism: Papers From a Symposium Held at the Frederick R. Weisman Museum, University of Minnesota, March 10–12, 2000* (ed. S. McNally; British Archaeological Reports International Series 941; Oxford: Archaeopress, 2001), 15–28, 19 and eadem, *Archaeology of Qumran*, 120.

[35] For discussion of the Qumran occupation and the development of the Qumran community from the larger DSS movement, see J.-D. Hopkins, "Sacrifice in the Dead Sea Scrolls: Khirbet Qumran, the Essenes and Cultic Spiritualization" (Ph.D. diss., The University of Manchester, 2005).

their reading. If this passage without οὐκ was correct, then the view that the Essenes were a sacrificing community suggests that they (the Essenes) sacrificed, but not in the temple at Jerusalem from which they were excluded or banned (εἰργόμενοι read passively which they suggest). Does this imply that the Essenes offered sacrifice elsewhere, away from the temple? In an attempt to smooth over this obvious difficulty, Black, who is followed by J. Baumgarten, suggested that the Essenes performed their sacrifices at the same temple to which they sent their ἀναθήματα (in Jerusalem).[36]

In his discussion on the view of Essene sacrifice, Black surmised that the most original reading of *Ant.* 18.19 lacked οὐκ. He conjectured that it may have been imported into the text from a misunderstood Latin translation. He suggests that Cassiodorus' translation ("in templo autem anathemata prohibent, sarificia vel hostias com populo non celebrant") could have indicated a negation in the sense that the Essenes do not celebrate sacrifices with the people, thus, rather, performing them by themselves. Black implies that the Essenes had free access to the temple based on an Essene Gate. He wrongly posits, however, that this Essene Gate allowed the group to bring their sacrifices to the temple in seclusion from the people.[37]

J. Baumgarten postulated that in view of priestly laxity in the temple (especially during a time when there was an attempt to achieve universality regarding temple ritual purity matters), the Essenes could have brought individual sacrifices, which like votive offerings had no fixed time at which to be offered.[38] Both Black's and J. Baumgarten's postulations fail to convince for a number of reasons: (1) both arguments fail to answer the question poignantly put forth by Thomas, if the Essenes regularly went to the temple, why would they send offerings? (2) As A.

---

[36] See M. Black, *The Scrolls and Christian Origins: Studies in the Jewish Background of the New Testament* (New York: Scribner, 1961), 40–41 and J. Baumgarten, "The Essenes and the Temple," 63–74.

[37] See Black's discussion in *The Scrolls and Christian Origins*, 40, also his n. 1.

[38] See J. Baumgarten, "The Essenes and the Temple," 63–74, who describes this matter. Baumgarten's position here may reflect the actions of the larger DSS movement only. However, Baumgarten appears to miss this point on account of he fails to recognize the difference between the larger DSS movement and the later Qumran community, which both reflected different cultic views. Also, as noted here, Baumgarten reads εἰργόμενοι as a passive participle which raises a number of difficult questions. With regard to the ideological distinctions between the larger DSS movement and the Qumran community, see n. 5 above.

Baumgarten insightfully notes,[39] both Black and J. Baumgarten fail to account for how they think the current temple authorities would allow a group which they banished (εἰργόμενοι read passively according to both) from the temple to have special privileges to the temple; (3) Black mis construes the location of the Essene Gate, which was located at the city wall, not the temple. Moreover, like the scholars above, both Black and J. Baumgarten fail to recognize that there seems to have been at least two Essene groups. As previously noted, although the larger DSS movement could have offered certain sacrifices in Jerusalem,[40] the group related to Qumran ceased sacrificing during the latter stages of its development. This is particularly evident in the Qumran archaeology as well as the *Rule of the Community* and 4QFlor. In these texts prayer and praise was likened as offerings and the community as temple is envisaged as a place which atones.[41]

3. *Εἰργόμενοι: Middle or Passive?*

Viewing εἰργόμενοι as grammatically passive has been predicated on reading *Ant.* 18.19 in the following way, without οὐκ:

> They send votive gifts to the temple but perform sacrifices with different purifications, which are customary; for this reason they were excluded from the public precinct of the temple, thus they perform sacrifices by themselves.[42]

Grammatically, εἰργόμενοι can be interpreted as either a middle or passive plural participle. As Klinzing notes,[43] those who have favoured οὐκ, usually read εἰργόμενοι as a middle participle, "they separated them-

---

[39] See A. Baumgarten, "Josephus," 171, and n. 8 there.

[40] As noted earlier, due to a calendar difference between Jerusalem's temple establishment and the DSS movement, only certain sacrifices were offered. See n. 5 above which also makes this distinction.

[41] Here sacrifice is observed in a more spiritualized way. See 1QS III:4–12(= 4Q255 ii 1–9+4Q257 iii 6–14+4Q262 1 1–4); IX:3–5, 26b; X:6a, 8b, 14b, and 4Q174 1 i, 21, 2 5b–7a respectively. With regard to the notion behind spiritualization see J.-D. Hopkins, "Hebrew Patriarchs in the Book of *Jubilees*: A Descriptive Analysis as an Interpretative Methodology," in *With Wisdom as a Robe: Qumran and Other Jewish Studies in Honour of Ida Fröhlich* (ed. K.D. Dobos and M. Kőszeghy; Hebrew Bible Monographs 21; Sheffield: Sheffield Phoenix Press, 2009), 239–252, 244 n. 22.

[42] My translation.

[43] See G. Klinzing, *Die Umdeutung des Kultus in der Qumrangemeinde und im Neuen Testament* (SUNT 7; Göttingen: Vandenhoeck & Ruprecht, 1971), 45 n. 14.

selves."[44] Those who have rejected οὐκ, generally favoured εἰϱγόμενοι as passive, "they were banned or excluded."[45] Exceptions, however, are found in the translations of Thomas, Lightfoot, Cross, Steckoll and Nolland;[46] each favour οὐκ while rendering εἰϱγόμενοι as grammatically passive. They roughly translate *Ant.* 18.19 in the following way:

> They send offerings/gifts to the Temple but do not offer sacrifices because of different purifications which should be used, and for this reason, having been excluded from the common precincts of the Temple, they perform their sacrifices among themselves.

It is interesting to note here that Lagrange offers yet another translation of this passage, which is different from the previous one mentioned. As noted above, he rejects οὐκ and renders εἰϱγόμενοι as grammatically middle.[47] His translation, too, fails to answer the question, "why would the Essenes send offerings to a temple which they regularly attended?"

As noted previously, J. Baumgarten contends that εἰϱγόμενοι should always be rendered passively in Josephus.[48] Strugnell suggests that the use of this verb as passive in Thucydides could have influenced how Josephus

---

[44] See the translations of those who favor the οὐκ and follow the middle reading of εἰϱγόμενοι: J. Baumgarten, "Sacrifice and Worship among the Jewish Sectarians of the Dead Sea (Qumran) Scrolls," *HTR* 46 (1953): 141–159, 155; Wallace, "The Essenes," 335–338; K. Schubert, *The Dead Sea Community: Its Origins and Teachings* (London: Black, 1959), 55; T.H. Gaston, *No Stone on Another: Studies in the Significance of the Fall of Jerusalem in the Synoptic Gospels* (NovTSup 23; Leiden: Brill, 1970), 120, also his n. 2; M. Petit, "Les Esséens de Philon d'Alexandrie et les Esséniens," in *The Dead Sea Scrolls: Forty Years of Research* (ed. D. Dimant and U. Rappaport; STDJ 10; Leiden: Brill, 1992), 139–155, 151; and D. Green, "To '... send up, like the smoke of incense, the works of the law': The Similarity of Views on an Alternative to Temple Sacrifice by Three Jewish Sectarian Movements of the Late Second Temple Period," in *Religion in the Ancient World: New Themes and Approaches* (ed. M. Dillon; Amsterdam: Hakkert, 1996), 165–175, 165.

[45] See Klinzing, *Umdeutung*, 45 n. 14 who also takes up this claim. Also see Marcus, "Pharisees," 158; Strugnell, "Flavius Josephus," 113; Josephus, *Ant.* 18.5 (Feldman, LCL); Black, *The Scrolls and Christian Origins*, 39–40; J. Baumgarten, "The Essene and the Temple," 62; H. Lichtenberger, "Atonement and Sacrifice in the Qumran Community," in *Approaches to Ancient Judaism*, vol. 2: *Essays in Religion and History* (ed. W.S. Green; BJS 9; Ann Arbor: Scholars Press, 1980), 159–171, 160; T.S. Beall, *Josephus' Description of the Essenes Illustrated by the Dead Sea Scrolls* (SNTSMS 58; Cambridge: Cambridge University Press, 1988), 115; and A. Baumgarten, "Josephus," 169–183.

[46] S.H. Steckoll, "The Qumran Sect in Relation to the Temple of Leontopolis," *RevQ* 6 (1967–1969): 55–69, 65; Cross, *The Ancient Library of Qumran*, 75–76 and Nolland, "Misleading Statement," 558.

[47] See n. 17 above.

[48] See nn. 28 and 29 above. Also see J. Baumgarten's reappraisal in "The Essenes and the Temple," 63.

used it.[49] Referring to K.H. Rengstorf's *A Complete Concordance to Flavius Josephus*, as well as its use in other Josephus passages, A. Baumgarten similarly asserts that the use of εἰργόμενοι is passive.[50]

Εἰργόμενοι most likely should be read as grammatically middle for three reasons: (1) this term is contained in a causal clause, which favours the negation in the context of *Ant.* 18.19; (2) if the Essenes were banned, it is unlikely that Josephus would have also mentioned the presence of an Essene teaching in the court of the temple (unless he was talking about a particular group of Essenes which he doesn't appear to indicate). On the basis of an Essene presence in the temple court, it is more meaningful to stress a middle reading of εἰργόμενοι, "they separated themselves," especially since they (the Essenes) would be free to frequent the temple whenever they wanted, like Judah the Essene;[51] and (3) as will be discussed later, reading εἰργόμενοι as a middle participle better harmonizes with the overall ideology of the DSS movement and later Qumran community, particularly in view of their strict purity and sacrificial regulations as recorded in their related texts.

The Essenes most likely excluded themselves from the temple both ideologically and physically.[52] Although it is not explicitly clear to which separation Josephus is referring, it is likely that the former is intended. Although the case for εἰργόμενοι as middle is preferred here, in view of an overall understanding of the Essene group, this term perhaps subtly conveyed a two-fold meaning, incorporating a passive understanding of this verb. The Essenes most likely separated from the temple because their approach to sacrifice was excluded or rejected from being practiced by the temple establishment. In view of this, it seems plausible to contend that the Essenes as a group were never rejected from the sanctuary per se. Rather, it seems more likely that it was their views on purity (θυσίας [οὐκ] ἐπιτελοῦσιν διαφορότητι ἁγνειῶν) and most sacrifices (ἐφ' αὑτῶν τὰς θυσίας ἐπιτελοῦσιν) that were excluded.

---

[49] See Strugnell who argues this case, "Flavius Josephus," 114 n. 34.

[50] See A. Baumgarten, "Josephus," 171 n. 6.

[51] See *J.W.* 1.78; *Ant.* 13.311. Also see *J.W.* 2.562–567, where John the Essene was appointed at a public meeting held at the temple.

[52] Although the larger DSS movement offered some sacrifice, perhaps only fully separating from the temple ideologically, the Qumran community completely separated from the temple, both ideologically and physically, especially during their Qumran settlement.

4. Ἐφ' αὑτῶν τὰς θυσίας ἐπιτελοῦσιν—They Sacrifice (What) by Themselves?

Josephus' further remark, ἐφ' αὑτῶν τὰς θυσίας ἐπιτελοῦσιν, seems to suggest that the Essenes, being separated from the temple, did perform sacrifices, thus enforcing the view that the more original reading of *Ant.* 18.19 lacked οὐκ. This reading allows for the possibility of interpreting θυσίας in both occurrences of this passage as meaning actual sacrifice. But this reading also raises two unsettling questions, 1) did the Essenes, having some special arrangement, indeed, sacrifice in the temple at Jerusalem? Or 2) did they sacrifice in their own community? Whereas J. Baumgarten and Black attempted to assert that the Essenes had a special arrangement in the temple, Feldman, followed by Strugnell, Cross and others inferred that the Essenes offered sacrifice in their own community away from the temple. As illustrated above, both arguments fail to fully convince. Therefore, on the basis of this, exactly what is the meaning of θυσίας in general, and in particular its meaning in the last line of this passage (ἐφ' αὑτῶν τὰς θυσίας ἐπιτελοῦσιν)?

The Meaning of θυσίας

θυσίας is a feminine plural noun that means "sacrifices" or "offerings."[53] The use of this term in the first clause of *Ant.* 18.19 seems to convey a different meaning than its use in the last line of this passage. In the first clause (according to the {Lat.} and {E} MSS), the Essenes do not sacrifice because of different purifications to which they adhere (θυσίας [οὐκ] ἐπιτελοῦσιν διαφορότητι ἁγνειῶν). The purification(s) that the Essenes observed (which most likely applied to a type of offering that they practiced), is different from the θυσίας and its purity regulations, which were practiced in Jerusalem's temple and by its authority. This notion is attested in both the first clause as well as in the last line of the passage: θυσίας [οὐκ] ἐπιτελοῦσιν διαφορότητι ἁγνειῶν and ἐφ' αὑτῶν τὰς θυσίας ἐπιτελοῦσιν.

Primarily based on the last line of *Ant.* 18.19, which is a continuing thought from the idea in the first clause (θυσίας [οὐκ] ἐπιτελοῦσιν διαφορότητι ἁγνειῶν), the Essenes offer different sacrifices than those offered in Jerusalem. If the Essenes offered the same sacrifices (sacrifices

---

[53] See LSJ s.v.

adhering to the same stipulations as required in Jerusalem's temple) elsewhere, this would be meaningless. The entire passage stresses that the
Essenes offered different sacrifices than those offered in Jerusalem, which
incorporated different purity regulations. On this basis, it seems acceptable to interpret these sacrifices as (1) sacrifices for non temple-approved
festivals, or those that were non-calendar binding (which correlates with
the ideology of the larger DSS movement), or (2) spiritualized sacrifices
or substitutes for sacrifice (which correlates with the ideology of the later
Qumran community).

J. Baumgarten translated the term θυσίας (in the last line of the
passage) as worship. Although it is more preferable to translate the
term as sacrifice, the idea behind his translation (which is followed by
others) is tenable. On the basis of accepting a more spiritualized view of
ἐφ᾽ αὐτῶν τὰς θυσίας ἐπιτελοῦσιν, an examination of the character of
Essene sacrifice is essential.

The Character of Essene θυσίας

It is possible that the Essenes's θυσία was the red heifer, which according
to the law (Num 19) was sacrificed outside the camp. As described
by John Bowman and others, although the rite of the red heifer was
called a sacrifice, it was not considered an actual sacrifice since it was
offered outside of the temple.[54] The Essenes could have performed these
sacrifices (θυσίας) outside of the temple camp on their own (ἐφ᾽ αὐτῶν
τὰς θυσίας ἐπιτελοῦσιν).

It is also possible that the Essenes viewed their θυσίας (in ἐφ᾽ αὐτῶν
τὰς θυσίας ἐπιτελοῦσιν), as meals, prayer, praise, and study. Milik[55] and
Kuhn[56] viewed θυσίας as referring to the Essenes' (thus, subsequently,
the Qumran community's) meals. With regard to study, perhaps Philo

---

[54] For a study on the red heifer, see J. Bowman, "Did the Qumran Sect Burn the Red
Heifer?" *RevQ* 1 (1958–1959): 73–84; J. Milgrom, "The Paradox of the Red Cow," *VT* 31
(1981): 62–72; J.M. Baumgarten, "The Pharisaic-Sadducean Controversies about Purity
and the Qumran Texts," *JJS* 31 (1980): 157–170; idem, "The Red Cow Purification Rites in
Qumran Texts," *JJS* 46 (1995): 112–119; A. Baumgarten, "The Paradox of the Red Heifer,"
VT 43 (1993): 442–451 and idem, "Josephus," 177–181.

[55] J.T. Milik, *Ten Years of Discovery in the Wilderness of Judaea* (trans. J. Strugnell;
SBT 26; Naperville: Allenson, 1959), 105 n. 2.

[56] K.G. Kuhn, "The Lord's Supper and the Communal Meal at Qumran," in *The Scrolls
and the New Testament* (ed. K. Stendahl; London: SCM Press, 1958), 65–93, especially 68
n. 15.

gives insight into the Essene view of sacrifice. As noted above in Charles Yonge's translation of *Prob.* 75, the Essenes thought that studying to preserve the purity and holiness of their minds was more acceptable to God than sacrificing animals.[57] Moreover, the importance of the idea of studying as a substitute for animal sacrifice is also conveyed in Philo's *Prob.* 80–82. In view of Philo's references, it is probable that in *Ant.* 18.19, the Essenes's viewed their θυσίας with διαφορότητι ἁγνειῶν as study: i.e. studying to preserve purity and holiness.

C. Summary: The Relationship between the Essene View of Sacrifice and the Movement Related to the Dead Sea Scrolls

As noted above, at least two streams of thought concerning Essene sacrifice exist. Although the variant views can only be seen in *Ant.* 18.19, it is probably more likely that, similar to *Prob.* 75, *Ant.* 18.19 reflects a more spiritualized understanding, which also coincides with the ideology of later Qumran community (an offshoot group from the larger parent Essene movement). As I have noted elsewhere:

> Before taking up residence at Qumran, which in view of the archaeological evidence at Qumran was after 100 B.C.E., the Qumran-related community seems to have embraced both a literal and figurative view of sacrifice. This can be attested in the various views of sacrifice as described in the *Damascus Document*. The *Damascus Document* makes explicit reference to sacrificial regulations (like in CD 16:13–17a) as well as emphasizing a more figurative view of sacrifice (i.e. that righteous prayer is equivalent to sacrifice noted in CD 11:18c–21a). When the community moved to Qumran, its view of sacrifice became predominantly spiritualized. This is attested in the descriptions of sacrifice in the *Rule of the Community* and *4QFlorilegium.*[58]

With regard to *Ant.* 18.19, when referring to θυσίας (in ἐφ' αὐτῶν τὰς θυσίας ἐπιτελοῦσιν) in a spiritualized manner, there has been the tendency to accept the οὐκ and read εἰργόμενοι as grammatically middle (they separated themselves).[59] It would seem that this spiritualized view

---

[57] See C.D. Yonge, *The Works of Philo Judaeus, the Contemporary of Josephus: Translated from the Greek* (4 vols.; London: Bohn, 1854–1855); repr. *The Works of Philo: Complete and Unabridged* (Peabody: Hendrickson, 1993).

[58] See Hopkins, "Hebrew Patriarchs in the Book of *Jubilees*," 243 n. 19. With regard to references in the *Rule of the Community* and 4QFlor, see n. 41 above.

[59] See n. 43 above.

of Essene ϑυσίας was initiated in light of the discovery of the scrolls. This, however, was not the case. Thomas and Lightfoot asserted a spiritualized view of *Ant.* 18.19 before the scrolls were discovered.

Understanding Josephus' description of Essene sacrifice in a more spiritualized way coheres with the view of sacrifice of the Qumran community, particularly during the later stages of its development; this is attested throughout their texts. Just like the Essenes (described above), the Qumran community, too, developed a more spiritualized understanding of sacrifice. Although the Qumran community revered both the temple and its sacrifice (which they viewed as impure and defiled), they viewed their own prayer, praise, and study as substitutes for sacrifice. Concerning prayer and praise, and a place which atones, the *Rule of the Community* asserts the following:

> When these exist in Israel in accordance with these in order to establish the spirit of holiness in truth eternal, in order to atone of the guilt of iniquity and for the unfaithfulness of sin, and for the approval for the land, without the flesh of grunt offering and without the fats of sacrifice—the offering of the lips in compliance with the decree will be like the pleasant aroma of justice and the perfectness of behaviour will be acceptable like a free will offering.[60]

In view of the above textual considerations, it seems clear that not only is Josephus in harmony with Philo's description of Essene sacrifice, but that the view expressed by these authors also is in harmony with the Qumran community, particularly during the latter stages of its development. As demonstrated above, Josephus notes that the Essenes offered a type of sacrifice that was different from the sacrifice performed at Jerusalem. This type of offering served as substitutes for actual sacrifices. According to Josephus, these sacrifices were performed by themselves according to different purity standards. Unfortunately, Josephus gives no description of how these sacrifices differed from those that were performed at the temple.

Philo perhaps provides insight into what some of these sacrificial substitutes looked like. He describes the Essenes as "studying to preserve the purity and holiness of their minds." The idea of studying is also picked up in the following passages of *Quod omnis probus liber sit*, particularly 80–82, which seems to reinforce the idea that studying which preserved

---

[60] 1QS IX:3–5a. Passage taken from F. García Martínez and E.J.C. Tigchelaar, *The Dead Sea Scrolls Study Edition* (2 vols.; Leiden: Brill, 1997–1998), 1:91.

purity and holiness was also viewed as a substitute for sacrifice, i.e. it was viewed as more important to God than sacrificing animals. Both Philo and Josephus imply that the Essenes revered the temple and sacrifice; however, they preferred to offer a more spiritualized type of sacrifice.

1 ENOCH IN THE CONTEXT OF PHILO'S WRITINGS

Ekaterina Matusova
Russian State University for the Humanities, Moscow

The discovery of many Aramaic and several Hebrew fragments of *1 Enoch* in Qumran Caves 1 and 4,[1] in conjunction with the importance of this text for other documents of the Qumran community, has led some scholars to the assumption that there was a special, almost sectarian, connection between Enochic literature and the Qumranites.[2] This reasoning is, to a certain extent, natural. As yet, no direct evidence has been found that Hellenistic Jewish groups other than the one at Qumran knew and read *1 Enoch*. We do have some fragments of the Jewish Hellenistic historian Eupolemus,[3] but they are very scanty and are not usually taken into consideration in answering the question of how widely disseminated and how significant *1 Enoch* was in Jewish society of the late Second Temple period. Even without direct literary support from the period, however, some scholars challenge the sectarian character of the Enochic literature, basing on the arguments from its content.[4]

We have the Greek translation of some parts of the book. The translation is known from one parchment (the Gizeh-Akhmim fragment) that contains *1 En.* 1–32, one papyrus (the Chester Beatty-Michigan papyrus)

---

[1] See J.T. Milik, *The Books of Enoch: Aramaic Fragments of Qumrân Cave 4* (Oxford: Clarendon, 1976). The Aramaic fragments of the so called *Book of Giants*, which forms part of the *Book of Watchers*, have also been commented upon by L.T. Stuckenbruck, *The Book of Giants from Qumran: Text, Translation, and Commentary* (TSAJ 63; Tübingen: Mohr Siebeck, 1997).

[2] G.W.E. Nickelsburg, *1 Enoch 1: A Commentary on the Book of 1 Enoch, Chapters 1–36; 81–108* (Hermeneia; Minneapolis: Fortress, 2001), 65; G. Boccaccini, "Introduction: From the Enoch Literature to Enochic Judaism," in *Enoch and Qumran Origins: New Light on a Forgotten Connection* (ed. idem; Grand Rapids: Eerdmans 2005), 1–14, 13.

[3] Ps.-Eup. frg. 1 (Eusebius, *Praep. ev.* 9.17.1–9) according to C.R. Holladay, *Fragments from Hellenistic Jewish Authors*, vol. I: *Historians* (SBLTT 20; Pseudepigrapha Series 10; Chico: Scholars Press, 1983), 170–175.

[4] See the articles by M. Himmelfarb, "Jubilees and Sectarianism," and J.S. Anderson, "Denouncement Speech in Jubilees and other Enochic Literature," in *Enoch and Qumran Origins*, 129–131 and 132–136, respectively.

that contains *1 En.* 97:6–104:13; 106:1–107:3; one tachygraph fragment from the Vatican (Vatic. 1809) containing *1 En.* 89:42–49, and partly from a transmission by Gregory Syncellus.[5] The first part of *1 Enoch*— the *Book of Watchers*—has been best preserved in Greek. In fact, some Greek fragments were also found at Qumran, but whether they belong to *1 Enoch* is still a matter for debate.[6]

The Greek translation has been variously dated. M. Black believed the translation had been made by Christians, while E. Larson thinks that it dates from the period between 150 and 50 B.C.E.[7] Of course, Christian literary sources are rich enough in allusions to the Greek *Enoch*, but, for the reasons mentioned above, no literary evidence has been brought in support of an earlier date.

This paper aims to show that the works of Philo of Alexandria can, when studied properly, serve as a reliable source of such evidence. Like many ancient authors, Philo prefers allusions to direct quotations, weaving themes and expressions into the texture of his narrative. It would also be inappropriate to expect that he, commenting upon the Septuagint, and not on *1 Enoch*, would prefer particular plotlines of the latter to those of the Septuagint where they differ. Therefore we have to look not for a commentary upon clearly formulated Enochic subjects, but for Philo's knowledge and use of these Enochic subjects as they are incorporated into his commentary upon the Septuagint.

Assuming that Philo would not have worked with any text but the Greek, I will confine this study to the extant Greek fragments of *1 Enoch* and to only two treatises of Philo, i.e. *De gigantibus (On Giants)* and *Quod Deus sit immutabilis (That God Is Unchangeable)*, which seem to be the most relevant to the Greek fragments.

I will start with an example. The treatise *On Giants* begins with the description of Noah's righteousness as against all other people—it is a commentary upon Gen 5:32–6:2. Philo says:

---

[5] See A.-M. Denis, *Introduction aux pseudépigraphes grecs d'Ancien Testament* (SVTP 1; Leiden: Brill, 1970), 17–20. The Greek fragments of *1 Enoch* have been collected and edited by M. Black, ed., *Apocalypsis Henochi Graece* (PVTG 3; Leiden: Brill, 1970), 3–44.

[6] See J. VanderKam and P. Flint, "Were New Testament Scrolls Found at Qumran?" in *The Meaning of the Dead Sea Scrolls: Their Significance for Understanding the Bible, Judaism, Jesus, and Christianity* (San Francisco: HarperSanFrancisco, 2002), 311–320.

[7] M. Black, *The Book of Enoch or 1 Enoch: A New English Edition with Commentary and Textual Notes* (SVTP 7; Leiden: Brill, 1985), 87; E. Larson, "The LXX and Enoch: Influence and Interpretation in Early Jewish Literature," in *Enoch and Qumran Origins*, 84–89.

> And no unjust man at any time *implants* (σπείρει) a masculine *generation* (γενεάν) in the soul, but such, being unmanly, and broken, and effeminate in their minds, do naturally become the *parents* of female children (θηλυγονοῦσι); having *planted* (φυτεύσαντες) no *tree* (δένδρον) of virtue, *the fruit of which must of necessity have been beautiful and precious*, but only trees of wickedness and of the passions, the *shoots* (βλάσται) of which are womanlike.[8]   (*Gig.* 4)

In this commentary the image of planting a tree predominates. Yet, the image is lacking in the Septuagint, except for a reference to the vine planted by Noah (Gen 9:20). Meanwhile, the italicized words and images are all used in *1 En.* 10 in connection with Noah:

> and his *seed* (σπέρμα) will last for all the generations of the age … and the plant of righteousness and truth will appear … it will be *planted* (φυτευθήσεται) with joy … then a tree will be planted (φυτευθήσεται δένδρον) … till they will have engendered (γεννήσονται) thousands … and all the trees (πάντα τὰ δένδρα) upon the earth will rejoice; it will be planted and they [i.e. all the righteous] will be planting (ἔσονται … φυτεύοντες) vines, … olive trees [with excellent, abundant fruits].[9]
>   (*1 En.* 10:3–19)

Philo also uses here the word βλάστη, "shoot," a word not found in Greek ethical language. But in *1 En.* 26:1 this word comes up in connection with and in the development of the image of a tree: "trees with branches that … bring shoots (βλαστούσας)." Thus, *1 En.* 10 explains the image employed by Philo, in regard both to Philo's argument and to his language. It associates Noah with the image of a tree, with the description of righteous men who plant fruitful trees, and with the idea of being fecund. In this description we see the four roots used also by Philo: σπείρω, δένδρον, βλάστη, φυτεύω. Only one of them—φυτεύω—is properly applied to Noah in the Septuagint (Gen 9:20).

Let us follow the text of *1 Enoch* chapter by chapter. *1 Enoch* 2; 3–5 talk about the unchangeableness of all created things in nature toward God: "Examine all the works in heaven, how they do not change (οὐκ ἠλλοίωσαν) their paths, …" (*1 En.* 2:1). In the subsequent lines the key expression οὐκ ἀλλοιοῦνται is repeated three times (2:2; 3–5:2, 3). At

---

[8] Here and below, the translation is according to C.D. Yonge, *The Works of Philo Judaeus, the Contemporary of Josephus: Translated from the Greek* (4 vols.; London: Bohn, 1854–1855); repr. *The Works of Philo: Complete and Unabridged* (Peabody: Hendrickson, 1993), sometimes with my emendations.

[9] Here and below, I quote the Greek text according to the edition of Black, *Apocalypsis Henochi Graece.* I have rendered it into English with consideration of the existing translations by Nickelsburg (*1 Enoch 1*) and Black (*Book of Enoch*).

the same time, one of Philo's main goals in *That God Is Unchangeable* is to show that the biblical descriptions of God do not contradict one of the main theological theses of Platonism, namely that God does not change (οὐκ ἀλλοιοῦται).[10]

In order to substantiate his claim, Plato says that even good organic things, for instance, plants, do not easily change under extrinsic influence (πᾶν φυτόν … ἥκιστα ἀλλοιοῦται), nor does a good human soul.[11] In *Deus* 33–48, Philo reproduces the whole chain of Plato's argument, but replaces the bare mention of "every plant" of the *Republic* with an extensive description of trees that never change their life course, bringing fruits in due time. As far as we can judge, it is only *1 En.* 2:1–3–5:4, that explicitly contrasts everlasting continuity and unchangeableness in nature with the non-continuity of human behavior toward God.[12] The verb ἀλλοιόω is only used in *1 Enoch* in this type of context. *1 Enoch* not only alludes to the heavenly bodies (2:1) (something common to other Jewish texts of the Second Temple period), but also extensively discusses the example of trees, which faithfully repeat their cycle of seasonal changes every year. Thus, the juxtaposition of thoughts in *1 Enoch* and the use of the key verb ἀλλοιόω, which was significant against the background of the Platonic tradition, strongly echoed the famous passage of Plato's *Republic*. Plato says: God does not change, because even organic objects do not change, nor do good human souls. The idea of *1 Enoch* is as follows: the heavenly bodies do not change; organic objects, although they are perishable, do not change the succession of their life stages, especially trees (an extensive description of a tree's life course follows); but you, humans, did not remain faithful, and changed your minds. There is a lacuna in the Greek text, which is easy to fill with the help of an extant Aramaic fragment (4QEnᵃ ar [4Q201] 1 ii 3): the lost text describes the previous stage in a tree's life, when it withers and sheds all its foliage. Philo, attentive as he was to every assonance between Platonic and Jewish tradition, would not have passed this parallel by. He also, like *1 Enoch*, proceeds in his description from a withering tree to excellent fruits. I think it is pos-

---

[10] This thesis goes back to Plato's *Republic* 380d–383b. It was later developed in *Metaphysics* and other treatises of Aristotle, and inherited by Middle Platonism.

[11] Plato, *Resp.* 380e–381a.

[12] Jewish texts of the Second Temple period often allude to the continuous revolutions of stars and planets, as well as to the turn of the seasons, in order to demonstrate the majesty of God (cf. Sir 16:26–28; 43; *Pss. Sol.* 18:10–12). As Jer 5:20–24 suggests, these images could be contrasted to human disobedience to God. But none of these examples contains an equally clearly formulated juxtaposition.

sible that the replacement of Plato's "every plant" with the description of a tree life course was made under the influence of *1 Enoch*.

1 Enoch 3–5, having mentioned the faithfulness of nature and the infidelity of humans, goes on to a description of the last judgment. This subject is introduced for the second time, the first mention being made in *1 En.* 1:6–9. The story of the flood, the sins and punishment of the giants, and the rescue of Noah (chs. 6–11) follows these introductory chapters as their natural consequence. It is important to note that the biblical narrative does not introduce the story of Noah as a story of judgment in the eschatological sense of the word: we do not find any mention of judgment in the Genesis account, which is rather archaic in form and in some points closer to Hesiod's story about the sufferings of earth. But we know that the flood story was set in the context of the last judgment, and viewed as a prefiguration of this event later, as Jewish eschatological thought grew.[13] Philo proceeds along the same line of argument: having discussed the behavior of created things and souls toward God, he turns to the discussion of the flood story, setting it in the context of the last judgment (κρίσις):

> On which account God now says, that Noah found grace in his sight, when all the rest of mankind, appearing ungrateful, were about to receive punishment, in order that he might mingle saving *mercy* (ἔλεος) with *judgment against sinners* (τῇ κατὰ ἁμαρτανόντων κρίσει). ... For if God were to choose to judge the race of mankind without mercy, he would pass on them a sentence of condemnation.   (*Deus* 74–76)

First of all, we should note that in these lines Philo speaks of κρίσις, and not of δίκη, which of itself is atypical of him in such a context. In Greek both words designate "judgment." But in Plato, who has his own idea of the forthcoming judgment, and whom Philo usually follows and alludes to when speaking about this event, the word δίκη is always preferred to designate the future trial. The word κρίσις is used by him, and, accordingly, by Philo, to designate the mental act of evaluation or "decision."[14] By contrast, in the Septuagint tradition the word κρίσις is preferred to designate every kind of trial, and accordingly, in the Greek translation of *1 Enoch* to designate the last judgment. In the whole corpus of Philo's works, this is the only place, where he speaks about

---

[13] Cf. Matt 24:36–40; Luke 17:26; 2 Pet 3:5–7.

[14] Philo applies the word κρίσις to the situation of a trial only in the *On the Special Laws*. But this trial is in no way the last judgment. Here Philo simply follows the language of the Septuagint text being interpreted.

the catastrophic judgment of sinners (ἡ κατὰ ἁμαρτανόντων κρίσις; cf. *1 En.* 1:7: κρίσις κατὰ πάντων; 3–5:6, 7, 8: οἱ ἁμαρτωλοί, ἁμαρτιῶν, ἁμαρτήσονται), setting it in connection with the flood story and using the word κρίσις—exactly as *1 Enoch* does. Moreover, Philo's mention of *mercy*, which God "exercises towards the good actions of even the unworthy" (*Deus* 76) corresponds to *1 En.* 3–5:6. In this context we are told that on the day of judgment "there will be *forgiveness of sins and all mercy* (λύσις ἁμαρτιῶν καὶ πᾶν ἔλεος)."

1 Enoch 14 tells us about the vision of Enoch, how he enters the heavenly house of God, sees Him sitting on the throne surrounded by cherubim and hears His word. The description of *1 Enoch* ends with God's address to Enoch: "Come here, Enoch, and hear My word (καὶ τὸν λόγον μοῦ ἄκουσον)" (14:24). Enoch obeyed, and he "heard" (ἤκουσα) (15:1) His voice, but "had his face bowed down" (14:25). In the same way, Philo in our treatise proceeds to the description of the Glory of God, exceeding all (*Deus* 77–81). His description too ends with a discussion on the word (ὁ λόγος) of God, which no human being can hear (ἀκούειν) as it is uttered (*Deus* 82–85, esp. 83).

Although the vision of Enoch is essentially modeled on the vision of Ezekiel and has other sources and counterparts in Jewish literature, it has a number of peculiar features, which set it apart from other similar descriptions. 1) Although all visions known to us compare the Glory of God with flame and splendor of fire, none compares it to the sun.[15] Here the image of the sun predominates: "its wheel was like the shining sun" (14:18), and, "He was surrounded by what appeared to be like the sun" (14:20). 2) Only in the framework of this vision is it stressed that it was absolutely impossible either to see or to approach God. It was equally impossible for "all flesh," and even for angels (14:19; 14:21: "And no angel could enter into this house and behold his face because of the majesty and glory. And no flesh could behold …"). 3) Only some of the angels surrounded God. They were close to Him and did not leave Him night or day (14:23). 4) There are two expressions in the text that are not very clear: ὄρος χερουβίν (14:18)—literally, "a mountain of cherubim," considered to be a mistranslation of the Aramaic original,[16] and τὸ περιβόλαιον αὐτοῦ, which was "like the appearance of the sun, more shining and whiter than snow." In this context, I prefer not to translate the word περιβόλαιον as having its more common meaning of "raiment." Enoch's vision avoids

---

[15] Cf. 1 Kgs 22; Isa 6; Ezek 1–2; Dan 7.
[16] Black, *Book of Enoch*, 149.

comparing God with a human being,[17] and it would be inappropriate to suppose that the notion of garments is introduced here, especially when we consider that other Greek translations of prophetic texts often use this word in a metaphorical sense of "something which is around" and "covers and protects."[18] In any case, Philo, when reading the text, would be strongly opposed to understanding this word in sense of clothes, because one of his main goals in interpreting Jewish writings was to clear them from any suspicion of anthropomorphism. I think that the meaning of "being surrounded," referring to the glory of God, is more appropriate here. But Philo may certainly have understood it in his own way. Let us look at Philo's text:

> for God exerts his power in an untempered degree towards himself, but in a mixed character towards his creatures; for it is impossible *for a mortal nature to endure his power unmitigated.* Do you think that you would be *unable to look at the unmodified light of the sun?* … but you are nevertheless able to gaze upon *those uncreated powers, which exist around him and emit the most dazzling light,* without any veil or modification. … but *what mortal* could possibly receive in this manner the knowledge, and wisdom, and prudence, and justice, and all the other virtues of God, in an unalloyed state? *The whole heaven, the whole world, could not do so.* Therefore the Creator, knowing in what exceeding plenty all that is best exists *around Him,* … It has been shown that the unmixed and unmingled and those *really supreme* powers exist only *around* the living God.   (*Deus* 77–81)

Although this text incorporates apparent allusions to Sir 43:1–5, nevertheless its basic structure is modeled on the pattern of a "vision." The image of the transcendent God, surrounded by powers (δυνάμεις), which in Philo's system often correspond to angels, underlies the whole description. It ends, like the other visions, with God addressing a human being. In this description, the impossibility of approaching, of seeing, of perceiving—in a word, of enduring the presence of God—is especially stressed.[19] Divine radiance is compared to the splendor of the sun, and the impossibility of perceiving it pure pertains both to "a mortal nature" and to "the whole heaven, the whole world," which, according to the platonising Philo, is an immortal and the most perfect living being. Thus, Philo's description reproduces the three main points of *1 Enoch*: the

---

[17] Cf. Nickelsburg, *1 Enoch 1*, 264.
[18] Job 26:6; Isa 50:3; Jer 15:12.
[19] Something which is in full accordance with the idea of *1 Enoch*, but differs from Sir 43:27–33, which talks about vanity of man's endeavors properly to describe the majesty and the deeds of God, because men do not have any idea of their real dimensions.

impossibility of direct perception of God, the comparison of God's splendor with the sun and the two categories of recipients (cf. *1 En*. 14:21: "no flesh could behold ... And no angel could enter ...").

Philo talks about "those uncreated powers, which exist around him, and emit the most dazzling light (περὶ αὐτὸν οὖσαι λαμπρότατον φῶς ἀποστράπτουσι)." Most probably, this sentence faithfully reproduces the expression of *1 Enoch*: "He was surrounded by what appeared to be like the sun (τὸ περιβόλαιον αὐτοῦ ὡς εἶδος ἡλίου)." The word τὸ περιβόλαιον was taken by Philo to mean something that περιβάλλει, i.e., "surrounds," God. He probably understood it to comprise those angels who continuously assist Him. The impression that Philo had in his mind the image of God, surrounded by ministering powers, similar to angels, is increased by the continuous repetition of the expression "around him" (περὶ αὐτὸν), which is not identical in the Greek with the normal possessive construction.

Several lines lower down, Philo says of these powers that they are "really supreme," or literally, "real summits" (τῷ ὄντι ἀκρότητες), which "exist only around the living God." It is not impossible that the definition of the virtue of God by means of ἀκρότης, "extreme" or "summit," which looks middle-Platonic, but is not fully orthodox from the point of view of this theology,[20] was suggested to Philo by the strange expression "a mountain of cherubim" (ὄρος χερουβίν), attested in the Greek text of *1 Enoch*.

In *On Giants* Philo says:

> ... he who is really a man (ὁ πρὸς ἀλήθειαν ἄνθρωπος) will never come of his own accord to those pleasures. ... For the saying, "Man, man," (ἄνθρωπος ἄνθρωπος) not once but twice, is a sign that what is here meant is not the man composed of body and soul, but him only who is possessed of virtue. For such a one is really a true man (ὁ ἀληθινὸς οὗτος),
> ...   (*Gig.* 33–34)

This is a commentary upon Lev 18:6–7, where the repetition of the word "man" is a mistranslation of the Hebrew איש איש, what means in this context "nobody." To explain the significance of this repetition, Philo introduces the idea of a "true man," ἀληθινὸς ἄνθρωπος. This collocation in itself is not impossible within the Platonic and Aristotelian

---

[20] In the Middle Platonic tradition the virtue of God can properly be described as transcending human virtue (cf. Aristotle, *Eth. nic.* 1145a26–36; *Mag. Mor.* 2.5.3), but the word ἀκρότης is used in terms of human ethics only (cf. Alcinous, *Epit.* 30.4).

tradition.[21] Nevertheless, in the framework of this tradition it is used only fairly occasionally and does not have the status of a philosophical concept (because within this tradition the true man is divine, rather than human). I think that Philo, when introducing such a commentary, had been inspired by 1 *En.* 15:1: "Oh, true man (ὁ ἄνθρωπος ὁ ἀληθινός), man of truth (ἄνθρωπος τῆς ἀληθείας), scribe, ... Enoch, true man (ἄνθρωπος ἀληθινός) and scribe of righteousness."

Note the three following points: the doubling of the word *man* in 1 *Enoch*, which is what makes this text relevant to the text being interpreted (Lev 18:6); the alternative expression ἄνθρωπος τῆς ἀληθείας which corresponds to Philo's expression ὁ πρὸς ἀλήθειαν ἄνθρωπος (it is very typical of him to repeat expressions in a slightly different form); in accordance with the idea of the exclusive righteousness of Enoch, Philo stresses the extreme virtuousness of a true man.

It is not difficult to see that Philo is always trying to reconcile the two traditions, the Platonic and the Jewish. In his view, the allusions he makes to Jewish writings are meaningful only if they correspond to something familiar to the Greek philosophical audience. The following examples therefore are all the more important for us, because they can be correctly appreciated only against the background of the Greek text of 1 *Enoch*.

1 *Enoch* 15 is absolutely indispensable for understanding what Philo says about the fallen angels and the giants in the *On Giants*. Commenting upon Gen 6:2–4, which talks about the sons of God, the daughters of men and the giants, Philo draws the following picture: The soul is identical with the angel. The daughters of men represent pleasure. Some of the angels/souls deliberately preferred pleasure and thus lost their spiritual existence and descended into the body. These are angels unworthy of their name (*Gig.* 17). The others "have not thought worthy to approach any one of the portions of the earth" (*Gig.* 12); they preferred to remain with God, being employed as intermediary spirits, heralds, announcing the will of God.

The interpretation is based upon the famous Platonic image of souls falling down from heaven into the body.[22] Nevertheless, compared with the Platonic doctrine, there are two important differences. Firstly, Plato does not mention souls that never fell. Such a class of "unfallen" souls either does not exist for him at all, or else does not interest him. He is focused on "anthropological" problems of the relation of the human soul

---

[21] Cf. Plato, *Pol.* 300 d 7; *Phileb.* 22 c; Diogenes Laertius 2.119.
[22] Plato, *Phaedr.* 248 a–e.

and God. As far as I know, the notion of unfallen souls was also never developed in later Platonism. Secondly, this downfall of the soul is, for Plato, in no way a deliberate choice, because nobody wants to be unhappy. It is rather an accident, dramatic and unavoidable.

Let us see what the Septuagint verses in question contain:

> 2 Now when the *sons* (οἱ υἱοί) of God (*bĕnē hā 'Ēl*) saw the daughters of humans, that they were fair, they took wives for themselves of all that they chose.
> 3 And the LORD God said, "My spirit shall not abide in these humans forever, because they are flesh, but their days shall be one hundred twenty years."
> 4 Now the *giants* (οἱ δὲ γίγαντες; *hannĕpīlīm*) were on the earth in those days and afterward. When the sons of God used to go in to the daughters of humans, then they produced offspring for themselves. Those were the *giants* (οἱ δὲ γίγαντες; *haggibbōrīm*) that were of old, the renowned humans.[23]
> (Gen 6:2–4)

Philo cites these verses with a significant difference: instead of the sons of God in Gen 6:2 he has angels of God, as do some of the Alexandrian manuscripts. But even if we take into account that his version of the Septuagint could have had the reading "angels" instead of "sons," we still have to maintain that the information contained in these Greek verses is absolutely insufficient to draw the picture that Philo is drawing.

Angels took wives for themselves. Not "some angels took wives" (and others did not), but simply "angels" as a genus. It is not said whether this was good or bad; there is no evaluation of the fact. We do not know what happened to the angels afterwards. The giants are introduced into the narrative not as a consequence of the angels' deed, but in a parallel and almost independent way (cf. Gen 6:4).

Some of the inconsistency of sense here is due to the inaccurate translation from the Hebrew. The Greek translator renders with one word, "giants," two Hebrew notions, *hannĕpīlīm* and the mighty men, *haggibbōrīm* (6:4). Thus, when reading the Hebrew text, one gets another sequence of events: the sons of God saw the daughters of men; after that God withdrew his favor from men, cutting off the days of their lives; in those days there were *hannĕpīlīm* upon the earth. The Hebrew version

---

[23] Translation by R.J.V. Hiebert in *A New English Translation of the Septuagint and the Other Greek Translations Traditionally Included Under that Title* (ed. A. Pietersma and B.G. Wright; Oxford: Oxford University Press, 2007).

also does not introduce this last statement explicitly as an outcome of the previous events. Nevertheless, the word itself facilitates such an interpretation and even demands it. Whatever the real etymology of the word *hannĕpīlīm*, it is natural to connect it with the root *npl* "to fall." This unexpected appearance of some fallen substances requires that we understand the preceding lines as containing the cause of that event. Thus, the fact that the sons of men took daughters of men as wives immediately appears to be the reason of their downfall and a matter for disapproval. And v. 4 says that the mighty men, i.e. the giants, were their children.

Thus we see how the Hebrew text contains the seeds, which were later developed into the interpretation we see in *1 Enoch*. According to *1 Enoch*, the angels who committed this sin were the bad ones; besides them there were also good angels, true to God, who preferred to remain with Him. *1 Enoch* makes a point of the fact that the angel-sinners had been incorporeal, pure spirits, who deliberately left heaven and changed their status to be like flesh and to engender flesh (that is the giants) (*1 En.* 12; 15). Consequently, God and Enoch, by order of God, justly reproaches these angels for their actions (*1 En.* 15:3, 6).

Thus, the interpretation we meet in Philo fully coincides with the interpretation of *1 Enoch* in those very points in which it differs from the Platonic teaching about souls coming down into bodies (the unfallen angels and the deliberate choice to fall). It is generally accepted that the Septuagint was the only version of the Bible accessible to Philo. But the Greek translation of Genesis could not have been his source for such an interpretation, because it dismisses all hints which could lead to it.

In *Gig.* 58–65 Philo identifies the giants with the men "born of the earth" (γῆς γεγόνασι ἄνθρωποι). In a formal way, such an interpretation is justified by Gen 6:4, because it is said there that the giants were "on the earth" (ἐπὶ τῆς γῆς). It is clear, however, that the expression "on the earth" does not have here a special or emphasized meaning. The earth is not contrasted to any other part of the cosmos; it is simply a word for the stage upon which events unfold. The notion of the "earthiness" of giants is much more heavily emphasized in *1 Enoch*, and in the very same manner in which we encounter it in Philo. In *1 En.* 15:8, after the fact that they left heaven has been pointed out, it is said: "but now the giants ... are mighty spirits upon the earth (ἐπὶ τῆς γῆς), and their dwelling is inside the earth (ἐν τῇ γῇ)." And later (*1 En.* 15:10): "the spirits who are born upon the earth (ἐπὶ τῆς γῆς τὰ γεννηθέντα), their dwelling shall be upon the earth (ἐπὶ τῆς γῆς)." Not only does the idea

that the giants have some intimate connection with the earth correspond
to Philo's description, but so does even the phrase in which the words
"earth" (γῆ) and "to be born" (γεγόνασι γεννηθέντα) collocate. A little
later on, Philo says:

> But the sons of earth ... removed their minds from the path of reason,
> and transmuted it into to the *lifeless and immovable* (τὴν ἄψυχον καὶ
> ἀκίνητον) *nature of the flesh* (σαρκῶν φύσιν), ... they *deserted* (ἔλιπον)
> from the better rank, which had been allotted to them as their own, to the
> worse rank, which was contrary to their original nature.   (*Gig.* 65)

Philo does not explain or comment on this statement. It would have
remained puzzling for us, if it did not completely correspond to what
is said in *1 En.* 15:

> For what reason have you *abandoned* (ἀπελίπετε) the high, holy, and
> eternal heaven? ... And you used to be holy and spiritual, possessing
> eternal life, but now you have defiled yourselves with the blood of women,
> and with the blood of the *flesh* (σαρκός), you have begotten children,
> you have lusted in the blood of men, like them producing blood and
> *flesh* (σάρκα), like those *who die and perish* (οἵτινες ἀποθνήσκουσι καὶ
> ἀπόλλυνται) ... But you, *formerly you were spirits, having eternal life* ...
>   (*1 En.* 15:3, 6)

As in Philo's passage, the fallen angels are reproached for leaving the
rank of spirits and deserting to the rank of flesh and blood. We see,
that the correspondence is very complete on the level of ideas as well
as on the semantic level: "like those who die and perish" echoes the
"lifeless and immovable nature"; ἀπελίπετε corresponds to ἔλιπον; and
σαρκός/σάρκα to σαρκῶν φύσιν. The only difference is that *1 Enoch*
talks about the fallen angels themselves, whereas Philo applies it to the
"sons of the earth," who, as we are told, are giants. The inconsistency
is easy to explain by the fact that Philo is strongly inclined to identify
the fallen angels with the giants in some way, allegorizing the offspring
of these angels as the miserable condition to which their souls had
degenerated.

Accordingly, the name of Nimrod, who in the Septuagint is said to have
been the first giant on the earth (Gen 10:8) is interpreted as "desertion"
(*Gig.* 66) (a word which is repeated several times with reference to the
bad angels in *1 Enoch*). Philo continues:

> for it was not enough for the thoroughly miserable soul to stand apart
> from both, but having gone over to its enemies, it took up arms against
> its friends (τῶν φίλων) and resisted them, and made open war upon them
> (ἀνθεστῶσα αὐτοῖς ἐπολέμει).   (*Gig.* 66)

This is, again, quite a mysterious assertion. Of course nothing of that sort is said about Nimrod in the Septuagint. What does "stand apart from both" mean? Who are the "friends" whom this "miserable soul" betrays? I think that we can find the answer at the end of the same chapter 1 *En.* 15. There the destiny of the giants is predicted, and it is said that the spirits which proceeded from their corpses will constantly insult men until the day of judgment. "These spirits shall rise up (ἐξαναστήσει) against the children of the people and against the women, because they have proceeded forth from them" (*1 En.* 15:12). If we take into consideration that the word τῶν φίλων, translated in Philo's text as "friends," can also designate a mother, father or other relatives, then the picture becomes clearer. The giants (Nimrod being one of them), proceeding from heavenly spirits and men, and so being something intermediate between them, did not stay "apart from both"— they betray humans as well, insulting those who gave them life, i.e., τοὺς φίλους. And even the verb "to resist" (ἀνθίστημι) is a variant of the verb "to rise up" (ἐξανίστημι) used in the Enochic text, differing from it only by a prefix.

Thus one gets the impression that Philo, allegorizing Gen 6:2–4, accurately alludes to every particular of *1 En.* 15.

We have in no way exhausted the material which *1 Enoch* gives us with respect to these two treatises, to say nothing of Philo's other writings. But it is neither possible nor necessary in the limited scope of an article. My goal is to show that Philo's text is full of allusions to *1 Enoch*; that these allusions lie at the deep levels of the text; that the extant parts of the Greek translation are semantically reflected in Philo's text.

This first of all, helps us in dating the Greek translation of *1 Enoch*, because it testifies to its existence at the turn of the first century B.C.E. Secondly, we are driven to a more general conclusion. We can now infer that by that time *1 Enoch* was already well known in the Greek speaking Diaspora, since it was obviously part of Philo's cultural background. That evidence contradicts the opinion that the connection between these books and the community at Qumran was exclusive. At least by the first century B.C.E., the book had already crossed the boundaries of any secluded community and became—or remained—a *commune bonum* of the Jews living in areas as widely distant as, for instance, Qumran and Alexandria.

WHERE DOES THE SHEKHINAH DWELL?
BETWEEN THE DEAD SEA SECT, DIASPORA JUDAISM, RABBINIC LITERATURE, AND CHRISTIANITY

NOAH HACHAM
The Hebrew University of Jerusalem

One of the well known theological conceptions of the Dead Sea sect is its approach to the Temple, its sanctity and the resulting question of the location of the One who was supposed to dwell therein. The sect denied the sanctity of the Temple of their time, claiming it did not function appropriately, and advocated withdrawing from it. The sect members perceived their own group, the "Council of the Community," as a spiritual substitute for the Temple in Jerusalem. As the *Community Rule* states: "The Council of the Community shall be truly established ... a house of holiness for Israel and a foundation of the holy of holies for Aaron ... chosen by God's will to atone for the land." And in the continuation of the *Rule*: "It shall be the tested wall, the costly cornerstone, its foundations shall neither be shaken nor be dislodged from their place. Holy of holies dwelling for Aaron ... and a house of perfection and truth in Israel."[1] This is patently based on Isa 28:16: "Thus said the Lord God: 'Behold, I will found in Zion, stone by stone, a tower of precious cornerstones,

---

[1] My translation of 1QS VIII:5–9: נכונה עצת היחד באמת ... בית קודש לישראל וסוד קודש קודשים לאהרן ... ובחירי רצון לכפר בעד הארץ ... היא חומת הבחן פנת יקר בל יזדעזעו יסודותיהו ובל יחישו ממקומם. מעון קודש קודשים לאהרן ... ובית תמים ואמת בישראל; and similarly: CD 6:11–12: "And all who were brought into the covenant (are) not to enter the sanctuary to light his altar in vain." וכל אשר הובאו בברית לבלתי בוא אל המקדש להאיר מזבחו חנם (J.M. Baumgarten and D.R. Schwartz, "Damascus Document [CD]," in *The Dead Sea Scrolls: Hebrew, Aramaic, and Greek Texts with English Translations*, vol. 2: *Damascus Document, War Scroll, and Related Documents* [ed. J.H. Charlesworth et al.; The Princeton Theological Seminary Dead Sea Scrolls Project; Tübingen: Mohr Siebeck, 1993], 4–57, 23). On the sect's attitude toward the Temple see, inter alia: B. Gärtner, *The Temple and the Community in Qumran and the New Testament* (Cambridge: Cambridge University Press, 1965), 16–46; L.H. Schiffman, "Community without Temple: The Qumran Community's Withdrawal from the Jerusalem Temple," in *Gemeinde ohne Tempel/Community without Temple: Zur Substituierung und Transformation des Jerusalemer Tempels und seines Kultus im Alten Testament, antiken Judentum und frühen Christentum* (ed. B. Ego, A. Lange, and P. Pilhofer; WUNT 118; Tübingen: Mohr Siebeck, 1999), 267–284, esp. 269–274.

exceedingly firm; he who trusts need not fear.'"[2] The parallelism is clear; but while the prophet speaks of "Zion," the sect identifies the "Council of the Community" as the subject of the prophecy, and believes that the sect itself realizes this prophecy regarding "Zion."[3] Clearly, then, if the sect is a "house of holiness," a "foundation of the holy of holies," the "holy of holies dwelling," and a "house of perfection," and its members are intended to "atone for the land," then it functions as a temple, the place of God.

God, therefore, is exiled from His place, and dwells among a community who, like Him, are exiled. The notion of disengagement from the physical place is obviously Diasporan; that is, it limits the importance of the tangible physical location, and enables the sect members to find God in their midst, though they are not bodily in the place of God. This idea constitutes an important component of the theology and self-perception of the scrolls sect, and has been extensively discussed within these contexts. The discovery of such a position among a group living in Judea in the second half of the Second Temple period makes a significant contribution to our understanding of the historical continuity of the manner in which the reality of the absence of the Temple was confronted.

In this paper I wish to present the development of this historical continuity, from its biblical beginnings to its later manifestations in rabbinic literature. My assertion is that this perception must also be examined diachronically, namely as an inner progression of Diasporan Judaism. To this end, I will focus special attention on two witnesses representing such a stance: one appearing in Hellenistic Jewish literature, and the other in rabbinic literature, and will examine the content and meaning of the testimony within this continuity.

---

[2] NJPS translation of: הנני יסד בציון אבן, אבן בחן פנת יקרת מוסד מוסד המאמין לא יחיש ...

[3] On the importance of this verse in this context see: D. Flusser, *Judaism and the Origins of Christianity* (Jerusalem: Magnes, 1988), 35–44, esp. 41–43; M. Kister, "Some Observations on Vocabulary and Style in the Dead Sea Scrolls," in *Diggers at the Well: Proceedings of a Third International Symposium on the Hebrew of the Dead Sea Scrolls and Ben Sira* (ed. T. Muraoka and J.F. Elwolde; STDJ 36; Leiden: Brill, 2000), 159–165; N. Hacham, "An Aramaic Translation of Isaiah in the *Rule of the Community*," *Leš* 67 (2005): 147–152 (Hebrew). In this paper I pointed to the affinity between several passages from the scrolls, all using the verb הזדעזע, and I suggested that an Aramaic translation of Isaiah that translates יחיש as יזדעזען was known to all these scrolls' authors. I regret that when writing my study I was unaware of Kister's important suggestions. He also pointed to the affinity between those passages, and noted that the word יזדעזען appears in the Aramaic translation of Isaiah. However, our conclusions differ; I find it reasonable to assume the existence of an Aramaic *Targum of Isaiah* in the first century B.C.E., while Kister does not find this satisfactorily proven.

The earliest source of the conception that the Lord dwells with His exiled people outside the Temple and the Land of Israel already appears in the Bible itself, in a text dealing with the start of the Babylonian exile. Ezekiel's depiction of the departure of the divine presence (ch. 11) from the Temple tells of the inhabitants of Jerusalem saying of their brethren, who were exiled to Babylonia by Nebuchadnezzar: "Remove yourselves from the Lord; the land has been given to us as a heritage" (11:15), that is, the exiles were taken from the land, and are therefore distant from the Lord and His Temple, and the land is given to those who remain in it. The prophet's response to this challenge begins with: "Thus said the Lord God: Though I have removed them into the midst of the nations and scattered them through the lands, and am but a small sanctuary for them in the lands into which they have come" (v. 16).[4] As Greenberg writes, "In this statement of deprivation, it is obliquely conceded that the exiles enjoy a measure of divine nearness even in the exile (contrary to the Jerusalemites' view)."[5] This means that the Lord's Presence is not dependent solely on the Temple, but mainly on the elect group of people: the exiles—that will return to the Land, and in the meantime, the Lord is with them, to a limited degree, in the different lands, as a "small sanctuary."

The dependence of the Lord's presence on the people is not, of course, Ezekiel's own innovation. It is a well-established biblical idea, as expressed, for example, in Exod 25:8 ("and let them make Me a sanctuary that I may dwell among them")[6] and 29:45 ("I will abide among the Israelites"; NJPS). However, while in these sources the Divine Presence within the Israelites is in or through a physical element—the Tabernacle—according to Ezekiel this is not contingent on a specific location and though the Temple might be absent, the Divine Presence resides within the people nonetheless.

This idea resurfaced, in various formulations, in Second Temple period. We are less interested in formulations such as "But God did not choose the people on account of the Place; rather, He chose the Place on

---

[4] English translation of both verses is based on M. Greenberg, *Ezekiel 1–20* (AB 22; New York: Doubleday, 1983), 185–186.

[5] Ibid., 190; see also D. Rom-Shiloni, "Ezekiel as the Voice of the Exiles and Constructor of Exilic Ideology," *HUCA* 76 (2005): 1–45, 17–18.

[6] See Sarna's commentary on this verse (N.M. Sarna, *Exodus* [The JPS Torah Commentary; Philadelphia: JPS, 1991], 158.)

account of the people" (2 Macc 5:19).[7] Nor will we focus on expressions
of the superiority of the people over the Temple as demonstrated by
2 Maccabees' (14:34) description of the priests praying "Him who has
always championed *our people*"[8] in contrast with the parallel description in 1 Maccabees (7:37) where the priests say: "you have chosen this
house to bear your name, to be a house of prayer ... for Your people."[9] Instead, I will focus on a single example that expresses the Jewish Diaspora concept that the Divine Presence was, specifically, in their
midst.

3 Maccabees, a Hellenistic Jewish composition, apparently from the
first century B.C.E., tells of two clashes between the Jews and King Ptole-
my IV Philopator. The first incident occurred in Jerusalem, when the
monarch sought to enter the Holy of Holies, and the second, in Egypt,
when the king attempted to destroy all of Egyptian Jewry. In both instances the king was unsuccessful, but the depictions of these failures are
very different. In Jerusalem, the Temple was saved, but the Lord did not
reveal Himself, and the king did not repent. In Egypt, on the other hand,
the people are saved, God is revealed, and the king recants. The following
comparison of the many parallels in the two narratives highlights the
superiority of the salvation in Egypt to that in Jerusalem.

The significance of the location of the epiphany cannot be disregarded.
One would expect that God be revealed in his place, in the Jerusalem
Temple, as indeed happens in the parallel story of Heliodorus' attempt
to plunder the Temple treasures (2 Macc 3:24, 30). This expectation
becomes stronger when the High Priest Simon requests "manifest Thy
mercy at this hour" (2:19).[10] Nevertheless, this expectation is not fulfilled. The epiphany of the God of Israel takes place in a pagan institution, the hippodrome of Alexandria (3 Macc 6:18), in order to save the
endangered people. At this point we read that "the Ruler of all ... manifest His mercy" (3 Macc 6:39).[11] The similar vocabulary indicates that the

---

[7] D.R. Schwartz's translation of: ἀλλ' οὐ διὰ τὸν τόπον τὸ ἔθνος, ἀλλὰ διὰ τὸ ἔθνος
τὸν τόπον ὁ κύριος ἐξελέξατο (2 *Maccabees* [Commentaries on Early Jewish Literature;
Berlin: de Gruyter, 2008], 248).

[8] Schwartz's translation of: τὸν διὰ παντὸς ὑπέρμαχον τοῦ ἔθνους ἡμῶν (ibid., 465).

[9] J.A. Goldstein's translation of: Σὺ ἐξελέξω τὸν οἶκον τοῦτον ἐπικληθῆναι τὸ ὄνομά
σου ἐπ' αὐτοῦ εἶναι οἶκον προσευχῆς ... τῷ λαῷ σου (*I Maccabees* [AB 41; New York:
Doubleday, 1977], 328).

[10] καὶ ἐπίφανον τὸ ἔλεός σου κατὰ τὴν ὥραν ταύτην.

[11] ἐπιφάνας τὸ ἔλεος αὐτοῦ ὁ τῶν πάντων δυνάστης. Both translations by M. Hadas,
The Third and Fourth Books of Maccabees (New York: Ktav, 1953).

Jerusalemite High Priest's prayer was indeed accepted, not on behalf of the temple in Jerusalem, but rather on behalf of the people in Egypt.

Epiphany is an important theme in 3 Maccabees and in Hellenistic literature as well. Words deriving from the verb ἐπιφαίνω appear several times in 3 Maccabees (2:9, 19; 5:8, 35, 51; 6:4, 9, 18, 39), revealing the essential function of epiphany in the book. In Hellenistic literature epiphanies often serve to legitimize political claims or function as propaganda for the importance of a certain place or cult.[12] It seems that the divine epiphany in 3 Maccabees is also propagandist in nature, for the sake of the elected and sanctified people.

Other points further demonstrate the presence of God with his people in Egypt. Simon's prayer ends with a request that the Jews be able to praise God after they are granted peace (ποιήσας ἡμῖν εἰρήνην, 2:20). However, peace is not granted to the Jews in Jerusalem. In contrast, in the story of the deliverance of the Egyptian Jews, the word "peace" (εἰρήνη) appears twice (6:27; 7:19), and a similar word expresses that the Jews celebrated and thereby expressed joy because of the peace (6:32: εἰρηνικός). Again, High Priest Simon's prayer is not fulfilled at the Temple in Jerusalem but rather by the deliverance of the Jews in Egypt.

The appearance of descriptions of holy and holiness illustrate the same phenomenon. The holy God is mentioned three times in the context of the events in Jerusalem (2:2, 13, 21), but this holiness was not made manifest at the time.[13] In the events in Egypt, on the other hand, God revealed His Holy countenance (6:18) and in addition, he is called "holy" four or five times more.[14] Respectively, according to the Jerusalemite high priest's prayer, God sanctified the *place* (τόπος, 2:16) for His name (2:9);

---

[12] On epiphanies in the Hellenistic world in general see: R. Bultmann and D. Lührmann, "ἐπιφαίνω, ἐπιφανής, ἐπιφάνεια," *TDNT* 9:7–10; F. Graf, "Epiphany," *Brill's New Pauly* (ed. H. Cancik and H. Schneider; Leiden: Brill, 2004) 4:1121–1123; on this theme in 2 Maccabees see: R. Doran, *Temple Propaganda: The Purpose and Character of 2 Maccabees* (Washington: Catholic Biblical Association of America, 1981), 98–104.

[13] Two of the references to God's holiness in Jerusalem are found in the High Priest's prayer, and the third (2:21: ἅγιος ἐν ἁγίοις) is a repetition of the appellation appearing in the first verse of the prayer. The verb εἰσακούσας following this appellation describes the listening to the prayer. In this repetition, the author emphasizes that the Holy among the holy ones, to whom the prayer is addressed, did hear it, but there is no description of an epiphany of his holiness. In Egypt, on the other hand, the references to God's holiness are the narrator's descriptions and not quotes of the book's protagonists. This may, perhaps, be accounted for as follows: in Jerusalem, God's holiness is a wish expressed in prayers but it is not apparent in the events, whereas in Egypt, the "objective" narrator tells innocently of the evident holiness of God.

[14] 3 Macc 5:13; 6:1, 29; 7:10, 16 (according to some of the manuscripts).

according to Eleazar's prayer, those sanctified to God are Jacob (including of course his sons too) and God's people.[15] Reference to the sanctity of the place is repeated in Simon's Prayer (2:14: τόπος; 2:18: οἶκος) and according to some manuscripts the Jerusalem priests' holy vestments are also described as holy (1:16).[16] The holiness of the people of Israel is mentioned again in Eleazar's prayer (6:9: τοῖς ἁγίοις Ισραηλ γένους) according to Codex Alexandrinus.[17] The people of Israel are called holy once in Simon's prayer (2:6)[18] and the city (πόλις) is called holy once in Eleazar's prayer (6:5). Thus, Simon emphasizes the holy place whereas Eleazar mentions the holiness of the people and does not mention the sanctity of the Temple at all, only that of the town. The result is that God's holiness is not revealed for the sake of the holy place, as requested by the high priest, but on behalf of the holy people as mentioned by the Egyptian priest Eleazar. The reason is obvious: God's presence is to be found with the people, His people, not in a place.

Comparison of the two prayers for salvation offered by a priest in both incidents would sustain this conclusion, and I will specify just three of the many points. In Jerusalem, it is Simon the High Priest who prays, and apart from his title, nothing more is said of him (3 Macc 2:1).[19] In the hippodrome in Egypt, it is Eleazar, one of the priests of the country. 3 Maccabees mentions some of his exalted qualities (6:1): a distinguished person among the priests of the country, who had attained an advanced age and whose life had been adorned with every virtue.[20] The priest in Egypt is therefore decidedly superior to his Jerusalem counterpart; consequently, according to 3 Maccabees, the Temple does

---

[15] 3 Macc 6:3: ἡγιασμένου τέκνα Ιακωβ, μερίδος ἡγιασμένης σου λαόν.

[16] See the apparatus criticus in R. Hanhart, ed., *Maccabaeorum liber III* (2nd ed.; Septuaginta: Vetus Testamentum Graecum Auctoritate Academiae Scientiarum Gottingensis 9.3; Göttingen: Vandenhoeck & Ruprecht, 1980), 43.

[17] See Hanhart, *Maccabaeorum liber III*, 63.

[18] True, Simon's prayer does not cancel or ignore the uniqueness of the people of Israel: The sanctity of the place derives from God's desire that his honor will be within the people of Israel (16), and the people of Israel are considered "your people" (2:6, 16), i.e., God's people. But this uniqueness is apparent on earth in the place that is holy for God's honor (14). And indeed, the house of Israel is described as the object of God's love (2:10), but the expression of this love is in listening to the prayers at the location of the Temple.

[19] For the versions of this verse see Hanhart, *Maccabaeorum liber III*, 44. On the superiority of the Lucianic version in this verse see: N. Hacham, "The Third Book of Maccabees: Literature, History and Ideology" (Ph.D. diss., The Hebrew University of Jerusalem, 2002), 69 n. 22 (Hebrew).

[20] Ελεαζαρος δέ τις ἀνὴρ ἐπίσημος τῶν ἀπὸ τῆς χώρας ἱερέων, ἐν πρεσβείῳ τὴν ἡλικίαν ἤδη λελογχὼς καὶ πάσῃ τῇ κατὰ τὸν βίον ἀρετῇ κεκοσμημένος.

not transform those who officiate in it into exemplary beings. Simon, in Jerusalem, does not use the Lord's title "Father" to describe God, and in the narrative of the attempted breaching of the Jerusalem Temple, He is simply the "forefather" (προπάτωρ, 2:21), an authoritative appellation charged with primeval greatness, lacking the connotation of the affinity between a father and his children. Eleazar, in contrast, addresses the Lord twice as "Father," (6:3, 8) and in three other instances during the course of the events in Egypt, God is portrayed as the Father of His people (5:7; 6:28; 7:6). This speaks of God's closeness to His people, who face danger in the hippodrome. Finally, Simon requests, at the end of his prayer, that the Lord put praises in the mouths of the downtrodden (2:20). Despite the rescue of the Temple, there is no mention of any thanksgiving prayer by the Jews of Jerusalem. After any rescue of the Jews of Egypt, however, even partial salvation, before their final deliverance, they praise and laud their God, who has come to their succor (5:13, 35; 6:32).

Several years ago, David S. Williams suggested that 3 Maccabees should also be regarded as an apologia by Egyptian Jews directed at the Jews of the land of Israel, as it conveys the contention that Providence exists with Diasporan Jews as well, thus legitimizing Diaspora Judaism. According to Williams, Palestinian Jews considered Diasporan Jews inferior. Therefore, the Diasporan author of 3 Maccabees stresses God's existence with them as well as the kinship of both groups.[21] This view was criticized by Gruen, who claims that "there is no evidence for criticism of Diaspora Jewry by those in Palestine."[22] Similarly, Cousland claims, "Jerusalem is not linked to the victory (= of the Jews in Egypt): the triumph remains purely Diasporan," and "how successful as an apologetic this implicit derogation of Jerusalem would have been to a Palestinian audience."[23]

However, in light of the discussion above, one cannot deny that Williams' hypothesis is basically correct, and that 3 Maccabees tries to bolster Diaspora Jewry. Moreover, it seems that Williams was overly careful by claiming that according to 3 Maccabees God is "also" with Diasporan Jews; indeed, the author's view is that God's revelation in the

---

[21] D.S. Williams, "3 Maccabees: A Defense of Diaspora Judaism?" *JSP* 13 (1995): 17–29.

[22] E.S. Gruen, *Heritage and Hellenism: The Reinvention of Jewish Tradition* (Berkeley: University of California Press, 1998), 233 n. 192.

[23] J.R.C. Cousland, "Reversal, Recidivism and Reward in *3 Maccabees*: Structure and Purpose," *JSJ* 34 (2003): 39–51, 40–41.

hippodrome in Egypt, to save His people, was greater than His manifestation in His Temple in Jerusalem. In other words, the Lord is with
the people, and not within the Temple. Thus the audience cannot be
the Jews of the land of Israel, but rather the Diasporan-Egyptian Jews,
who were bothered by their alleged inferior status and needed encouragement in relation to their religious status and their closeness to their
God.[24]

The overall picture is clear: in different historical contexts, from Babylonia in the late first Temple period to Hellenistic-Roman Egypt[25] and
the Judean Desert in the second or first century B.C.E., Jews assert that
God is with them, within their group, and not in His official place—the
Temple in Jerusalem.

The element common to all these sources is that they represent groups
that were geographically distant from the Temple, and/or clashed to some
degree with the center in Jerusalem. Ezekiel speaks of those who were
exiled against their will and had to wrestle with the theological meaning
of this forced exile, though the Temple remained at that stage intact.
Regarding Hellenistic Jewry, the factor of compulsion is absent and
other factors are prominent in its stead. The Jews outside Judea lacked
physical affinity to the Temple, though many identified with it. This lack
of a feeling of closeness to the Temple meant remoteness from God. A
believer desirous of intimacy with God would have difficulty in accepting
any remoteness from Him, and would accordingly seek solutions for this
religious alienation. He therefore would offer various substitutes for the
Temple, so that God would be close to him, as well. The religious ideology
of the Dead Sea sect regarded the Temple as a sinful site, which served
as an additional reason for disassociating from it. As regards the range of
opinions expressed in these sources, the more priestly sources—Ezekiel

---

[24] For a detailed discussion on this approach of 3 Maccabees see: Hacham, "The Third
Book of Maccabees," 65–144.

[25] For other Jewish-Hellenistic sources of this view see e.g.: Philo, *Spec.* 1.66–67; *Somn.*
1.149; *Sobr.* 66; and C. Werman, "God's House: Temple or Universe," in *Philo und das
Neue Testament: Wechselseitige Wahrnehmungen: I. Internationales Symposium zum Corpus Judaeo-Hellenisticum 1.–4. Mai 2003, Eisenach/Jena* (ed. R. Deines and K.W. Niebuhr;
WUNT 172; Tübingen: Mohr Siebeck, 2004), 309–320. On the *Letter of Aristeas* in this
context see my note in "Exile and Self-Identity in the Qumran Sect and in Hellenistic
Judaism," in *New Perspectives on Old Texts: Proceedings of the 10th International Symposium of the Orion Center for the Study of the Dead Sea Scrolls and Associated Literature, 9–
11 January, 2005* (ed. E.G. Chazon and B. Halprin-Amaru; STDJ 88; Leiden: Brill, 2010),
3–21, 6–7, and note also that according to the *Letter of Aristeas* God is with the translators
in Egypt.

and the Dead Sea Scrolls—strip the abandoned and defiled Temple of all sanctity, while Hellenistic Jewish sources afford it limited holiness, and differ as to the degree of its sanctity. For all, sanctity and the Divine Presence are contingent on the chosen group, and if this elect group is not in the place of the Temple, then the latter's sanctity diminishes or is abrogated, and the Divine Presence shifts from the place to the people. As for the geographical location of the groups arguing the Divine Presence's exile, we should add that Ezekiel's claim relates to a situation at the eve of the Temple's destruction and physical exile from the Land of Israel. In the case of Hellenistic Jewish authors, in contrast, the Temple stood and functioned, but they lived outside Judea. Sect members who maintained that that Temple did not function at all, on the other hand, actually lived in Judea itself, that is, not in geographical exile, not far from the existing Temple. In other words, even someone who lived in the Land of Israel could contend that the Divine Presence was in exile, and the existence of the Temple did not hinder the formulation of such a stance among those alienated from it.

In light of these facts, we should not be surprised by the presence of similar views, both in early Christianity and in rabbinic literature. Christianity did not forge the conception of the Divine Presence being with the community, nor did the rabbis *ex nihilo* create this model for coming to terms with the Destruction or as a reaction to the emerging Christian religion. Both took their ideas from a rich tradition that was prevalent in the Jewish world of the Second Temple period, which they fashioned in accordance with their specific needs. This understanding is of great importance, both on the fundamental level and for the history of scholarly research. Fundamentally, despite the earth-shattering crisis that the Jewish world experienced upon the destruction of the Second Temple, the following time should not be viewed as a new world unconnected with what preceded it. The transition between periods is not a sudden change, but rather gradual processes, and the religious existence and self-definition of the Jewish people without a Temple had already been fashioned throughout a lengthy span in the Second Temple period, during the course of which an important and lively Jewish Diaspora existed in the Hellenistic-Roman world. The Destruction obviously posed a theological and spiritual challenge to the Jewish world in general and particularly to the Jews of the Land of Israel, but the tools for contending with this dilemma were already present in the Jewish world's treasury of religious thought, and both the rabbis and the early Christians took their positions from this ready treasury.

In terms of scholarly research history, several leading scholars apparently do not share this insight. For example, Ephraim Elimelech Urbach and Shalom Spiegel discuss the concept of the Shekhinah in exile in rabbinic literature, in the context of consolation following the destruction of the Second Temple and the theological-philosophical tension between "His presence fills all the earth" (Isa 6:3) and the limited place of the Divine Presence.[26] Indeed, we should not underestimate the importance of a phenomenological inquiry of these issues by themselves, and their inclusion in the limited and immediate historical context of the events close to the appearance of these conceptions among those groups. Nonetheless, we should not disregard the diachronic context.

Let us turn to a discussion of rabbinic literature and Christianity. The Tannaitic midrash *Sifre* on Numbers (161) teaches:[27]

> R. Nathan says: Israel are beloved, for every place where they were exiled, the Shekhinah went into exile with them. They were exiled to Egypt—the Shekhinah was with them, as it is said (1 Sam 2:27): "I revealed Myself to your father's house in Egypt when they were subject to the House of Pharaoh;" they were exiled to Babylon—the Shekhinah was with them, as it is said (Isa 43:14): "For your sake, I have sent to Babylon;" they were exiled to Elam—the Shekhinah was with them, as it is said (Jer 49:38): "And I will set My throne in Elam, and wipe out from there king and officials;" they were exiled to Edom—the Shekhinah was with them, as it is said (Isa 63:1): "Who is this coming from Edom, in crimsoned garments from Bozrah." And when they return, the Shekhinah returns with them, as it is said (Deut 30:3): "Then the Lord your God will return [with] your captivity"—it does not state "*ve-heshiv*" [and He shall bring back] but "*ve-shav* the Lord your God" [and He shall return].

This midrash is meant to encourage and console the exiled people. Furthermore, Arnold Goldberg notes that the consolation is reinforced by the ending in which redemption is assured for both the people and God.[28] Within the framework of our discussion, however, this obviously is not all this midrash is saying. As Urbach stated, this exposition relates to an actual theological problem that greatly intensified after the Destruction.

---

[26] E.E. Urbach, *The Sages: Their Concepts and Beliefs* (Jerusalem: Magnes, 1979), 54–57; S. Spiegel, *Fathers of Piyyut: Texts and Studies toward a History of the Piyyut in Eretz Yisrael* (New York: Jewish Theological Seminary of America, 1996), 308–353 (Hebrew). This view is widely accepted; see also, e.g., N.J. Cohen, "Shekhinta Ba-Galuta: A Midrashic Response to Destruction and Persecution," *JSJ* 13 (1982): 147–159.

[27] English translation is mine.

[28] A. Goldberg, *Untersuchungen über die Vorstellung von der Schekhinah in der frühen rabbinischen Literatur (Talmud und Midrasch)* (Berlin: de Gruyter, 1969), 163.

The conception current among Palestinian Jewry saw the Temple as the locus of the Shekhinah, that is, as the place in which God causes His glory to dwell and in which it is revealed. Thus, for example, Flavius Josephus (*B.J.* 5.459) writes that the rebels believed that the Temple would yet "be saved by Him who dwelled therein." The destruction of the Temple meant the departure of the Shekhinah from the Temple. The simple concept states that if the place of God is devastated, God no longer dwells in the earthly realm. This idea is confirmed by many sources, such as *Sifre Zuta* 35:33:[29]

> R. Nehorai said: "For I the Lord abide" (Num 35:34)—[does this mean] in exile? Scripture teaches: "in the land." Or, [He abides] in the Land, while you are in exile? Scripture teaches: "among the Israelite people"—while the people are in the Land, and not when they are outside the Land.

The notion that the Shekhinah did not ascend to heaven and is present on earth, which established the exiled people of Israel as the alternative "place" of the Shekhinah during the Exile, seems to be an innovation in the world of the Pharisees and their successors, the rabbis.

We should highlight the dialectic embodied in this source. The Shekhinah is with the people, but it is in exile. This means that this is not its preferred place, and it will eventually return, but in the meantime, it is in the midst of the people. This emphasis is not pronounced in Jewish Hellenistic sources, which are mainly concerned with the question of the current location of the Divine Presence, without stressing that this place is exile. Furthermore, in contrast to Jewish Hellenistic sources, this rabbinic teaching does not limit itself to specifying the current location of the Shekhinah, but also speaks of the future: the restoration of the Shekhinah to its place in Jerusalem.

As part of a prevalent tendency to view the rabbinic dicta as an anti-Christian polemic, it was proposed that this idea should be regarded in a similar light, on the background of the Destruction and the rise of Christianity, and the latter's claims of God's abandonment of Israel and the abrogation of the covenant with it.[30] Moreover, the idea of God's being with Israel could fundamentally be understood as the inversion of the common claim by the early Church that God is present in their

---

[29] English translation is mine. For other formulations of the same idea see e.g., *b. Roš Haš.* 31a; *Mek. de Rabbi Yishmaʻel*, tractate Pisḥa, 1 (ed. Lauterbach p. 2).

[30] In addition to the above-mentioned studies in n. 26, see also: M. Eyali, "God's Sharing in the Suffering of the Jewish People," in *Studies in Jewish Thought* (ed. S.O. Heller Willensky and M. Idel; Jerusalem: Magnes, 1989), 29–50 (Hebrew).

community. Thus, for example, we find in Paul's letter to the Ephesians
the following statement addressed to those Gentiles (2:19–22):[31]

> So then you are no longer strangers and sojourners, but you are fellow
> citizens with the saints and members of the household of God ... being
> the cornerstone, in whom the whole structure is joined together and grows
> into a holy temple in the Lord; in whom you also are built into it for a
> dwelling place of God in the Spirit.   (RSV)

In other words, the Gentiles who join the Christian community become
the dwelling place of God, a sort of temple. This is also stated in several
sources like the first epistle of Peter (1 Pet 2:5): "and like living stones be
yourselves built into a spiritual house, to be a holy priesthood, to offer
spiritual sacrifices acceptable to God ..." (RSV).[32] Thus, the temple is
simply the community, and the people are the dwelling place of God.
Put differently, the Divine Presence is in the congregation, since the Lord
chose it as His elect.[33]

This common Christian argument might have been addressed by the
Tannaim in their teaching cited above, as if to say: yes, the chosen people
are the dwelling place of God, and not the destroyed Temple. These
human beings, however, are not the Christians, but the Lord's chosen
people, the people of Israel, exiled in Edom. And indeed, the Babylonian
Talmud (*Yoma* 57a) contains a disagreement on this question between
R. Hanina (first generation of Palestinian Amoraim) and a *min*, most
likely a Christian:[34]

> The *min* said to R. Hanina: Now you are surely unclean, for it is written
> (Lam 1:9); "Her uncleanness clings to her skirts." He [R. Hanina] replied:
> Come and see what is written concerning them (Lev 16:16): "which abides
> with them in the midst of their uncleanness"—even when they are unclean,
> the Divine Presence is among them.

Although the contrasts between the worldview of the rabbis and that of
the Christians are unmistakable, we cannot learn from these sources that

---

[31] ἄρα οὖν οὐκέτι ἐστὲ ξένοι καὶ πάροικοι, ἀλλὰ ἐστὲ συμπολῖται τῶν ἁγίων καὶ
οἰκεῖοι τοῦ θεοῦ ... ὄντος ἀκρογωνιαίου ... ἐν ᾧ πᾶσα οἰκοδομὴ συναρμολογουμένη
αὔξει εἰς ναὸν ἅγιον ἐν κυρίῳ, ἐν ᾧ καὶ ὑμεῖς συνοικοδομεῖσθε εἰς κατοικητήριον τοῦ
θεοῦ ἐν πνεύματι.

[32] καὶ αὐτοὶ ὡς λίθοι ζῶντες οἰκοδομεῖσθε οἶκος πνευματικὸς εἰς ἱεράτευμα ἅγιον,
ἀνενέγκαι πνευματικὰς θυσίας εὐπροσδέκτους θεῷ ...

[33] On this passage in 1 Peter and its meaning and implications see commentaries ad
loc.

[34] Translation is mine, based on I. Epstein, ed., *The Babylonian Talmud: Translated into
English with Notes, Glossary and Indices* (35 vols.; London: Soncino, 1935–1952).

these arguments were generated within the Jewish-Christian polemic. In light of the sources cited earlier, it seems that the conception of the Lord dwelling with His exiled people originated neither in Christianity nor with the Tannaim, but much earlier.

Indeed, many years ago David Flusser discussed the connection between the above passage from 1 Peter and the passage we cited from the *Community Rule*, and the reliance of both on Isa 28:16.[35] On the one hand, the early Christians drew their ideas from a Diasporan sect that had preceded them: the Dead Sea sect; while on the other (as was observed by numerous scholars, such as Marcel Simon), these notions were influenced also by the Jewish-Hellenistic nature of nascent Christianity. It will suffice, in this context, to allude to the speech (Acts 7) by the Hellenistic Jew (τῶν Ἑλληνιστῶν; Acts 6:1) Stephen, who declared that the ideal condition was the wandering sanctuary, meaning that the Lord is present everywhere. In other words, as regards Christianity as well, the question of distance from God, the withdrawal from the Temple, and the Jewish Hellenistic model intrinsically influenced the development of this conception.

Accordingly, we should not view either the Christians or the rabbis as the originators of this idea. This is an early concept, and although the stance of the rabbis might be related to the Christian conceptions, to which it responds, the rabbis took an already existing concept, one that was popular among Hellenistic Judaism and the Dead Sea sect. Thus, the Dead Sea Scrolls can be viewed as a link completing the picture of the Diasporan perception of the Second Temple period and afterwards on the dwelling place of God.

The sources reviewed in this article reveal the conception of the Divine Presence dwelling among the people, as a theological development deriving and resulting from the Diasporan state—a state of distance or detachment from the location of the nation's religious center. Though Hellenism indeed exercised a great deal of influence over the development of these perceptions in the Jewish world,[36] the term מקדש ("Sanctuary") as denoting the presence of God with his people, removed from the physical Temple, appears already in the Bible, towards the end of the First Temple period, long before Hellenism, in the context of the eve of the destruction of this Temple. Moreover, even in the Jewish Hellenistic world, these

---

[35] Flusser, *Judaism and the Origins of Christianity*, 35–44, esp. 41–43.
[36] See D.R. Schwartz, *Studies in the Jewish Background of Christianity* (WUNT 60; Tübingen: Mohr Siebeck, 1992), 40.

perceptions appear not solely on account of the Hellenistic culture but
should also be attributed to the fact that Hellenistic Jewry was Diasporan, distanced as such, from the Temple. The combination of the Diasporan need with the Greek way of thinking enabled the Jews of the Land
of Israel, many generations later, to deal with the destruction of the Second Temple and the national center in the Land of Israel. These historical
circumstances allowed the Diaspora to permeate the Land of Israel. An
examination of the ongoing history of the concept of the Divine Presence
in the Diaspora during the talmudic period may also reveal aspects of the
Land of Israel's influence on the Diaspora—but this is a topic for another
article.

11QMELCH IM SPIEGEL DER WEISHEIT

ULRIKE MITTMANN
Universität Osnabrück

In der Qumranforschung gehört 11QMelch (11Q13)[1] zu denjenigen Texten, bei denen es scheint, als würden sie um so rätselhafter, je länger sich die Wissenschaft bemüht, sie zu verstehen und sachgemäß auszulegen. Dass das Rätsel der Melchisedekgestalt in 11QMelch noch lange nicht gelöst ist, zeigt auch die Vielzahl jüngerer Veröffentlichungen zum Thema.[2] Zumeist werden dabei die Menschensohnvorstellung nach Dan 7 und den Bilderreden Henochs (*1 Hen.* 37–71)[3] oder verschiedene Engelsvorstellungen zum Vergleich herangezogen. Nur am Rande diskutiert wird die Möglichkeit, dass Melchisedek als Personifikation der Weisheit zu verstehen sei. I.R. Tantlevskij spricht in seiner 2004 erschienenen Studie „Melchisedek *Redivivus* in Qumran" vorsichtig von „a Divine hypostatisation [*sic*] through which the transcendent Lord-Creator realizes His relative immanence in regard to the created world",[4] aber er ordnet diese genuin weisheitliche Aussage nicht theologiegeschichtlich ein. Die Aussage, dass Melchisedek eine göttliche Hypostase sei, wird als These präsentiert, ohne dass dieselbe in den Gesamtrahmen alttestamentlicher und frühjüdischer Hypostasenvorstellungen integriert würde. Dies gilt insbesondere für den Kontext weisheitlicher Personifikationen, wie sie von der persischen bis in die hellenistische Zeit das

---

[1] Zum Text s. F. García Martínez, E.J.C. Tigchelaar, and A.S. van der Woude in *DJD* XXIII (1998): 221–241 mit Tafel XXVII.

[2] Dies betrifft auch den vorliegenden Sammelband, in welchem drei Beiträge 11QMelch gewidmet sind. S. Anm. 34.

[3] Deutsch: S. Uhlig, *Das äthiopische Henochbuch* (JSHRZ V/6; Gütersloh: Gütersloher Verlagshaus, 1984), 573–634; Englisch: E. Isaac, „1 (Ethiopic Apocalypse of) Enoch (Second Century B.C.—First Century A.D.): A New Translation and Introduction," in *OTP* 1:5–89, 29–50.

[4] I.R. Tantlevskij, *Melchizedek* Redivivus *in Qumran: Some Peculiarities of Messianic Ideas and Elements of Mysticism in the Dead Sea Scrolls* (The Qumran Chronicle 12; Kraków: Enigma Press, 2004), 24–25.

weisheitliche Denken konstitutiv bestimmen.[5] Ja, es fällt auf, dass in der
Qumranforschung—obwohl der weisheitliche Hintergrund des Qumranschrifttums ein gründlich erforschtes Gebiet ist[6]—die Frage nach der
Personifikation der Weisheit und der eschatologischen Implikationen des
weisheitlichen Personverständnisses bis heute nicht oder nur am Rande
gestellt wurde. Das gilt auch für die große Monographie *Melchisedek e
l'angelologia nell'epistola agli ebrei e a Qumran* von F. Manzi,[7] in welcher „Melchisedek" als göttlicher Titel klassifiziert wird,[8] ohne dass dabei
der weisheitliche Rahmen vor Augen gestellt würde, innerhalb dessen
eine solche Klassifikation allein möglich ist.[9] Das soll in diesem Beitrag
nachgeholt werden. Dabei geschieht die Annäherung an 11QMelch vom
nichtqumranischen Vergleichsmaterial her, in welchem sich die priesterliche Personifikation der Weisheit bis hin zur Identifikation der Sapientia
mit Melchisedek dokumentiert findet.

1. Melchisedek im Hebräerbrief

Die messianologische bzw. christologische Besonderheit des Hebräerbriefes innerhalb des Neuen Testaments besteht darin, dass Christus
nicht nur als der Messias im Sinne der davidischen Messianologie und

---

[5] Im Folgenden werden im Blick auf die irdische Manifestation der Weisheit die
Begriffe „Hypostase" und „Person" bzw. „Hypostasierung" und „Personifikation" bedeu-
tungsgleich verwendet. Dabei wird der Personbegriff allein auf die Selbstentäußerung
Gottes im Akt des Zur-Welt-Kommens Gottes und auf die Manifestation Gottes im Irdischen bezogen. Die häufig geübte Vermischung eines hypostatischen Personbegriffs mit
rein literarischen Personifikationsmustern, wie sie etwa die aus jüngster Zeit stammende
große Monographie zum Thema von J.R. Dodson prägt (*The „Powers" of Personification:
Rhetorical Purpose in the Book of Wisdom and the Letter to the Romans* [BZNW 161; Berlin: de Gruyter, 2008], s. bes. 51–118), hat in der Forschung mit dazu beigetragen, die
weisheitliche Personvorstellung zu verdunkeln, statt sie zu erhellen.

[6] S. J.J. Collins, *Jewish Wisdom in the Hellenistic Age* (OTL; Louisville: Westminster
John Knox, 1997), 112–131, und A. Lange, „Die Weisheitstexte aus Qumran: Eine Einleitung," in *The Wisdom Texts from Qumran and the Development of Sapiential Thought*
(ed. C. Hempel, A. Lange und H. Lichtenberger; BETL 159; Leuven: Peeters, 2002), 3–30.

[7] F. Manzi, *Melchisedek e l'angelologia nell'epistola agli ebrei e a Qumran* (AnBib 136;
Rom: Päpstliches Bibelinstitut, 1997).

[8] Ibid., 63–96.

[9] Statt dessen verweist man auf die Hypostasenspekulationen der späteren rabbinischen Literatur. Vgl. A.F. Segal, *Two Powers in Heaven: Early Rabbinic Reports about
Christianity and Gnosticism* (SJLA 25; Leiden: Brill, 1977), 23, 260–261. Dass dieselben
in der alttestamentlich-jüdischen Weisheit wurzeln, kommt dabei nicht in den Blick.

der sie weiterführenden Menschensohnerwartung[10] angesehen wird, sondern gleichzeitig als der himmlische Hohepriester[11]. Die in Qumran auseinandertretende Erwartung eines königlich-davidischen und eines priesterlichen Messias (CD 19:10–11; 19:33–20:1; 1QS IX:9–11; 1QSa [1Q28a] II:11–22; 4QTest [4Q175])[12] sind in Christi Person vereinigt. In dieser Vereinigung der Traditionsstränge wird nun allerdings interessanterweise das Priestertum Christi nicht auf Aaron und das levitische Priestertum zurückgeführt, sondern auf Melchisedek. Christus ist—so nennt ihn der Verfasser des Hebräerbriefes—„Priester nach der Ordnung Melchisedeks" (Heb 5:6, 10; 6:20; 7:11, 15, 17), ἀρχιερεὺς κατὰ τὴν τά- ξιν Μελχισέδεκ. Diese Titulatur verdankt sich Ps 110:4, wo der davidische König als „Priester auf ewig nach der Ordnung Melchisedeks„ proklamiert wird. Psalm 110:4 seinerseits ist nur verständlich vor dem Hintergrund von Gen 14. Hier erscheint Melchisedek als der königliche Urpriester auf dem Zion, dem Abraham sich mit der Übereignung des Zehnten unterstellt (Gen 14:17–20). Dabei zielt die einzigartige Darstellung Abrahams als eines territorial weit ausgreifenden Kriegsherrn ebenfalls auf das davidische Zionskönigtum, genauer auf die Begründung des Großreiches Israel durch David.[13] Wenn daher in Ps 104—im Rückbezug auf die in Gen 14 *narrativ* vermittelte Urtradition vom Jerusalemer Königpriestertum—die Inthronisation des davidischen Königs als Einsetzung zum Priester nach der Ordnung Melchisedeks besungen wird, dann geschieht dies zum einen wegen der messianologisch bedeutsamen Vorordnung des Zion vor den Sinai: Die kultische Verehrung des einen und wahren Gottes auf dem Zion wird für eine Zeit fixiert, in welcher die Gottesoffenbarung auf dem Sinai und die Einsetzung Aarons zum Priester Israels noch in weiter Zukunft liegen. Sie geschieht zum anderen um der eschatologischen Signifikanz des Urgeschehens willen: Als Garant für die kultische Integrität des Volkes, dessen Herrscher er ist, verbürgt der Priesterkönig nach der Ordnung Melchisedeks Israels Heil auf ewig.

---

[10] S. H. Gese, „Der Messias," in idem, *Zur biblischen Theologie: Alttestamentliche Vorträge* (3. Aufl.; Tübingen: Mohr Siebeck, 1989), 128–151.

[11] Heb 2:17; 3:1; 4:14–15; 5:1, 5, 10; 6:20; 7:26–28; 8:1, 3; 9:7, 11, 25; 10:21.

[12] Einen Überblick über den gegenwärtigen Stand der Forschung bietet H.-J. Fabry, „Die Messiaserwartung in den Handschriften von Qumran," in *Wisdom and Apocalypticism in the Dead Sea Scrolls and in the Biblical Tradition* (ed. F. García Martínez; BETL 168; Leuven: Peeters, 2003), 357–384.

[13] M. Delcor, „Melchizedek from Genesis to the Qumran Texts and the Epistle to the Hebrews," *JSJ* 2 (1971): 115–135, 119–120 greift theologisch zu kurz, wenn er die Verankerung der Zehntabgabe in der Väterzeit als den Skopus von Gen 14 benennt.

Bereits in alttestamentlicher Tradition findet sich also die messianologische Zusammenführung von Königtum und Priestertum bezeugt als
ein Vorstellungskomplex ohne Verbindung zum aaronitisch-levitischen
Priestertum (vgl. 1 Chr 21:26).[14] In diesen gleichzeitig urzeitlichen und
endzeitlichen *davidischen* Traditionszusammenhang ordnet der Autor
des Hebräerbriefes das Christusgeschehen ein, wenn er Christus als König und Hohepriester identifiziert und dabei das Priestertum Christi auf
Melchisedek zurückführt.

Der Hebräerbrief aber geht in der Adaption der Traditionen noch
einen Schritt weiter. Und er *muss* weitergehen, da er das Königpriestertum Christi nicht als ein irdisches, sondern als ein himmlisches Priestertum klassifiziert. Auf welcher Grundlage diese Klassifikation erfolgt,
zeigt die Analyse der Beschreibung Melchisedeks in Heb 7:1–3. Hier wird
Melchisedek zunächst in Anlehnung an Gen 14 als Priesterkönig von
Salem vorgestellt; was aber folgt, hat keine Parallele in Gen 14. In V. 3
heißt es von Melchisedek: „Er ist vaterlos, mutterlos, ohne Geschlechts-
register (d.h. ohne jedwede Vorfahren) und hat weder Anfang der Tage
noch Ende des Lebens" (ἀπάτωρ ἀμήτωρ ἀγενεαλόγητος, μήτε ἀρχὴν
ἡμερῶν μήτε ζωῆς τέλος ἔχων). Wie kommt der Verfasser des Hebräerbriefes zu dieser Charakterisierung Melchisedeks und welche Vorstellung
wird hier auf Melchisedek übertragen?

Um zu einer Antwort zu gelangen, muss man sich klarmachen, was
es bedeutet, wenn im Hebräerbrief Melchisedeks Existenz als ewig charakterisiert wird. Denn nichts anderes besagen die genannten Adjektive
in ihrer Gesamtheit. Ewigkeit—das bedeutet im Blick auf die Zukunft
Unsterblichkeit, das bedeutet im Blick auf die Vergangenheit Präexistenz. Melchisedek ist also *wesenseins mit Gott*. In der alttestamentlich-
jüdischen Tradition aber gibt es nur eine „Person" neben Gott, die in
dieser Weise charakterisiert wird: die Weisheit. Melchisedek ist im Hebräerbrief die irdische Manifestation der Weisheit.

Um allerdings diesen Text sowie im Anschluss auch den Text
11QMelch der weisheitlichen Tradition theologiegeschichtlich zuordnen
zu können, muss man das Gesamtbild der weisheitlichen Entwicklung
von der persischen bis in die hellenistische Zeit vor Augen haben. Dies
soll, da in der Qumranforschung der personale Aspekt der Weisheit in

---

[14] Zum Priesterdienst Davids und seiner Nachkommen vgl. auch 2 Sam 6:12–19 (David); 1 Kön 8:5 (Salomo); 2 Sam 8:18 (Söhne Davids); 2 Kön 16:12–13 (Ahas).

der Diskussion der Weisheitsschriften kaum erörtert wird, hier in aller Kürze und im Rückgriff auf Vorarbeiten zum Thema geschehen.[15]

EXKURS 1:

DIE ENTWICKLUNG DER WEISHEITLICHEN PERSONVORSTELLUNG
VON DER PERSISCHEN BIS IN DIE HELLENISTISCHE ZEIT

Bereits in Prov 8 erscheint die Weisheit als eine personale göttliche Größe. Ihr Wesen wird lokal und temporal im uneigentlichen, d.h. den Begriff von Raum und Zeit transzendierenden, Sinne qualifiziert. Sie erscheint als eine Person der Vorzeit (Prov 8:22–29), deren „Ort" bei Gott ist (Prov 8:30). Die Weisheit ist— in systematisch-theologischer Terminologie—göttlicher Natur und präexistent. Die Personifizierung dieser göttlichen, aber von Gott selbst unterschiedenen Größe entspricht dem Personsein Gottes und der personalen Struktur der Offenbarung vom Sinai her, wo Gott aus seiner transzendenten Verborgenheit heraus- und in den irdischen Raum der Geschichte eintrat.

Die Frage, warum es überhaupt zur Vorstellung einer göttlichen, aber von Gott unterschiedenen Person kommt, findet ihre Antwort im Schöpfungsgedanken, der ein Sein und Handeln des ewigen und jenseitigen Gottes in Zeit und Raum impliziert. Die Erkenntnis einer gleichzeitig verborgenen und irdisch manifesten Existenz Gottes führt im Zuge der theologischen Systematisierung zur Unterscheidung des für-sich-seienden, irdisch unverfügbaren Gottes von Gott als demjenigen, der sich im Schöpfungsakt in Beziehung zur Welt und zum Menschen setzt und daher auch weltlich erkannt werden kann. Man könnte auch sagen: Die Weisheit ist die Anwesenheitsform Gottes im Irdischen; sie ist die Form, in welcher Gott immanent fassbar und erfahrbar wird. Daher wird bereits in den Texten aus persischer Zeit die Weisheit als das Ordnungsprinzip identifiziert, das der Schöpfung zugrunde liegt. Als solches durchwaltet sie alle Bereiche des Irdischen, d.h. als physikalisches Grundprinzip den Bereich der Natur (Prov 8:22–31), als ethische Norm den menschlichen Bereich, der wesenhaft durch die Beziehung zu Gott und damit durch das Wort der Tora konstituiert ist (Prov

---

[15] U. Mittmann-Richert, „Thesen zur offenbarungsgeschichtlichen Grundlegung der Christologie," in *Heil und Geschichte: Die Geschichtsbezogenheit des Heils und das Problem der Heilsgeschichte in der biblischen Tradition und in der theologischen Deutung* (ed. J. Frey, S. Krauter und H. Lichtenberger; WUNT 248; Tübingen: Mohr Siebeck, 2009), 307–331; eadem, „Joseph und Asenath: Die Weisheit Israels und die Weisheit der Heiden," in *Biblical Figures in Deuterocanonical and Cognate Literature: Conference of the ISDCL at Tübingen, Germany, 30 June – 4 July 2007* (ed. H. Lichtenberger und U. Mittmann-Richert; Deuterocanonical and Cognate Literature Yearbook 2008; Berlin: de Gruyter, 2009), 239–279. Die genannten Beiträge gründen in der wegweisenden Studie von H. Gese, „Die Weisheit, der Menschensohn und die Ursprünge der Christologie als konsequente Entfaltung der biblischen Theologie," in idem, *Alttestamentliche Studien* (Tübingen: Mohr Siebeck, 1991), 218–248.

8:12–21). Da in diesem Sinne die Weisheit beide Bereiche vertritt—den himmlischen und den irdischen Bereich—, wird sie zur Mittlerin Gottes an den Menschen. Die Weisheit gibt dem Menschen Anteil an Gott, sie lässt ihn gleichsam
an Gott teilnehmen. Gott selbst vermittelt sich in seiner Schöpfungsordnung an
die Welt, und in der menschlichen Erkenntnis dieser Schöpfungsordnung als
Erkenntnis der Weisheit kommt diese Vermittlung zu ihrem Ziel.[16]

Entscheidend für die Weiterentwicklung der Weisheit im frühjüdischen
Schrifttum der hellenistischen Zeit ist die Personalität der Weisheit und die
Worthaftigkeit der weisheitlichen Vermittlung Gottes an den Menschen. Sie ist
entscheidend, weil auch in den Geschichtstraditionen Israels die Personalität
der Offenbarung und ihr Wortcharakter das Offenbarwerden des Gottes vom
Sinai kennzeichnen. Daher wird nun die Weisheit als Mittlerin nicht nur der
Schöpfung, sondern auch der geschichtlichen Offenbarung am Sinai erkannt,
mehr noch: als das Wort Gottes selbst. Dabei werden die Sinai- und die Zions-
tradition zusammengeführt in der Vorstellung von der irdischen Einwohnung
der mit Gottes Wort identifizierten Weisheit in Zion (Sir 24:3–12). So wird die
Weisheit automatisch auch zur kultischen Größe und konsequenterweise mit
der Schekinah identifiziert.[17] Das aber bedeutet: Die Weisheit wird erkannt als
der auf Erden offenbare Gott. Sie *ist* der im Wort der Selbstteilgabe auf Erden
in Person dem Menschen gegenübertretende Gott, der *deus praesens*. Es liegt in
der Konsequenz dieser Entwicklung, dass in einem letzten Schritt die Person der
Weisheit im Bereich des Irdischen visionär und auditionär manifest wird. Dies
belegt insbesondere die Weisheit Salomos, die im Fortlauf dieser Analyse noch
ausführlich zur Sprache kommt, da sie den theologischen Bezugspunkt für die
Identifikation sowohl Christi als auch Melchiseks im Hebräerbrief darstellt.
Hier genügt es, festzuhalten, dass die neutestamentliche Identifikation Melchiseks mit der Weisheit ein *personales* Weisheitsverständnis voraussetzt, wie es
in den alttestamentlichen und frühjüdischen Weisheitsschriften die Grundlage
sowohl der Schöpfungs- als auch der Geschichtstheologie bildet. In diesen beiden Zusammenhängen ist die Weisheit ausnahmslos personhaft gedacht. Die
Erkenntnis Gottes erwächst aus der Begegnung mit Gott als dem, der sich in
Gestalt der Weisheit als Schöpfer der Erde und Herr der Geschichte offenbart.

Der Hebräerbrief steht im alt- und neutestamentlichen Gesamtzusammenhang der Traditionen zeitlich am Ende der weisheitlichen Entwicklung und markiert innerhalb des Neuen Testaments einen Schlusspunkt.
Bemerkenswert ist, wie tief diese späte neutestamentliche Schrift in der
frühjüdischen Weisheitstheologie verwurzelt ist und wie selbstverständlich sie von einer sichtbaren und hörbaren Manifestation der Person der

---

[16] Vgl. Gese, „Weisheit,“ 218–226.

[17] Vgl. B. Janowski, „Gottes Weisheit in Jerusalem: Sir 24 und die biblische *Schekina*-
Theologie,“ in *Biblical Figures in Deuterocanonical and Cognate Literature*, 1–29; Gese,
„Weisheit,“ 226–231.

Weisheit ausgeht, wenn sie Melchisedek Präexistenz und ewiges Sein zuschreibt und ihn auf diese Weise mit der Weisheit identifiziert. Das aber heißt: *Melchisedek ist der offenbare Gott in Person.*

Dass im Hebräerbrief genau dies die Vorstellung ist, zeigt auch die zweite Vershälfte von Heb 7:3. Hier heißt es: „Er gleicht dem Sohn Gottes und bleibt Priester in Ewigkeit" (ἀφωμοιωμένος δὲ τῷ υἱῷ τοῦ θεοῦ, μένει ἱερεὺς εἰς τὸ διηνεκές). Der Sohn Gottes—das ist im Hebräerbrief der mit Gott wesenseine Christus, der in seiner irdischen Existenzform Gott selbst auf Erden offenbar gemacht hat. Christus wird also auch als irdische Erscheinungsform der Weisheit identifiziert und Melchisedek an die Seite gestellt. Die Doppelheit der Personen ist Ausdruck einer heilsgeschichtlichen Differenzierung: Melchisedek ist die irdische Erscheinungsform der Weisheit in der Zeit des alten Bundes, Christus die irdische Erscheinungsform der Weisheit in der Zeit des neuen Bundes. So kommt für den Verfasser die irdische Selbstoffenbarung Gottes zu ihrem Ziel in Person der mit seinem Sohn Jesus Christus identischen Weisheit.

Dass in der Tat im Hebräerbrief auch Christus mit der Weisheit identifiziert wird, bestätigt der Anfang des Briefes, Heb 1:1–3:

1 Πολυμερῶς καὶ πολυτρόπως πάλαι ὁ θεὸς λαλήσας τοῖς πατράσιν ἐν τοῖς προφήταις

2 ἐπ' ἐσχάτου τῶν ἡμερῶν τούτων ἐλάλησεν ἡμῖν ἐν υἱῷ, ὃν ἔθηκεν κληρονόμον πάντων, δι' οὗ καὶ ἐποίησεν τοὺς αἰῶνας·

3 ὃς ὢν ἀπαύγασμα τῆς δόξης καὶ χαρακτὴρ τῆς ὑποστάσεως αὐτοῦ, φέρων τε τὰ πάντα τῷ ῥήματι τῆς δυνάμεως αὐτοῦ, καθαρισμὸν τῶν ἁμαρτιῶν ποιησάμενος ἐκάθισεν ἐν δεξιᾷ τῆς μεγαλωσύνης ἐν ὑψηλοῖς.

1 Viele Male und auf vielerlei Weise hat Gott einst zu den Vätern gesprochen durch die Propheten;

2 in dieser Endzeit aber hat er zu uns gesprochen durch den Sohn, den er zum Erben des Alls eingesetzt und durch den er auch die Welt erschaffen hat;

3 er ist der Abglanz seiner Herrlichkeit und das Abbild seiner Person [Hypostase]; er trägt das All durch sein machtvolles Wort, hat die Reinigung von den Sünden bewirkt und sich dann zur Rechten der Majestät in der Höhe gesetzt.

Die Motivik dieser Verse ist typisch weisheitlich: Christus ist der Schöpfungsmittler und daher rechtmäßiger Inhaber des göttlichen Throns (vgl. Sir 24:4). Er ist dies aber als der von jeher mit Gott wesenseine Sohn. In diesem Zusammenhang ist ausdrücklich auf den hier verwendeten Begriff ὑπόστασις, „Hypostase" hinzuweisen (Heb 1:3). Dass Christus dabei nicht direkt als göttliche Hypostase bezeichnet wird, sondern als

Abbild der göttlichen Hypostase, hängt mit der schon erwähnten heilsgeschichtlichen Unterscheidung der Erscheinungsform der Weisheit zusammen: als Melchisedek zur Zeit des alten, als Christus zur Zeit des
neuen Bundes. Der Begriff „Hypostase" meint dabei nichts anderes, als
was im bisherigen Verlauf der Argumentation mit „Person" bezeichnet
wurde. Es geht um die Selbstentäußerung Gottes und sein personales
Offenbarwerden in Schöpfung und Geschichte im Sinne der Unterscheidung des irdisch offenbaren Gottes von dem in transzendenter Verborgenheit existierenden Gott.

Die Relevanz, die diese weisheitliche Melchisedek-Christus-Reflexion
des Hebräerbriefes für das Verständnis von 11QMelch hat, ergibt sich an
dieser Stelle aus der Tatsache, dass der Autor des Briefes ausdrücklich Bezug nimmt auf das frühjüdische Schrifttum. Heb 1:2–3 ist ein freies Zitat
aus dem großen Lob der Weisheit in Weish 7, wo es in V. 24–26 heißt:

24   πάσης γὰρ κινήσεως κινητικώτερον σοφία,
     διήκει δὲ καὶ χωρεῖ διὰ πάντων διὰ τὴν καθαρότητα.
25   ἀτμὶς γάρ ἐστιν τῆς τοῦ θεοῦ δυνάμεως
     καὶ ἀπόρροια τῆς τοῦ παντοκράτορος δόξης εἰλικρινής·
     διὰ τοῦτο οὐδὲν μεμιαμμένον εἰς αὐτὴν παρεμπίπτει.
26   ἀπαύγασμα γάρ ἐστιν φωτὸς ἀιδίου
     καὶ ἔσοπτρον ἀκηλίδωτον τῆς τοῦ θεοῦ ἐνεργείας
     καὶ εἰκὼν τῆς ἀγαθότητος αὐτοῦ.

24   Denn die Weisheit ist beweglicher als alle Bewegung,
     sie geht und dringt durch alles wegen ihrer Reinheit.
25   Denn sie ist ein Nebelschleier der Macht Gottes
     und eine Emanation der lauteren Herrlichkeit des Allmächtigen;
     darum kann nichts Unreines in sie hineinkommen.
26   Denn sie ist der Abglanz des ewigen Lichts
     und der fleckenlose Spiegel der Wirksamkeit Gottes
     und das Ebenbild seiner Güte.

Die Identifikation Christi mit der Weisheit findet im Hebräerbrief in der
direkten Übertragung der Wesensbeschreibung der Weisheit nach Weish
7:25–26 auf Christus statt. Wenn daher in Heb 7:3 von Melchisedek
gesagt wird, er gleiche dem Sohn, dann zielt dies auf Christi Identität
mit der Weisheit und erklärt, warum Melchisedek als von jeher und
in Ewigkeit existierend vorgestellt wird. Die Gleichheit mit dem Sohn
Gottes manifestiert in diesem Zusammenhang sein göttliches Wesen.

Von besonderer Bedeutung im Blick auf Christi und Melchisedeks
priesterlichen Status ist bei der Übertragung von Weish 7 auf Christus
die Aussage über die Reinheit der Weisheit in Weish 7:24–25. Sie zielt,
ähnlich wie in Sir 24:10–11, auf die kultische Integrität der gesamten

Schöpfung, welche die Weisheit garantiert. Auf die Frage nach der kultischen Funktion der Weisheit läuft in Heb 1:3 die gesamte Argumentation des Textes zu. Denn der Abschnitt endet mit dem Hinweis auf das Sühnewirken des mit der Weisheit identifizierten Schöpfungsmittlers. Er wird kombiniert mit einer zitatartigen Anspielung auf Ps 110:1 und damit gerade auf denjenigen Psalm, der ebenfalls von Melchisedek als dem Urbild des davidischen Priesterkönigtums handelt (Ps 110:4).

Der Autor des Hebräerbriefes greift in der Identifikation des Priesterkönigs Melchisedek mit der präexistenten Weisheit allerdings nicht nur auf Weish 7 zurück, sondern auch auf Weish 18, wo die Weisheit als Weltenpriester auf Erden erscheint und Sühne schafft für Israel.

2. Die priesterliche Personifikation der Weisheit in Weish 18

Die Bedeutung von Weish 18 für die Rekonstruktion der Entwicklung der Weisheit in hellenistischer Zeit wurde lange Zeit verkannt,[18] weil innerhalb dieser Weisheitsschrift ein Umbruch der Weisheitskonzeption und der Terminologie stattzufinden scheint und fraglich ist, ob in Kapitel 18 überhaupt von der Weisheit die Rede ist.[19] Denn nach dem Preis der Weisheit in Weish 7 erscheint in Weish 18 der auf Erden offenbare Gott plötzlich in männlicher Form hypostasiert bzw. personifiziert, und statt der weiblichen Bezeichnung „Sophia" ist nun der männliche Begriff „Logos" verwendet (Weish 18:15). Dass dabei allerdings Logos und Sophia miteinander identifiziert werden (vgl. Weish 9:1–2),[20] zeigt

---

[18] S. Mittmann-Richert, „Joseph und Aseneth," 260–263, wo Weish 18 erstmals in die Rekonstruktion miteinbezogen wurde.

[19] Die Fülle der Literatur zur Weisheit Salomos ist groß. Um so auffallender ist, dass in vielen Veröffentlichungen zum Thema die Frage nach einem möglichen Zusammenhang der Konzepte nicht einmal gestellt wird. Beispielhaft sei hier auf die Monographie zum Thema von M. Nehr, *Wesen und Wirken der Weisheit in der Sapientia Salomonis* (BZAW 333; Berlin: de Gruyter, 2004), verwiesen, in welcher Weish 18 gar nicht behandelt wird und ohne weiteren Kommentar als offensichtlich nicht zum Thema gehörig aus dem weisheitlichen Gesamtzusammenhang ausgeschlossen wird.

[20] Gegen H. Hübner, *Die Weisheit Salomons* (ATD Apokryphen 4; Göttingen: Vandenhoeck & Ruprecht, 1999), 215.—Zu bestreiten ist in diesem Zusammenhang auch die These von H. Engel, *Das Buch der Weisheit* (Neuer Stuttgarter Kommentar Altes Testament 16; Stuttgart: Katholisches Bibelwerk, 1998), dass die Personifikation sowohl der Weisheit als auch des Logos als „literarische Personifikation" zu deuten sei und „nicht eine selbständige personhafte Gestalt ‚neben' oder gar außerhalb von Gott" bezeichne (247; vgl. 283).

sich daran, dass es vom Logos heißt, sein Herabkommen auf die Erde
geschehe von seinem himmlischen Thron aus (Weish 18:15). Die himmlische Throngenossin Gottes zu sein, aber ist bereits in den alten Weis-
heitstexten das Charakteristikum der Weisheit (Prov 8:30; Sir 24:4). Die
Identifikation von Weisheit und Logos ist schon deshalb konsequent,
weil vom Sinai her das *Wort* das Offenbarungsmedium Gottes ist, durch
welches Gott als Person erkennbar wird, weshalb, wie bereits erwähnt,
die Weisheit, als Norm der Gottesbeziehung, im offenbarungsgeschichtlichen Kontext auch mit der Tora identifiziert werden kann. In der Weisheit Salomos ist daher der vom himmlischen Thron steigende Logos die
Personifikation des göttlichen Offenbarungswortes und somit identisch
mit der Weisheit. Wie konkret diese Personifizierung werden kann, zeigt
die Tatsache, dass in Weish 18:15 der Logos (ὁ παντοδύναμος ... λόγος) als „harter Kriegsmann" (ἀπότομος πολεμιστής) betitelt wird. Dieser Titel hängt mit der Funktion zusammen, die der Logos im fraglichen
Zusammenhang hat: Er muss Gericht halten und Gottes Recht auf Erden
durchsetzen. Geschichtlich ist dabei zunächst auf Israels Zeit in Ägypten
angespielt und wird das Gericht als Strafe an den Ägyptern verstanden,
der Macht, die Israel versklavt. Ägypten steht hier, wie in anderen alttestamentlichen und frühjüdischen Texten auch, für das Urböse, das am
Anfang der Geschichte Israel in Gefangenschaft hielt und zum Typos der
gegengöttlichen Macht wurde.

Im Blick auf 11QMelch ist Weish 18 aus zweierlei Gründen interessant:
Zum einen erscheint auch in 11QMelch Melchisedek als der Gerichts-
herr, der das Gericht an Belial und seiner Gefolgschaft vollstreckt und
die von Belial Versklavten und Gefangenen befreit (1QMelch II:4–6, 9,
13–14, 21–23); zum anderen verbindet die beiden Texte das priesterliche
Element. Denn im Anschluss an die Gerichtsszene erscheint in Weish
18:21 die wiederum männlich verkörperte Weisheit nun in priesterlicher Funktion und entsühnt Israel. Die Entsühnung wird im genannten
Zusammenhang notwendig, weil in V. 20 auch von Israel gesagt wird,
dass es den Gotteszorn auf sich gezogen habe.

Allerdings ergibt sich an dieser Stelle im Blick auf die weisheitliche Gesamtkonzeption des Kapitels ein Problem: Denn die Weisheit
erscheint hier, da Logos und Weltenpriester einander gegenüberstehen,
in doppelter Personifikation. Wie ist diese personifizierte Doppelheit des
göttlichen Wirkens auf Erden zu verstehen? Da die Antwort nur auf der
Grundlage der in Weish 18 rezipierten Tradition gegeben werden kann,
soll die Verstehensgrundlage dieses Textes in einem zweiten Exkurs erar-
beitet werden. Er führt die in Exkurs 1 ausgezogene Linie traditions-

geschichtlich weiter und schließt den Überblick über die weisheitliche Gesamtentwicklung ab.[21]

EXKURS 2:
DIE DOPPELTE MÄNNLICHE PERSONIFIKATION DER WEISHEIT IN WEISH 18

In Weish 18 zeigt sich, dass die Vorstellung von der Weisheit als einer personalen göttlichen Größe, wie sie in hellenistischer Zeit am eindrücklichsten Sir 24 und 1 Hen. 42:1–2 dokumentieren, im Kontext der ägyptischen Diaspora nochmals eine Weiterentwicklung erfahren hat hin zu einer Konkretisierung ihres irdischen Erscheinens: Die Weisheit wird auf Erden visuell und auditionell manifest. Dies belegt gleich am Anfang des Kapitels die Schilderung des Herabkommens des Logos von seinem göttlichen Thron:

14 ἡσύχου γὰρ σιγῆς περιεχούσης τὰ πάντα
  καὶ νυκτὸς ἐν ἰδίῳ τάχει μεσαζούσης
15 ὁ παντοδύναμός σου λόγος ἀπ᾽ οὐρανῶν ἐκ θρόνων βασιλείων
  ἀπότομος πολεμιστὴς εἰς μέσον τῆς ὀλεθρίας ἥλατο γῆς
16 ξίφος ὀξὺ τὴν ἀνυπόκριτον ἐπιταγήν σου φέρων
  καὶ στὰς ἐπλήρωσεν τὰ πάντα θανάτου
  καὶ οὐρανοῦ μὲν ἥπτετο, βεβήκει δ᾽ ἐπὶ γῆς.

14 Denn als tiefes Schweigen das All umfing
  und die Nacht in der ihr eigenen Geschwindigkeit ihre Mitte erreichte,
15 da fuhr dein allmächtiges Wort vom Himmel herab, vom königlichen
    Thron,
  als harter Kriegsmann, mitten in die Zerstörung der Erde,
16 und trug als scharfes Schwert deinen unmissverständlichen Befehl
  und stellte sich hin und erfüllte das All mit Tod;
  dabei berührte es den Himmel, schritt aber auf der Erde einher.

Der Logos erscheint als Kriegsmann, der auf der Erde in Ausübung seines Richteramtes einherschreitet, dabei aber weiterhin den Himmel berührt. Er ist also derjenige, der gleichzeitig den irdischen und den himmlischen Bereich vertritt, was ebenfalls auf seine Identität mit der Sophia schließen lässt. Nicht weniger konkret ist das Auftreten des Weltenpriesters in Weish 18:21–25 geschildert:

---

[21] Es sei an dieser Stelle angemerkt, dass Exkurs 2 die verkürzte Übernahme des entsprechenden Exkurses aus dem in Anm. 15 bereits genannten Beitrag „Joseph und Aseneth" darstellt. Die nochmalige Präsentation im vorliegenden Kontext geschieht um des besseren Verständnisses der auf 11QMelch zulaufenden Argumentation willen, aber auch deshalb, weil die Forschungsbereiche, in welchen die aus Weish 18 gewonnenen Ergebnisse relevant werden, relativ weit auseinander liegen und der Kreis der jeweiligen Rezipienten nicht deckungsgleich ist.

20c οὐκ ἐπὶ πολὺ ἔμεινεν ἡ ὀργή·
21 σπεύσας γὰρ ἀνὴρ ἄμεμπτος προεμάχησεν
τὸ τῆς ἰδίας λειτουργίας ὅπλον
προσευχὴν καὶ θυμιάματος ἐξιλασμὸν κομίσας.
ἀντέστη τῷ θυμῷ καὶ πέρας ἐπέθηκε τῇ συμφορᾷ
δεικνὺς ὅτι σός ἐστιν θεράπων·
22 ἐνίκησεν δὲ τὸν χόλον οὐκ ἰσχύι τοῦ σώματος,
οὐχ ὅπλων ἐνεργείᾳ,
ἀλλὰ λόγῳ τὸν κολάζοντα ὑπέταξεν
ὅρκους πατέρων καὶ διαθήκας ὑπομνήσας.
....
24 ἐπὶ γὰρ ποδήρους ἐνδύματος ἦν ὅλος ὁ κόσμος,
καὶ πατέρων δόξαι ἐπὶ τετραστίχου λίθων γλυφῆς,
καὶ μεγαλωσύνη σου ἐπὶ διαδήματος κεφαλῆς αὐτοῦ.
25 τούτοις εἶξεν ὁ ὀλεθρεύων.

20c Aber der Zorn [Gottes] währte nicht lang.
21 Denn ein Mann ohne Fehl eilte herbei und kämpfte für sie
und hatte mitgebracht die Waffe seines *eigenen* [priesterlichen] Dienstes:
Gebet und sühnendes Räucherwerk.
Er widerstand dem Zorn und machte dem Unheil ein Ende
und zeigte so, dass er dein Diener ist.
22 Er überwand aber den Zorn nicht mit Körperkraft
und nicht mit Waffengewalt,
sondern unterwarf den Strafgewaltigen mit dem Wort,
indem er an die den Vätern geltenden Eide und Bundesschlüsse erinnerte.
....
24 Denn auf seinem fußlangen Gewand befand sich die ganze Welt,
und die Doxa der Väter stand eingraviert auf dem vierreihigen Schmuck
von Steinen,
und deine Majestät war auf dem Diadem seines Hauptes.
25 Davor wich der Verderber.

Die Zusammengehörigkeit der beiden Personen zeigt schon die Tatsache, dass beide allein durch das Wort als das Medium der Selbstoffenbarung Gottes auf Erden handeln (V. 16, 22). Äußerlich scheint der Textabschnitt Weish 18:20–25 auf Num 17 anzuspielen, wo die Rede ist vom Aufbegehren Israels gegen Gott in der Wüste und von der Vernichtung großer Teile der Gemeinde. Sie endet durch das Einschreiten Aarons, der zwischen die Toten und die Lebenden tritt und für Israel Sühne wirkt. Die sprachlichen Bezüge aber zeigen, dass hier ein ganz anderer Text im Vordergrund steht, nämlich 1 Chr 21. Es ist dieser Text, der die Personenkonstellation in Weish 18 erhellt.

Auch in 1 Chr 21 geht es um ein Strafhandeln Gottes an Israel; der Grund des göttlichen Zornes ist in diesem Fall aber nicht das Volk, sondern David, der mit einer Volkszählung Gottes Eigentumsrecht an Israel verletzt hat. Wegen dieses Vergehens sendet Gott, als irdischen Repräsentanten seiner selbst, einen Strafengel nach Jerusalem, um die Stadt zu vernichten (1 Chr 21:14–15). Dass das, was nun geschieht, dem Verfasser der Weisheit Salomos das Grundmuster der theologischen Reflexion in Weish 18 geliefert hat und das Kapitel insgesamt—nicht nur der von der Entsühnung Israels handelnde zweite Teil—von 1 Chr 21 her konzipiert ist, ergibt sich aus der Tatsache, dass die Beschreibung des Logos, der als Kriegsmann vom Himmel steigt, im ersten Teil des Berichts genau der des Strafengels entspricht. Dieser Engel steht zwischen Himmel und Erde und hält in der Hand ein Schwert, ausgestreckt über Jerusalem (1 Chr 21:16). Dies ist in der oben zitierten Stelle Weish 18:16 aufgenommen, wo es heißt, dass der Logos mit dem Schwert in der Hand als Vollstrecker des göttlichen Gerichts sein Werk tut, indem er in Person Himmel und Erde verbindet.

Die Ersetzung des Strafengels durch den Logos ist theologiegeschichtlich hochbedeutsam. Sie eröffnet einen Einblick nicht nur in die Entwicklung der Weisheit, sondern auch in die Entwicklung der Angelologie. Denn in dem Maße, wie in hellenistischer Zeit die Vorstellung vom himmlischen Heer in eine hochdifferenzierte, aber in sich vielfältige Engelslehre überführt wird, tritt die Vorstellung vom Engel des Herrn als dem Boten Gottes auf Erden in den Hintergrund. Und sie *muss* in den Hintergrund treten, da das himmlische Heer der geschaffenen Welt zugehört und die ihm angehörenden Engel trotz ihrer transzendenten Existenz in ihrem Sein und Wesen von Gott unterschieden sind, während der Engel des Herrn (מלאך יהוה) die irdische Erscheinungsform Gottes selbst ist: der offenbare Gott. Am deutlichsten zeigt sich dies in Exod 3, der Erzählung von der Berufung des Mose, wo es im Visionsteil zunächst der Engel des Herrn ist, der Mose am Dornbusch im Feuer erscheint (Exod 3:2), in der Audition aber Gott selbst, der zur Mose spricht und sich ihm offenbart (Exod 3:4–15). Der Unterschied ist ein schöpfungstheologischer. Da gleichzeitig im Bereich der Weisheit—im Zuge ihrer offenbarungsgeschichtlichen Aufweitung in hellenistischer Zeit—die Person der Weisheit als der auf Erden offenbare Gott erkannt wird, ist es traditionsgeschichtlich konsequent, wenn in den Texten der Spätzeit die Weisheit an die Stelle des Engels des Herrn tritt. Es ist nun die Weisheit, die Gottes Willen offenbar macht und in der Kraft des Wortes durchsetzt. So auch in Weish 18:14, wo der Strafengel aus 1 Chr 21 als der vom himmlischen Thron herabfahrende Logos betitelt ist.

Entscheidend für das Verständnis von Weish 18 aber ist das, was in 1 Chr 21 auf das Auftreten des Strafengels folgt: Angesichts der Unzahl derer, die in Israel dem Schwert des Engels zum Opfer fallen, bekommt Gott, obwohl er selbst den Strafengel ausgesandt hat und in dessen Handeln wirksam ist, Mitleid mit seinem Volk und gebietet dem Engel Einhalt (1 Chr 21:15b, 27). Das heißt: Gott stellt sich gegen Gott. Gott stellt sich gegen sich selbst und hebt den Richterspruch auf. Da aber die Aufhebung des Richterspruches die Entsühnung Israels voraussetzt, weist Gott David an, auf einem von ihm eigens dazu bestimmten Stück Land einen Altar zu bauen und Opfer darzubringen. Das Stück Land (die Tenne Ornans) ist der Grund und Boden des späteren Jerusalemer Tempels. Und David, der Gott ja eigentlich den Anlass für sein Strafhandeln geliefert hat, fungiert hier als Priester, der das Opfer darbringt, das Israel entsühnt. Es handelt sich in 1 Chr 21 also um nicht weniger als die Gründungserzählung des Jerusalemer Tempels und Kultes, in welcher David als Priesterkönig auftritt. Während allerdings in 1 Chr 21 Gott die Entsühnung Israels durch David vollziehen lässt, wirkt er in Weish 18:21–24 selbst die Entsühnung. Dabei ist—wie schon im Fall des Gerichtswortes Gottes—auch das Wort, das den Strafbefehl aufhebt, personifiziert: Es kommt ein „Mann ohne Fehl" (ἀνὴρ ἄμεμπτος), wie es in Weish 18:21 heißt, und das bedeutet: Es kommt ein Priester. Dass diese priesterliche Gestalt kein irdischer Mensch ist, sondern der seinem Volk in Liebe und Erbarmen zugewandte Gott in Person, zeigt sich an zweierlei: 1. Der Priester trägt ein Gewand, auf welchem die ganze Welt ist (ὅλος ὁ κόσμος). Er ist der Garant der kultischen Integrität der Schöpfung und daher niemand anderes als die Weisheit in Person, die als *principium* der Schöpfung und als *principium* der im Kult manifesten Offenbarung die Welt durchwaltet. 2. Die Entsühnung Israels geschieht nicht durch irdisch vollzogene Opfer, sondern allein durch das Wort (Weish 18:22), wie auch der als strafender Richter auftretende Logos das Gericht allein durch das Wort vollzieht (Weish 18:16). Die beiden Aspekte des Wirkens Gottes nach außen, sein Gerichtshandeln und sein Gnadenhandeln, sind hier in zweifacher Weise hypostasiert bzw. personifiziert, wobei im Gesamtkontext der Weisheit Salomos klar ist, dass es sich in beiden Fällen um die Weisheit Gottes handelt, deren universelle richterliche und kultische Funktion in Weish 7 vor Augen gestellt wurde und die in Weish 18 zur Garantin der göttlichen Weltordnung wird. Dass dabei das Gnadenhandeln Gottes sich in der Entsühnung Israels vollzieht und daher die Weisheit priesterlich personifiziert erscheint, entspricht ganz Sir 24:10, wo die Weisheit ebenfalls das priesterliche Amt auf dem Zion ausübt.

So zeigt sich gerade an der Doppelheit der göttlichen „Personen" in Weish 18, die im Gegenüber Gottes Gerichts- und Gnadenwillen repräsentieren, wie selbstverständlich man in hellenistischer Zeit die theologische Reflexion von der Hypostasenvorstellung her betrieb, die in den alten Texten ihr Pendant in der Vorstellung vom Engel des Herrn als der irdischen Erscheinungsform Gottes selbst hat.

Zieht man von hier aus zunächst wieder die Linie zum Hebräerbrief aus, so zeigt sich, dass die spezifische Konzeption der Weisheit als einer irdisch manifesten und in dieser Manifestation priesterlich wirkenden Größe das Rückgrat der christologischen Reflexion bildet. Für den Autor des Hebräerbriefes konnte Weish 18 deshalb zum Anknüpfungspunkt seiner weisheitlich-priesterlichen Melchisedek-Christologie werden, weil hier das priesterliche Sühnewerk, das nach 1 Chr 21 David vollbringt, *Gott in Person der Weisheit selbst vollzieht.* Aufgrund von Ps 110:4, wo das Davidkönigtum als ewiges Königtum nach der Ordnung Melchisedeks und demnach als Priesterkönigtum klassifiziert wird, konnte Melchisedek als derjenige erscheinen, welcher nach Weish 18 die Entsühnung des Kosmos vollzieht, und d.h. als die irdische Erscheinungsform der Weisheit. Richtet man aber, unabhängig vom Hebräerbrief, von Weish 18 aus den Blick auf die bis heute umrätselte Figur Melchisedeks in 11QMelch, dann ist folgende Erkenntnis von grundlegender interpretatorischer Bedeutung: Die Vorstellung von der Weisheit als einer irdisch manifesten göttlichen Person, die auf Erden den Priesterdienst verrichtet und die kultische Integrität nicht nur Israels, sondern des ganzen Kosmos garantiert, die ferner im eschatologischen Kontext heilstiftend wirkt, ist eine schon Mitte des zweiten Jahrhunderts v.Chr. im Judentum fest verankerte Vorstellung. Die Lösung des Rätsels der Melchisedekfigur in 11QMelch ergibt sich von hier aus schon deshalb von selbst, weil Melchisedek göttlich qualifiziert wird (11QMelch II:10; vgl. 11QMelch II:24–25). Der Rahmen der theologischen Reflexion in 11QMelch ist damit eindeutig kein angelologischer, sondern ein weisheitlicher. Die Frage ist nur, welche besondere Form die weisheitliche Personvorstellung im Kontext des Qumranschrifttums gewinnt.

3. Melchisedek in 11QMelch

Wenn im Folgenden die Interpretation von 11QMelch im traditionsgeschichtlichen Bezug auf die frühjüdischen Weisheitstexte, besonders auf Sir 24 und die Weisheit Salomos, gleichzeitig auf den neutestamentlichen Hebräerbrief vollzogen wird, so geht es—dies sei ausdrücklich angemerkt—nicht darum, literarische Abhängigkeiten zu etablieren oder direkte Bezüge nachzuweisen.[22] Solche Verbindungen der Texte untereinander sind schon wegen der zeitlich, geographisch und theologiegeschichtlich ganz unterschiedlichen Entstehungsbedingungen der Schriften auszuschließen. Es geht vielmehr darum, für die Interpretation von 11QMelch Denkmöglichkeiten in den Raum zu stellen, die in der Qumranforschung bislang nicht oder nur am Rande diskutiert wurden. Vor einer Neuinterpretation des Textes müssen allerdings die bisherigen Lösungsmöglichkeiten erörtert und auf ihre Gültigkeit hin überprüft werden.

Zwei Interpretationsansätze beherrschen gegenwärtig die Forschung zu 11QMelch: zum einen die Identifikation Melchisedeks mit einem Engel, zum anderen die Identifikation Melchisedeks mit dem Menschensohn nach Dan 7. Im letztgenannten Fall wird die Deutung noch dadurch

---

[22] Die These einer direkten Verbindung zwischen dem Autor des Hebräerbriefes und essenischen Kreisen, wie sie etwa Y. Yadin, „The Dead Sea Scrolls and the Epistle to the Hebrews," in *Aspects of the Dead Sea Scrolls* (ed. C. Rabin und Y. Yadin; ScrHier 4; Jerusalem: Magnes, 1958), 36–53, 38; C. Spicq, „L'Épitre aux Hébreux, Apollos, Jean-Baptiste, les Hellénistes et Qumran," *RevQ* 1 (1959): 365–391, 390, und Delcor, „Melchizedek," 126–127, vertraten, ist nicht zu halten.

erschwert, dass auch die Frage, was für eine Gestalt der Menschensohn sei, höchst umstritten ist und von den meisten Forschern die Antwort ebenfalls im Rahmen der Angelologie gegeben wird. Weil dennoch die Begründungsmuster ganz unterschiedlich sind, sollen im Folgenden die beiden Deutungsansätze gesondert betrachtet werden.

3.1. *Melchisedek als Engel*

Bei der generellen Identifikation Melchisedeks mit einem Engelwesen,[23] verweist man gemeinhin auf die Völker- oder Erzengelvorstellung. Zumeist wird in diesem Zusammenhang Melchisedek mit Michael identifiziert (vgl. Dan 10:13).[24] Allerdings entsteht bei dieser Klassifikation Melchisedeks als eines Engelwesens eine Schwierigkeit. Sie liegt in der offensichtlichen Überordnung Melchisedeks über das gesamte himmlische Heer (11QMelch II:14).[25] An zwei Stellen wird, wenn man der gängigen Textrekonstruktion folgt, Melchisedek sogar ausdrücklich „Gott" genannt: אלוהים (11QMelch II:10, 24–25), was nicht sofort interpretatorisch relativiert und umgedeutet werden sollte.[26] Denn auch wenn der Terminus אלוהים in anderen Kontexten wie den Sabbatliedern als Bezeichnung für die im himmlischen Heiligtum priesterlich dienenden Engel verwendet werden kann, so ist damit doch nie ein einzelnes Engelwesen bezeichnet. אלוהים *als Singular* findet sich—mit Ausnahme der Belege in 11QMelch—nur als Bezeichnung für Gott selbst, gerade

---

[23] S. z.B. F. García Martínez, *Qumran and Apocalyptic: Studies on the Aramaic Texts from Qumran* (STDJ 9; Leiden: Brill, 1992), 176. Wie selbstverständlich man Melchisedek als Engel klassifiziert, zeigt der Beitrag von G.G. Xeravits, „Wisdom Traits in the Qumranic Presentation of the Eschatological Prophet," in *Wisdom and Apocalypticism in the Dead Sea Scrolls and in the Biblical Tradition*, 183–192, der zu Beginn seiner Analyse von 11QMelch Melchisedek als „angelic protagonist" vorstellt, ohne diese Klassifikation inhaltlich zu begründen (188).

[24] So bereits A.S. van der Woude, „Melchisedek als himmlische Erlösergestalt in den neugefundenen eschatologischen Midraschim aus Qumran Höhle XI," *OtSt* 14 (1965): 354–373, 368–373. S. auch Delcor, „Melchizedek," 125; García Martínez, *Qumran and Apocalyptic*, 369; J.C. VanderKam, *The Dead Sea Scrolls Today* (Grand Rapids: Eerdmans, 1994), 171; J.R. Davila, „Melchizedek, Michael, and War in Heaven," *SBLSP* 35 (1997): 259–272; P. Alexander, *The Mystical Texts: Songs of the Sabbath Sacrifice and Related Manuscripts* (Library of Second Temple Studies 61; London: T&T Clark, 2006), 56–57.

[25] Vgl. Heb 1:4, wo ausdrücklich die Überordnung des mit der Weisheit identifizierten Christus über die Engel festgestellt wird und damit die *Un*gleichheit des Wesens.

[26] Vgl. J.A. Fitzmyer, „Further Light on Melchizedek from Qumran Cave 11," *JBL* 86 (1967): 25–41, 32. Gegen G.J. Brooke, „Melchizedek," *ABD* 4:684–688, 685.

auch in den *Sabbatopferliedern*.[27] Und ebenso häufig wie mit dem Plural
אלוהים[28] werden in den *Sabbatopferliedern* die Engel mit dem Plural
אלים[29] benannt.

Dass überhaupt die Engel als אלוהים bezeichnet werden können, verdankt sich Ps 29:1; 89:7 (vgl. Exod 15:11) und setzt traditionsgeschichtlich die Auseinandersetzung mit den heidnischen Göttern voraus, deren
Depotenzierung und gleichzeitige angelologische Integration das Bemü-
hen Israels zeigt, innerhalb des monotheistischen Gottesglaubens das
Verhältnis der himmlischen Wesen zu Gott genau zu bestimmen.[30] Gerade weil aber die göttliche Betitelung der Engel in der jüdischen Tradition *nicht* auf die Wesensgleichheit Gottes und der Engel zielt, sondern,
ganz im Gegenteil, auf die Unterscheidung ihres Wesens von dem des
ungeschaffenen, ewigen Gottes, wird in dem Maße, wie man in hellenistischer Zeit nicht nur in Qumran, sondern im Judentum allgemein
die Angelologie immer stärker entwickelt und systematisiert, immer ein-
dringlicher auch auf die Geschöpflichkeit der Engel hingewiesen. Dass
sie der geschaffenen Welt angehören, unterscheidet die Engel grundsätzlich von Gott (vgl. 4Q403 1 i 35–36; *Jub.* 2:2).[31] In dieser angelologischen
Systematik hat freilich die Vorstellung vom Engel des Herrn als der irdischen Erscheinungsform Gottes selbst keinen rechten Platz mehr. Daher
ist es nur konsequent, wenn an die Stelle des Engels des Herrn eine andere
Größe tritt, die terminologisch nicht mehr der Engelwelt zugerechnet
wird: die Weisheit als der in Person auf Erden offenbare Gott. Die Integration der Angelologie in die Schöpfungstheologie und die Integration
der Offenbarungstraditionen Israels in die Weisheit gehen Hand in Hand.
Und wo in den Schriften gleichwohl der *angelus interpres* dem Menschen
erscheint und als Offenbarer des göttlichen Willens fungiert (Dan 7:16;

---

[27] 4Q400 2 8; 3 ii+5 8; 4Q401 1–2 2; 16 1; 4Q402 1 2; 4 7–8, 12; 9 2; 4Q403 1 i 2, 4–6,
10, 30, 32, 34, 37, 39, 42, 45; 1 ii 18, 20, 25–26; 4 5; 4Q405 4–5 2; 6 6, 9; 8a–b+9 2; 14–15
i 3; 11Q17 I:7; II:4, 6 (rek.); III:3 (rek.); IV:3; VII:9 (rek.), 10; VIII:5–6.—Auch von daher
ist der von Alexander, *Mystical Texts*, 22, 43, 56–57, für die Sabbatlieder vorgenommenen
angelologischen Einordnung Melchisedeks nach 4Q401 11 3; 22 3 zu widersprechen.

[28] 4Q400 1 i 2, 5; 1 ii 7; 2 2–3, 5; 3 i 3; 4Q401 1–2 5; 11 2; 5 4; 14 i 8; 28 1; 4Q402 3 i 2,
4, 6, 11–12; 4 9–10, 14; 4Q403 1 i 2, 31–33, 36, 44; 1 ii 5–6, 12, 20; 4Q404 3 3; 4 3; 4Q405
4–5 1, 4; 6 5; 14–15 i 5–7; 15 ii–16 4; 11 Q17 I:7; VIII:4.

[29] 4Q400 1 i 4; 1 ii 9, 17; 2 1, 7; 4Q401 14 i 5, 7; 16 1; 30 1; 4Q402 4 8; 9 2; 4Q403 1 i
14, 18, 21, 26, 31, 34–35, 38; 1 ii 26, 33, 35; 4Q404 2 2; 4 6–7; 4Q405 4–5 1–3; 13a–b 2,
5; 14–15 i 3; 11Q17 IV:3, 10 (rek.); VIII:7. Vgl. auch 11QMelch II:14.

[30] Dazu ausführlich M. Hengel, *Judentum und Hellenismus: Studien zu ihrer Begegnung
unter besonderer Berücksichtigung Palästinas bis zur Mitte des 2.Jh.s v.Chr.* (3. Aufl.;
Tübingen: Mohr Siebeck, 1989), 424–425.

[31] S. Alexander, *Mystical Texts*, 19, 29.

8:17–19; 9:21–22 u.ö.), tut er dies zwar als Abgesandter der himmlischen Welt, der dem Menschen ihre Geheimnisse vermittelt, bleibt dabei aber das dem Wesen nach unterschiedene Geschöpf Gottes. Er ist nicht die Erscheinungsform Gottes selbst.[32]

Die nicht nur in der Qumranforschung, sondern auch in der biblisch-exegetischen Forschung und in der Forschung am griechischsprachigen frühjüdischen Schrifttum mehrheitlich undifferenzierte Verwendung des Engelbegriffs macht eine konzeptionelle Klärung des Problems dringend notwendig.[33] Diese Klärung kann wegen der Integration der alten Vorstellung vom Engel des Herrn in die Weisheit, wie sie auch die Transformation der Engelvorstellung von 1 Chr 21 in Weish 18 belegt, nur in Auseinandersetzung mit der frühjüdischen Weisheitsvorstellung geschehen.

3.2. *Melchisedek als der Menschensohn*

Die konzeptionell undifferenzierte Betitelung himmlischer Personen beherrscht auch die Menschensohndiskussion, welche im Blick auf 11Q-Melch das terminologische Problem noch verschärft. Denn man kann Melchisedek nur dann als den Menschensohn klassifizieren, wenn man in dieser Gestalt ein Engelwesen im Sinne der geschöpflichen Engelhierarchien erblickt.[34] Gerade diese Deutung des Menschensohnes aber muss als höchst zweifelhaft gelten. Der Menschensohn ist in der alttestamentlich-jüdischen Tradition nie als genuin himmlisches Wesen dargestellt; er ist stets der *von der Erde* in den Transzendenzraum Gottes gelangende *Mensch* (Dan 7:13).[35] Dies zeigt schon der Titel der so benannten escha-

---

[32] Einen Grenzfall stellt Dan 10 dar. Allerdings wird hier die Gestalt, die Daniel am Fluss Tigris erscheint, gerade nicht als Engel betitelt. Dazu ausführlich Mittmann-Richert, *Joseph und Aseneth*, 257.

[33] Vgl. auch Mittmann-Richert, *Joseph und Aseneth*, 269 Anm. 53 in Auseinandersetzung mit G.J. Brooke, „Men and Women as Angels in *Joseph and Aseneth*," *JSP* 14 (2004–2005): 159–177.

[34] Stellvertretend für andere Untersuchungen seien die entsprechenden Beiträge des vorliegenden Sammelbandes von J.H. Ellens, „The Dead Sea Scrolls and the Son of Man in Daniel, *1 Enoch*, and the New Testament Gospels: An Assessment of 11QMelch (11Q13)," und P. Bertalotto, „Qumran Messianism, Melchizedek, and the Son of Man," genannt.

[35] Vgl. nochmals Gese, „Messias," 138–145. Die Wolken, auf denen nach Dan 7:13 der Menschensohn in den himmlischen Lebensbereich Gottes gelangt, manifestieren in alttestamentlich-jüdischer und auch christlicher Tradition stets die Grenze zwischen Himmel und Erde. Sie sind daher in entsprechenden Kontexten das adäquate Medium der Grenzüberwindung, markieren im Blick auf den Menschensohn also seine *irdische* Herkunft.

tologischen Figur (aram. בר אנש; hebr. בן אדם). Der Menschensohn ist der eschatologische Menschheitsrepräsentant, der trotz der göttlichen Herrschaftsübertragung *nie*—auch in den *Bilderreden* Henochs nicht— als wesensgleich mit Gott gedacht wird. Ja, in den *Bilderreden* Henochs ermöglicht allein die Tatsache, dass die göttliche Weisheit ihren „Wohn-ort" im Menschensohn nimmt, die Übertragung der Herrschaft im trans-zendenten Gottesreich auf den Menschensohn (*1 Hen.* 49:3; vgl. 48:7). Dass diese eschatologische Herrschaftsgestalt wie in 11QMelch II:10, 24–25 den Titel אלוהים tragen könnte, erscheint schon angesichts des Titels „Menschensohn" als undenkbar. Die herrscherliche Wirksamkeit des Menschensohns umfasst auch nie ein priesterliches Sühnehandeln, wie es in 11QMelch II:6–9 für Melchisedek ausdrücklich festgestellt wird.

3.3. *Melchisedek als Personifizierung der Weisheit*

Die einzige „Person", auf die in den zeitgenössischen Quellen alle Epi-theta Melchisedeks in 11QMelch passen, ist die Weisheit. Die Weisheit ist göttlichen Wesens, sie ist der auf Erden offenbare Gott in Person, der in der Gestalt der Weisheit die Erde königlich regiert, das Gericht über den Menschen vollzieht und um der Integrität des Kosmos willen selbst das Werk der Entsühnung vollbringt.[36] Wie im christlichen Hebrä-erbrief erscheint auch in 11QMelch Melchisedek als die Verkörperung der Weisheit. Ihre der Tradition nach gleichzeitig königlich-richterliche und priesterliche Funktion konnten schon deshalb ohne weiteres auf die Person des Priesterkönigs aus Gen 14 übertragen werden, weil in Ps 110:1 das Sitzen zur Rechten Gottes im eschatologischen Zusammen-hang als ein *gemeinsames* himmlisches Thronen Gottes und des Priester-königs „nach der Ordnung Melchisedeks" gedeutet werden konnte und offensichtlich gedeutet wurde. Auch wenn in den erhaltenen Resten von

---

[36] Den Vorbehalt, den M. de Jonge und A.S. van der Woude, „11Q Melchizedek and the New Testament," *NTS* 12 (1966): 305–306, gegenüber der priesterlichen Funktion Melchisedeks in 11QMelch äußern, relativiert schon der Name „Melchisedek", mit dem sich von Haus aus bestimmte Vorstellungen verbinden. Der gemeinsame Nenner der biblischen Melchisedeküberlieferungen ist das König-Priestertum Melchisedeks, wes-halb eine Rezeption dieser Figur im eschatologischen Kontext unter Ausblendung ihrer priesterlichen Funktion als unwahrscheinlich gelten kann. Die Abtrennung der Aussa-gen über die Schuldbefreiung (11QMelch II:6) und Entsühnung der „Männer des Loses Melchisedeks" (11QMelch II:8) von den Aussagen über Melchisedeks Gerichtshandeln an den Frevlern des Bundes (11QMelch II:13–14) entbehrt der traditionsgeschichtlichen Grundlage.

11QMelch Ps 110 nicht explizit zitiert wird, hat doch das Ende dieses
Psalms ganz offensichtlich die Gerichtsvorstellung von 11QMelch beein-
flusst (Ps 110:5–6):

5   Der Herr ist zu deiner Rechten!
     Er zerschmettert Könige.
6   Am Tag seines Zorns (ביום אפו) hält er Gericht.
     Mit Leichen füllt er die Täler,
     zerschmettert Häupter auf weitem Gefilde.

Und allein dieser Psalm erklärt auch, warum in 11QMelch II:9 die Mel-
chisedekerwartung mit Jes 61:1–3 verbunden wird, wo Israel das Erlass-
jahr angekündigt wird und die Auslösung des Volkes aus seinen Fesseln
(vgl. auch 11QMelch II:14). Denn in Jes 61:2 ist die Verkündigung der
Freilassung und Sündenvergebung verbunden mit der Ankündigung des
Tages der Rache, יום נקם, was ganz der Ankündigung des Gerichts über
die gottfeindliche Welt am Tage des Zornes Gottes in Ps 110:6 entspricht.

Gegen die hier vorgeschlagene Identifikation Melchisedeks mit der
Weisheit kann nicht das irdische Auftreten Melchisedeks nach Gen 14
ins Feld geführt werden, das—wie beim Menschensohn—die irdische
Herkunft Melchisedeks impliziert. Denn Gottes Erscheinen in Person
der Weisheit ist dort, wo sie sich irdisch manifestiert, notwendig ein
Erscheinen in Menschengestalt, wie es der alten Vorstellung vom Auftreten des Engels des Herrn entspricht. Dies ist am Beispiel von Weish
18 hinreichend deutlich geworden. Dabei kann, wie es der Hebräerbrief
dokumentiert, im Prozess der theologischen Reflexion eine menschliche
Figur auch nachträglich als Personfikation der Weisheit „erkannt" werden. Einen ganz ähnlichen Vorgang bezeugt auch die ägyptische Diaspo-
raschrift *Joseph und Aseneth*, deren weisheitliches Profil wegen der ein-
seitigen Fixierung der Forschung auf die Angelologie bislang ebenfalls
viel zu wenig beachtet wurde.[37] Dass Melchisedek in der frühjüdischen
und christlichen Tradition im Rahmen der Weisheit als die Erscheinungsform Gottes selbst erkannt wurde, ist von Ps 110 her zu verstehen,
wo das Thronen des Priesterkönigs zur Rechten Gottes in dem Moment
die Zugehörigkeit Melchisedeks zur göttlichen Welt implizierte, in dem
der Psalm nicht mehr auf das irdische Thronbesteigungsritual bezogen,
sondern eschatologisch interpretiert wurde.

---

[37] S. Mittmann-Richert, „Joseph und Aseneth."

4. Resümee

Die These, dass Melchisedek in Qumran als eine weisheitliche personale Größe zu verstehen ist, impliziert eine grundsätzliche Neuausrichtung der Forschung zur Weisheit in Qumran. Auch wenn an dieser Stelle keine Einordnung von 11QMelch in den Gesamtrahmen der Weisheitsschriften aus Qumran vorgenommen werden kann, sollen am Schluss doch zwei Anmerkungen die hier durchgeführte Richtungsänderung in der Interpretation von 11QMelch untermauern.

1. Angesichts der unbestrittenen weisheitlichen Grundausrichtung der essenischen Gemeinschaft wäre es verwunderlich, wenn die in der Tradition verbreitete und seit persischer Zeit konstitutive Vorstellung von der Weisheit als einer göttlichen Hypostase im Denken der Gemeinschaft keine Rolle gespielt hätte.[38] Die einseitige Ausrichtung der Forschung auf die sogenannte Spruchweisheit deckt nur ein Segment der alttestamentlich-jüdischen Weisheit ab und ignoriert das große Feld der im Bereich der Weisheit beheimateten schöpfungs- und offenbarungstheologischen Reflexion, die gerade in hellenistischer Zeit zur Integration der Geschichtstraditionen in die Weisheit führt.[39]

---

[38] Einen ersten Schritt in die angedeutete Richtung unternimmt B.G. Wright, „Wisdom and Women at Qumran," *DSD* 11 (2004): 240–261, der die Frage nach der weiblichen Personifikation der Weisheit in Qumran stellt, dabei aber nicht zu einem endgültigen Ergebnis kommt. Die Frage ist, ob nicht die männliche Verkörperung der Weisheit in Gestalt Melchisedeks und die eschatologische Funktion dieser Figur die weibliche Personvorstellung zurückgedrängt haben. Zum Problem s. auch G.J. Brooke, „Biblical Interpretation in the Wisdom Texts from Qumran," in *The Wisdom Texts from Qumran and the Development of Sapiential Thought*, 201–220, 219.

[39] In diesem Zusammenhang stellt sich auch die Frage, in welchem Verhältnis andere Texte, die von einer eschatologischen priesterlichen Figur sprechen, zu 11QMelch stehen. Vgl. etwa 4QapocrLevi[b]? ar (4Q541) 9 i 2–7 im Zusammenhang mit 4Q541 7, wo von der Öffnung der Bücher der Weisheit die Rede ist: אדין יתפתח[ו]] ספרי חכמ[תא; vgl. auch in 4Q541 2 ii 6 den Hinweis auf die Weisheit einer im näheren Kontext nicht eindeutig zu identifizierenden Gestalt. Ob das Fragment tatsächlich levitisch geprägt ist, wie man gemeinhin vermutet, oder sogar „the future Levi" ankündigt (G.J. Brooke, *The Dead Sea Scrolls and the New Testament* [London: SPCK, 2005], 145), ist im weisheitlichen Gesamtrahmen zumindest neu zu prüfen. Vgl. auch Alexander, *Mystical Texts*, 35–37, zur siebenfachen Manifestation der göttlichen Gegenwart auf den sieben himmlischen Thronen im 10. Sabbatopferlied (4Q405 15 ii–16 1–8 + 11Q17 9–12 i 3–10 + 4Q405 17 1–9 [?]). Und schließlich muss man im Blick auf die *Sabbatopferlieder*, in denen Melchisedek in priesterlicher Funktion in das himmlische Gesamtbild integriert zu sein scheint (4Q401 11 3; 11Q17 II:7), generell die Frage stellen, ob Melchisedek im Gegenüber von Gott und seinen Engeln nicht auf Seiten Gottes zu stehen kommt. S. dazu bereits Anm. 27.

2. In den biblischen und frühjüdisch-außerbiblischen Schriften wird
strikt und konsequent unterschieden zwischen der personalisierten
göttlichen Weisheit und dem davidischen und/oder priesterlichen Messias bzw. Menschensohn, und zwar im Blick auf ihre göttliche bzw.
menschliche Herkunft. Daher müssen auch im Qumranschrifttum die
eschatologischen Vorstellungen deutlicher voneinander differenziert
werden.[40] Auch wenn die These von Tantlevskij, dass Melchisedek als
göttliche Hypostase zu verstehen sei, grundsätzlich als Fortschritt in der
Interpretation von 11QMelch zu werten ist, so ist es doch unmöglich,
diese himmlische priesterliche Gestalt, wie der Autor es tut,[41] gleichzeitig
mit dem messianischen Freudenboten in 11QMelch II:18 zu identifizie-
ren. Hier werden Konzepte vermischt, die theologiegeschichtlich streng
voneinander zu unterscheiden sind. Der jesajanische Freudenbote ist in
allen Quellen stets ein von Gott zum Amt der Verkündigung berufener
irdischer Mensch, nie eine Personifikation Gottes, wie sie der Hyposta-
senbegriff impliziert. Die in Weish 18 vollzogene Hypostasierung bzw.
göttliche Personalisierung des nach 1 Chr 21 von David vollzogenen
priesterlichen Sühnehandelns zeigt einerseits den Entsprechungscharak-
ter zwischen dem Handeln Gottes und dem seines irdischen Repräsentanten, es zeigt andererseits aber auch die zwischen Immanenz und
Transzendenz verlaufende Grenze. So muss auch in 11QMelch das Ent-
sprechungsverhältnis zwischen Melchisedek und dem erwarteten Messias als ein Verhältnis zwischen Gott und seinem irdischen Repräsentanten verstanden werden. David ist nach Ps 110:4 Priester nach der

---

[40] Als Schritt in die falsche Richtung ist der Beitrag von R. van de Water, „Michael
or Yhwh? Toward Identifying Melchizedek in 11Q13," JSP 16 (2006): 75–86, 85–86,
zu bewerten, in welchem der Autor vorschlägt, „Melchisedek" in 11QMelch als Sam-
melnamen für ganz unterschiedliche eschatologische Figuren zu klassifizieren bzw. die
Person Melchisedeks als eine Figur zu verstehen, in welcher die Vorstellung vom messianischen Freudenboten und die Menschensohnvorstellung mit der rabbinisch beleg-
ten Vorstellung von der personal doppelten himmlischen Präsenz Gottes zusammengeführt wurden. Eine solche Zusammenführung der Konzepte unter der Prämisse eines
multiplen hypostatischen Heraustretens Gottes aus sich selbst ist im Blick auf all jene
Traditionskomplexe undenkbar, in welchen die eschatologische Erwartung sich auf eine
menschlich-irdische Gestalt wie den Messias bzw. den Menschensohn richtet.—Unbe-
friedigend bleibt auch die Bestimmung Melchisedeks als „a superior being of some sort"
bei F.L. Horton Jr., *The Melchizedek Tradition: A Critical Examination of the Sources to the
Fifth Century A.D. and in the Epistle to the Hebrews* (Cambridge: Cambridge University
Press, 1976), 79. Vgl. auch C. Gianotto, *Melchisedek e la sua tipologia: Tradizioni giudai-
che, cristiane e gnostiche (sec. II a.C.–sec. III d.C.)* (Supplementi alla Rivista Biblica 12;
Brescia: Paideia, 1984), 74–75.
[41] Tantlevskij, *Melchizedek* Redivivus, 21–23.

Ordnung Melchisedeks, aber *er ist nicht Melchisedek selbst*. Diese letzte personale Identifizierung zwischen der priesterlichen Person der Weisheit und dem davidischen Messias und Menschensohn wird erst im christlichen Rahmen vollzogen, und zwar auf der Grundlage der Vorstellung von der gleichzeitig göttlichen und menschlichen Natur Christi. Die Vereinigung göttlichen und menschlichen Wesens ist im antik-jüdischen Traditionsrahmen nicht denkbar! Hier liegt der Unterschied zur christlichen Melchisedekrezeption, die gleichwohl durch die frühjüdische Weisheitstheologie vorbereitet wurde und ohne Kenntnis der frühjüdischen theologischen Entwicklung, die auch 11QMelch dokumentiert, nicht verstanden werden kann.

THE "HEART" IN THE DEAD SEA SCROLLS: NEGOTIATING BETWEEN THE PROBLEM OF HYPOCRISY AND CONFLICT WITHIN THE HUMAN BEING

LOREN T. STUCKENBRUCK

Princeton Theological Seminary

INTRODUCTION

Since the discoveries of documents from Cave 1, readers and students of the Dead Sea Scrolls have noted dualistic features in many of the texts.[1] Not infrequently, the writers and first readers of the materials defined themselves in relation to dualistic oppositions such as those between light and darkness, good and evil, God and Belial, spirits of truth and iniquity, and the present age of wickedness and future age of salvation. These contrasts are all the more interesting because they do not, strictly speaking, correspond to the more conventional socio-religious distinction between those who are righteous and those who are wicked. This may come as a surprise especially in documents that *prime facie* appear to draw unmistakable boundaries between insiders and outsiders.

---

[1] The literature is abundant. In particular, one may see the following: J.H. Charlesworth, "A Critical Comparison of the Dualism in 1QS 3:13–4:26 and the 'Dualism' Contained in the Gospel of John," *NTS* 15 (1968–1969): 389–418, repr. in *John and the Dead Sea Scrolls* (New York: Crossroad, 1991), 76–106 (esp. 76–89); H.W. Huppenbauer, *Der Mensch zwischen zwei Welten: Der Dualismus der Texte von Qumran (Höhle I) und der Damaskusfragmente: Ein Beitrag zur Vorgeschichte des Evangeliums* (ATANT 34; Zürich: Zwingli Verlag, 1959) and P. von der Osten-Sacken, *Gott und Belial: Traditionsgeschichtliche Untersuchungen zum Dualismus in den Texten aus Qumran* (SUNT 6; Göttingen: Vandenhoeck & Ruprecht, 1969); J.G. Gammie, "Spatial and Ethical Dualism in Jewish Wisdom and Apocalyptic Literature," *JBL* 93 (1974): 356–385; D. Dimant, "Qumran Sectarian Literature," in *Jewish Writings of the Second Temple Period: Apocrypha, Pseudepigrapha, Qumran Sectarian Writings, Philo, Josephus* (ed. M.E. Stone; CRINT 2.2; Assen: Van Gorcum, 1984), 533–536; J. Duhaime, "Dualistic Reworking in the Scrolls from Qumran," *CBQ* 49 (1987): 32–56; and, especially, J. Frey, "Different Patterns of Dualistic Thought in the Qumran Library: Reflections on their Background and History," in *Legal Texts and Legal Issues: Proceedings of the Second Meeting of the International Organization for Qumran Studies, Cambridge 1995* (ed. M. Bernstein, F. García Martínez, and J. Kampen; STDJ 23; Leiden: Brill, 1997), 275–335.

It is in the *Treatise of the Two Spirits* that most of these stark contrasts converge into a complex of interwoven ideas.[2] While "the sons of light" (1QS III:24, 25; or "of righteousness" III:20, 22; "of truth" IV:6) and "the sons of iniquity" (III:19, 21) are referred to as distinct groups, the remaining dualistic categories are more profound. The Prince of Lights and Angel of Darkness each have dominion over separate spheres in the cosmos; the Angel of Darkness, however, is the one whose influence lies behind the sins, iniquities, guilt and deeds of transgression committed by "the sons of righteousness" (III:23–24). Thus the catalogue of virtues and vices in 1QS IV:2–8 and 9–14 does not actually describe the sons of light and the sons of darkness *per se*, but rather the "paths" or "ways" (IV:2, 10, 11; cf. IV:17, 19) in which they walk when engaged in corresponding activities.

Now this instruction about the two paths is given "to illuminate the heart of man" (IV:2) and to "establish fear in his heart for the judgements of God" (IV:2–3).[3] Indeed, in the present world order the battleground of conflict between truth and iniquity does not so much lie between definable communities of the righteous and wicked; instead, it is "the heart of man"—that is, the heart of all human beings—in which the spirits of truth and iniquity contend against one another (IV:23), and it is here where the separation of outsiders from insiders will, at the visitation of God (IV:18–19), ultimately take place.

The discussion to follow shall return to this same *Treatise of the Two Spirits*, though after what shall first be a brief survey of the "heart" in the Dead Sea Scrolls and a brief consideration of the use of this term in relation to both biblical tradition and evolved usage in the later texts. Second, and in particular, I shall examine several texts which refer to activity "with a double heart." By exploring this motif, we shall be in a better position to understand how "the heart" functions in two contemporary, yet very different, modes of discourse and to see what this means for the theological anthropologies adopted by the writers of the texts.

---

[2] Only the contrast between God and Belial, which dominates the discourse in 1QS I–III (I:16–19, 21–24; II:4–9, 19–26), is not upheld. In the *Treatise* God is portrayed as transcendent. He is posed above the opposition between "the Angel of Darkness" and "the Prince of Lights" (1QS III:20–25), though it is God—as well as "the Angel of Truth"— who comes to the aid of the sons of light when they stumble because of the malevolent influence of the Angel of Darkness.

[3] Translations in the present contribution are my own, unless otherwise indicated.

1. "Heart" in the Dead Sea Scrolls: A Brief Survey

To a considerable degree, much of the language about the "heart" in the Dead Sea texts can be traced back to the influence of several recurring motifs in the Hebrew Bible. Below I list some of the more prominent turns of phrase that reflect or draw upon biblical tradition:

a. obedience with "the whole heart" (CD 15:9, 12; 4Q266 8 i 3; 1QS V:9; 4Q256 IX:7; 4Q257 i 1; 4Q258 I:6; 1QH^a VI:37; VII:23; 4Q504 1–2 ii 13; 11Q5 XXII:12; 11Q19 LIV:13; LIX:10; 4Q196 ar 17 ii 1 [Tobit])
- see the *Shema'* in Deut 6:5; further, cf. 2 Kgs 23:25; 2 Chr 6:14, 38; 22:9; 30:19; 34:31; Jer 24:7; Prov 3:5

b. walking in "stubbornness of heart" (CD 2:18; 3:5, 12; 7:8, 19; 19:20, 33; 20:10; 4Q266 5 ii 11; 1QS I:6; II:14, 26; III:3; V:4; VII:19, 24; IX:10; 4Q257 III:5; 4Q258 I:4; 4Q266 5 ii 11; 1QH^a XII:16; 4Q393 3 3, 5)
- Deut 29:18; Jer 7:24; 9:13; 13:10; 16:12; 18:12; 23:17

c. a perfect/peaceful heart (CD 1:10; 1QH^a VIII:25, 35)
- 2 Chr 12:39; 25:2

d. a pure heart or purity of heart (4Q436 1a+b i 10 par. 4Q435 2 i 1; 4Q525 2 ii + 3 1; 4Q542 ar 1 i 10)
- Pss 51:12; 73:1; Prov 22:11

e. melting the heart (1QM VIII:10; IX:9; X:6; XIV:6; 1QH^a X:8, 30; XII:33; XXII:33; 4Q432 3 5; 11Q19 LXII:3, 4)
- Deut 1:28; 20:8; Josh 14:8; 2 Sam 17:10; Isa 13:7; 19:1; Ezek 21:7, 15

f. strengthening the heart (4Q421 9 2; 4Q422 III:7, 11; 4Q504 1–2 vi 9)
- Pss 10:17; 104:15; cf. 2 Chr 16:9

g. harden the heart (4Q365 4 2)
- Exod 4:21; 7:3; 14:4; Isa 63:17

h. "thoughts of the heart" (1QH^a XII:14 [God's heart]; 4Q511 63–64 ii 3)
- Ps 33:11; cf. Ps 139:23

i. "double heart" (1QH^a XII:15; 4Q452 1 i 9)
- Ps 12:3(2)

j. "heart of stone" (1QH^a XXI:12, [13–14]; 4Q427 10 3)
- Ezek 11:19; 36:26; cf. 1 Sam 25:37; Job 41:24

k. circumcise/circumcision of the heart (1QpHab XI:13; 4Q434 1 i 4; 4Q435 1 1; 4Q504 4 [11]; 4Q509 287 [1]); cf. 1QS V:5
- Deut 10:16; 30:6; Jer 4:4, 9:25

   l. "heart of man"/"human heart" (1QS IV:2, 23)
    - Prov 12:25; 19:21; 20:5
   m. "wise ones of heart" (4Q418 81 + 81a 20; 4Q468a 1 2)
    - Exod 28:3; Job 37:24
   n. "those upright in heart" (4Q266 5 i c–d 2); cf. (o) below
    - 2 Chr 29:34; Pss 7:11; 11:2; 32:11; 36:11(10); 64:11(10); 94:15; 97:11; cf. Ps 119:7; 78:72
   o. "uprightness of heart" (CD 8:14; 19:27; 1QS XI:2)
    - Deut 9:5; 1 Kgs 9:4; 1 Chr 29:17
   p. turn the heart aside (from God) (11Q19 LVI:19)
    - 1 Kgs 11:9
   q. "heart of deceit" (4Q525 2 ii + 3 3; 5 7; cf. 4Q381 85 3)
    - Jer 23:26; cf. Job 15:35; Prov 12:20; Sir 1:30
   r. "an evil heart" (4Q370 1 i 3; 4Q525 5 6)
    - Prov 25:20

While biblical tradition has undeniably shaped the language about "the heart" in the Scrolls, there are a number of expressions and phrases among the Scrolls texts which, in their precise form, mark a departure from language preserved in the Hebrew Bible. Supplied with the closest approximations from the Hebrew Bible, these include the following:

   a. "foolish ones of heart" (1QH^a IX:39; 4Q418 58 1; 69 ii 4, 8; 205 2); cf. Qoh 10:2
   b. to bring/give/open up understanding to/teach the heart (1QH^a VI: 19; XXII:31; 4Q372 3 3, 5; 8 4; 4Q423 7 7; 4Q426 1 i 4; 4Q444 1–4 i + 5 3; 4Q511 18 ii 8; 48–49 + 51 1); cf. Ps 51:8(6) and Prov 2:10
   c. a good heart (4Q385 6 2); cf. Deut 6:5
   d. open the heart (1QH^a XIII:35; XVIII:33); no examples in the Hebrew Bible, though see Acts 16:14 and 2 Cor 6:11
   e. heart of knowledge/knowledge of the heart (4Q511 63–64 ii 3; 11Q5 XXVI:12; cf. 1QH^a X:20); no examples with the substantive "knowledge" in the Hebrew Bible
   f. illumination of the heart/enlighten the heart (1QS II:3; IV:2; XI:5; 4Q511 18 ii 8)
   g. "Belial I will not keep in my heart" (1QS X:21; 4Q260 V:2)
   h. "spirit of holiness" placed by God in the heart (4Q435 2 i [2]; 4Q436 1 ii [1]); cf. Ps 51:8(6)
   i. "walk in the way of your [God's] heart" (1QH^a XII:18, 22, 25; XIV:9– 10; cf. 1QH^a XII:14; 1Q35 1 11; 4Q266 2 i 15; 4Q428 10 5); cf. Deut 10:12; Josh 22:5; 1 Kgs 2:4; 8:23; 9:4; 2 Chr 6:14
   j. make upright in heart (4Q432 3 1)

A cursory glance of and comparison between the two lists just provided makes clear that most developments in the Dead Sea texts can still be interpreted in relation to biblical traditions. Nevertheless, in the Scrolls, formulations that involve the "heart" take several new directions: (1) the language, which previously has been primarily related to human beings (though cf. 2 Sam 7:21; Job 10:13; Ps 78:72), now refers to the heart of God, whose adherents "follow in the way of your (viz. God's) heart"; (2) Belial, an opponent to or counterpart of God, can reside in the human heart and, therefore, the pious one can seek to remove him (g); (3) a "spirit of holiness" can be placed in the heart (h); (4) the heart can be "opened" to divine revelation (d); and (5) and (6) the heart is a place within the human being that can be enlightened by or receive light from God (f).[4]

On the basis of these differences, one should be cautious in drawing up a synthesis that can be assigned to a coherent worldview on the part of the authors with often distinguishable aims. Motifs (f) and (g), however, can be explained in relation to a dualistic framework that contrasts respectively between light and darkness and between God and Belial. Furthermore, even where the language is shared with biblical tradition, its meaning can often be transformed in its newly acquired contexts. With dualistic categories in mind, I would like to examine the degree to which such transformation may or may not be observed in relation to two motifs of the first list: (i) and (l). In such an examination, the significance of examining the Scrolls within broader streams of tradition during the Second Temple period becomes apparent.

2. ACTIVITY WITH A DOUBLE HEART (1QHᵃ XII:15 AND 4QTQAHAT AR [4Q542] 1 i 9–10)

In the Scrolls, activity "with a double heart" (לב ולב) occurs twice: once in a sectarian Hebrew text and once in an Aramaic text. The biblical passage behind this language is Ps 12:3(2):

> they utter lies to each other; with flattering (lit. smooth) lips (שפת חלקות)
> and a double heart (לב ולב) they speak   (NRSV)

In the psalm, falsehood and deceit are marks of those who are without piety (12:2[1]). The synonymous counterpart in the text to speaking with

---

[4] Cf. Eph 1:18; 4 Ezra 14:25.

"double heart" is the expression "flattering (lit. smooth) lips" (שפת חלקות).
The text does not merely have in view humanity as a whole (cf. 12:2[1]),
but builds a profile that seems rather to refer to those among God's
covenant people who oppress the poor (עניים מאנקת, 12:6[5]), whose
cause the psalmist is taking up. In 12:4(3), the text expresses a longing
that God will cut off "all flattering lips" (כל שפתי חלקות) which are
further described with the collective expression, "a tongue which says
great things" (NRSV: "makes great boasts"). Taking the context into
consideration, we may infer that a "double heart" implies that those with
smooth lips say one thing and do another. There is no hint, however,
that there is any conflict *within* them, that is, that a "double heart"
refers to two conflicting principles that reside within the human being.
Instead, double-hearted speech, in terms of theological anthropology, is
in itself treated as a culpable characteristic that applies to persons as a
whole.

"Double hearted" behaviour is picked up in the Hebrew text of the
Hodayot at 1QHª XII:8–15. In the edition of the text by H. Stegemann
and E. Schuller, the translation prepared by C. Newsom reads as follows:[5]

(8) ... Deceitful interpreters (מליצי רמיה) led them astray and they came
to ruin without understanding, for [　]
(9) with delusion their deeds, for (I) have been rejected by them. They
have no regard for me when you show your strength through me,
for they drive me away from my land
(10) like a bird from its nest. All my friends and my relatives are driven
away from me, and they regard me like a broken pot. But they are
lying interpreters (מליצי כזב)
(11) and deceitful seers (חוזי רמיה). They have planned devilry (בליעל)
against me to exchange your law, which you spoke repeatedly in
my heart, for slippery words (בחלקות)
(12) for your people. They withhold the drink of knowledge from the
thirsty and for their thirst they give them sour wine to drink so
that they may gaze on
(13) their error, acting like madmen on their feast days, snaring themselves in their nets. But you, O God, despise every devilish plan
(מחשבת בליעל)
(14) and it is your counsel that will stand, and the plan of your mind
that will be established forever. But they, the hypocrites (נעלמים),
concoct devilish plans (זמות בליעל יחשובו)
(15) and seek you with a divided heart (וידרשוכה בלב ולב).

---

[5] H. Stegemann, E. Schuller, and C. Newsom in *DJD* XL (2009): 157–166 (for text,
critical notes, and translation).

One term for the hymnist's description of the "deceitful interpreters" (line 8; cf. line 10) is translated by the editors as "hypocrites" (line 14), which more literally refers to being "clandestine," that is, to engaging in non-transparent behaviour. The writer regards such people as seeking God "with a divided (lit. double) heart" (line 15), and goes on to declare that they are "not established in your truth" (line 15). As far as the expression "double heart" is concerned, the text does not substantially deviate from what we have observed in Ps 12: all doubled-hearted activity is calumnious.

Nonetheless, four details in this text show particular interests on the part of the hymnist that move beyond the biblical tradition. First, the oppressors of the pious are more specifically described as "deceitful interpreters" (line 8) and "lying interpreters" (line 10). In this and a previous hymn (1QHᵃ X:33) the writer seems again to have referred to this group as "lying interpreters" (מליצי כזב; perhaps an interpretation of Ps 12:3(2): שוא ידברו "they speak deception").[6] The writer of that previous hymn, in thanking God for having "delivered me" from his opponents, caricatures them under the influence of Ps 12 as "the congregation of those who seek smooth things" (עדת דורשי חלקות). Second, in another, earlier hymn, the same writer not only refers to "erring interpreters" (מליצי תעות, X:16) and also calls them "seekers of smo[oth things" (דורשי חל[קות, X:17), but—in a departure from Ps 12—marks himself out as the divinely appointed "expert interpreter of wonderful mysteries" (מליץ דעת ברזי פלא, X:15). In this role, the writer regards himself as the arch-opponent of those who seek (God) with a double heart. By applying the term "interpreter" to himself, that is, the same word he has used to designate the opponents, the writer admits that the teachers of error share his Torah tradition, but have changed it (להמיר תורתכה, XII:11) and so interpret it wrongly. The negative momentum of the writer's invectives against the detractors does not allow him to stress what they all hold in common, but rather erects and reinforces hard boundaries between his inspired instruction and their false teaching. Third, in thanking God for deliverance from the congregation of smooth things, the hymnist also refers to himself as "the poor one" (אביון, X:33). The poor ones whom the

---

[6] Exegetically, the term for "interpreters" reflects an interpretation of the more general verb דבר ("say, speak") which is associated with flattery and double-heartedness in Ps 12 (vv. 3[2] and 4[3]).

flatterers oppress in Ps 12 (called עניים and אביונים, Ps 12:6[5]) are transformed by the writer into a self-designation. The fourth difference to
notice is that the division between the flatterers and the hymnist is cast
against the backdrop of categorical opposition between Belial (who lies
behind the plots of the mediators of deceit, X:16–18) and God (who,
the writer claims, is the revealer of his own knowledge and instruction;
X:15, 19–20).[7] Significantly, in the lines immediately following the passage quoted above, this contrast is rearticulated with reference to "heart"
language: the opponents' "stubbornness of heart" corresponds to their
inability to choose, recognize and walk "the way of your (viz. God's)
heart" (XII:18, 19, 22, 24; see also XIV:10, 24 and the language of 4QD[a]
[4Q266] 2 i 15).[8]

Thus, on the one hand, Ps 12 accounts for several features retained
in the web of rhetoric employed in several of the *Hodayot* (flattering
or smooth things, double hearted activity, oppression of the poor, and
speech). On the other hand, the opposition between the poor ones and
those engaged in double-hearted speech is recast as an opposition between *the Poor One* (the hymnist) and the double-hearted and fraudulent interpreters of the Torah who have irretrievably placed themselves
on the side of Belial. In neither the biblical tradition nor the *Hodayot*
passage does the expression "double hearted" have anything to do with
an interiorizing theological anthropology. If anything, despite the tradition shared by the poor and the flatterers, the notion of double heartedness marks out the wicked as *wholly deceptive* and counterfeit, while
the hymnist aligns himself wholly with the Torah which accords with the
plan of God's heart (XII:14, מחשבת לבכה; cf. lines 18–19) and which God
has etched into his heart (XII:11, שננתה בלבבי). The language of the psalm
has been interpreted within a more dualistic framework which, in turn,
is placed in service of the hymnist's claim to inspired interpretation in
the face of opposition.

---

[7] Newsom's translation frequently renders בליעל as "devilish," as is the case here. Even
if the word can be taken this way, the notion of Belial as a malevolent being behind the
opponents schemes is not remote; the next hymn opens, for example, with a reference to
"the council of deception and the congregation of Belial" (X:24).

[8] Ideologically close to this is the language of the *Damascus Document* at CD A 1:10–
11, according to which God raised up a "Teacher of Righteousness" for those who sought
after God "with an undivided heart (בלב שלם) ... in order to direct their way on the path
of his heart" (בדרך לבו) par. 4QD[a] [4Q266] 2 i 15).

The other occurrences of "double heart" are preserved within the Aramaic text of 4QTQahat ar (4Q542) 1 i 7–10. The patriarch instructs Amram and his siblings as follows:

(7) ... Grasp the word of Jacob
(8) your father, and take hold of the judgments of Abraham and of the righteous deeds of Levi and of myself. Be holy and pure
(9) from every manner of mingling, grasping the truth and walking (אזלין) in uprightness, not with a double heart (ולא בלבב ולבב)
(10) but with a pure heart (להן בלבב דכא) and with a truthful and good spirit.

Here, the expression is associated with the verb "to walk" and, as such, is contrasted with "walking in uprightness." The notion of walking "in a double heart" is a fixed expression for the disobedient who mingle what they have with foreigners (cf. lines 5–6: "do not give your inheritance to foreigners or dispossess yourselves to mixed kinds") and do not conduct themselves with purity. Unlike the *Hodayot* text discussed above, this passage is not shaped by a reading of Ps 12. Instead, the preserved text, if anything, may have its counterpart in the influential exhortation of the *Shema'* to "love the Lord your God with your whole heart and with all your soul and with all your strength" (Deut 6:5), in which the human heart, soul, and strength are summoned to undivided covenant obedience. The *Testament of Qahat* also differs from the *Hodayot* in its emphasis on the problem of social intercourse with non-Jews. The scope of the *Hodayot* is more sectarian and focuses more on the contrast between a *single* person (the hymnist!) and his opponents. Nevertheless, as in the *Hodayot*, the expression "double heart" has nothing to do with an interior state of being. Both passages share a view of double-heartedness as a disposition that is not even capable of pursuing righteousness. Although there is some hint of cosmic dualism in the *Testament of Qahat* (i.e. a possible contrast between darkness and light in the fragmentary text of 4Q542 2 11–12), the writer makes no apparent attempt to integrate the language of double heartedness into such a system of ideas.

3. Double-Heartedness in Other Second Century B.C.E. Literature (Ben Sira, Exhortation of Enoch)

The precise connotations of the phrase "double heart" in the *Hodayot* and *Testament of Qahat* are not simply to be understood against the background of biblical interpretation. The expression is further illuminated if we draw into consideration two further writings composed during the second century B.C.E. and also extant in fragments amongst the Dead Sea Scrolls: Ben Sira[9] and the Enochic Exhortation in *1 En.* 91:1 10, 18–19.[10]

In Ben Sira, the idea of a "double heart" occurs almost at the outset. Whereas in the *Hodayot* the expression applies to opponents who, though once associated with the hymnist, are outsiders to his community, the language of Ben Sira, as *Testament of Qahat*, is less sectarian. At 1:28, which is not preserved in any of the Hebrew materials, the Greek translation exhorts:

> Do not disobey the fear of the Lord and do not approach him in a double heart (μὴ ἀπειθήσῃς φόβῳ κυρίου καὶ μὴ προσέλθῃς αὐτῷ ἐν καρδίᾳ δισσῇ).

As the surrounding context shows (1:28–30), this exhortation has the worshipping assembly in view. Ben Sira thus admits that it is possible to participate in the assembly without actually fearing God (1:28, 30; cf. 1QS II:11–14). To have a "double heart," then, is tantamount to hypocrisy (1:29, μὴ ὑποκριθῇς): one is not to act pretentiously "in human mouths" while being watchful over ones "lips." As with the *Hodayot*, the language of Ps 12 (vv. 2–3[1–2]) may well lie in the background. In addition, similar to the *Hodayot*, being double hearted is equivalent to having "a heart full of deceit" (1:30, ἡ καρδία ... πλήρης δόλου). Ben Sira goes on to develop this understanding with a related expression, "double-tongued" (δίγλωσσος), which functions as the virtual equivalent for "the sinner" (ὁ ἁμαρτωλός; cf. 6:1 and further 5:14; 28:9, 13).

As in the Dead Sea texts, the "double heart" in Ben Sira categorically distinguishes the one who is wicked from the one who is pious without suggesting at all that the wicked experience an *inner* moral

---

[9] Cf. 2Q18, two fragments corresponding to a few words, respectively, from Sir 6:14–15 (or possibly 1:19–20) and 6:20–31; 11QPs^a [11Q5] XXI–XXII (to Sir 51:13–19, 30). For a brief summary on Ben Sira among the Scrolls, see P.W. Flint, "'Apocrypha,' Other Previously-Known Writings, and 'Pseudepigrapha' in the Dead Sea Scrolls," in *The Dead Sea Scrolls after Fifty Years: A Comprehensive Assessment* (ed. P.W. Flint and J.C. VanderKam; 2 vols.; Leiden: Brill, 1998–1999), 2:24–66 (here 35–37).

[10] 4QEn^g (4Q212) 1 ii 13–21 (lines 13–17 have no precise equivalent, while 18–21 correspond to *1 En.* 91:18–19); see L.T. Stuckenbruck, *1 Enoch 91–108* (Commentaries on Early Jewish Literature; Berlin: de Gruyter, 2007), 153–154, 173 and 182.

conflict.[11] The larger context of this language, however, is more compli-cated. More explicitly than in either the *Hodayot* or *Testament of Qahat*, the exhortation of Ben Sira in 1:28 may be comprehended in relation to instruction about the "two ways" or "paths."[12] In 2:12, the writer pro-nounces a "woe" against "a sinner who traverses on two paths" (ἁμαρ-τωλῷ ἐπιβαίναντι ἐπι δύο τρίβους). If these two paths have to do with good and evil, respectively, then here we have a mild admission on the part of the author that "a sinner" might indeed live a life that includes what is good. This makes room for a degree of ambiguity or at least allows for the possibility that the boundaries between the pious and sin-ners are porous, a point that Ben Sira does not attempt to develop. To be sure, he does make conceptual space for dualistic principles set up by God for the created order (33:15; 42:24–25). Although these princi-ples of good and bad remain exterior to human nature, human beings are neither caught up in a conflict between the two[13] nor are the righ-teous and the wicked aligned, respectively, with the one sphere or the other. Humans are treated as essentially whole beings who, at any one time, are either wholly sinners or wholly pious. Despite this correspon-dence with the *Hodayot*, the language of double-heartedness in Ben Sira, which can be correlated to existence on "two paths" (so 2:12), does not result in as clear-cut a division between the righteous and wicked.

This point is augmented by a further consideration of the wider con-text of Ben Sira's presentation: for the writer, the "righteous one" is not "sinless" in any way; it is, rather, a classification that includes those who have sinned, have repented and have been forgiven (23:2–3). The distinc-tion between "the sinners" and "the godly" is, strictly speaking, not so much descriptive as it is socio-religious in orientation. Broadly, there are those who ignore the Torah (41:8; 42:2), are lacking in wisdom (37:21) and misuse wealth (34:21–27); and then there are those who, on the other hand, take a proper attitude towards their own sin by seeking forgiveness

---

[11] We shall see below that in the *Treatise on the Two Spirits*, an *inner* conflict draws on a different linguistic idiom.

[12] 1QH[a] XII:18–19 refers twice to "the way of your (God's) heart" without, however, contrasting it with the opposite path.

[13] They are endowed with freedom of choice and can alternatively choose at any one time to do what is right or wrong (Sir 15:14, 16–17; cf. 15:11–12, 20). See the treatment of 15:11–20 by M. Gilbert, "God, Sin and Mercy: Sirach 15:11–18:14," in *Ben Sira's God: Proceedings of the International Ben Sira Conference, Durham—Ushaw College 2001* (ed. R. Egger-Wenzel; BZAW 321; Berlin: de Gruyter, 2002), 118–135 (esp. 119–121).

(cf. 2:11; 3:3, 14–15; 5:6–7; 23:4) and adhere to Ben Sira's repeated summons to acquire wisdom and obey the Torah (1:14–27; 9:15; 15:1–10; 19:20–24; 21:11; 24:23–34; 35:1; 38:34–39:11).

The language of Ps 12 only shapes the way Ben Sira appropriates the "double heart" motif in a limited sense. Like the psalm, Ben Sira implies that double-hearted disposition manifests itself in speech (1:29), though precisely which kind of speech is not explicitly stated. There may, however, be some analogy with what happens in the *Hodayot* where, as we have seen, the writer recasts the double-hearted and flattering speech of the biblical text to his opponents' activities as fraudulent interpreters of the Torah. To this extent, Ben Sira envisions those who would be likely to speak in assemblies (1:30) and should take care that what they say not be a matter of pretence (1:29). But whereas the writer of the *Hodayot* texts in 1QHᵃ X and XII applies Ps 12 to a sectarian situation in which opposing communities are already completely separate, Ben Sira envisions double-heartedness as an ever present problem within the worshipping community.

The other text to consider, *1 En.* 91:3d–4b, occurs near the beginning of an Exhortation (91:1–10, 18–19) composed in the form of a testamentary address by an Enochic author to his offspring (i.e. Methuselah and his brothers). The text, which is only preserved in Ethiopic, can be translated as follows:

> Love uprightness and walk in it.
> And neither draw near to uprightness with a double heart (*ba-kel'ē leb*),
> nor associate with those who have a double heart (*'ellā ba-kel'ē leb*);
> instead, walk in righteousness, my children,
> and it will lead you in the ways of goodness,
> and righteousness will be your companion.

Similar to Ben Sira, the Enochic text conceives of "a double heart" in terms of drawing near (*'i-teqrabu*, 91:4a) and co-ordinates this with a socio-ethical distinction between the righteous and the wicked. But whereas Ben Sira thinks of an approach (μὴ προσέλθῃς, 1:28) to God in the worshipping assembly, the Exhortation seems more explicitly fixed on ethics: "neither draw near to *uprightness* with a double heart."

Indeed, a comparison between the Exhortation (including its wider literary context), Ben Sira, and the Dead Sea texts makes further differences of emphasis apparent. For one thing, the opposition between the righteous and the wicked is nowhere linked up with other dualistic language (e.g. God versus Belial, light versus darkness, principle of good versus bad in the created order). Moreover, and much in contrast to Ben Sira in particular, neither the writer of the Exhortation nor the writers of the *Epistle of Enoch* that follows (*1 En.* 92:1–5; 93:11–105:2) allow for any ambiguity as far as the origin of sin and the possibility of the pious sinning (or of the sinners doing pious acts) are concerned.

Throughout *1 En.* 91–105 (including the *Apocalypse of Weeks* in 93:1–10 and 91:11–17), the Enochic writers emphasize categorical opposition between the two "ways" or "paths." The instructions on these distinct paths are most clearly set forth in *1 En.* 91:3–4, 18–19, and 94:1–5. Though some mention is made that the wicked offer instruction based on a tradition shared with the Enochic author and his adherents (cf. 98:9–99:2; 104:10–13?), these teachings are branded as "false words" and "lies" (98:15) and as departures from "the words of truth" and "the eternal law/covenant" (99:2; cf. 1QH^a XII:11: the opponents are accused of changing God's Torah).[14] The existence of shared traditions between the writer(s) of the *Epistle* and the "sinners," however, remains implicit; unlike Ben Sira, nothing is said about any socio-religious connections between the righteous and the wicked. Rhetorically, the two groups are distinct in every way. It is possible that this strict differentiation is teleological: the righteous and wicked are distinct because that is what will happen when the rewards and punishments are meted out to humanity at the time of eschatological judgement. The righteous ones are so clearly presented as downtrodden, enslaved, and oppressed in contrast to the wicked ones who are wealthy and socially elite, however, it is reasonable to infer that for the *Epistle* (and probably the Exhortation that precedes it), being righteous is a matter of transparency in the present socio-religious order of things. Ben Sira's possibility of someone being "on two ways" at once is excluded by the Enochic authors from the start. Not only are the Enochic readers exhorted not to draw near to uprightness with a double heart, they are not even to associate with those who are of such a disposition (*1 En.* 91:4; see the same emphasis in the *Epistle* at 97:4; 99:10; 104:6). Thus, without invoking an opposition such as that between God and Belial and without drawing on the language of Ps 12, the author comes close to the *Hodayot* text in treating his readers and those whom he counts among the wicked as carrying out their respective forms of religiosity in largely separate spheres.

---

[14] For a more sustained discussion of the text and theological argument of *1 En.* 98:9–99:2 and 104:9–105:2, see Stuckenbruck, *1 Enoch 91–108*, 351–381 and 582–605.

Sociologically, the *Hodayot* have their nearest parallel in the way the Enochic tradition developed the motif of "double heartedness." The Enochic texts show, in particular, how such language could be placed in service of a group which, appealing to a two-ways instruction, is at least in the process of separating from a larger socio-religiously dominant community. On the other hand, the *Testament of Qahat*, for all its interest in the retribution of sinners at the final judgement (4Q542 1 ii 6, 8), does not reflect a social context in which a community has either separated itself from others or is being summoned to do so. As noted above, one of the fragments (2) does seem to draw on a dualistic distinction between darkness and light, but the insufficiently preserved text does not allow us to determine whether or how this was related to socio-religious circumstances of the writer's community.

4. "The Heart of Man" in the *Treatise of the Two Spirits*

We return to the *Treatise of the Two Spirits* mentioned in the introduction above. The anthropologically significant phrase, "heart of man" (בלבב גבר, 1QS IV:23; לב איש, IV:2), occurs several times in the biblical tradition, though only in Proverbs and only in the form לב איש (12:25; 19:21; and 20:5). In the Proverbs texts, the expression denotes the affective side (12:25) and cognitive activity (19:21; 20:5) of the human being. In the *Treatise of the Two Spirits* the term "heart" is more comprehensive in scope: it is almost synonymous with human nature as a whole and, as such, is the place acted upon by cosmic powers. In Proverbs, moreover, the human heart is capable of knowing anxiety, devising plans, and directing the individual in this or that course of action. The occurrences in Prov 19:21 and 20:5 are consistent with the way the expression functions in 1QS IV:2: the enlightened "heart of man" manifests itself in a long list of virtues (IV:2–8), as opposed to a list of vices assigned to "the spirit of iniquity" (IV:9–14; רוח עול, line 9). These virtues and vices are, in turn, associated with contrasting "paths" (III:26–IV:1, 15) reminiscent of the widespread two ways instruction as found, for example, in *1 En.* 91:4, 18–19 and 94:1–5.[15] Both here and in the wider context (cf. 1QS III:17–IV:1 and IV:15–17), however, these ethical contrasts are

---

[15] For discussions of the wide impact of the two ways discourse in Second Temple Jewish literature, see K. Niederwimmer, *The Didache: A Commentary* (Hermeneia; Minneapolis: Fortress, 1998), 59–63; H. van de Sandt and D. Flusser, *The Didache:*

aligned with two opposing spirits ("spirit of truth/holiness" versus "spirit of iniquity/darkness/impurity") or angels ("Prince of Lights"/"angel of his truth" vs. "Angel of Darkness") whom God has placed within the created order (III:17–19). It is ultimately these cosmic forces that contend in "the heart of man" (IV:23).

This combination of the two ways with two cosmic forces offers a tension not dissimilar to the one we have observed in Ben Sira: the juxtaposition of human free choice, on the one hand, with a God-given opposition between good and evil, on the other. The predetermined opposition in the *Treatise of the Two Spirits* between two angels with separate dominions over light and darkness (1QS III:18–IV:1) both crystallises and intensifies Ben Sira's more general emphasis that God has arranged the universe from the very beginning to consist of pairs, both good and bad (Sir 42:24–25; 33:15). Moreover, the *Treatise* moves well beyond Ben Sira's oppositions by developing them along cosmological (i.e. light and darkness), theological (Prince of Lights verses Angel of Darkness), and anthropological (conflict within the person) lines. By focusing on and interweaving each of these oppositions, the *Treatise of the Two Spirits* goes a significant step further. It is not that these contrasting influences are at work at different times, so that a person conducts him- or herself in wholly one way or the other (as presented in *Hodayot*, *Testament of Qahat*, *1 En.* 91–105, and even Ben Sira); instead, these oppositions are *concurrent and overlapping*.[16] To be sure, the righteous can be called "sons of truth" (1QS IV:6), "sons of light" (III:25), and "sons of righteousness" (III:20, 22), while the wicked can be called "sons of iniquity" (III:21). But unlike the Enochic tradition and even Ben Sira, this classification between two sorts of people is never going to be fully transparent in the present world order (IV:15–26). Whereas in Ben Sira, the pious person can remedy

---

Its Jewish Sources and its Place in Early Judaism and Christianity (CRINT 3.5; Assen: Van Gorcum, 2002), 55–111; and M. Del Verme, *Didache and Judaism: Jewish Roots of an Ancient Christian-Jewish Work* (London: T&T Clark, 2004), esp. 126–130.

[16] Some precedent for opposing angelic powers vying for power over a human may be found in the Aramaic *Visions of Amram* (4Q543–547, 4Q548?): two angels who, together, have authority over all humanity are presented as trying to gain control over the patriarch Amram. The angel associated with darkness is named "Melki-resha'," while the other (unnamed) angel who speaks with the patriarch is associated with light (4Q544 1 10–14). Since the patriarch is asked to choose between the two (4Q544 1 12), the pre-deterministic strain found in the *Treatise of the Two Spirits* is absent here. On the fragments, see P.J. Kobelski, *Melchizedeq and Melchireša'* (CBQMS 10; Washington: Catholic University of America Press, 1981) and their publication by É. Puech in *DJD* XXXI (2001): 283–405.

wicked behaviour by repenting from sin, in the *Treatise* the problem of sin persists within the human being until the time of God's visitation, when the conflict between the "divisions" within humanity shall come to a decisive end (IV:15–20). All human beings, whether socially on the inside or outside of the righteous community, provide the battleground wherein the conflict between the opposing powers is, in effect, carried out; the boundaries between wickedness and righteousness are neither discernible (*contra* Ben Sira) nor socially delineated (*contra* Exhortation in *1 Enoch, Hodayot, Testament of Qahat*).

The possible charge of hypocrisy against sinners who carry out their activities "with a double heart"—so *Hodayot*, Ben Sira, and the Enochic Exhortation—is, if not altogether absent, demoted to being one of the many vices that characterise the "spirit of iniquity" (IV:9–11, including רום לבב "haughtiness of heart" and כיבוד לב "hardness of heart" which, along with the other vices, are associated with "paths of darkness"). The more conventional problem of hypocrisy gives way in the *Treatise* to a dualistic web of oppositions that explains *inconsistent behaviour as endemic to the "heart of man," that is, to human nature itself.*

Conclusion

Discourse concerned with "hypocritical" behaviour in the *Hodayot*, the Exhortation of *1 Enoch* and Ben Sira is less interested in anything happening within the human being than with marking out those whose claims to piety should not be confused with authentic religiosity. In keeping with the tradition in Ps 12, the demarcation between those who are pious, on the one hand, and the sinners, on the other, is visible, that is, the writers assume that this is a socially discernible contrast. We have seen that the motif of double-heartedness is a feature of such discourse. A different line of thought is taken up in the *Treatise of the Two Spirits*: a visible distinction "the sons of light/righteousness" and "the sons of iniquity" is not guaranteed. Here "the heart" of each human being is regarded as a combat zone for powers that struggle to assert their control. The principled opaqueness of insiders and outsiders—which stands in contrast with much of the remainder of the *Community Rule*—is only temporary. As God has apportioned to each human being a certain measure of each spirit, whether of "truth" or "iniquity," so an apocalyptic act of divine cleansing at the end will reveal the people of God as they have been predetermined to be from the beginning.

These differing modes of discourse should not in each instance be mistaken as systematic reflections of those who adopted them. It is likely, for example, that the writers of the *Hodayot*, Sirach, and the Exhortation in *1 Enoch* were aware that they themselves, as well as members of their communities, might be confronted by ambiguities that would cast into doubt their identity of being "amongst the pious." For them to have reflected or elaborated on such possibilities, however, would have run counter to the reasons they wrote, whether such reasons involved the shoring up of sectarian identity (*Hodayot*), the admonition of pious readers with straightforward advice (Ben Sira), or the provision of a voice to a group of those being oppressed by the social and religious elite (*1 En.* 91–105). It is the *Treatise of the Two Spirits* which ventures into the arena of principled ambiguity, though even here—as its incorporation into the Qumran *Community Rule* may attest—the writer(s), who did not develop the implications of the instruction to their logical end, may have belonged to a sectarian community that had physically separated itself from others.[17]

Thus, while the dualistic language, explored here in relation to the motifs of double-heartedness and the human heart as a battle zone, should not be mirror-read or mapped straightforwardly onto socio-religious equivalents, it does communicate something about where, in terms of theological anthropology, writers were locating the religious tensions in their communities and about how they attempted to negotiate them in relation to their communities' ideals.

---

[17] For the view of the *Treatise* as an originally separate document from the rest of the *Community Rule* (and therefore reflecting a different ideology), see, conveniently, A. Lange and H. Lichtenberger, "Qumran," *TRE* 28:45–79; H. Stegemann, *The Library from Qumran: On the Essenes, Qumran, John the Baptist, and Jesus* (Leiden: Brill, 1998) 108–110; and Frey, "Different Patterns of Dualistic Thought," 279–280.

SUPPLEMENTS TO VETUS TESTAMENTUM

115. BERGSMA, J.S. *The Jubilee from Leviticus to Qumran*. A History of Interpretation. 2006. ISBN-13 978 90 04 15299 1. ISBN-10 90 04 15299 7
116. GOFF, M.J. *Discerning Wisdom*. The Sapiential Literature of the Dead Sea Scrolls. 2006. ISBN-13 978 90 04 14749 2. ISBN-10 90 04 14749 7
117. DE JONG, M.J. *Isaiah among the Ancient Near Eastern Prophets*. A Comparative Study of the Earliest Stages of the Isaiah Tradition and the Neo-Assyrian Prophecies. 2007. ISBN 978 90 04 16161 0
118. FORTI, T.L. *Animal Imagery in the Book of Proverbs*. 2007. ISBN 978 90 04 16287 7
119. PINÇON, B. *L'énigme du bonheur*. Étude sur le sujet du bien dans le livre de Qohélet. 2008. ISBN 978 90 04 16717 9
120. ZIEGLER, Y. *Promises to Keep*. The Oath in Biblical Narrative. 2008. ISBN 978 90 04 16843 5
121. VILLANUEVA, F.G. *The 'Uncertainty of a Hearing'*. A Study of the Sudden Change of Mood in the Psalms of Lament. 2008. ISBN 978 90 04 16847 3
122. CRANE, A.S. *Israel's Restoration*. A Textual-Comparative Exploration of Ezekiel 36–39. 2008. ISBN 978 90 04 16962 3
123. MIRGUET, F. *La représentation du divin dans les récits du Pentateuque*. Médiations syntaxiques et narratives. 2009. ISBN 978 90 04 17051 3
124. RUITEN, J. VAN and J.C. VOS DE (eds.). *The Land of Israel in Bible, History, and Theology*. Studies in Honour of Ed Noort. 2009. ISBN 978 90 04 17515 0
125. EVANS, P.S. *The Invasion of Sennacherib in the Book of Kings*. A Source-Critical and Rhetorical Study of 2 Kings 18-19. 2009. ISBN 978 90 04 17596 9
126. GLENNY, W.E. *Finding Meaning in the Text*. Translation Technique and Theology in the Septuagint of Amos. 2009. ISBN 978 90 04 17638 6
127. COOK, J. (ed.). *Septuagint and Reception*. Essays prepared for the Association for the Study of the Septuagint in South Africa. 2009. ISBN 978 90 04 17725 3
128. KARTVEIT, M. *The Origin of the Samaritans*. 2009. ISBN 978 90 04 17819 9
129. LEMAIRE, A., B. HALPERN and M.J. ADAMS (eds.). *The Books of Kings*. Sources, Composition, Historiography and Reception. 2010. ISBN 978 90 04 17729 1
130. GALIL, G., M. GELLER and A. MILLARD (eds.). *Homeland and Exile*. Biblical and Ancient Near Eastern Studies in Honour of Bustenay Oded. 2009. ISBN 978 90 04 17889 2
131. ANTHONIOZ, S. *L'eau, enjeux politiques et théologiques, de Sumer à la Bible*. 2009. ISBN 978 90 04 17898 4
132. HUGO, P. and A. SCHENKER (eds.). *Archaeology of the Books of Samuel*. The Entangling of theTextual and Literary History. 2010. ISBN 978 90 04 17957 8
133. LEMAIRE, A. (ed.). *Congress Volume Ljubljana*. 2007. 2010. ISBN 978 90 04 17977 6
134. ULRICH, E. (ed.). *The Biblical Qumran Scrolls*. Transcriptions and Textual Variants. 2010. ISBN 978 90 04 18038 3
135. DELL, K.J., G. DAVIES and Y. VON KOH (eds.). *Genesis, Isaiah and Psalms*. A Festschrift to honour Professor John Emerton for his eightieth birthday. 2010. ISBN 978 90 04 18231 8
136. GOOD, R. *The Septuagint's Translation of the Hebrew Verbal System in Chronicles*. 2010. ISBN 978 90 04 15158 1
137. REYNOLDS, K.A. *Torah as Teacher*. The Exemplary Torah Student in Psalm 119. 2010. ISBN 978 90 04 18268 4
138. VAN DER MEER, M., P. VAN KEULEN, W. TH. VAN PEURSEN and B. TER HAAR ROMENY (eds.). *Isaiah in Context*. Studies in Honour of Arie van der Kooij on the Occasion of his Sixty-Fifth Birthday. 2010. ISBN 978 90 04 18657 6
139. TIEMEYER, L.-S. *For the Comfort of Zion*. The Geographical and Theological Location of Isaiah 40-55. 2011. ISBN 978 90 04 18930 0
140/1. LANGE, A., E. TOV and M. WEIGOLD (eds.). *The Dead Sea Scrolls in Context*. Integrating the Dead Sea Scrolls in the Study of Ancient Texts, Languages, and Cultures. 2011. ISBN 978 90 04 18903 4
141. HALVORSON-TAYLOR, M.A. *Enduring Exile*. The Metaphorization of Exile in the Hebrew Bible. 2011. ISBN 978 90 04 16097 2